The Better Practices of Project Management

Based on IPMA competences

Other publications by Van Haren Publishing

Van Haren Publishing (VHP) specializes in titles on Best Practices, methods and standards within four domains:
- IT and IT Management
- Architecture (Enterprise and IT)
- Business Management and
- Project Management

Van Haren Publishing offers a wide collection of whitepapers, templates, free e-books, trainer materials etc. in the **Van Haren Publishing Knowledge Base**: www.vanharen.net for more details.

Van Haren Publishing is also publishing on behalf of leading organizations and companies: ASLBiSL Foundation, CA, Centre Henri Tudor, Gaming Works, IACCM, IAOP, IPMA-NL, ITSqc, NAF, Ngi, PMI-NL, PON, The Open Group, The SOX Institute.

Topics are (per domain):

IT and IT Management
ABC of ICT
ASL®
CATS CM®
CMMI®
COBIT®
e-CF
ISO 20000
ISO 27001/27002
ISPL
IT Service CMM
ITIL®
MOF
MSF
SABSA

Architecture (Enterprise and IT)
ArchiMate®
GEA®
Novius Architectuur Methode
TOGAF®

Business Management
BABOK® Guide
BiSL®
EFQM
eSCM
IACCM
ISA-95
ISO 9000/9001
Novius B&IP
OPBOK
SAP
SixSigma
SOX
SqEME®

Project, Program and Risk Management
A4-Projectmanagement
DSDM/Atern
ICB / NCB
ISO 21500
MINCE®
M_o_R®
MSP™
P3O®
PMBOK® Guide
PRINCE2®

For the latest information on VHP publications, visit our website: www.vanharen.net.

The Better Practices of Project Management

Based on IPMA competences
3rd revised edition

John Hermarij

Van Haren
PUBLISHING

Colophon

Title:	Better Practices of Project Management based on IPMA competences - 3rd revised edition
Series:	Best Practice
Author:	John Hermarij, Dhirata BV, Ouderkerk a/d Amstel, The Netherlands
Cultural reviewer:	Leo Kwarten, Arabist and anthropologist, The Netherlands: www.leokwarten.com
English translation:	Tineke Bruce-Feijen, TENNET Translations, The Netherlands: www.tennettranslations.nl
Publisher:	Van Haren Publishing, Zaltbommel, The Netherlands, www.vanharen.net
ISBN Hard copy:	978 90 8753 717 3
ISBN eBook:	978 90 8753 796 8
ISBN ePub:	978 94 018 0559 9
Edition:	Third edition, first impression, February 2013
	Third edition, second impression, October 2014
Lay-Out:	John Hermarij
Cover design:	CO2 Premedia bv, Amersfoort

All rights reserved. No part of this publication may be reproduced in any form by print, photo print, microfilm or any other means without written permission by the publisher.

For any further enquiries about Van Haren Publishing, please send an e-mail to: info@vanharen.net.

Although this publication has been composed with most care, neither Authors nor Editor nor Publisher can accept any liability for damage caused by possible errors and/or incompleteness in this publication.

FOREWORD

In front of you is a book, which, in my opinion, you are not going to read but use. It is a particularly informative and useful book, the content of which you not only need, but also must know, in order to become a better project manager. This book provides a significant contribution to achieving that. The profession and your skills are elaborated on from various viewpoints, also from an international perspective.

The project management profession, and with it the development of the project manager, has taken a significant forward step in recent years. As well as the project manager's knowledge and experience, the understanding has developed that, in particular, the project manager's professional behavior is essential to ensure the success of a project.

For this purpose, IPMA has developed three competence groups; technical project management competences, behavioral competences, and competences that determine the relationship between the projects and the organizational context.

The number of IPMA certified Project Managers is rapidly increasing, and furthermore, more and more organizations are choosing the IPMA model as the standard for the quality and development of the project manager.

This is the first international book covering all subjects and competences of the IPMA Competence Baseline (ICB), which makes it not only unique, but also important. This book offers every project manager the opportunity to learn, understand and apply the project management competences. It is self-evident that, if you want to successfully achieve international IPMA certification, this book is indispensable.

Projects and project managers can be found everywhere, and every different type of project contains its own complexities. You can devise as many methodologies as you like, but every country or continent has its own culture. Project managers, and their projects, are successful within their own culture and values, and when they understand their own stumbling blocks and political power relationships within another culture they can be successful everywhere.

John Hermarij has succeeded in combining his substantial knowledge of the project management profession with his international experience, and to look at the world of project management and the competences of the project manager from an intercultural perspective.

Over recent years, I have witnessed John Hermarij in many different roles; as trainer, coach, IPMA assessor and especially also as a positive critical conscience for IPMA and the advancement of the profession. John is able to put things into perspective, and is also sharp, but above all else, he always radiates pleasure. In my opinion it is this combination of qualities that has enabled John to compile this book.

Foreword

I wish you a lot of pleasure and success with your further development in our fascinating profession of Project Management.

Joop Schefferlie

President of the Board

IPMA Netherlands

Table of Content

Introduction XXVII
The IPMA Competence Baseline XXVII
An intercultural view XXIX
Reader's Guide XXX
The website with the book XXXII
Project management as a discipline for life XXXII

1. TECHNICAL COMPETENCES 1

1.01 Project Management Success 3
  1.01-1 Definitions 4
  1.01-2 Introduction 5
  1.01-3 Process steps 7
    1. Analyze before accepting 7
    2. Develop the approach 7
    3. Resolve conflicts and integrate 8
    4. Agree upon the approach 8
    5. Execute the management plan 8
    6. Collect, interpret and report 9
    7. Apply lessons learned 9
    8. Other standards and guidances 10
  1.01-4 Special Topics 11
    1. Initiation documents 11

1.02 Interested parties 13
  1.02-1 Definitions 14
  1.02-2 Introduction 15
  1.02-3 Process Steps 16
    1. Prioritize interested parties 16
    2. Analyze their interests 16
    3. Communicate 16
    4. Develop a strategy 17
    5. Add strategy to PM plan 17
    6. Opportunities and threats 18
    7. Identify decision authority 18
    8. Satisfy them in each stage 18
    9. Deploy the strategy 18
    10. Communicate change 18
    11. Apply lessons learned 19
    12. Other standards and guidances 19

Table of Content

1.02-4 Special Topics 20
   1. The project environment 20
   2. Interested parties 21
   3. Analysis of Interested parties 23
   4. Sensitivity...26

1.03 Requirements and objectives 27
   1.03-1 Definitions 28
   1.03-2 Introduction 30
   1.03-3 Process steps 31
     1. Document requirements..31
     2. Justify the project 31
     3. Document project goals 32
     4. Manage progress 32
     5. Validate requirements 33
     6. Assess compliance 33
     7. Set up a review process 33
     8. Apply lessons learned 33
   1.03-4 Special topics...34
     1. Refining versus changing..34
     2. The Business Case...34
     3. The GAP principle 37
     4. Value Management 37
     5. The project review..39

1.04 Risk and opportunity 41
   1.04-1 Definitions 42
   1.04-2 Introduction 45
   1.04-3 Process steps 47
     1. Identify and analyze 47
     2. Plan Responses 48
     3. Incorporate responses 50
     4. Assess attainability objectives 50
     5. Track and monitor risk profile 50
     6. Track and monitor responses 51
     7. Apply lessons learned 51
     8. Other standards and guidances..51
   1.04-4 Special Topics 53
     1. Checklists..53
     2. Risk Breakdown Structure 53
     3. Risk matrix 53
     4. Qualitative scale of impact 54
     5. Variance 56
     6. Decision trees 57
     7. Risk log or Register...58
     8. The 'insurance premium'...60

    9. Monte Carlo Simulation..60
    10. Sensitivity analysis 61
    11. The Successive Principle 61

1.05 Quality...65
  1.05-1 Definitions 66
  1.05-2 Introduction 70
  1.05-3 Process steps 71
    1. Develop a quality plan..71
    2. Select, build and test...71
    3. Approve the final version...71
    4. Assure and check..71
    5. Log tests and get approval..72
    6. Correct and repair 72
    7. Apply lessons learned 72
    8. Other standards and guidances...72
  1.05-4 Special topics 74
    1. The quality gurus 74
    2. The quality system of a project 75
    3. Product quality 76
    4. The cost of quality...76
    5. Benefits/cost consideration 77
    6. Standards..79
    7. Assessments and audits 80
    8. The seven tools of quality 81

1.06 Project Organization 89
  1.06-1 Definitions 90
  1.06-2 Introduction 92
  1.06-3 Process steps 93
    1. Determine organization..93
    2. Determine teams..93
    3. Determine roles...94
    4. Define project procedures 94
    5. Acquire resources 94
    6. Manage interfaces 94
    7. Communicate decisions...95
    8. Improve the organization 95
    9. Apply lessons learned 95
    10. Other standards and guidances...95
  1.06-4 Special Topics 97
    1. The organization chart 97
    2. Roles in the project 97
    3. RACI table...99

Table of Content

1.07 Teamwork 101
   1.07-1 Definitions 102
   1.07-2 Introduction 103
   1.07-3 Process Steps 104
      1. The forming stage 104
      2. The storming stage 104
      3. The norming stage 105
      4. The performing stage..105
      5. The adjourning stage 105
      6. Apply lessons learned...105
   1.07-4 Special Topics 107
      1. Success factors..107
      2. Team structure 107
      3. Team roles according to Belbin..108
      4. Problems with teams..109

1.08 Problem resolution...111
   1.08-1 Definitions 112
   1.08-2 Introduction 113
   1.08-3 Process Steps 114
      1. Add problem procedure..114
      2. Identify problems 114
      3. Determine the cause 115
      4. Apply creative methods 115
      5. Evaluate and select solutions 115
      6. Implement the solution...115
      7. Apply lessons learned..115
   1.08-4 Special Topics 116
      1. Brainstorming...116
      2. Force field analysis 116
      3. Manage towards consensus 117
      4. System thinking..117

1.09 Project structures..123
   1.09-1 Definitions 124
   1.09-2 Introduction 125
   1.09-3 Process steps 126
      1. Defining PPP breakdown 126
      2. Determine responsibilities...127
      3. Determine requirements 127
      4. Decompose and analyze 129
      5. Maintain and communicate 131
      6. Apply lessons learned..131
   1.09-4 Special topics...133
      1. Work Breakdown Structure 133
      2. OBS: Organization Breakdown 138

X

Table of Content

    3. RAM: The Responsibilities Matrix 138
    4. RBS: Resource Breakdown Structure...140
    5. Product oriented planning 140

1.10 Scope and deliverables 143
  1.10-1 Definitions 144
  1.10-2 Introduction 145
  1.10-3 Process steps 146
    1. Define requirements...146
    2. Agree on deliverables 146
    3. Define and control the scope 146
    4. Update scope and deliverables 147
    5. Control the quality 147
    6. Formal handover 147
    7. Apply lessons learned..148
    8. Other standards and guidances...148
  1.10-4 Special Topics 149
    1. Configuration Management...149

1.11 Time and project phases..151
  1.11-1 Definitions 152
  1.11-2 Introduction 154
  1.11-3 Process steps..155
    1. Define and sequence activities 155
    2. Estimate the duration 155
    3. Schedule the project or phase 156
    4. Allocate and balance..159
    5. Compare target, planned and actual dates...159
    6. Control the time schedule 160
    7. Apply lessons learned..161
    8. Other standards and guidances...161
  1.11-4 Special Topics 162
    1. Concepts of time 162
    2. Gantt Chart 162
    3. The principle of phases..164
    4. Various methods of staging...165
    5. Estimation methods 166
    6. PERT 168

1.12 Resources...169
  1.12-1 Definitions 170
  1.12-2 Introduction 171
  1.12-3 Process steps..172
    1. Decide on the need..172
    2. Schedule the resources 172
    3. Reach an agreement 173

Table of Content

  4. Apply change control 173
  5. Manage assignment..174
  6. Process impact of change...175
  7. Escalation in time 175
  8. Use experience 175
  9. Apply lessons learned 175
 1.12-4 Special Topics 176
  1. Critical Chain...176

1.13 Cost and finance 179
 1.13-1 Definitions 180
 1.13-2 Introduction 181
 1.13-3 Financial Process 182
  1. Analyze financing options 182
  2. Negotiate the potential funds 182
  3. Select the source of finance 183
  4. Allocate budgets 184
  5. Calculate cash flows 184
  6. Document and authorise..184
  7. Take care of the audit systems 184
  8. Validate and manage budgets 185
  9. Apply lessons learned 185
 1.13-4 Cost Process..186
  1. Choose a cost control system 186
  2. Estimate and evaluate costs 186
  3. Define monitoring and control 187
  4. Define cost objectives 187
  5. Calculate actual costs 187
  6. Include changes and claims 188
  7. Carry out a variance analysis 188
  8. Make a forecast 188
  9. Take corrective measures 189
  10. Update the cost estimate 189
  11. Apply lessons learned 189
  12. Other standards and guidances..189
 1.13-5 Special Topics 190
  1. Structuring the costs 190
  2. Islamic Financing 190
  3. Sarbanes-Oxley 191
  4. Public Private Financing 191
  5. Price risks 192

Table of Content

1.14 Procurement and contract 193
   1.14-1 Definitions 194
   1.14-2 Introduction 196
   1.14-3 Process steps 198
      1. Make-or-buy analyses 198
      2. Select suppliers 199
      3. Set up contract management 199
      4. Manage contract changes 200
      5. Discharge and close contracts 201
      6. Apply lessons learned 202
      7. Other standards and guidances 202
   1.14-4 Special Topics 203
      1. Selecting suppliers 203
      2. Full Analytical Criteria Method 203
      3. Outsourcing 205
      4. Contract pricing 206
      5. Public and Private tendering 207

1.15 Changes 211
   1.15-1 Definitions 212
   1.15-2 Introduction 213
   1.15-3 Process steps 215
      1. Define change control policy 215
      2. Identify changes 215
      3. Determine the impact 216
      4. Arrange authorisation 216
      5. Get acceptance or rejection 217
      6. Apply changes and report 217
      7. Monitor changes 217
      8. Apply lessons learned 218
      9. Other standards and guidances 218
   1.15-4 Special Topics 219
      1. Issue register and report 219
      2. Prioritizing changes 220

1.16 Control and reports 221
   1.16-1 Definitions 222
   1.16-2 Introduction 223
   1.16-3 Process steps 224
      1. Set up a monitoring system 224
      2. Measure status & performance 224
      3. Analyze deviations 224
      4. Plan alternatives 224
      5. Take corrective measures 224
      6. Adjust project objectives 224
      7. Report to the stakeholders 224

Table of Content

    8. Apply lessons learned 225
    9. Other standards and guidances 225
  1.16-4 Special Topics 227
    1. Earned Value Method 227
    2. Slip Chart 230

1.17 Information and documentation 233
  1.17-1 Definitions 234
  1.17-2 Introduction 235
  1.17-3 Information Process 236
    1. Develop a PMIS 236
    2. Adhere to the company policy 237
    3. Ensure it is implemented...239
    4. Control the information 239
    5. Apply lessons learned 239
  1.17-4 Documentation Process 240
    1. Develop a plan 240
    2. Keep to the existing rules...240
    3. Classify the documents 241
    4. Issue documents 241
    5. Save the documents 241
    6. Manage the versions...242
    7. Archive 242
    8. Apply lessons learned 242
    9. Other standards and guidances...242
  1.17-5 Special topics 244
    1. Documents in projects 244

1.18 Communication..247
  1.18-1 Definitions 248
  1.18-2 Introduction 249
  1.18-3 Process steps 250
    1. Set up a communication plan 250
    2. Identify the appropriate style..250
    3. Determine the timing..251
    4. Decide on the method...251
    5. Plan and prepare 251
    6. Check the infrastructure..252
    7. Measure the effectiveness...252
    8. Evaluate and take action 252
    9. Apply lessons learned 252
  1.18-4 Special Topics 253
    1. The communication model...253
    2. Verbal and Non-Verbal 254
    3. The five axioms of Watzlawick 256
    4. Four aspects - Schulz von Thun 258

- 5. Levels in group discussions 261
- 6. Presentation Skills 262
- 7. Meeting 265

1.19 Start-Up 271
- 1.19-1 Definitions 272
- 1.19-2 Introduction 273
- 1.19-3 Process steps 274
  - 1. Initiate the project start up 274
  - 2. Communicate project goals 274
  - 3. Develop a mission and vision 274
  - 4. Draw up a PM plan 274
  - 5. Gain acceptance for the plan 275
  - 6. Ensure co-operation 275
  - 7. Secure all resources 275
  - 8. Ensure a start up per stage 275
  - 9. Apply lessons learned 276
  - 10. Other standards and guidances 276

1.20 Close-out 277
- 1.20-1 Definitions 278
- 1.20-2 Introduction 279
- 1.20-3 Process Steps 280
  - 1. Start to use the deliverables 280
  - 2. Formalise the completion 280
  - 3. Obtain customer feedback 281
  - 4. Plan the handover 281
  - 5. Assure warranty conditions 282
  - 6. Close contracts 282
  - 7. Finalize financial transactions 283
  - 8. Hold a close-out meeting 283
  - 9. Release resources and assets 284
  - 10. Archive the project file 285
  - 11. Issue final report 285
  - 12. Apply lessons learned 285
  - 13. Other standards and guidances 286
- 1.20-4 Special topics 287
  - 1. Project evaluation 287

2. BEHAVIORAL COMPETENCES **289**

2.01 Leadership 291
- 2.01-1 Definitions 292
- 2.01-2 Introduction 293
- 2.01-3 Process steps 294
  - 1. Determine the leadership style 294

Table of Content

    2. Know your own abilities 295
    3. Apply the chosen style 295
    4. Modify the style if required 295
    5. Develop your competence 295
    6. Develop this also in your team..296
    7. Continuously improve 296
    8. Apply lessons learned 297
  2.01-4 Special Topics 298
    1. The development of management 298
    2. Leadership in a multicultural perspective.......................................299
    3. Blake & Mouton's Grid 300
    4. Situational Leadership - Fiedler 301
    5. Hersey & Blanchard 302
    6. Power - Hersey & Blanchard..305
    7. Manfred Kets de Vries 306
    8. Delegating...307
    9. Feedback 308

2.02 Engagement 309
  2.02-1 Definitions 310
  2.02-2 Introduction 311
  2.02-3 Process steps 312
    1. Be aware of those involved..312
    2. Explain your ability to 'serve'...312
    3. Investigate the possibilities...312
    4. Understand the engagement 313
    5. Appreciate and communicate...313
    6. Be proud of achievements 313
    7. Identify changing demands 314
    8. Apply lessons learned 314
  2.02-4 Special topics..315
    1. Being Accountable 315
    2. Delegating and empowerment..315
    3. Motivating..315
    4. The Maslow needs hierarchy 316
    5. Theory X, Theory Y...318
    6. Motivation-Hygiene Theory 319
    7. Dealing with opposition 320
    8. Coaching leadership 322
    9. Enthusing 323
    10. Positive attitude..323
    11. Images 324
    12. The Creation Spiral 324

2.03 Self-control 327
2.03-1 Definitions 328
2.03-2 Introduction 329
2.03-3 Process steps 330
1. Analyze a stressful situation...330
2. Analyze working behavior 330
3. Provide adequate resources and skills to the project team 330
4. Produce a SWOT of the team..331
5. Act to reduce stress 331
6. Communicate open and honest 331
7. Share tasks, responsibilities and authorities..332
8. Be well organized yourself and demonstrate appropriate behavior.............332
9. Apply lessons learned 332
2.03-4 Special topics 333
1. Emotional Intelligence 333
2. Personality 333
3. Cognitive dissonance...334
4. How people learn 335

2.04 Assertiveness..337
2.04-1 Definitions 338
2.04-2 Introduction 339
2.04-3 Process Steps..340
1. Determine and record project goals and results 340
2. Determine what can lead to discussion 340
3. Prepare counter-arguments..340
4. Assess viewpoints, interests and relationships...341
5. Prepare meetings and discussions 341
6. Present project interests in a calm and self-assured manner......................342
7. Value others 342
8. Build up sustainable relationships with others 342
9. Apply lessons learned 343
2.04-4 Special Topics 344
1. The cultural dimension...344
2. Persuasiveness...345
3. Diplomacy 346
4. Pillars of self-esteem..346
5. RT, RET and REBT..347
6. The will..351

2.05 Relaxation..355
2.05-1 Definitions 356
2.05-2 Introduction 357
2.05-3 Process Steps..358
1. Detect tensions or fatigue 358
2. Be proactive in discovering the reason for tensions 358

XVII

Table of Content

    3. Remove the cause, and set up an action plan 359
    4. Relax at a location away from the workplace 360
    5. Meet regularly as a team, and involve everybody 360
    6. Apply lessons learned 361
  2.05-4 Special Topics 362
    1. From tension to overstressed 362
    2. Possible Causes of Stress 364
    3. Humour 365
    4. Balancing private life and work 366

2.06 Openness 369
  2.06-1 Definitions 370
  2.06-2 Introduction 371
  2.06-3 Process steps 372
    1. Develop a policy on openness 372
    2. Start with informal contacts 372
    3. Welcome information 372
    4. Ask open questions 372
    5. Create opportunities to stimulate openness in the team 373
    6. Praise positive input 374
    7. Apply lessons learned 374
  2.06-4 Special topics 375
    1. Skills to improve openness 375
    2. Model I versus Model II 377
    3. Defensive Routines 377
    4. The skilful discussion 379

2.07 Creativity 381
  2.07-1 Definitions 382
  2.07-2 Introduction 383
  2.07-3 Process Steps 384
    1. Recognise situations 384
    2. Determine contributors 384
    3. Bring people together 385
    4. Generate many ideas 385
    5. Prioritize ideas 385
    6. Make a choice 386
    7. Plan and execute 386
    8. Apply lessons learned 386
  2.07-4 Special topics 387
    1. Culture 387
    2. Think holistically 387
    3. Intuition 388
    4. Creativity techniques 389
    5. Edward De Bono 391
    6. The Cartesian Product 392

Table of Content

2.08 Results orientation 395
   2.08-1 Definitions 396
   2.08-2 Introduction 397
   2.08-3 Process steps 398
      1. Define results unambiguously 398
      2. Arrange results into interest groups 398
      3. Explicitly manage expectations 399
      4. Determine and communicate the critical path 399
      5. Finalize the project plan, communicate it and get it approved 400
      6. Repeating the previous steps for as many times as is necessary 400
      7. Striving for a continuous result improvement 400
      8. Communicating project performances and results 400
      9. Compare project performance and results against the plan 401
      10. Apply lessons learned 401

2.09 Efficiency 403
   2.09-1 Definitions 404
   2.09-2 Introduction 405
   2.09-3 Process Steps 406
      1. Actively seek to improve 406
      2. Plan, obtain and assign 406
      3. Determine priorities 407
      4. Look for sustainable efficiency 407
      5. Look for improvements 407
      6. Follow, monitor and compare 408
      7. Estimate resources 408
      8. Report, and propose measures 409
      9. Propose and evaluate 409
      10. Apply lessons learned 409
   2.09-4 Special Topics 410
      1. Long term efficiency 410
      2. Benchmarking 411
      3. Time management 411
      4. Take account of your rhythm 412
      5. Core Quadrants 413

2.10 Consultation 415
   2.10-1 Definitions 416
   2.10-2 Introduction 417
   2.10-3 Process Steps 418
      1. Analyze situation and context 418
      2. Identify goals 418
      3. Listen to arguments 419
      4. Determine similarities and differences 419
      5. Diagnose problems and choose solutions 419
      6. Come to an agreement on differences 419

Table of Content

    7. Consider consequences; document and communicate them 420
    8. Apply lessons learned 420
  2.10-4 Special Topics 421
    1. Build up arguments 421
    2. Toulmin..422

2.11 Negotiation 425
  2.11-1 Definitions 426
  2.11-2 Introduction 427
  2.11-3 Process steps...428
    1. Determine the desired outcome and the absolute minimum 428
    2. Develop a negotiation strategy 429
    3. Explore and analyze the situation..430
    4. Address issues and suggest alternatives...431
    5. Consider alternatives to achieve a win-win situation 431
    6. Focus on the agreements 431
    7. Discuss viewpoints of both parties 432
    8. Apply lessons learned 432
  2.11-4 Special Topics 433
    1. The Harvard Method 433
    2. Negotiation styles 435
    3. Rapport 435
    4. Dealing with manipulation 437
    5. Developing this competence 437
    6. Thirty-Six Stratagems 437

2.12 Conflicts and crisis...449
  2.12-1 Definitions 450
  2.12-2 Introduction 451
  2.12-3 Process steps...452
    1. Predict reactions 452
    2. Don't become involved...452
    3. Consider all points of view 452
    4. Choose a suitable approach 453
    5. Balance interests 453
    6. Agree upon solutions 453
    7. Apply lessons learned 453
  2.12-4 Special Topics 454
    1. Diagnosis of conflicts 454
    2. Stages of the conflict..457
    3. Conflict styles...462
    4. Solving conflicts 464
    5. Crisis approach 465

2.13 Reliability 467
   2.13-1 Definitions 468
   2.13-2 Introduction 469
   2.13-3 Process steps 470
      1. Use good planning techniques 470
      2. Communicate to stakeholders 470
      3. Know their dilemmas..470
      4. Be respectful, honest and open 471
      5. Engage stakeholders 471
      6. Mitigate and clarify 471
      7. Reach agreement 471
      8. Work systematically 472
      9. Apply lessons learned..472

2.14 Values appreciation 473
   2.14-1 Definitions 474
   2.14-2 Introduction 475
   2.14-3 Process steps 476
      1. Communicate your values 476
      2. Look after values, opinions, ethics and interests 476
      3. Comply with the values 477
      4. Discuss about values 477
      5. Amend viewpoints 477
      6. Respect and value others 477
      7. React quickly to changes 477
      8. Apply lessons learned..478
   2.14-4 Special Topics 479
      1. Building a relationship...479
      2. Ethics and Cultural dimensions..480
      3. Customs..481

2.15 Ethics..487
   2.15-1 Definitions 488
   2.15-2 Introduction 489
   2.15-3 Process steps 491
      1. Ensure conformity 491
      2. Address ethical issues 491
      3. Involve interested parties 492
      4. Be explicit..492
      5. Escalate when needed...493
      6. Deal with the consequences 494
      7. Apply necessary 495
      8. Apply lessons learned..495
   2.15-4 Special topics...496
      1. Declaration of Human Rights 496
      2. Cairo Declaration 497

Table of Content

    3. Project Management Ethics 498
    4. Ethical dilemmas 498

3. CONTEXTUAL COMPETENCES 501

3.01 Project orientation 503
  3.01-1 Definitions 504
  3.01-2 Introduction 505
  3.01-3 Process steps 507
    1. Assess whether there is a need to carry out projects 507
    2. Culture and process analysis in relation to projects 508
    3. Make the business case for project management 509
    4. Implement project management 510
    5. Monitor progress and record learning experiences 510
  3.01-4 Special Topics 511
    1. The Project Management Office 511
    2. Project management Methods 511

3.02 Programme orientation 519
  3.02-1 Definitions 520
  3.02-2 Introduction 521
  3.02-3 Process steps 522
    1. List and prioritize improvements 522
    2. Confirm there is a justification 522
    3. Quantify the benefits 523
    4. Align with the strategic goals 523
    5. Assess the benefits 523
    6. Change the organization, culture and processes 523
    7. Initiate relevant programmes 524
    8. Apply lessons learned 524
  3.02-4 Special Topics 525
    1. Available Standards 525
    2. Kurt Lewin 527
    3. Kotters Eight Stage Process 527
    4. Change in Five Colors 528
    5. Change is inevitable 531

3.03 Portfolio orientation 535
  3.03-1 Definitions 536
  3.03-2 Introduction 537
  3.03-3 Process steps 538
    1. Identify and prioritize 538
    2. Balance and allocate 540
    3. Standardize processes 541
    4. Track and monitor 541
    5. Remove components 542

Table of Content

    6. Add components 542

3.04 PPP implementation 543
   3.04-1 Definitions 544
   3.04-2 Introduction 545
   3.04-3 Process steps 546
    1. Decision to consider PPP as a continuous improvement process 546
    2. Determining the current capability of the organization 547
    3. Developing the PPP concept for the organization 547
    4. Proving the feasibility through a pilot 548
    5. Assessing the pilot 548
    6. Determining the implementation speed of the maturity path 548
    7. Implementing company wide 548
    8. Apply lessons learned 548
   3.04-4 Special Topics 550
    1. OPM3 550
    2. ISO 21500 Guidance 552

3.05 Permanent organization 555
   3.05-1 Definitions 556
   3.05-2 Introduction 557
   3.05-3 Process steps 558
    1. Understand the structure, goals and working methods 558
    2. Take account of structure, goals and working methods 558
    3. Monitor the project-line interface 558
    4. Identify similarities and differences 559
    5. Consider the different options and their consequences 559
    6. 6. Discuss, decide, communicate and implement 559
    7. Apply lessons learned 559
   3.05-4 Special Topics 560
    1. Formal and informal 560
    2. The organization architecture 560
    3. Line verses Project 563
    4. Henry Mintzberg 565
    5. Porters Value Chain 567
    6. Management of change 567
    7. The learning organization 568
    8. The coping curve 569
    9. Adjusting change strategy to company culture 570

3.06 Business 571
   3.06-1 Definitions 572
   3.06-2 Introduction 573
   3.06-3 Process steps 574
    1. Align project an line organization 574
    2. Understand strategic standards and guidelines 574

Table of Content

    3. Verify whether standards and guidelines have been met 575
    4. Satisfy the business case requirements 575
    5. Provide feedback on the existing PPP implementation 575

3.07 Systems, products and technology 577
   3.07-1 Definitions 578
   3.07-2 Introduction 579
   3.07-3 System Application Process 580
    1. Analyze the structure, definition and environment 580
    2. Make a feasibility analysis, and produce a business justification 581
    3. Determine customers and functionality 581
    4. Determine goals and components 581
    5. Design production and supply chain for the distribution 581
    6. Authorise the design and production 582
    7. Test and Optimize the system 582
    8. Validating against the requirements in the "business case" 582
    9. Put into operation 582
    10. Manage the life cycle 582
    11. Apply lessons learned 583
   3.07-4 Systems Development Process 584
    1. Define the development as new project 584
    2. Define the customers and the required functionality 584
    3. Connect to the existing systems, products and technology 584
    4. Design production and distribution 585
    5. Calculate the costs 585
    6. Optimize in accordance with the requirements 585
    7. Hand over to the organization 585
    8. Determine opportunities for further strategic improvement 585
    9. Apply lessons learned 585
   3.07-5 Special topics 587
    1. EFQM 587
    2. Deming's fourteen points 588
    3. Standards 589
    4. Process impeovement with Six Sigma 591

3.08 Personnel management 593
   3.08-1 Definitions 594
   3.08-2 Introduction 595
   3.08-3 Process steps 596
    1. Set the requirements for employees 596
    2. Employ, or keep, the right people 596
    3. Explain your expectations to the team members 598
    4. Check the planned and actual performance per employee 598
    5. Monitor changes in the staff 598
    6. Monitoring staff motivation 599
    7. Maintain contact with the responsible HR person 599

Table of Content

 8. Discharge the team members personally at close-off 599
 9. Apply lessons learned 599
 3.08-4 Special Topics 600
  1. Competence development 600
  2. Professional Development Plan 601
  3. The appraisal cycle 602

3.09 Health, Security, Safety and Environment 605
 3.09-1 Definitions 606
 3.09-2 Introduction 607
 3.09-3 Process steps 608
  1. Determine applicable laws and regulations 608
  2. Determine the risks that are present 608
  3. Evaluate the actual situation 609
  4. Plan and develop processes 609
  5. Monitor and control effectiveness 610
  6. Report issues and risks 610
  7. Record and apply learning points 610
 3.09-4 Special Topics 611
  1. Sustainability 611
  2. Health 612
  3. Security 613
  4. Safety 614
  5. Environment 617

3.10 Finance 619
 3.10-1 Definitions 620
 3.10-2 Introduction 624
 3.10-3 Process steps 625
  1. Recognise the financial environment of the project 625
  2. Define the business case 625
  3. Implement the financial administration and reports 625
  4. Provide the financial reports 626
  5. If applicable, schedule financial audits 626
  6. Obtain financial discharge on close-out 627
 3.10-4 Special Topics 628
  1. The annual report 628
  2. Accounting 630
  3. Cost allocation 632
  4. OPEX and CAPEX 635
  5. Ratios 635
  6. Investment appraisal 638

Table of Content

3.11 Legal 643
  3.11-1 Definitions 644
  3.11-2 Introduction 645
  3.11-3 Process Steps 646
    1. Set up legal standards 646
    2. Identify legal aspects 646
    3. Initiate compliance 646
    4. Manage contracts adequately 646
    5. React to unions and works councils 647
    6. React to from 'whistle-blowers' 647
    7. Apply lessons learned 647
  3.11-4 Special Topics 648
    1. Law sources 648
    2. Different Legal systems 648
    3. Contract law 649
    5. Incoterms 650
    4. Intellectual property 653

Index 655

Introduction
The primary objective I want to achieve with this book is to provide an overview of the project management competence that is as complete as possible. A book, in fact, that I would have liked to have had when I experienced my first adventures as a project manager in the early 1980's.

> In 2002 together with Clemens Bon and Rinse van der Schoot, just like me, both IPMA assessors in the Netherlands we wrote a Dutch book based on the National Competence Baseline. The years following I've been expanding my vision more internationally, resulting in the need for book with an intercultural view on project management.

The IPMA Competence Baseline
My starting point was the IPMA Competence Baseline (ICB), which covers the crucial elements of the project management competence. These elements are divided into three main areas: technique; behavior; context.

Technique
In the first 20 elements, the ICB describes the most essential technical project management competences:

ICB	Topic
1.01	Project management success
1.02	Interested parties
1.03	Requirements & Objectives
1.04	Risks & Opportunity
1.05	Quality
1.06	Project organization
1.07	Teamwork
1.08	Problem resolution
1.09	Project structures
1.10	Scope & deliverables
1.11	Time & Project phases
1.12	Resources
1.13	Cost & Finance
1.14	Purchase & contract
1.15	Changes
1.16	Control & Reporting
1.17	Information & Documentation
1.18	Communication
1.19	Start-Up
1.20	Close-out

These twenty elements form the basis of what good project management is. As a project manager, when you have a command of the major part of these techniques, you can be assured that you are in a position to structure your project soundly, and to maintain this structure for the duration of the project. This is an important condition for success, but it is not enough.

Introduction

Behavior

The ICB then covers the following 15 behavior elements:

ICB	Topic
2.01	Leadership
2.02	Engagement & Motivation
2.03	Self control
2.04	Assertiveness
2.05	Relaxation
2.06	Openness
2.07	Creativity
2.08	Result orientation
2.09	Efficiency
2.10	Consultation
2.11	Negotiation
2.12	Conflict & Crisis
2.13	Reliability
2.14	Values Appreciation
2.15	Ethics

Here, the ICB does something which, in my opinion, is a stroke of genius, by describing for 15 behavior elements how these could be expressed in terms of a project management function. In this way, they accomplish a connection between, on the one hand technique, and on the other hand behavior. I shall make this clear, by way of a few examples.

The element 2.06 Openness: *"is the ability to make others feel they are welcome to express themselves, so that the project can benefit from their input, suggestions, worries and concerns"* i.e. a competent project manager ensures that within the project team, there is sufficient room for contributions to the plans he draws up. In this way, he achieves a qualitatively much better schedule than when he produces the schedule himself from behind his laptop. The technical element "Time and Project phases" is in this instance linked to the behavior element "Openness".

Element 2.08 Results orientation: *"to focus the team's attention on key objectives to obtain the optimum outcome for all parties involved",* also demonstrates a link between the hard and soft sides within a project.

When we look at element 2.09 Efficiency, this link becomes even clearer: *"the ability to use time and resources cost-effectively to produce the agreed deliverables and fulfil the interested parties' expectations".* Here, the technique of Project Control is linked to efficient behavior - a competent project manager acts efficiently!

Context

There is not one single project that exists in a vacuum, sometimes there are other projects battling for the same resources, sometimes there are commercial interests, which determine whether or not the project gets priority, and at other times something goes amiss in the operations of one of the parties involved in the project, whereby your project cannot progress any further.

Introduction

In order to understand this, as project manager you need a certain amount of management knowledge, and that is what the third part of the ICB is about. In total the last 11 elements:

ICB	Topic
3.01	Project orientation
3.02	Programme orientation
3.03	Portfolio orientation
3.04	PPP Implementation
3.05	Permanent Organization
3.06	Business
3.07	Systems, Products & Technology
3.08	Personnel management
3.09	Health, Security, Safety & Environment
3.10	Finance
3.11	Legal

The first four are related to the professional implementation of project management in an organization, and the last seven are related to general knowledge about companies and organizations.

A complete picture
To the best of my knowledge, there is currently not a more complete description of the necessary project management knowledge and skills available anywhere in the world. For this reason the choice of layout for this book was quickly made. In the following 46 chapters, I cover all of these subjects one by one, always using the ICB as my guiding principle. Because the Dutch IPMA is one of the associations in Europe that is very far advanced in putting the ICB into practice, I have used their exam terms in the choice of the various techniques, models and insights covered. Although some of them are only known in the Netherland, I'll think they will be of help to you.

An intercultural view
This book has been written to support every project manager in the world, who can get along with the English language, so for those whose native language is English, and also for those whose second language is English. This has consequences for the style in which this book has been written; in straightforward and accessible English. For this, I am extremely grateful to Tineke Bruce-Feijen, who has translated my Dutch text.

In addition, the book had to be applicable to groups of project managers originating from diverse cultures. This is not a book that tells how a Westerner must behave in an Arab or an Asian country, but one which, from a number of cultures, looks at the different subjects covered in the ICB. For example, time in Western society is "*a line that goes from left to right in an upward slope*", whereas in an Arab country it is much more "*a circle that finishes back at it's starting point*". It is clear that this has an effect on the way in which you draw up a schedule, but also on how you cope with stress. For this intercultural aspect, Leo Kwarten, a well-known Arabist in the Netherlands, has carried out important work.

Introduction

Furthermore, I went in search of non-western management literature and, where applicable, I have used this in describing the different elements, with the goal of trying to rise above the various cultures. This also makes the book suitable for training purposes, where the participants originate from different cultures, as long as they are able to read English. I have already successfully used this book for a number of years in such training groups.

Reader's Guide
This is a book that, when I was first starting out as a project manager, I would have liked to have had, and also a book that serves as support for the IPMA certification exams (therefore I have used the end terms available), for both the trainer and the exam candidate. This book consists of more than 600 pages, and I can well believe that you are asking yourself where you can best make a start.

As I have chosen to keep to the same sequence as the ICB, this may come across as slightly confusing, and I am, therefore, proposing a number of reader's guides:

- The junior project manager
- The experienced project manager
- The IPMA certification candidate
- The project management training programme developer

The junior project manager
As a first-time project manager, the most important aspect of all is to ensure that your project is well-structured, and the first 20 chapters cover this. If you have little knowledge of project management, then I would concentrate on the following chapters, and read them in this sequence: 1.01; 1.02; 1.19; 1.05; 1.09 to 1.13; 1.15 to1.17; and finally chapter 1.20. When you look at a chapter, you will see that it always consists of four sections:

1. Definitions
2. Introduction
3. Process Steps
4. Special Topics

Initially, you should read through the first three sections and concentrate on the process steps. In this way you can form a picture of the things you have to organise in such an element. Once you have formed that picture, the fourth section provides you with more in-depth information.

Each chapter is written in such a way that you can read each one separately. Chapters 2.01 to 2.15 are about behavior and you should look at the contents of these chapters to see what you need from them. The same applies to the last 11 chapters (3.01 till 3.16) about the contextual aspects, although if you are just starting out in the profession, you can best leave these alone to start with.

The experienced project manager
Each chapter is written in such a way that you can study each one separately. You will see that the process steps that I have adopted from the ICB, form, as it were, a "mini methodology" for each competence element.

As you are experienced, you already have an overview of the profession, and you could just read the book all the way through from start to finish. An alternative, and much more efficient, way, is firstly to make a choice as to where your primary requirement lies. I would then suggest making a choice between:

- Technique
- Behavior
- Context

Dependent on this, you can again look at the contents of the relevant chapters and make your choice from these. Then read a chapter right the way through and use what is relevant for you in practice.

An IPMA certification candidate
This book contains practically every subject that could arise in the IPMA theory exams. Given the IPMA structure (central organization with autonomous country associations), it is impossible to be up-to-date with all the terms. You should, therefore, always contact your own national IPMA association. In addition you should look for a good trainer. The bureau, to which the author is associated, (Dhirata, info@dhirata.nl), also provides English language training courses for the IPMA certification, and has a large number of training modules, which enable a training to be customized to meet your specific requirements.

When studying all the chapters, you should focus your attention predominantly on the various different techniques and models covered, as it is precisely these that can be examined on.

A project management training programme developer
The author has training modules available for all chapters, and these can be acquired on a license basis, and we can also develop new ones for you if required, in line with the IPMA standard. Please do not hesitate to contact us on these aspects (info@dhirata.nl).

If you want to develop a training yourself on the basis of this book, then it is absolutely essential that you also purchase an ICB (download via www.ipma.ch), and preferably also the national version (NCB) from the country where you want the actual certification to take place. Make sure that you are also well informed about the end terms applicable there.

Introduction

As a reading guide, we advise you firstly to read the process steps (third section) in all the chapters, in order to form a picture of the complete field of the discipline. Following this, you can successively study in more depth the technique, the behavior and finally the context chapters.

The website with the book
For this book, there is a section for trainers and students in the interactive learning environment www.e-dhirata.nl. Please contact info@dhirata.nl for more information.

Project management as a discipline for life
There are a lot of people, who from their profession are involved with project management, and initially, this book has been written for them. When you think about it some more, however, every person who wants to be successful in life, needs some of the project management skills. The organization of a removal, a wedding, a holiday with a family of three children, or the funeral of a parent, requires someone who consistently and in a structured way, knows how to keep a cool head. All these characteristics are embodied in a competent project manager.

I wish you a lot of pleasure in reading and applying what is contained in this book.

John Hermarij

1. Technical Competences

1.01 Project Management Success

NOT EVERYONE THINKS THE SAME ABOUT THIS

What is success and what is failure? Ask this of ten interested parties.

Everyone one of them will have his/her own view. Success or failure is that what each particular interested party perceives it to be.

You'll just have to accept that.

1.01-1 Definitions

Project Management assessment	An assessment of the work carried out, and the performance achieved, by the project management team.
Project Management plan	The plan for carrying out a project, which describes how the project will be carried out and monitored.
Project Management success	The appreciation of the project management results by the relevant interested parties.
Project Management success and failure criteria	The criteria against which the success or failure of the project management in a project can be measured.
Project Management success and failure factors	The factors, which, to a large extent, contribute to the success or the failure of the project management of a project.
Project success	The extent to which, within the set requirements and the agreed restrictions, the actual result delivered is in accordance with the result expected, as seen from the perspective of the relevant interested parties.
Project success and failure criteria	The criteria against which the success or failure of a project can be measured.
Project success and failure factors	The factors which strongly contribute to either the success or the failure of a project.

1.01-2 INTRODUCTION

The 1996 *PMBOK Guide* version of the American Project Management Institute provides the following definitions of project management[1]: *Project management is the application of knowledge, skills, tools and techniques to ensure that the project activities fulfil, or exceed the expectations.*

The extent to which we exceed the expectations of the stakeholders, determines the extent to which they perceive the project as being successful. A later version of the *PMBOK Guide* is more precise and defines project management[2] as: *Project management is the application of knowledge, skills, tools and techniques to ensure that the project activities deliver the desired result.* 'Exceed' has been removed, because it could be a justification for giving in to customer demands for additional requirements without any limits. Project success here means that the project team delivers what has been agreed, no more and no less. As more people are involved, leading, therefore, to more expectations, you are confronted with different views on the alleged success of a project. This means that even though the project sponsor ultimately discharges the project manager and his team, it is not sufficient just to take account of him; there are more parties.

It is quite a job to ensure that all interested parties perceive the project as being a success. Even if project plans have been approved, and the packages of requirements have been unambiguously established, it does not mean that this is exactly what the interested parties expect. This process, in which you, as project manager, must constantly monitor to ensure the expectations still tally with what was agreed at the outset, is often referred to as *"managing the expectations"*.

A lot of literature talks of project success as being when the end result has been delivered on time, according to specifications, and within the agreed budget. The focus of this definition is on the product or the result of the project. A narrow definition, because you can also look at the way in which that result has been achieved. In this case, success is about the product delivered, and *also* about the process that led to it. There is only real success, when both of these are successful.

In his thesis T. van Aken[3] gives a simple definition of project success:

> *Project success is the extent to which the project result satisfies the actors involved.*

---
1 (1996), *A guide to the Project Management Body of Knowledge,* THE PROJECT MANAGEMENT INSTITUTE INC.
2 (2004), *A guide to the Project Management Body of Knowledge, PMBoK 3rd edition,* THE PROJECT MANAGEMENT INSTITUTE INC.
3 (1996), *De weg naar projectsucces,* T. v. Aken, ELSEVIER/DE TIJDSTROOM

1.01 Project Management Succes

With this definition, he covers both factors in one go. Before I go into more detail on the various actors and the elements that contribute to satisfaction, it is interesting to summarize the most important findings from his research:
- For projects which are not so tangible, structuring is required.
- For tangible projects the opposite is true, less structuring is required.
- A goal-oriented style of working has a positive influence on project success.
- The more tools that are used, the less chance there is of project success.

These conclusions have to do with the way in which a project manager manages his projects. In short, when you, as project manager, aim directly at your goal, adapt the structure to what is needed, and do not lean too much on all different kinds of tools (such as super deluxe planning tools and very heavy methodologies), then you have already laid an important foundation for project success.

Research carried out by the Standish Group[4] into successful ICT projects, names the following success factors and the extent to which these contribute to success:

- User involvement — 20%
- Senior management support — 15%
- Clear business goals — 15%
- Experienced project manager — 15%
- Small milestones — 10%
- Fixed basis of requirements — 5%
- Competent members of the project organization — 5%
- Good planning — 5%
- Involvement — 5%
- Various other factors — 5%

The first three factors alone are responsible for 50% of the project success. T. van Aken's research shows a number of other correlations:
- Small projects have a higher success rate than larger projects.
- Projects with a shorter time scale have a higher chance of success.
- Projects with a small team have a higher chance of succeeding than those with a large team.

In summary, it comes down to the fact that a smaller project has a higher chance of success, which, if you think about it for a while, is a logical conclusion.

Even though the *project manager's success*, to a large extent, depends on the success of the project, it is not the same. It is possible that the project manager does an excellent job, but a business justification can no longer be found for it. In such a case, a decision is made to stop the project and you can not talk of a project success, but on the other hand, you can say that the project management was successful.

---

[4] (1999), *Chaos : a recipe for Success*, THE STANDISH GROUP INTERNATIONAL INC.

1.01-3 Process steps[1]

1. Analyze before accepting.
2. Develop the approach.
3. Resolve conflicts and integrate.
4. Agree upon the approach.
5. Execute the management plan.
6. Collect, interpret and report.
7. Apply lessons learned

1. Analyze before accepting

The time at which a project manager becomes involved in the project differs per organization. It is best to do at an early stage, but in practice this is not always possible. This means that the project manager is often confronted with decision making, which in practice cannot be executed in the way in which the decision makers had thought.

It is now important, that, as project manager, you take the time to study this decision making and the information on the proposed project, to analyze whether or not you see the possibility of carrying out this project successfully. Also, if you take the project over from someone else, you have to "mark time" so to speak, in order to create the conditions required to make the project a success.

The following are essential conditions a project has to satisfy:
- A *decision* from line management has been made to achieve this 'job' in the form of a project.
- It must have an *overall objective* and an intended *result*.
- It intends to achieve a *pre-defined* result.
- It is *temporary*, with a defined beginning and end.
- There is *pre-defined work* to be carried out.
- There is an own *project organization*.
- There must be **resources** required, i.e. it doesn't just happen by itself.
- It is often a *unique combination* of activities, which if take separately may well have a routine character.
- There has to be a *project sponsor*, someone who is interested in the end result, and who makes the resources available.
- The project sponsor is the person, who, as representative of the regular organization or customer, ensures that the project gets the priority required to bring it to a successful conclusion.

2. Develop the approach

The project manager must now translate the broad outline of the assignment into a workable approach. This, in fact, cannot be done properly until the core of his project team has already been formed, and ideally this should be done before the actual start of the project execution. We do not live, however, in an ideal world, and often the team members are not yet available. In this case, the project manager must realize that, when his team is complete, he might have to adapt his approach. An approach, in which the people carrying out the work have had a say, has more chance of success than one which the project manager has thought out himself, whilst sitting behind his notebook.

The project approach consists of *pragmatically* applying methods, techniques and tools:
- A method[2] is a systematic, carefully thought-out way of working in order to reach a result that contributes towards a goal.
- A technique is a way in which a certain activity or piece of work is carried out.

---

[1] Although process steps are based upon the IPMA Competence Baseline we have adapted them to some extend.

[2] (2011) *Wegwijzer voor methoden bij projectmanagement, 2de druk*, VAN HAREN PUBLISHING, Zaltbommel.

- Tools are resources which help with this.

I consciously put the emphasis on the pragmatic application, keeping one of the conclusions from Van Aken's research cited previously in the back of my mind: *In projects which are not so tangible, structuring is required, and for tangible projects the opposite is true*. Complex projects require more structure than simple ones. *Over structuring* leads to a focus on the management of the project, whereas, the focus should be on the end result. On the other hand, *under structuring* leads to 'messy work', that is why I speak of *pragmatic structuring*.

3. Resolve conflicts and integrate

It is inevitable that each project has its discrepancies, and the project manager and his team must find a way to solve them. We are then talking about integration!

There may be discrepancies in the interests of the parties involved, but also between the requirements of senior management and the possibilities the project team has. Other projects may be competing to include the same people in their teams. In short, many "potential" conflicts of interest, which the project manager must try to resolve.

Many of these conflicts of interest are normal for each project, and I have already mentioned a few of them above. The project manager, therefore, has to identify them beforehand and include them in his approach. Foresight is the essence of good management!

4. Agree upon the approach

There has to be something like a document in which the requirements for the project deliverables have been defined. That alone is not enough, because apart from the requirements which have been explicitly set out, there are often expectations which have not been voiced for both the end result, and the approach. Success is only possible when, in his approach, the project manager manages to find the biggest common denominator for all the different expectations. A good analysis of these expectations, and a translation of them in the approach to the project, will, therefore, contribute to the success of the project.

The project manager, therefore, starts (in cooperation with his team if it already exists) to incorporate this information in his approach. He defines the global deliverables and the approach in the project management plan and ensures these are approved by the project sponsor, and, where possible, by the most important stakeholders. The plan functions as a mandate for him to work accordingly.

5. Execute the management plan

The project management plan contains a description of the way in which the team will achieve the desired results. It contains a description of the duration and costs, scope, project organization, quality plan, risk management, change management and suchlike.

It is the "*soldiers' manual*" for which the most important interested parties have given their approval, and it is the basis for carrying out the work involved in the project. Putting it into writing is one thing, but it is, of course, all about the execution. A project management plan is on the desks of the interested parties and not in a binder under a layer of dust; it is a working document.

We can hold an interesting discussion about the number of pages the plan should contain. Although that depends very much on the project, the plan must provide the reader with an insight into the project in a relatively short space of time. A plan containing a few dozen pages achieves that aim better than one of a hundred pages. You may well ask yourself whether the project sponsor's signature on such a bulky document, which he probably has not read, is worth anything?

The project manager has ensured that all interested parties are aware of the parts of the plan which are relevant for them, and he must check that they keep to these.

6. Collect, interpret and report

Nothing goes according to plan as originally conceived and the reality will supersede calculated estimates and the planned approach. A good project manager will have set up an information system, which allows him to see in a *timely fashion* where things might *possibly* go wrong. The words *timely fashion* and *possibly* have deliberately been put in italics, because in that way I can emphasise the project manager's proactive predictiveness, as opposed to the fire-fighting reaction when something goes wrong.

Note the difference between the following two statements of a project manager:

- We are running three months over time.
- If we don't do something, we'll end up running three months over time.

The first statement is reactive, the second pro-active.

Project managers, who only determine their progress by asking their employees for the actual figures (and overruns), haven't understood it very well. Project management is prediction; anticipating unwanted events and taking action on them at the right time.

As well as interpretation and prediction, there is also the reporting to relevant parties, and this provides us with an interesting dilemma. When do you report? Remember that you are continuously busy analyzing and clarifying uncertainties and arbitrariness in order to be able to preventively act on these. The chance of something unwanted happening does not necessarily mean that this will actually come about.

Take the example of running three months over time, if you do not take any measures. Do you have to inform the project sponsor about this now? A lot of people will answer "yes" to this, but as I have a more considered point of view, if only because of the fact that the time overrun is just as uncertain as delivering on time.

You report it when the parties involved can influence the uncertainty with their input, or when they, as a result of the uncertainty, have to take measures that are outside the scope of the project. You also report it when there is virtually no uncertainty left, and it is almost certain that the negative event will happen. In this case, the time to report it is now, immediately.

Further, you report actions you have taken to prevent the uncertain event from happening. You could report the example of the three months time overrun as follows: *In the last period we have worked overtime, and through this we have managed to achieve a deadline. If we hadn't done that, we would have overrun by three months.*

7. Apply lessons learned

It is remarkable fact that a lot of people learn little from their mistakes or from history. This is a pity, because "re-inventing the wheel" always takes a lot of time and energy. Usually people keep to a certain approach without looking for new ways of working. Change quite often means admitting failure in the past.

1.01 Project Management Succes

You cannot look at **project management success** without looking at the experience you have gained as a project manager in the past. You only learn from your experience when you try to fathom out what the reasons are for your success or failure. This is knowledge you then apply once more in the following project.

In job interviews, I always ask the candidate for his biggest failure as project manager. The manner in which he then explains how he has learnt from his mistakes, has a significant influence on my decision whether or not to hire someone.

8. Other standards and guidances

The process steps as identified by IPMA are only a suggestion. The process steps described in the *ISO 21500 Guidance*, the *'guide to the Project Management Body of Knowledge'* (the *PMBOK Guide*) from the Project Management Institute, and in the popular PRINCE2 Project Management method are much more "binding". Without discussing it in detail I shall name, as a comparison, a number of items from these standards that are related to this competence element. What will be noticeable is the high level of similarity and overlap.

Both the ISO Guidance and the 5th edition of the *PMBOK Guide* contain a subject which cannot easily be fitted into the IPMA framework. It is the subject of Integration, which, because of its importance for project management success, will be discussed here.

ISO 21500
The processes in the ISO 21500 Guidance are differentiated as follows:
- Develop project charter.
- Develop project plans.
- Direct project work.
- Control project work.
- Control changes.
- Close project phase or project.
- Collect lessons learned.

It is immediately clear that these processes are spread across the IPMA framework.

PMBOK Guide
The processes covered in the 5th edition of the *PMBOK Guide* correspond, to a large extent, with those in the ISO Guidance. PMI differentiates the following processes:
- Develop project charter.
- Develop project management plan.
- Direct and manage project execution.
- Monitor and control project work.
- Perform integrated change control.
- Close project or phase.

As with the ISO Guidance, these processes are spread over the IPMA framework.

1.01-4 SPECIAL TOPICS

1. Initiation documents

This first chapter is about project management success, by which we mean: how the different people involved in the project rate the way in which the project was managed.

A condition for achieving this is to ensure that it is clear in advance:
- What the project team will deliver.
- The way in which this will be achieved.

The decision makers will assess these aspects from the perspective of:
- The expected benefits.
- The uncertainties present in this.

In addition to all the initiating discussions and meetings prior to the execution, it is good practice to document the approach in a collection of so-called initiation documents. This is derived from the PRINCE2 methodology[3], which requires that all important decisions are tested against the so-called Project Initiation Documentation (PID). This consists of the project management plan and a documented business case.

The project management plan provides an overall impression of[4] the:
- Project life cycle.
- Customized project management processes
- The execution of the work.
- Procedures for changes and configuration management.
- The way in which project performance is made transparent.
- The manner of stakeholder management.
- The most important decision points in the project.

Obviously, in the project management plan we also find:
- Planning baseline.
- Budget.
- Scope description.

For a sizeable project it is often not possible to sum everything up in one plan, and the underlying detail plans are then added to the initiation documents, in this case providing plans for managing the:
- Scope.
- Requirements.
- Schedule.
- Budget.
- Quality.
- Process improvements.
- Personnel policy.
- Communication.
- Risks.
- Purchases.

By documenting these plans, decision makers can form a picture beforehand as to whether a lot of thought has been put in to managing the project, and whether or not they can agree with it. Furthermore, these plans are a basis for the project manager and his team for the daily management of the project.

We describe the documented business case in a different chapter.

---

3 (2009) *Managing Successful Projects with PRINCE2tm*, OGC, UK
4 (2013) *A guide to the Project Management Body of Knowledge – Fifth Edition*, PROJECT MANAGEMENT INSTITUTE INC. USA

1.01 Project Management Succes

1.02 Interested parties

EVERYONE WHO (THINKS THAT HE) HAS AN INTEREST IN THE RESULT

Every project has an influence on people.

Everyone with an interest in the project is an interested party[1].

All of these interested parties together form the environment of the project.

These are not only the project staff and the users, but also the project sponsor and the project manager himself.

The management of this environment requires political skills.

---
[1] **Interested parties** (is the ISO approved term adopted in here; 'stakeholders' is a synonym used for interested parties; 'client' and 'customers' are also used in the text to identify a subset of interested parties) are people or groups, who are interested in the performance and/or success (or failing) of the project, or who are constraint by the project.

1.02 Interested Parties

1.02-1 DEFINITIONS

Culture	Everything that characterizes an organization in all its activities and actions.
Environment of a project	The totality of the external factors and interested parties having an influence on the project.
Interested party	Person, or group, who has an interest, or wishes to have an interest, in the performance or the success of an organization.
Support	The extent to which the interested parties support a subject.

1.02-2 INTRODUCTION

Projects do not take place in isolation. However annoying it can sometimes be, you are involved in the big "*game of interests*". In the first instance, there is, of course, the project sponsor who has an interest, but don't forget yourself and your team members, and what about people who are involved in the way in which your team carries out the project? Ultimately there are also the people who make use of the project deliverables and who, therefore, also have an interest. A specific group consists of the people who believe that they have an interest.

You often hear novice project managers moaning and groaning under the weight of the project's *social, cultural and political environment*. This is what this competence-element is all about, because if you find that the environment is working against you, then in most instances it has come about because you have not recognized the different interests.

Being a good project manager is all about having the political skills to deal with the different interests. It is possible to do that with integrity, and indeed, I think that integrity is the only way to survive as a project manager without too much damage to your own feelings.

1.02-3 Process Steps

1. Prioritize interested parties.
2. Analyze their interests.
3. Communicate approach.
4. Develop a strategy.
5. Add strategy to PM plan.
6. (Include) Opportunities and threats.
7. Identify decision authority.
8. Satisfy them in each stage.
9. Deploy the strategy.
10. Communicate changes
11. Apply lessons learned

1. Prioritize interested parties

Van Aken[1] makes a distinction between the following interested parties: project sponsor, project manager, project team, internal and external suppliers, users, line management, direct and indirect interest groups and social groupings.

It is necessary to identify and analyze all interests, and when prioritizing these, you should look at:
- The *influence* that can be exercised on the execution of the project.
- The *consequences* of the project for the interested parties.

There are different techniques for this, and these will be explained later.

Many authors use the term *"Stakeholders"* to mean interested parties.

2. Analyze their interests

When the various interested parties and each of their interests has been identified, it is necessary to analyze all of them. Their (future) behaviors can be interpreted and deduced from the interests they have, which can be focussed on the result, or on the way in which the project is executed.

There are different types of interests, and Licht/Nuiver[2] differentiate the following:
- *Business interests*, which can be firmly expressed in terms of money.
- *Idealistic interests* that are connected to someone's principles.
- The *political interests*; how the results can influence someone's position.
- *Management interests*; the necessity of following a consistent course of action.
- *Loyalty interests*, which are linked to personal relationships.
- *Emotional interests*, related to an affinity with, or aversion to, certain themes.

You may add to this cultural interests especially when operating in an environment in which parties with different values systems need to cooperate.

Those involved often have more, and sometimes opposing, interests. The interests of especially the most influential people play a role in the project. If the project manager and his team have analyzed these well, they can also anticipate them.

3. Communicate

The way in which the project copes with the interested parties is dependent on the influence that someone has on the project and the interest that he has.

The way of communicating can be:
- Strong involvement.
- Consultation.
- Informing.

The greater the influence and stake someone has, the more useful it is to involve him

---

[1] (2009) *De weg naar projectsucces,* Teun van Aken, vierde druk, VAN HAREN PUBLISHING, Zaltbommel

[2] (2001) *Projecten en Beleidsontwikkeling,* Hans Licht en Hans Nuiver, VAN GORCUM, Assen

1.02 Interested Parties

in the project. I can best illustrate the way in which the actors will act during the project by using the diagram below.

Because of their interests, they will provide support and set demands on the project. The project translates this support, and the demands, into the final result to be delivered, and also the approach to be used to achieve it.

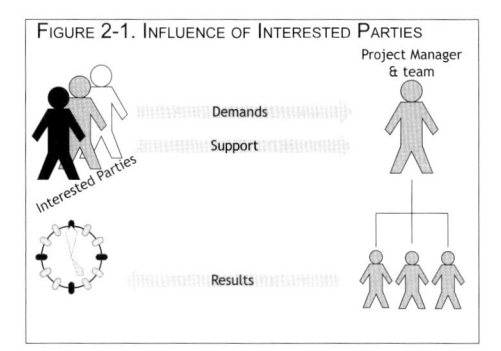

FIGURE 2-1. INFLUENCE OF INTERESTED PARTIES

The extent and speed with which the team, in the perception of the interested parties, takes account of their interests, determines whether the support is maintained, or whether the demands are increased. Communication plays an important role in this. When everyone is working hard to satisfy the interests, but does not communicate this sufficiently, it can result in the interested parties gaining the impression that their interests are not being sufficiently looked after.

In connection with this, I would like to mention the importance of *managing the expectations,* meaning: the project manager actively intervenes when the expectations of the different interested parties look like deviating from what the project team is actually going to deliver.

4. Develop a strategy

As well as the extent to which the interested parties set requirements and provide support to the project, there are also less tangible issues such as the trust the interested parties have in the project manager, the project sponsor and the operational project staff, and the way in which the project is executed.

This trust also impacts the demands and the support given. The greater the trust, the higher the level of support, and the lesser the trust, the more the demands increase. In addition, the question arises as to how much the project manager will notice any of this. Sometimes you don't notice it until you meet resistance, and then it is often too late.

It is advisable to develop a strategy to get the most important stakeholders involved in how the project will be carried out by the project manager. This builds trust, as the strategy (approach) has, after all, been agreed collectively. In this way, the project manager also gets an idea of '*which way the wind blows*' in the organization; who is really in charge, and where the 'informal' leaders are situated.

The key word in developing a strategy is always TRUST! When you have gained the trust of the parties involved, then even those who don't agree with you will also approach you with a more open attitude.

The IPMA code of conduct anticipates this situation by stating that a member of IPMA in the Netherlands[3]:

> *Acts in a way which commands trust from both the professional group and customers.*

You win trust by meeting commitments and fulfilling expectations.

---

3 (2005) *Code of conduct* IPMA NEDERLAND

5. Add strategy to PM plan

In the project management plan you establish this approach and you have this plan signed by the steering committee. Preferably, such a steering committee consists of representatives of the most important stakeholders, who have the power to decide.

In any event, the plan is a means to sort out your authority in advance. If you need the cooperation of other interested parties, who are represented on the steering committee, then you must ensure that you also involve them in determining the approach.

6. Opportunities and threats

Everyone involved looks at the project in a different way, based on his own interests. For him, the project may be an opportunity, but could also pose a threat. An opportunity when it makes his work easier, or if he can develop himself further, and a threat if, for instance, he loses his job as a result of the improvements in efficiency achieved through the project.

You get support when the interested parties feel that the project offers them an opportunity, and when the potential threats have been sufficiently addressed. Depending on their influence, you give priority to proactively working on those opportunities and threats. Whether or not you do this well becomes evident from any changes in the balance of requirements/support from the third process step (more support and fewer requirements).

7. Identify decision authority

In advance, you consider how decision-making has to be arrived at. This translates itself into defined decision points in the planning, which make clear who has to take a decision and when. It also makes clear who can, and who must, take certain decisions, and when.

Because, as project manager, you may be confronted with conflicting interests, it is necessary to consider how the team will cope with this. Together with the interested parties, you establish the way in which, for certain issues, you will initiate an escalation.

8. Satisfy them in each stage

Acceptance comes in small chunks. As the project progresses the influence of the interested parties diminishes. At the end of each stage, there is a moment of "reflection" allowing the interested parties to formally decide the extent to which there still is a justification for the project, and, therefore, if they want to carry on with it.

Staging is also a tool to help in obtaining this acceptance. At the start you ensure that it is clear at which stages acceptance is required. The satisfaction of the interested parties at the end of a stage increases the support for the final result. Satisfaction then has a positive effect on the requirements/support balance.

9. Deploy the strategy

Developing a strategy is one thing, carrying it out is something else. Once the above mentioned points have been established, and you have decided on a strategy, it is important to carry this out, or if it does not appear to be working, to adapt it to the reality.

Management of the interested parties means that you are continuously busy influencing the parties involved. This is politics. Senior project managers spend a great deal of time on this, and are always up-to-date with the current state of affairs and what this means for the interested parties personally.

10. Communicate change

It may be necessary to change this strategy during the course of the project. When this is the case, then you go through the same steps again as in the initial analysis. You have to involve the different parties again to ensure the support you already have is continues, and to possibly adapt the strategy. The steering committee then has to approve any changes to the plans, and you communicate the changes to the parties involved.

11. Apply lessons learned

During, and after, the conclusion of the project, it is good practice to record what you have learned from this project. This political skill grows over the years. However, it is possible to speed up this learning process by learning from the experience from others. The best sources can be found in history; it is here we see the impact certain actions have had on the course of history.

12. Other standards and guidances

The process steps as identified by IPMA are only a suggestion. The process steps described in the *ISO 21500 Guidance*, the *'guide to the Project Management Body of Knowledge'* (the *PMBOK Guide*) from the Project Management Institute, and in the popular PRINCE2 Project Management method are much more "binding". Without discussing it in detail I shall name, as a comparison, a number of items from these standards that are related to this competence element. What will be noticeable is the high level of similarity and overlap.

ISO 21500

The Guidance deals with this topic in the subject group Stakeholder and differentiates between the following two processes:
- Identify stakeholders.
- Manage stakeholders.

PMBOK Guide

The 5th edition of the *PMBOK Guide* has somewhat more processes than the ISO Guidance:
- Identify stakeholders.
- Plan stakeholder management.
- Manage stakeholder engagement.
- Control Stakeholder management.

PRINCE2

PRINCE2 does not contain a separate topic on stakeholders. That does not mean the method does not give any consideration to it, but it is primarily covered in the topic of Organization. The following steps are named here:
- Identify stakeholders.
- Produce and analyze stakeholder profiles.
- Define stakeholder strategy.
- Plan their involvement.
- Involve the stakeholders.
- Measure the effectiveness.

1.02-4 SPECIAL TOPICS

1. The project environment

Projects are not carried out in isolation, and normally all the external factors that could influence a project are designated as being part of the project environment. These external factors consist of the following elements:
- Political
- Economic
- Sociological
- Technical
- Legal
- Environmental

These elements are sometimes abbreviated to the acronym PESTLE[4] (**P**olitical, **E**conomic, **S**ociological, **T**echnical, **L**egal and **E**nvironmental). I shall briefly describe each of these categories in turn.

Political

In the first instance, you are involved with political decision-making in a country where the project is being carried out. The way in which the power is divided can have a big influence on public projects. For large projects with a lot at stake, it is important that the project organization maintains good ties with the government, and lobbying is a part of this.

Due to the different ways in which things in different countries come into effect, when you are involved with projects that extend across country boundaries, the project organization can find itself caught between two stools. What people in one country find as being totally normal, people in another country can consider as being unacceptable or impermissible. There is really no good solution to this, and if, as project manager, you are confronted with such a situation, you have to ensure that you understand the different expectations, so that you can make a choice or decision yourself.

Another challenge is the political (in)stability in a country where you carry out a particular project. Such risks are difficult to assess in advance, but that does not remove the need to take stock of them and monitor them during the project.

Economic

Decisions are also dependent on the economic circumstances in which the organization involved in the project find themselves. When suppliers or sub-contractors get into financial difficulties during a recession, this can have immediate consequences for your project. As project manager, you can do little about this, and if one of your suppliers goes bankrupt, it has a direct impact on your project. What you can do, however, is to keep an eye on developments in the situation.

The more suppliers you have, the greater the risk. On the other hand, a worsening economy also offers opportunities, because of the associated pressure on prices. It may then be possible to acquire qualified staff, or purchase materials, for a lower price, which will deliver a cost saving. As project manager, this is something you must always try to do, because, when your own organization or that of the customer hits hard times, you can anticipate that enforced savings will have to be made, and you can continue trying to assess what risks the project runs.

Sociological

This is about the way in which people interact with each other; the prevailing morals and beliefs. Is it a collective, or rather an individualistic oriented society? In one country it is fully acceptable to voice your disagreement to a senior manager, whereas

---
[4] (2006) *APM Body of Knowledge 5th Edition*, ASSOCIATION FOR PROJECT MANAGEMENT, UK

in another country it is totally unacceptable. Primarily, this happens in projects where you cross cultural boundaries, and it can be stated that when you become involved with this, you have to really study how a particular environment works. Not that this necessarily has to involve an international project, as even within one country you can find many different cultures you need to take account of. The maxim is always: *wait with your judgement, and realize that you are the guest.*

Technical
Technology can seriously influence the progress of the project i.e. new technology that has many teething problems, or a project for which no technology has been developed, or one where the technology is obsolete or outdated. As an experienced project manager, you are often divorced from the technology, and you have to ensure you become informed about it by experts.

Legal
Legislation can impose all sorts of constraints related to what is, and what is not, permitted. Not infrequently, you need permits or licenses to build something or to allow people to work overtime, matters which you would rather not be bothered by. This does not alter the fact, however, that you are legally obliged to handle these matters, and so you have to include them in the project.

Environment
As well as environmental law that applies in a country, and which I shall cover later, with respect to the environment there is also something called moral responsibility. You have to realize what it feels like, when, as project manager, you are responsible for pollution or contamination, which will affect future generations for years to come.

2. Interested parties

The project sponsor
He represents the 'business interests' in the project. Preferably, this is a line manager with sufficient hierarchical power in the organization. He is the person, who, in consultation with the project manager, translates the strategic choices i.e. the project objective, into the project result.

His main interest is:
- That the project provides value for money.
- A cost-conscious approach in relation to a timely delivery.
- A balance between the interests of the organization, suppliers and users.

As well as these obvious interests, there are always personal interests that play a role; something that is the case for all the parties involved.

The project manager
Obviously, the project manager is also one of the stakeholders in the project. That is for the most part a personal interest; the successful conclusion of the project reflects on his professional recognition and further career.

The same applies to failure which may be considered as a personal failure an in some cultures even loss of face.

The project management team
The project management team consists of the project manager, various experts who support him, and the sub-project managers of the different sub-projects which are included in the project. The team carries out the daily operational management of the project.

1.02 Interested Parties

Within such a team, the interests may differ. Apart from all personal interests:
- The project manager will look for an optimum balance between the progress, cost and quality of the result, whereas…
- The experts will emphasize the importance of a qualitative solution, and …
- The sub-project managers will, above all, protect the (sub-optimum) importance of their sub-project.

Whereas the project sponsor weighs up the interests between the project and the organization, the project manager considers the different interests between the team members.

The internal and external suppliers
These are the operational project staff, who carry out the work that is coordinated by the sub-project managers from the project team. There is a distinction to be made between internal and external suppliers.

In principle the internal line manager's interest should be in line with that of the project, as both are, in fact, working for the same organization. Experience, however, tells a different story, because the focus of the project manager is only on the project, whereas the internal line manager has to ensure an optimum staffing for his unit. Despite all the developments in the area of priorities, programme management and portfolio management, this remains a problem which is difficult to solve.

The difference between project interest and that of an external supplier can be large.

In 1513 Machiavelli[5] already wrote about mercenaries: *"When someone bases his power on mercenaries, he will never be able to feel strong and safe"*. And further: *"They want to be your soldier as long as you do not go to war, but as soon as war breaks out, they make ready to flee and make a run for it"*.

External suppliers have a different interest in a project than the project manager. For them it is all about keeping the margin of profit as high as possible, or to force a certain solution through, etc., whereas, the project manager is looking for a solution with the best price/performance ratio.

The users
These are the people who will be using the final project result. Their interest is the quality of the project result. It is possible to divide up user groups further as follows:
- The operational users, who work with the system.
- The functional users, who work with the output of the system.
- The supporting users, who are responsible for maintenance and management.

If the financing does not come from within the user department, then this group will have a one-sided interest. Quality costs money, but the end user often doesn't feel that in his wallet. This results in him specifying a lot of new requirements when the project releases its deliverables. This in turn conflicts with the interest of the project manager (which is to deliver on time, within budget and according to the expected quality).

The line managers
The line managers allocate resources. We already met them when we discussed the internal suppliers. The interest line managers have in making resources available is optimum staffing, and in line with that, an optimum cost coverage. If projects are carried out in a matrix organization, there is a cer-

---
5 (1513) *Il Principe*, Machiavelli

1.02 Interested Parties

tain amount of tension between the interests of the project manager and those of the line manager. The interests of the line manager are long term; the continuation of the organization. The interests of the project manager are short term; meeting the deadlines! The project staff are in between these.

Not necessary but important
The following groups, as opposed to the previous groups, are not directly necessary for the achieving the project result. This does not make them any less important, because when they feel involved with a project, they can have a big influence on it.

DIRECT INTEREST GROUPS
These are people or groups of people who are involved in the project result in another way as mentioned before. Examples are: local village councils, a ministry, the quality department and in some countries the works council and unions.

INDIRECT INTEREST GROUPS
People who are not involved in the execution of the project, but are confronted with the consequences of it. For example the people living around a building project.

With these groups we are confronted with the local initiatives of interested parties, they may form a temporary action committee.

SOCIAL MOVEMENTS
These groups (like Greenpeace) looks similar to the previous one, but are further removed from the project result. They are organization with societal objectives, which they feel that project violates.

The difference with the indirect interest groups is that the social groups have more backing, and can mobilise more resources to slow a project down, or even prevent it from happening.

3. Analysis of Interested parties

This analysis goes hand in hand with the identification. With the help of various matrices that will be covered shortly, an insight is provided into the influence, effort, interest, agreements and support of the different interested parties.

Matrices are useful tools for analyzing the different people involved in the project. The essence of these instruments is that you always weigh-up two dimensions against each other, for example:
- Influence versus interest.
- Influence versus involvement.
- Dedication versus importance.
- Agreement versus trust.

As well as these matrices we also have:
- The environment chart

The influence matrix
With the help of this matrix, you make an overview of the different interested parties on the project, and the influence they have on the different issues. We can find an example of this matrix in Milosevic[6], which I've adapted a little.

---

6 (2003) *Project Management Toolbox,* Dragan Z. Milosevic, JOHN WILEY & SONS, Hoboken – New Jersey.

1.02 Interested Parties

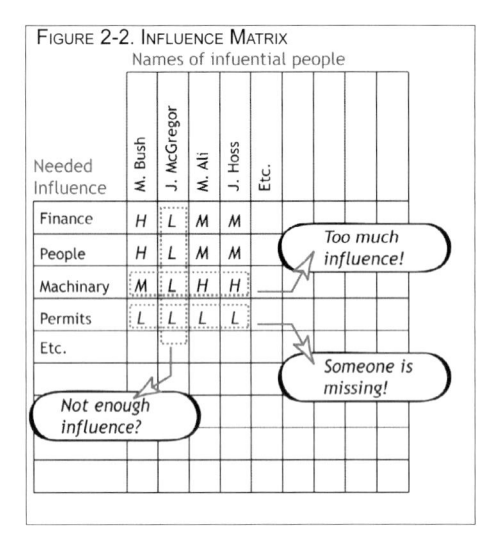

FIGURE 2-2. INFLUENCE MATRIX

(Names of influential people: M. Bush, J. McGregor, M. Ali, J. Hoss, Etc.)

Needed Influence	M. Bush	J. McGregor	M. Ali	J. Hoss	Etc.
Finance	H	L	M	M	
People	H	L	M	M	
Machinary	M	L	H	H	
Permits	L	L	L	L	
Etc.					

- Too much influence!
- Someone is missing!
- Not enough influence?

For each interested party, you fill in a line and determine the influence (H, M, L) this person has on: the resources, the requirements, the project processes and the assessment and reward of the various performances. It is a laborious process, but it helps you to think of all the factors.

After completion, you carry out a vertical and horizontal analysis of matrix.

VERTICAL ANALYSIS

This analysis is aimed at determining how great the total influence of a person is. A lot of **H's** on a column indicate this. The more influence, the more important the person is for the project.

HORIZONTAL ANALYSIS

This analysis determines where the potential risks are in the decision making on certain project parameters.

A row containing many **H's** may be an indication that you will have to deal with a laborious decision making process, as there are a lot of people who have an influence on that parameter. A row containing mainly **L's** on the other hand, is an indication that in the project organization you potentially have too little decision making power with respect to the subject in question.

Stake Matrix

This 3x3 matrix compares the influence of the interested parties with the stake they have in that project.

When there is a lot at stake for someone with a lot of influence, then you deal with that in a different way to when there is little at stake for an unimportant interested party. Top left in the matrix you involve, and bottom right you inform.

This matrix is useful in the development of the communications plan.

Effort matrix

This matrix compares three dimensions with each other:
- How important the person is for the success of the project.
- The effort this person shows.

The third dimension, which can be seen from the size of the circles, is:
- The influence that someone has.

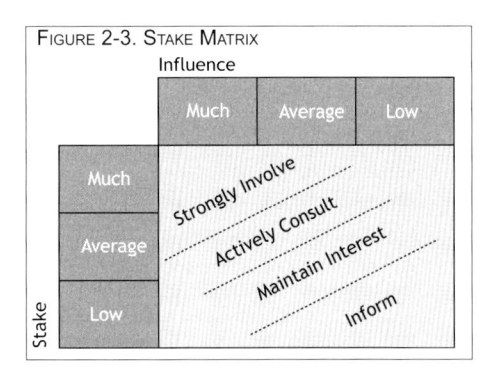

FIGURE 2-3. STAKE MATRIX

Stake \ Influence	Much	Average	Low
Much	Strongly Involve		
Average		Actively Consult	Maintain Interest
Low			Inform

The matrix is a tool for determining the extent to which interested parties should be involved, more actively or less actively, with the project.

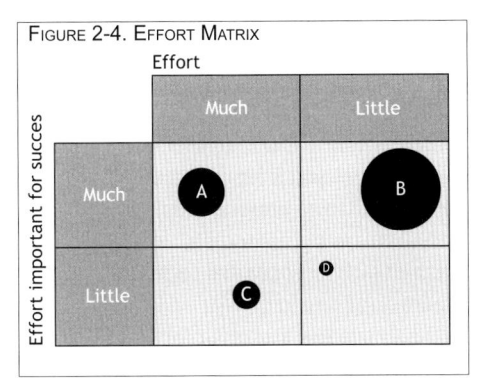

FIGURE 2-4. EFFORT MATRIX

The environment chart
Using this chart, you can map out the various relationships between the interested parties.

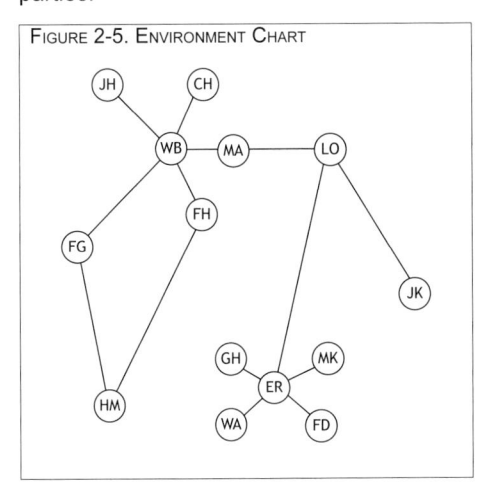

FIGURE 2-5. ENVIRONMENT CHART

It forms a useful addition to the previous matrix, and you use it to determine which interested parties you are going to use in order to exert influence for the benefit of the project.

Trust versus agreement matrix
This matrix has been developed by Peter Block[7] and is applicable when analyzing the various parties you need to have in order to get "your own way" in a particular situation.

There are two dimensions that you use in this analysis:
- The extent of the **trust** that the different parties have in you as a person.
- The extent to which the different parties **agree** with you.

There are five groups that exist: allies, opponents, adversaries, bedfellows and fence sitters. Each group requires its own approach, the essence of which is that you negotiate on the basis of both trust and agreement.

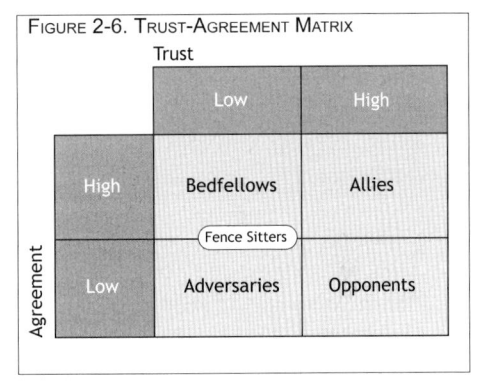

FIGURE 2-6. TRUST-AGREEMENT MATRIX

Allies:
- Confirm the agreement that there is.
- Emphasis what you think of the relationship.
- Be open about the doubts that you have.
- Ask for advice and support.

Opponents:
- Emphasise the trust that exists in both directions.
- State clearly what you want to achieve.

---
[7] (1987) *The Empowered Manager*, P.Block, JOSEY-BASS, San Francisco

Adversaries:
- State clearly what you want to achieve.
- Summarize their point of view (in so far as you understand it) in a neutral manner.
- Recognize your own role in the 'difficult' relationship.
- Afterwards, ensure that they are informed of your plans but do not specify any requirements.

Bedfellows:
- Confirm the agreement that there is.
- State the concerns you have over the relationship.
- Be clear about what you expect from the cooperation.
- Ask what they expect from the cooperation.
- Try to get agreement on the way in which, between you, you will cooperate.

Fence sitters:
- State clearly what you want to achieve.
- Ask for their point of view.
- Use some slight pressure to enable them to take a point of view.
- Ask them to think about their position.
- Ask them what is needed to gain their support.

4. Sensitivity

Sensitivity has to do with your capacity to project yourself into someone else's feelings. There are different forms of sensitivity:
- *Empathy*, the capacity to project yourself into someone else's feelings.
- *Social Sensitivity,* capacity to empathise with what is, and what is not possible, within a group.
- *Political Sensitivity,* judging how the formal and informal decision making works within an organization.

EMPATHY
Empathy is a road that leads to understanding the inner world of another person. During a discussion you let your own experience resonate with that of the other person. In this way, you feel and understand what the other person feels and understands.

You can further apply this capacity to empathize with others to groups and organization, thus creating the two other forms of sensitivity.

SOCIAL SENSITIVITY
You need this in order to assess which interventions, will, and which will not, work within a group. Instead of "*being like a bull in a china shop*", you take account of the existing values and standards that exist within a group.

POLITICAL SENSITIVITY
Here, you estimate what the chance is of getting people to agree with your point of view. There is a difference between being right and getting agreement to you being right. This sensitivity has to do with the power structures within an organization and knowing how to make beneficial use of this knowledge.

- Look for a common solution (in so far as this is possible).

1.03 Requirements and objectives

AN APPROACH LEADING TO A RESULT WHICH IS USEFUL TO USE

A project manager is responsible for delivering the project results. These results will help the line organization to achieve the objectives defined in their strategy.

We have to choose the right approach so that the results, and the way in which they are achieved, contributes to the strategic objectives of the organization.

During the execution, one of the central questions is: Are we delivering the results that the organization is expecting?

1.03 Requirements and objectives

1.03-1 Definitions

Acceptance criteria	A defined value, on the basis of which can be determined whether or not a requirement has been fulfilled.
Business case	The justification of the investment decision.
Constraint	Restriction applied to the project objectives.
Fit for use/purpose	The product responds to customer needs, in addition, quality includes freedom from failures, plus good customer service if failures do occur.
Project approach	The way in which the project deliverables will be realized.
Project goal	The effect that the project sponsor wants to achieve through the project deliverables.
Project goal (in a narrow sense)	Achieving the project deliverables in accordance with in the defined requirements and constraints.
Project objectives	Criteria with respect to the execution of the project, against which project management success can be measured
(Project) Requirement	Explicit requirement (compulsory or optional) (either self-evident or not) regarding the to-be-delivered results.

1.03 Requirements and objectives

Project review	An review of the feasibility and desirability of the project, taking due consideration of the business case.

1.03 Requirements and objectives

1.03-2 INTRODUCTION

In one way or another, every project begins with a need, which can be a shortcoming, a necessity, a wish, a statutory provision or just an arbitrary idea that arises in a manager's brain. Sometimes these are vague, and sometimes clearly defined. In order to achieve the wish, there is a great temptation to begin immediately, or as I once heard a project sponsor say in the first week of the project: "Where are the programmers?" This is understandable, but unfortunately not how things work, as we have realized through trial and error. Shortcomings, necessities, wishes, laws, and ideas change, and the hunter who shoots at the cornered hare, sees the hare move and suddenly change into a deer, a lion or an elephant, leading him initially to think about what is happening. Running around over the project terrain like a blind chicken does not lead to the desired success.

We have to consider the translation of a customer's vague wishes into defined requirements, and translate these into even better defined objectives, and so well defined that following the delivery, we can say: *This is exactly what we wanted to have, nothing more and nothing less.*

We translate the needs into requirements, which have everything to do with the environment in which the organization investing finds itself i.e. the opportunities and threats it is faced with. This project delivers a solution, for a certain price, within a certain time and then preferably also with an eye to the risks surrounding the project. All of these taken together we call the project objectives.

So Project Management is proactive working, therefore, and that is another aspect that belongs here; the project manager considers beforehand how he is going to achieve the objectives and indeed, how he is going to ensure that what his team delivers, corresponds to the original requirements. As the human mind does not excel in accuracy, it is a good habit to specify and record all of this.

With each solution, however, we again introduce a new challenge, in this case with the recording of the requirements and objectives. The pitfall involved is related to the translation of needs into requirements and the further translation of the requirements into objectives, for example with respect to the quality to be delivered. After all, with each translation round, we distance ourselves further from the original need, and it is questionable whether or not we deliver according to specification and also still then satisfy the original need. There have been whole books written on this subject, but in my opinion not satisfactorily, as we are still searching, especially for the less tangible projects such as an organizational change. I do not believe this is a reason, however, why we should not do it, as presently we do not have anything better, and so we make the best use of the instruments we have.

1.03-3 PROCESS STEPS

1. Document requirements.
2. Justify the project
3. Document project goals.
4. Manage progress.
5. Validate project requirements.
6. Assess compliance.
7. Set up a review process.
8. Apply lessons learned

1. Document requirements

The programme of requirements is a document describing the criteria to which the project result has to comply. It is not sufficient just to specify what the customer wants.

Not all stated requirements are absolutely necessary, though some are; and besides, there may be additional wishes and even implicit expectations. It is, therefore, advisable to make sure all expectations are made explicit as far as possible. After that, one should apply some sort of prioritization (e.g. must-haves, should-haves, would-haves and nice-to-haves).

When drawing up a programme of requirements, it is important to clearly understand the strategic objectives of the organization. The strategic plan of the organization, division or unit can then be used as a control to ensure that what is delivered is in line with the organization's objectives.

We speak of constraints when we are talking about specific requirements set by the interested parties (the environment) for either the project result or the execution. Rules and regulations come into play here, and examples of these are: compliance with certain standards or environmental legislation; the project results having to be available before a certain date, or budget limits which must not be exceeded.

In order to draw up a good programme of requirements, it is important to know which parties have a stake and an influence on the project. These stakeholders of course, you have to involve in this process. The stakeholder analysis is an important prerequisite for drawing up the list of requirements. Those with much power and much at-stake are more involved that those with little power and/or less stakes.

2. Justify the project

Before the project sponsor draws up a programme of requirements, there has to be a reason for the project. That reason is the basis for the **goal** (note that this is different from the project objectives).

You now have to differentiate between:

- The GOAL IN THE BROAD SENSE: this is what the project sponsor (or the organization receiving the result) wants to achieve with the help of the project result.
- The PROJECT GOAL IN THE NARROW SENSE: this is what the project team delivers under the responsibility of the project manager. These are the requirements mentioned earlier, translated into a specific end result.

EXAMPLE 3-1 GOAL IN NARROW AND IN BROAD SENSE

The team is responsible for a promotion campaign for a new collection of scented fabric softener on the first day of the Dubai Shopping Festival. This is the project goal in the narrow sense of the word. Before noon, they have to hand out about 300,000 samples at 75 shopping centres and other locations in the city. This is also a project goal in the "narrow sense" of the word. The overall objective of the fabric softener manufacturer is to achieve a 10% turnover increase. So this is the project goal in the broad sense.

1.03 Requirements and objectives

- The PROJECT OBJECTIVES: criteria with respect to the execution of the project, against which project management success can be measured.

We combine these three into what is now popularly called the "business case". In this, we underpin the effort (documented in the objectives), which is necessary to achieve the results, the benefits (documented in the goal in the broad sense) the organization will achieve from it, and the extent to which the benefits stack up against the costs.

> EXAMPLE 3-2 WHATEVER IT TAKES
> The project sponsor told the project manager: "Whatever it takes, it has to work." The project manager set to work with total dedication, duration was now the most important controlling variable.
> Half a year after the project sponsor took him of the project, the project manager still wonders why the project sponsor had been so angry about the cost of the project.

With respect to the responsibilities, there is a separation of the roles; the project manager is responsible for delivering the project result within the defined objectives, and in his turn, the project sponsor is responsible for using the result in such a way in his organization that it achieves the goal of the project.

3. Document project goals

Traditionally the following objectives were always documented in a project plan:
- The scope of the project.
- The duration.
- The costs.

These three together formed the so-called "*triple constraint*", a three-sided constraint we impose on the project team. Nowadays this concept has been extended with: quality, risk, and customer satisfaction.

The separate elements always have an influence on one another: the scope has an influence on the costs, reducing the duration means higher costs for overtime, etc.

At the start of the project the project sponsor considers which of the three is the most important. Based on this consideration, the objectives are set. The consideration selected now becomes indicative for the execution of the project. Of course, when for instance time is the most important indicator, this does not mean that you do not have to monitor the costs anymore.

The result of this consideration, and the way in which the team is going to realize this, is documented in the project plan and in any underlying detailed plans. When the parties involved have given their approval, you, as the project manager, cannot make any more changes to these objectives, without submitting a formal change request.

4. Manage progress

Progress is delivering results according to the requirements on time for the agreed costs. The project objectives provide the starting point for making the progress measurable. As the project manager, you ensure that during the execution, the progress is kept to, as agreed at the start of the project.

This topic, therefore, involves reporting on the performance the project delivers against the agreed requirements. By new insights as the project advances, it can be that certain requirements are no longer needed (the foundation of the project changes), or are no longer feasible. This means a change in the project, which has to be implemented in a *structured* way, and which always requires the approval of the most important stakeholders (represented in a steering committee).

The communication to the stakeholders has to be well-timed, because they must have the opportunity to make a well-considered decision.

5. Validate requirements
Acceptance comes in small steps, and, during the transition from one stage to the next, and possibly also at other points in time, the stakeholders are always given the opportunity to check whether or not the (interim) results still conform to the defined requirements and their expectations.

The way in which you plan in these acceptance points depends on what the project team is delivering. As you can imagine, there are less control points required when, from the outset of the project, the required end result has been clear, or when there is a lot of support. In other cases, it may be advisable to insert several "smaller" control points.

6. Assess compliance
The requirements have been translated into the project plan and the specifications, and the project team commences its work. This process step is discussed in detail in "Control and Reports". It is, however, essential that you plan points in advance when the most important stakeholders are able to assess to what extent the project performance is in line with the expectations.

We find these so-called pre-defined decision points as a minimum at the transition from one stage to another, but it is also very possible to have very specific reviews carried out in between.

7. Set up a review process
For this, a review process is needed in which the team subjects the project and the project deliverables to a critical test. If necessary, an external party can do this. The project manager describes this process in advance, and he makes sure that it is adhered to.

In order to design the review process, he uses a series of Deming cycles, namely:
- *Plan* what you want to achieve.
- *Do* what you planned.
- *Check* against plan.
- *Act* on your findings.

For all critical requirements, a cycle has to be implemented, ensuring that we do deliver what we have to deliver.

8. Apply lessons learned
There are organizations that suffer from the "changes syndrome". At the start of the project, little time is used to think about what is needed; the consensus is "let's get going". That works for a while until the first deliveries take place. The requirements of the parties involved evolve or grow with the deliveries, and when this happens, an important learning experience presents itself with regard to this competence element.

You can only start a project when you know what you want! It is better to take your time to document the requirements well, as opposed to just starting and seeing where it leads you. Many projects fail because the project sponsors, customers, and users, constantly change their requirements, and you then end up with an uncontrollable whole. An often used excuse is that the "market is asking for it". This remains to be seen, as there are two options: it really is true, or they just don't know what they want.

In both cases you have to make small steps allowing for the possibility of re-direction. With respect to this subject, learning to cope with changed requirements and translating these in a structured manner into the project execution, can give an organization an important competitive advantage.

1.03-4 SPECIAL TOPICS

1. Refining versus changing

There is a difference between refining and changing the requirements.

At the start of the project, stakeholders often cannot define their requirements in as much detail as during the course of the project, and so the extent of the detail will increase as the project progresses. The danger lying in wait is: when is something a refinement, and when is it a change?

EXAMPLE 3-3 REFINING THE REQUIREMENTS

Half a year before the actual move, the requirement states that there have to be at least 250 workplaces in the new office.

After a month of searching, an office has been found that can house the required number of people. The unit heads now discuss how they want to organise this.

---

2. The Business Case

The business case provides the connection with the organization, and is one of the driving forces behind the project control. Another name by which the business case is known, is the 'cost/benefit analysis'.

The business case is a tool for controlling the decision-making around projects. It contains many more uncertainties than a project plan, which contains a clear definition of the result, time and money. The business case looks further than the project horizon and considers the whole life cycle of the project result to be delivered.

At the outset, this tool ensures that the 'crystal ball gazing' is carried out in a responsible way, and is more than just using intuition.

The business case considers:
- The reason for, and the purpose of, the project.
- The assumptions that have been made.
- The method for setting up the business case.
- The expected benefits, and the reasoning behind them.
- The extent of sensitivity for external change that the outcomes will have.
- The risks of the proposed undertaking.

The ultimate responsibility lies with either the project sponsor or a steering committee consisting of members of the senior management, who are often supported by financial specialists. It is preferable to ensure that the costs and benefits are, as far as possible, expressed in financial terms. This is not always possible, but the aim should always be to make this as specific as possible.

The business case is recorded in a document, which, after approval, forms the justification for the project, and the foundation for all other planning activities. During the planning, a number of iterations are needed to also 'finish off' or complete the business case.

At all major stage transition points during the execution of the project, a review is carried out to determine whether or not the project performance provides grounds for amending this foundation. Furthermore, the project sponsor looks at changes in the environment of the project, which might have an impact (positive or negative) on the business case. In an ideal situation, this would be carried out from the portfolio management function.

One of the project methods that strongly emphasizes the use of the business case is

1.03 Requirements and objectives

PRINCE2[1], and this method even goes as far as saying that this is a part of the definition of a project:

A project is a temporary organization that is created for the purpose of delivering one or more business products according to an agreed Business Case.

Although at first sight this appears to be a bit strange, when you look at it from a control viewpoint it is not at all bad. A project is about delivering something that the customer can use. That is, in fact, what you write down in the business case, and is, therefore, something you must continuously keep sight of. This definition necessitates that the project manager also pays more attention than usual to the business case for the project.

The business case is two things, on the one hand it is the reason why we carry out the project, and on the other hand it is a (decision) document in which we record this. This leads to the question as to which subjects have to be considered in the business case?

I would say (adapted from PRINCE2):
- A summary for the decision makers.
- A description of the reasons for the project.
- The different alternatives that have been studied.
- The benefits and disadvantages of the different alternatives.
- A summary of the project plan (time, money and quality).
- The most important risks.
- A qualitative and quantitative assessment of the investment.

These could be the different paragraphs of this document, which is leading for all important decisions both at project commencement and during the project. I have to make one comment that, of course, there must be something for the project sponsor to choose. A decision document with only one option is not sufficient, as that is a choice to either do something or not do it, without any alternative options.

As a minimum, therefore, we describe the zero option, describing what the benefits and disadvantages are if we do not carry out the project at all, and giving us something to assess the other option(s) against. It is now a question of how many options you include, and this will be different for each project, as it is strongly dependent on the expectations of the various people involved. The stakeholder analysis already produced, should provide an insight into the support there is for a particular solution. Every solution has its own scenario, and it is good practice to describe the main one.

We then get the following options:
- The zero option.
- One or more in-between options.
- The option with the most support.

The eventual choice is one that must be made by senior management, often represented by the project sponsor. Sometimes there are a number of project sponsors, and either agreement between them must be sought, or simply what the person with the most power wants.

Who is responsible
Senior management is responsible for the business case, and this is always a manager in a line organization, because the business case extends over the project boundaries and once the project is completed there is no longer a project manager to oversee,

---
1 (2009) *Managing Successful Projects with PRINCE2™,* TSO, United Kingdom

1.03 Requirements and objectives

monitor and maintain everything. I always say that "a project manager does not have to make any important decisions" and that certainly applies to the business case.

This does not alter the fact that we regularly come across project managers, who produce a business case. In this way they support senior management on the technical side of such a document, but the final responsibility belongs in the line organization. Involving the project manager in this process results in him becoming more involved in the reasons behind the project, enabling him to experience the importance and urgency of the project. This requires the project manager to have some knowledge of the environment in which the project will take place.

Assessment of the benefits

Much of the professionalization in projects was always aimed at the project manager and his team, and then strongly towards having a good project definition and delivering on schedule, within budget and according to the specifications. With the addition of the business case and a shift towards a "fitness-for-use" quality concept, the realization that the success of a project will be partly determined by what happens after the project has permeated through to the project manager's job responsibilities.

A new area of expertise has arisen, going under the name of Benefits Realization Management[2], and a part of this is formed by monitoring the effectiveness of the product (or result) delivered by the project, and in how far this project also delivers the projected benefits. PRINCE2 even prescribes that the project manager produces a plan early on in the project defining how these benefits should be assessed both during and after the project.

The following subjects are then addressed:
- The general vision.
- The dependencies between the various benefits.
- The method of measuring and reporting.
- How the benefits correspond to the strategy of the organization.
- The time schedule.
- The responsibilities.
- The assumptions within the total business case.

There is something more to be said about this last point. At the commencement of a project, we often have an optimistic picture of the future, because we underestimate the costs and overestimate the benefits. Although, as far as possible, we try to make things measurable and preferably also financial, we must realize that everything is based on assumptions. My supposition now is that as well as managing the achievement of the benefits, it is furthermore important that we continuously track and monitor the assumptions made.

McGrath and MacMillan[3] have developed discovery driven planning, whereby line management continuously keeps track of whether or not the assumptions included in the original decision are still applicable to the project. When a change in these occurs, it can mean that a decision is made to stop after all, or, where possible, correct accordingly.

Such an approach allows the organization to keep the plan and reality in line with each other, also following project completion.

---

2 (2010) *Benefits Realization Management,* Gerald Bradley, GOWER PUBLISHING LTD, SURREY ENGLAND

3 (2009) *Discovery Driven Growth*, Rita Gunter McGrath en IAN C MacMillan, HARVARD BUSINESS PRESS, BOSTON US

1.03 Requirements and objectives

Please note that this no longer has much in common with project management in its original sense.

Business justification for commercial project management

When a supplier takes on a project, you will become involved in two (possibly conflicting) business cases; one from the customer, and one from the supplier. As the supplier's project manager, you may be faced with a dilemma; do you side with the customer (from your professional standpoint, you might be inclined to do this), or do you side with the supplier (your employer)? Such dilemmas are not easy to handle, and demand a significant level of seniority to resolve them.

3. The GAP principle

People are often far too positive about the benefits of a project, which, of course, makes the review less precise.

This can, however, be overcome by evaluating the foundation based on three scenario's:
- Most positive scenario (Good).
- Most probable scenario (Average).
- Most pessimistic scenario (Poor).

This approach ensures that the person or group making the decision obtains a good insight into the feasibility of the project. The difference between positive and pessimistic says something about the uncertainty of the benefits to be expected. This so-called GAP scenario analysis (good-average-poor) then provides a good insight in the extent to which the estimations are realistic.

4. Value Management

Value Management is a structured approach in which the project team, in consultation with the key stakeholders, focuses on the value of the project deliverables.

Everyone has an idea of the concept of value; it is more than money. A kilo of gold costs more than a liter of water, but the value changes when you're floating around for a few days on a life raft i.e. value depends on the situation you are in. Furthermore, it is about what you have to spend. Imagine, you are on the raft with someone who has two bottles of water and is prepared to sell you one bottle for € 10,000; unfortunate for you, as you do not have that money. The bottle of water has no value for you. If you were to have exactly the amount of money being asked for, then the bottle has great value. Should you have € 1,000,000 in your pocket, then the value of the bottle is less, because you can afford to buy it quite easily.

The concept of value is well expressed in the diagram, whereby the project team looks for the optimum balance between the quality delivered compared to the quality expected, and the resources available compared to the resources required.

EXAMPLE 3-4 SELECTING VALUABLE FUNCTIONS

Suppose that the result to be delivered consists of the following functions 1 till 3. This is also the order of importance that the customer attaches to the various functions. After some investigation, there appear to be two possible solutions:

Function	Alternative 1	Alternative 2
1	100,000	75,000
2	50,000	90,000
3	25,000	10,000

The cost of alternative 2 for function 2 is relatively too expensive, it is clear that, based on the importance that the customer attaches to the different functions, the preference must be for alternative 1.

1.03 Requirements and objectives

Analogous to the story of the persons on the raft, we can now state that:

Value	Quality coefficient	Resources coefficient
Excellent	> 1	= 1
Good	> 1	> 1
	= 1	= 1
Poor	< 1	≥ 1
None	≤ 1	< 1

In order to find the right balance, the team concentrates on the functions required to meet the needs of the parties involved. This already happens fairly early in the project during that part of the development stage where we determine the requirements for the project. What is special about this approach is that the team does not yet look at the technical solutions or the actual project deliverables, but focuses on which functions these deliverables will soon have to fulfil.

The functions are described by a *verb* and a '*measurable*' noun. For example:
- Houses a family
- Carries a weight
- Relocates a weight
- Archives personnel files

If the focus had been on the technical solutions, then we would have talked of:
- A house
- A chair
- A lorry
- A filing cabinet

In value management, we consciously delay this until later. Firstly we focus on the functions the customer needs, and, after that, we search for the technical solutions. If you concentrate directly on the solutions from

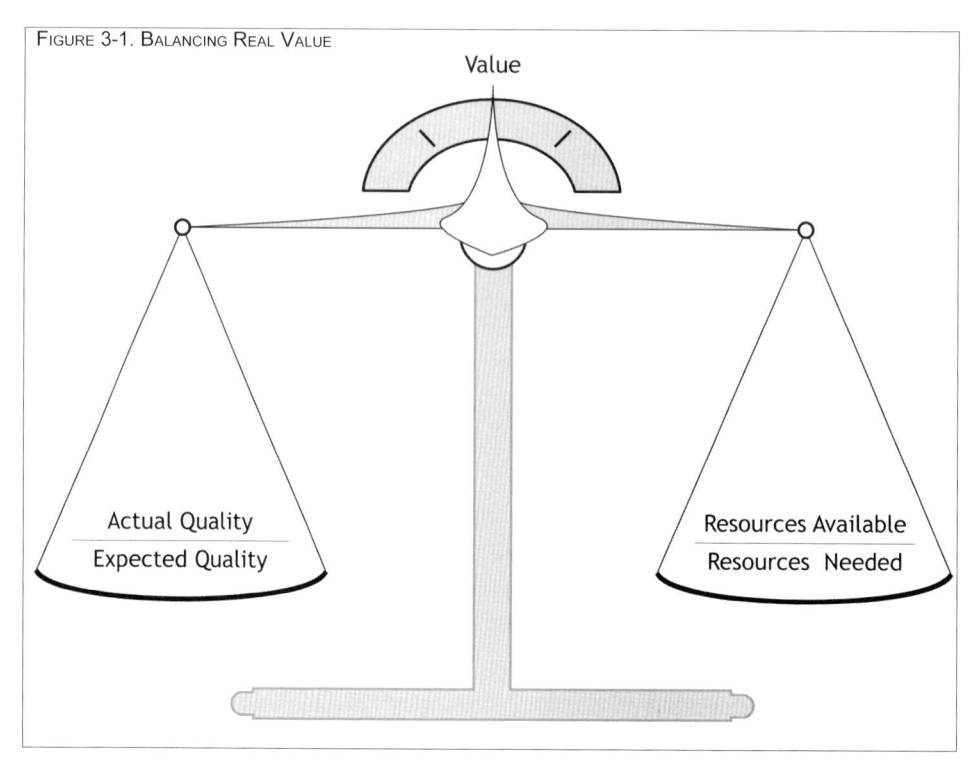

FIGURE 3-1. BALANCING REAL VALUE

the outset, then you lose sight of other potentially more valuable solutions.

The complete approach consists of the following steps:
- Describe the need.
- Translate this into functions.
- Generate alternative solutions.
- Make a cost-benefit analysis.

Which the participants work through in a number of workshops. You could say that the functions generated in this way are the benefits of the project, which are weighed against the costs of the alternatives. According to the British Office of Government Commerce[4], Value Management has the following advantages:
- A better understanding of the business need and the desired flexibility.
- A simple and clear definition of the needs of the stakeholders.
- All options, alternatives and innovations are taken into consideration.
- The best value for money, whilst meeting the users needs.
- Prevention of unnecessary expenditure on waste and inefficiency.
- A better co-operation is achieved through having common ownership of the solution.

5. The project review

The project goal and the project result have been defined. The project sponsor, assisted by the project manager, must now, on the basis of clear criteria, keep track of whether the project is on course, and whether or not the (expected) result still contributes towards the bigger picture. He already did this at the start, but it is good practice to repeat this several times during the project. The aim of an interim review is to check whether or not the project still meets the basic criteria.

---

4 (2007) *Risk and value management*, OGC, London

Review points
During a project there can be a number of points in time when an review is held, and the first of these takes place before approving the project. In this, the project sponsor pays particular attention to how the project fits in with the organization, and contributes to achieving the strategic objectives.

Further reviews also take place at important transitions between stages, and also in the event of large changes (or an accumulation of small changes) and calamities. The project sponsor should take the initiative, and if he doesn't, the project manager does, at the same time remaining attentive to the support of the sponsor, who is the person ultimately making the decision at the review.

Organizing a project review
A review has to be prepared carefully, in order to arrive at a clear decision-making process. The final meeting is actually about making decisions on bottlenecks, and a good preparation is obviously required. Particular attention has to be paid to:
- Making a list of all the bottlenecks.
- Preparing alternatives.
- Making agreements in advance with the team members and the ultimate users to ensure that all views are known.
- Keeping focus on the more important problems.
- Preventing the session from becoming too informal.
- Ensuring the decision-making is explicit.

Results of a project review
There can be one of four results from a review, and at it's conclusion, the decision must be clear. The four possibilities are:
- OK, continue.
- OK, continue, but implement specifically mentioned changes.

1.03 Requirements and objectives

- Examine a few more specific alternatives, and then come back.
- Stop.

Next, it must be clearly indicated who is responsible for carrying out the follow-up actions. The project manager often plays an important part in this. During the post-project review the following is determined:
- Whether or not the expected benefits have been achieved.
- Whether or not certain products cause problems.
- Potential adjustments or amendments.

Special reviews
Apart from the general reviews there are also reviews, which have a specific objective. These look at the total project, but then from a specific angle.

A number of examples are:
- HAZOP (Hazardous and Operability study, focussed on components).
- FMECA (Failure Mode, Effects and Criticality Analysis, the same as above, but focussed more on functions and processes).
- Design reviews, very common in complex technical projects.
- Risk Analysis.
- Environmental impacts.
- Internal project audit (project assurance; is the project being managed professionally in accordance with the agreements).
- Survey.

Methods for reviews
There are different methods for holding reviews. This mainly concerns the working procedure during the preparation of the reviews. A number of approaches are:
- Brainstorm (limited in structure and less suitable for well planned reviews).
- Delphi method (everybody is asked individually for their opinion about a subject and the results are fed back anonymously until ultimately there is a convergence of the answers).
- Fraternal audit (peer review, a colleague assesses your work).
- Official auditors.
- Second opinion.

Based on the available knowledge, the objective of the review and the culture of the organization, the project manager makes a choice from the options.

1.04 Risk and opportunity

NOTHING VENTURED, NOTHING GAINED

Projects are surrounded by risks and opportunities.

The success of a project depends on the ability to anticipate risks, and to react effectively when they occur.

1.04 Risk and Opportunity

1.04-1 DEFINITIONS

Business risk	A risk, which has an impact on that which the customer wants to achieve with the project deliverables.
Disaster plan	A plan made in advance to control the consequences when a risk occurs.
Expected monetary value	The expected value expressed in a unit of currency.
External risk	A risk, which has its cause outside the scope of the project and/or outside the responsibility of the project organization.
Expected value	The size of the risk calculated by multiplying the probability (opportunity) by the impact of the risk.
Fall back plan	A plan to fall back to the original starting point, when a risk manifests itself.
Impact	Compared to the status quo or plan, the change as a result of a risk or opportunity when one of these occurs.
Internal risk	A risk, for which the cause lies within the scope of the project and/or within the responsibility of the project organization.
Opportunity	The probability that a fact or circumstance will occur in the future, and the extent to which this will have positive effects on the project.
Project risk	A risk, which may have negative consequences on the achievement of the project result.

Residual risk	The risk remaining after carrying out the risk containment measures.
Response plan	The plan for carrying out the agreed risk containment measures.
Risk	The probability that a fact or circumstance will occur in the future, and the extent to which this will have negative effects on the project.
Risk analysis	The investigation of the risks, including risk identification, risk assessment, and determination of suitable responses.
Risk assessment	Assessment of the probability and the possible impact of the risks.
Risk aversion	The negative attitude of the management with respect to a risk.
Risk category	A group of similar risk causes.
Risk cause	The possible event or condition which causes the risk.
Risk identification	Identifying potential risks.
Risk log	A log containing the registration of all relevant risks registered during the project.
Risk management	The totality of management activities that have to be carried out to control the risks.
Risk owner	The person who within the project organization has the ownership and responsibility for a certain risk.

1.04 Risk and Opportunity

Risk profile	A graphical representation of the probability (%) and the impact of a risk.
Risk response	An activity to control the risk of a possible event or condition.
Risk term	The potential term over which, and the period within which, a risk may occur.
Risk tolerance(line)	The boundary, within which risks are acceptable for the management.
Scenario planning	A planning technique that is aimed at possible alternative future scenarios and the related management response.
Sensitivity analysis	Analysis of the relative effects certain variables may have on the end result.
SWOT analysis	An analysis of the strong and weak points within an organization or project compared against the opportunities and threats from the surroundings.
Successive Principle	A method of decreasing the uncertainty, by splitting up the uncertain aspects further step-by-step.

1.04-2 INTRODUCTION

Risks and opportunity go hand in hand, as both contain an amount of uncertainty. Your project sponsor wants to do something with the project result and both the result, and the road leading to it, may ultimately be better than expected, or may prove disappointing. You are playing a game of uncertainty.

A risk or opportunity is an uncertain event or condition, which has potential negative or positive consequences. Usually project managers focus on the risks instead of on the opportunities, whereas the focus should be on both.

A key supplier on the project increases his rates, meaning you cannot remain within your budget.

Event:	*Impact*:
An increase of the rates	Exceeding the budget

At the commencement of the project, the users have specified a programme of requirements. It is questionable whether or not these requirements represent want they really want.

Event:	*Possible impact*:
New requirements	Exceeding the budget

In these examples, it can be seen that the impact is the same for both events. That is why in normal speech, we sometimes confuse impact and risk with each other, and state that exceeding the budget is one of the risks on the project, which is incorrect. Suppose that both refer to the same project, then that would mean we are dealing with two risks:

A key supplier who may increase his rates causing us to exceed the budget.

Users, who during the project, may come up with new requirements which we have to accept, causing us to exceed the budget .

This may sound like a play on words, but by focussing on the uncertain event you are closer to the origin of the risk, which sets you on the track of responses to reduce the chance of that event happening.

Agreements have been made regarding the availability, however, it is almost certain that the employees will have insufficient time available to spend it all on the project.

1.04 Risk and Opportunity

Condition:	**Possible impact:**
Employees are not available full-time on the project	Exceeding the original duration

It is the unfavorable condition of not obtaining resources who can be allocated full-time to the project, which might have a negative impact on the duration. It is not yet certain whether or not this will happen, and also not to what extent.

An important sub-division is:

- *Project risks* which have to do with the project deliverables, and issues (the project goal in the narrow sense), which may have a (negative) impact on the project execution.

- Furthermore, there are *business risks* related to the expected advantages (the project goal in the broad sense), which can be achieved with the project deliverables. Think of the *risks* an organization runs, when a project is not implemented successfully.

In the review of the project, you include the risks together with the costs and benefits in the considerations. The extent to which people are willing to run a risk, and to make use of opportunities, has a significant influence on the ultimate decision whether to start the project.

1.04-3 PROCESS STEPS

1. Identify and analyze.
2. Plan responses.
3. Incorporate responses.
4. Assess attainability objectives.
5. Track and monitor risk profile.
6. Track and monitor responses.
7. Record and apply experience.

1. Identify and analyze

Identification
Identification can be top-down as well as bottom-up. In the top-down method, the focus is on similar projects and experiences gained from the past, which are then applied to the current project. This can be done by using checklists or brainstorming techniques. This top-down approach is best suited to the start of the project development stage.

Bottom-up is a much broader method, which is used at the end of the planning stage. Use is then made of the different products delivered during this stage, such as, for example:
- The *product description;* to a large extent, the result to be delivered determines the risk. For example, a project with a tangible result, such as a piece of technology which has proven itself over time, will bring with it less of a risk than a project, for which the end result is the merger of two organizations.
- The *estimates of costs;* the way in which the process of estimation has been carried out is an important indication for the level of this risk. If the estimation has been on the basis of little information, you run a high risk that the estimate is wrong, resulting in the budget being exceeded.
- *Planning people and resources;* how many irreplaceable people have been planned into key positions, and to what extent can they be employed full-time. Also the knowledge and experience of the allocated people may pose a risk.
- The *purchased and outsourced* products and services; how sharp have the negotiations been, and what level of quality can you expect from your external suppliers.

It is, therefore, only possible to conclude the risk identification process successfully once the above points have been clarified.

As well as these sources, you can also look at the historical information (if this is available within the organization), i.e. project files from similar projects, commercial databanks and, obviously, the knowledge and experience of the various project members.

Analysis
The following dimensions are defined in the risk analysis:
- The event or the condition.
- The origin or cause.
- The probability that the event will occur.
- The possible consequences.
- Signals, which are an indication of the occurrence.
- The period within which the risk might manifest itself (proximity).

The *event* or *condition itself* has already been described during the identification. During the analysis, the project manager must describe this as clearly as possible. As long as you are not able to phrase it properly, you have not got a clear picture of the event or condition. A clear description is the foundation on which you can build further.

The second dimension the project manager has to investigate is the *origin* or *cause*. This partly determines the possible responses

1.04 Risk and Opportunity

you can take. Prevention is better than cure, should be an important motto.

As always, one difficulty is estimating the probability and the impact level, is there a low, medium, or high risk, and if high, how is this defined? This is highly dependent on the attitude the parties involved have towards the risks. Most people unconsciously make choices which are contrary to their long term objectives[1]. You do the project decision makers a favour by making the risk management process as rational as possible.

When the event or the condition manifests itself, this will have an impact on:
- The costs.
- The duration.
- The quality of the result.

As well as these, Groote and others also mention[2]:
- The quality of the information the project provides to the parties involved.
- Not being able to meet other requirements and standards set.

Also, of course, the impact on achieving the objective the project sponsor wants to attain with the result delivered.

You do not estimate *probability* and *impact* on your own, but in consultation with the main stakeholders and the most important operational staff, who provide the so-called expert opinions.

You estimate both probability and impact in two steps:
- Qualitative (high, medium and low).
- Quantitative (70% probability and the damage is usually divided by an average of € 100,000 and a standard deviation of € 1,000).

Following the *qualitative* analysis, you can make a first selection between issues to be further investigated, and issues you leave for what they are. You investigate this first group further, by making actual estimates, which then provide the *quantitative* analysis. The results of this form the basis of the decision as to which responses you have to take.

The last dimension you have to analyze is at what point in time the event or the condition may manifest itself (proximity), and the 'early warning' signs which are an indication of this time approaching.

2. Plan Responses

The ICB[3] mentions the following responses in projects:
- Exclude (or use for an opportunity).
- Mitigate (or increase for an opportunity).
- Share.
- Transfer or insure.
- Develop disaster plan.
- Passively accept.

Exclude (or avoid) the risk, means that you take measures which have the effect of preventing the risk from occurring (again). The most rigorous form is not carrying out activities which have the risk attached to them, because when you doing nothing, nothing can go wrong. By taking this approach, you often introduce new risks. A patient who has to undergo a heart operation runs a certain risk that if the operation goes wrong, he can die. When he decides to avoid this risk, he still has an increased risk of having a heart attack and dying anyway.

It is much better to change the activities

---

1 (2001) *Risk and decision analysis in projects*, J. Schuyler, PROJECT MANAGEMENT INSTITUTE, Newton Square, USA.
2 (2007) *Projecten leiden* – Groote e.a., SPECTRUM, Utrecht

3 ICB Version 3

1.04 Risk and Opportunity

in such a way that risk disappears, for example when a certain part has to be transported from one city to the other and there is a threat of strikes by lorry drivers. The risk can be eliminated by transporting by plane (if available), or by changing the schedule in such a way that the part concerned is not needed until much later.

Use is the equivalent for the responses you take when an opportunity occurs. This means that you ensure the opportunity in question does actually arise.

Mitigate responses are responses taken by the operational organization to decrease the probability or the impact of risks. When, for instance, one of the risks is exceeding the deadline, which can cause a lot of damage, tight progress control can reduce that risk. Obviously the costs of such responses must be compared with the potential consequences of such a risk. If, for instance, you make additional costs of €100,000 for progress control, then this is only sensible when the consequences of such a risk are a lot higher than this amount..

Increasing responses do the opposite and are connected with grasping opportunities. For instance, by working overtime for two weekends, you are in a position to deliver a month earlier, which may give the project sponsor an interesting advantage if the company is the first to bring a new product onto the market.

But what do you make of one month of extra design to add a piece of extra functionality to a product, which will distinguish it from many other similar products on the market.

Sharing impact have to do with agreements you make with parties involved to share either the risks or the opportunities. For example, so called 'incentive' contracts in which the customer and the supplier share cost reductions, or when the supplier receives an extra bonus if he delivers a part of a product one month earlier.

When *transferring*, the consequences of the risk are passed on to another party. For example, in a fire insurance the possible financial consequences are passed on to the insurance company. In this way there is still the same risk, but an important part of the consequences are carried by someone else. Take note that in some Islamic countries insurance differs from the most commonly used contracts.

A fixed price contract is another example. Here you pass the price risk on to the supplier, and in this situation, it is good practice to place this risk with the party that is also able to control it.

Developing a disaster plan: In advance, you think about what to do in the event of certain disasters. In this way, you can limit the damage when disaster strikes. You draw up a plan you can activate immediately the risk actually manifests itself. By having this plan, you are prepared, and are able, to limit the impact of the risk to a certain extent.

When parties involved are in danger, it is important to hold a 'fire drill' (simulate and act out the disaster).

Although the ICB only speaks of *passive acceptance*, the *PMBOK Guide* makes a distinction between *passive* and *active* acceptance. The difference is that with active acceptance, you separate out a part of the budget to use when the risk manifests itself, whereas you do not do this with passive acceptance.

Every response has a price tag, with which the decision makers have to agree. The outcome of the risk analysis determines the choices the decision makers have to make with respect to the responses the project manager must, or is allowed to, take. You are then left with a *residual risk,* which the organization can accept.

3. Incorporate responses

Now it is a question of incorporating the different responses into the planning. These responses form part of the basis of the management cycle implemented by the project manager.

The response exclude will, in all probability, result in a change in the size (scope) of the project. We can identify the response mitigate by an increased control on the execution, or in the form of disaster plans added to the project plan as sub-plans. The response *transfer* may possibly be translated into a *"make or buy decision"* or by insuring the risk through an insurance company or broker. The response *acceptance* can be recognized in the form of extra budget (in the event of active acceptance) or as an assumption (in the event of passive acceptance) in the pre-conditions or conditions on which the planning is based.

EXAMPLE 4-1 RISK RESPONSE PLANNING
Not having sufficient capacity available in time is an uncertain condition for a project. Even though agreements have been made (conditions) with the line managers, they cannot give any assurance.
One of the responses the project manager makes is to study the employees' time sheet records to see whether or not there is a change in their work activities. He does this on a weekly basis and this response is explicitly described in his project plan.

We have to differentiate here between the owner of the risks, and the team member who has to execute the actions related to the planned responses; the latter is the so-called action holder (actionee). The owner is ultimately responsible for tracking and monitoring the risk i.e. the changes in probability and impact. He can be the actionee himself, but it is also possible for him to delegate this to someone else.

Does this exempt the project manager from managing the so-called residual risk that remains when all responses have been implemented? I believe not; suppose that the risk owner does not carry out his work properly, or the actionee neglects to implement the responses? It is then ultimately the project manager who must ensure there is a solution. Besides what you have organized and agreed, it remains necessary for you, as project manager, to keep a very close watch on the risk profile of your project.

4. Assess attainability objectives

After the risk analysis and the planning of the responses, the organization must again assess to what extent the project objectives (costs, duration and quality of the result) are still attainable, and also to what extent the goal the project sponsor wants to achieve with the project still fits within the scope, which may possibly have changed, and the new risk profile. It is also possible that through this, the investment decision will ultimately be made based on other reasons.

The stakeholders, who have the power to make decisions, must assess this attainability at set times, which as a minimum are the times of transferring from one stage to the next. As time goes on, the future of the project becomes increasingly clear, with respect to both the attainability and the expected benefits to be derived from it.

5. Track and monitor risk profile

The risk analysis is carried out at the start of a project, but also during the execution, attention continuously needs to be paid to the risks. The nature and size of the risks change during the life cycle of the project and therefore, during the execution of the project, you will have to update the initial risk plan.

In fact this means that during the whole project, you are actively busy monitoring the risks. At certain points in time during the project, it is advisable to carry out a formal re-evaluation of the risks. These points in time are:
- After an *important change* has taken place in the project environment or in the organization in which, or for which, the project is being carried out.
- At *important milestones*, which are logical points to review the risks again.
- Before *important decisions* that have to be taken during the project.

6. Track and monitor responses
As well as monitoring the opportunities and risks themselves, you must also check to what extent the responses actually have an impact. The big problem with risk management is that it is nothing more than an exercise in 'rational fortune-telling'. The same applies to the planned responses. During the execution of the project you continuously have to test these assumptions.

7. Apply lessons learned
As always it is an open door, but only if you are consciously thinking about the impact of your actions, can you actually learn. This is also true for risk management, but there is more to it than that.

When you work in an organization that carries out a lot of projects, you will notice that it is often the same things that cause projects to go wrong. That is why we have the Risk Breakdown Structure, which is explained later.

This **RBS** already contains all problems that frequently occur, divided into categories. Every project manager has to study this RBS at set times, and decide which risks might arise for his or her project. At the end of a project, the RBS can be updated again.

8. Other standards and guidances
The process steps as identified by IPMA are only a suggestion. The process steps described in the *ISO 21500 Guidance*, the *'guide to the Project Management Body of Knowledge'* (the *PMBOK Guide*) from the Project Management Institute, and in the popular PRINCE2 Project Management method are much more "binding". Without discussing it in detail I shall name, as a comparison, a number of items from these standards that are related to this competence element. What will be noticeable is the high level of similarity and overlap.

ISO 21500
The Guidance deals with this topic in the subject group Risk, and differentiates between the following processes:
- Identify risks.
- Assess risks.
- Treat risks.
- Monitor and control risks.

PMBOK Guide
Again, the processes in the 5th edition of *PMBOK Guide* are very similar to those of the Guidance, although the naming convention is slightly different. The following processes are included:
- Plan risk management.
- Identify risks.
- Perform qualitative risk analysis.
- Perform quantitative risk analysis.
- Plan risk responses.
- Control risks.

1.04 Risk and Opportunity

PRINCE2

For Risks, PRINCE2 contains a separate topic, in which the following steps are covered:
- Identify
- Assess
- Plan
- Implement
- Communicate

1.04-4 SPECIAL TOPICS

1. Checklists

Based on lessons learned from other similar projects, checklists are used, in which certain questions are asked that could put you on the trail of potential risks.

A number of examples of such questions for a system development project are:
- Are the end users being interviewed?
- Do end users participate in the acceptance test?
- Are the documentation standards described?
- Has an acceptance procedure been agreed?

Organizations can make their own lists of questions, or use standard lists.

One of the PMI[4] publications gives an extensive list of specific project risks, which is divided up into the following groups:
- External, unpredictable and uncontrollable.
- External, predictable but uncontrollable.
- Internal, not technical but in general controllable.
- Technical and in general controllable.
- Legal and in general controllable.

Checklists work fast and are easily applicable to similar projects. The main objection to this method is that new risks are not automatically recognized. In a checklist of this type, you build further on the errors made in similar projects in the past, but that doesn't mean that a future risk profile is the same.

2. Risk Breakdown Structure

A special checklist is the so-called Risk Breakdown Structure, in which the checklists are grouped hierarchically.

The specific risks can then be included under the last blocks.

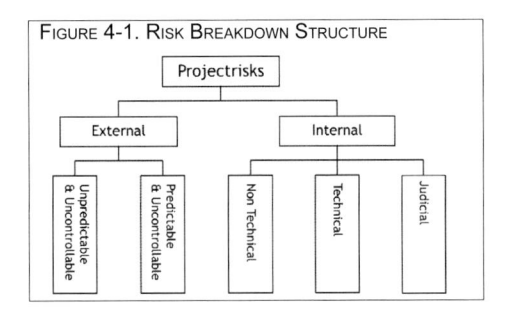

FIGURE 4-1. RISK BREAKDOWN STRUCTURE

3. Risk matrix

The risk matrix is a tool which is used during the qualitative analysis, and it provides a number of handles for classifying the identified risks. It looks as follows:

FIGURE 4-2. RISK MATRIX

Impact / Probability	Low	Med.	High
High	Med.	High	High
Medium	Low	Med.	High
Low	Low	Low	Med.

The probability is then either the probability of the uncertain event, or the probability that a certain condition will have a negative impact on the results of the project.

---

4 (1992), *Project and Program RISK MANAGEMENT*, R.Max Wideman, THE PROJECT MANAGEMENT INSTITUTE INC.

1.04 Risk and Opportunity

FIGURE 4-3. QUALITATIVE SCALE OF IMPACT

	Impact				
	Very Low	Low	Medium	High	Very High
Measurement / Control factor	0,05	0,10	0,20	0,40	0,80
Costs					
Duration					
Scope					
Quality of the result					

4. Qualitative scale of impact

A problem with the qualitative analysis is that every participant has a different view of the concepts high, medium and low. Therefore, before you carry out an impact analysis with the team, it is advisable to first calibrate the different views of the participants.

PMI[5] has defined a yardstick for measuring the level of impact that particular uncertain events may have on a project. The cells now contain a global quantification of the cell in question. For instance a low impact on the cost is described as *less than 10% budget overrun*. The calibration now consists of agreeing a description for each impact that is to be qualified during the analysis. Together you decide which description to use.

Set Priorities

The risks having the highest probability and impact for the product should get the most attention. Both in terms of preventing them, as in cushioning the blows should they happen anyway.

Prioritizing can also be carried out both qualitatively and quantitatively. The general guideline for qualitative priorities is:

	Probability			Impact		
	H	M	L	H	M	L
1	x			x		
2		x		x		
3	x				x	
4		x			x	
5			x	x		
6			x		x	
7	x					x
8		x				x
9			x			x

Quantitatively prioritization is based upon sorting the number "*probability* x *impact*".

---

5 (2004) *A guide to the Project Management Body of Knowledge 3rd Edition*, THE PROJECT MANAGEMENT INSTITUTE INC.

Other methods

The following methods are based on a team, in which the various members each score the risks separately. For example:
- Each team member puts the risks in sequence. After that, all the separate ranking numbers are added together and the list is sorted.
- Each team member divides 100 points over the risks. Add these up and sort again.
- Each team member gives a mark from 1 to 5 for probability and for impact and multiplies both, after which the scores of the various participants are put into sequence.

EXAMPLE 4-2 QUALITATIVE PRIORITATION

A pharmacist has invested tens of millions of Euros in the development of a new medicine and approval has been given to start testing it on humans. In this next stage, a request will be sent out to general practitioners to look for patients who want to participate in the research. The research will then take place within this stage in four iterations.

The following risks have been identified and qualitatively analyzed.

Probability	Event description	Impact	Impact description
M	1. Not enough patients participate	M	Size of random sample not representative
L	2. Patients drop out	M	Size of random sample not representative
M	3. Medicine has side effects	H	Medicine cannot be put onto the market

Using the prioritization table, a qualitative prioritization then looks as follows:

Probability	Event description	Impact	Impact description
M	3. Medicine has side effects	H	Medicine cannot be put onto the market
M	1. Not enough patients participate	M	Size of sample not representative
L	2. Patients drop out	M	Size of sample not representative

The basic assumption of this approach is that within the team there is consensus on the scores. Furthermore, this guideline assumes that a higher impact carries more weight than a higher chance.

5. Variance

> EXAMPLE 4-3 VARIANCE
>
> We have the following estimate for duration: making the ground ready for building on will take between 10 and 15 months. The actual **uncertain** result will be somewhere in the 'middle'. However, our project sponsors will want to know how much grip the project manager has on this uncertainty, and a level of statistical knowledge is necessary for this. I will explain this concept by using the example "making the ground ready for building on". The key question is: with how much certainty can the project manager say that making the ground ready for building on will take between 10 and 15 months? The estimate has been determined by investigating thirty projects and processing the outcomes in the following table, of which we show a part (note: projects 3 to 28 are hidden but are included in the totals).
>
> | | 1
Duration | 2
Duration -/- Average | 3
(Column 2)^2 |
> |---|---|---|---|
> | 1 | 12 | 0 | 0 |
> | 2 | 9 | -3 | 9 |
> | .... | .... | .... | .... |
> | 29 | 13 | 1 | 1 |
> | 30 | 16 | 4 | 16 |
> | Average | 12 | 5 | 603 |
>
> In *column 1* we see how the project manager has calculated the average. To obtain an impression of the extent to which the different durations vary from the average (the variation), he calculates the difference between the duration and the average in *column 2*. As some of these results are negative, the sum of this column does not mean that much, this is solved by multiplying every difference by itself (squaring) to make everything positive. The total of the third column now does mean something: the higher this number, the further, in general, the different durations are away from the average.
>
> Statisticians use this number (603) as starting point to determine two criteria for the variation of the different durations. The first is the **variance**, this is equal to the total of the third column divided by the number of durations minus one, which in this case is 603/(30-1) = 20.8. The second often used is the **standard deviation**, which is the square root of the variance, or in our example: 4.6. The normal distribution helps us answering the question regarding the extent of certainty there is that the duration will fall between 10 and 15 months.
>
> From the normal distribution you can derive a table, with which you can determine the probability that an outcome will be under a certain value. To do this you first have to convert the boundaries in the 'number' of standard deviations from the average. The standard deviation is 4.6: the 10 months boundary (2 months before the average) is 2/4.6 = 0.4 standard deviations before the average. The 15 months boundary (3 months after the average) is 3/4.6 = 0.7 standard deviations after that. By using a Z table, we can read off the related chances. The columns always give the first number behind the comma, and the chances are in the cells. In our example: The chance the duration will be less than 15 months is 75,8%. We are looking for the chance between 10 and 15, and therefore we must still subtract the chance that it will be less than 10 months from it. The chance that the duration will be between 10 and 15 months is 75.8% - 34.5% = 41.3%. It is now up to the project sponsor to determine whether or not this is acceptable.
>
> | Z | 0.0 | 0.1 | 0.2 | 0.3 | 0.4 | 0.5 | 0.6 | 0.7 | 0.8 | 0.9 |
> |---|---|---|---|---|---|---|---|---|---|---|
> | -2.0 | 0.0228 | 0.0179 | 0.0139 | 0.0107 | 0.0082 | 0.0062 | 0.0047 | 0.0035 | 0.0026 | 0.0019 |
> | -1.0 | 0.1587 | 0.1357 | 0.1151 | 0.0968 | 0.0808 | 0.0668 | 0.0548 | 0.0446 | 0.0359 | 0.0287 |
> | -0.0 | 0.5000 | 0.4602 | 0.4207 | 0.3821 | 0.3446 | 0.3085 | 0.2743 | 0.2420 | 0.2119 | 0.1841 |
> | 0.0 | 0.5000 | 0.5398 | 0.5793 | 0.6179 | 0.6554 | 0.6915 | 0.7257 | 0.7580 | 0.7881 | 0.8159 |
> | 1.0 | 0.8413 | 0.8643 | 0.8849 | 0.9032 | 0.9192 | 0.9332 | 0.9452 | 0.9554 | 0.9641 | 0.9713 |
> | 2.0 | 0.9772 | 0.9821 | 0.9861 | 0.9893 | 0.9918 | 0.9938 | 0.9953 | 0.9965 | 0.9974 | 0.9981 |

1.04 Risk and Opportunity

When we make an estimate for the duration of a certain activity, it is often not possible to do this with any certainty. In fact, it is better to take an upper and lower limit between which the possible result can lie.

When we now count how often a certain duration occurs and put this in a histogram, then it could look like the diagram.

The normal distribution

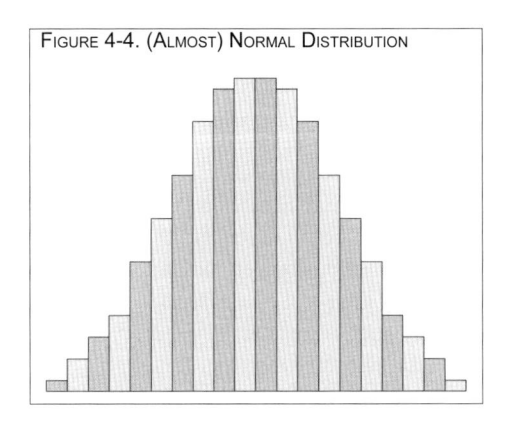

FIGURE 4-4. (ALMOST) NORMAL DISTRIBUTION

The standard deviation is, next to the average, one of the parameters that determines the shape of this distribution.

In our case, the highest bar is now exactly above the average and the greater the standard deviation becomes, the higher the bars further away from the average will also be.

If we were to measure it precisely to the second, we would get a graph that looks like the well-known normal distribution.

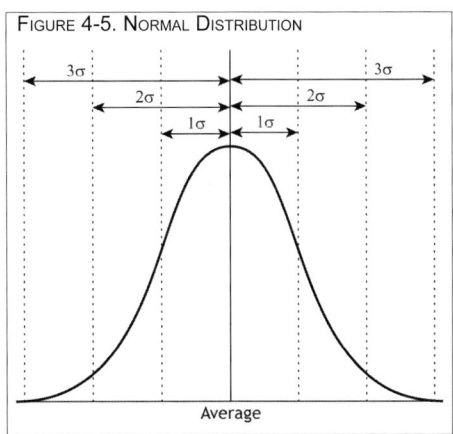

FIGURE 4-5. NORMAL DISTRIBUTION

6. Decision trees

Now consider the following option: the risks on a project have been analyzed. One of the risks concerns a probability of 50% of exceeding the costs for a certain cost component by € 100,000. This percentage can be reduced to 10% by responses which will cost a total of € 30,000, and there is a budget available. Do the responses have to be applied or not? This can be decided with the help of a decision tree.

A square represents a choice; in this case the project manager must decide whether or not he will apply responses. If he does this, he has to spend € 30,000 of his budget on doing it. A circle represents a possible effect. There is only be a 10% probability left of exceeding the costs of € 100,000 and a 90% probability of not exceeding the costs. Should he decide not to apply the responses, then he incurs no extra costs. The probability of the costs being exceeded then remains at 50%.

57

1.04 Risk and Opportunity

FIGURE 4-6. DECISION TREE

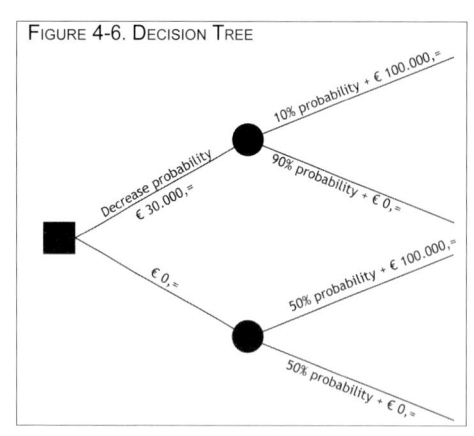

The decision tree shows the structure of the decision he has to make. Before the project manager takes the decision, he can consider four possible outcomes:
- He decides to apply the responses, without these having any effect.
- He applies the responses, and these do have the intended effect.
- He does not apply the responses, and the costs are exceeded.
- He does not apply the responses, and the costs are not exceeded.

When he calculates the monetary value of each decision, it is not difficult to see which choice he should make.

The monetary value (economic monetary value, expected monetary value or EMV) of the choice to apply the responses is:

€ 30,000 for the responses + 10% of € 100,000 + 90% of € 0, which comes to € 40,000

The monetary value of the choice not to apply responses is:

€ 0 + 50% of € 100,000 + 50% of € 0, which comes to € 50,000

This shows that the choice to apply the responses is the most profitable, as in that case you only take the 'lowest'.

7. Risk log or Register

There is a need for a tool to track and monitor risks over the duration of the project. We often see risks listed as a table in a project management plan, or added in this way to the appendices. The danger of this is that you lose sight of the risks, and therefore it is better to construct a separate register, which you regularly look at to check whether the suppositions made at the start of the project are still valid.

It is best to construct such a register in the form of a spreadsheet or a database, as in this way you are in a position to make quick selections, and yet still retain an overview. It is a good idea to include the following columns in such a register:
- Description of the risk.
- Status.
- Cause.
- Event.
- Uncertainty and impact before responses:
  - Uncertainty of the event.
  - Impact on the costs.
  - Impact on the duration.
  - Impact on the quality.
  - Impact on other projects.
- Responses implemented.
- Responses deadlines.
- Risk owner.
- Risk actionee.
- Uncertainty and impact after responses:
  - Uncertainty of the event.
  - Impact on the costs.
  - Impact on the duration.
  - Impact on the quality.
  - Impact on other projects.
- Warning signs.
- Proximity of the risk.

1.04 Risk and Opportunity

- Underlying assumptions.
- Proximity of assumptions.
- Reporting level.
- History.

The register is one of the first things you construct and functions as a "repository" with respect to risks.

USE DURING THE PLANNING STAGE
There is a risk as soon as someone thinks of one, and although that does not mean you have to actually do something with it, initially you should record each risk in the register. A risk can have the following status:
- Identified.
- Qualitatively analyzed.
- Quantitatively analyzed.
- Responses proposed.
- Responses approved.
- Proximity.
- Occurred.
- Analyze again.
- Accepted.
- Closed.

This is self-explanatory and the more the status develops, the more information on the risk becomes available. Once you have recognized the risk, you analyze how big it is and make proposals for implementing responses. The status changes from "analyzed" to "responses proposed". If a steering committee or project sponsor decides not to implement any responses, then the risk changes to the "accepted". If you then leave the risk in the register, you cover yourself against accusations from management should the risk occur. Acceptance of risks is a decision that should be taken by a steering committee.

USE DURING THE EXECUTION
Risk is another word for 'uncertainty', with the consequence that you, as project manager, must regularly look at the analyses you made at the start of the project to make sure that the risks are still valid. Dependent on the project and the required control cycle, you look at the risk register at fixed times (weekly or monthly). The recommendation is to choose a fixed time to do this (for example, always after a project meeting), thus ensuring that you do not forget, because of the everyday pressures, to look forward.

In the first instance, you look at the deadlines for the responses to be implemented, and, when necessary, you speak to the risk owners and actionees. Next, you look to see if there are any new risks, and if that is the case, you carry out a new analysis with accompanying responses. By sorting the risks in order of proximity, you obtain an overview of the most urgent risks. The risk register also contains a column with possible warning signs you have to look out for. When a risk threatens to occur, it has consequences for the complete risk profile and possibly also for the responses implemented.

As well as keeping an eye on the risks, you must also check whether or not the assumptions are still valid. Just as with the manifestation of warning signs, the risk profile also changes when certain assumptions are no longer valid. For each risk, an entry is made in the register of the level that has to be reported to. In this way, the risk register is a useful instrument for monitoring risks during the execution, and ensuring these are handled adequately.

AT THE CLOSE-OUT OF THE PROJECT OR THE END OF A STAGE
It is advisable to enter the history of the risks in the register. You can then use this data when you carry out an evaluation at the end of a stage or the project, on how well the project has gone and has been managed.

8. The 'insurance premium'

When probability and consequence can be expresses in figures, this can serve as the basis for determining an extra risk reservation. We explain this further by using the following example.

Description of risk event & consequence	P	Impact	EMV
Product milestone does not meet the specifications, whereby a part of it must be done again.	10%	€ 25k	€ 2,5k
Product is delivered too late, whereby a loss in turnover can be expected.	50%	€ 100k	€ 50,0k
Total reservation to cover the risk.			€ 52,5k

The column 'Impact' contains an estimate of the amount that must be used to finance the consequences of the risk. In the column 'EMV' you find the result of multiplying the costs of the consequence by the probability percentage. By totalling these you arrive at the insurance amount for the recognized risks. This premium has to be included in the project's financial plan. It would, however, be a mistake for the project manager to see this as an amount to be used for unexpected expenses. In the example above, this amount would indeed be insufficient if the risk of were to manifest itself. It would be better if the organization were to take account of a 'setback', which is equal to the total of all risk reservations for all the projects in existence.

The complete risk analysis is an iterative process in which we identify risks, estimate the probability and consequence, and on the basis of this, define responses, whereby the probability and consequence change. Before taking the risk premium as an insurance, we must adjust this amount based on the risk responses that have been taken.

This amount should be taken in to consideration in the investment decision. It does not, however, form part of the budget the project manager has to spend.

9. Monte Carlo Simulation

The Monte Carlo simulation is a statistical technique, in which with the help of random numbers, a particular event is simulated. It's name is taken form the casinos in the capital of Monaco, because roulette is one of the simplest random number generators there is that exists. In each round, roulette generates a number between 0 and 36 inclusive. Other "random number generators" are the dice (1-6) or a coin (1-2). Every spreadsheet contains a **random** (aselect) function.

We look at the activity: "make a project plan", for which there is some uncertainty about the duration. You could do a Monte Carlo simulation in which you have to ask yourself the question how the results would be distributed when you and another 99 'doubles' of you write the same report at the same time. In this case, we are then looking for the statistical distribution.

There are various statistical distributions available, for example:

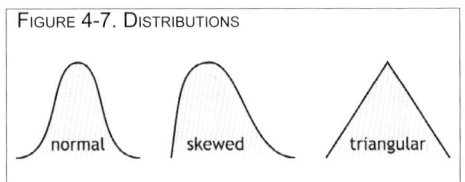

FIGURE 4-7. DISTRIBUTIONS

normal   skewed   triangular

We choose for the normal distribution. The average duration to produce a project plan is 30 days. The results are distributed according to a normal distribution, for which the

1.04 Risk and Opportunity

standard deviation is three days. In a normal distribution, 68% of all results lie between one standard deviation below and above the average, and 95% lie between two standard deviations below and above the average.

For a Monte Carlo simulation, you can make use of a random number generator, spreadsheets, or software applications specially developed for this.

The benefit of a Monte Carlo simulation lies in a number of factors. Because you have to consider beforehand which distribution you use, you become more aware of what the distribution of the risk is, and the determination of the standard deviation indicates how certain or uncertain you are. It gives a handle on working out how much extra time you must plan in to provide a particular amount of "certainty" of success.

10. Sensitivity analysis

With a sensitivity analysis, we investigate which risks have the largest consequences for the project. We input the various uncertainty factors into a arithmetical model. We then repeatedly change one of the factors, each time keeping the other factors constant, allowing us to determine which factor has the most effect on the end result.

11. The Successive Principle[6]

This principle of step-by-step refinement is a risk analysis method for handling risks in a proactive manner. The method is applicable in all management areas where uncertainty is a significant factor. It combines hard statistical techniques with the softer aspects, such as an open and honest atmosphere with respect to uncertainty.

---

6 (2000) *Proactive Management of Uncertainty using the Successive Principle*, Steen Lichtenberg, POLYTEKNISK PRESS, Kopenhagen

There are two stages that I will cover in summary, which you, as project manager, have to take account of when you want to apply the method.

The qualitative stage

FORM THE ANALYSIS GROUP
There are two important conditions which must be satisfied before you can begin with this approach:

1. The relationship with the project sponsor is such that you can confront him openly and honestly with the reality.

2. It is possible to form a team with competent members, who are prepared to enter into an open and honest discussion about the uncertainties in the project.

As well as competent members, it is important that the analysis team also contains the different team roles (e.g. from Belbin) that are necessary. In my opinion, an ideal team should contain at least the following team roles:
- Both a RESOURCE INVESTIGATOR (existing ideas) and a PLANT (new ideas).
- A number of MONITOR EVALUATOR (to warn).
- A number of specialists.
- A CHAIR to lead the team.

The chair should be chosen above the Belbin team role of 'former', as the latter has the tendency to steamroller over others, whereas it is important in this method that the members can discuss everything openly and honestly.

Firstly, the team makes a description of the project that they will analyze for uncertainty.

1.04 Risk and Opportunity

The description of the scope should be sufficient for this. During the various meetings, and especially in the beginning, the project sponsor can participate in the process.

IDENTIFY ALL SOURCES OF UNCERTAINTY
Even before checklists or risk breakdown structures are used, a number of brainstorm sessions must be held on the uncertainties that are present.

These brainstorm sessions generally result in a list with numerous so-called "General Points for Attention", and often it is useful to classify these in a matrix.

Next, the general points for attention are divided in such a way that independent groups are created. These "Overall influences" form input for the qualitative analysis which follows. For example, the sphere of influence of "legislation" with respect to "technique".

For each group, the following is now determined:

- The "*base-case*" definition, which is the starting point on the basis of which the further analysis will be carried out
- The "*future case*" which is the deviation from the base-case definition which is expected.

> EXAMPLE 4-4 BASE/FUTURE CASE
> "*base-case*": current employees.
> "*future-case*": declining labour market conditions

Following this, the first stage of the process is completed and a deeper analysis is carried out in the quantitative stage.

The quantitative stage
In the stage, the team starts work on the actual calculations. To do this, they use the list of "Overall influences" and also the scope description as described in the Work Breakdown Structure.

THE WORK BREAKDOWN STRUCTURE
The elements from the first WBS level form the basis for the first calculation. For each element, the analysis team makes a three-point estimate:

- The most likely (W).
- The most optimistic (O).
- The most pessimistic (P).

The average is now calculated using the following formula: (P + 3xW + O)/5.

The standard deviation is then: (P-O)/5.

The priority number, or the variance, of a WBS element is the square of the standard deviation. When we do this for the cost estimates we make a calculation sheet consisting of two parts. The first part contains the cost estimates under normal circumstances, as described in the base-case definition.

Look for example at the next table, the following estimates (x €10k). In this table the uncertainty included in the rates under normal circumstances has been taken into account, but not yet the uncertainties that are present according to the *actual-future* definition.

		O	P	W	V	S	P
1	Design	2	8	4	4.4	1.2	1.4
2	Build	16	32	20	21.6	3.2	10.2
3	Test	4	12	8	8.0	1.6	2.6
4	Implement	2	6	3	3.0	0.8	0.6
	Total				37.4	6.8	46.24

For this purpose, we shall make a correction table.

CORRECTIONS
When we take the example above, and the *actual-future* definition foresees a sharp rise in the rates as a result of the labour short-

age, then the following correction could be applied for the build.

		O	P	W	V	S	P
2	Build	2	4	3	3	0.4	0.16
	Total						

REFINING STEP-BY-STEP
After this, the actual step-by-step refining or detailing of the recognized uncertainties begins. When we carry on with our example, we research further those uncertainties with the highest priority numbers. On the basis of the WBS we look further.

		O	P	W	V	S	P
2	Build	16	32	20	21.6	3.2	10.2
2.1						1.2	1.44
2.2						0.6	0.35
2.3						0.8	0.64
	Total 2				21.6		

The effect of this action is that the variance/ the priority number (a criterion for the variation) of the components is, in general, a lot smaller than the total, which also makes the uncertainty smaller and, therefore, more controllable.

There comes a point when refining no longer really provides any improvement (i.e. extra certainty).

CREATING AN ACTION PLAN
Ultimately there is a risk profile left over, on the basis of which we can determine the required responses. The complete risk management process then carries on further as described.

1.04 Risk and Opportunity

1.05 Quality

QUALITY COSTS MONEY

Quality is a concept that is difficult to describe. Everybody knows what it is, but there is not one single definition that does the concept justice.

Quality has not only something to do with satisfaction, but also with price (better quality is more expensive).

Quality also has to do with the extent to which expectations are exceeded, and with the delivery of a certain level of service.

1.05 Quality

1.05-1 DEFINITIONS

Audit	Systematic, independent and documented process for collecting proof and assessing objectively, in order to determine to what extent the totality of policy guidelines, procedures or requirements are being met.
Concession	Permission to use or release a product, which does not comply with the specified requirements.
Continuous improvement	Coordinated activities aimed at the increasing the ability to comply with the requirements.
Corrective measure	Measure to effect the correction of an observed deviation, or other unwanted situation.
Defect	Non-compliance with respect to the intended or specified use, in terms of meeting a requirement
Detection measure	Measure to determine whether or not a product complies with the specifications and other required situations.
Deviation (from a specification)	Non-compliance with a requirement.
Effectiveness	Extent to which planned activities are realized, and scheduled results achieved.
Evaluation	A subsequent Investigation to determine points for improvement.

1.05 Quality

Failure costs	Costs for rectification and corrective measures.
Feature	A distinguishing characteristic.
Preventative costs	The costs made to remove causes of a possible future deviation or other unwanted situations in order to prevent it, or them, from occurring.
Preventative measure	Measure to remove the cause of a possible future deviation, or any other unwanted situation, in order to prevent it from occurring.
Process quality	The extent to which a totality of the features and characteristics of a process conforms to the requirements.
Product quality	The extent to which a totality of the features and characteristics of a product satisfies the requirements.
Project quality	The extent to which a totality of the features and characteristics of the project result satisfies what the customer wants.
Quality	The extent to which a totality of the features and characteristics satisfies the requirements.
Quality assurance	The implementation, maintenance, testing and evaluation of the project quality system.
Quality control	Coordinated activities aimed at complying with the quality requirements.

1.05 Quality

Quality costs	Those costs caused by effecting and ensuring the required quality, and the losses that are incurred if a required level of quality is not achieved.
Quality feature	Intrinsic distinguishing characteristic of a product, process, or system with respect to a requirement.
Quality improvement	Coordinated activities aimed at increasing the ability to comply with the quality requirements.
Quality register	A log containing the registration of all planned and executed quality assessments during the project.
Quality management	Coordinated activities to direct and control an organization with respect to quality.
Quality management system	The totality of coherent elements, or elements influencing each other to direct and control an organization with respect to quality.
Quality manual	Document specifying an organization's quality management system.
Quality plan	Document specifying how the project will comply with the quality requirements.
Quality policy	General aims and direction of an organization with respect to quality, as formally made known by the management.

1.05 Quality

Release	Permission to carry on to the next step in the process.
Review	Qualitative assessment of certain areas of attention carried out by a number of experts.
Specification	A precise description of (sub-) deliverables, products and services.
Validation	By providing objective proof, confirming that the requirements for a specific intended use, or specific intended application, have been met.
Verification	By providing objective proof, ascertaining that the specified requirements have been met.

1.05 Quality

1.05-2 INTRODUCTION

Quality is an interesting subject, because everyone has a certain view of it, but when you try to find a definition for quality, this turns out to be very difficult. In the 20th century, quite a lot was talked and written about quality, and broadly you could deduce the following meanings from the discussion about it:

- Delivered in accordance with the specifications.
- Fit for use.
- At minimum costs for society.
- Satisfies all expectations.
- A good feeling.

The last meaning has the greatest importance when we speak of a disappointing quality. Quality is mainly an emotional issue, and as project manager you can't do a lot with that, so you look for the possibilities to make quality measurable. In itself, there is nothing wrong with that, as long as you don't forget that the feeling people have about it determines the actual quality experienced.

There are a number of steps in this process of making quality measurable. We have already seen that needs translate into requirements that the customer stipulates for the delivered product, or project result. However, something always gets lost in the translation process, because no matter how precisely you define everything, the initial expectations of your customer will always be playing a background role.

It is, therefore, not sufficient to just write good specifications, as during the project you must also develop an effective quality management process. 'Effective' means that what is delivered matches expectations, and that this process, from the start, helps the customer to match his expectations to what is possible within the agreed budgets and time frames.

Ultimately, quality is a good feeling.

1.05-3 Process steps

1. Develop a quality plan.
2. Select, build and test.
3. Approve the final version.
4. Assure and check.
5. Log tests and get approval.
6. Correct and repair.
7. Apply lessons learned.

1. Develop a quality plan
First think, and then act! If we have an idea of the requirements, we investigate what the quality requirements are. The first step is thinking about the way in which we are actually going to achieve this quality. The project quality plan describes how the team organizes the quality of the result.

This plan contains:
- Quality expectations and acceptance criteria.
- Responsibilities.
- Relevant standards.
- Quality processes/procedures.
- Change management procedures.
- Configuration management plan.
- Possible tools.

2. Select, build and test
Depending on the required quality and the available skills within the organization, the parties involved select the required solution. This can mean doing the building yourself, have the building carried out by someone else, or a combination.

Building has to be viewed in a broad perspective, and it has nothing to do with a physical product. For carrying out a particular service, you can also think of some designing work (selection of the required solution). The preparations in order to actually carry out the service are then the building and testing. Before actually carrying out the service, you go through the description of the service to be delivered with the project sponsor. The delivery is then the actual service.

3. Approve the final version
Testing the result to be delivered is usually carried out in a number of steps, whereby each version delivered moves a step closer to the final result. The last test, also called the acceptance test, is a formality in which the customer tests whether or not the predefined acceptance criteria have been met.

4. Assure and check

Quality Assurance
Assurance contains all scheduled activities to ensure that the employees use the available quality procedures. The diagram shows that when the team has delivered accepted results, and these are under 'configuration management', then the change procedure serves to protect and assure the quality already achieved.

Quality control
During the complete (historical) development of products, and the further life cycle of a product, the quality has to be kept under control. This is shown in the quality circle above and everything that happens with a product is managed this way. That means there will be no chance, or casual, actions,

> The risk of ignoring quality is that of not achieving the project objectives

but that each step that does something with a product will be considered by the appropriate people.

The quality circle is the basis for the project quality plan. This ensures that all steps in the circle are managed uniformly.

5. Log tests and get approval
Within the project team, it is good practice to document the course of events in tests in a so-called test log. This allows you to keep an eye on the complete course of events in the test, and afterwards to be able to reconstruct the testing stage.

The responsible sub-project leaders approve their team member's tests, and ultimately the users have to approve the final version.

6. Correct and repair
During the tests the testers find deviations from the specifications, or defects. Both must either be corrected or repaired, but before this is done, the impact on other parts of the project has to be studied and this work has to be re-planned if necessary.

7. Apply lessons learned
In this paragraph it is good to refer to a statement from one of our most well-known specialists in the area of quality, W. Edwards Deming[1], who said:

"Experience alone, without theory, teaches management nothing about what to do to improve quality and competitive position, nor how to do it."

You must always put experience into a theoretical framework, and there are a number of reasons that illustrate this. When certain things in a project do not run as smoothly as you would like, you must sometimes improve them and in other situations definitely not. This is all about coincidental and structural causes, and is the theory of uncertainty. In addition, it is useful to be aware of what innovations have already been thought of before re-inventing the wheel yourself, and in this aspect, cost effectiveness is a consideration.

Practical experience and theory always go hand in hand, and they reinforce each other. Furthermore, a lot of theory is formulated out of the practical experience of others who went before you, and why should you not make use of that experience in your own project. Learning from experience in the area of quality means, therefore, that you go and investigate how others have delivered quality in similar situations. Read what is available in the area of quality, as this is a pre-condition for improving the competitive position of your organization, and it is not only Deming who thinks this.

Furthermore, learning from experience is not something which you just do following completion of the project. Applying experience is something you begin with even before you start the planning of a project.

8. Other standards and guidances
The process steps as identified by IPMA are only a suggestion. The process steps described in the *ISO 21500 Guidance*, the *'guide to the Project Management Body of Knowledge'* (the *PMBOK Guide*) from the Project Management Institute, and in the popular PRINCE2 Project Management method are much more "binding". Without discussing it in detail I shall name, as a comparison, a number of items from these standards that are related to this competence element. What will be noticeable is the high level of similarity and overlap.

---

1 (1982) Out of the Crises, W.Edwards Deming, MIT, USA

ISO 21500
The Guidance deals with this topic in the subject group Quality and differentiates between the following three processes:
- Plan quality.
- Perform quality assurance.
- Perform quality control.

PMBOK Guide
The processes of the 5th edition of *PMBOK Guide* are identical to those of the Guidance:
- Plan quality.
- Perform quality assurance.
- Perform quality control.

PRINCE2
There is a separate topic that pays a lot of attention to determining the desired quality, and the way of securing this for the project's duration. The different activities are divided into quality planning and control.
- Quality planning:
- Clarifying the quality expectations.
- Defining the acceptance criteria.

Documenting of expectations and criteria in product descriptions.

Formulating the Quality Management Strategy.
- Producing a Quality Register.
- Quality control:
- Executing the quality methods.
- Maintaining quality and approval records.
- Obtaining acceptance.

1.05-4 Special topics

1. The quality gurus

In the previous century, a number of gurus from the quality movement shone their light on this concept, and provided handles to deal with this difficult to describe concept.

In chronological order, they were:
- Deming (1900-1993).
- Juran (1904-2008).
- Taguchi (1924-1987).
- Crosby (1926-2001).

W. Edwards Deming
According to Deming, quality is *"the continuous improvement of performance"*. The well-known Deming cycle has been named after him:

- *Plan*, which improvement has to be applied.
- *Do*, the actual implementation.
- *Check*, study the results of the improvement.
- *Act*, adjust and amend when necessary.

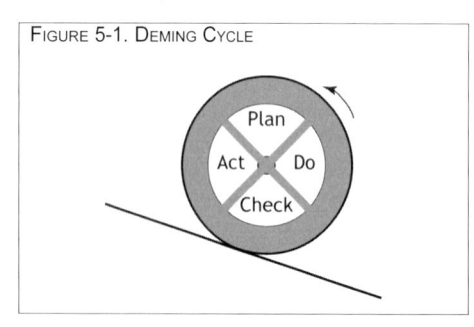

FIGURE 5-1. DEMING CYCLE

This is a continue process through which an organization, in steps, improves the quality of its service provision (*continuous improvement*).

According to Deming, management is responsible for 85% of the problems in the area of quality. The big problem is that managers are not able to interpret the information concerning variation in the operational process. It is now essential for improvement to statistically check the various processes, in order to recognise deviations in time, and to implement process improvements.

The so-called Statistic Process Control (SPC) is a statistical method to assess whether the deviations of a process are random, or have a specific (and assignable) cause. He is still considered to be the founder of the quality movement.

Joseph Juran (1904-2008)
For Juran, quality means *'fitness-for-use'*, in short *'can the customer make use of the product'*. He made the Pareto Principle (80% of the problems arise from 20% of the causes) popular. Furthermore, as well as the statistical approach, he also emphasized the human side. At the core of his thinking is the so-called Quality Trilogy used as a route map for quality improvement:

Quality planning:
- Identify the customer.
- Determine his need.
- Translate this need.

Quality control:
- Produce a product in which the customers needs, and those of the delivering organization, are optimized.
- Develop a process for producing the product.

Quality improvement:
- Optimize the process.
- Prove that the process is capable of producing the product.
- Start using the process.

Philip Crosby (1926-2001)
Crosby sees quality as 'being in agreement with the requirements' (conformance to

specification). Just as Deming, he reaches the conclusion that the main responsibility lies with the senior management. In his view it is key to do things right straight away, with the emphasis on prevention (zero defects).

His thinking can be summarized in[2]:
- Quality is *being in agreement* with the requirements.
- The quality system is PREVENTION.
- Standard performance is zero defects.
- The criterion for quality is conformance.

Genichi Taguchi (1924-1987)
Taguchi defines quality as the variance compared to a pre-determined goal. This is different from contemporary methods, which see quality as a result lying between lower and upper limits (tolerance). For loss of quality, he does not only look at the supplier for the cost of non-conformance, but also at the costs made by the ultimate customer. In short, the loss *'the society as a whole suffers'* by not being in agreement with the specified goal.

Basic thoughts with his methods are:
- Quality already starts with the design.
- Quality is achieved by deviating as little as possible from the goal.
- The cost of quality is measured throughout the system by looking at the deviation.

In order to create a 'robust' design which, in the production process, was as independent as possible from factors in the environment, he developed a series of techniques to efficiently experiment with design prototypes.

He did this for the:
- *System design*; the design for a prototype of both the product, and the production line.
- *Parameter design;* in experiments, the ideal settings for the controllable process variables is cleverly determined (ortagonal series) by testing different variables at the same time.
- *Tolerance design,* by reducing the tolerances for variables with the highest impact on the end result.

Parameter design ensures a decrease in costs (you do not then have to use the most expensive materials any more), and tolerance design increases the costs because the production process becomes more complex. Tolerance design is carried out, when the first two appear not to be sufficient.

Through the clever way of testing the environmental variables and their impact on the end result, you design quality into both the product and the production process.

2. The quality system of a project
Projects are a part of a larger entity and, with respect to quality, are concerned with several quality systems:
- With that of the own organization.
- With that of the customers organization.
- With that of the suppliers.
- With that of partners.

Based on these systems and the specific project requirements, the project team designs its own quality system, which is sufficient to achieve the required quality. It is, therefore, important that a project manager makes himself familiar with the quality policies and the standards used by the organizations involved.

---
2 (2002) *Business – The Ultimate Resource*, BLOOMSBURRY, London

1.05 Quality

> **EXAMPLE 5-1 IMPLICIT REQUIREMENTS**
> A refinery had a new factory built. Completely computerised, so that the control room could regulate everything. Local indicators and such-like were no longer needed, because you didn't have to be in the factory any more to open the valves and start the engines. After delivery of the factory, the operators had meters installed anyway. The reasoning was: "you do not expect me to walk through a factory not knowing what is going on inside? I only have to go there in case of disasters and then I want to know how critical it is!" The designers had overlooked this aspect.

Determining the quality

The user documents the characteristics of the project result in a programme of requirements, ensuring that these explicit requirements are clear at the start. Furthermore, there are also implicit requirements (you can sail with a boat), and it is important that the team is also completely aware of these. To ensure that the team delivers the required quality, it must be ensured that:
- The specifications are produced.
- The tests of (intermediate) products are planned and carried out.
- The acceptance tests are carried out.

The project sponsor has to make the main requirements clear. Next, you as project manager get to work with your team to put everything together in a clear specification, and there are several ways of ensuring the necessary clarity:
- Firstly, come to an agreement on the project result to be ultimately delivered by the project. A clear agreement on the project result, the ultimate contribution of the result to the organization, is best.
- Make a clear list of what is out-of-scope.
- State the conditions, so that the project sponsor has a clear idea of the world in which the project manager thinks he is living.
- State what the project sponsor has to do in the project.
- Be clear about the norms and standard specifications to be used, in order to exclude the possibility of any confusion about this.
- Ensure, by drawing up acceptance criteria, that it is clear when the customer is satisfied.

Research[3] shows that one of the most important conditions for the successful completion of IT projects is the participation of users.

Delivering quality

Before the team provides the (sub-)deliverables, it has to make a number of decisions regarding the quality. The first decision is whether or not the result complies to the specifications set (*conformance to specification*). If this is not the case, it has to be checked whether or not it can be used (*fitness for use*)[4]. To make this decision, knowledge of the following is needed:
- The user.
- The way in which he uses the product.
- Risks for the product, safety and environment.
- The urgency of the delivery.
- What impact the alternatives have on the customers' company.

Next to these two concepts, there is also the extent to which the product to be delivered enables the user to achieve his (benefits) goals (*fitness for purpose*).

4. The cost of quality

Achieving quality is initially an investment and this may either be to prevent mistakes, or to solve them. This so-called *cost-of-qual-*

---

3 (1999) *CHAOS: A recipe for Success*, THE STANDISH GROUP
4 (1998) *Juran's Quality Handbook – fifth edition*, Joseph Juran, McGRAW-HILL, New York

ity consists of[5]: the costs of an impeccable delivery, and the so-called failure costs.

Cost of a perfect delivery
Prevention costs, all expenditure to ensure that the result is perfect, for example:
- Quality planning
- New-products review
- Process planning
- Process control
- Quality audits
- Supplier quality evaluation
- Training

Appraisal costs, all expenditure to assess whether or not processes and their (sub-) deliverables contribute to a perfect delivery, for example:
- Incoming inspection and test
- In-process inspection and test
- Final inspection and test
- Document review
- Balancing
- Product quality audits
- Maintaining accuracy of test equipment
- Inspection and test materials and services
- Evaluation of stocks

Failure costs
Internal costs for failures; all costs required to repair the product before it goes to the customer, for example:
- Scrap
- Rework
- Lost or missing information
- Failure analysis
- Scrap and rework - supplier
- One hundred percent sorting inspection
- Reinspection retest
- Changing processes
- Redesign of hardware

- Redesign of software
- Scrapping of obsolete product
- Scrap in support operations
- Rework in internal support operations
- Downgrading
- Variability of product characteristics
- Unplanned downtime of equipment
- Inventory shrinkage
- Variation of process characteristics from best-practice
- Non-value-added activities

External costs for failures; all costs post delivery. A number of the costs mentioned under failure are also included here, and furthermore the following:
- Warranty charges
- Complaint adjustment
- Returned material
- Allowances
- Penalties due to poor quality
- Rework on support operations
- Revenue losses in support operations
- Customer defections
- New customers lost because of quality
- New customers lost because of lack of capability to meet customers' needs

If you take Taguchi's definition, you also have to include the costs incurred by the customer.

Every organization, whether it is an existing organization or a project organization, has to consider how much it is willing to invest to achieve a certain level of quality. This means weighing-up the costs for a perfect delivery, against the failure costs. An optimum can always be found.

5. Benefits/cost consideration
In the investment, there always has to be a weighing-up of the prevention of mistakes compared to the costs of repair. The choice

---
5 (1991) *Quality Management for Projects and Programs,* Lewis R. Ireland, PROJECT MANAGEMENT INSTITUTE INC.

1.05 Quality

is then between:
- What does the control of the quality risk cost? and,
- What does acceptance of the quality risk provide?

We work this out in an example on the next page.

EXAMPLE 5-2 CONSIDERATION QUALITY COSTS AND BENEFITS

The organization Efficiency Boosters B.V. manufactures a machine for the process industry to improve the efficiency of factories. It works by placing 'boosters' at several places in the factory. It is an ingenious machine and applicable almost everywhere, so, a real miracle tool.

The production of the 'boosters' currently costs € 30,000 per project, and, because they are custom made, an extra € 10,000 in design costs always has to be added to this. As it is never completely certain whether or not a 'booster' will work, inspection is important. Each project gets an additional of € 5,000 allocated to it for inspection costs. 20% of the 'boosters' don't make it through this inspection and eventually about 15% have to be replaced after installation at the customer.

The new project manager is considering whether or not the quality can be improved. Together with his team, he brainstorms on this. If they spend three times as much time beforehand on the design (€ 30,000), the production costs will be halved (€ 15,000). By tightening up the inspection (€ 7,500), it should then be possible to reduce the percentage of waste from 20% to 5%, and the number of 'boosters' to be replaced at the customer from 15% to 1%.

Is it worth it?		Currently		Alternative	
Production Costs			30,000		15,000
Design costs			10,000		30,000
Inspection costs			5,000		7,500
Percentage of waste	20%		6,000	5%	750
Replacing defective units installed	15%		4,500	1%	150
			55,500		53,400

The set up above shows that it is worth it from a cost point of view, as the alternative provides a saving in costs of € 2,100. This is not much, but together with the increase in customer satisfaction, it is worth doing (or not?).

Certainly, if one of the key assumptions you make for the quality costs, is also to take into consideration the costs the customer has to make (Taguchi).

Note here that this decision is made on the assumption that the intended savings will actually be achieved.

Prior to, and during, the project, the team has to make several considerations regarding quality. In the example above, we weighed up the costs and the quality, and, there is of course also the consideration of duration versus quality.

The production time has been reduced from 20 days to 15 days, and the time for the design has gone from 15 to 45 days, and the inspection from 4 to 5 days. In total this results in an increase in the duration of 26 days. The consideration now is whether or not these 26 extra days are worth a reduction in the cost of € 2,100. If customers find this duration too long it is probably not worth it, but if on the other hand there are a lot of complaints about the quality of the product, and these might affect the competitive advantage of the organization, it might be worth it after all.

6. Standards

When determining the project requirements and describing the quality, quite often standards are involved which constrain the way in which the project team can, and is allowed to, carry out certain tasks.

A *standard* is a mandatory regulation laid down by a (inter)nationally recognized body. In essence standards are product oriented, and result in all kinds of specifications, which products have to comply with. Not all standards are prescribed by law. There are standards and regulations in the area of:

- Design and build of the project result.
- Rules and regulations.
- Health and Safety.
- Environment.
- Security.
- Taxation.

The Value of Standardization

For many reasons, organizations use standardization. By complying with certain standards in their service provision or products, they can differentiate themselves from competitors who do not. Some markets cannot even be entered into without complying with certain standards. By using standard components, a reduction in costs can be achieved, because you are no longer dependent on one supplier, and parts are interchangeable.

Quality standards

There are a number of (inter)national standards specifically for quality; some for quality control at a company level and some specifically for projects.

- ISO 9001-2000 (International Standard Organization): Quality standards for an organization. Mainly aimed at using processes in a controlled way, with limited improvement objectives (2000).
- ISO 21500: Project Management Quality in projects.
- EFQM: Approach for continuously improving the organization. Has a scoring system to check how far you are.
- Branch systems: Consequences of the above, usually aimed at ISO.
- Malcolm Baldrige Award: Approach for continuously improving the organization. Has a scoring system to check how far you are.

These standards are often the basis of an organization's custom made quality system. In this way, an organization can test to what extent it works in conformance with the procedures so drawn up. The best known of these is the ISO certification.

The ISO standard is arranged in such a way that all risks that could occur in the production process are identified and covered, and if an organization complies with this, then it gets the ISO certificate. Through the certificate, the organization demonstrates that it is competent in producing products or providing services in accordance with the specifications.

The certificate says to what extent an organization observes the rules of the quality system. Systems like Malcolm Baldrige, EFQM and INK go much further, and also look at the culture, the leadership, etc. These, therefore, provide a much better indication of the quality an organization delivers and are much more a path for development that an organization follows, whereas obtaining an ISO certificate can be viewed as a step on that development path.

The organization's quality system often also applies to the project. Depending on what is already available, the project manager will have to gear this specifically to his project. In

1.05 Quality

general, fewer rules are not allowed, whereas having more rules is dependent on the project needs.

7. Assessments and audits

A once only assessment of the project management at the start is not sufficient. Depending on the importance of the project, the decision can be made to assess the project management either preventively or correctively. We make a distinction between assessment and audit; the former is about measuring how things are done, whereas the latter is also about trying to discover the underlying causes. If necessary an audit report will also identify solutions for the problems acknowledged. Furthermore, a distinction can be made between a project management audit, and the project audit.

Project Management audit

This is concerned with assessing to what extent the agreed project management processes are effective and efficient. Topics looked at are:
- Is what is stated in the project management plan being carried out?
- How are the estimates arrived at?
- How are the work methods determined?
- Is use being made of prescribed methods and standards?
- How is the progress being measured?
- Are reactions to deviations in the plan timely?
- How is it ensured that the right people work on the project?
- How are suppliers managed?
- How are contractual commitments satisfied?

The audit can be very general, or a specific topic can be singled out; the essence is that it is not about the project, but about how the project manager (and his team) manages the project. The preference is for a pragmatic approach, meaning that if processes do not work, they are replaced.

Project audit

A project audit is about the performance of the project, and the auditors now look at:
- Are the deliveries in accordance with the schedule?
- Compare the costs to the budget?
- Is the project ahead of, or behind, schedule?
- Is sufficient quality being delivered
- Is there enough capacity?
- Do the original assumptions still apply?

The project audit is separate from the normal progress report the project manager has to produce in the frame of project control. It is an extra check, which serves as reassurance for the decision makers.

Carrying out an Audit

There are different ways of carrying out an audit. It may have been included beforehand in the planning, allowing the project manager to take account of the work required for the audit. It is also possible, however, that the management of an organization decides to put the project under the microscope.

Before the responsible auditor starts his work, it has to be clear:
- What the goal is.
- What the investigation should focus on.
- How long it should take.
- How much manpower should be deployed on it.
- How reporting should take place.

Auditors can collect the required information by:
- Interviewing the project manager.
- Interviewing team members.
- Interviewing other involved parties.
- Attending meetings.
- Holding a group discussion.

1.05 Quality

- Studying the management documents.
- Studying actual data.

Although the project manager can carry out an audit himself, it is better to have this done by an outsider, who has no interests in the outcome of the investigation.

Lay-out of the Audit Report
An audit report contains the following subjects:
- Management summary.
- Aspects investigated.
- Observations.
- Causes.
- Recommendations.
- Appendix containing the detailed data.

Attitude with regard to the audit
In most cases, an audit means extra work for the project manager and his team. It is understandable, therefore, that project managers often display some resistance to audits. Auditors should understand this, and decision makers should always consider whether or not the remedy could be worse than the disease. When the audit is taking place, as project manager, you can best embrace it as an instrument, which allows you to manage your project even better. An outsider is often better at identifying a team's blind spots than you are.

8. The seven tools of quality
The following tools, which in general are called the basic quality tools, are pre-eminently suitable for detecting problems and looking for solutions:
- Check sheet.
- Histogram.
- Cause and effect diagram.
- Scatter Diagram.
- Control Chart.
- Flow diagram.
- Pareto analysis.

Check sheet
A check sheet is a form, which, for instance, is kept by a machine operator to keep a count of defects. For example:

	Defect	Total
Machine A	/ / / /	4
Machine B	/ / / / / / / / /	9

Cause and effect Diagram
The cause and effect diagram is also known as the Ishikawa (the inventor) or fishbone diagram. There are different types, but one that is used a lot looks as follows:

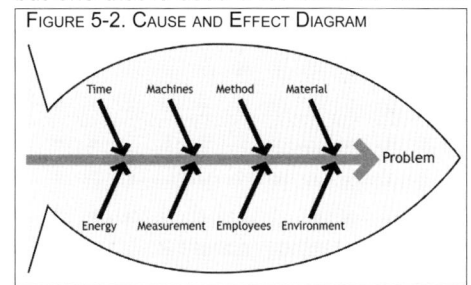

FIGURE 5-2. CAUSE AND EFFECT DIAGRAM

The approach starts with naming the problem. A multi-discipline team solves the problem together. By brainstorming, they go searching for possible causes.

This can be done in different ways:
- Randomly, in one session, the team names causes in all different categories.
- Systematically, a session per category.
- Process analysis, the team firstly maps out the complete process, and then looks, per process step, at the extent to which the various categories contribute to the problem.

The causes are placed in the 'side branches' of the different categories.

1.05 Quality

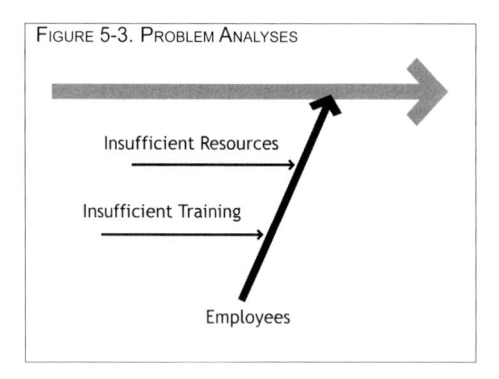

FIGURE 5-3. PROBLEM ANALYSES

- Insufficient Resources
- Insufficient Training
- Employees

It may be that the team members in the category 'employees' identify two important causes for the problem. There are insufficient staff, resulting in too much pressure on the individuals.

The steps you take, together with a team of specialists, to arrive at the diagram[6] are:
- Define the problem to be solved.
- Brainstorm to find all the possible causes for the problem.
- Group these results into categories.
- Draw a fishbone diagram showing the various relationships.

If required you can draw extra branches (or leaves) on the side branches. When all causes have been determined in this way, the corrective actions necessary to solve, or prevent, the problem are determined. The 'fishbone' can also be used to help set out the corrective actions required, and assess the overall effect of them.

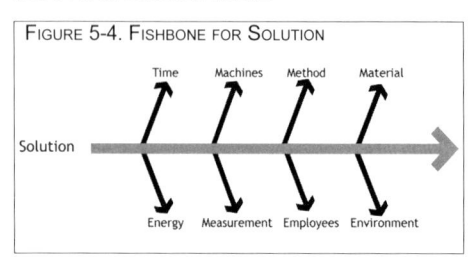

FIGURE 5-4. FISHBONE FOR SOLUTION

Solution — Time, Machines, Method, Material, Energy, Measurement, Employees, Environment

---

6 (2001), *The Six Sigma Handbook*, Thomas Pyzdek, MCGRAW-HILL

Histogram

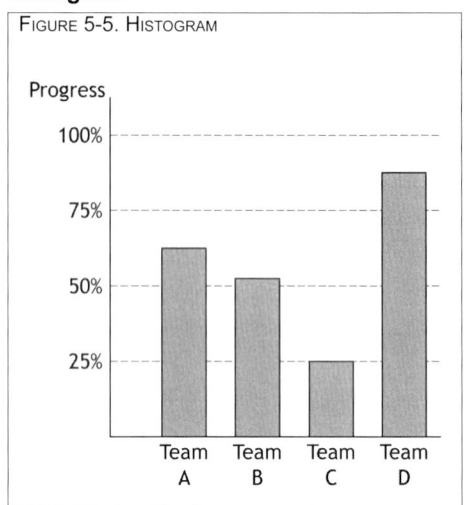

FIGURE 5-5. HISTOGRAM

Progress
- 100%
- 75%
- 50%
- 25%

Team A, Team B, Team C, Team D

The histogram provides insight into the differences between certain categories.

Scatter Diagram

A scatter diagram has the objective of showing a relationship that may exist between two variables.

EXAMPLE 5-3 SCATTER DIAGRAM

Suppose you suspect a relationship between the outside temperature, and the number of errors made by the service engineers.

You check the log with error reports per day and measure these against the temperatures you received from the weather forecast bureau. The horizontal axis gives the temperatures, the vertical axis the number of errors.

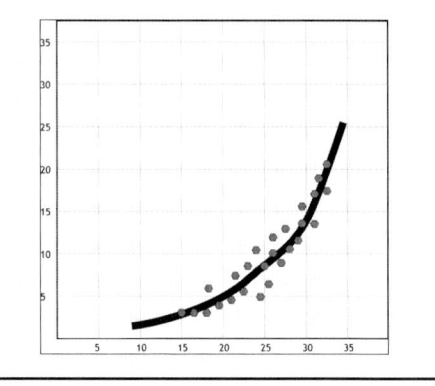

1.05 Quality

Control Charts

The control chart belongs to the Statistical Process Control approach, and is predominantly useful when certain activities in a project have to be carried out more than once. By mapping out the outcome of these actions (or process), it is now possible to see whether or not the process is under control.

When you carry out a certain activity a number of times, one after the other, the outcome will not be the same every time. The results have a certain randomness, and we can say that they are spread around the average. A measurement for this spread is the standard deviation, which can be calculated in Excel using the function Stdev.

EXAMPLE 5-4 CONTROL CHART

The following control chart concerns a maintenance project, in which a certain part has to be changed in all machines installed by a machine manufacturer. As the manufacturer has installed about 15,000 machines of this type worldwide, it is important to develop a standard method of operation and, during the execution, to keep track of to what extent the replacement process is under control. The following control chart shows in graphical form the duration measured for each of 21 installations.

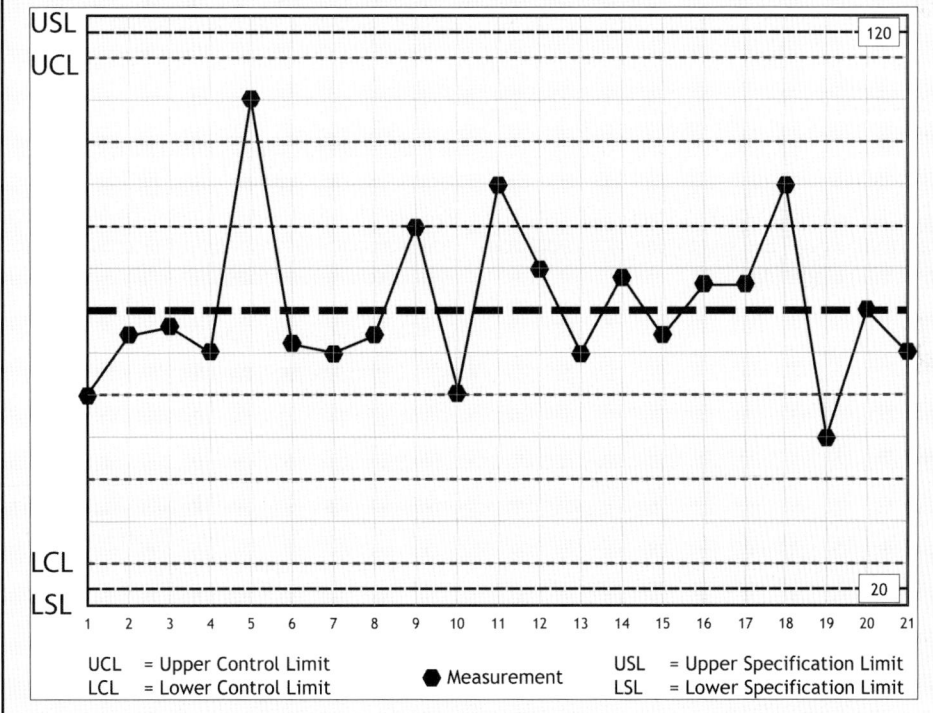

| UCL | = Upper Control Limit | ● Measurement | USL | = Upper Specification Limit |
| LCL | = Lower Control Limit | | LSL | = Lower Specification Limit |

The horizontal lines are of interest for the analysis of the diagram.

The bottom and the top line are the Upper and Lower Specification Limit respectively. They refer to the maintenance period agreed in the maintenance contract. In this contract, it is stated that the manufacturer is allowed to carry out between 20 and 120 minutes of maintenance on a machine per month.

The middle line shows the average of the series of measurements; in this case 69 minutes. Two more line are of importance here, the Upper and Lower Control Limit. These limits are, respectively, plus and minus three standard deviations removed from the average.

1.05 Quality

The way in which the outcomes are spread around the average is based on a statistical formula, of which the normal distribution is best known, and which we have seen before. The control charts are based on the assumption that the random outcomes follow this normal distribution.

FIGURE 5-6. NORMAL DISTRIBUTION

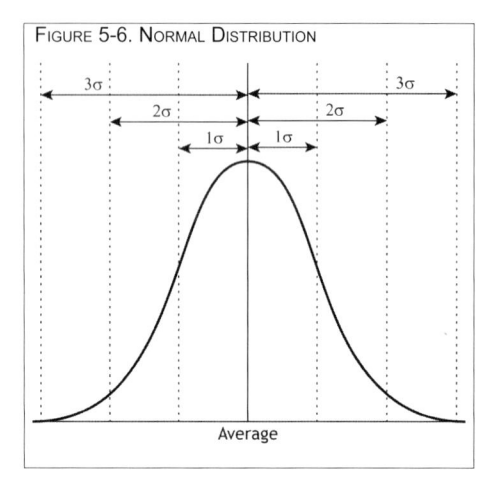

There is no cause for concern when:
- Most points are near to the average.
- A few points are close to the UCL and LCL.
- No point is above UCL and LCL.
- UCL and LCL are within the USL and LSL range.

The chart gives an indication of when we have a cause for concern.

The control chart gives an indication as to when the deviations are no longer random. What this method does not do, however, is indicate where the problem is. The primary objective is to indicate when certain measurements are statistically unlikely. It prevents you reacting to random 'peaks', but lets you know when something is really wrong.

The control chart is now used to determine to what extent the outcomes are randomly (normal) distributed.

By comparing the control (UCL and LCL) and the specification (USL and LSL) limits with each other, it is possible to say something about the maturity of the process. We use two formulas for that:

- $C_p = (USL - LSL)/6\sigma$
- $C_{Pk} = |(Average - Nearest\ SL)/3\sigma|$

FIGURE 5-7. CONTROL CHART - HUGGING

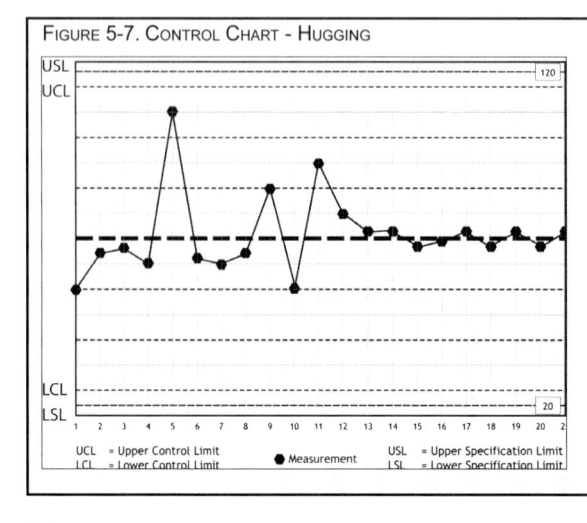

When a series of points is near the central line or close to one of the limits, it is called hugging the line. If that is the case, then this is often because the measurement data is contaminated with other data, and it is then best to check the measuring method.

1.05 Quality

The process capability; the generally accepted guidelines for Cp are:
- 1.33 - the process is well within the specifications of the customer.
- 1.33 > CP > 1,0 - improvements to the process are required, the process is only marginally acceptable.
- Cp< 1,0 - the process is unacceptable, improvements are necessary.

The second criterion is of importance for assessing to what extent the process is within both of the specification limits. As CPk approaches 1, the process provides more results in line with the customer specifications.

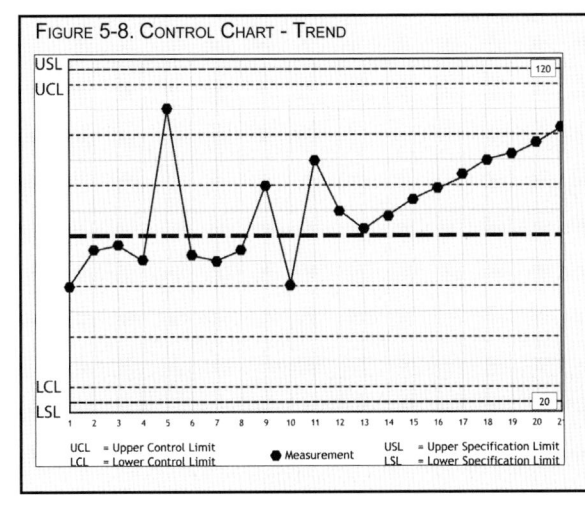

FIGURE 5-8. CONTROL CHART - TREND

Another situation which is a cause for concern is the trend. This occurs when seven or more measurements show an ascending or descending line. The following chart is an example of that. From eleven measurements onwards, we see an (ascending) trend.

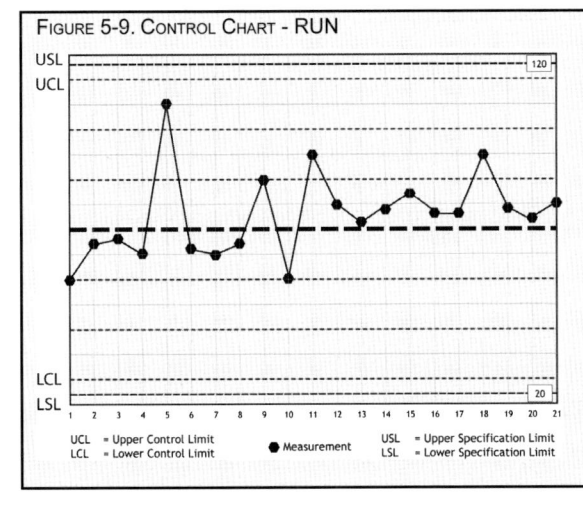

FIGURE 5-9. CONTROL CHART - RUN

When more than seven consecutive points lie on one side of the line, we talk of a "run". This is the case from measurement 11 onwards.

85

1.05 Quality

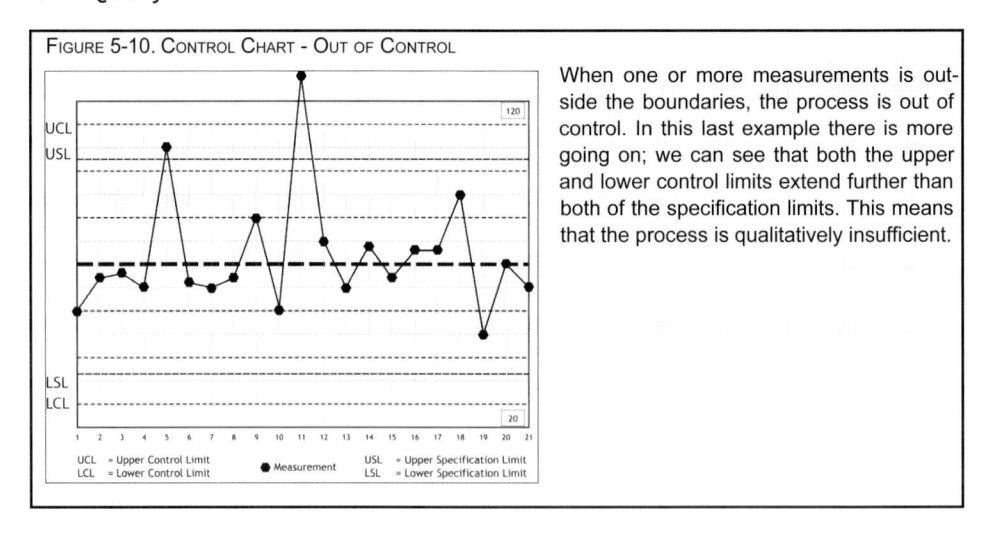

FIGURE 5-10. CONTROL CHART - OUT OF CONTROL

When one or more measurements is outside the boundaries, the process is out of control. In this last example there is more going on; we can see that both the upper and lower control limits extend further than both of the specification limits. This means that the process is qualitatively insufficient.

Flow diagram
With a flow diagram you illustrate a particular process schematically.

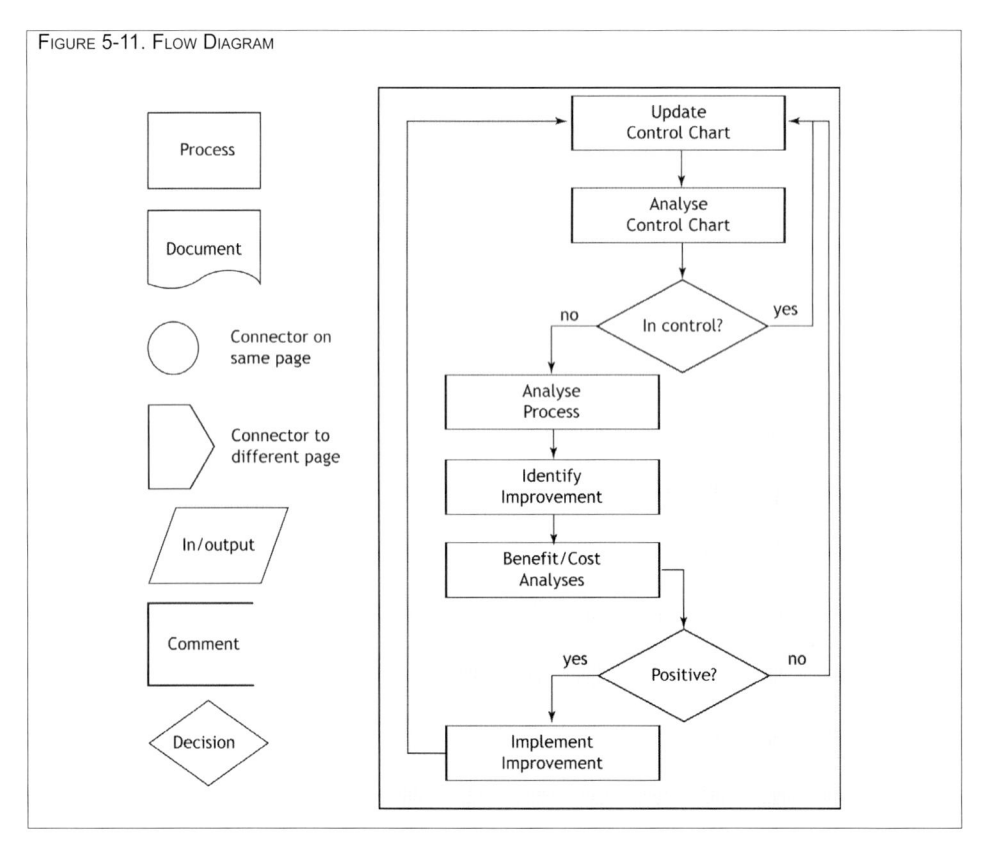

FIGURE 5-11. FLOW DIAGRAM

Pareto Analysis

The Pareto analysis makes use of the histogram. Once again I shall explain this by using an example.

EXAMPLE 5-5 PARETO ANALYSES

The average time it takes eight engineers to install a certain part within the scope of a maintenance project is measured. In order to keep within the budget, the project manager wants to investigate where he has to initially intervene to achieve a required increase in speed. In the chart to the right, he has entered the different measurements.

Engineer	Average installation in minutes	Fraction	Cummulated
B	450	45,0%	45,0%
C	350	35,0%	80,0%
A	100	10,0%	90,0%
F	50	5,0%	95,0%
G	20	2,0%	97,0%
I	10	1,0%	98,0%
E	10	1,0%	99,0%
H	5	0,5%	99,5%
D	5	0,5%	100,0%
	1000	100%	

He calculates the fraction of the total, and accumulates this in the far right-hand column. He sorts the chart from high to low. Based on this chart, he can make the standard Pareto Diagram.

The approach is now to initially tackle the engineers who contribute most to the time overrun. From the diagram on the left, it can be clearly read-off that these are B and C.

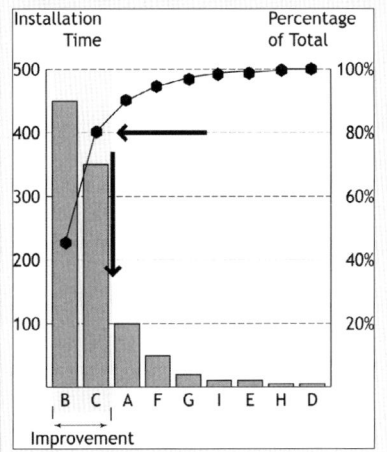

Let us assume that the project manager replaces these two engineers with X and Y. After this corrective action, the diagram now looks as follows.

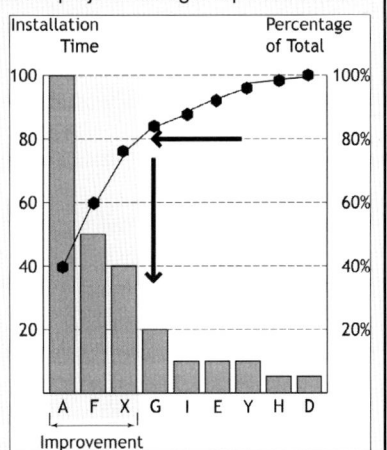

Based on this new graph, a new Pareto Analysis can (if required) be carried out, as often as necessary until the required result is achieved.

The essence of the technique is that, in order to solve problems, you firstly concentrate on those factors which contribute the most to the solution of the problem. Often only 20% of the factors contribute to 80% of the problems.

1.05 Quality

1.06 Project Organization

THERE ARE JUST AS MANY PROJECTS AS THERE ARE PEOPLE INVOLVED

In a project, people work together in mutual interrelationships which they did not have previously.

Agreements, therefore, have to be made as to how the different people are going to work together.

Everyone is allocated a so-called role within the project.

1.06 Project organization

1.06-1 DEFINITIONS

Customer	Organization or person receiving the project deliverables.
Organization chart	Schematic representation of the project organization structure.
Project (management) team	The project manager and everybody reporting directly to him.
Project assurance	The responsibility of the project sponsor / steering committee to ensure that the project is properly organized and carried out.
Project employee	A person who, with respect to content (execution), provides a contribution within the project.
Project manager (project leader)	The person responsible for the day-to-day management of the project.
Project Office	An entity that is put together to carry out certain administrative services for one or more projects.
Project organization	A temporary organization for realizing a project.
Project organization structure	Overview of the roles in the project organization and the delegation and reporting lines.
Project sponsor	The customer's representative in the project.

Project support	An administrative role within the project management team, supporting the project manager and the sub-project leaders in the areas of planning, archiving and administration.
Project team	The project manager and the employees working on the project.
Responsibility assignment matrix	An overview of tasks and responsibilities linked to individuals or groups (RACI).
Sub-project manager	The person within the project, who, in terms of both content and process, is responsible for a part of the work, and who reports on this to the Project Manager.
Supplier	Organization or person that provides a product or service.
User	Everyone who is going to use, manage, maintain or otherwise be involved with the final project deliverables.

1.06 Project organization

1.06-2 Introduction

A project is a temporary organization in which people work together on the realization of a unique product, service or result. For this temporary cooperation, we have to organise a temporary organization form in which the various people, departments, companies and/or organizations know what they have to do within the scope of the project.

This competence element consists of designing and maintaining the correct:

- Roles
- Organization structures
- Tasks and authorities
- Skills

Required for the project.

There is a relation with other technical competence elements, namely:

- Interested parties: to determine which parties and/or people have to be involved in the final project organization, the approach and the ultimate result.
- Project structures: the structure of the project deliverables.
- Resources: to determine how many people are needed, and which 'suppliers' can provide them.
- Purchasing and contract: the people the project involves from outside the own organization and the contracts through which the responsibilities are organized.
- Project start: to ensure the people involved have a clear picture of the way in which they, together, have to go about the project.
- Teamwork: getting the various people involved in the project organization working (together).
- Conclusion: the dissolution of the project organization and returning the team members involved to their organization (units).

Note
Even though there is a close connection with the competence: *"Resources"* there is a fundamental difference. The *"Project organization"* determines which functions are required, and *"Resources"* relates to calculating the required capacity, and actually acquiring the required people.

1.06-3 Process steps

1. Determine organization.
2. Determine teams.
3. Determine roles.
4. Define project procedures.
5. Acquire resources.
6. Manage interfaces.
7. Communicate decisions.
8. Improve the organization.
9. Apply lessons learned.

1. Determine organization

Based on the scope, the project manager and a number of key players consider the ideal way of cooperating. From the analysis of the interested parties, the project manager has formed an idea of the most important people, their interests and the way in which these can best be involved.

With the help of the WBS, the (sub-)deliverables have been structured, and there is some insight into what the project team can or cannot do, and what additional resources are required, such as: ICT, project rooms, meeting rooms, tools, etc.

2. Determine teams

Both technology and the power structures present have an influence on the way in which you must divide up the project organization into parts. The project organization must consist of at least the following parts:
- A decision making body.
- The operational management.
- Executing body.

In the simplest form, these are respectively the project sponsor, the project manager and the employees that carry out the actual work. This three-way split is a condition for success. Each form of combining these brings with it certain risks. In principle, I would state that combining these is undesirable.

In the next table, the possible mixes are described:

Combination	Risk
A line manager manages a project using his own line budget.	The project is not in line with the overall strategy of the organization, but is a 'hobby' of the project sponsor.
A line manager is project sponsor, but also provides a contribution to the content of the project.	The project manager is caught in a pincer construction as he has to 'manage' his project sponsor.
The project manager is busy with the content of the project and also delivers content.	When under time constraints, he either produces an unsatisfactory end result (when he is leading the project) or he does not manage (when he uses all his time to deliver the content).

Decision making body
The decision making body (project sponsor or steering committee) provides the hierarchic power required to direct the project. It is the place where problems are escalated to, which cannot be resolved within the project, and where decisions are made.

Operational management
The project manager himself, or in case of a more complex project, the project manager and the sub-project managers of the various teams working on the project. In the event of the latter, we then speak of the project management team.

Executing body
This consists of the various team members, possibly divided over the various sub-project teams. They are the experts with respect to content; the technicians, the workers, the people carrying out the work.

1.06 Project organization

3. Determine roles
For all functions, there is a (global) description of the tasks, authorities, responsibilities, competences and experience required within the scope of the project. This is necessary as they can deviate from the daily line responsibilities. Furthermore, the experience required of the various incumbents is described.

This description serves as a basis for the actual acquisition of the necessary people and, therefore, forms a link between the project (what) and the existing organization (who).

4. Define project procedures
There are separate procedures for the way in which we:
- Make decisions
- Hire people.
- Report on progress.
- Escalate.
- Hold meetings.
- Release work.
- Approve and plan changes.
- Make purchases.

You make as much use as possible of what is already available in the organization in which the project is carried out. Where things are missing, you yourself provide the necessary project standards. Obviously, there needs to be support for this.

5. Acquire resources
This can be an expedition in itself, dependent on the knowledge and experience you have with the project, and the organization within which the project takes place. The outcome of the analysis of the interested parties provides pointers for this issue.

It is important that you, as project manager, play an active role in this process. I often come across the misunderstanding that the project sponsor has to organise the 'resources'. This is not true! The project sponsor provides the conditions (*the necessary priority*) whereby the project manager is put in a position to organise the necessary people and means.

The project manager indicates which resources he needs and, because the project sponsor (and the other main interested parties) ensures the necessary priority, the line managers involved are, therefore, able to provide these resources to the project.

Realize that this will take a number of iterations, in which the project manager together with the line managers of the resources in question gradually arrives at a good capacity planning.

6. Manage interfaces
As project manager, you must identify and describe everything that is nonstandard. It is at the interfaces where things go wrong. From the start, therefore, you must consider what the dependencies of the teams on each other are. As well as the technical interfaces there are also the organizational interfaces, each of which forms a risk that we have to address. A quick look at the organization chart is often sufficient to see what can go wrong.

The regulation of the interfaces can be carried out in different ways, i.e.:
- Formal discussion.
- 'Collect' and 'deliver' obligation.
- Escalation procedures determined beforehand.

Collect and deliver obligation
When a particular team (team A) has to deliver a sub-deliverable that another team (team B) is waiting for, then the first team (A) has a *'deliver' obligation* meaning that the leader of the sub-project must state when he expects to deliver. The *'collect' obliga-*

1.06 Project organization

tion is with the receiving team (B), who must not passively wait until something is 'thrown over the wall', but raise the alarm when the delivery is not on time.

7. Communicate decisions

You describe the project organization in the project plan. But in itself a plan is passive, and needs to be approved and implemented. When the plan has been approved by the major parties involved (in any case the project sponsor and the major resource suppliers), you have to ensure that everyone is informed.

It is not sufficient to send the plan as an appendix to a mail message. Active communication is necessary. We often see this happening during the kick-off, in news bulletins and in one-to-one conversations.

Next to actively communicating, there is also the matter of supervising the project organization, which means ensuring that everything is going to plan and, where needed, making corrections and anticipating unexpected problems, risks and changes.

8. Improve the organization

No project organization is set in stone; when necessary, you adapt (in consultation with the other parties involved) the organization. Continuous improvements are necessary to achieve an efficient execution.

9. Apply lessons learned

You learn from experience when you consciously work on the above. You are prepared to gain insight and to let go of certain assumptions when this leads to better cooperation. You convert the learning gained from the experience with this specific project organization into an experience which you can also apply later.

10. Other standards and guidances

The process steps as identified by IPMA are only a suggestion. The process steps described in the *ISO 21500 Guidance*, the *'guide to the Project Management Body of Knowledge'* (the *PMBOK Guide*) from the Project Management Institute, and in the popular PRINCE2 Project Management method are much more "binding". Without discussing it in detail I shall name, as a comparison, a number of items from these standards that are related to this competence element. What will be noticeable is the high level of similarity and overlap.

ISO 21500

The Guidance deals with this in the subject group Resource where differentiates between the following processes:
- Establish project team.
- Estimate resources.
- Define project organization.
- Develop project team.
- Control resources.
- Manage project team.

PMBOK Guide

The 5th edition of the *PMBOK Guide* deals with this under the knowledge area Human Resources and also has a few less processes then the Guidance:
- Plan HR management.
- Acquire project team.
- Estimate activity resources.
- Develop project team.
- Manage project team.

PRINCE2

PRINCE2 has a separate topic on Organisation, which forms a part of the backbone of the method that is based, among other things, on a Management by Exception philosophy. Whereas IPMA, ISO and the 5th edition of *PMBOK Guide* do not comment on

95

1.06 Project organization

the organisation form, PRINCE2 provides a clear Guidance for it. There are three levels: Project Board as the directing level.

- Project Manager as the managing level.
- Team Manager as the delivering level.
- The setting up of the project organisation then takes place during the process Starting up a Project, in the following activities:
- Appoint the Executive and the Project Manager.
- Design and appoint the project management team.

1.06-4 SPECIAL TOPICS

1. The organization chart
The diagram below shows the basic organization chart for a project:

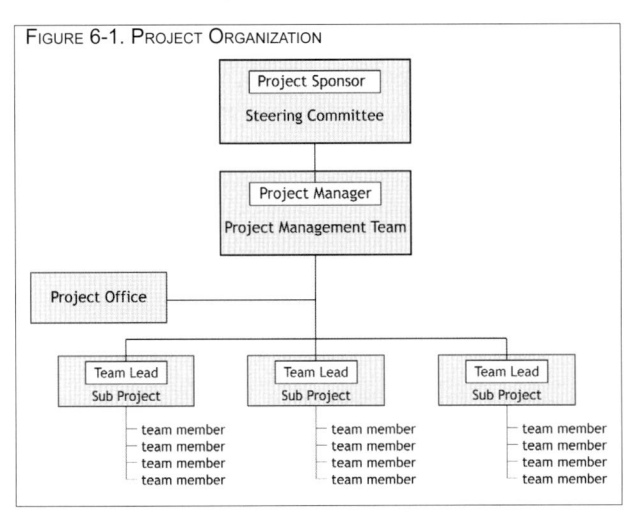

FIGURE 6-1. PROJECT ORGANIZATION

[Organization chart showing: Project Sponsor / Steering Committee at top, connected down to Project Manager / Project Management Team, with Project Office branching off to the side, and three Team Lead / Sub Project boxes below, each with four team members.]

There are guidelines to which a project organization must conform, and each time this conformance cannot be achieved, there is a certain risk involved.

Hierarchy
A good project organization is a hierarchy containing a clear line of authority. Any form of matrix construction within a project organization is undesirable (but not always unavoidable).

Power of the steering committee
The steering committee, or the decision making body, consists of line managers with sufficient hierarchical authority over the people and means in the executing body. As a minimum, the management (in the person of the project sponsor), the users and the suppliers must be represented.

Linking pin
Each part of the organization is represented in a higher part of the hierarchy. It is possible to start a theoretical discussion as to whether a project manager is a member of the steering committee or not. This discussion is not important, as long as he is there.

2. Roles in the project
Many of the agreements on roles in a project are custom built. This is because each project is different, and because you try to make the best possible use of the personal qualities of the players involved. Roles can also be combined, for example a combination of user and project sponsor can well be possible. A number of roles are better not combined. A project manager, who himself carries out the project assurance, is not really desirable, as you do not want to let someone check on himself.

The essence of each role is that it represents a specific interest that is essential for the project. *Consider firstly, therefore, the interests that have to be kept in balance and then determine the roles.* It is possible that one person will carry out more than one role.

Steering committee
The steering committee has the ultimate responsibility for the project and consists of managers, who have hierarchic authority over all resources coming under the control of the project manager. As well as the *Project Sponsor*, there is a representation of the users and the suppliers.

From the nature of their interests, the *User* and the *Supplier* have the inclination to make the project more expensive. It is also possible that a number of different people are needed to fulfil the interests of the user or supplier, and the composition of the steer-

1.06 Project organization

ing committee can change over the duration of the project.

The project sponsor is continuously looking for a balance, which is shown in the business case, and which is acceptable to him. The steering committee does not function on the basis of a consensus model. The project sponsor is the decision maker, and includes the opinions of the other steering committee members in his considerations.

Project manager
The *Project Manager* is responsible for ensuring the project is carried out well, on time, within budget and to the agreed quality. In order to accomplish this, he has the day-to-day management over all project activities. He is accountable to the project sponsor, mainly in the steering committee. Bilaterally, he keeps in regular contact with the steering group in order to discuss and agree actions on the various day-to-day problems arising.

Sub-project manager (team lead)
Sub-project manager is a role; it is possible that the project manager himself leads one or more teams. *Sub-project managers* are, therefore, not always assigned. Sub-project managers come into the picture only when the number of participants in a project is so large that direct management by the project manager becomes a problem. They are often referred to as sub-project manager, and have the same responsibility as that of a project manager, but then only for a much smaller part of the project. The sub-project manager reports to the project manager.

Project office
The *Project Office* plays a supporting role. The size of it can vary greatly, from solely a project secretary to a group of experienced staff in the areas of planning, budgeting, risk management, cost monitoring, configuration management and suchlike. The office relieves the project manager of a number of tasks, whereby he can work more effectively and manage larger projects. By combining together the project offices of all projects, an effective and permanent high quality group can be set up, benefiting all projects.

Project controller
If there are many projects, a project controller is often allocated, who is responsible for all of the project administrations. This person has the task of monitoring the finances of the projects and to report on these to the project manager and the other management. He also makes proposals on the potential to save costs and reduce risks.

Project assurance
Project assurance is a specific role (PRINCE2), which demonstrates that attention will be paid to the agreements made in the plan of approach, in particular the work procedures, and ensure that these are adhered to. The ultimate responsibility for this role lies with the members of the steering committee. They can carry out the assurance function themselves, or involve an external party, independent of the project, to do this. An organization's quality assurance department often carries out the work in this area.

Customer organization
It is essential that the project manager reasons from the customer's position. In fact he must identify with the project sponsor and achieve a high return from a small as possible investment. If the project manager comes from the supplier's organization, he will have the tendency to use more capacity, which can bring the business case into danger.

1.06 Project organization

Not to be forgotten rules

When agreeing the roles, you must not lose sight of the following issues:
- The project sponsor is responsible for the complete project, including the company benefits.
- The project sponsor is the chairman of a steering committee if it exists.
- The project manager carries out the day-to-day management.
- The project manager must think from the customer's, whose business case it is, position.
- The interests of the user and the supplier must be brought into, and kept in, balance.
- You have to take care in building up a good relationship with your key-stakeholders, if not they probably will overwhelm you with irrelevant demands during the execution stages of the project.
- Teams work autonomously within their own clearly defined work packages.

Communication must be organized so as to be unambiguous. Nothing is more annoying than people communicating at cross-purposes, holes in the communication appearing and untruths circulating all over the place. The rules of the game for responsibilities are as follows:

Role	Responsible for communication with
Project manager.	Project sponsor.
Sub-project manager.	Project manager.
Employee.	Sub-project manager or project manager.
Steering committee.	Company.
Steering committee.	Interested parties, unless explicitly delegated to the project manager.

3. RACI table

For the WBS elements, the RACI table shows who:
- Carries out the work (*R*esponsible)
- Checks and approves the work (*A*ccountable)
- Must give advice (*C*onsult)
- Must be informed (*I*nformed)

EXAMPLE 6-1 RACI TABLE

	Project manager John Winner	Sub-project manager Michel Leader	Designer Chris Nice	User John Hopeful
2.1 Design Office	A	R		
2.1.1 Office landscape		A	R	C
2.1.2 Furniture		A	R	C
2.1.3 ICT Front-ends		A		C
2.1.4 ICT Infrastructure		A		I

From the above, we can deduce that:

John Winner as Project manager	Must approve the design for the office.
Michel Leader as Sub-project manager	Combines the partial results into the final design. Manages, among others, Chris Nice to achieve this.
Chris Nice as Designer	Produces the design for the office landscape and the Furniture.
John Hopeful as User	Is consulted by the people carrying out the work 2.1.1, 2.1.2, and 2.1.3, and is informed about 2.1.4.

1.06 Project organization

1.07 Teamwork

THE END RESULT IS A REFLECTION OF THE PROJECT TEAM

The plan has been produced, the project sponsor has agreed it, and there is support from within the organization.

The meeting structure is clearly detailed and the specification of the project deliverables cannot be bettered.

It is people that must deliver the required result. An alternative definition of a project is, therefore:

A project is a collection of people, who, over a defined period of time, work together to achieve the project deliverables.

1.07 Teamwork

1.07-1 DEFINITIONS

Teams	A number of people who in connection with their work have regular contact with each other and who together in mutual task dependency co-operate to achieve a common goal, or result.
Teamwork	The concept that people work together as a team.

1.07-2 INTRODUCTION

Dependent on the complexity of the project and the size of the project organization, the composition and management can lie with a number of people. Ultimately it is the people who deliver the results, as they carry out what you have designed and described in the form of project procedures. This competence element goes hand in hand with "project organization", where the emphasis is put on responsibilities and structure as opposed to teamwork which is about taking responsibility and co-operation.

We often say that the total is more than the sum of the parts, and the project manager applies his "teamwork" skills to get more out of his team than just a well-oiled machine. This is about leading the team in such a way that the inherent potential in all the characters manifests itself in an optimum way.

The project manager is ultimately responsible. He begins by selecting the sub-project leaders, who in turn select their team members. It is stating the obvious to say that you go and look for the best people, in terms of both experience and personality. You look for the right combination of specialist and social skills.

The composition of the team is usually built upon the basis of specific knowledge, experience and /or skills of the team members. It is exactly these differences in expertise and skills that ensures the existence of synergy between the team members.

1.07-3 Process Steps

1. The forming stage.
2. The storming stage.
3. The norming stage.
4. The performing stage.
5. The adjourning stage.
6. Apply lessons learned.

This is in line with the Tuckman model. The essence of the model is that each team must go through each of the stages listed. Tuckman talks of forming, storming, norming and performing.

1. The forming stage
When the team first comes together, some time is necessary for the participants to become aware of the objectives, and the way in which they can best work together. It is a time of uncertainty, and questions in the area of emotions that arise are:
- Who is the boss here?
- What is actually expected of me?
- Are the people friendly?
- Am I able to carry out my task?

As project manager in this stage, you have to employ a directive style of management, so that it is clear to the team the direction they must take, and who the leader is (you!). This style ensures that the uncertainty does not get a chance to develop into all sorts of inefficiencies.

In addition you have to provide the team with clarity on the:
- Objectives they have to work to achieve.
- Way in which the co-operation is organized.

After a while, you stimulate the team to move on to a next stage, and you do this by increasing the pressure, for example by:
- Formulating a common goal.
- Continuously clarifying what the result of the project must be.
- Taking account of the team roles during the selection.
- Clarifying the need for the project.
- Clearly communicating the time pressures.
- Stimulating the co-operation.
- Asking someone to play devil's advocate.

2. The storming stage
For many project managers, this is one of the more difficult stages to guide the team through. This is the stage where the objectives are questioned, the project plan challenged, and normally where friction between the team members arises. This is a reaction to the uncertainty of the previous stage, and is unavoidable. There is a great temptation to move ahead too quickly to the following stage, and if you let this happen, the potential conflicts are repressed and cannot be brought out into the open and discussed. You will then be confronted with these at a later point in time when you don't need them. It is now, at the beginning of the project, that all your options are still open and it also gives everyone the chance to resolve their differences with each other.

In this stage you hone the personal characters such that they, communicatively, are on the same wavelength. You do this by stimulating discussion between them. In order to co-operate, people have to know each other and you have to know them as well. This may take a while, until you decide to steer the team into the next stage.

You could do this by making the following interventions:
- Obtain a common understanding of the objective.
- Accept that, during this phase, the team is still wrestling with itself.

- Trigger discussion about this without getting too much involved yourself.
- Agree on a number of performance indicators and targets.
- Encourage members to share insights and information with each other.
- Make clear how you expect everyone to co-operate.
- Make clear that in case of conflict you are the ultimate arbitrator.

3. The norming stage

In this stage, the team lays the foundation for an efficient and effective co-operation. The result of the conflicts from the previous stage is group cohesion that you as leader facilitate in a participating manner. It is important that the team members are in discussion with each other over the way in which they are going to carry out the project. Carefully you release your level of control for the realization.

Interventions to guide the team into the following stage are, for example:
- Work on a shared responsibility for the project results.
- Translate the common goal into measurable performance units.
- Effect consensus with respect to the goal and approach.
- Keep the focus on the external relationships, support, the feedback from the work floor and a potentially changed environment.
- Take risks to improve performance.
- Celebrate success, share rewards.
- Continuously evaluate the results of the team.

Challenge the team to take over the control themselves, so that in the following stage you can employ a delegating style of leadership.

4. The performing stage

If the previous stages have been passed through successfully, you now have, after a number of weeks, a good team with everyone working for each other. This is real team building, and something other than an outing of 'paintball shooting'. There is nothing wrong with the latter, but it does not contribute very much if you don't take the above to heart.

Many project managers whom I have spoken to, have let their teams go through the various stages too quickly. As the team is then not yet 'ripe', it will quickly fall back into a previous stage, with the result that you, as project manager, cannot adopt a consistent style of management.

If you allow the team the time to resolve a specific problem belonging to a particular stage, then they will evolve fairly naturally into this 'maturity' stage. The style of management that accompanies this is delegating, and consequently you, as project manager, have more time on your hands. In this stage, the team achieves independently the required results, solves the problems, works together in mutual interrelationships and develops a high level of group cohesion.

5. The adjourning stage

At the end of the project, the uncertainty increases once again. After all, it is now the question as to whether the team members will get the chance of another such project, which is as good and challenging as this one. The style of management applicable here is again, therefore, directive, whereby you clearly state how the close down, or 'adjournment' is to take place.

6. Apply lessons learned

Managing teams is a career long activity, in which we learn from one another, and in which you, as project manager, accumu-

1.07 Teamwork

late people knowledge and knowledge of group processes. As project manager, you must read up a lot about group dynamics, to continuously improve in the skill of leading teams.

1.07-4 SPECIAL TOPICS

1. Success factors

Following the selection of the employees, work begins on creating a successful team.

There are six success factors[1] that need to be present to ensure a team functions well:
- *Clear objectives,* whereby the team is fully aware of the required result, and the challenge involved in achieving it. The objectives also form the basis for making clear agreements.
- *Joint responsibility,* whereby team members support one another in their tasks, and which forms the basis for real co-operation.
- *Open communication,* there is transparency and clarity, team members are informed, and there is an open, honest and direct form of communication.
- *Mutual respect,* differences in age, culture, lifestyle and background form a source of energy; there is trust between everyone and a basis for consensus exists.
- *Flexibility,* the team strives towards a continuous improvement in their performance, and adapts itself to the environment and to changes in circumstances.
- *Show initiative,* by thinking ahead, and encouraging creativity and self-management.

As project manager, you must continuously keep an eye on all six of these factors and take action on them when necessary. Teamwork is also continuously keeping everyone focussed, and training the team members in co-operation.

There are different ways of achieving the desired situation; the formal approach through the kick-off or project start-up, but of course also via an informal get-together or drink.

EXAMPLE 7-1 TEAMBUILDING IN SCOTLAND

After the joint-venture between a Saudi and a British company had been set-up, a project manager was made responsible for overseeing the compilation of the first joint financial report. That was not an easy task as there were strongly divergent opinions between the two financial departments. These were aggravated by bad communication due to the geographical distance. Soon serious conflicts erupted. To deal with this situation, the project manager invited all Saudi and British staff to attend a survival course in Scotland. After a week of hiking, wood-cutting, hunting and fighting off insects the bonds of mutual dependency and friendship that had emerged were so strong that the compilation of the financial report was now seen as just a holiday.

In this case, you let the people do something together that is completely different and separate from their daily work. In this way they get to know each other in other circumstances, and realize that the others involved are also just ordinary people. Just doing that helps more than any number of talks or discussions.

In this example, team building has been approached proactively.

2. Team structure

As well as the knowledge and experience of the different team members, the team structure, which is dependent on the task that the team has to fulfil, influences how effectively it functions. I describe below a number of considerations for designing an effective structure.

---

1 (2001), *Managers en teams,* Korevaar, Politiek, Spruit, SAMSOM

For this, I use the work of Mintzberg[2] as a basis, and have applied that to organizing project teams.

- *Organizing according to knowledge, skills and function,* all designers in one team, the builders in another team, etc.
- *Organizing according to time,* all designers and builders who are involved in the first stage in one team, likewise for the second stage, etc.
- *Organizing according to the result to be delivered,* designers and builders of sub-system A in one team, likewise for sub-system B, etc.
- *Organizing according to user group,* each team is responsible for representing the interests of a particular user group.
- *Organizing according to location,* dependent on where the team members are stationed.

According to Mintzberg, when designing the right structure you take account of *the relationships within the work to be carried out.* These relationships can be determined on the basis of mutual facilities that are used, but also on the basis of the sequence of the mutual dependencies within the areas of work. The best approach is then to design the structure in such a way that the costs for co-ordination and communication are kept as low as possible.

Other criteria are:
- The size, when a particular team can only function well within a particular size, this becomes the main principle for the structure. Therefore, you see, for example, one project office for multiple projects, or multiple projects grouped together in one programme.
- The social coherence, straight to the point, this means that you put the people together in a team who can get along with each other.

3. Team roles according to Belbin

Dr. R Meredith Belbin's book on *Management Teams*[3] has had a large influence on the way in which we perceive the co-operation between various team members. His research shows that an efficient team has members who play nine very different roles in the team. Each role has an important, but different, function in the group dynamics.

Management roles

These roles covered under this heading are:
- SHAPER, the charismatic, extrovert manager, who is actively busy in influencing and 'shaping' the situation to his way of thinking.
- CO-ORDINATOR or CHAIR, a good co-ordinator keeps control over the team and particularly in critical moments, he tries to maintain unity. He succeeds in this because people respect him. He is the manager who gets the best out of his people.

Creative roles

Here we have the:
- RESOURCE-INVESTIGATOR, who knows how to establish contacts and finds solutions for problems within his network.
- PLANT, who comes with his (own) creative solutions to problems.

Operational roles

These are the:
- MONITOR-EVALUATOR, who quickly recognizes whether or not a certain direction for a solution will work.

---

2 (1983), *Structures in fives: designing effective organizations,* Henry Mintzberg, PRENTICE HALL Inc.

3 (1981) *Management Teams,* R. Meredith Belbin, BUTTERWORTH-HEINEMANN, Oxford

- TEAM WORKER, ensures there is a good atmosphere in the group.
- COMPLETER-FINISHER, maintains a high standard of quality and ensures that work is completed.
- IMPLEMENTOR, is strong in planning and organizing activities the team has to carry out.
- SPECIALIST, brings his own particular specialism into the team.

The Belbin team roles are especially useful for fathoming out the group dynamics and the role that each member plays. In addition, they can be useful in composing the team at the commencement of the project.

4. Problems with teams

Dysfunctional behavior in a team
Co-operation only works when people really do "work together". There are various types of dysfunctional behavior within a team, and a number are stated below:
- Starting on something without discussion first.
- Setting unclear objectives.
- Keeping something that's frustrating you to yourself.
- Employing a hidden agenda.
- Manipulation.
- Letting someone else down.
- Rumor mongering.
- Letting a team member muddle on, when you have the solution.
- Acting uninterestedly.
- Pointing out guilty parties.
- Unwillingness to take responsibility.
- Holding information back.
- Looking for a scapegoat.
- Mocking and gloating.
- Glossing over mistakes.
- Making a new idea look absurd.
- Always pointing to problems.

You should tackle dysfunctional behavior as soon as it arises. "They act just like children", is what I heard one project manager say, and he had a point. When team members display this sort of behavior within the team, you are confronted with a low level of task maturity in the area of co-operation, and the appropriate style of management to use is then a directive style.

Dysfunctional teams
Sometimes, it is unavoidable that a team becomes "blocked" in their co-operation.

Symptoms of this are[4]:
- Loss of energy or enthusiasm.
- A feeling of helplessness.
- Lack of purposefulness and identity.
- Lacklustre, non-constructive and one-sided discussions with no openness.
- Meetings for which the agenda is more important than the result.
- Cynicism and mistrust.
- Personal attacks behind someone's back towards, and in the presence of, outsiders.
- The pointing of accusatory fingers at top management and the rest of the organization.

In one way or another you have to break through such a deadlock. A first step is to go back to the starting point; why the team exists, and what the objectives of the team are. It is also possible to remove a number of dysfunctional team members, or to motivate them to provide a constructive contribution to the team. A change in the strategy can jolt the team awake. You give them a new challenge and motivate them to tackle it. An external coach can also be brought in to get the team going again.

---

4 (2001), *Managers en teams*, Korenvaar e.a., SAMSON

1.07 Teamwork

In a very serious situation, you can decide to replace the whole team, and if you do not do this, the project sponsor may well do it himself, or maybe even take you off the project.

Group blindness
A separate phenomenon is group blindness. This arises when a group of people are under pressure to achieve consensus on all of their decisions. The pressure on unity is then so great that no-one dares to bring an opposing opinion into the team. After a while, differences in opinion are not even recognized any more.

Symptoms of teams suffering from this are:
- The illusion of invulnerability.
- A negative attitude towards competitors.
- The unshakable belief in the right to exist.
- The holiness of reaching agreement.
- Setting up a protective shield.

History is full of examples. A well known example of group thinking is the decision making of the committee that advised Kennedy on policy during the Cuba crisis. Parallels can also be found in more recent history.

The danger within a project is that team members are no longer aware of what is happening around the project. Everyone is busy, so to speak, dragging the project to the finishing line and forgets that there is in fact no longer a business case present. When the company management then pull the plug on the project, everyone is surprised and outraged.

1.08 Problem resolution

PART OF THE SOLUTION, OR PART OF THE PROBLEM

There are two types of problems:

1. Problems which get worse if you do nothing about them.

2. Problems which will go away by themselves if you do nothing about them.

There is only one way to find out which type of problem we are dealing with.

To wait.

1.08 Problem resolution

1.08-1 DEFINITIONS

Brainstorming	A creativity technique with the objective of generating many new ideas on a particular problem or issue.
Lateral thinking	Rearranging existing information (differently) in order to create new information.
Limitation	A situation for which a change is desirable, but which is not possible within the boundaries set.
Problem	A situation for which a change is desirable and conceivable.
Problem resolution	An approach to changing a situation in the direction desired.

1.08-2 INTRODUCTION

There is no project in which everything goes according to plan. Problems are part of projects. The extent to which a project team is capable of anticipating, preventing and resolving problems, partly determines their success as a team. Some problems are easy to solve, others require a lot of creativity from the team. It is necessary to have a system to record problems and to monitor the status of the solution. Such a system may be a simple file, or an advanced database in which you carefully record the progress. Which system you select depends on the complexity of the project.

Problem resolution has an overlap with "creativity", in the sense that you often have to be creative to arrive at the solution to a specific problem. Where the two do not overlap, is in the type of solution. Creative means something new and original, whereas for a specific problem it is completely acceptable, and maybe even preferable, for you to opt for a solution that already exists (non-creative).

1.08 Problem resolution

1.08-3 PROCESS STEPS

1. Add problem procedure.
2. Identify problems.
3. Determine the cause.
4. Apply creative methods.
5. Evaluate and select alternatives.
6. Implement the solution.
7. Apply lessons learned

1. Add problem procedure

The diagram below contains a flow diagram for dealing with errors or faults. The problems register consists of the following headings:
- Reference number, date and author.
- Description.
- Seriousness of the issue.
- Responsible team member.
- History of the decision making.
- Actual status.

2. Identify problems

This may seem obvious, but very often it is difficult to admit that there is a problem. After a while, such "blindness" in the project management results in team members no longer reporting problems, which is obviously not desirable. As project manager, you have to ensure that all problems are made visible.

So identifying starts with an open mind and atmosphere. When a problem is visible, you have to decide to what extent you need to deal with it. If it is a relevant problem, you document it in the problem register.

The immediate question that then arises is: What is relevant? A problem is relevant when it poses a risk for the project if it is not solved. This is the first check, which can be carried out in different areas of the project organization. This is only possible when the staff are in a position to assess the problem,

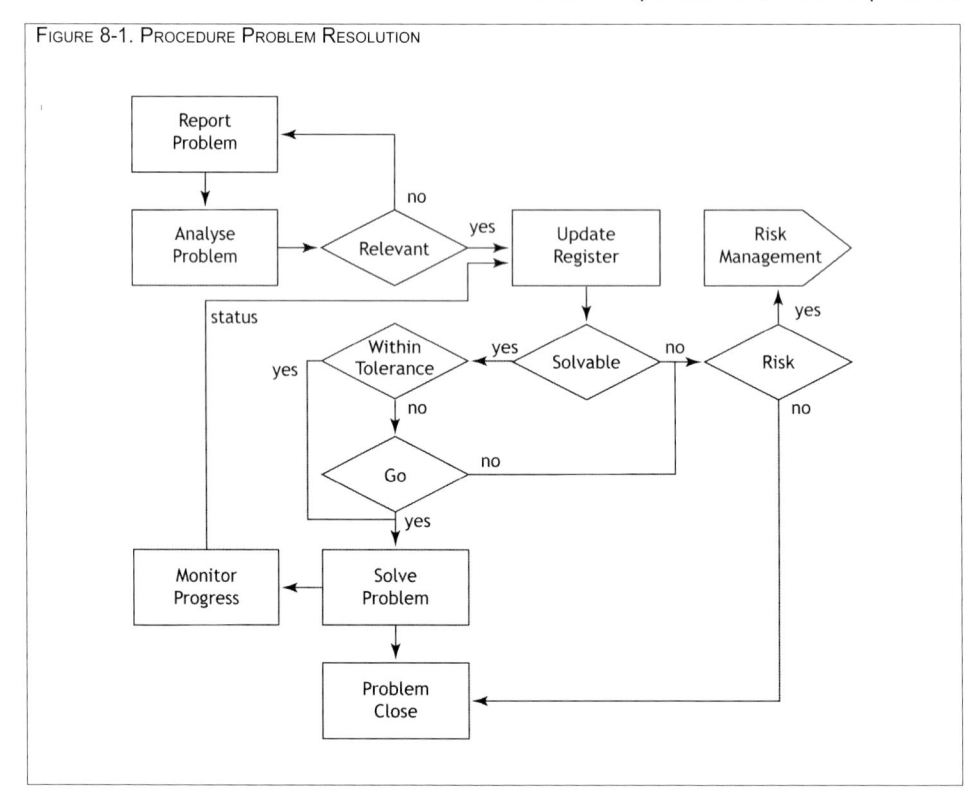

FIGURE 8-1. PROCEDURE PROBLEM RESOLUTION

1.08 Problem resolution

based on the information they have received on the objectives of the project and the deliverables.

As well as problems there are also limitations. This distinction is important because there is no solution for a limitation. The limitation must be included in the risk management process in order to be able to take measures there to mitigate the impact of the risk caused by the limitation.

3. Determine the cause
Now it has been determined whether or not the problem is relevant, the problem has to be analyzed. There are several tools for this, and the seven tools for quality are well-known, namely:
- *Check sheet:* keep a tally of each problem; this makes it easy to measure its development over time.
- *Ishikawa*, also called a cause and effect diagram, helps you to structurally analyze a problem to find out its possible causes.
- *Control Chart*, in which you can identify statistical deviations in repeated processes.
- *Flow diagram*, to schematically show the various steps in a process, and, if necessary, make changes to it.
- *Histogram*, to compare various outcomes with each other (this is, in fact, a graphical form of the first tool).
- *Pareto Analysis*: 20% of the functions causes in 80% of the problems; a prioritizing tool for problems.
- *Scatter diagram*, identifying the correlation between two variables.

In addition to these, there are also tools such as the force field analysis, system thinking, thinking hats and lateral thinking.

The principle: think first act later applies to a lot of the project management techniques, and the same applies to resolving problems: firstly analyze, then come up with the solution and finally implement the solution.

4. Apply creative methods
In the previous process step, a number of methods have been mentioned for solving a problem creatively. Creatively means in an original way or innovative i.e. not following the traditional paths. Many problems are insoluble, because people keep going round in circles leading to any solution only making the problem worse.

5. Evaluate and select solutions
Together with the interested parties, the project manager selects a solution, which in terms of cost/revenues is the most effective and efficient. You also determine the impact on other work and this is also part of the consideration for the choice the parties involved have to make.

6. Implement the solution
When the parties involved have selected the solution, you have to plan it in and allocate people to it. This, of course, has an impact on other work with respect to priorities and possible changes in priorities.

7. Apply lessons learned
We learn from problems at two levels. Firstly, directly on the project, when a certain problem occurs for which the cause can be found in the manner in which the work is carried out. In this case, you have to change that process.

Secondly, in the long term you learn how to organise a problem solving process, how certain techniques work and when they are applicable and when not.

Just as with all other competence elements, you have the professional obligation to share your experience with others.

1.08-4 Special Topics

1. Brainstorming
There are different brainstorming techniques. They all have the objective of stimulating the creativity of the participants. A number of rules apply to brainstorming:
- A start and finish time.
- A clear objective or goal.
- A time in which everyone can call out their ideas.
- A time in which the attendees can evaluate the ideas.
- The production of a list of actions and decisions.

During the collection of ideas, there must be no discussion on the feasibility. Every idea is O.K., also the impossible ones, as these can potentially help the other participants think of an idea that is feasible. We talk about "dumping" ideas, and after the "dump", the participants look to see if somewhere in the "rubbish" there are some worthwhile ideas – which turns out often to be the case.

Another form of brainstorming is the "yes, and …" variant, in which the participants stimulate each other to build further on the last idea. That happens by always starting the next sentence with "yes and …" and then to immediately say what is in your thoughts. The danger is that, because you think of a stupid idea, you become stuck, but that is precisely the intention; to get you to think laterally and step outside your normal boundaries.

You can easily apply the "yes and …" technique in a meeting, without the need for it to be a formal brainstorm session. When the discussion stalls, you can propose that the participants always react by beginning with the words yes and … and then they make their point. The effect on the meeting is amazing.

At the beginning of the meeting you discuss the procedure, if that has not already been done in one way or another. You say when particular subjects can, and can no longer, be raised. In advance, the chairman works towards agreement on the way in which the meeting will run. When the meeting has to take decisions, you firstly seek agreement on the way this will happen. This prevents people returning at a later stage to decisions already taken. If it is not possible to reach agreement, you can, as project manager (when you have the power to do so) take the decision yourself. If necessary, you can minute the fact that some team members only accepted the decision under protest, which in any case allows the meeting to continue further. To prevent repetitive discussion, you can decide to also record the arguments for particular decisions taken.

During the meeting, the chairman is continuously mindful of two aspects; the task of running the meeting, and the relational side. This is a very intense task, whereby it is almost impossible to also take part in the subject matter of the discussion. If this does become necessary, it is best to mention this during the meeting, and, if necessary, let someone else temporarily take over the chairmanship of the meeting.

2. Force field analysis
In the force field analysis we look at a problem situation by making two lists; one list with forces which advance the solution, and another list with forces which hinder the solution. You go through the following steps, together with the team that has to solve the problem:
- Formulate the problem in unambiguous, clear and comprehensible words.
- Formulate both the current and desired situations.

1.08 Problem resolution

- Make a list of forces which advance the solution.
- Make a list of forces which hinder the solution.
- Discuss the different forces in the team, and add new ones if necessary.
- Determine the relationship, and sort on importance, degree of difficulty and clarity.
- Determine actions to reduce hindrances and to increase strengthening forces.
- Plan the actions and allocate them.

3. Manage towards consensus

It can happen that for a particular solution, you want to achieve as much consensus as possible.

According to Oomkes[1] you point out the following basic principles to your team members:

- Recognize that your own knowledge is insufficient.
- Other team members can fill in the gaps in your knowledge.
- For each opinion, determine whether it is based on expertise, common sense or guesswork.
- Share opinions and knowledge in order to influence the team positively.
- Listen to other team members and allow yourself to be influenced.
- Avoid votes, agreeing compromises, or yielding, just to keep the peace.
- Differences of opinion can be helpful.

Achieving consensus may be a lengthy process, as both parties must take their time to get to know each other better, and strive for a win-win situation.

Oomkes names the following starting points:
- Both parties realize that their own possibilities are incomplete.
- Both parties can fill these gaps.
- Are opinions based on expertise, common sense or guesswork?
- Share information to stimulate co-operation.
- Parties are prepared to be influenced by each other.
- Do not cover up difficult topics and do not avoid them either.
- Differences of opinion are useful.

4. System thinking

Definitions

In the system approach, specific attention is paid to the greater picture, the totality; it is a holistic view of situations. A number of definitions:

Holism *(<Gr), o., biological-philosophical theory which assumes the life forms to be determined by the totality of the living, which is more than the sum of the parts.*

Holism *[biological-philosophical teaching] -after 1950- derived from gr. Holos [whole]*

A number of quotes:
- A system is a way of looking at the world.[2]
- A discipline through which we can learn to see the whole. It is the attitude to see mutual relations instead of things, to see patterns of change instead of statistical snapshots in time.[3]
- Depending on the objective set by the researcher, a system is a collection of elements which are distinguishable within the total reality. These elements

---

[1] (1998), *Training als beroep*, F R. Oomkes, BOOM

[2] (1975) *An introduction to General Systems Thinking*, Gerald M. Weinberg, JOHN WILEY & SONS, New York

[3] (1990) *The Fifth Discipline*, Peter M. Senge, DOUBLEDAY

1.08 Problem resolution

have mutual relationships and (possibly) relationships with other elements from the total reality.[4]

As a great deal of project management consists of dividing the larger whole up into smaller parts, this competence is important for retaining an overview of the situation.

The system approach has a long history. In Bertalanffy[5] came with the notion of thinking in terms of systems, and his definition of this was:

> *A coherent totality of elements that represents the characteristics of the whole, which cannot be connected to one of the separate elements.*

Systems try to maintain a stable condition. Take man for instance; anatomically, he can be divided into all number of different parts. If, however, you just look at the bones or an organ, it is no longer a human being. When it is cold in his environment, man will do whatever he can to keep his body temperature at the right level. A lot of things happen automatically and are taken care of by the body itself, but other things are not, such as when someone consciously puts on warm clothes. But instinctively there is always an urge to return to a stable situation.

Apply this to a project; when things are not clear, people start guessing, and they invent clarity in the form of gossip and rumors. When the management tries to invalidate or refute the gossip or rumors, there is a chance that they will not be believed; the management is holding things back, and is not reliable. See how the system is back in balance again; the conflict between the information from the flow of rumors, and that from the management, is resolved by describing the management as unreliable.

The system approach is a way of looking at the world around you in general, and at a project in particular. On the one hand, it divides the world up into smaller sub-systems, and at the same time it doesn't lose sight of the links between these sub-systems.

The description of a system

To clarify the working of a system, the elements of the system, and the relationship between these elements, is described. This can be done for both technical and organizational systems. The basis of the description is defining the boundaries of the system, as this determines what will be investigated and what will not. What falls outside these boundaries is the environment, or the universe.

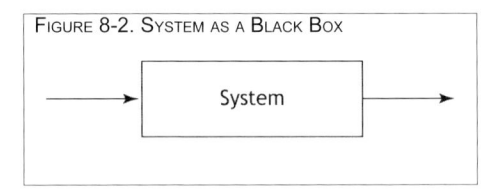

FIGURE 8-2. SYSTEM AS A BLACK BOX

The relationship or interfaces of the system with the environment is described. The researcher sees the system as a black box and does not yet concern himself with what the content of it is. There is input received by the system, and output delivered by the system. The way in which the 'transformation' takes place is only important in the second instance, when the black box is opened.

---

4 (1993) *Oriëntatiecursus bedrijfs- en bestuurskunde,* OPEN UNIVERSITEIT, Heerlen
5 (1969) *General System Theory,* Ludwig von Bertalanffy

1.08 Problem resolution

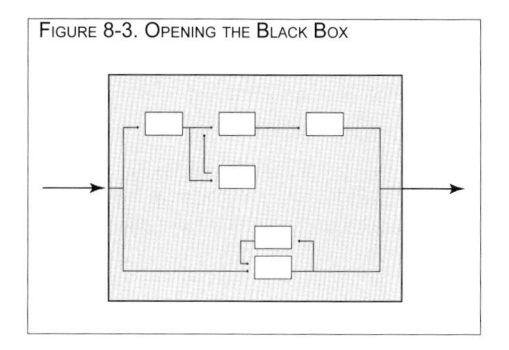

FIGURE 8-3. OPENING THE BLACK BOX

Each system can be divided into sub-systems. Each sub-system is also a black box with its own input and own output. The arrows show the presence of a relationship or an interface, which must also be described.

The total system is under control when it delivers the output that is required. Usually this does not happen by itself and is it necessary to organise a control loop for it. By implementing such a loop, the quality of the input or the output can be measured and compared with standards already implemented earlier.

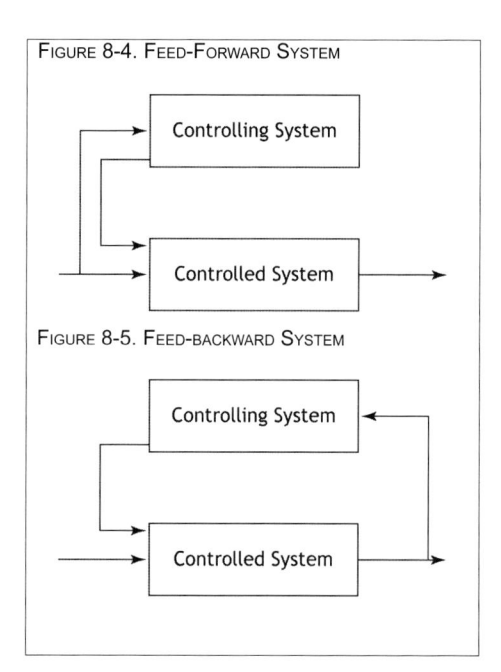

FIGURE 8-4. FEED-FORWARD SYSTEM

FIGURE 8-5. FEED-BACKWARD SYSTEM

On the basis of this comparison measures can be taken. We speak of a feed-forward loop (prevention) when the input is measured, and of a feedback loop (correction) when the output is measured.

In general we find problems in the common ground or interfaces between the sub-systems. The output of one is the input of the other, and there is an interface problem when these do not match each other. The absence of a good interface specification is potentially the cause of this problem.

Another problem is that one system is waiting for the output of another system before it can carry on. Here, a **collect** and a **deliver** obligation could ensure that the receiver does not just sit and wait for input.

System approach and problem solving
The system approach is a way of looking at problems. We have already done something of that with the fishbone diagram and the force field analysis, when we introduced these as methods for solving problems. The system approach is something similar to these.

The following step-by-step plan systematically indicates which steps you have to take to use this technique for solving problems in your project:
- Study and describe the problem, and do not yet look for causes.
- Define the system.
- Select the major trends and patterns.

EXAMPLE 8-1 WHO'S TO BLAME
Two teams in a project have a serious conflict with each other. The one is blaming the other for not being able to start because a certain specification had been received too late. The other team defends itself by stating that it had been ready a long time, but nobody had asked for it.

1.08 Problem resolution

- Determine the underlying systems and structures.
- Build a model.
- Check the model.
- Identify possible actions.
- Carry out the actions.
- Repeat the cycle.

Thinking in systems is something which can only really be learned by practicing it. Sometimes it is referred to as a helicopter view. Peter Senge calls systems thinking the cornerstone of a learning organization[6].

---

6 (1990) *The Fifth Discipline*, Peter M. Senge, DOUBLEDAY

1.08 Problem resolution

EXAMPLE 8-2 BOB THE PROJECT MANAGER

Bob, a project manager who has just finished the one day course "Managing projects successfully" at the training company WWSR.

Bob is keen to go, his first real project. He will show everyone what it means to manage a project successfully. He remembers the words of Jean-Claude the trainer who said: "*Cut the crap, and get down to work, that is the standard rule in project management*". Full of enthusiasm he gets going with his team. The next release which will be delivered on the 1st of December contains a large amount of functionality, it is an ambitious date, but not impossible.

Halfway through the project Bob notices that not everything is going as well as he would have liked. This doesn't look good, and Bob is very worried. He wonders how he is going to get himself out of this. He surfs on the internet and, among other things, he reads the Chaos report from the Standish group; putting more people into the team is not going to work. This means that there is only one solution left. People will have to work overtime. In the months following, this intervention seems to have worked.

In the following month, he is faced with a number of people reporting sick, whereby the production falls seriously behind. An attempt to force the team to work even more overtime results in an enormous argument, after which the team no longer wishes to work under Bob. How it all ended Bob doesn't know anymore, because he has now been at home for six months without a job. The only thing he heard was something about an certified project manager who finished the project off. Actually, he is not that interested, project management is not something he aspires to anymore.

What did Bob overlook? Approach this question by looking at this case as a system.

FIGURE 8-6. SYSTEM: MOTIVATION

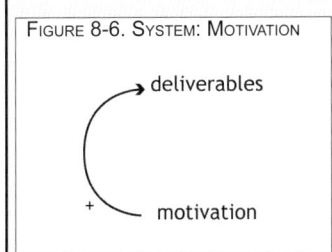

Bob tells the staff at the start of his project what he expects of them, and what the objectives are.

For a large part, the performance is determined by the motivation of the team. The more motivated the team is, the more results they deliver.

Then Bob notices that the team is falling behind in the production. He momentarily considers putting more people into the team, but for well argued reasons, he decides against this. So working overtime it is then the solution.

The diagram shows how systems thinking works. More people means fewer functions, more work means an increase in the capacity of the team and therefore more functions. It all seems to go well until he is faced with people reporting in sick. Because Bob's picture of his project system is that more overtime results in more functions, he decides to make that intervention again, with disastrous results as we have read. Bob's picture of the system wasn't complete, he overlooked one factor.

FIGURE 8-7. SYSTEM: OVERTIME

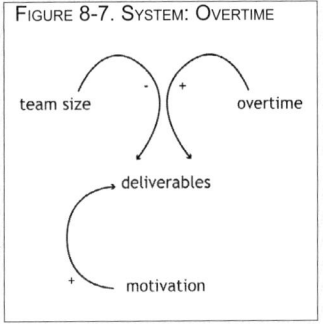

The intervention to work overtime has another effect, which does not show up until later. It is a negative effect on the motivation of the employees.

FIGURE 8-8. SYSTEM: DEMOTIVATION

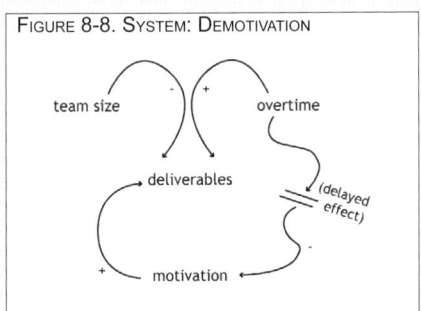

Once this ball started rolling, it was not possible to stop it. When Bob forced the team to work even more overtime, he was faced with the highly dominant effect of the demotivation. If he had understood his system, he would have been better able to address the problems he was faced with.

(Adapted and changed from Pascal Van Cauwenbergh, Bob the project manager thinks about systems, www.nayima.be).

1.08 Problem resolution

1.09 Project structures

IN SMALL PARTS

According to a saying, it is easy to eat an elephant, as long as you do it
bite by bite.

Project structures are a collection of techniques to create order in a project by representing certain aspects in a structured manner.

1.09 Project Structures

1.09-1 Definitions

Product Breakdown Structure (PBS)	Schematic representation of a hierarchic breakdown of the products in a plan.
Product Description	Description of the objective, the composition, the origin, the responsibilities and the quality requirements and assessment of a product.
Product Flow Diagram (PFD)	Schematic representation of the sequence and the mutual dependencies of the products.
Project structure	Schematic representation of the products and/or activities of a project.
Work Breakdown Structure (WBS)	Result oriented breakdown of the work that has to be delivered to achieve the project objectives and at the same time deliver the required results.
WBS dictionary	Document in which every component of the WBS is described.
Work package	The lowest level of the WBS.
Work package description	Total of information and agreements required to achieve and control a work package.

1.09-2 INTRODUCTION

If there is something a good project manager does, it is bring structure to chaos. You structure by splitting larger entities into smaller parts, without endangering the underlying cohesion. The two techniques you have at your disposal to do that are:

- Breakdown structures.
- Matrices.

You use the breakdown structures to split up entities into smaller parts. We have:

- WBS: Project Work Breakdown Structure.
- OBS: Organization Breakdown Structure.
- CBS: Cost Breakdown Structure.
- FBS: Functional Breakdown Structure.
- PBS: Portfolio Breakdown Structure.
- PBS: Problem Breakdown Structure.
- PBS: Product Breakdown Structure.
- PWBS: Programme Work Breakdown Structure.
- RBS: Resource Breakdown Structure.
- RBS: Risk Breakdown Structure.
- SBS: Stakeholder Breakdown Structure.

It is confusing, because some of the abbreviations for different breakdown structures are the same. Although not all of these structures will be addressed in this chapter, the principles discussed are applicable to all structures. Represented graphically, a breakdown structure looks most like an organization chart in which the divisions are visible. You divide up until you have found a size that is controllable. The breakdown structures often go hand in hand with an accompanying dictionary, in which the different structure elements are described briefly and to the point. Of all these structures, the Work Breakdown Structure is the most important, and is the basis for practically all scheduling, budgeting and control activities that the project manager has to carry out. The other structuring technique we come across are the matrices we use for linking various breakdown structures together. For instance we have:

- The Stakeholder matrices.
- The RACI Matrix.
- The Responsibilities Matrix.
- The Risk Impact Matrix.

All matrices are two dimensional tables with a breakdown structure on each axis, and in which the link can be made in the overlapping cells. Sometimes (as with the RACI matrix, which will be discussed elsewhere), different symbols are used to achieve even more depth.

1.09-3 PROCESS STEPS

1. Define PPP breakdown.
2. Determine responsibilities.
3. Determine requirements.
4. Decompose and analyze.
5. Maintain and communicate.
6. Apply lessons learned.

1. Defining PPP breakdown

A lot of organizations use so-called cost centres to compare budgets and actual costs. These are included in the administration as ledger accounts, and are used to assess the line managers in terms of how they control the costs of their unit. The different accounts are included in the so-called chart of accounts. This chart of ledger accounts is also a breakdown structure, but then for the permanent organization.

Something similar is also required for the whole structure of projects. The mistake often made is that projects are included in the existing accounting systems, and what is then often overlooked is the fact that an accountant looks back, whereas as project manager you need a system with which you can look forward. Furthermore, a line organization's control cycle (monthly) is insufficient for a project (one to two weeks). Therefore, the project manager needs his own administration.

What the chart of accounts is to the permanent organization, the PPP breakdown structure is to the organization of projects. PPP stands for all portfolios, programmes and projects which are active in an organization. Such a PPP structure might look like the figure below.

At the lowest level we find the projects (P01 up to P29 and the Tour Event Project), which have been grouped in a certain way, either in programmes (for related projects), or in a sub-portfolio which is, for instance, linked to certain strategic objectives. In the accompanying programme and project management plans, an even deeper breakdown is then made for detailing a programme and/or a project breakdown structure (respectively PWBS and WBS) in depth.

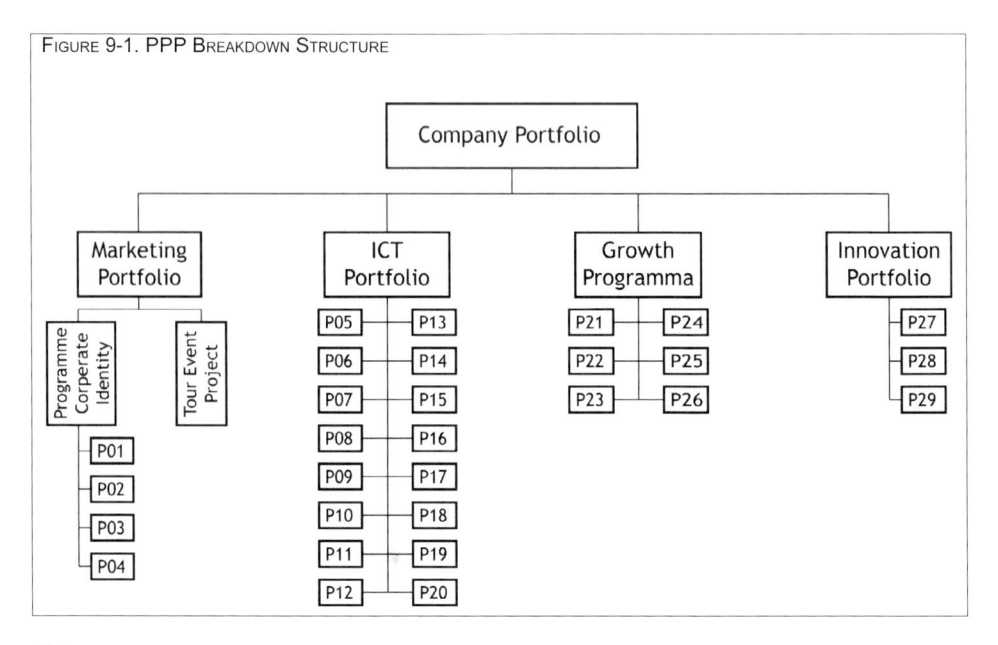

FIGURE 9-1. PPP BREAKDOWN STRUCTURE

1.09 Project Structures

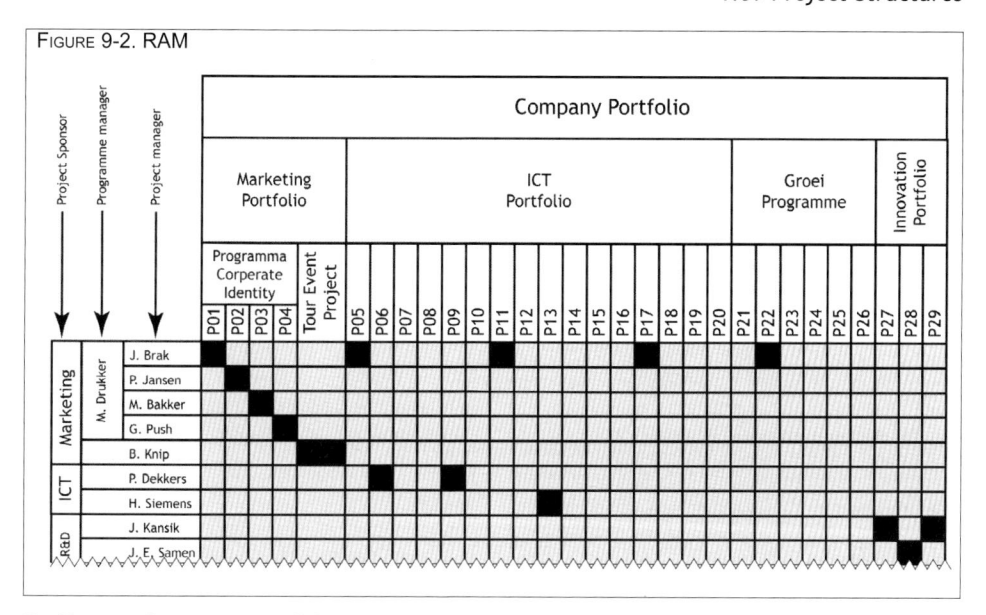

FIGURE 9-2. RAM

2. Determine responsibilities

A next step is to appoint the responsible job holders. In the PPP structure, these are the managers for the different portfolios, programmes and projects. Portfolio managers are line functions, and the other two (programme and project manager), have been appointed for the duration of the programme or the project.

To establish the link, a breakdown structure of the organization is needed (an OBS), which we link to the so-called PPP breakdown structure in a matrix (the so called RAM: Responsibility Assignment Matrix). We find the PPP breakdown structure in the columns, and the OBS in the rows of the matrix. For the previously illustrated structure, this could, for example, look as above.

The various projects and programmes have project sponsors and suppliers in the form of line managers, a programme manager and a number of project managers. For projects being carried out in the permanent organization, you have to ensure that the final project sponsorship always resides with a line manager, and this ensures there is a link with the permanent organization.

The accounts which we want to have control of at this level have been colored black, and are called Control Accounts. For such a Control Account, we appoint someone who is responsible for all the work included in this account. We will see this same principle again, when we split up the project using a WBS.

3. Determine requirements

The way in which an organization wants to have control over its projects, determines the way in which it will put together the PPP breakdown structure, and this has consequences for all projects and programmes, as they are a part of this superstructure. With respect to the WBS per project or programme, agreements must be made on:

- The representation.
- The depth.
- Standard divisions.
- The number of control accounts.
- Compulsory matrices.
- Span-of-control allowed.
- Set of tools.

127

1.09 Project Structures

- Numbering.
- Standard templates.
- Link to ledger accounts.

and in this way, the underlying connection remains intact.

There are two quality principles for a good WBS[1]:
- The minimum that has to be present.
- The demands of the project

I will discuss a number of minimum requirements for putting together a WBS in more detail.

A WBS is a delivery oriented breakdown of the work to be delivered. One of the most common mistakes is including activities in the WBS.

When making the WBS, the focus is on what the team delivers during the project, and not on which activities the project team has to carry out, that comes later. The elements of the WBS can best be described by *adjectives and nouns*.

The WBS is about the WHAT, and not yet about the HOW.

> EXAMPLE 9-1 WBS - NO ACTIVITIES
> RIGHT:
> Functional Design
> Technical Design
> Build
> Acceptance
> WRONG:
> Make Functional Design
> Make Technical Design
> Build the System
> Accept the System

The WBS can be presented as a diagram, text or as a table. Although in most examples you see a graphic representation, you will notice that in practice this is difficult with a large WBS, as you very quickly need a large size of paper to print the WBS.

Initially, it is preferable to do this on a large sheet of wrapping paper, during a brainstorm with *the most important parties involved,* and *the staff who will have to deliver the work!* If this is not possible, then in any case with a representative group of them. In this first team, by doing this, you "live through" the scope.

Initially, the breakdown is a top down approach, which will continue with "cutting up" to a level at which it is easily possible to *identify the activities to be carried out by the team,* and to make realistic estimates. That lowest level is called a work package.

When splitting up, we also look at how we will be managing, as this determines the control accounts in the intermediate levels. The breakdown is *a hierarchic structure*. Taken together, all work packages form *100%* of the element above it, and that also applies to the intermediate elements.

There is yet another consideration for splitting up, and this has to do with the frequency in which you want to measure the progress. When this is done on a two weekly basis, the work package (lowest level of the WBS) would, on average, also have a duration of about two weeks. In this way, the status of a work package is always one of the following:

- Not yet started.
- Started in the last period.
- Finished in the last period.
- Finished in previous periods.

---

1 (2006) *Practice Standard for Work Breakdown Structures*, PROJECT MANAGEMENT INSTITUTE

1.09 Project Structures

By using such a splitting up process, you have a strong instrument to measure progress. This is better than an activity which is 25% completed, as you cannot do enough with that when controlling your projects. People are inclined to estimate the progress positively.

EXAMPLE 9-2 WBS
1. Functional Design
    1.1. Function description
        1.1.1. Input function
        1.1.2. Processing function
        1.1.3. Printing function
    1.2. Control functions
2. Technical Design
    2.1. TD Sub-systems
        2.1.1. TD Input
        2.1.2. TD Processing
        2.1.3. TD Print
    2.2. Interface Specifications
    2.3. Hardware

Etc.

Note: the above is not staging! It is possible that when input function 1.1.1 is ready, the team immediately starts with 2.1.1 TD input.

What is good about this method, is that you actually have the proof that something is finished. Once the WBS has been approved, it forms the basis for measuring the progress of the delivered parts of the scope. The team only delivers what is in the WBS, no more and no less.

The link with the different operational units, which have been sub-divided with the help of the OBS, is carried out by using a responsibility matrix (RAM: Responsibility Assignment Matrix). What we have shown earlier for the company portfolio, must also be carried out for the project in such a way that from top to bottom, the work always has one person who is responsible.

4. Decompose and analyze

Here I will discuss in outline the elaboration of three structures which, as a minimum, must be present a project:
- The WBS, in which the scope has been split up.
- The OBS, in which the project organization has been split up.
- The RAM, in which the WBS and the OBS are linked.

Depending on the stage of the project, and the clarity that is present or not regarding the project deliverables, there are a number of techniques for developing the WBS. These are:
- Top-down approach.
- Bottom-up approach.
- According to company standards.
- WBS templates.

Developing the WBS – Top-down

If you have to start anywhere, then the best way is to start at the top, at the end result. Ask yourself the question: *"What will be working when the project has been completed successfully?"* The top-down approach provides a good insight into the most important sub-deliverables, and because you start top-down, it is possible to do this with the main parties involved i.e. the project sponsor, representatives of the supplier and the various user groups. The WBS process ensures support from them with respect to the scope to be delivered.

Developing the OBS and RAM

Because you started top-down, you can already take account of which party is responsible for certain deliveries. The first contours are created of an organization which has to deliver the different results, and you involve both internal and external suppliers in this. In consultation, the OBS and RAM are developed alongside each other, enabling sup-

1.09 Project Structures

port to be created for the responsibilities carried during the execution of the project.

Bottom-up iterations
As soon as the main levels of WBS and OBS are clear, and the responsibility structure in the RAM has been described in outline, we involve representatives of the people carrying out the work in the process. The technical experts have to provide their input, and this creates support for the technical feasibility of the project. Where these are compulsory, we make use of the available standards and templates, thus ensuring that the relationship between line organization and the project organization is maintained. In the line organization, support is generated for the way in which we will carry out the project.

From the time we go bottom-up, it is possible that we have to return to the higher levels of both structures. A number of iteration cycles arise, which will possibly be intensified by the other scheduling processes such as:
- Budgeting.
- Planning the duration.
- Risk analysis and responses to be taken.

Frequent amendments will have to be made in the WBS leading to an end result which has to be: a WBS in which all project deliverables have been specified.

One of the possible outcomes of this process is that there is not yet sufficient information available to describe a certain section in detail. In this case, we are confronted with a *"rolling wave"* planning of the scope to be delivered, and we have to divide up the first level of the WBS into stages. In this event, it is important to explicitly indicate that a certain element is a stage. The packages that can't be broken down because a lack of information are called planning packages.

At the end of each stage, you can split up the WBS further, and there is a point in time at which the project sponsor has to decide whether or not to continue with a following stage. In this way, we obtain support for the project deliverables and the developing plans.

This so-called go-no go decision is needed, because at the end of a certain stage, there is enough information available to provide a proper budget and time estimate.

Analyzing the breakdown structures
In one respect, this is done during the setting up of these structures, and for each version you ask as a minimum, the following questions:
- Has the 100% rule been adhered to?
- For the WBS: only adjectives and nouns.
- For the OBS: is the responsible team leader for each unit known?

Analyzing the matrices
There are always two analyses you have to carry out:
- A vertical analysis.
- A horizontal analysis.

You have to apply this to the responsibilities matrix (RAM), in which the different WBS elements are shown in the columns, and the

---

EXAMPLE 9-3 WBS AND STAGING
1. Stage1: Functional Design
   1.1. Function description
      1.1.1. Input function
      1.1.2. Process function
      1.1.3. Print function
   1.2. Control functions
2. Stage 2: Technical Design
3. Stage 3: Build
4. Stage 4: Acceptance

Compare this to the example on the previous page, where the technical design has been split into more detail. The team firstly finishes stage 1 before commencing stage 2.

responsible organization units, with their managers, in the rows.

The vertical analysis shows whether all units always have just one person with the ultimate responsibility, and the horizontal analysis shows the span of control of the different people responsible.

5. Maintain and communicate

A number of the structures used form the starting point, from which the project manager controls the progress of his project. I have already mentioned the three structures, which should as a minimum be present in a project: the WBS, the OBS and the RAM. These form a part of the project management plan, and have been accepted by the main parties involved prior to the start of the project execution. From then on, they come under change control, meaning that when a change is required, this has to be preceded by a (fast) decision making process.

The project manager now communicates to his team members when they can start a series of work packages, and in the work package description we find:
- Which activities.
- Which dependencies.
- How critical it is.
- When it has to be completed.
- Various work agreements.

This process is handled by a work authorisation system the project manager is using.

During the project, the insights change, and sometimes it may be necessary to change the structures. You have to take this into account during the set up, so that the breakdown structures and matrices can be properly maintained. Problems arise when you adopt the WBS in a scheduling software, where you detail it further into activities. You then are confronted with some challenges.

Maintaining the OBS / RAM
This problem arises because you let yourself be tempted into allocating the management responsibility to a relatively low level. This leads to a lot of control accounts, and a heavy reporting structure. The number of control accounts is a good indicator for the effectiveness of the structure introduced. Too many means too many different responsibilities, resulting in a non-transparent reporting structure, something you should try to avoid. When you leave the control accounts at a higher level, this problem will appear less, and the maintenance will also be less time consuming.

Software often assumes ABS
With scheduling software, just as with the WBS, it is possible to introduce a hierarchic structure, where you are dealing with activities and summary tasks. Scheduling software assume a breakdown of activities (Activity Breakdown Structure), and not a breakdown of work.

It is best to adopt the work breakdown as summary tasks, as the work package is then the lowest summary task under which the actual activities can then be identified.

6. Apply lessons learned

The experience of an organization is embedded in the standards used, and in the templates available for the breakdown structures and matrices. The danger of standards is that project managers adopt them without thinking. The method then takes on a more importance than common sense, and that is not the intention. Each project has its own needs, and you have to be able to adapt standards to the specific needs of the project. Every organization should regularly give some thought to the question as to whether or not existing standards are still satisfactory.

1.09 Project Structures

The pre-eminent breakdown structure for recording the experience is the Risk Breakdown Structure (RBS). In this we find a grouping of the risks, which experience has shown to often be the causes of things going wrong within the organization. By including these aspects in the standard RBS, we ensure that other project managers do not make the same mistakes as before.

1.09-4 SPECIAL TOPICS

1. Work Breakdown Structure

The WBS is the starting point for:

- Refining the scope.
- Identifying the various activities.
- The scheduling.
- The production or purchase decisions.
- The budget.
- The allocation of the work.
- The risk analysis.
- The progress control and reports.

The WBS is a breakdown of the project deliverables, or in short the "work", and as stated before, not the activities. In the following WBS we have split up the "*Tour Event*" project further.

At the lowest level we find the so-called work packages. Note that we do not include activities; the WBS is about the "what" and not yet about the "how", which comes later. The activities carried out within the scope of a work package do not belong to the WBS, but we use them for planning the duration.

The breakdown can take place in different ways:

- Physical structure of the result.
- Processes leading to the result.

The physical structure has preference, because the WBS can then be used for measuring the progress, which is then also visible by way of its physical character. The sub-deliverables of the WBS are described per level. Each element is allocated a unique number which indicates its place in the hierarchy (2.1. is the first element at the second level of the second element at the first level).

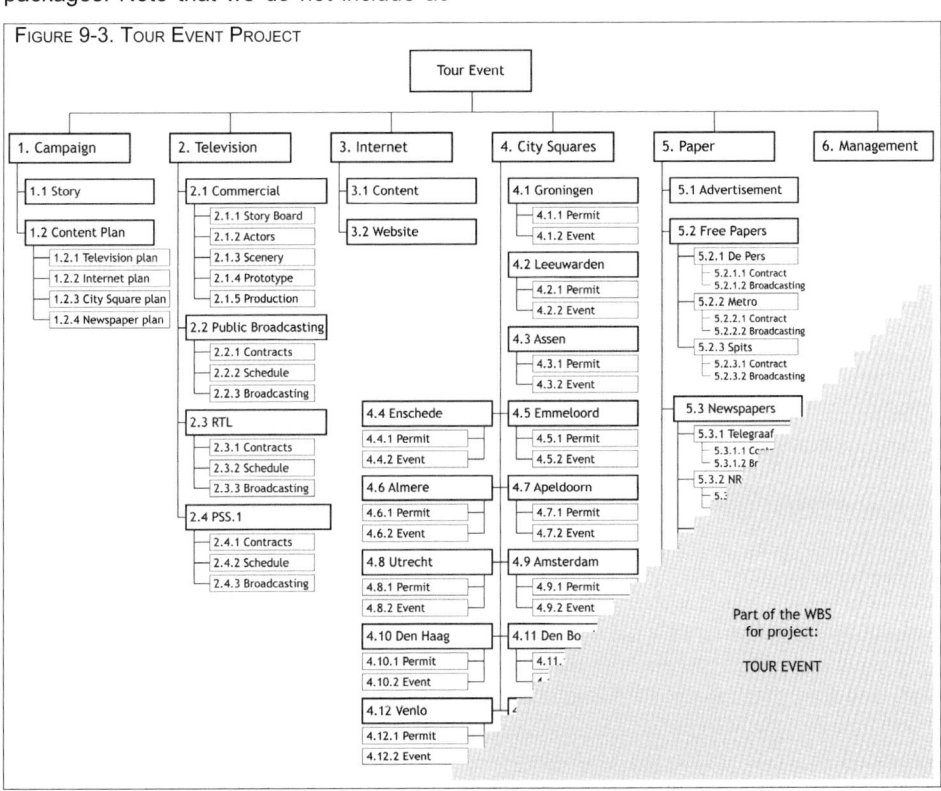

FIGURE 9-3. TOUR EVENT PROJECT

Tour Event

1. Campaign
- 1.1 Story
- 1.2 Content Plan
  - 1.2.1 Television plan
  - 1.2.2 Internet plan
  - 1.2.3 City Square plan
  - 1.2.4 Newspaper plan

2. Television
- 2.1 Commercial
  - 2.1.1 Story Board
  - 2.1.2 Actors
  - 2.1.3 Scenery
  - 2.1.4 Prototype
  - 2.1.5 Production
- 2.2 Public Broadcasting
  - 2.2.1 Contracts
  - 2.2.2 Schedule
  - 2.2.3 Broadcasting
- 2.3 RTL
  - 2.3.1 Contracts
  - 2.3.2 Schedule
  - 2.3.3 Broadcasting
- 2.4 PSS.1
  - 2.4.1 Contracts
  - 2.4.2 Schedule
  - 2.4.3 Broadcasting

3. Internet
- 3.1 Content
- 3.2 Website

4. City Squares
- 4.1 Groningen
  - 4.1.1 Permit
  - 4.1.2 Event
- 4.2 Leeuwarden
  - 4.2.1 Permit
  - 4.2.2 Event
- 4.3 Assen
  - 4.3.1 Permit
  - 4.3.2 Event
- 4.4 Enschede
  - 4.4.1 Permit
  - 4.4.2 Event
- 4.5 Emmeloord
  - 4.5.1 Permit
  - 4.5.2 Event
- 4.6 Almere
  - 4.6.1 Permit
  - 4.6.2 Event
- 4.7 Apeldoorn
  - 4.7.1 Permit
  - 4.7.2 Event
- 4.8 Utrecht
  - 4.8.1 Permit
  - 4.8.2 Event
- 4.9 Amsterdam
  - 4.9.1 Permit
  - 4.9.2 Event
- 4.10 Den Haag
  - 4.10.1 Permit
  - 4.10.2 Event
- 4.11 Den Bo
  - 4.11.
- 4.12 Venlo
  - 4.12.1 Permit
  - 4.12.2 Event

5. Paper
- 5.1 Advertisement
- 5.2 Free Papers
  - 5.2.1 De Pers
    - 5.2.1.1 Contract
    - 5.2.1.2 Broadcasting
  - 5.2.2 Metro
    - 5.2.2.1 Contract
    - 5.2.2.2 Broadcasting
  - 5.2.3 Spits
    - 5.2.3.1 Contract
    - 5.2.3.2 Broadcasting
- 5.3 Newspapers
  - 5.3.1 Telegraaf
    - 5.3.1.1 Co..
    - 5.3.1.2 Br
  - 5.3.2 NR

6. Management

Part of the WBS for project:

TOUR EVENT

1.09 Project Structures

All the work to be delivered is included in the WBS, and these are:
- *Internal results:* that which we deliver, and for which no approval is needed.
- *External results*: that which we deliver, and which has to be approved by parties involved.
- *Interim results*: intermediate products, which are necessary for the production process.

Interim results
These interim results are divided up into:
- Analysis elements.
- Integration elements.
- Process elements.

Analysis elements are such things as a building plan, a system design and suchlike. Integration work is, for example, connecting to the sewerage system, system testing etc. After the work has been delivered, you actually do not find anything from the interim results in the end result, whereas without that work, an operational end result would not be possible, and so you have to include these interim results in the WBS.

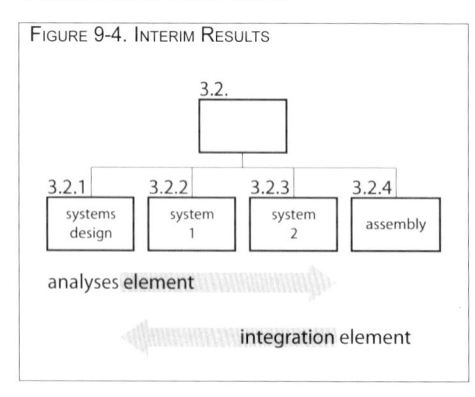

FIGURE 9-4. INTERIM RESULTS

```
                    3.2.
        ┌────────┬────┴────┬────────┐
      3.2.1    3.2.2     3.2.3    3.2.4
     systems   system    system   assembly
     design      1         2
```
analyses element
integration element

You include both analysis and integration elements at the level under the parent they belong to. You mention the analysis elements first, and they are related to the elements that follow on. The integration elements are included at the end, and these are related to the ones that come before. In the example 3.2.1 is an analysis element, and 3.2.4 an integration element.

Matters such as project management, a newsletter, progress reports, and meetings are process elements, as is necessary work (and that is why you include them in the WBS).

Adding control accounts
During the splitting up of the WBS, you already take account of the way you are going to organise the control. A number of considerations play a part in this:
- How are you going to manage the parties involved?
- At what level can you collect progress and actual costs?

This depends on the project organization you ultimately choose for the project. For instance, when you make use of an external agency which delivers 2.1 Commercial, you get the progress presented at work package level, but probably the costs at one level higher. In that case you select 2.1 Commercial as one of the control accounts in the WBS. In the responsibilities matrix (RAM), you record the link between the WBS and the OBS.

The WBS dictionary
A description of the different elements should be included in the WBS. Together with the graphical representation, this document forms a description of the scope to be delivered for the project (scope-baseline).

Aggregation of the costs in the WBS

EXAMPLE 9-4 AGGREGATION OF COSTS

2.1	Commercial	80k
2.1.1	Story Board	25k
2.1.2	Actors	15k
2.1.3	Decors	10k
2.1.4	Prototype	30k
2.2	Public Broadcasting	50k
2.2.1	Etc..	

Next to the schematic representation, it is also possible to present the WBS in the form of a table. From the example above, I have presented a part of the WBS in which the budget is aggregated from bottom to top. Initially, this may look confusing, as the totals are above the details.

The chosen breakdown and the previously mentioned control accounts depend on how you want to control the costs of the project.

Measuring progress with the WBS

Progress consists of results delivered by the team in a particular time period. We do not report partial progress, but report 100% when it is all actually finished. *Something is finished when it has been completed, no sooner and no later.*

Analyzing the WBS

When you are checking a WBS, you should pay attention to the following points:
- Each WBS element must represent one single tangible result.
- Each WBS element is the sum of the underlying WBS elements (the children).
- Each lower level element has precisely one parent or higher level WBS element.
- The various results are unique and distinguishable from each other.

EXAMPLE 9-5 PRIOGRESS AND THE WBS

We look at task 2. Television for the "Tour Event" project. Together with the employees who will deliver the work, an estimate of the duration is made. For the Commercial, these estimates are shown in the table below:

2.1	Commercial	6 w
2.1.1	Story Board	1 w
2.1.2	Actors	2 w
2.1.3	Scenery	1 w
2.1.4	Prototype	2 w

Together, the work packages under 2.1 Commercial, take six weeks. Be aware that, because we have not yet determined the sequence, we cannot say anything about the planned duration of the intermediate elements of the WBS. The duration, together with the work package, has now become a unit of progress (result/duration).

Each week stands for (1/6) 16.6% of the total work (6 w) to be done in 2.1 Commercial. When you now see the following status at the end of a period:

2.1	Commercial		Status	Progr.
2.1.1	Story Board	1 w	Completed	16,6 %
2.1.2	Actors	2 w	On-going	0,0 %
2.1.3	Scenery	1 w	Completed	16,6 %
2.1.4	Prototype	2 w	Not yet started	0.0 %

then the progress of 2.1 Commercial is now 33.3%. The work package 2.1.2 is work-in-progress, but has not yet been completed.

- The production of the WBS must be a flexible process.
- The WBS must be complete (also management results).

The above are the minimum requirements for a good WBS.

There are a number of other criteria[1] we can look at, in order to assess the quality of the

---
1 (2006) *The Earned Value Management Maturity Model*, R.W. Stratton, MANAGEMENT CONCEPTS

1.09 Project Structures

WBS. With each of these criteria, it is difficult to indicate whether what is right or wrong, but the thought process behind this provides pointers for improving the WBS. The following criteria can only be determined when budgets and sequence are known.

We are then talking about:
- Control Accounts versus Project budget.
- Value per WBS level.
- The Fan-Out ratio.
- Span of Control.

Control Accounts and Project budget
To maintain sufficient control over the project budget, you must have enough Control Accounts, but also not too many.

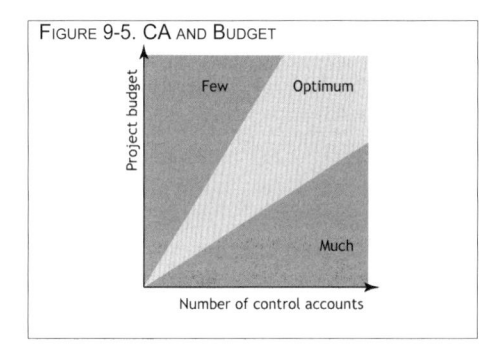

FIGURE 9-5. CA AND BUDGET

For each Control Account, you appoint a responsible Control Account Manager. When there are too few Control Accounts, the budget is insufficiently divided up into sub-budgets, and during the execution there may not be enough control applied to the budget spend and the development of the costs.

When there are too many Control Accounts, you place a lot of pressure on the various figures that, as project manager, you must report, and for which you have to keep an administration. This is then a situation of micro management.

Value per WBS Level
When you compare the costs of the different WBS elements per level with each other, you can quickly see when certain elements are atypical, and this is something which can be undesirable.

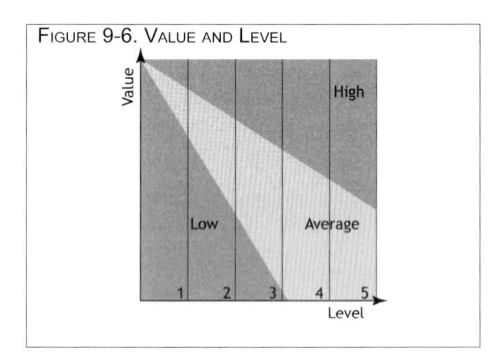

FIGURE 9-6. VALUE AND LEVEL

Elements with a relatively high value compared to the brothers and sisters at the same level, are candidates for dividing up further, whereas elements with a low value are candidates to be combined together.

It is preferable to ensure that the values of the different elements at a certain level are comparable in size.

The Fan-Out Ratio
The further you come in the lower levels of the WBS, the better it is to split out less downwards. In this way, you prevent micro management, and the fan-out ratio can be used as a measure for this. You calculate this by dividing a number of elements for a level by the number of elements of the previous level. In the following table, this has been done for the Tour Event project.

At each level you see the fan-out ratio becoming smaller, and that indicates that the WBS designed for this aspect is of sufficient quality.

EXAMPLE 9-6 FAN-OUT RATIO

WBS Level		
N+1	N	Fan-Out Ratio
6	1	6/1 = 6.0
26	6	26/6 = 4.3
60	26	60/26 = 2.3
32	60	32/60 = 0.5

Span Of Control

When you allocate Control Accounts in the responsibilities matrix (RAM), and then look to see which Control Account Managers in a certain period are responsible for a series of work packages, it is, of course, a good idea to restrict the number of work packages to someone's span of control. A good guideline is (dependent on someone's experience) somewhere between the five and nine work packages simultaneously (seven plus or minus two).

In this way, you use the WBS, RAM and duration schedule to keep the work pressure on your team leaders within acceptable limits.

Problems[1] as a result of a wrong WBS

A wrong WBS can give rise to the following problems:
- Missed deadlines and durations.
- Budget overruns.
- Products delivered being unusable.
- The scope not being manageable.
- The project not being able to be finished off.
- Confusion about the responsibilities.
- Not all of the planned work having been carried out.

Each problem has a number of possible causes in the WBS.

___

[1] (2006) *Practice Standard for Work Breakdown Structures*, PROJECT MANAGEMENT INSTITUTE

Missed deadlines and durations:
- Not all deliverables are included in the WBS.
- The description is not specific enough.
- The WBS does not support the use of Earned Value.

Budget overruns:
- The WBS does not support the use of Earned Value.
- Control Accounts are illogical.

Products delivered are unusable:
- Breakdown has been stopped too quickly (work packages are at too high a level).
- WBS elements are not result oriented.
- The points in time of integration and assembly are not included in the WBS.
- Training has not been included in the WBS.
- Implementation has not been included in the WBS.

The scope is not manageable:
- No WBS has been produced.
- The complete scope has not been divided up into work packages.
- The WBS is inflexible.
- The WBS has not been updated with changes.
- The WBS has not been brought under change control.

The project cannot be finished off:
- The close-off has not been included in the WBS.

Confusion about the responsibilities:
- Control Accounts are illogical.
- Breakdown has been stopped too quickly (work packages at too high a level).
- The points in time of integration and assembly are not included in the WBS.
- There are overlapping responsibilities.

1.09 Project Structures

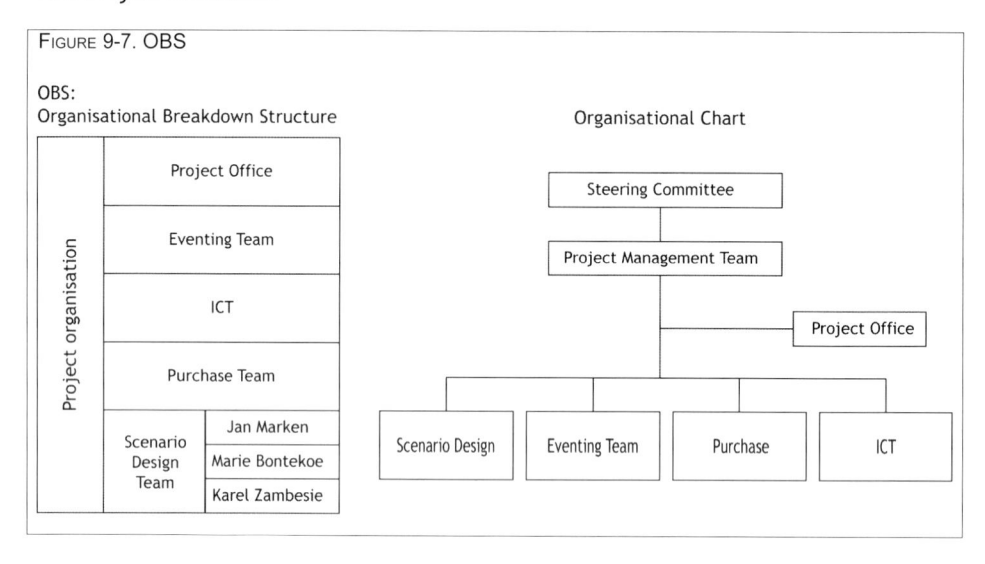

FIGURE 9-7. OBS

OBS:
Organisational Breakdown Structure

Project organisation:
- Project Office
- Eventing Team
- ICT
- Purchase Team
- Scenario Design Team: Jan Marken, Marie Bontekoe, Karel Zambesie

Organisational Chart

- Steering Committee
  - Project Management Team
    - Project Office
    - Scenario Design
    - Eventing Team
    - Purchase
    - ICT

- Work packages deliver intangible results.
- Not all key figures have been involved in producing the WBS.

Not all of the planned work has been carried out:
- Breakdown has been stopped too quickly (work packages at too high a level).
- WBS elements are not result oriented.
- The complete scope has not been divided up into work packages.
- The breakdown has been done after the schedule has been produced.

2. OBS: Organization Breakdown

Just as in the WBS, we can split up the project organization, but be aware that this is something other than an organization chart of the project organization. As opposed to the OBS, the project organization contains the reporting lines. In the diagram below, we have provided an example of both.

3. RAM: The Responsibilities Matrix

This matrix connects the WBS to the OBS, with the objective of ensuring that all the work has a responsible manager or team leader. We place the responsibilities on the Control Accounts, (abbreviated to CA), and within this technique, we call the responsible persons the Control Account Managers (abbreviated to CAM).

You can differentiate between a simple matrix, in which you only show the link, and a more complex matrix in which you also say something about the nature of the link. An example of this is the RACI or RASCI table.

Next, we have included a part of the RAM for the Tour Event project.

Analysis of the RAM

The analysis of any RAM taken at random always follows these steps:
- Horizontal analysis.
- Vertical analysis.

HORIZONTAL ANALYSIS

For the RAM, you look at the level of the Control Accounts, and go through the table row for each of the responsible persons. In the Tour Event example, it is directly evident that for 2.1 Commercial, all Control Accounts at the work package level have been defined. This is possibly a situation of micro manage-

1.09 Project Structures

FIGURE 9-8. RAM FOR TOUR EVEN PROJECT

		Tour Event												
		1. Campaign					2. Television							
			1.2 Content Plan				2.1 Commercial					2.2 Public Broadcasting		
		1.1 Story	1.2.4 Newspaper plan	1.2.3 City Square plan	1.2.2 Internet plan	1.2.1 Television plan	2.1.5 Production	2.1.4 Prototype	2.1.3 Scenery	2.1.2 Actors	1.1.1 Story Board	2.2.3 Broadcasting	2.2.2 Schedule	2.2.1 Contracts
Project organisation	Project office													
	Eventing Team							■						
	ICT													
	Purchase Team									■	■	■	■	■
	Scenario Design Team		■	■	■	■	■		■		■			

ment, and in any case this requires a better structure. You can now consider combining the two work packages 2.1.4 and 2.1.5 under a new level.

VERTICAL ANALYSIS
For the RAM, The vertical analysis uses the rule that there can only be one person responsible for each Control Account. For 2.1.4 this is not the case, and we have to investigate why this is so, and where necessary make an amendment.

THE NEW WBS
After both analyses, the project manager has thought up a better WBS:
- Actors and Scenery have been brought under one new Control Account.
- The same applies to the Prototype and Production, and note that the naming has also been changed.

- The Story Board has been brought under 1.2.
- What cannot be seen directly from the WBS, but can in the new RAM, is that one team member is managed, for the Prototype, by the team leader of the Scenario Design Team.

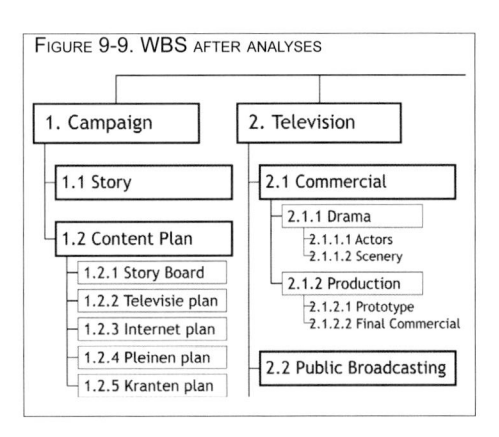

FIGURE 9-9. WBS AFTER ANALYSES

1. Campaign
- 1.1 Story
- 1.2 Content Plan
  - 1.2.1 Story Board
  - 1.2.2 Televisie plan
  - 1.2.3 Internet plan
  - 1.2.4 Pleinen plan
  - 1.2.5 Kranten plan

2. Television
- 2.1 Commercial
  - 2.1.1 Drama
    - 2.1.1.1 Actors
    - 2.1.1.2 Scenery
  - 2.1.2 Production
    - 2.1.2.1 Prototype
    - 2.1.2.2 Final Commercial
- 2.2 Public Broadcasting

139

1.09 Project Structures

4. RBS: Resource Breakdown Structure

The RBS structures the various resources. The most usual arrangement has been applied to the Tour Event project, as shown in the diagram.

As well as the people, we also distinguish the tools that the operational team members use during the project.

The material/machines task consists of "hard" items that the team delivers. Furthermore, it is also customary to include a separate task for fees the project must pay during the project (such as administrative charges and permits).

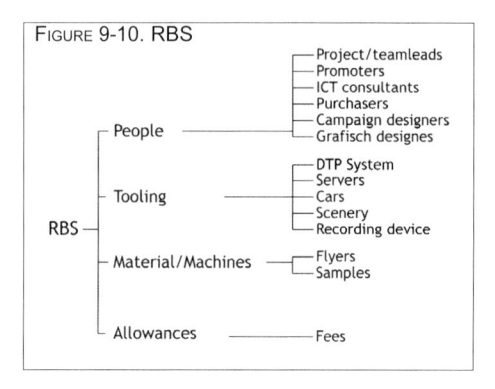

FIGURE 9-10. RBS

RBS
- People
  - Project/teamleads
  - Promoters
  - ICT consultants
  - Purchasers
  - Campaign designers
  - Grafisch designes
- Tooling
  - DTP System
  - Servers
  - Cars
  - Scenery
  - Recording device
- Material/Machines
  - Flyers
  - Samples
- Allowances
  - Fees

5. Product oriented planning

Whereas the WBS places the emphasis strongly on the basic structure of the planning, the PRINCE2[1] method, which is particularly popular in Europe, places more emphasis on the definition and delivery of products, and then predominantly on the quality requirements. Furthermore, the terminology is different to that which we use when drawing up a WBS.

Although the emphasis, in both the WBS and PRINCE2, is on products instead of activities, the latter is much more concerned with exactly what you deliver, and the quality requirements that have to be satisfied. In that sense, this subject has many more common ground with quality than the WBS has. Product oriented planning forms one of the basic principles of PRINCE2.

Once the customer's general quality expectations have been converted into measurable acceptance criteria, you translate these into a so-called Project Product Description; a document that describes, in broad terms, the scope of the deliverables. The product description strongly resembles that which we would include in the WBS dictionary.

The following elements are covered in the project product description:
- Title.
- Purpose for the user.
- Composition.
- Derivation.
- Required development skills.
- Customer's quality expectations.
- Acceptance criteria.
- Quality tolerances at project level.
- Acceptance method.
- Acceptance responsibilities.

Here, the importance of specifying the quality in advance clearly emerges, as well as what the customer expects, and the way in which he wants to establish this. By tolerances is meant the permitted deviations in the area of the quality.

You produce this description before a project has even been established, and it forms a part of the project proposal, or so-called Project Brief, on the basis of which a decision is then made as whether to proceed or not. If that is positive, the project manager can spend time and money on the planning phase of the project (in PRINCE2 terms, we now talk of the "Initiation of the Project").

---

[1] (2009) *Managing Succesful Projects with PRINCE2,* TSO, UK

1.09 Project Structures

The team divides up this description further into product descriptions consisting of:
- Title.
- Purpose for the user.
- Composition.
- Derivation.
- Format and presentation.
- Required development skills.
- Quality criteria.
- Quality tolerance.
- Methods for determining the quality.
- Skills required to do that.
- Quality responsibilities.

You can see that a lot of attention is paid to quality aspects. By ensuring beforehand that it is clear what the different products have to satisfy, and the way in which you on the one hand ensure that this is the case (process quality) and on the other hand that you can objectively measure that they satisfy the requirements (product quality), the chance of satisfaction is, of course, much greater.

PRINCE2 makes a distinction between the role of the project manager and that of the so-called team manager. The first one manages and the second one delivers. The project manager is responsible for the product descriptions, whereas the team manager is responsible for delivering the different products. Somewhere in the whole management process comes a point in time that the project manager gives the product descriptions to the team manager for the execution.

This is carried out by using work packages. In PRINCE2 the work package is a collection of information about one or more products that the team manager (or if there is no team manager, then a team member) can work on. As well as the product descriptions themselves, the work packages contain various work agreements between the project manager and the team manager (or team member).

141

1.09 Project Structures

1.10 Scope and deliverables

THAT WHICH HAS BEEN AGREED, NO MORE AND NO LESS

How many projects, when you honestly look back at them, haven't delivered something completely different from what was initially intended.

For many of these projects, not enough time was spent at the beginning to determine the scope of the project; what we do and what we do not do.

1.10 Scope and deliverables

1.10-1 DEFINITIONS

Configuration	The functional and technical features of a product, as described in the technical documentation and realized in the product.
Configuration baseline	The configuration of a product, formally established at a certain point in time, which serves as the reference for further work.
Project result	The product or service to be delivered.
Scope	The delimitation of the totality of the products and services to be delivered, and the activities to be carried out.
Scope-creep	The changing of the scope in small steps, each of which taken separately does not appear to justify re-defining scope, but added together may have far-reaching consequences.

1.10-2 INTRODUCTION

The ICB[1] defines the scope as the boundaries of the project. It is the sum of all projects products.

The guide to the Project Management Body of Knowledge[2] from the Project Management Institute defines it as: the sum of the products, services, and results to be provided as a project. The project scope is: The work that must be performed to deliver a product, service, or result with the specific features and functions.

The APM Body of Knowledge[3] states that the scope comprises the project deliverables and the work associated with producing those deliverables.

So: The product(s) you deliver, and the work carried out by the team to achieve this. The scope is everything we are going to deliver and carry out within the framework of the project. It is essential to define and document this in advance.

---

1 (2006) *IPMA Competence Baseline version 3.0*, IPMA
2 (2008) *A guide to the Project Management Body of Knowledge 4th Edition*, THE PROJECT MANAGEMENT INSTITUTE INC.
3 (2006) *APM Body of Knowledge 5th Edition*, ASSOCIATION FOR PROJECT MANAGEMENT, UK

1.10-3 Process steps

1. Define requirements.
2. Agree on deliverables.
3. Define and control the scope.
4. Update scope and deliverables.
5. Control the quality.
6. Formal handover.
7. Apply lessons learned

1. Define requirements
On the basis of the existing (ist) and the required situation (soll), the organization defines the changes that have to be made. Based on that, a number of possible solutions (project deliverables) are generated, and the management of the organization assesses which of those solutions will contribute the most to the required objective (project selection).

The scope is determined by the objective the organization wants to achieve with the project deliverables, and the organization uses the result to achieve that objective.

2. Agree on deliverables
You can only make a schedule and a budget once the scope has been determined. The project cannot start if there is no agreement on what it should deliver, how long it should take and how much it will cost. In one way or another, the work has to be defined.

When determining the scope you produce a definition, which, on the one hand accommodates the required level of control from a project management standpoint, and on the other hand, accommodates the required contribution to the objective as seen from the viewpoint of the receiving organization. A definition which is too narrow may result in a project delivering the agreed result on time and within budget, but if that result cannot be applied because it is too limited, you can hardly speak of the project being successful.

On the other hand, a definition which is too broad will result in the project never being completed and being too expensive.

If, at the commencement of a project, it is not possible to make a clear definition, it is better to define a preliminary project, which has as its most important result, the determination of the scope. Only when this is clear, can you start with the actual project.

3. Define and control the scope
The scope describes the project result, how the products are put together, what we do and what we do not do. You also specify the boundary with other projects or departments in the vicinity of the project.

A good scope description contains the following elements:
- Name, date.
- Business objective.
- Project deliverables.
- Description of the work.
- Project deliverables through a PBS or WBS.

And furthermore, you have to do with:
- *Out of scope*, the aspects that you do not do.
- *Assumptions*, uncertain and not controllable aspects you take for certain for planning purposes.
- *Conditions*, those subjects the project sponsor has to organise to assure a successful execution of the project.
- *Constraints* (or *project requirements*), issues that restrict the team in its choices, such as: deadlines, budget constraints, statutory regulations, etc.

Realize that you are dealing with a progressive insight into the scope. At the commencement of the project, the required end result is not as clear as in later stages, and this is the process of refining. Make sure that

1.10 Scope and deliverables

this does not degenerate into 'scope-creep', slowly extending the scope (a lot of small ones make one big one).

In the scope definition, the requirements and interests of the various interested parties in the project are, as far as possible, taken into account. Once the scope has been determined, a plan and a budget can now be made. The budget is directly linked to the scope, and changes in the scope can, in principle, mean changes to the budget, duration and quality of the final result.

4. Update scope and deliverables
When the scope has been determined, it comes under change control, which means that the application of changes is not automatically allowed. Every required change has to be analyzed for the impact that change has on the total project. When the change is within your room to manoeuvre as project manager, you can let it be carried out and if it is not, then you have to let the project sponsor take care of it.

5. Control the quality
In a project, the quality of products must be well organized from the beginning up to and including the delivery of the project.

The quality circle indicates how you define the required quality and keep it under control. Procedures which connect well to each other are essential for this. The project manager draws these up, and checks that everyone keeps to them.

In practice, this means working with product descriptions, in which at least the following is documented:
- The specification of the product.
- The quality criteria.
- The way in which the quality will be measured.
- The product acceptance criteria.

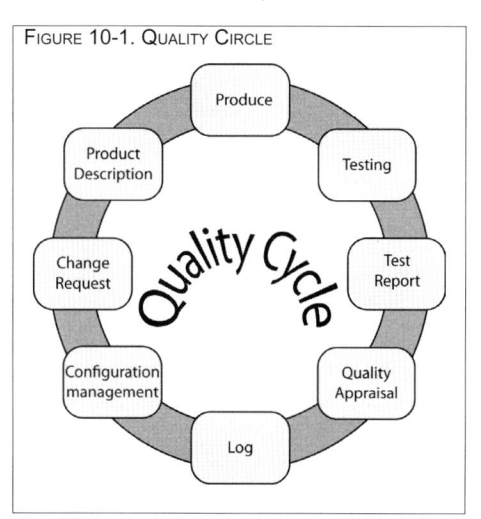

FIGURE 10-1. QUALITY CIRCLE

Quality Cycle: Produce, Testing, Test Report, Quality Appraisal, Log, Configuration management, Change Request, Product Description

- The way in which the acceptance of the result is carried out.

Having the products tested by the user organization, prior to their release is essential. All information regarding the testing of a product is recorded in the quality register. Sometimes that is an archive in which all test documents per product are collected, which has the advantage that the details can still be looked up.

After a successful test the product comes under configuration management, and, in principle, it cannot be changed anymore. The user has agreed to the product and in the end does not want to get something else. Only with the approval of the user, is it possible to amend the product description and then, with the change implemented, go round the quality circle again.

6. Formal handover
Because a project has a defined time-frame, it is necessary that a formal handover takes place, in which the responsibility for the further use and management of the deliverables is transferred to a user, or support organization.

1.10 Scope and deliverables

7. Apply lessons learned
During, and at the end of the project, the project manager documents the experience gained and distributes this to colleagues.

8. Other standards and guidances
The process steps as identified by IPMA are only a suggestion. The process steps described in the *ISO 21500 Guidance*, the *'guide to the Project Management Body of Knowledge'* (the *PMBOK Guide*) from the Project Management Institute, and in the popular PRINCE2 Project Management method are much more "binding". Without discussing it in detail I shall name, as a comparison, a number of items from these standards that are related to this competence element. What will be noticeable is the high level of similarity and overlap.

ISO 21500
The ISO 21500 Guidance describes the following processes:
- Define scope.
- Create Work Breakdown Structure.
- Define activities.
- Scope control.

With IPMA, this is spread over a number of different competence elements.

PMBOK Guide
The 5th edition of the *PMBOK Guide* has somewhat more processes than the ISO Guidance:
- Collect requirements.
- Define scope.
- Create WBS.
- Define activities.
- Verify scope.
- Control scope.

With IPMA, this is spread over a number of different competence elements.

PRINCE2
PRINCE2 does not have a separate topic for Scope, but deals with it extensively in the topic Plan, in which three steps are explicitly named:
- Produce one project product description for the total project.
- Produce a product composition structure.
- Produce product descriptions of the components.

This appears very similar to producing a Work Breakdown Structure, but for this PRINCE2 has provided its own interpretation in the form of Product Oriented Planning, which, by the way, is worth studying.

1.10-4 SPECIAL TOPICS

1. Configuration Management

By using configuration management, you ensure that everyone works with the same version of the products and that the "value" of the products remains at the required level. Furthermore, it is clear where each product is at any given time, and who is working on it or is responsible for it.

The Configuration management (plan)
This defines the following:
- What is included in configuration management.
- Roles and responsibilities.
- Procedures for approval and delivery of versions.
- Verification (is the information about the current configuration correct).
- The procedure for applying changes to a product.

Responsibilities
In the framework of configuration management, the responsibilities are as follows:
- The project manager is ultimately responsible, and he draws up the configuration management plan.
- The configuration manager prevents working on the wrong versions, checks the correctness of the versions (administrative check) and verifies that everyone is keeping to the rules.
- All deliveries are to the configuration manager (with the appropriate signatures).

1.10 Scope and deliverables

1.11 Time and project phases

TIME IS A SUCCESSION OF ANXIOUS MOMENTS[1]

Even though many project sponsors look mainly at the cost aspects, a lot can be said for TIME being the most important drivers in projects.

This is based on the supposition that an organization only carries out those projects that contribute to the strategy.

Each month that delivery is early, means more revenue, and the execution costs of the project are often just a fraction of this.

---

1 (1956) Freely translated from *La tentation d'exister,* Emil Ciorin

1.11 Time and Project phases

1.11-1 DEFINITIONS

Bar chart	A schematic representation of a time schedule, in which the duration, and start and end date of activities are shown positioned along a time bar.
Critical path	The longest sequence of activities to be carried out in a (part of a) time schedule.
Decision point	Pre-determined point in the project at which the project sponsor decides whether or not to carry on with the project.
Free slack (or float)	The total amount of time an activity can be delayed, without any subsequent activity being delayed.
Margin	A contingency included due to a legitimate inaccuracy of an estimate.
Milestone	Important event in the project.
Network diagram	A schematic representation of a time schedule, in which the activities are shown as junction points, or the connections between junction points in a network.
Project life cycle	All the phases a project goes through, from the project contract up to and including its conclusion.
Project phase	A discrete time period within a project, separated from other time periods, and having a pre-defined sub-deliverable.

1.11 Time and Project phases

Schedule	Activities and events in time.
Stage boundary	Assessment of, and conclusion of, the current stage, and authorisation to start the following stage.
Total slack (or float)	The total amount of time by which an activity can be delayed, without increasing its shortest duration.

1.11 Time and Project phases

1.11-2 Introduction

In the classical concept, project management is the management of project activities to ensure that a certain result is delivered within a certain time, for acceptable costs and to a pre-determined level of quality. This concept proves the relevance of this competence element. Delay in the delivery of projects costs organization a lot of money, and time, therefore, is usually the factor in a project which is the most important to control.

The critical path method is one of the techniques a project manager must master. First manually, to get a feel for how the method works, and then, with the help of time scheduling software, to gain insight into his time schedule and which activities (the critical ones) he has to pay careful attention to.

1.11-3 PROCESS STEPS

1. Define and sequence activities
2. Estimate the duration.
3. Schedule the project or phase.
4. Allocate and balance.
5. Compare target, planned and actual dates.
6. Control the time schedule.
7. Record and distribute experiences.

1. Define and sequence activities

The WBS work packages are the basis for drawing up a schedule. Such a work package has a clearly described end result, and sometimes it is necessary to divide these up further into activities required to deliver this end result.

It is advisable to describe the activity in the schedule with a verb, as this indicates that something has to happen. Take, for instance, the example of planning a re-location. At a certain point in time, you will have to pack removal boxes. Compare the following two descriptions of this activity:
- Removal boxes
- Pack removal boxes

Because it lacks a verb, the first description is unclear. It could mean: collect removal boxes, transport removal boxes, or pack removal boxes. The second description is more accurate, and we immediately see what activity is involved. Also make sure that everyone means the same thing.

Define dependencies

Activities may depend on each other, and some can only start when another one is completed. This is important in the process of time scheduling.

We separate out the following dependencies:
- FS: Finish-to-Start; an activity starts only after completion of the previous activity.
- SS: Start-to-Start; an activity can only start after another one has started.
- FF: Finish-to-Finish; the activity can only complete once another one has completed.
- SF: Start-to-Finish; the activity can only stop after the other one has started.

A number of examples:

EXAMPLE 11-1 DEPENDENCIES

Design Kitchen-FS-Build kitchen

The building of the kitchen can only start once the design has been completed.

**Flying in the quartermasters
- SS+ 3 months- Flying in the troops**

The troops can only be flown in three months after the quartermasters have been flown in.

**Design prototype
-FF-Build prototype**

Designing and building the prototype is carried out in parallel. The build, however, can only be completed once the design is has been finished.

**Connect up new security system
-SF-Disconnect old security system**

The old system can only be disconnected once the new system has been connected up.

---

2. Estimate the duration

Estimating the duration presents us with a problem. Preferably, you would like to ask the people who will be carrying out the activities for an estimate, but often, they are not yet available. What you do need, however, are experts who can provide some sensible input on the duration.

Because they are often afraid of making a commitment to it, most people are wary of stating a duration. This fear is, of course, somewhat justifiable. Because they 'hang

1.11 Time and Project phases

themselves" by guessing their own deadline.

The best thing is to make a so-called three-point estimate, by asking the experts to give you an optimistic, a pessimistic and a most-likely estimate. The weighted average is then included in the schedule.

3. Schedule the project or phase

Implement phases
The most important reason for implementing phases in a project has to do with uncertainty. The further you have to estimate ahead, the more uncertain the accuracy of these estimates. Therefore, it is necessary to build in a number of decision points, at which time sufficient information is available to re-assess the project again.

Such a decision point is then the end of a phase at which point the project sponsor can decide, based upon the available information, whether or not he wants to continue with the project. At the end of such a phase you, as project manager, provide a detailed time schedule of the next phase, and an updated time schedule for later phases.

Make a network
To make the structure of the time schedule in a phase clear, the project manager can show the dependencies in a network diagram.

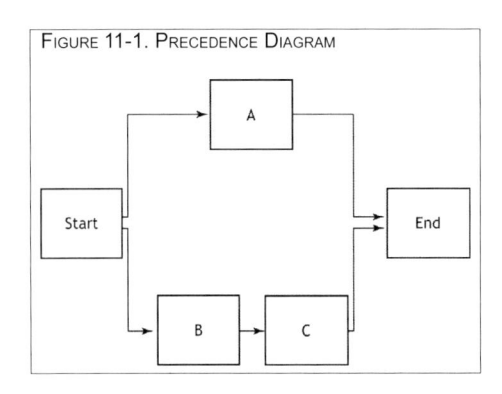

FIGURE 11-1. PRECEDENCE DIAGRAM

If you study the network above, you can see two paths you can follow to get to the end point. The activities B and C on one side and the activity A on the other side. Each path has a duration, and the longest determines the duration of the project. If, in this example, A takes three weeks, B takes three weeks and C takes two weeks, then the duration of the project is five weeks (duration A (3) < duration B (3) + duration C (2)).

This also means that for the total duration of the project, it does not matter if activity A overruns its time. There is a slack, or float, of two weeks before this has an impact on the end date of the project. That will not be the case if, for instance, either activity B or activity C overruns its time. If activity B takes four weeks and C three weeks, then the total duration will be seven weeks instead of five, an overrun of two weeks. It is the path B – C, therefore, that determines the duration of the project.

The activities on which the duration of the project depends, are called *critical activities* and taken together, they form the *critical path*. Every time when you are busy with the schedule, you look at the critical path; these are the activities which you need to pay the most attention to in order to control the time.

It is possible that the critical path will change during the project, as a result of activities, which initially were not critical, overrunning their time.

HARD AND SOFT LOGIC
With the help of the network, we make mutual dependencies clear. This so-called project logic can be dependent on the technique, for example: you can only start building the house once the foundations have been laid, and prior to this, the ground must first be prepared. We call this form of logic; hard

1.11 Time and Project phases

logic. However you go about things, this is the sequence in which you have to work.

Another form is the so-called soft logic, and we use this term when there is a dependence on resources. For example, when you technically could carry out two activities in parallel, but you need the same machine for both activities and only have one available.

Determining Critical path

The calculation of the critical path (the minimum duration of the project) is carried out in a number of steps:

1. For each activity, calculate the earliest possible start and end time (*forward pass*).

The earliest possible start for A is 0 and the earliest time this activity can be finished is the end of the third week.

The earliest possible start for B is 0 and, at the end of the third week, B is finished and C can start. At the earliest, C can be finished at the end of week five.

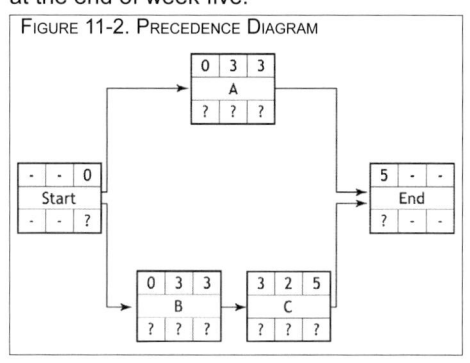

FIGURE 11-2. PRECEDENCE DIAGRAM

Therefore, this project can at the earliest be finished at the end of week five.

2. We count back from the end to the beginning (*backward pass*).

The latest possible end date of activity C is the end of week 5. This activity therefore has no slack; every delay means that the project will overrun. The whole of the path from B to C has no slack.

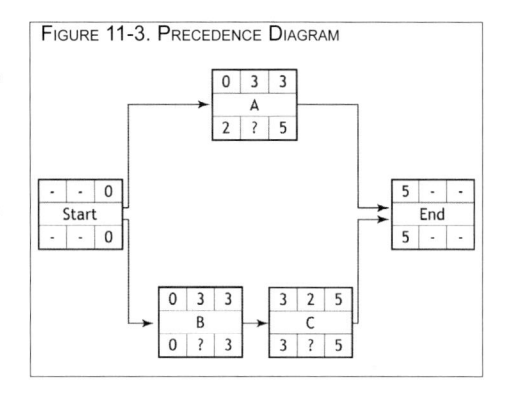

FIGURE 11-3. PRECEDENCE DIAGRAM

To do this, we use the bottom lines from the rectangles.

3. Calculating the slack (float).

Next, we calculate how much slack time, or float, the different activities have. That is different from the path going via A, which has a slack of 2. So A only has to be finished at the end of week 5 before there is a danger that the project finish will not be on time.

When we put the slack in the network diagram we get:

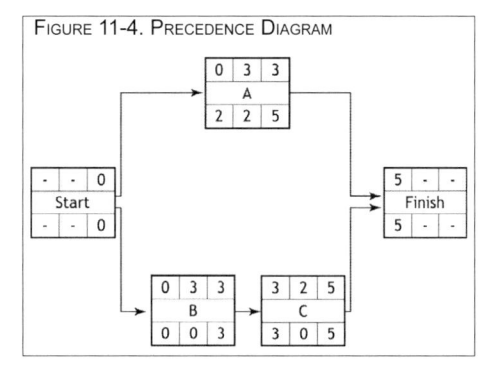

FIGURE 11-4. PRECEDENCE DIAGRAM

157

1.11 Time and Project phases

There are two types of slack:
- *Slack* is the time an activity can overrun in time without the total duration of the project being delayed.
- *Free slack* indicates when a further overrun in time will delay the start of other activities.

Note that as already indicated, float is another word that can be used for slack. The technique we have used is a *precedence diagram* or an *activity-on-node (AON)*. This is the most frequently used technique, which is supported by almost all known scheduling software.

The calculations of the forward and the backward pass are now shown in the rectangles:

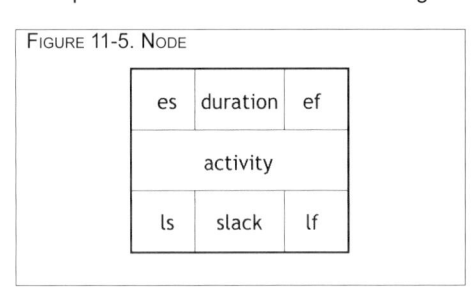

FIGURE 11-5. NODE

es	duration	ef
	activity	
ls	slack	lf

- ES = earliest start.
- EF = earliest finish.
- LS = latest start.
- LF = latest finish.

The more complicated relationships, such as FS, SF, SS and FF are drawn as follows:

WHEN A IS FINISHED B CAN START (FS)
FIGURE 11-6. FINISH-TO-START

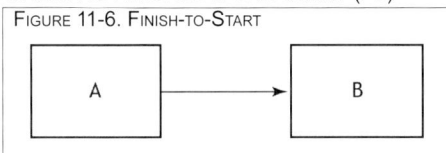

A → B

B CAN START AFTER A HAS STARTED (SS)
FIGURE 11-7. START-TO-START

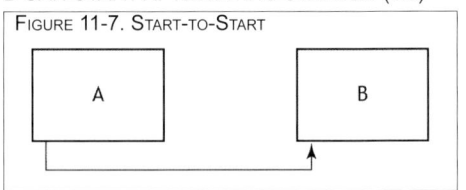

A   B

B CAN STOP AFTER A HAS STARTED (SF)
FIGURE 11-8. START-TO-FINISH

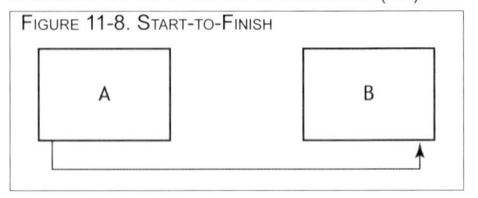

A   B

B CAN FINISH AFTER A HAS FINISHED (FF)
FIGURE 11-9. FINISH-TO-FINISH

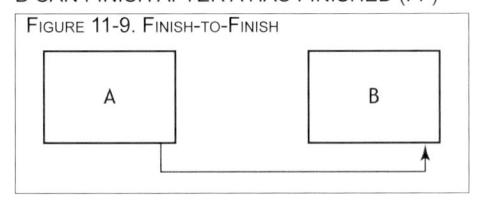

A   B

Applying these dependencies and limitations in the network make the calculations during the forward and the backward pass more complicated. Fortunately, scheduling software does this automatically.

The critical path is dependent on the availability of the resources

When making a critical path schedule, no account is taken of the availability of resources. In the event of limited resources being available, it is possible that activities which could be carried out in parallel, have to be carried out by the same person and, therefore, have to be executed one after the other. This will change the critical path, and the process of balancing is called the "levelling of resources". The new critical path is called the *Critical Chain*. I will discuss this in a coming chapter.

1.11 Time and Project phases

Adding milestones and decision points
The start of certain activities often depends on milestones or decision points, and these are also included in the network diagram. As a decision point, or a milestone, doesn't take time, you include it as an activity with a duration of **zero**. However, for the actual decision making, time is usually planned.

Lead and Lag
It is also possible that a so-called lead or lag time exists in the relationship between two activities. We speak of a lead time when two activities that are dependent can overlap, whereas, a lag time means that there is a gap between two activities.

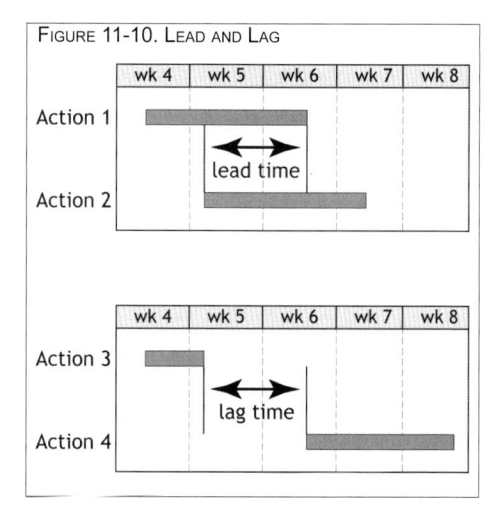

FIGURE 11-10. LEAD AND LAG

4. Allocate and balance
The technique discussed above assumes that there are sufficient resources available to carry out the different activities. In addition, it does not allow at all for idle time, sickness and holidays. This results in an ideal schedule, and now we have to think of an optimum allocation of the available resources. This will be discussed in the following chapter.

5. Compare target, planned and actual dates
Indicative for the final optimized schedule are the required dates, which have often been communicated to the project manager as constraints. Scheduling software offers tools to include these requirements in the calculation of such a schedule.

Indication of systematic constraints
Every project has activities which have constraints on the way in which they are scheduled. Examples of these types of **constraints** are:
- ASAP: Start as soon as possible.
- ALAP: Start as late as possible.
- Must: Must definitely start or end on a certain date.
- S/FNET (start/finish not earlier than): Start or finish after a certain date.
- S/FNLT (start/finish not later than): Must definitely start or end before a certain date.

The project manager and his team determine for each activity to what extent these constraints exist.

Negotiating the schedule
Making a schedule is a combined action between the team members and project manager, and also between the project manager and project sponsor. There often is a tension between team members, who want more time, and a project sponsor who wants things carried out faster.

There are two techniques to reduce[1] the duration of an activity:
- Crashing; using this technique, you look at the relationship between costs and durations, and when a project has to be finished earlier, you may decide

---
1 (2002), *A Guide to Project Management Body of Knowledge,* THE PROJECT MANAGEMENT INSTITUTE

159

to put more people on the critical path. That does mean, however, that the costs will probably be higher (more people, more overhead). Sometimes it is possible to change the order of activities, and you could also propose to reduce the content of the required end result.
- Fast-tracking; with this, tasks originally planned to be carried out one after the other, are now carried out in parallel. The result is that the planning telescopes, but by applying this technique, you introduce a number of extra risks which may make it necessary further along the path, to redo work. This could push up the costs, but if it means the project will be finished earlier, it might be considered as being acceptable.

Visualizing the time schedule
In a Gantt Chart, the duration of the project is graphically displayed as bars. These have to be levelled, as the schedule now also takes into account the availability of resources.

Levelling the Gantt-Chart is done by slowing down or speeding up certain activities. Often, the whole process of levelling the Gantt Chart means that one or more of the process steps mentioned earlier will have to be repeated until an acceptable Gantt-chart has been achieved.

Rescheduling during the project
The following process step can potentially result in measures being taken, which lead to certain parts of the schedule having to be carried out again.

6. Control the time schedule
A number of issues are important for controlling the schedule, and these are covered successively:

- The critical path.
- Uncertain paths and potential risks.
- Scope creep.
- "Monument building".
- External dependencies.

The critical path
This is the path in which every overrun of an activity on it results in the whole project overrunning. This has a number of consequences in the way in which you manage these issues.

On a daily basis, you keep an eye on which activities on the critical path are soon to be completed, and which still have to be started. As each estimate contains a level of uncertainty, you have to ensure that the person delivering indicates this in time (especially when he is finished earlier), so that the next person, who has to carry on the work, can take over immediately. Whatever time you can gain here is a bonus, and whatever overruns you have to win back later.

Uncertain paths and potential risks
As well as the critical path, you also have to watch the non-critical paths that have an uncertain duration, because in the event of a significant time overrun (when they use up their slack), they may become critical. A part of the risk analysis should, therefore, also include an analysis of the different paths in the network diagram.

Scope creep
These are the many small changes which, unnoticed, can jeopardise the project. It is tempting to permit these types of changes, without sizing up the overall effects of them on the duration, money and/or quality. But remember, many small changes can add up to the equivalent of one large change.

"Monument building"
This phenomenon exists when you let technicians do their own thing, things are never good or elaborate enough. However, one of the principles of working on the basis of a project approach, is that you deliver what has been agreed in the scope; no more and no less.

External dependencies
When you have to deal with external dependencies, which are outside your sphere of influence, then these are included in the schedule as assumptions, and you can include them in your schedule as milestones. Every assumption is a risk that you have to monitor separately and provide with counter measures.

7. Apply lessons learned
You cannot assume that the project team is immediately up to speed. At the start, you therefore have to make room in the schedule for some learning time. The experience certain team members gain, has to be documented and distributed to the other members of the team, so that they can learn from it during their work.

Transcending the project, it is advisable following completion to evaluate the whole planning and scheduling process, and to check how accurate the estimates and schedules were.

8. Other standards and guidances
The process steps as identified by IPMA are only a suggestion. The process steps described in the *ISO 21500 Guidance*, the *'guide to the Project Management Body of Knowledge'* (the *PMBOK Guide*) from the Project Management Institute, and in the popular PRINCE2 Project Management method are much more "binding". Without discussing it in detail I shall name, as a comparison, a number of items from these standards that are related to this competence element. What will be noticeable is the high level of similarity and overlap.

ISO 21500
The Guidance differentiates between the following processes for this subject:
- Sequence activities.
- Estimate activity durations.
- Develop schedule.
- Control schedule.

PMBOK Guide
The 5th edition of *PMBOK Guide* is somewhat more comprehensive than the Guidance, and differentiates between the following processes:
- Define activities.
- Sequence activities.
- Estimate activity resources.
- Estimate activity durations.
- Develop schedule.
- Control schedule.

PRINCE2
PRINCE2 makes a very clear differentiation between the project plan and the different stage plans. The project manager always needs approval to execute a stage plan. The following activities are addressed in the topic Plan:
- Draw up plan.
- Define and analyse products.
- Produce the project product description.
- Produce the product breakdown structure.
- Produce the product descriptions.
- Produce the product flow diagram.
- Identify activities and dependencies.
- Make estimates.
- Produce the timetable.
- Analyse risks.
- Document plan.

1.11 Time and Project phases

1.11-4 SPECIAL TOPICS

1. Concepts of time

It should be added that there is a cultural element here. The American anthropologist Edward T. Hall[2] coined the term polychronic to describe cultures in which people are able to attend to multiple events at the same time, e.g. chairing a meeting and answering a telephone call. In these cultures, which we find in Latin America and the Middle East, people working on a project can easily deal with three or four activities at the same time without feeling overwhelmed or loosing control. They are driven foremost by people and not by tasks. Agendas are fluid. So making an appointment with a business contact in the short term is easy, but if you forget to reconfirm it may well be that your appointment has been deleted from his agenda by the time you arrive. Opposed to polychronic cultures are the monochronic cultures of North-West Europe and the United States. Here people tend to handle activities one-by-one. Continuous interruptions by people with requests, telephone calls or other distractions that put pressure on their agenda make them nervous. Appointments with business contacts are highly reliable though and you can plan tasks for weeks or even months ahead.

MONOCHRONIC	POLYCHRONIC
Does one thing at a time	Does many things at the same time
Keeps strictly to agreements	Does not keep strictly to what has been agreed
An agreement is more important than relationship	Relationship is more important than an agreement
Keeps rigidly to the original plan	Waits and sees where something may lead to

2. Gantt Chart

In 1919, Henry Laurence Gantt[3] (1861-1919) introduced a revolutionary management instrument, which made it possible to represent project schedules graphically. The objective of this instrument was to assist the manager, as a good steward, in handling the people and resources he had available. Currently, this type of diagram goes under various different names: Bar Chart or Gantt Chart. The Gantt Chart consists of a number of parts:
- Table
- Timescale
- Schematic view

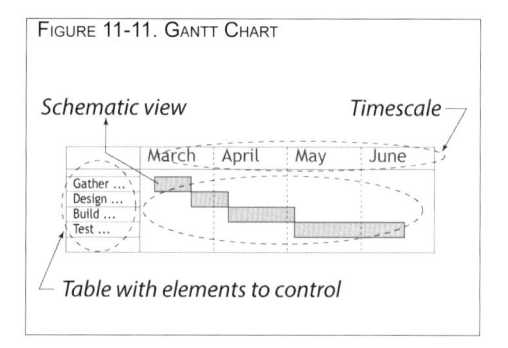

FIGURE 11-11. GANTT CHART

TABLE

On the left-hand side of the chart, you will find a table with rows in which you list the elements to be managed. Normally, planners include the complete WBS in this. You can then stop at work package level, or, if a detailed schedule is required, go on to include activities. In many scheduling software, use is still made of tasks, which is in fact an old-fashioned term for what we nowadays know as WBS elements. Another possibility is, in the place of the WBS, to list the people and resources in the table, and we then talk of a resource Gantt Chart.

In the figure you can see a table with one detail per activity, in this case the name of the

---

2 (1959) *The Silent Language,* E.T. Hall, BANTAM DOUBLEDAY DELL PUBLISHING GROUP

3 (1919), *Organizing for Work,* Henry Laurence Gantt

1.11 Time and Project phases

activity. But you do not have to make do with just this; you can extend the table columns with the duration, effort, dependencies, resources to be applied and so on. In this way you obtain a good overview of the various characteristics of a particular activity.

TIMESCALE
This consists of a ruler showing what the timescale represents. The lengths of the bars in the drawing area correspond with this scale, it equates to the duration. In the figure only one tier of timescale is used, but in practice you also see Gantt Charts with more tiers enabling you to increase the clarity of the schedule.

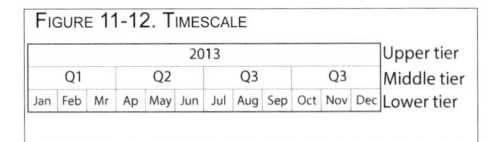

FIGURE 11-12. TIMESCALE

2013				Upper tier
Q1	Q2	Q3	Q3	Middle tier
Jan Feb Mr	Ap May Jun	Jul Aug Sep	Oct Nov Dec	Lower tier

SCHEMATIC VIEW

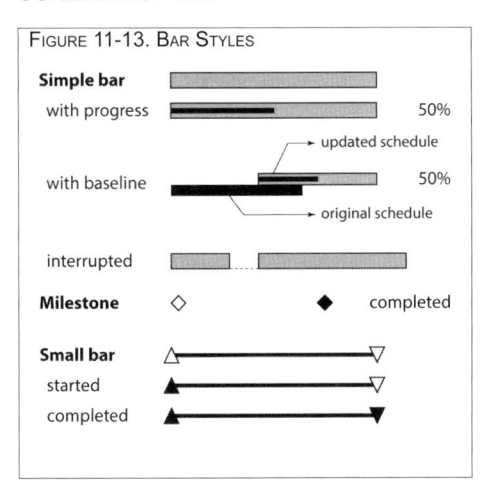

FIGURE 11-13. BAR STYLES

- Simple bar
- with progress — 50%
  - updated schedule
- with baseline — 50%
  - original schedule
- interrupted
- Milestone ◇ ◆ completed
- Small bar
- started
- completed

This view consists of bars, which run from a start date to an end date, the length being dependent on the timescale chosen. On account of these bars, such a diagram is also sometimes called a bar chart. The style of the bars is highly dependent on the planner's personal preferences, and the options available in the chosen scheduling software.

The use of multiple symbols does provide more insight, but at the same time less of an overview. You must, therefore, always ask yourself for whom the Gantt Chart is intended.

During the execution of the project, it is possible to add a status line to the chart.

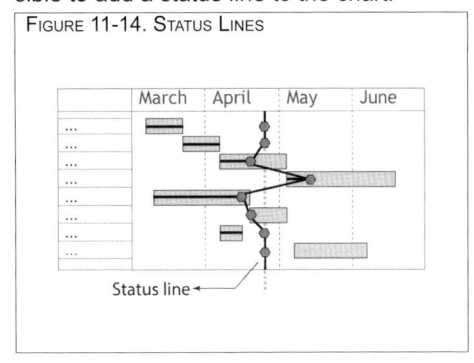

FIGURE 11-14. STATUS LINES

Status line ←

You start with this line at the top on the date for which you are reporting the project status. There is a node point on each row, which, if a particular activity is on schedule, lies on the date for which you are producing the status report. For those activities that are ahead of, or behind, schedule, you "pull" the line to the appropriate position on the bar in question. In the previous diagram, the third, fifth and sixth activities are behind schedule, the fourth activity is ahead of schedule and the remaining activities are on schedule.

IDEALISM
The Gantt Chart is one of the oldest project management techniques we have. It was developed in the time of the Scientific Management movement, a movement that as well as achieving a greater efficiency, also aspired to an ideal.

Gantt wrote in his first chapter:
"It is this conflict of ideals which is the source of the confusion into which the world is driving headlong. The community needs service first, regardless

1.11 Time and Project phases

of who gets the profits, because its life depends upon the service it gets."

Many of the project management techniques, and certainly the Gantt Chart, have the ultimate goal of delivering a good service. For project managers that means: delivering the project result on time, within budget and according to expectations, ensuring that the project result is worthy of the investment made.

3. The principle of phases
The following phases are the bare minimum:
- Initiation phase.
- Execution phase.

Creating phases contains a large number of concepts, and the next diagram shows the relationship between these concepts.

A project is a set of connected activities, which, at the end, delivers as a minimum the end product. Depending on the agreements made, a part making the end product operational may be included in the project. The greater the "making operational" part, sometimes referred to as commissioning, that is included in the project, the more the project shifts towards being a programme.

A phase is a part of the project with a clear decision point, that is marked by making a choice whether or not to continue. Sometimes it is a choice of how to carry on, and it is essential that a decision at a higher level is required. The division into phases is intended to limit the risk of a project. Creating phases with clear decision points from management is a tool for being able to take necessary actions earlier.

A milestone is an important event during a project and usually this is marked by the delivery of an important product. Often, the milestone is the point at which part of the contract price is paid. The milestone plays an important part in establishing an image of the project for the project team and the surrounding environment, and as such it also has a psychological value.

In general a critical decision point falls together with end of a phase. Only in the event of significantly large amendments, will you get an interim decision point. Decisions regarding a go/no-go, assess the project on the basis of the current, updated business case. Input for this is the up-to-date project plan (past and future) and the summary of all risks.

Advantages and disadvantages
Creating phases not only has advantages, but also disadvantages, and when choosing the phases, account should be taken of this.

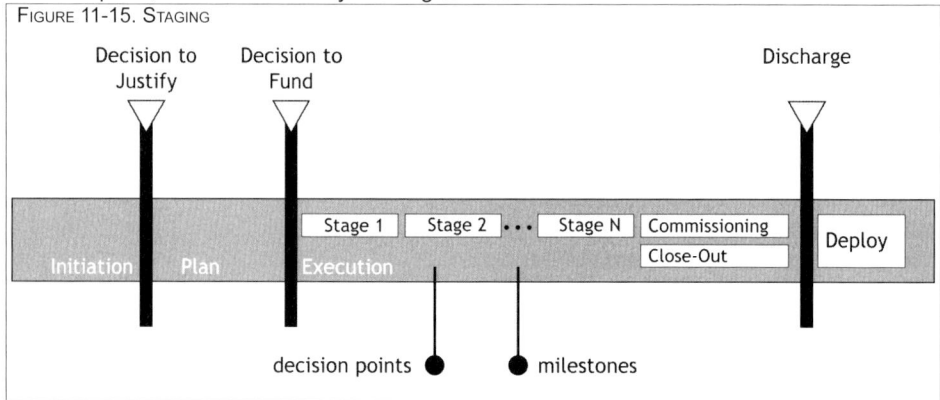

FIGURE 11-15. STAGING

1.11 Time and Project phases

ADVANTAGES:
- Well organized chunks.
- Schedule only what reasonably can be kept track of.
- Clear decision points.

DISADVANTAGES:
- Loss of the total picture.
- Too loose an estimate of the later phases.
- Later decision points are can be seen as "fakes", as due to the high investments, you cannot really go back anymore.

4. Various methods of staging

There are many types of staging, or phasing, possible. It is important that the division into phases really does require management action. The choice of the phases is strongly determined by the type of project.

What you want to keep under control is leading: is the technical development the most important, or, for example, keeping the finances under control. This is because at the end of each phase, you want to be able to make a considered decision as to whether or not to carry on. In fact, the phases indicate the points in time at which the project sponsor at the least will want to see the total picture.

There are different options for creating phases:
- Waterfall method.
- Cyclical phases.
- Versions.
- Management phases.

The Waterfall Method

This method has two foremost principles:
- The result is delivered in one go.
- The production process determines the phases.

In general such a phased schedule will look as follows:
- Stage 1: Establish the requirements.
- Stage 2: Design.
- Stage 3: Build.
- Stage 4: Test.
- Stage 5: Handover.

The end of each phase is followed by a go/no go decision. Only after the handover has an operational whole been delivered.

Cyclic phases

With this method, the cycle is gone through several times: requirements, design, build and test, whereby a cycle is often restricted in time (time-boxed). The advantage is that future users gain an insight into the functionality of the result at a relatively early phase.

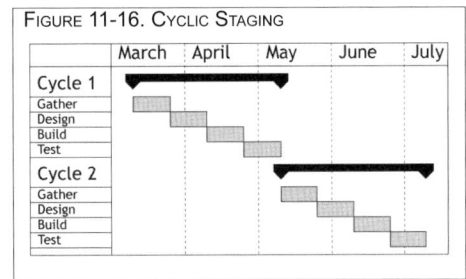

FIGURE 11-16. CYCLIC STAGING

	March	April	May	June	July
Cycle 1					
Gather					
Design					
Build					
Test					
Cycle 2					
Gather					
Design					
Build					
Test					

Versions

This form strongly resembles the waterfall method, and the final result required is delivered after a number of earlier versions. However, as opposed to creating phases using the cyclic method, each version delivers a working result which is ready for production.

Management Stages

For the methods mentioned for creating phases, our starting point has always been the production process. Such a way of creating phases has the drawback that it does not connect with the control cycle of the permanent organization within which the project is being carried out. We can find the solution to this in the use of management phases.

165

1.11 Time and Project phases

A management phase then corresponds, for example, with the annual or quarterly cycle of the organization.

Characteristics of a phase
A phase is characterized by the following elements:
- It delivers a defined result, which is used as input for the next phase.
- The budget is released per phase or sometimes for a complete project, with a re-evaluation at each phase, which, with regard to content, is close.
- Sometimes (for example with DSDM or time-boxes) time and budget are held on tightly to, but the scope or the quality is left variable (so this provides a flexible result!).

The general rule is: the less clear, or the less predictable, the project is, the shorter the phases. This makes it possible to make timely adjustments, which are needed more frequently for these types of projects than for other projects.

5. Estimation methods
For estimations, the quality of the estimate improves by doing them in various different ways, and often. There are many ways to make an estimate, such as:

Feedback
By making an estimate, and then obtaining the actual value through feedback, you learn to improve the quality of your estimates. By using this consciously, you can provide yourself with many learning moments. If, for all kinds of issues and activities, you firstly estimate the values yourself, and then subsequently verify them, you develop a skill in estimating.

Databases
The experience from the past is a good basis for predicting the future. Especially in the building industry, a lot experience has been gained and collected, which has resulted in standards being developed for the consumption of materials and time for all types of work.

Logic
Usually, the current project is not precisely the same as another project, but it often looks that way. By analyzing the similarities and differences, we can make a logically reasoned estimate about the current situation.

Calculating
The building industry in particular has a lot of experience with this. By dividing the project up into various activities and necessities, an accurate prediction can be made based on past performances and the current prices.

Segmenting
Using this method, the object to be estimated is divided in a number of smaller elements and an estimate is then made for these smaller parts. Working in too much detail does not always help, as the sum of small parts is simply not equal to the larger whole. Estimates carried out on the basis of details and segmenting seem to be accurate, but they must be supported by estimates made in other ways. A good WBS provides the required segmentation.

Delphi method
If there is no practical experience with new technologies, market introductions or cultural changes, then this is a useful method to apply. Using the Delphi method[4], you involve experts, usually over a number of rounds.

Some characteristics of this method:
- Anonymity.
- The experts give anonymous answers.

---
4 (1969) *The Delphi Method: An experimental study of group opinion,* Norman C. Dalkey, RAND

1.11 Time and Project phases

- Over a number of rounds, the experts give their opinions or expectations.
- After this, feedback and steering/narrowing of the phrasing of questions takes place.

Statistics
By analyzing the answers of the experts statistically, you get an impression of the spread of the various answers. This also influences the predicted value.

Obviously a lot depends on the choice of experts, as their knowledge and quality determines the quality of the estimation. Experts are often thin on the ground, have clear likes and dislikes and often also specific interests. The advantage, however, is that in this way an estimation and risk analysis can be obtained, which would be difficult to achieve in any other way.

Function point analysis
Function point analysis is a method for measuring the functional size of an information system. It measures this by looking at the product to be delivered (information system). You count the functions and (logical) collections of data, which are relevant for the user. The measuring unit of this method is the function point. The function point is the only measuring unit for which the size of the information system to be developed can, in advance, be discussed concretely and, to a large extent, objectively.

A quote such as: *"It is a system of about 1100 function points"* provides a better footing than *"It is a reasonably large system"*.

Unfortunately, the function point is an abstract quantity. To assure the objectivity of the measurement, user groups have published standard counting guidelines.

If it is known from previous experiences how many hours are needed to realize one function point (the productivity), then the formula below can be used to form the basis for a project budget:

Size (number of function points)
x Productivity (hours per function point)
= Budget (number of hours).

Function point analysis is a simple method, which, with adequate documentation, can be carried out quickly. A function point analysis can be carried out as soon as the functional specifications for a system are globally known. Function point analysis is not a scheduling technique. With function point analysis, a statement can only be given on the size of a project and the total hours required. Function point analysis does not provide a verdict on what the duration of a project will then be, but you can use it to compare the outcomes of the other estimates.

Suppliers
It is also possible to ask a supplier to make an estimate by inviting him to produce a proposal. If an actual investment is being considered, or a comparison of pros and cons between *'make or buy'* has to be made, this is then of course the obvious method. There are also companies who use suppliers to validate their own estimates and assumptions.

1.11 Time and Project phases

> **EXAMPLE 11-2 TEN WEEKS PROJECT**
>
> Suppose the expected duration is 10 weeks with a standard deviation of 1 week. There is a probability of 50% that the project will indeed be achieved within the expected duration. That probability becomes greater (84%), when you take one more week (= one standard deviation). This can be read-off from a so-called Z table.
>
> | Z | 0.0 | 0.1 | 0.2 | 0.3 | 0.4 | 0.5 | 0.6 | 0.7 | 0.8 | 0.9 |
> |------|-------|-------|-------|-------|-------|-------|-------|-------|-------|--------|
> | -3. | .0013 | .0010 | .0007 | .0005 | .0003 | .0002 | .0002 | .0001 | .0001 | .0000 |
> | -2. | .0228 | .0179 | .0139 | .0107 | .0082 | .0062 | .0047 | .0035 | .0026 | .0019 |
> | -1. | .1587 | .1357 | .1151 | .0968 | .0808 | .0668 | .0548 | .0446 | .0359 | .0287 |
> | -0. | .5000 | .4602 | .4207 | .3821 | .3446 | .3085 | .2743 | .2420 | .2119 | .1841 |
> | 0. | .5000 | .5398 | .5793 | .6179 | .6554 | .6915 | .7257 | .7580 | .7881 | .8159 |
> | 1. | .8413 | .8643 | .8849 | .9032 | .9192 | .9332 | .9452 | .9554 | .9641 | .9713 |
> | 2. | .9772 | .9821 | .9861 | .9893 | .9918 | .9938 | .9953 | .9965 | .9974 | .9981 |
> | 3. | .9987 | .9990 | .9993 | .9995 | .9997 | .9998 | .9998 | .9999 | .9999 | 1.0000 |
>
> In order to determine the required chance, you carry out the following steps:
> 1. Determine how many standard deviations the related duration lies from the expected time.
> 2. This can be a negative distance (before) or a positive distance (after).
> 3. Determine the row by looking in the Z table for the first numeral before the comma.
> 4. Determine the column by looking in the Z table at the next numeral after the comma
> 5. The required number is on the cross-point.
>
> In our example of 10 weeks with a standard deviation of 1 week, we find the probability that the project is completed within 12½ weeks (this is 2½ times the standard deviation above 10) in the cell in the table 2, + 0.5 which is 0.9938 and therefore 99.38%.

6. PERT[5]

Pert (Program Evaluation and Review Technique) was developed during the 1950's by the American Navy to manage the Polaris Missile Program, with the objective of producing reliable estimates.

Every estimate contains a degree of uncertainty. When you have carried out a particular activity more times, you can give a statement on the: optimistic time (O); Most likely time (M) and; Pessimistic time (P)

We determine the duration of the activity with the help of the following formula:
$V = (O + 4M + P) / 6$

This is then done for all the activities in a project, after which the activities are put into a network, and a critical path analysis carried out. One of the assumptions in PERT is that optimistic and pessimistic duration are 6 standard deviations apart. So the formula for standard deviation becomes: Stdev = (P-O)/6.

Another important assumption is that the duration of the critical path follows a normal distribution. With the help of the standard deviation, which can be calculated, it is possible to make statements on the probability of a certain duration being achieved.

---

[5] *The Polaris System Development - Bureaucratic and Programmatic Succes in Government,* Harvey M. Sapolski, HARVARD UNIVERSITY PRESS, USA

1.12 Resources

IT DOESN'T GET EXCITING UNTIL PEOPLE JOIN THE PROJECT

Before you can start planning resources, you have to know how much/many you need and when.

Estimates and assumptions are used to determine what/who and how much is needed.

This always involves uncertainty.

1.12 Resources

1.12-1 DEFINITIONS

Feeding buffer	The reserve available at the end of every non-critical chain of activities, before this chain becomes part of the critical path.
Project buffer	The reserve at the end of the critical path, which is a buffer between the scheduled end date of the activities, and the date of delivery.
Required resources	All people, tools, materials and provisions required to deliver a particular performance.
Resource plan	Plan for the allocation of resources.
Rules of thumb file	A file with indicators for allocation of the necessary capacity, and the duration of work to be carried out.
Scheduling resources	Identifying and allocating the required resources in order to allocate them optimally at the right time, within the given constraints, and taking account of the availability.

1.12-2 Introduction

The allocation of resources is the link between the plan and the actual situation. Up until now, we have only thought about the project in terms of the schedule. A stakeholder analysis has been made, the requirements have been listed, priorities have been set, the scope has been defined, the resources needed on the project have been considered, as well as the way in which we shall deliver the results.

Now we have to find and allocate the required resources, because without doing that, not a lot will happen. We do this using the resource plan we have made. This plan is not nearly finished though, because you still have to wait and see if you actually get the resources you assumed in the previous step. You are involved in a negotiation with line management.

In most cases, as project manager, you do not yet have any resources, and you have to acquire them. You have to "*go shopping*", or better said, "*go to the line managers*" to find them. You are dealing with a division in functions; you use resources, and the line manager manages them. You must indicate *what* has to be delivered at a certain time (*when*), and the line manager will indicate *who* and *how*. This point at which you need to acquire the required capacity, is in fact a checkpoint to test the actual priority your project has.

1.12 Resources

1.12-3 PROCESS STEPS

1. Decide on the need.
2. Schedule the resources.
3. Reach an agreement.
4. Apply change control.
5. Manage assignment.
6. Process impact of changes.
7. Escalation in time.
8. Use experience.
9. Apply lessons learned.

1. Decide on the need
There are a number of starting points for determining the capacity requirements:
- The scope and project deliverables.
- The project organization.
- The schedule.

The project deliverables and the project organization provide an idea of the type of resources needed. The overall plan completes the picture by providing information on when the resources are needed, and, on this basis, we can make an initial resource schedule.

2. Schedule the resources
When, for the next stage, we schedule the number of required resources, we obtain a resource diagram.

It is advisable, if necessary, to move bring certain activities forward or move some back, in order to arrive at an optimum resource allocation. You also watch out for something which is not taken account of sufficiently in the critical path analysis, and that is an overstaffing of resources. This process is called resource levelling.

Another representation of the required capacity is the so-called S curve, in which the hours for all team members have been accumulated over time.

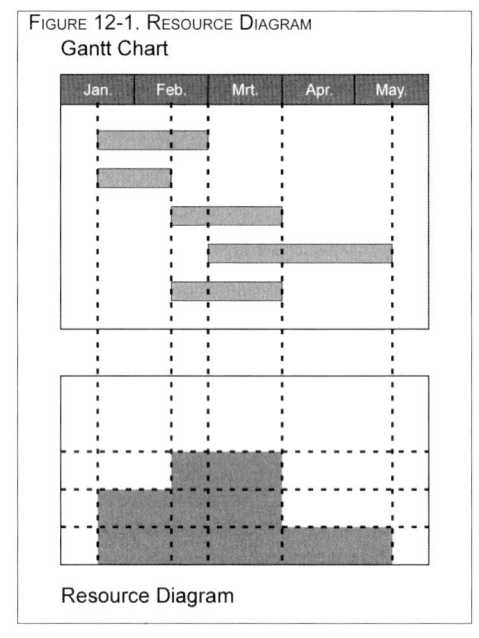

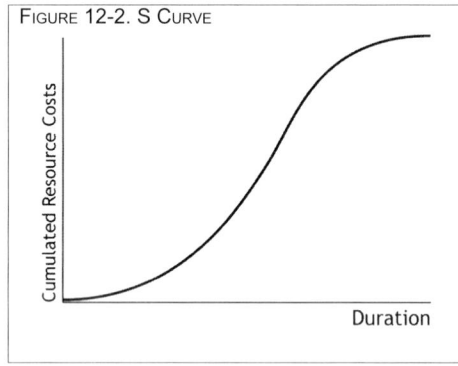

FIGURE 12-1. RESOURCE DIAGRAM
Gantt Chart

Resource Diagram

FIGURE 12-2. S CURVE

When you study the chart, you see that in the first weeks of the project, the curve climbs a bit more slowly than in the middle part, and then levels off somewhat again at the end of the project. This is because in the beginning you are starting up the project, and you use fewer resources than in the middle part, where the most resources are working and where the S curve will climb faster. The curve levels off again at the end of the project when resources start leaving the project.

3. Reach an agreement

The project manager will have to recruit the required people and resources from somewhere. In general he will have to work together with line or resource managers. Even if both work for the same organization, their interests may still be very different, which is something that may be very frustrating for you as project manager. There are two planning cycles which continuously have an influence on one another.

Annually, the management sets objectives for the organization, and the responsible managers use these to create the plans for their department. This also includes a resource schedule, detailing the people they need. This is the circle on the left.

In addition to these regular line activities, there are the projects, which also need resources. The project managers go "shopping" with their resource plan to the different line managers, and this is the circle on the right. Negotiation is carried out in the middle.

In situations in which the availability of the resources is limited, it is important to negotiate early to get commitments on the assignment of the required resources. Often there are more projects submitting a claim for the same resources, and conflicts such as these are very common and all part of the game.

When there are no "internal" resources available, the project manager can look for an external party who can provide them. You also often see constructions in which the line manager concerned does this, whereby for the project manager, it is just the same as hiring an "internal" person.

4. Apply change control

The estimates you produced for the required capacity and the resources acquired (assignments) should be placed under change control.

This sounds strange.

Usually it is customary to only place the scope and the specifications under change control, because many small changes often result in a schedule slippage or budget overrun. We therefore need to keep close track of this during the project, and control it.

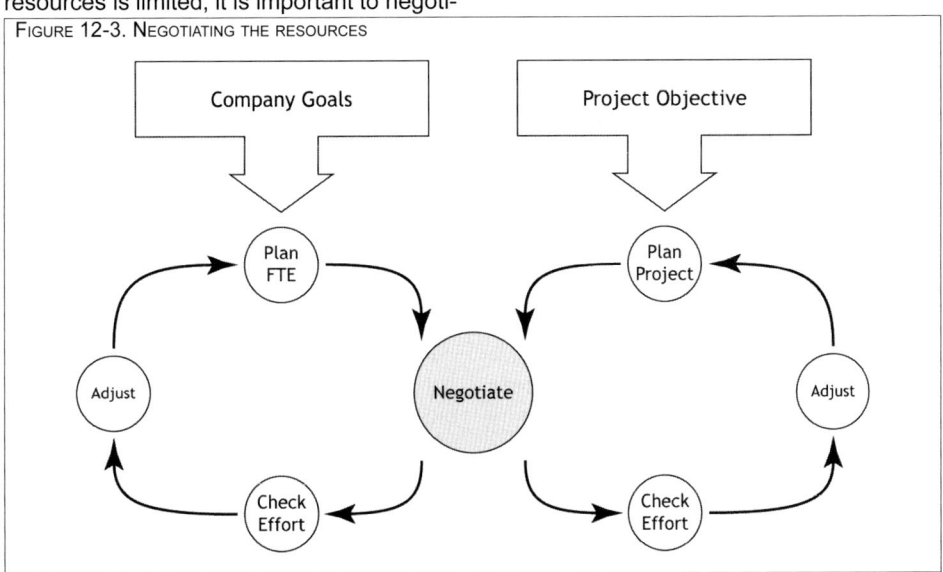

FIGURE 12-3. NEGOTIATING THE RESOURCES

1.12 Resources

For the same reason you also place the estimates and assignments under change control, because if the estimates are wrong, this can also often lead to slippages or overruns. The same reasoning applies to the assignments. When you do not get the agreed resources, this will definitely have a negative impact on the duration, and possibly also on the actual costs incurred.

What does this mean in practice?

THE ESTIMATE PROVES TO BE WRONG
After some time the team has built up new insights into the work they have to deliver. This may mean that the team members reach the conclusion that certain activities can be done faster, or will need more time. When this relates to a number of weeks in duration, and not just to a few days, it is advisable to take another look at the total plan.

In accordance with the change procedure, a request for change is drawn up for this part of the plan. This may be as a result of activities which have already been carried out (in which case it has been discovered during the progress control), but also for future work (in which case it is at the suggestion of a team member). In the change process the project manager, together with his team, analyses what effects this has on the total plan and on the way they have to deploy the various resources. If this stays within the tolerance the project manager has, he can decide himself what he does, and otherwise approval of the project sponsor or the steering committee must be sought.

ASSIGNMENT IS NOT BEING EFFECTED
This is much the same story. The progress report shows that certain people are not putting in the hours agreed with their unit manager. An analysis is also made here as to whether or not the impact falls within the margins of the project manager, and when this is not the case, he should recognise this, think up alternatives, and present these to the project sponsor or steering committee.

THE ADVANTAGE OF THIS APPROACH
Doing this together with the other requests for change has the advantage that all changes, whether these have to do with the result to be delivered, the time of delivery, or the price, are now being controlled integrally.

5. Manage assignment

Agreed is agreed, but reality and agreement still differ sometimes. Certainly when resources have been assigned to the project on a part-time basis, you run the risk that someone works less than specified in the schedule. Furthermore, working part-time results in a certain inefficiency (it is a form of multi-tasking).

There are different ways of keeping an eye on the assignment:
- Ask how much time someone has spent during the last period.
- Study the time sheets.
- Keep track of the actual progress.

It is useful to come to agreements with the employees about when they will deliver certain results. Ensure that they (at least emotionally) enter into a commitment with you to deliver the results, and in that case it does not matter too much if they spend less time on the project, as long as they deliver results (on time).

The S curve is a useful tool for keeping an eye on whether or not the allocation of resources is line with the agreement (the dotted curve). Next to the curve for the planned allocation of resources, you now also include a curve for the actual allocation (the continuous curve).

1.12 Resources

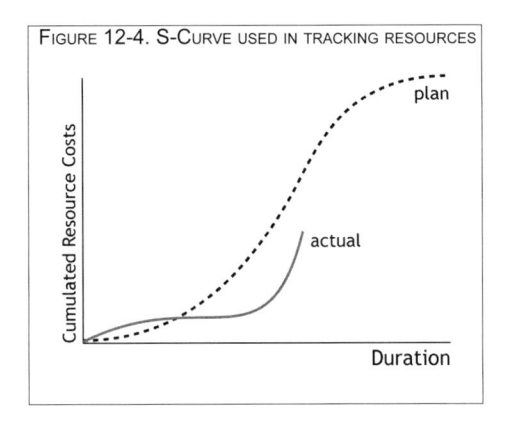

FIGURE 12-4. S-CURVE USED IN TRACKING RESOURCES

The example shows that the project starts off slightly slower than planned, but that it is catching up.

6. Process impact of change

Most changes in durations "creep" into the project unnoticed, causing you only to notice them when it is already too late, and this is obviously not desirable. All the work is under change control, and for each change, you determine the impact a potential change may have on the:
- Durations.
- Costs.
- Quality of the result.

When the durations change, you have to adjust the plan, and that means that you will need certain resources at a different time. It goes without saying that you communicate such a change to the team members involved. And possibly renegotiate their assignment.

Time that you do not use is time you waste, which is the opposite of cost, because if you do not spend money, you also do not lose it.

7. Escalation in time

You have to escalate serious underestimates, which fall outside your margins as project manager and which you cannot off- set in any other way, to the steering committee. Actually you are expected to see these overruns coming, and, therefore, the escalation should actually be raised before the overrun has happened. With the escalation, you should also provide a proposal for the countermeasures to be taken, giving the steering committee time to react and take action.

8. Use experience

Often we find it difficult to make an estimate, which is partly because many organizations fail to keep an estimates bank. Especially when the organization carries out a lot of projects, it is a useful tool for improving the accuracy of the estimates over the course of time.

9. Apply lessons learned

As well as the estimates databank from the previous process step, you have to evaluate together with your team members with whom you did the estimate how this was arrived at and how accurate it was. In this way, you contribute to improving the level of professionalism with which estimating is carried out in the organization.

1.12-4 SPECIAL TOPICS

1. Critical Chain

Eliyahu Goldratt's Critical Chain method is described in his management book: "The Critical Chain"[1] and it solves a number of important problems, which are not taken into account in the critical path method.

These problems are:
- The student syndrome.
- Uncertainty in estimates.
- Multi-tasking.
- Resource availability.

The student syndrome
When you give people a certain task, they are inclined to start at the last possible moment. This is the *student syndrome.*

If you compare this with the habit of project managers to schedule all activities as early as possible, it is not hard to see that this practice leads to wasting valuable time.

Uncertainty in estimates
Most estimates we ask our team members to do are one point estimates (with the exception of the PERT approach). Furthermore, we confuse accuracy with certainty and that arises due to the way in which we ask people to provide estimates. This means that people play it safe, and what we obtain are estimates which are then much too high. Everyone knows the situation whereby the executing team member estimates a certain activity to take three days, and then adds an extra two just to be sure. As project manager you know from experience that this activity, which has now been estimated to take a week, runs the risk of extending, and to be certain, you add another week. The result is that an activity which could have been done in three days is now already planned in for two weeks. The employee, who is suffering from the student syndrome, will probably start as late as possible and see a self-fulfilling prophecy come true.

Multi-tasking
Sometimes it is tempting to let people do several things at the same time. We call this multi-tasking.

The diagram shows the effects of it. The top three bars of the Gantt-chart form the single-tasking variant. An employee only carries out one task at the time and does not start the next one until the previous one is finished.

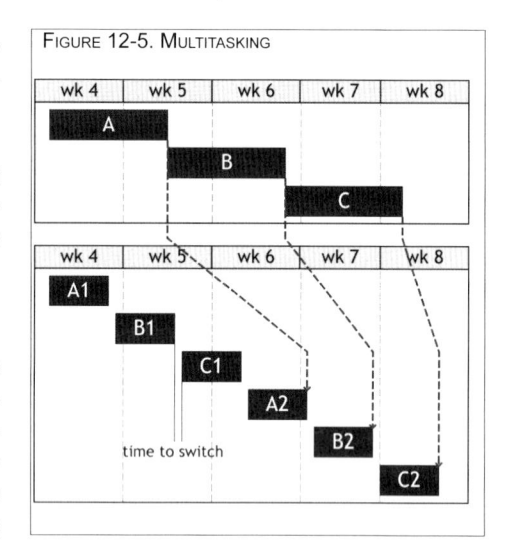

FIGURE 12-5. MULTITASKING

When we look at the bottom six bars, we see how the employee initially works on the first half of activity A. Halfway through that he starts activity B, repeats this for C and then carries on with A, B and C with the result that all activities, except for C, are finished later than in the single-tasking variant.

An argument can be made for not carrying out more than two activities at the same time. In this case, the team member can work on another activity, in the event that he temporarily loses motivation on the first activity.

---
1 (1997) *The Critical Chain*, Eliyahu Goldratt, GOWER

1.12 Resources

Resource availability
When two activities running in parallel make use of the same resources, the critical path method will not take this into account. The only solution is, with the help of soft logic (inserting a dependency), ensuring that this is the case.

The suggested solution
With Critical Chain Project Management you plan as late as possible (ALAP) to prevent the student syndrome, and in addition you estimate with a 50% level of certainty and provide for a potential overrun on the time schedule, which now happens more frequently, by building in buffers. This does demand a certain culture change. Compared to the classical method, you now do not put people under so much pressure to achieve their schedule. If, however, you do do this, people will increase their estimates to raise the level of certainty. What is very important now is 'handing over the baton' to the next person in the chain.

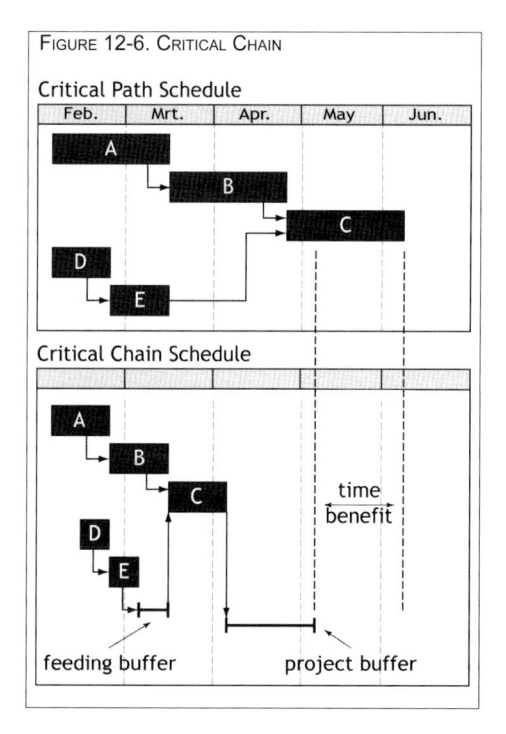

Multi-tasking is also no longer carried out; as soon as an employee has to begin an activity in the critical chain, he stops doing all his other work. The critical chain is the critical path that takes account of resource availability.

In the two Gantt charts, you can see the difference between both methods.

You can see how activities D and E are planned as early as possible. As we are concerned here with a schedule that has been arrived at in the traditional way, the estimates contain too much certainty. If we 'transform' this schedule into a Critical Chain schedule, then this will look approximately like the second Gantt Chart.

All durations are halved, and at the end of the project a *project buffer* containing half of the total project duration is added. In addition, the non-critical activities are planned as late as possible, and there where they enter into 'the critical chain', they are separated by a so-called *feeding buffer*. This is shown in the second Gantt Chart.

For the progress report, the project manager now only has to report on how much of the various buffers have been used.

FIGURE 12-6. CRITICAL CHAIN

1.12 Resources

1.13 Cost and finance

AS BEFITS A PRUDENT MAN

Project managers work with the organization's money, that money belongs to the owners of the organization.

Each project is an investment in a 'better future'!

Budgeting is the process in which a 'limited' amount of money is made available for the project manager.

That money does not just materialise out of thin air, but is financed.

The budget does not have to be used up; it is permitted to have money left over.

1.13 Cost and Finance

1.13-1 DEFINITIONS

Budget	An authorised amount or summation of amounts to achieve a result.
Budgetary control	Checking for expenditure either not included in the budget, or which exceeds the budget.
Budgeting	The setting up of a budget.
Cost control	Estimating, budgeting and monitoring the expenditure, and taking the required actions to achieve the result within the agreed budget.
Cost estimating	Identifying and quantifying the expected cost of the various parts of the project.
Financing	Obtaining the money required for a project.
Management reserve	A budget entry to potentially supplement the agreed budgets, should they unexpectedly turn out to be insufficient for the activities foreseen. This is under the management of the project sponsor.

1.13-2 INTRODUCTION

A budget is a *plan* for spending money. It regulates who is *authorised* to make *specified payments at certain points in time*. By approving the proposed budget of the estimate, the project sponsor can transfer this *responsibility* to a project manager.

By imposing discipline and deadlines, the budget, drawn up as tasks specified in a plan for the financial future helps to keep the financial behavior under control, and it also provides controlling options by comparing the budget with reality. By comparing pre-determined costs with actual costs, the budget process can continuously be improved.

This competence element is made up of two parts:

- *Financial Management*: organizing the required finances.
- *Cost Control*: keeping the actual expenditure within budget.

The respective processes for financial management and cost control will be discussed successively.

1.13 Cost and Finance

1.13-3

FINANCIAL PROCESS

1. Analyze financing options.
2. Negotiate the potential funds.
3. Select the source of finance.
4. Allocate budgets.
5. Calculate cash flows.
6. Document and authorise.
7. Take care of the audit systems.
8. Validate and manage budgets.
9. Apply lessons learned.

1. Analyze financing options

There are two ways to finance the expenditure on a project:
- Internal
- External

Organizations often finance projects *internally*, which means that money comes from the cash flows generated within the company. With *external* financing, an extra incoming cash flow is required, and is provided through a share issue, an investment company (more risk-bearing), or a bank (less risk-bearing). Ultimately, the organization will have to pay this money back somehow, and furthermore, remuneration in the form of dividend or interest will be owed on it.

In general the project sponsor ensures the finances are provided. A project manager can assist in this, especially with respect to defining the project and reducing the uncertainty potential investors may have. As it is dependent on the total finance requirements of an organization, the manner of financing is a decision senior management must take.

The following forms of *external* financing exist:
- Low risk financing.
- High risk financing.

LOW RISK FINANCING
- Short term loan or bridging loan.
- Medium term loan of between 1 and 10 years, geared to the economic lifespan.
- Bonds
- Long term or mortgage.
- Current account.
- Leasing of machines, buildings, etc.
- Factoring, where a bank takes over the payment risks of the debtors.

HIGH(ER) RISK FINANCING
These can be banks, investment companies, governments or other investors:
- Shares.
- Subordinated loan.
- A-loan.
- Regional Development Banks like the: African Development Bank, Asian Development Bank, European Investment Bank, Arab Fund for Economic and Social Development, Islamic Development Bank, etc.
- Government guaranteed loan scheme for small and medium-sized enterprises.
- Venture capital.

2. Negotiate the potential funds

Depending on the organization's financial options, the funds are negotiated, although this is not something the project manager is responsible for. His contribution to the total financing process consists of providing the estimates for the required funds.

When the organization is not able to finance the project from its own means and, as a result, opts for an external financing source, the sponsors or financial backers will want a degree of certainty. Initially, they will look at the extent to which the organization can meet its obligations in the short term (liquidity), followed by the long term (solvability).

1.13 Cost and Finance

Both the organization's liquidity and the solvability can be derived from the organization's balance sheet, and in addition they will look into the impact the project has on the organization's cash flows and the extent to which the organization is capable of meeting its obligations with respect to interest and repayments.

If this does not provide sufficient certainty, the investors will often ask for additional guarantees in the form of preferential creditorship. If the organization is not in a position to meet its commitments, then, in advance, certain assets are designated and the receipts from the sale of these are first allocated to the preferential creditor. The most well-known example is a mortgage, whereby if we cannot meet our repayments, the bank is entitled to sell the assets in order to recover its money.

3. Select the source of finance
At top management level, the choice is made as to which finance source is best for the organization. This choice is dependent on the organization's general financial situation.

Above, I stated that a financial backer assesses this financial situation on the basis of the annual accounts. This can have a significant disadvantage, since the organization is now, with all its assets, accountable for the repayment of the debt to the financial backer. There are situations whereby this is undesirable, and a different construction called "Project financing" has been introduced to provide an acceptable alternative solution.

Project financing
We see this form of financing predominantly in large-scale projects in the areas of: energy generation, pipelines, mines, public and private co-operation, toll roads, development projects etc.

The basis of this construction is the setting-up of a separate legal entity (Special Purpose Vehicle), which as a fully-fledged company goes searching for a source of finance. Through this construction, the only certainties are: the expected cash flows, and the assets of the project company. For the sponsors this provides the advantage that they do not carry more risk than their participation in the project.

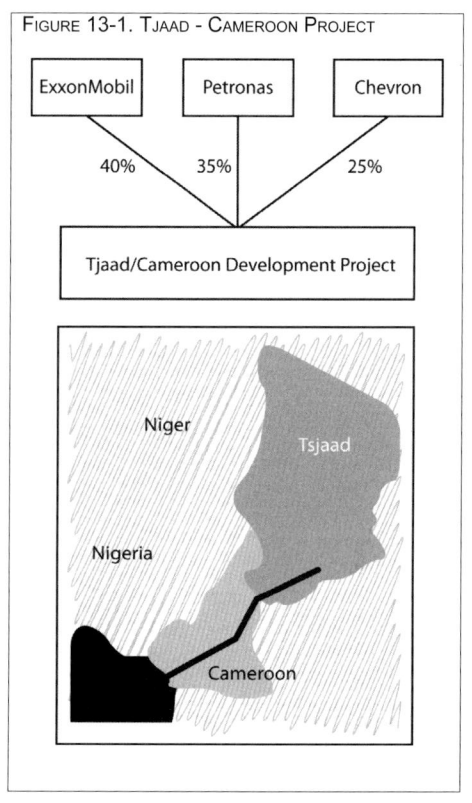

FIGURE 13-1. TJAAD - CAMEROON PROJECT

```
ExxonMobil      Petronas        Chevron
    40%           35%             25%
         Tjaad/Cameroon Development Project
```

Niger
Tsjaad
Nigeria
Cameroon

Seen from the sponsors' standpoint, project financing has many advantages[1]:
- Limited liability for the sponsors.
- Debt remains outside their balance sheet.
- Better ratio of debt to assets.
- Limited influence on other transactions.
- Better terms and conditions.

---
1 (2008) *The Law and Business of International Project Finance*, S.L. Hoffman, CAMBRIDGE UNIVERSITY PRESS, New York

1.13 Cost and Finance

- Higher returns.
- Political risk is restricted to the project.
- Risk sharing between the sponsors.
- Provision of security is restricted to the project.
- Higher level of involvement from the sponsors.
- Security provisions can be diversified.
- More credit possibilities.

There are of course also a number of disadvantages:
- A more complex risk allocation.
- More risk for the financial backer.
- Higher interest rates.
- Supervision of the financial backer.
- Detailed reporting requirements.
- Higher Insurance premiums.
- Encourages the taking of political risks.

4. Allocate budgets

Once the choice has been made, the budgets can be allocated. As the forecasts that the project manager has made are based on the times at which the work will take place, there can be a discrepancy between the times at which the money actually comes in, and the times when it is needed.

Some suppliers demand payment in advance, even before the actual work has been carried out, and for this reason a projected cash flow has to be made.

5. Calculate cash flows

The cash flow overview is important for both the final investment decision and the projected cash flow. The organization must ensure that the necessary funds are available at the point in time that the project manager approves an invoice for payment.

In its simplest form, a cash flow summary looks like this:

	Period				
	1	2	3	4	5
Capital investments					
Hiring third parties					
Etc.					
Cash flow out					

For each row, you show the type of cost in the same way as asked for by the existing organization, and you also do the same for the period. Note that such a summary can only be made properly by using a planning tool.

6. Document and authorise

All procedures the project has to follow are described or named in the project management plan. This also applies to the payment of costs incurred within the scope of the project.

The project sponsor must ensure that all parties involved have sufficient authority to be able to carry out the required financial dealings in the project. However, for project managers working in a matrix organization, this does not mean they actually get power of attorney (i.e. the authority to pay invoices). Usually you see a construction in which the project manager checks and initials invoices, on the basis of which the authorised manager authorizes the invoice to be paid.

7. Take care of the audit systems

Every organization has its own audit systems that a project has to comply with. Organizations listed on the stock exchange in the United States, must comply with the Sarbanes-Oxley legislation, an act aimed at preventing new accounting scandals from occurring. When a project in any way, directly or indirectly, has an impact on the financial accounts of an organization, it is subject to this act.

IT projects
If the software developed by the organization provides numbers from which the accountants obtain their data, they will definitely ask questions on the way in which it has been developed.

Questions you can expect are:
- What software has been changed?
- Who has changed the software?
- Why was the software changed?
- What has been changed (compared to the previous version)?
- Who approved the software to be released for production use?

8. Validate and manage budgets
Managing the budgets is one of the project manager's on-going activities (see process steps for cost control). Validating the budgets and covering the costs incurred is primarily the project sponsor's activity.

The validation of a budget usually takes place at the start of each new stage. At that time, the project manager produces a statement for the project sponsor or steering committee containing the following sums of money:
- The actual costs to date.
- An estimate of costs for the whole project.
- A specified budget for the next stage.
- The external commitments that will be taken on.

The decision-makers now make a choice as to whether or not they want to continue with the project, and they do this on the basis of the costs and income still to be expected. In fact, the decision to fund is repeated at the start of each new stage. Even though the costs incurred and income received may be interesting, the decision-makers should not include these sums in their consideration to either continue or terminate the project. We are dealing with "sunk costs/profit", and whatever happens these cannot be changed. The same applies to the commitments entered into, which cannot be reversed, and it is, therefore, of no use to include them in the consideration.

If the decision is positive, the budget for the following stage is made available to the project manager, and he is mandated to enter into external commitments on behalf of the organization.

Ultimately, there must be an income against the costs incurred, and this is something other than the finance for ensuring sufficient liquidity to pay the invoices on the project. Covering the costs is about earning back the investment with a good profit, and this income must, in one way or another, be made attributable to the project.

9. Apply lessons learned
Learning occurs in many places, but here especially through the planned and unplanned financial audits carried out on the project. The project manager will process the findings from the audits in his project.

1.13-4 COST PROCESS

1. Choose a cost control system.
2. Estimate and evaluate costs.
3. Establish monitoring and control.
4. Define cost objectives.
5. Calculate actual costs.
6. Include changes and claims.
7. Carry out a variance analysis.
8. Make a forecast.
9. Take corrective measures.
10. Update the cost estimate.
11. Apply lessons learned.

1. Choose a cost control system

The cost control system is the collection of control measures you take to control the costs. This is dependent on the results of the risk analysis. If the risk that the costs will go up is high, or if the estimates show a large amount of uncertainty, it is necessary to have a '*stricter*' control than when this is not the case.

Another factor is the way in which the organization views the costs. Organizations doing well economically, are less inclined to pay attention to this than organizations not doing so well, who therefore have to carefully monitor their cash flows.

2. Estimate and evaluate costs

The WBS is the basis for estimating the costs, and we produce these for each work package. It is important to know how accurate and certain it is. How correct the estimation (method) was, can be subsequently determined by making a comparison with the actual costs.

Depending on how detailed the WBS and the specifications which provide an insight in the required quality are, you can make use of different estimation techniques:

- The analogy method: this is a very rough estimate, whereby you look at similar projects and apply this experience to the current project.
- The top-down approach: whereby you "chop up" the whole into chunks and estimate each one separately.
- The bottom-up approach: this is a very detailed approach, whereby you estimate each work package on its own and aggregate it from bottom to top.
- An expert estimate: here, you involve people with a lot of experience of these types of projects and make an estimate based on their opinion.
- Making use of standards and models: when an organization has a lot of experience with a certain type of project, then they have processed their experience in advanced models which can be used for estimating the project.

The above mentioned techniques are not mutually exclusive, and usually you see a joint application of a number of these techniques.

A trap which you can easily fall into, is to just focus on the project costs. You then go for the best price/quality ratio, but you forget to look further then the boundaries of the project. It is better to look at the Total Cost of Ownership, as it may be possible to make savings during the project execution by choosing a cheaper version of a certain part, even though it is much more expensive in maintenance. In **cost conscious design**, you take all costs into account.

1.13 Cost and Finance

When the cost estimate has been done three entries are missing:
- Contingency reserve.
- Management reserve.
- Risk premium.

The first two reserves enable the project manager and the project sponsor to, if necessary, initiate certain activities without making a new budget application. There is always a lot of discussion as to whether or not you have to provide your project sponsor with insight into the reserves. I believe you do, because if reserves are invisible, then they cannot be controlled, and this has the consequence that the project organization usually also spends them.

When the reserves have been calculated, you have to wait for approval, after which the estimate/assessment becomes the budget.

Contingency reserve
This is a sum the project manager can use to offset setbacks. It is possible that, in advance, this amount is designated for a specific purpose (for example for applying small changes), in which case you can only use it for that. Another term we come across is the *"tolerance"* or *"foreseen, but not yet named"*.

Management reserve
This is the project sponsor's tolerance. By having this, he does not immediately have to go to his managers in the event of exceeding the budget.

Risk premium
This is the total monetary value of the remaining risks once all the measures have been processed in the budget and the plan. Although, this amount is part of the project budget, the project manager cannot use it. The totality of the risk premiums for all projects within an organization must be controlled the portfolio management function.

3. Define monitoring and control
Once the estimate has been approved, then the budget has been fixed, and this means that it is available to the project manager. The budget is the cost baseline or yardstick, the measure with which we compare the actual performances during the execution of the project.

Often, and definitely when the project is carried out in a matrix organization, the project manager is not an authorised signatory. We see that the project manager checks and initials invoices on the basis of which the financial department makes the invoices payable.

4. Define cost objectives
This is another way of saying that the budget has been fixed. As project manager, you have to be well aware that what you have belongs to someone else. Personally, I have a problem with expressions such as "spending the budget" or "using the budget" because they suggest that you are unrestricted in spending money. Based on the budget, it is much better to look at where you can further tighten up on these cost objectives.

For all work packages, there are objectives related to both cost and quantity, and these have to be realistic and challenging to be effective. Where necessary, it is advisable that they are accepted by the staff or contractors carrying out the work, as that increases the support and has a motivating effect. If this has not yet been done, then you need to do it as soon as possible.

5. Calculate actual costs
The project manager obtains information on the actual costs in various ways, initially from the organization's own administration

1.13 Cost and Finance

(accounts payable department). However, they often lag behind, and the project manager has to set up his own system in order to react in time to developments in the area of costs.

The costs are compared to the original plan (the baseline) and based on that, any necessary corrective actions can be taken. Often, based on the current development, forecasts of the expected costs are produced.

6. Include changes and claims
The following special entries have already been named:
- Contingency reserve.
- Management reserve.

These are derived from the risk analysis. It is important to allow for the possibility of:
- Changes
- Claims

Risk analysis plays an important role in these as well. It does no harm, in advance, to include these explicitly in the reserves.

Changes have an impact on the budget, and the project manager has to therefore include accepted changes in the budget, because otherwise, the comparison does not hold good any more. Also when claims are to be expected, he has to include them in the overviews.

7. Carry out a variance analysis
When comparing the plan with the reality, both the costs incurred and the obligations entered into are important. When reporting financial data on project, the following aspects are important:

Totality of obligations	Obviously these must be kept up to date to prevent any unpleasant surprises.
Invoiced / invoices received.	These are the invoices, which have already been sent, and those that have been received and approved.
To be invoiced.	These are the invoices which have to be sent, and invoices yet to be received.
Previous period.	Obligations related to the previous period.
Current period.	Obligations related to the current period.
Coming period.	Obligations related to the coming period.
Maximum Work In Progress.	The maximum monetary sum of work in progress.
Work In Progress already released.	The monetary sums for Work In Progress from the previous periods which have been released.
To be released from the current period.	The monetary value of Work In Progress that will be released in the current period.
Remaining Work In Progress.	The remaining Work In Progress. This is equal to the maximum possible WIP, less the WIP monetary sums released.

This information can often be found in the columns of the project reports, with a line for each (part of a) project. The reports are especially revealing, if the Estimate to Complete is also included.

8. Make a forecast
Good and correct project management is pro-active, this means that the cost control system is implemented in such a way that the project manager, or the project bureau, is able to estimate where the project, with respect to the cost, will end up. When there is a view of the cost trend, it is also possible

to take measures to either turn a potentially negative trend around, or to strengthen a positive trend.

9. Take corrective measures

When necessary the project manager, in consultation with his team and/or project sponsor, takes corrective measures. This may be working more effectively, purchasing more cheaply, or suchlike.

10. Update the cost estimate

"Stop hoping for a different past" is what I would like the motto for this part to be. What is very important is to realize that all costs made in the past can no longer be undone. A frequently made mistake is illustrated in the following column lay-out of a progress report:

Work packages	Actual	Still needed	Budget
1.3.2	30k	15k	45k

At first sight, not much seems to be wrong with this, but this is not the case. The column "still needed" really means "still left", and has been calculated by subtracting the actual costs from the budget. The following would be better:

Work packages	Budget	Actual	Forecast Still needed	Forecast Actual costs	Variance
1.3.2	45k	30k	20k	50k	-10k

In any case this is something you have to report on, and when the impact of this overspending works through, and as a consequence means that the whole project will turn out to be more expensive than the budget available to you as project manager, you have to escalate the situation.

11. Apply lessons learned

For lengthy projects, this is easier to do than for shorter projects, but it is advisable to regularly check with the various team members whether certain things can be done better (*cheaper*). Actually, you should continuously be aiming to learn from your experience. For this subject, it means that you will continuously find more efficient ways to deliver the result.

12. Other standards and guidances

The process steps as identified by IPMA are only a suggestion. The process steps described in the *ISO 21500 Guidance*, the *'guide to the Project Management Body of Knowledge'* (the *PMBOK Guide*) from the Project Management Institute, and in the popular PRINCE2 Project Management method are much more "binding". Without discussing it in detail I shall name, as a comparison, a number of items from these standards that are related to this competence element. What will be noticeable is the high level of similarity and overlap.

ISO 21500

In this topic, the Guidance differentiates between the following processes:
- Estimate costs.
- Develop budget.
- Control costs.

PMBOK Guide

The 5th edition of *PMBOK Guide* contains the following processes:
- Estimate costs.
- Determine budget.
- Control costs.

PRINCE2

The method does not contain a separate topic on costs. The determination of costs is described in the topic Plan.

1.13-5 SPECIAL TOPICS

1. Structuring the costs
In principle there are two ways to structure the costs. With the help of the:
- Cost Breakdown Structure
- Work Breakdown Structure

Cost Breakdown Structure
A well-known classification of cost types looks as follows:
- Costs for raw and ancillary materials.
- Costs for human labour.
- Costs for durable machinery
- Costs for land.
- Cost for third party services and taxes.
- Interest costs.

It is important to be specific in a project. Only then does the budget offer the possibility to actually control the financial running of the project. When you now clarify the project costs in such a way, you can talk of a *Cost Breakdown Structure*.

The Work Breakdown Structure
In the following WBS, the costs of the different work packages have been aggregated to the higher levels.

WBS with the reserves added
When we extend the WBS with the entries mentioned earlier, it will look as follows:

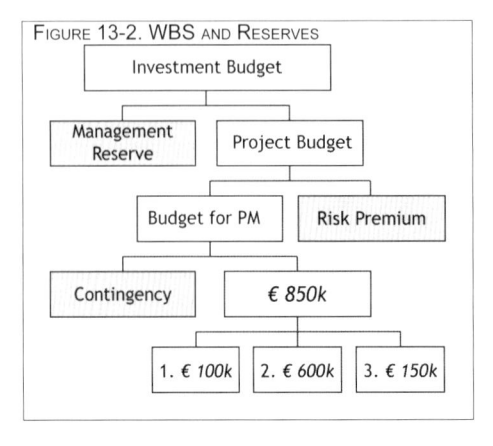

FIGURE 13-2. WBS AND RESERVES

Investment Budget
├── Management Reserve
└── Project Budget
    ├── Budget for PM
    │   ├── Contingency
    │   └── € 850k
    │   ├── 1. € 100k
    │   ├── 2. € 600k
    │   └── 3. € 150k
    └── Risk Premium

2. Islamic Financing
The financing of projects according to Islamic principles is emerging strongly. Compared to more traditional forms, this imposes a number of ethical restrictions, which are:
- No interest (riba)
- Uncertainty in contracts (gharar)
- Speculation (masir)

Riba means that you cannot pay any interest, but also not receive it. Money is a virtual active (asset), and no one is allowed to earn money from it. Gharar means that parties are only able to close a contract containing clear (and certain) matters, and/or things that people possess. It is, for example, forbidden to sell a building before the construction has commenced. Masir forbids gambling and speculation, whereby the covering of price risks through options (futures) is not allowed.

As well as a profit objective, the investor must also strive to achieve a social or an ethical goal, and he cannot invest in matters that are concerned with gambling, alcohol or drugs.

These three principles have consequences for the way in which you can finance a project. Various constructions have been developed that satisfy these principles. As Islamic laws are taken very seriously, a so-called Sharia committee (board) assesses in each case in how far the construction is permitted.

The following financing forms are permitted:
- *Mudarabah*: a partnership, whereby one party provides the finances, and also carries all the losses, and the other party provides the business skills. In advance an agreement is made as to how the profits are to be shared between the parties.

- *Musharakah*: both parties provide capital and share the profit according to an agreed apportionment formula. Losses are shared in proportion to the capital provided.
- *Murabaka*: the bank purchases the goods and sells these on at a profit. The customer pays the amount off in a number of instalments.
- *Salam*: the investor pays an agreed price in advance that (in all probability) is lower than the market price at the time of delivery, and in this way extracts his profit. To prevent gharar, the quality of the delivery must be clearly defined.
- *Ijarah*: the investor remains the owner of the asset, and leases this to the entrepreneur, who has a financing need. In this case the investor, therefore, carries no risk.
- *Istisna'ah*: a turnkey contract with a fixed price agreement.

In all of these forms, the underlying principle is always that the investor only receives reimbursement for the risk he runs as a result of "real" matters and the "real" services he provides.

3. Sarbanes-Oxley

In the Spring of 2002, the American Senator, Paul Sarbanes defended his legislative proposal for sound company management, but due to the strict and drastic measures proposed, he received little support. His colleague, Michael Oxley, proposed a milder version. The climate only changed after the first scandals (WorldCom, Enron, etc.) came to light. Both proposals were compared to each other, and thus formed the basis for the well known Sarbanes-Oxley (SOx) act, which came into force on the 30th of July 2002.

The act imposes a large number of rules on companies listed on the American stock exchange, in order to enforce sound company management and prevent new scandals. These companies do not, therefore, specifically have to be of American origin.

The most important articles are:
- **Article 302:** the management periodically reports on the set up and the effects of the audits on the distribution of information.
- **Article 404:** sets rules for the internal audit and the financial reports. The management is annually obliged to provide an explicit statement on the reliability of the internal audits used in the company.

The annual financial report, therefore, also contains a chapter which evaluates the internal audit on the correctness of the figures quoted. For the company directors, the law holds out the prospect of imprisonment and fines, if they do not comply with the conditions of sound company management.

The question as to what a project manager has to do with these articles is easy to answer: *Everything in the project having an effect on the financial reporting of the company is subject to the legislation mentioned.*

4. Public Private Financing

For large infrastructure projects, for which a government cannot or will not provide investment, we see forms of public-private partnerships, whereby the government grants a concession to a private party to exploit, for example, a toll road or a port. The risks then lie predominantly with the private party, and in this way, the government is able to acquire the desired infrastructure for its inhabitants.

1.13 Cost and Finance

There are now various contract forms that have become known under the acronyms:
- BOOT: build, own, operate en transfer.
- BOO: build, operate en own.
- BOT: build, operate en transfer.

The differences with respect to BOOT are on the one hand in the ownership, and on the other hand in the transfer of everything to the government at the end of the concession period.

5. Price risks

A problem arises with international projects where you incur costs in different currencies. Through exchange rate fluctuations, the budget may be insufficient. A way to prevent this is by taking an opposite position on the future exchange market. How this is done can best be shown with the help of a simplified calculation example.

The project budget is set in euros, and a number of costs involve purchases in dollars. When, in the intervening period, the value of the dollar goes up against the euro, then the budget is exceeded. Depending on the risk, you may decide to take out a contingency reserve for that, or you cover the currency risk ("hedging").

EXAMPLE 13-1 HEDGING	
Project budget	**Futures market**
In 3 months time, you have to pay an invoice of $ 100,000 In your project budget, you included an amount of € 78,000 (at an exchange rate of $1 = € 0.78).	Take out a forward exchange transaction to exchange € 78,000 for $ 100,000 in three months time. You will pay a relatively small premium to do this.
3 months later you have to pay the invoice of $100,000. The exchange rate has gone up, which means you have to pay € 85,000 (at an exchange rate now of $1 = € 0.85). An extra cost of € 7,000.	By effectuating the forward exchange transaction you can exchange € 78,000 for $ 100,000. Because the dollar has gone up, this transaction has a positive result on the budget of € 7,000
Both results counterbalance each other; the only cost you make is that of the premium you pay for the futures transaction, but that is not in proportion to the total amount. In this way it is possible to cover all kinds of price risks, as long as there is a future exchange market for it.	

1.14 Procurement and contract

WHAT CAN WE ACTUALLY DO OURSELVES

When the scope has been determined, the question arises:

Do we do it ourselves, or do we let someone else do it?

The make-or-buy decision.

1.14 Procurement and Contract

1.14-1 DEFINITIONS

Back-to-back agreement	This is a particular form of sub-contracting, whereby the main contractor lets part of the accepted contract be carried out by a third party, and the rights and obligations are transferred to the sub-contractor on a one-for-one basis.
Contract	Oral or written agreement.
Contract award criteria	Criteria, on the basis of which, the ultimate contract is awarded.
Contract management	Managing, observing and archiving contracts.
Contract manager	Person responsible for the contract management.
Contract structure	Schematic overview of all contracts to be entered into and their interrelationships.
Outsource	Having work carried out by third parties.
Pre-contractual stage	Period of the first contact between the customer and the supplier up to the signing of the agreement.
Procurement	Acquiring products or services from third parties.

1.14 Procurement and Contract

Request for Information (RFI)	Request to potential suppliers to indicate which relevant products and services and/or resources they have available to satisfy the potential request of the customer.
Request for Proposal (RFP)	Invitation to parties through a tendering process to submit a proposal for the delivery of a specific service or product.
Request for Quotation (RFQ)	Invitation to parties through a tendering process to submit a quotation on the basis of fixed specifications.
Selection criteria	Criteria, on the basis of which, the suitable suppliers are selected in a pre-selection phase.
Tendering	Procedure whereby a project sponsor makes known that he wants a contract to be carried out and requests companies to submit a proposal.

1.14 Procurement and Contract

1.14-2 INTRODUCTION

During the development of the project plan and the required management approach at the start of, or during, the execution of the project, the project manager must sometimes carry out a *'make or buy'* analysis. This analysis provides an answer to the question of which products, services, sub- deliverables and tools we already have available and which we have to procure.

With procuring, there is a commercial transaction between the project team and a third party for certain products or services that the team itself cannot, or will not, produce or carry out. The agreements that are then made form the contract (often put into writing), which is legally enforceable.

The project manager has to come to agreements with the supplier on a large number of issues. The most fundamental of these are:

- What level of control the project manager has over the supplier.
- Who carries certain risks.

At the outset, the parties have to agree these issues, and have to ensure that the execution of this contract is carried out in accordance with the agreement.

With regard to services we can differentiate between:

- Procurement and
- Outsourcing

With procurement, the project manager has full responsibility for controlling the work. He has, as it were, brought resources into the project from outside, which he then controls himself.

It is different for outsourcing, as here an important part of the control is in the hands of the supplier's management. Because there is now less opportunity to exercise direct control, you will want to set down contractually a lot more points in advance.

Both forms have their advantages and disadvantages, which I will discuss later, but the basic principle for this consideration must always be: which party is most able to control the work. As this has everything to do with the risks a project carries, this choice can only be made after carrying out a detailed risk analysis.

That brings us to the question of who carries what risks. In looking for this answer, as project manager, you will come to the conclusion that this is actually the wrong question. It is better to ask the question as follows:

Who carries the impact of certain risks?

1.14 Procurement and Contract

There are risks which negatively influence the quality of the project result, by causing a cost overrun, or by endangering the delivery date, and often it is a combination of both. How much of this can be transferred to a supplier? Actually, just the financial consequences of the wrong delivery, because when the delivery date is too late, your project is endangered whichever way you look at it. The same applies to disappointing quality, because as project manager, you will also here pay a higher price than the supplier. To counteract these risks, contracts contain agreements on prices and also penalty clauses.

This competence element is about taking the right *"make or buy"* decision, and about recording the purchase in a legally enforceable agreement, where the responsibilities lie with the party who can best carry them.

1.14 Procurement and Contract

1.14-3 PROCESS STEPS

1. Make-or-buy analyses.
2. Select suppliers.
3. Set up contract management.
4. Manage contract changes.
5. Discharge and close contracts.
6. Apply lessons learned.

1. Make-or-buy analyses

A principal decision precedes the procurement or outsourcing of projects(parts), products or services: *"buying or making"*. This may be a strategic choice, but it doesn't have to be. The buy decision has a number of advantages and disadvantages:

Advantages:
- Suppliers can bring in specific knowledge and skills, which are not available in the project team.
- Suppliers can broaden the product offering of the main contractor.
- Availability of resources is more flexible.

Disadvantages:
- Authority and influence of the project manager is less in the supplier's organization.
- The project sponsor is worried when large parts of the project contract are outsourced to sub-contractors.
- Greater dependency on the suppliers.
- The supplier has less knowledge of the organization.

With projects, the procurement of resources is usually done via the purchasing department of the permanent organization. Usually there are fixed procedures, and there will already be (framework) agreements in place with preferred suppliers. At the start of the project these are issues to consider.

The input for this activity is the scope breakdown in the form of the WBS. The project management team now determines which parts they want to outsource, and which they will do themselves. For example, in the WBS shown below, the choice was made to outsource the complete second branch.

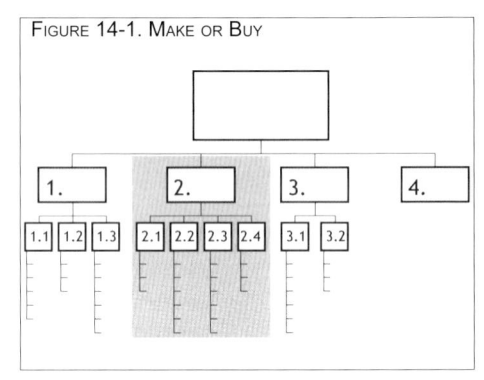

FIGURE 14-1. MAKE OR BUY

This part of the WBS (the grey area) is called the Contract Work Breakdown Structure (CWBS), which forms the basis for a good definition of that part for which the supplier is responsible. The supplier should now further develop that part in his own WBS.

A procurement plan is required for the project, in which the specific procurement processes are described. The plan will address the following topics:
- Where and how to make use of suppliers?
- Which issues do we have to consider when involving suppliers?
- What are the advantages connected with this?
- What are the risks involved?
- How do we establish contact with the project team?
- How do we co-ordinate the work of the suppliers?

How the contracting will be done, is one of the issues you have to decide upon at the start of each stage. You design the required documents (when these are not available as

standard), which will support the complete procurement process, such as:
- Contracts.
- Standard procurement forms.
- Selection criteria checklists.
- Request for information (RFI).
- Request for proposal (RFP) or sometimes called a Request for quotation (RFQ).
- Confidentiality agreements.
- Non-competition clauses.

2. Select suppliers

Suppliers can be invited through a tender, an advert, or based on a shortlist of possible suppliers. Many large organizations now have a list of preferred suppliers, and in such a case, you can only do business with suppliers of your own choice if management is willing to make an exception.

In addition, the team draws up the selection criteria for the assessment of the various tenders. Certainly when the situation involves a complex product or service, it is advisable to think in advance about the criteria and the decision making process.

Possible selection criteria can be:
- The extent to which the suppliers understand the project requirement.
- The total costs (both investment and exploitation).
- The expertise of the suppliers with regard to what is delivered.
- The management approach of the supplier.
- The technical approach of the supplier.
- The financial strength of the supplier.
- The production capacity of the supplier.
- The extent to which the supplier owns the intellectual property.
- The size of the supplier's organization.
- References.

It is important to also look at the terms and conditions under which the supplier delivers his products or services. Obviously in the case of complex contracts, it is preferable that the project manager is supported by a legal expert. A first check however, can be carried out on the basis of the following checklist:
- *The status of the offer*, without obligation, fixed, the validity period.
- *Delivery*, term of delivery.
- *Non-extendable term*, if the deadline is not met, does this automatically result in default or breach of contract?
- *Transport costs*, for whose risk, costs and responsibility?
- *Guarantee*, payment terms.
- *Payment*, discount arrangement, fines, collection charges, bank guarantee and non-payment.
- *Transfer of ownership*, and also the transfer of the risk.
- *Liability*, for what, limitations and exclusions.
- *Force majeure*.
- *Dissolution of the agreement*, for which events and in what way?
- *Damages*, when, how, the amount and exclusions.
- *Arbitration arrangement*, which law is applicable, and for which law will be chosen?

3. Set up contract management

Contracting external parties always has a legal side, and the project manager, therefore, must ensure that on the one hand the supplier fulfils the obligations in the contract entered into, but on the other hand that he and his team are aware of the implications of the various contractual agreements in the project that they also have to keep to.

Contract management or monitoring concerns those activities that ensure that both parties meet their obligations. Especially

1.14 Procurement and Contract

with complex contracts, it is recommended to make a member of the team, who has legal knowledge, responsible.

Contract management includes:
- Translating the contractual obligations into concrete actions.
- Checking that the agreed deliveries actually take place.
- Carrying out formal assessments, inspections and audits.
- Assessing progress reports from the supplier.
- Arranging payments.
- Fulfilling own contractual obligations.
- Administration of claims.
- Management of the formal documentation.

The WBS is the starting point for controlling the different sub-contractors. In the example below, the decision has been made to outsource the second branch (the grey area) of the WBS. These are the sub-deliverables the supplier is responsible for.

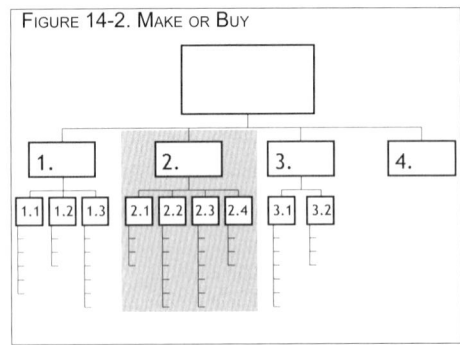

FIGURE 14-2. MAKE OR BUY

The controlling and monitoring from the project is now carried out, as a minimum on the sub- deliveries 2.1, 2.2, 2.3 and 2.4., for which agreements have been made regarding the delivery times and costs. Depending on the risks, a decision can be made to implement controls at one level deeper.

In consultation with the supplier's contact person, you make sure that the agreed deliveries are on time. As indicated in the above, this must be done at 'some distance', because the supplier does not always want his customers to look into his 'kitchen'. That does not mean that it is not desirable to have insight into how the supplier has organized his part of the project. This should already have been part of the negotiations prior to awarding the contract.

Problems may occur in the quality of what is delivered when the supplier overruns his own internal budget, or when he is in danger of missing certain deadlines. When you, as project manager, have a good relationship with the supplier's coordinators, via informal communication, you can often see issues coming before the supplier officially reports them. Very often you can then, on a friendly basis, find a solution together with the supplier's project leader, without resorting directly to all sorts of escalation processes.

4. Manage contract changes

One thing a written contract with a supplier results in, is a clear definition of the responsibilities, particularly when the contract contains penalty clauses and "*fixed price*" agreements. This makes it more difficult for the customer to make changes to the outsourced part of the project. The advantage is that with the outsourcing, you create a safety barrier against changes, and through that you resist the slow expansion of the scope (*scope creep*). The disadvantage, however, is that when a quick change is needed, you have to renegotiate a part of the contract, and that takes time. During the risk analysis it is important to consider which parts we want to buy, and which parts we do not.

1.14 Procurement and Contract

Contract changes come from two sides, and each need to be handled in their own way:
- From the project management team.
- From the supplier.

From the project management team
The project manager's role here is on behalf of the customer, and in this role he may be the source of a string of changes the supplier has to process. In any event, the project manager has to deliver the changes structurally, and obviously he has to administer what changes he has submitted and whether or not they have been processed. In advance, a change control procedure, specifically for the supplier has to have been agreed.

The approach used here is: *agree, administer and propose structurally*.

It is desirable to keep this to a minimum and in advance, when the contract is drawn up, to take sufficient time to also define the supplier's scope.

From the supplier
The supplier himself can also take the initiative for a change. You have to ensure that changes are only carried out if you agree to them, and if they remain within the scope of the project. An undesired situation arises if the supplier makes changes without agreement. This danger mainly exists when, in case of a fixed price agreement, he looks like overrunning his budget and starts 'tinkering' with the quality, or just delivers less. Therefore you, as project manager, have to agree in advance with the supplier how you will monitor the quality and the progress of his work.

The approach used here is: *agree, monitor and approve*.

5. Discharge and close contracts

A contract can be closed-out in a number of ways:
- According to agreement.
- Terminated in mutual consultation.
- Breach of contract.

According to agreement
This is the most common situation in which a contract will come to an end. As project manager you then have to check the following issues:
- Has everything been delivered?
- Has the adopted acceptance procedure been adhered to?
- Has the delivery been in accordance with specification?
- Have all deliverables been accepted?
- Does the result do what it should do?
- Has the accompanying documentation been delivered?
- Has there been (if required) a proper transfer to operational management?
- Has the guarantee been arranged?
- Are there any deficiencies?

When this has been carried out in the way it should, the last payment and the formal handover can take place. Often the project manager then also has to run through a number of administrative procedures, in order to conclude everything within his own organization.

A problem may arise if the supplier alleges to have concluded his part, and the project manager disagrees. This has to be handled carefully, as it is better to negotiate a solution at this point than to enforce it legally, which is usually a much more expensive route to take.

Terminated in mutual agreement
It is also possible that over the course of the contract new facts occur, making it sensible not to continue further. In this case, the proj-

ect manager and supplier must negotiate on how the contract will be terminated.

Breach of contract
A breach of contract situation arises when one of the parties does not keep to contractual agreements. In principle this is not allowed, as both parties have bound themselves to each other contractually to undertake certain obligations with respect to one another.

However, this does not mean you should not consider it, it remains to be seen whether or not the supplier wants to enforce his rights in court. When you, therefore, only look at the result, a conscious breach of contract could be a realistic alternative. A legal process takes a long time and costs a lot of money, so possibly the supplier will decide against this course of action. Although you can place ethical question marks here.

6. Apply lessons learned
The experiences with certain suppliers are recorded for use in other projects. This is something that is highly dependent on what has been arranged in the organization with regard to recording such experience.

You should listen to the comments of both sides by looking at both the perception of the supplier, and to that of your project team, paying particular attention to what have you learned, and what you would do differently the next time.

When there has been a negative experience, it is important that the organization is well aware of what the issue has been. If necessary, senior management could even decide that the organization is not permitted to do business with a particular supplier again.

7. Other standards and guidances
The process steps as identified by IPMA are only a suggestion. The process steps described in the *ISO 21500 Guidance*, the *'guide to the Project Management Body of Knowledge'* (the *PMBOK Guide*) from the Project Management Institute, and in the popular PRINCE2 Project Management method are much more "binding". Without discussing it in detail I shall name, as a comparison, a number of items from these standards that are related to this competence element. What will be noticeable is the high level of similarity and overlap.

ISO 21500
The Guidance deals with this topic in the subject group Procurement and differentiates between the following processes:
- Plan procurements.
- Select suppliers.
- Administer procurements.

PMBOK Guide
The 5th edition of *PMBOK Guide* contains the following processes:
- Plan procurement management.
- Conduct procurements.
- Control procurements.
- Close procurements.

PRINCE2
Although PRINCE2 is based on a customer/supplier relationship, it says little about procurement. It does state that the project board has to represent the suppliers' interests, but not how you have to select suppliers.

1.14-4 SPECIAL TOPICS

1. Selecting suppliers
When we select suppliers, we want to be as objective as possible. After we have determined the criteria we determine a weight per criteria, and a good method is to compare the different criteria in pairs with each other, and to work it out as follows.

Suppose that we want to compare costs, duration and references during the selection process. We compare the criteria in pairs with each other, and in consensus reach the following conclusions:
- Duration is much more important than costs.
- References are just as important as duration.
- References are more important than costs.

2. Full Analytical Criteria Method
We determine the weighting factors by producing the following table:

	Costs	Time	Ref.
Costs			
Time	10		
References	5	1	
Total			

For each selection pair, the following values are always possible: 10, 5, 1, 1/5 and 1/10 respectively: much more important, more important, as important, less important and much less important.

Once the above table has been completed, we add two extra columns.

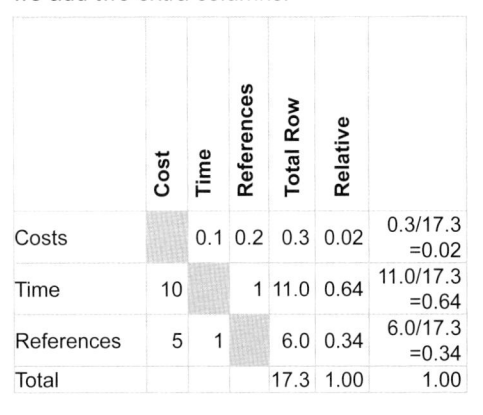

	Cost	Time	References	Total Row	Relative	
Costs		0.1	0.2	0.3	0.02	0.3/17.3 =0.02
Time	10		1	11.0	0.64	11.0/17.3 =0.64
References	5	1		6.0	0.34	6.0/17.3 =0.34
Total				17.3	1.00	1.00

This method works well in situations with up to six selection criteria, and requires prior consensus from all decision makers on the relative importance of the different criteria in relation to each other.

Once the tenders have been received, the time comes for selection. It is, of course, possible to instinctively assess which supplier has preference and not infrequently "*wanting to award someone something*" plays a part. But ultimately it is better to make a rational decision.

We have three criteria with their weighting factors, namely costs (0.02), time (0.64) and references (0.34).

In a similar way, we now compare, option by option, the different proposals. Suppose that three proposals have been submitted, by suppliers X, Y and Z.

1.14 Procurement and Contract

Cost evaluation
We now get the following table:

	X	Y	Z	Total Row	Relative
X		0.1	1	1.1	0.06	1.1/17.3 =0.06
Y	10		5	15.0	0.87	15.0/17.3 =0.87
Z	1	0.2		1.2	0.07	1.2/17.3 =0.07
Total				17.3	1.00	1.00

Of the proposals, the costs for Y were much more favorable than those for X. Z and X score equal as far as costs were concerned, and Z scored less compared to Y. The calculation shows that of all the proposals, Y scores the best for the cost aspect.

Duration evaluation

	X	Y	Z	Total Row	Relative
X		5	10	15.0	0.73	15.0/20.5 =0.73
Y	0.2		5	5.2	0.25	5.2/20.5 =0.25
Z	0.1	0.2		0.3	0.02	0.3/20.5 =.02
Total				20.5	1.00	1.00

Of all proposals, Y is slightly worse than X as for duration, Z is a lot worse than X and slightly worse than Y. The table shows that of all the proposals, X has the most favorable duration.

Reference evaluation
Now we only have to compare the references of the different suppliers, and we get the following table:

	X	Y	Z	Total Row	Relative
X		0.2	0.1	0.3	0.01	0.3/25.5 =0.01
Y	5		0.1	5.2	0.20	5.1/25.5 =0.21
Z	10	10		20.0	0.79	20.0/25.5 =0.78
Total				25.5	1.00	1.00

When investigating the references, those of Y are better than X, and those of Z much better than X but also a lot better than those of Y.

Final evaluation
The last step is now to weigh up the different outcomes, and we do this by multiplying the outcomes of the three tables above with weighting factors calculated previously.

We then get the following table:

	Costs 0.02	Time 0.64	References 0.34	Total Row
X	.06 X .02 = 0.0012	.73 X .64 = 0.4672	.01 X .34 = 0.0034	0.4718
Y	.87 X .02 = 0.0174	.25 X .64 = 0.1600	.21 X .34 = 0.0714	0.2448
Z	.07 X .02 = 0.0014	.02 X .64 = 0.0128	.78 X .34 = 0.2652	0.2794
				1.0000

From which we can deduce that, objectively speaking, the proposal of supplier X takes preference.

This method, starting from the weighting factors per criterion, up to and including calculating the ultimate ranking order, is called the *full analytical criteria method*.

This method can be applied particularly in the following situations[1]:
- Limited number of decision makers (3 to 8 people).
- Not too many alternatives (5 to 10 options).
- Not too many criteria (3 to 6).
- The decision makers have to reach consensus.
- A lot is at stake if the project fails.

The advantage of this approach, is that subjective preferences are pushed somewhat to the background when the decision is made. The discussion in order to arrive at the pairings consideration, also leads to consensus and a better understanding of the different proposals and how they compare with each other.

3. Outsourcing

Outsourcing always involves the consideration between:
- *Core* processes, and processes dictated by the *environment*.
- *Critical* processes and *noncritical* processes.

Core processes are those activities, which differentiate an organization from others, and is that which ensures an organization has a competitive advantage. The processes dictated by the environment are those normally expected in the market.

The more successful an organization, the bigger the attraction, and other organizations will try to match this. This means that when an organization does not innovate, the differentiating capacity will slowly disappears. Because of the market pressure, core processes almost always develop into processes which are being dictated by the environment.

You can draw a parallel for public bodies. For them, it is not so much the market, which dictates the process, but politics forcing the public body to adapt its process to the current standards.

With core processes, an organization has the freedom to organise these themselves, and for non-core processes, the environment sets requirements. In general, you can say that core processes are *not suitable* for outsourcing, whereas processes dictated by the environment are just that.

A second consideration for determining which processes to outsource and which not, is the consideration between critical and noncritical processes. Critical processes are those processes in an organization which must not go wrong. When such a process does go wrong, the company immediately suffers damage from it.

Based on this categorization of processes, you can say that, in principle, you do not outsource critical processes to third parties.

Outsourcing has advantages:
- Capital tied-up is lower.
- More room to concentrate on the core activities.

And some disadvantages
- Coordination costs.
- Quality control costs.
- External personnel is less committed.

It is happening more and more frequently that companies outsource the most obvious activities. These can be transport, catering, cleaning and security. There are also a lot of public bodies which are partially, or completely, outsourcing more and more activities.

---

1 (1994) *Philips Quality Memory Jogger*™, PHILIPS INTERNATIONAL B.V, Eindhoven, NL

1.14 Procurement and Contract

At the basis of an outsource agreement is the **S**ervice **L**evel **A**greement, in which it is clearly documented what levels of service can be expected. Such an SLA contains the following parts[2]:
- The objective of the agreement.
- The parties involved.
- The service to be provided.
- The period of service provision and notice term.
- Arrangement for measuring and checking the level of service provision.
- Escalation procedures.
- Procedures in event of non-performance.
- Change procedures
- Input of the user.
- Consultation and communication structures.
- Reimbursement and insurance premiums.

4. Contract pricing

After a party has been chosen for the delivery, agreements will be recorded in a contract. There are different ways of grouping contracts. A well-known one, is to base it on whichever party carries the price risk, and in general we see the following three main forms:
- Fixed price.
- Cost reimbursable.
- Time and materials.

Fixed price

Fixed price or 'lump-sum" contracts mainly apply to a product that can be well defined in advance, and the price risk lies completely with the supplier. Sometimes we see bonus/penalty conditions for either meeting or not meeting certain deadlines, or for exceeding the expectations.

ADVANTAGES:
- Predictable price.
- Clear who will take on any extra costs.
- Motivates a cost saving execution of the work.
- Supplier has more freedom.

DISADVANTAGES:
- Requires specialist knowledge of the results to be delivered.
- Requires extra time and costs for developing specifications.
- Might frighten off some qualified suppliers.
- Higher costs because of risk contingencies.
- Possible loss of quality when the supplier exceeds his budget.

There are different forms of fixed price contracts:
- Normal (FFP: Firm Fixed Price): The Buyer always pays an amount, which has been agreed in advance.
- With bonus (FPIF: Fixed Price Incentive Fee): Parties agree a ceiling. The buyer never pays more than the ceiling. When the supplier delivers for less than the agreed target amount, the saving is apportioned according to an allocation formula agreed in advance.
- With price correction (FP-EPA: Fixed Price with Economic Price Adjustment): As well as a fixed price, parties also agree to what extent the price can increase in line with the general rise in prices.

Cost reimbursable

The basis of cost reimbursable contracts is that the actual costs are invoiced.

ADVANTAGES:
- Maximum flexibility.
- Minimizes the supplier's profit.

---

2 (2002) *Business – The Ultimate Resource*[TM] page 502-503

- Simplifies the negotiations.
- Faster start and, therefore, earlier completion.
- Offers more possibility to select the best qualified supplier instead of the cheapest.

DISADVANTAGES:
- No clear view of the ultimate costs.
- No financial motivation to minimise time and costs.
- Allows large changes, resulting in a longer duration and higher costs.

There are three variations possible:
- Plus fee (CPFF: Cost Plus Fixed Fee; CPVF: Cost Plus Variable Fee):
  o *With fixed fee*: All allowed costs including a pre-determined fixed amount as fee.
  o *With variable fee*: All allowed costs, increased by a pre-determined percentage over the costs as a fee.
- Plus performance fee (CPIF: Cost Plus Incentive Fee): In advance, parties agree a target amount for the costs and the normal fee. If the supplier comes in under that amount, the supplier receives a percentage over the savings as a performance fee.
- Plus reward (CPAF: Cost Plus Award Fee): All allowed costs. On top of that, the supplier can earn a reward, which depends on a number (often subjective) of pre-agreed criteria.

Time and materials
Time and material, or bill of quantity, contracts are a mix of the forms mentioned above. Agreements on rates have now been made (fixed price), but because at the start it is not yet known how many products the customer will purchase, the total investment has not yet been determined.

The choice for the form of contract depends on the type of assignment, and in general the risks are laid down in the contract to be with the party who can exercise the most influence on them.

5. Public and Private tendering
What makes tendering in the public sector special, is the fact that the forces at play are different than in the private sector.

During the procurement process, public officials have to take account of a more complex (decision making) environment, limited procurement supporting services, tools and formal regulations. As a result, the interaction between the authorities as potential project sponsor and the companies (suppliers), is also different. During a game of golf (paid for by a potential supplier), a public official cannot casually mention that he would like to see an emphasis on certain points in a tender. He has the duty, in a competitive system, to ensure the procurement process runs as smoothly and correctly as possible.

Public tendering in Europe
To advance the internal market, the European Community has established regulations for issuing tender invitations. The regulations consist of guidelines, which have been laid down in the national legislation. The objective of the guidelines for public procurements is to open up public procurements to all companies within the EC, irrespective of their nationality.

The guidelines have the following objectives:
- Public disclosure, public procurements must be made public to the whole of the European business trade.
- Transparency, the invitation to tender has to be carried out using fixed procedures, and the complete process

1.14 Procurement and Contract

Comparison Public and Private tendering

Topic	Public tender invitation	Private tendering
Decision making processes.	As well as internal decision making, also external political decision making effects.	Almost solely internal decision making.
Procurement arguments.	As well as best proposals, all kinds of specific rules and key policy areas have an influence on the choice.	Usually the best proposal, unless other interests are involved, such as existing relationships, participations.
Co-operation of the parties during the process.	Due to the tender regulations, the authorities often struggle to come to a good interaction with the market parties.	There are no regulations.
Who does the procurement.	Many more civil servants carry out procurements than is realized.	It is always known who does the procurement and how.
Contract freedom.	Within the tender regulatory framework.	Completely free.

must be clear to everyone (for instance unambiguous requirements).
- Non-discrimination, objective criteria must be used for the selection of the best tender(s).

The basic premise is that every tendering company in the European Community must have a fair chance of being awarded the contract for a public procurement. The guidelines for that are the official rules of play which apply for both contracting authority and the bidding parties.

The rules for European Tenders apply to all cases in which the authorities play the role of project sponsor. The concept "authorities" is broader than you would initially think, as the guidelines also apply to all public organizations. These are companies and organizations in which the authorities have a lot of influence, for example when the authorities (partly) finance, (partly) manage this organization, or when the board of directors is appointed by the authorities.

Public procurements which in value exceed threshold amounts, must be put out to tender.

The estimation of the value of the order is a task and responsibility of a contracting authority inviting tenders. This authority has the obligation to be able to underpin the calculation objectively and demonstrably. Special attention is paid to the ban on (artificially) splitting orders, or making improper use of special regulations, in order to stay under threshold amounts and thus avoid the tender regulations.

There are two European Tender guidelines published: for public procurements (2004/17/EC) and for special sectors (2004/18/EC). These are related to procurements which:
- Come above a certain (jointly) estimated amount, the so-called threshold values.
- Do not come under the exceptions mentioned in the guideline.

1.14 Procurement and Contract

PUBLIC PROCUREMENTS
Procurements for: province, municipality/council, water authorities, regulatory institutions, or a joint venture of these authorities or regulatory institutions. The content and scope of the concept regulatory institution is still to be significantly developed.

SPECIAL SECTORS
Special sector companies are, for example, providers of fixed grids for gas or heat, electricity, drinking water and public transport, or ports, or postal services.

PUBLIC PROCUREMENT PROCEDURES[3]
There are different public procurement procedures: the open procedure, the restricted procedure, the negotiated procedure, and the competitive dialogue.

THE OPEN PROCEDURE
In an open procedure, any interested economic operator may submit a tender.

The minimum time limit for the receipt of tenders is 52 days from the date on which the contract notice was published. If a prior information notice has been published, this time limit can be cut to 36 days. In no case may the time limit for the receipt of tenders be less than 22 days.

THE RESTRICTED PROCEDURE
In the case of restricted procedures, any economic operator may request to participate and only candidates invited to do so may submit a tender.

The time limit for the receipt of requests to participate is 37 days from the date of the contract notice. The contracting authority then, simultaneously and in writing, invites the selected candidates to submit their tenders. There should be a minimum of five candidates. The minimum time limit for the receipt of tenders shall be 40 days from the date on which the invitation is sent. If a prior information notice has been published, this may be shortened to 36 days. The minimum time limit for the receipt of tenders may not be less than 22 days. Exceptionally and when urgency requires, the contracting authority may set a minimum time limit of 15 days (10 days if the notice is sent electronically) for requests to participate and of 10 days for the receipt of tenders.

THE NEGOTIATED PROCEDURE
In a negotiated procedure, the contracting authority consults the economic operators of its choice and negotiates the terms of the contract with them.

The following cases justify the use of the negotiated procedure with prior publication of a contract notice:
- Following another procedure which revealed the presence of irregular tenders, insofar as this new procedure does not substantially alter the original terms of the contract.
- In exceptional cases, when the nature of the contracts or the risks attaching thereto prevent prior pricing.
- In the field of services, for intellectual services which do not permit the use of an open or restricted procedure.
- For works which are performed solely for purposes of research or testing.

The following cases justify the use of the negotiated procedure without prior publication of a contract notice:
- For all types of contract: when no tenders have been submitted in response to an open procedure or a restricted procedure; when, for technical or artistic reasons, or for reasons connected with the protection of exclusive rights, the contract may be executed only by a particular economic

---
3 http://europa.eu

1.14 Procurement and Contract

operator; in cases of extreme urgency brought about by unforeseeable events.
- For supply contracts: when the products involved are manufactured purely for the purposes of RTD; for additional deliveries over a maximum period of three years where a change of supplier would oblige the contracting authority to acquire material having different technical characteristics; for supplies quoted and purchased on a commodity market; for purchases of supplies under particularly advantageous conditions from an economic operator definitively winding up his business activities or in receivership.
- For public service contracts, when the contract is awarded to the successful candidate in a design contest.
- For works and service contracts: up to 50 % of the amount of the original contract, for additional works or services which are not included in the initial project and have become necessary through unforeseen circumstances; for new works or services consisting in the repetition of similar works or services entrusted to the initial economic operator for a maximum of three years.

THE COMPETITIVE DIALOGUE

A contracting authority may make use of the competitive dialogue for complex contracts if it is not able to define by itself the technical solutions to satisfy its needs or is not able to specify the legal and/or financial make-up of a project. Large infrastructure projects would seem to lend themselves to this type of dialogue.

The contracting authority publishes a contract notice that includes the award criteria. The minimum time limit for receipt of requests to participate is 37 days. The contracting authority then, simultaneously and in writing, invites the selected candidates (a minimum of three) to conduct a dialogue. The discussion commences, may take place in stages and continues until the (technical and/or economic and legal) solutions have been defined. The contracting authority ensures equal treatment of all tenderers and protects the confidentiality of the information. At the end of the dialogue, the candidates submit their final tenders. These tenders may be specified, but without changing the basic features of the contract. The contracting authority awards the contract in accordance with the award criteria set and on the basis of the most economically advantageous tender.

1.15 Changes

MANY SMALL ONES MAKE ONE BIG ONE

From the conviction that the customer and the project sponsor must be satisfied, the tendency develops to gradually amend the scope as the project progresses.

Many small changes can make a project uncontrollable and a deliver a result, which is no longer in line with the original objective.

Change control, therefore, is very important. Not because no changes may be made, but to ensure that these are carried out structurally and in a controlled manner.

1.15 Changes

1.15-1 DEFINITIONS

Baseline	Defined and approved status of a project, based on which the progress is determined.
Change	Every change to a formally defined status.
Change authority	The person or group who is authorised to approve changes (under certain conditions).
Change budget	Budget available to be spent on changes.
Change control	The management of (potential) changes.
Change logbook	A logbook containing the registration of all project issues which have been recorded during the project.
Change request	A request to change a formally defined status.

1.15-2 INTRODUCTION

One of the hardest things to do in management is make decisions in the present, which have consequences for the near or distant future. That future is uncertain, and the effect of management decisions is uncertain. When the project sponsor discusses all the plans with the project manager at the start of the project, the project manager expects an approval before he starts work. Sometimes the project sponsor hesitates to do that, because he then ties himself down by giving such approval and what if the circumstances require a change? What if uncertainty turns into certainty?

The project manager in turn wants stability in the required end result he will deliver with his team. Nothing is more annoying than changes which pile up into an uncontrollable collection of work. Many project managers will therefore discourage changes, but what if what has been delivered according to plan, no longer meets the requirements at that point in time? How successful has the project then been?

Project managers do not like changes that come from outside. From inside it is often different, because when, during the execution, something goes wrong, or deviates from the original plan, you also have a change, but that is, according to the project manager, either necessary or unavoidable. How do you get a grip on this situation as project sponsor?

How do we find a balance between the uncertainty of the project sponsor, and the desire the project manager has for stability? Also, how do we find a balance between the technical need to apply changes, and the project sponsor's need for control and manageability? The answer to that question comes in parts:

- Use staging, so that what you are currently doing has a high degree of certainty.
- Structure how you deal with changes.

I have discussed the first topic in another chapter. Staging is the means to deal with uncertainty in a controlled manner. The effect of staging is that the team is clear about what the project result for the current stage has to be, and in this way we prevent becoming faced with an endless stream of changes that during the current stage. What we then have to make sure of, is that we can deal with the changes that do occur in a structured and controlled manner, and we do this with the help of the change control procedure covered in this chapter.

1.15 Changes

Changes come from different directions:

- The project sponsors.
- The users.
- The internal suppliers.
- The external suppliers.
- The project management team itself.
- The project environment.

The approach is structured pragmatism, which means that all requests are seriously considered, but that we keep sight of the agreed end result. We have an open mind to the environment of the project, but there is a limit. What is possible is possible! What is not possible, we will not do - not even under pressure!

1.15-3 PROCESS STEPS

1. Define change control policy.
2. Identify changes.
3. Determine the impact.
4. Arrange authorisation.
5. Get acceptance or rejection.
6. Apply changes and report.
7. Monitor changes.
8. Apply lessons learned.

1. Define change control policy

A change procedure is a part of the project management plan, and this has been agreed with the project sponsor in advance. There is agreement on how we deal with changes related to:
- The project result.
- The budgeted costs.
- The agreed progress.
- The chosen management approach.

The people submitting changes are:
- The project sponsors.
- The users.
- The internal suppliers.
- The external suppliers.
- The project management team itself.
- The project environment.

It is clear that not every person submitting a change has the same power to enforce a certain change. You can also differentiate between changes which are necessary, and changes that are not.

The change control policy for the project describes:
- The issues that are included in change control.
- The procedure that has to be followed for changes.
- Who can submit changes.
- Who gives approval.
- Which forms have to be used.
- How the team reports on the progress.
- How changes have to be dealt with in cases of emergency.

In many cases, a certain change control procedure is already present in an organization, and if so, you use this.

2. Identify changes

The identification of changes is *always* done on a change control form, which, for example, contains the following headings:
- Date of the request.
- Identification number.
- Author information (name, e-mail, telephone number, unit, organization).
- Proposed change.
- Reason for change.
- Amendment of the scope or a repair.
- Expected benefits of the change.
- Priority of the change.

The priority can be:
- Low priority.
- Normal.
- High.
- Show-stopper.

The latter concerns a change the team has to apply, because otherwise the result will probably not be accepted.

Apart from the above, the change control form also consists of headings which are concerned with the further handling and execution of the request, and these are:
- Impact of the change.
- Sharing common ground with other parts/projects.
- Necessary work.
- Costs and planning.
- Required speed of decision making.
- Approval or rejection.
- Reason for rejection.

These headings are filled in further during the change control procedure.

1.15 Changes

3. Determine the impact
Each change has consequences for the project, for better or for worse. That is one of the first things you have to work out. You have to realize that the operational parties are busy executing the project, and all disruptions to their work will lead to a hitch in the efficient execution, and you have to try and prevent that.

You determine the impact by successively answering the following questions:
- What does this change mean for my project?
- What does this change mean for other projects?
- How do I make a workable decision document?

The consequences for my project
The starting point is the original plan, and especially the work packages, the underlying activities and resources allocated. If you have constructed a good planning model, and have entered this into the scheduling software, it will now prove its worth in carrying out "*what if*" analyses.

As a result of the change, you are confronted with:
- The work involved in the change itself.
- The costs of the change.
- The end date of the stage (and, therefore, also the project).
- A changing schedule, whereby you might have to reschedule people.
- Risks as a result of this change.
- A changing level of support from the project sponsor and users.

The consequences for other projects
As a project is not an island, there is more to it, and so the next step is to evaluate the consequences for other projects, because it is possible that the impact of your change in itself implies a change for another project. The project manager of that project, therefore, will also have to work through the above list.

If it is difficult to analyze the consequences for other projects, it is usually an indication that the way the organization has split up the project portfolio is not good. A possible solution is to group related projects in a programme, thus ensuring explicit attention for these dependencies. You would then have to suggest this to your project sponsor.

The decision document
There has to be something to decide, as a minimum a Go or a No Go for this change. It is, therefore, desirable to include a number of alternative solutions, and in order to prepare for good decision making, the consequence of these solutions must be clear:
- How much will it cost?
- How long will it take?
- What will I get in return?
- How does this influence the business case?

4. Arrange authorisation
With regard to changes, there are the following levels at which you arrange authorisation:
- In advance with the help of tolerances.
- Approval from the project sponsor required.
- Approval outside the project sponsor's sphere of influence.

Arranged in advance with tolerances
Tolerances are permitted deviations from the plan. The tolerances can be found in many forms, for example under the terms: unforeseen expenditure, contingency reserve, risk surcharge and suchlike. These are a result of responses made following the risk analysis. However, you have to be careful to only use them for changes, as they have been allocated to compensate for uncertainties in

the original scope. With a change we often change something in the specifications of the project result (actually we change the scope somewhat), and when you do that at the cost of the tolerances mentioned, you corrupt the original responses. It is better to make use of a change budget, which is allocated beforehand specifically to cover such a situation. Such a budget ensures that if there are changes, they are at least limited.

Approval from the project sponsor
When the project manager is not able to absorb a change within his tolerances, then the approval of the project sponsor, or the approval of someone who has been authorised by him (change authority), is required.

Approval outside the sponsors influence
It would be nice if you could agree everything with the project sponsor, but that is often not possible. You have to ensure that you are aware of all people who could have an influence on your project. I briefly refer to the analysis of interested parties you carried out at the start of the project, in which possible stakeholder strategies such as *"strongly involve"* and *"consult"* can arise. You might consider involving certain interested parties in the decision as to whether or not to implement a change.

5. Get acceptance or rejection
Within his tolerances, the project manager can only accept, but not reject, changes. If he does not think a certain change is desirable, he will have to convince the project sponsor who takes the decision of this, and so it always falls outside the project manager's authority.

For all decisions involving changes that fall outside the authorisation of the project manager, we are faced with the time it will take to make the decision. Waiting for the decision results in the people who are carrying out the work being hesitant of continuing, as due to the change, they might have to do the work again, or they may end up doing the work to no avail. Delayed decision making, therefore, always endangers the efficiency of the execution, and in order to prevent this, it is a good thing when submitting the request, to also indicate the impact of delayed decision making.

6. Apply changes and report
When a change has been approved, the project manager ensures that it is carried out. One or more work packages are added, therefore, and these he has to:
- Schedule.
- Have carried out and delivered.
- Check, to ensure they are done.
- Take action on, when necessary.

Using the impact analysis, the project manager amends the plan, and allocates the resources concerned, possibly rescheduling other activities.

The approved changes need more attention than the original work, not because they are more important, but because the risk that the people carrying out the work might forget them is higher. Therefore, an extra Deming cycle (plan-do-check-act) is required for changes.

Also with regard to the reporting, changes get extra attention. Without changes, the project manager reports with respect to the baseline (for the original scheduling, scope description and budget). As the request was explicitly for a change to that, you also have to report both to the usual channels, and also to the person requesting the change, that you will implement that change.

7. Monitor changes
The classic risk on projects is the continuing expansion of the project scope (*scope*

1.15 Changes

creep). One of the tasks of the project manager is to monitor this, and that is why we make plans and have them approved. Everything that has been approved becomes a so-called baseline, a point of reference for the project manager, which he and his team keep to.

This requires your continuous pro-active attention. It starts when you become responsible for the project, and does not stop until the project sponsor discharges you for the project. It means that you:
- Refer the team members to the agreed scope.
- Involve the project sponsor and users sufficiently when determining the scope.
- Structure the scope with the help of the WBS.
- Check whether or not team members stay within the scope.
- Keep a check on the project environment for possible developments.
- Discourage changes without locking the door.

8. Apply lessons learned

A change control procedure must be workable. It may be that during the project the need arises to amend this, for example to allow the team to work more efficiently. You always have to consider that and discuss it with the people who are authorised to make decisions.

Furthermore, you have to evaluate whether or not the change has actually delivered what was intended, whether or not the people who submitted the change are happy with the result, whether or not side-effects have occurred, and whether or not the estimates have been exceeded.

9. Other standards and guidances

The process steps as identified by IPMA are only a suggestion. The process steps described in the *ISO 21500 Guidance*, the *'guide to the Project Management Body of Knowledge'* (the *PMBOK Guide*) from the Project Management Institute, and in the popular PRINCE2 Project Management method are much more "binding". Without discussing it in detail I shall name, as a comparison, a number of items from these standards that are related to this competence element. What will be noticeable is the high level of similarity and overlap.

ISO 21500
Deals with this subject in the process:
- Control Changes

PMBOK Guide
Deals with this subject in the process:
- Perform Integrated Change Control

PRINCE2
The method has a separate topic for this and makes a differentiation between configuration management and issue/change management. An issue is everything that could possibly lead to a change in the Plans. Configuration management ensures that changes take place in a tidy and structured way. The following four steps are present:
- Plan
- Identify
- Control
- Monitor status
- Verification and audits

The procedure for issue and change control looks as follows:
- Collect
- Assess
- Propose
- Decide
- Implement

1.15-4 SPECIAL TOPICS

1. Issue register and report

The PRINCE2[1] method which is much-used in Europe looks at potential changes from a much broader perspective than you would expect from the subject "changes". Instead of looking at change requests, a close watch is kept on those events that are not planned, but for which a management action is necessary. These events are the so-called "issues", of which there are three types:
- Change request.
- Deviation from the specification.
- Problem or concern.

All issues are logged in the so-called issue register. That can be on paper, a card-index box, spreadsheet, database or a special software application developed for this purpose. In this register, you record the following information:
- Identification.
- Issue type.
- Date submitted.
- Author.

---

1 (2009) *Managing Successful Projects With PRINCE2*, OGC, London

> EXAMPLE 15-1 RISK, PROBLEM AND ISSUE
>
> Someone who voices his concerns over the way in which the residents have been consulted, submits an issue. After consideration, the realization arises that if the residents form themselves into an action committee, this could lead to problems in the form of protests. Note the words "could lead to", because this is not yet certain, and it is, therefore, a risk which has to be thought about.
>
> The concern expressed is recorded as a line in the issue register, possibly accompanied by an issue report. During the consideration of it, it is decided to include it as a risk in the risk register, together with the required responses. Should this risk, despite all the responses made, arise, then without doubt it becomes an issue and a problem.
>
> A risk is, therefore, something that has not yet occurred, whereas by definition, an issue is something that has occurred.

- Reference to the issue report.
- Description.
- Priority.
- Seriousness.
- Status.
- Closure date.

When you record an item in the register, you always assess whether direct action is necessary, or whether you can wait until the next meeting with those involved. The priority indicates how important it is, whereas the seriousness indicates which level of management can and should make the decision (sub-project leader, project manager, steering committee or senior management).

The most important benefit of this register is that in this way you keep your sights on all events that could have an effect on the current schedule. Depending on the priority and seriousness, different management actions can be taken, such as:
- Approving or rejecting the desired change.
- Postponing the decision.
- Requesting more information.
- Having the project plan amended.
- Ensuring the specifications are adhered to anyway.
- Accepting the deviation from the specifications.
- Providing advice on how to progress further.

The issue register is nothing more than a "table of contents"; the issues themselves are described in a more detailed report. Such an issue report contains the following information:
- Identification.
- Issue type.
- Date submitted.
- Author.
- Description.
- Impact analysis.

1.15 Changes

- Recommendation.
- Priority.
- Seriousness.
- Decision.
- Approval.
- Decision date.
- Completion date.

As well as a detailed impact analysis, which clearly describes the consequences of the various options the decision-maker has, you write a recommendation of the preferred option, as seen from the project. In addition, you record the decision made, allowing what happened during the project to be reconstructed at a later stage.

2. Prioritizing changes

In the event of multiple changes or requirements, for which it is not yet certain if there will be enough time or budget to achieve them all, prioritization is required. A much used method carries the acronym MoSCoW. The consonants stand for:

M	Must haves	Requirements which must be met
S	Should haves	An equivalent alternative can also be used
C	Could haves	Only if there is enough time
W	Won't have now	Not part of this project, we'll do them later

By setting these priorities in advance, the project manager and his team have some margin, also sometimes called "tolerance", in the delivery of the actual end result.

1.16 Control and reports

A HELMSMAN MUST ABANDON SHIP
IF HE NO LONGER FEELS THE RUDDER IN HIS HANDS[1]

Regularly checking
the progress and the use of resources
is essential for managing the project
and informing the project sponsor.

---
1 Neerlands Hoop in Bange Dagen

1.16 Control and Reports

1.16-1 DEFINITIONS

Control Instruments	The procedures and instructions for project control.
Earned Value Analysis (EVA)	Method to measure the progress of a project on the basis of the budgeted costs of all the work carried out.
Measuring the performance	Determination of what has been achieved so far, compared with the resources used.
Measuring the progress	Determination of what has been achieved so far, compared with the time schedule.
Plan	Document describing who has to carry out what, where, when and how, in order to achieve the intended result or goal.
Project Control	All activities required to execute the project in a controlled manner.
Reporting	Providing an oral or written report.
Tolerance	Agreed margin in a plan, within which it is not necessary to report to the next level of senior management.

1.16-2 INTRODUCTION

Progress is delivering a result on time for acceptable costs and quality. A project manager has a project under control when this progress is in line with what has been agreed at the start. A Control Cycle means that the project manager, or his sub-project leaders, periodically keeps track of whether or not this is still the case. Furthermore, the Control Cycle contains a reporting function, which ensures that all parties involved are kept up-to-date with the progress.

1.16-3 PROCESS STEPS

1. Set up a monitoring system.
2. Measure status & performance.
3. Analyze deviations.
4. Plan alternatives.
5. Take corrective measures.
6. Adjust project objectives.
7. Report to the stakeholders.
8. Apply lessons learned.

1. Set up a monitoring system

As a minimum, the project manager must report on:
- The project deliverables.
- Quality achieved.
- Actual costs compared to the budget.
- Forecast costs compared to the budget.
- Milestones achieved compared to the plan.

To do this, he agrees a reporting system in advance with the most important stakeholders, ensuring that they receive enough information on the situation to base the decisions relevant to them.

2. Measure status & performance

The core of project control is the Control Cycle; regularly checking whether or not everything is still going according to plan. The basis for all Control Cycles is always the well-known Deming-Cycle (plan-do-check-act).

Periodically you look at the:
- Actual deliverables.
- Planned results.
- Costs incurred.

But, in addition, you can also look at the:
- Hours spent.
- Foreseen risks.
- New risks.
- Problems that have arisen.

3. Analyze deviations

It is necessary to have a view of the progress and the use of resources. By comparing the performance delivered to date with the performance which should have been delivered according to the plan, you can gain an insight into this, and based on this information, you can determine what corrective actions are required to deliver the required result within budget and on time.

Everything that has been planned in advance, can serve as a baseline. In the event of a deviation occurring or threatening to occur, you must analyze this situation.

Questions you should ask are:
- Is the measurement correct?
- What are the possible causes?
- Will a trend continue?
- What will happen if we do something or do nothing?

4. Plan alternatives

Following the analysis, and in consultation with your team, you develop alternative ways to resolve deviations. If necessary you build a simulation model which you run, or you do a mental exercise to assess the effect of a certain action. Ultimately, you make a choice as to which action is the most suitable.

5. Take corrective measures

The choice from the previous process step is implemented.

6. Adjust project objectives

Sometimes, if there is no other way, all you can do, in consultation with the project sponsor and the steering committee, is amend the objectives of the project.

7. Report to the stakeholders

Project control consists partly of recognizing and reacting to changes compared to the

1.16 Control and Reports

plan, and partly in keeping the stakeholders updated on progress.

Progress is the essence of projects. If the project manager reports insufficiently, there is a chance that the stakeholders get the idea nothing is happening. On the other hand, it is also not the intention that stakeholders become inundated with reports. Here, the "happy medium" is best. At the start, the various reports are specified in the project plan.

Layout of a progress report
A good progress report to the project sponsor or the steering committee, consists of a number of A4's containing:
- Impression of the progress.
- Financial paragraph:
  o Earned Value Analysis.
  o Forecasts.
- Duration versus results:
  o Milestones achieved in the previous period.
  o Milestones for the coming period.
  o Forecast.
- Risks:
  o Manifested risks.
  o Changed risks.
  o Corrective responses.
- Various.

This report contains a summary of the situation.

Exception report
- Describes a deviation outside the tolerances.
- Analyses causes and possible solutions.
- Requires approval from a senior management echelon.

Stage end report
- Special report from the PM to the steering committee.
- Information for deciding on a (no) go for the next stage.

Project end report
- Final report from the PM to the steering committee.
- Analysis of the actual performance compared to the planned performance.

Lessons learned report
- Describes the experience gained.
- Available for other projects.

8. Apply lessons learned

It has already been mentioned a few times, but you learn by doing. Project control shows what can go wrong, and carrying out corrective measures is, of course, also a form of learning.

9. Other standards and guidances

The process steps as identified by IPMA are only a suggestion. The process steps described in the *ISO 21500 Guidance*, the *'guide to the Project Management Body of Knowledge'* (the *PMBOK Guide*) from the Project Management Institute, and in the popular PRINCE2 Project Management method are much more "binding". Without discussing it in detail I shall name, as a comparison, a number of items from these standards that are related to this competence element. What will be noticeable is the high level of similarity and overlap.

ISO 21500
Deals with this subject in the process:
- Control Project Work

PMBOK Guide
Deals with this subject in the process:
- Monitor and Control Project Work

PRINCE2
PRINCE2 contains a separate topic on the Progress of the project, and in this way pro-

1.16 Control and Reports

vides the control on the project. Progress is monitored in the following six areas:
- Time
- Costs
- Scope
- Risk
- Quality
- Benefits

The control takes place by making use of three levels, and determining at each level which tolerances the responsible manager has. These three levels are:
- The project board at project level
- The project manager at stage level
- The team manager at work package level

The PRINCE2 control is based on Management by Exception, so that the main points are periodically reported, and only when there is a danger the tolerances will be exceeded, is an Exception Report sent.

1.16-4 SPECIAL TOPICS

1. Earned Value Method

An important method for measuring the progress is the Earned Value Method, a method which originated in the USA at the Department of Defence (DoD). In Anglo-Saxon countries it is customary that projects invoice, and are paid, based on this method using C/SCSC (Cost/Schedule Control System Criteria). Earned Value uses a number of concepts.

BCWS or PV	Budgeted Cost of Work Scheduled (=Planned Value)
BCWP or EV	Budgeted Cost of Work Performed (= Earned Value)
ACWP or AC	Actual Cost for Work Performed (=Actual Cost)
SV	Schedule Variance
CV	Cost Variance

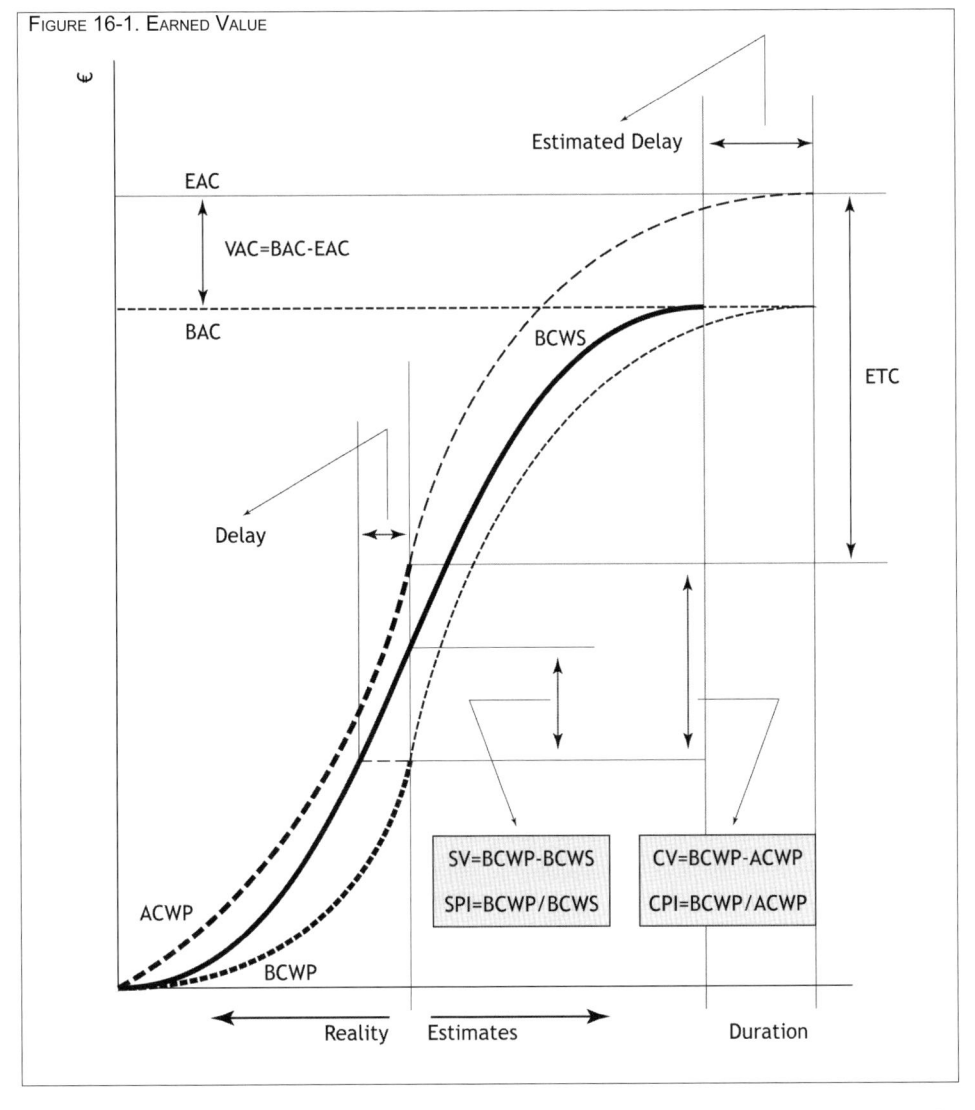

FIGURE 16-1. EARNED VALUE

$$SV = BCWP - BCWS$$
$$SPI = BCWP / BCWS$$
$$CV = BCWP - ACWP$$
$$CPI = BCWP / ACWP$$
$$VAC = BAC - EAC$$

1.16 Control and Reports

BAC	Budget at Completion
ETC	Estimate to Complete
EAC	Estimate at Completion
VAC	Variance at Completion
CPI	Cost Performance Indicator
TCPI	To-Complete Cost Performance Indicator
SPI	Schedule Performance Indicator
ETAC	Estimated Time at Completion

BCWS
= Budgeted Cost of Work Scheduled
The project is based on a schedule. The costs for the planned work come out of this.

At the end of the project, the BCWS is always equal to the project budget.

Based on the schedule, we know, for each point in time, what the *planned costs are for the work which should have been finished at the relevant point in time*.

BCWP
= Budgeted Cost of Work Performed
Probably, however, not all the work that should have been finished according to the schedule is actually finished. Also important are *the planned costs for the work actually finished at the point in time of the measurement*. In fact, this is the budget you could have used for the work carried out.

The BCWP is also called *Earned Value*, it is the amount you have "earned" for your project sponsor.

ACWP
= Actual Cost of Work Performed
What is the total project cost at the point that the measurement is made? In addition, *the actual costs of work carried out up to the point in time of the measurement* are of importance here i.e. the actual costs of the activities carried out.

EXAMPLE
At a certain point in time, the following data for a project is known:

BAC (total budget)	1,000,000
BCWS	500,000
BCWP	400,000
ACWP	550,000
Duration	12 months

SV
= Schedule Variance = BCWP – BCWS
Both BCWP and BCWS relate to the budgeted costs, so that is the constant factor. The schedule is the variable factor.

The schedule variance shows whether we are doing better or worse compared to the schedule.

The SV in the example is:

SV = 400,000 - 500,000 = - 100,000, so the project is behind schedule.

CV
= Cost Variance = BCWP - ACWP
Both BCWP and ACWP relate to work completed. The deviation is budget minus the actual value.

The CV in the example is:
CV = 400,000 - 550,000 = -150,000, so the project is exceeding budget.

Meaning of SV and CV

Variance	<0	=0	>0
SV	Behind schedule	On schedule	Ahead of schedule
CV	Over budget	On budget	Under budget

BAC
= Budget at Completion

This is the total project budget, or the BCWS at the end of the project.

ETC
= Estimate to Complete

The amount needed to complete the project. There are three alternative options to calculate this:

- On the basis of a new estimate, when the original estimate was incorrect.
- BAC - BCWP, when the actual costs up until now (ACWP), for all sorts of external reasons, prove either better or worse than anticipated, and it is expected that the further progress will go according to plan.
- (BAC – BCWP)/(BCWP/ACWP), when it is expected that the actual costs will continue to follow the same pattern.

EAC
= Estimate at Completion
= (ACWP / BCWP) x BAC

This is the extrapolation of the trend that has occurred up until now, based on the assumption that the rest of the project will not be very much different.

If the trend is continued, the EAC will be higher than budgeted at the commencement of the project, and is:

EAC = (550,000/400,000) x 1,000,000 = 1,375,000.

VAC
= Variance at Completion
= BAC – EAC

Indicates whether the project will finish under or over budget.

The forecast deviation is, therefore:
VAC = 1,000,000 – 1,375,000 = -375,000. Therefore, there will be an overrun on the original budget.

SPI
= Schedule Performance Indicator
= BCWP/BCWS

Indicator: how good is the performance in terms of time?

The SPI in the example is, therefore:

SPI = 400,000/500,000 = 0.80.

ETAC
= Estimated Time At Completion
= (BAC/SPI)/(BAC/Duration)

This formula can be simplified to: duration/SPI

A rough estimate of the total duration of the project.

If the trend is continued, the project will be finished after: 12/0.8 = 15 months.

CPI
= Cost Performance Indicator
= BCWP/ACWP

Indicator: how good is our performance as far as costs are concerned?

The CPI of the example is, therefore:

CPI = 400,000/550,000 = 0.73.

1.16 Control and Reports

Meaning of SPI-CPI

	<1	1	>1
SPI	Behind schedule	On schedule	Ahead of schedule
CPI	Over budget	On budget	Under budget

TCPI
= To-Complete Performance Indicator
= (BAC-BCWP)/(BAC-ACWP)

Indicator: what CPI do we have to achieve, to still attain the original budget (BAC)?

The TCPI of the example is, therefore:

TCPI = (1,000,000 – 400,000)/
(1,000,000 – 550,000) = 1.33

FIGURE 16-2. MILESTONE SLIP CHART

2. Slip Chart

The Slip Chart is a simple tool for providing an insight into the progress of the project. There are a number of variants, and I shall cover a few of these.

Milestone Slip Chart

In the Slip Chart on the left, three milestones have been entered in. Along the horizontal axis, we enter the various Control Cycles, and along the vertical axis the corresponding forecast for the three milestones. In each period, the project manager forecasts when he expects to achieve each of the three milestones.

Each milestone has its own symbol (circle, honeycomb, and star). The original schedule was week 5, week 23 and week 30. We connect the symbols each time using a slip curve.

When the project manager produces his report in week 4, he concludes that the first milestone may overrun by one week. At the end of week 7, the first milestone has been achieved (the line now dissects the diagonal), and he reports this in week 8. There is a slip in this milestone of 2 weeks (7-5).

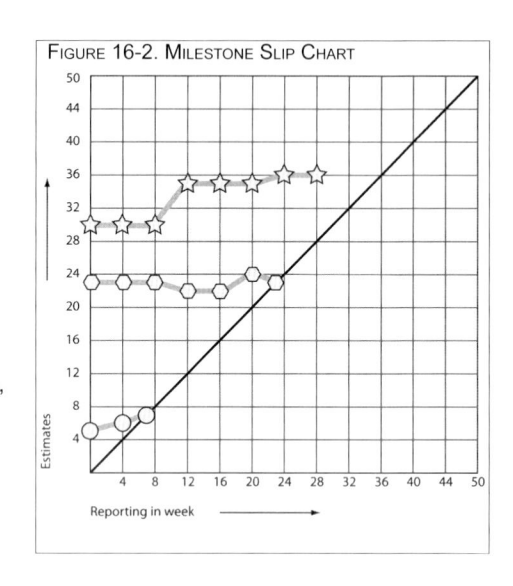

In week 12, there is something strange going on; the project manager forecasts that the second milestone will be achieved in week 22 and the third milestone in week 35. In his accompanying text, he explains the reasons.

Relative Slip Chart

A Slip Chart that is slightly more difficult to fathom out, sets out for each Control Cycle the relative amount of time (or cost) used against the time (or cost) that is necessary.

Let's have a look at such a Slip Chart related to the duration. The project has a planned duration of 52 weeks, and there are four Control Cycles (week 13, 26, 39 and 52).

1.16 Control and Reports

FIGURE 16-3. RELATIVE SLIP CHART DURATION

The original budget for this project is € 1,000k and the data for the successive periods are:

Period	Actual	Forecast
wk 13	200k	1,100k
wk 26	400k	1,100k
wk 39	750k	1,500k
wk 52	1,000k	1,600k

Also in this case, the diagonal line indicates when the project is on schedule.

FIGURE 16-4. RELATIVE SLIP CHART COSTS

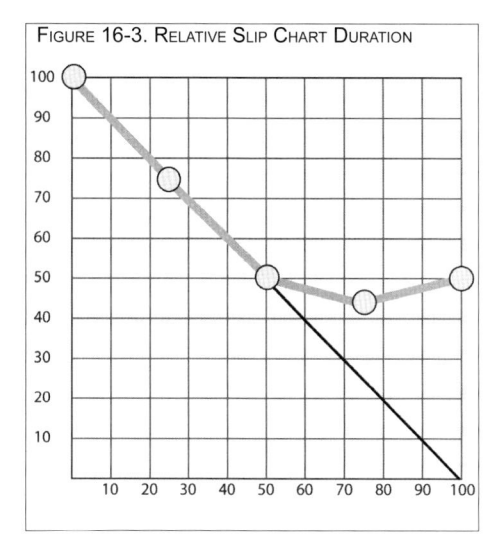

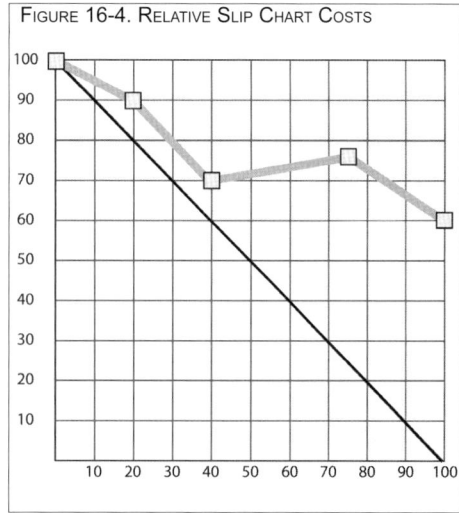

As opposed to the milestones Slip Chart, in which the diagonal shows that the milestone has been achieved, this slip curve shows where we should be if we are on schedule. In our example project, we can see that this is the case for the first two Control Cycles, after which the project starts to delay. Above the line is, therefore, bad, and under the line is good.

A similar Slip Chart can also be made for the budget. For the same project as before, the 'used' and 'still needed' parts are set out against each other.

EXAMPLE 16-1 CALCULATIONS RELATIVE SLIP CHART
Duration

Data		Calculation			
Period	Forecast	% used		still needed	% still needed
wk 13	wk 52	13/52 = 25%		52 – 13 = 39	39/52 = 75%
wk 26	wk 52	26/52 = 50%		52 – 26 = 26	26/52 = 50%
wk 39	wk 10 next year	39/52 = 75%		52 + 10 – 39 = 23	23/52 = 44%
wk 52	wk 26 next year	52/52 = 100%		52 + 26 – 52 = 26	26/52 = 50%

The percentages 'used' and 'still needed' are determined each time compared to the original duration.

Budget

Data			Still needed	
Period	Actual	Still needed	% used	% still needed
wk 13	200k	1,100k	200/1,000 = 20%	(1,100 – 200)/1,000 = 90%
wk 26	400k	1,100k	400/1,000 = 40%	(1,100 – 400)/1,000 = 70%
wk 39	750k	1,500k	750/1,000 = 75%	(1,500 – 750)/1,000 = 75%
wk 52	1,000k	1,600k	1,000/1,000 = 100%	(1,600 – 1,000)/1,000 = 60%

1.16 Control and Reports

Benefits of Slip Charts

The most important benefit of the Slip Chart compared to the Earned Value diagrams is the simplicity. The calculated indicators are fairly straightforward, whereas the EVA indicators are somewhat more difficult to understand.

A benefit that the Slip Chart shares with the EVA graphs is that the development over time is visible, and you can clearly see how effective certain interventions have been. In the above project, the project manager has carried out an intervention at the end of week 13 with respect to the costs, which has ensured that for the following period, the project is again back on schedule (the slip curve runs parallel to the diagonal). After week 26, the project goes completely off track in terms of both duration and cost, at least it does if you compare it with the original plan. We can see this through the slip curve diverging from the diagonal. In about week 39, the project manager carries out a new intervention, which has some effect on the costs (the slip curve begins to converge with the diagonal again), but not on the schedule for the duration (the slip curve diverges even further from the diagonal).

By showing the performance of the project in this way, you actually have an evaluation of the total project each time up to the respective Control Cycle point.

1.17 Information and documentation

BECAUSE WE FORGET SO QUICKLY

For a brief period at the beginning of the computer era, there existed the illusion of a paperless office.

Nothing could be less true, as the PC has allowed people to record and distribute enormous amounts of text.

Not infrequently, we hear people sigh under the quantity of e-mails with accompanying appendices.

We live in an era of a profusion of information.

The old adage also applies to this topic:

Think first, then act.

1.17 Information and documentation

1.17-1 DEFINITIONS

Data	Raw facts or symbols.
Information	Data which has meaning for the receiver.
Presentation	Verbal information transfer.
Documents	Information recorded in writing.
Reporting	Providing an account verbally or in writing. Providing agreed information at the agreed times.
Report	Written account to the person to whom we are responsible.

1.17-2 INTRODUCTION

The word *information* comes from Latin and means giving form to, moulding and/or instructing. It is often confused with *data* and/or *knowledge*. Even though the concepts are related, information is the *meaning* certain data has for someone. What is just data to one person, can be information to another person.

Someone who has no knowledge of the Earned Value technique will find little information in an EVA report. Someone who does have that knowledge, sees at a glance a lot important information on the status of the project. Through his knowledge, the report has actually become meaningful, and the content of the report has become *information*.

A good document is tailored to the target group, so that it contains information instead of just data. The essence of this competence element is the processing of this data into information. It is, in any event, about:

- Storing the data.
- Moulding the data into information.
- Storing the data, which has been processed into information in documents.
- Making these documents with information available.

But that is not all, sometimes the permanent organization in its compulsion for improvement, leads the project manager into a morass of standard templates and reports, in which no one can find any information. I once heard an experienced project manager sigh: *"I fill in the form anyway, just to keep my manager happy."* The organization had just completed a lengthy improvement project, but this could certainly not have been the intention.

If templates do not lead to information, they are wrong. When you fill in the forms, they should be there to help you. The whole process of transforming data into information using the available templates ensures that you live through the progress and the actual status of the project in such a way that it becomes part of you, as it were. Sometimes it is a bit of give-and-take between what the technocrats force on you, and that what you actually need to carry out your project, but that is part of the job.

This competence element is also about setting up an information system that you, as project manager, can work with. An information system which is up-to-date and accurate. Such a system does not just appear from nowhere, it is one of those success factors which you, as project manager, have to ensure it is there at the start of the project.

1.17 Information and documentation

1.17-3 INFORMATION PROCESS

1. Develop a PMIS.
2. Adhere to the company policy.
3. Ensure it is implemented.
4. Control the information.
5. Apply lessons learned

1. Develop a PMIS

PMIS stands for: project management information management system.

Even before the actual start of the project, as project manager you (in consultation with your team and other interested parties), make an inventory of the information needs within the project. The starting point is the analysis of all the parties involved.

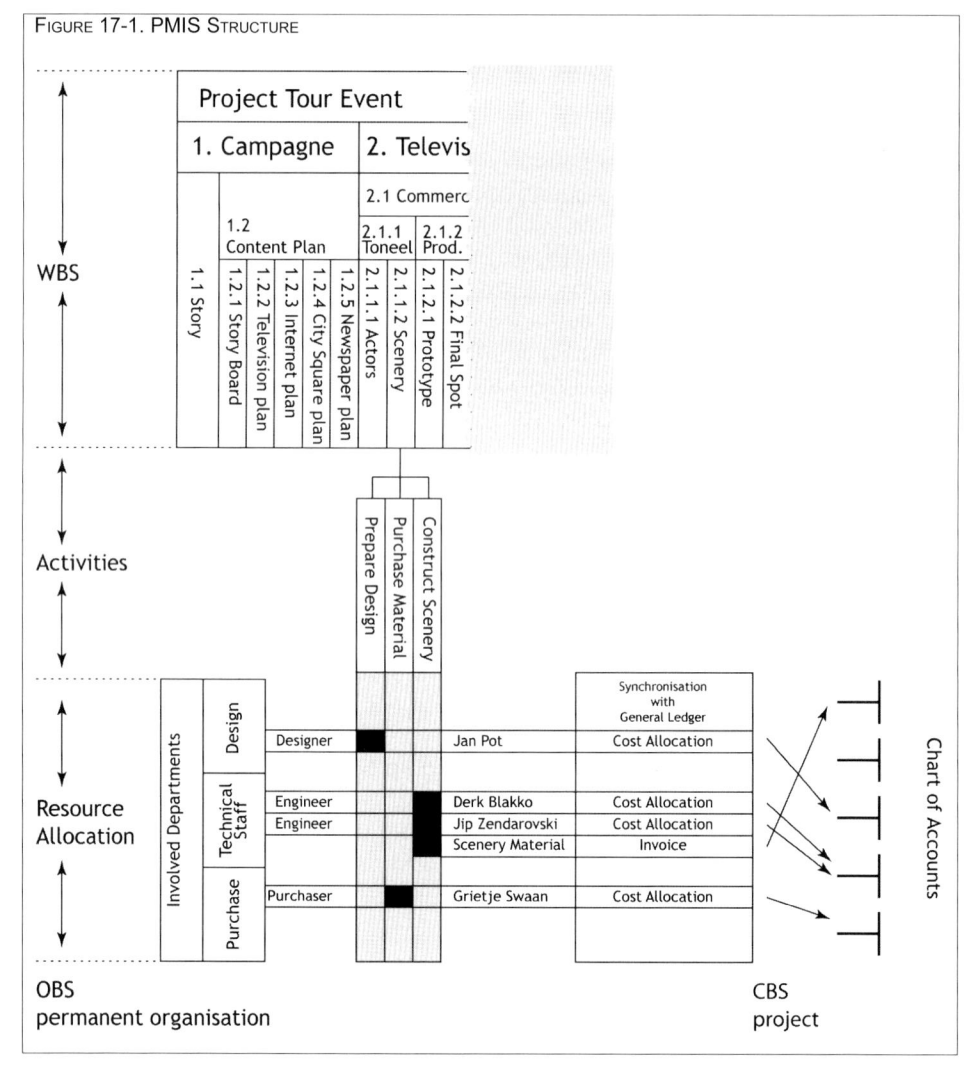

FIGURE 17-1. PMIS STRUCTURE

1.17 Information and documentation

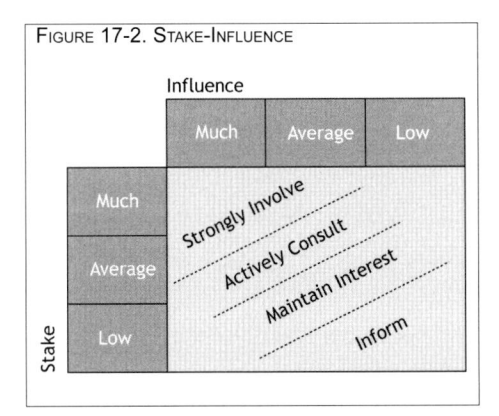

FIGURE 17-2. STAKE-INFLUENCE

Based on what is at stake for them, you determine what information they need. After that, you ask yourself what data you need to be able to provide this information. The amount of influence says something about the frequency with which you have to provide information, and derived from that, when you need certain data in order to mould it into information. In advance, you discuss the reports in question with the different parties.

The influence matrix gives an insight into those matters, which the person concerned can influence. With the help of this information, you determine the sort of information someone needs.

FIGURE 17-3. INFLUENCE

Needed Influence	M. Bush	J. McGregor	M. Ali	J. Hoss	Etc.		
Finance	H	L	M	M			
People	H	L	M	M			
Machinery	M	L	H	H			
Permits	L	L	L	L			
Etc.							

In the example shown, M. Busch has a need for financial information and the deployment of people. On the other hand, M. Ali and J. Hoss require information about the machines that have been commissioned for use.

The reports, therefore, depend a lot on the target group you want to reach with them. Standard templates form a good basis, but these are insufficient to cover all the information needs on the project.

As well as the information needs of these parties, as project manager you also have your own need for information, and a risk analysis is an important starting point for this. You want to know how certain risks are developing, and it can be that one of the restricting responses requires that you monitor the efficiency of the different teams. As a gauge of this, you measure the daily progress a team makes, and compare it with the other teams.

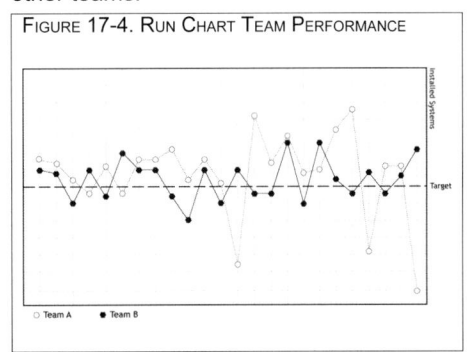

FIGURE 17-4. RUN CHART TEAM PERFORMANCE

Two teams have been plotted on the graph above. When you look carefully, you can see that team B controls its process much better than team A.

Such a graph, therefore, provides a lot more information than two tables with the data for the separate teams. A picture often says more than a thousand words.

2. Adhere to the company policy

Information
Time after time, the connection with the permanent organization turns out to be a big

237

1.17 Information and documentation

challenge. Because, in general, the administration of the permanent organization looks backwards, and the project looks forward. The project manager often has to set up his own information system, and link it to that of the organization. Furthermore, it is possible that the project is involved with several permanent organizations (for example several suppliers, own organization, a customer organization), and this generates a need for a co-ordinating structure.

Furthermore, the organization will have its own requirements for requesting resources, cost accountability, etc. The following is a table of the different structures that as project manager, you have to make a link between:

Project structures	Organization structures
Cost Breakdown Structure	Chart of accounts
Resource Breakdown Structure	Organization structure

If possible, for managing the project you adopt, in as far as is possible, the structure of the permanent organization. In this way, you have the least work to do when checking whether or not both administrations comply with each other. The CBS then links the WBS to the chart of accounts, whereas the RBS links to the actual units of the different permanent organizations involved.

By recording these connections, it is always possible to make a link from the project management information system to the systems used by the permanent organization. All these links can be recorded in the scheduling package, thus making it possible to plot these in time.

Documentation

In a project management environment we find the following documents[1]:
- Project management schedules.
- Project management reports.
- Project records and logs.
- Business documents.
- Technical documents.

It is necessary that all of these documents can be easily found when required.

There is a big difference between a software development project with staff spread over the whole world, and that for a local council, where a number of policy officials have to produce an advice for the council committee.

> EXAMPLE 17-1 WRONG TECHNOLOGY CHOICE
>
> The project team is in the design stage. The designers have convinced the project manager that a certain package is the best for the related design task.
>
> When the progress proves to be disappointing, the project manager speaks with the main designer. *"The memory in the PC is too small and it is also difficult to copy pictures into Word, and that is the reason we are overrunning."*
>
> To the question whether he could not have known that in advance, he answers that this is the first time he has used this application.

The choice for the technology to be used depends on[2]:
- The *urgency* with which the information has to be made available.
- The *availability* of the technology.
- The *composition* of the team.
- The project *duration*.
- The project *environment*.

For his choice, the project manager has to let himself be guided by the principle that

---
1 (2004) *The Complete PROJECT MANAGEMENT OFFICE Handbook,* Gerard M. Hill, AUERBACH PUBLICATIONS, New York
2 (2004) A guide to the Project Management Body of Knowledge 3rd Edition- het Project Management Institute, Pennsylvania

1.17 Information and documentation

technology is a means to an end, and not a goal in itself. The more technology, the more risk you run that it will work against you.

If it can be done simply, then it is best to keep it simple.

3. Ensure it is implemented
A plan is more than a good intention. What I said before about connecting to the permanent organization is only useful when someone is waiting for the information. That is why the interested parties in the project are looked at first. The project management information system has to contribute to the controllability of the project.

If the implementation of the system thought up is problematic, or fails, it is almost always due to the system, and not due to unwilling project staff. Opposition may have to do with *not being able* in place of *not wanting*. The basic principle for the documentation of data is that it assists the team members with the execution of their activities. If this is the case, you achieve support for the reporting system. If that is not the case, the implementation will not succeed, and it is then tempting to force staff to report, resulting in the wrong data being filled in.

We often see an obsessive utilisation of micro management, whereby the project management team concentrates more on data than on information. Success is dependent on the system being thought through in advance, also taking into account the workability and the courage to change when something does not work.

4. Control the information
This is concerned about the following issues:
- Gathering together the data.
- Moulding the data into information.
- Distributing the information.

This happens at every management level in the project, which means that what is information for an underlying level is data for the higher level. Each level processes this data into information for the next level. If the person you report to is not interested in what you provide, it is a signal that something is wrong with the moulding of the data.

Controlling is, therefore:
- Ensuring you gather the right information, and enable the staff who report to you to turn that data into information.
- Processing their reports into your progress report in such a way that you make this information suitable for the management level above you.

This transformation has an important function, which transcends the reporting function. In the transformation process, you have to fathom out the actual status of the project, and that understanding ensures that you are better able to manage the project.

5. Apply lessons learned
During the project, the team learns from what is happening. This experience gained within the project must be made available to all team members, and therefore, in the cycle of moulding the data into information, there is a stream of experience lessons you have to include in the further development. What one team has possibly discovered should be passed on to other teams, insofar as this could be of use to them.

1.17-4 Documentation Process

1. Develop a plan
2. Keep to the existing rules
3. Classify the documents
4. Issue documents
5. Save documents
6. Manage the versions
7. Archive
8. Apply lessons learned

1. Develop a plan

The number of different documents within a project can be overwhelming and, for this reason alone, it is worthwhile to consider the way in which you are going to organise these during project start-up. If you do not do this, then during the project execution you will have a jumble of documents with an accompanying lack of clarity on their status.

In principle there are two types of documents:
- Project results.
- Project Management results.

The first group contains documents that the team must provide as part of the total delivery, and these are predominantly specialised or technical documents, e.g. the manual for a computer system, the "as-built" documentation for a factory, or an agreed SLA (= Service Level Agreement) for the maintenance of the delivered system.

The basis of the plan for these documents is the WBS and the descriptions of the various work packages and/or products the team has to deliver during the project. It should be clear from this where technical documentation has to be delivered.

The second group relates to the project management results, whereby you have to consider the management documents that are needed to manage the project, for example project plans, completed checklists, reports and suchlike, which all form part of the project documentation. The recording of these documents is not only useful and helpful over the duration of the project, but also in the unlikely event that a disagreement or conflict with the customer arises, which then ends up in court, where a forensic analysis of the project documentation is carried out.

The documentation plan consists of at least the following parts:
- Naming.
- Method of numbering versions.
- Example templates and explanation.
- Location of the documents.
- Responsibilities.
- Approval procedure.
- Archiving moment.

A much used instrument is the previously mentioned RACI table, in which the following is stated for each document: who is responsible, who is accountable and who has to be consulted or informed.

2. Keep to the existing rules

On the one hand, as project manager, you are concerned with:
- Legal requirements.
- Customer standards.
- The standards of the supplying organizations.

On the other hand, you are concerned with what is necessary for the project, and you have to reconcile any differing viewpoints with each other. This means you must at least keep yourself informed on the various requirements that exist with respect to the documentation, and to achieve this it is necessary to have some knowledge of the line of business and the type of project.

1.17 Information and documentation

3. Classify the documents
Not every document is subject to the same regime, and it is, therefore, necessary to introduce a certain classification system. We have already seen above a simple categorisation into project and project management results.

A somewhat more detailed classification could be as follows:
- Management documents.
- Project plans.
- Technical plans.
- Technical documentation.
- Contract documentation.
- Minutes and reports.

A number of examples of these are given below. In this way, it is possible to define the rules for each category.

Management documents
Daily log, risk register, issue register, project management plan, action list, etc.

Project plans
Planning, budget, quality plan, etc.

Technical plans
Safety plan, security, environment, construction plan, support plan, etc.

Technical documentation
Programme of requirements, design documents, user manuals, etc.

Contract documentation
Proposals, contracts with the customer, contracts with suppliers, change requests, etc.

Minutes and reports
Progress reports, minutes of meetings, decisions, etc.

4. Issue documents
Dependent on the type of document, there is a point in time that a document changes status from draft to definitive, or is actualized, and this happens in a structural way. Although possibly supported by a project office, the project manager ultimately has the final responsibility for issuing a document.

Before issuing can take place, the document must be checked for:
- Consistency; it must not contain any internal or external inconsistencies.
- Actuality; it must reflect the reality of the actual situation.
- Completeness; it must contain all the information that should be in the document.
- Accuracy; attuned to the needs of the target group.

The production of documents must always have an objective and a target group. If no-one uses the document it is better to bring up the usefulness of it for discussion.

5. Save the documents
Documents must be traceable and accessible. There are various instruments available for doing this, often dependent on the organizations for which the project is being executed. The simplest form is a network folder, but more complex systems are available. As you do not want to introduce extra complexity into the project, it is important to

---

EXAMPLE 17-2 CHANGE HISTORY TABLE

This example relates to a WBS dictionary, in which one of the elements (2.1) is replaced by a different component to the one originally considered.

Date	Author	Authorized by	WBS	Description
29/01	JH(PM)	MH(Sponsor)	2.1	Replace drainage system Xipion v3 by Xendor 14.

1.17 Information and documentation

choose a method that fits in with the current way of working.

6. Manage the versions

A form of version control is always necessary for documents, and overlaps with change and configuration management described elsewhere. For documents, this is certainly important, as a document is easy to change, and if a number of people are working simultaneously on a document, it quickly becomes unclear which version is the right one.

One of the simplest ways to do this is to include a table at the beginning of the document in which the change status and history can be recorded. As well as the date, you include details of who has made the change and where it has been authorised, and a short description of the change. You can now save the document in two ways; one document with the complete new text, and a second document in which the changes applied are referenced against the previous version. If you then make PDF copies (that cannot be changed), you have the possibility later to check up on the history of the document.

7. Archive

Archiving takes place in two stages:
- Archiving during the project.
- Archiving after the project.

In the first instance, "archiving" should be construed as saving in a place where it can be found without having to spend time trying to find it using the pc's search function, but by knowing precisely where you have saved the document in question. This is described in the documentation plan.

At a certain point in time, certain documents are no longer needed, but must be retained. These are then stored in an archive. Some documents can be removed, but others not.

At the end of a project we hand over the documents required to the permanent organization. In so doing, we take account of the policy and any other rules in force.

8. Apply lessons learned

The way in which documentation is organized must fit in with the working practices of the project team and others involved. Sometimes you may have thought of a particular procedure for document management in advance. Real life practice, however, is the best way of checking if something is usable. If during the execution of the project it appears that there is a better method, you can assess with the team whether it is worth the trouble of changing the working practice with respect to documentation.

9. Other standards and guidances

The process steps as identified by IPMA are only a suggestion. The process steps described in the *ISO 21500 Guidance*, the *'guide to the Project Management Body of Knowledge'* (the *PMBOK Guide*) from the Project Management Institute, and in the popular PRINCE2 Project Management method are much more "binding". Without discussing it in detail I shall name, as a comparison, a number of items from these standards that are related to this competence element. What will be noticeable is the high level of similarity and overlap.

ISO 21500

The Guidance deals with this topic in the subject group Communication, through the following three processes:
- Plan communications.
- Distribute information.
- Manage communications.

PMBOK Guide

The 5th edition of *PMBOK Guide* is almost the same as the Guidance, only the naming convention is different:
- Plan communications management.
- Manage communications.
- Control communications.

PRINCE2

During the process Initiating a Project, the project manager draws up the communication strategy.

1.17 Information and documentation

1.17-5 SPECIAL TOPICS

1. Documents in projects

Project management plans

One of the first documents to be produced is the project mandate (or charter). This (short) document may consist of the following topics[3]:
- Project sponsor.
- Objective and result.
- Constraints.
- Interfaces.
- Quality expectations.
- Global business justification.
- Reference to relevant documents.
- Project manager and his authority.

Depending on the size of the project, details are further worked out in separate plans. If the project is large enough, we come across the following plans[4]: project definition, scheduling, budget, quality plan, resource plan, communication plan, risk plan and procurement plan. In these plans it is worked out at a detail level how these aspects have been organized within the project.

Furthermore, we find stage plans, in which a certain stage of the project is described in detail. In the case of a project with sub-projects, it is possible that each project leader of such a sub-project writes a plan for his own specific part. In such a case, the overall project plan shows the consolidated data.

One point of warning is required: the more documents, the less clear the whole becomes. It is therefore a good idea at the start to think hard about the structure of the different plans. Not too many and not too few!

---

[3] (2002) Managing Successful Projects with PRINCE2, OFFICE OF GOVERNMENT COMMERCE,
[4] (2004) *A Guide to the Project Management Body of Knowledge – Third Edition,* THE PROJECT MANAGEMENT INSTITUTE

Project management reports

Here we are dealing with all progress reports sent by the different people in the project organizations. As well as the standard progress reports, there is the question of interim exception reports, memos documenting agreements and other correspondence regarding the project management process.

Project reports and logs

This covers minutes of meetings and logbooks detailing events, which have occurred during the project.

For instance, the PRINCE2 methodology differentiates the following:
- Daily log, in which the project manager keeps a diary of matters which are important, but which cannot be found in other documents.
- Issue Register, a list of project issues submitted during the project, including change requests.
- Lessons log, a list in which all experience also useful to other projects, is kept.
- Quality register, registers all scheduled quality reviews, the details of when these took place, who participated in them and what the outcome was.
- Risk register, a document in which the identification, assessment, impact assessment and the responses of all risks of the project are recorded.

Business documents

Business documents such as proposals, contracts and suchlike must be securely saved. As these documents, compared to those previously mentioned, are not usually available digitally and are often signed, they have to be stored in a paper archive.

Technical documents

These are all documents related to products and/or services that the project either has

1.17 Information and documentation

to deliver, or which are used for the project work. Examples are technical specifications, designs, configuration descriptions, etc.

1.17 Information and documentation

1.18 Communication

ONE CANNOT NOT COMMUNICATE[1]

When two people come into contact with each other in one way or another, there is communication.

Even when they do not say anything.

Every form of behavior, or in fact refraining from certain behavior, has a communicative value.

---

1 (1967) *Pragmatics of human communications,* Watzlawick, NORTON & COMPANY, New York

1.18 Communication

1.18-1 Definitions

Closed question	A question, which can be answered with a simple yes or no, or with a single answer.
Communication	The process by which people try to convey a certain concept from one impression framework (the sender) to another (the receiver), by means of information which, by agreement, refers to that concept.
Non-verbal communication	Communication other than through the spoken word.
Open question	A question, which cannot be answered with a simple yes or no, or with a single answer.
Rhetorical question	A question to which the questioner does not really expect an answer.
Suggestive question	A question with a hidden message.
Verbal communication	Communication through the spoken word.

1.18-2 INTRODUCTION

There is a relation between this topic and the technical competence elements *"control & report", "information & documentation"*. Whereas these deal with the formal side, this chapter deals with getting the "planned" communication working. You can record as much as you like in advance on the way you communicate with each other, but the moment people actually make contact, or on the contrary do not, often provides you with unexpected challenges.

It is impossible not to communicate. From the first contact onwards, or the lack of it, communication is started, and as project manager, you have to deal with it on a daily basis. Just think of which message you communicate, when you:

- Are too late with your progress report.
- Come to work sloppily dressed and with bags under your eyes.

The point is that you, as project manager, have to consider carefully the way in which you communicate.

1.18-3 Process steps

1. Set up a communication plan.
2. Identify the appropriate style.
3. Determine the timing.
4. Decide on the method.
5. Plan and prepare
6. Check the infrastructure.
7. Measure the effectiveness.
8. Evaluate and take action.
9. Apply lessons learned

1. Set up a communication plan

The formal communication plan is included as part of project management plan, but the informal plan is in the back of the project manager's mind. The formal plan has already been covered previously, but the informal plan not yet, so I want to cover it here, as part of the consideration of this competence element.

With communication, it's all about thinking first and then acting. It is necessary for you to be aware of the "communicating value" that certain behavior can have on the parties involved with the project.

Such an "informal" communication plan then consists of:
- Identifying the target groups.
- Deciding how you will communicate.
- Determining when you will communicate.
- Choosing the communication medium.

Is this necessary? That is dependent on how effective you are in your communication; some people find it easier than others. If you fall into the last category, then as well as making a formal communications plan, I would also advise you to plan the informal communication.

2. Identify the appropriate style

If communication is the same as behavior, then your target group is everyone who sees you acting in the framework of this project. This "broad" definition of communication means that you must ask yourself what the effect of your behavior/communication is on other people. It is often the packaging (i.e. behavior) that either brings about what you want to achieve, or has the opposite effect.

There are certain matters you should tackle, and others you should leave alone. You communicate more through your deeds than with your words, and this is certainly true when you are dealing with people from other cultures. It is a good idea to invest time in understanding other cultures and to bear these differences in mind, because other people can easily take your behavior the wrong way.

Determining how you are going to communicate now comes down to considering what you are, and what you are not, going to do. It is a fact that the way you behave has to be appropriate to the way you are, because otherwise you will not come over as being "genuine".

Your spoken word, intention and deeds all have to be in line with one another. This first dimension, the spoken word, speaks for itself; it is the words that you speak and the language that you choose. But the spoken word is only one aspect. It is the intention, which is the underlying emotion, which also has to match the message, otherwise the receiver will not believe the message. The spoken word and the intention, therefore, should correspond with each other.

But what do you think of the following example?

> EXAMPLE 18-1 CORRESPONDENCE IN COMMUNICATION
> The CEO of a banking institution issues a request to the staff to forgo their bonuses, whilst at the same time he hires a new manager, who receives a bonus in advance. The staff cannot understand this at all, and it de-motivates them.

If the deeds do not correspond with the words and intention, then the message does not come over and is not understood. As project manager, you have to consider: are these three aspects in harmony with each other?

3. Determine the timing
This is all about timing! For formal and informal communication, there is a plan in which the various different communication moments are attuned to one another.

In practice, however, there are subtle distinctions which must be applied:
- When do you report on a time overrun?
- When do you report that the budget may be exceeded?
- When do you mention the lucky breaks?

It is, of course, always possible to agree "fixed" rules for these situations, however that is less effective. As project manager, you are expected to develop some sensitivity as to when to raise, and when not to raise, certain issues. Continuously ask yourself what the effect is of the matters you are communicating. It is just like a game of chess, in which you have to think out a number of moves in advance; often, the other person will surprise you.

4. Decide on the method
There are various possibilities: personally, by telephone or electronically (e-mail, MSN, Twitter). The first method provides you with the most control over the communications process and the last less.

> EXAMPLE 18-2 EMPLOYER FIRES MANAGER VIA SMS
> (This is a true story)
> An employer has fired an employee by using sms text message, but the courts have ruled against this. A prime example of how this should not be done.
>
> The man who was suspended, was surprised when he received an sms from his manager with the text: *'You don't have to come to work on Monday'*. The man requested a temporary injunction and won his case. His employer had to re-instate him in his function. The court found that the employer should have followed the official procedure.
>
> I am interested to know if the communication between the employee and his manager has improved since this.

The basic principle is that you must fit the means to the content of the message. If you make a mistake in this, then the means will work against you, as shown in the example alongside.

The danger of telephone or e-mail is that this technology provokes "impulsive" communication. What I mean is that, as there is no direct contact, the reaction will come directly from impulse, and you are no longer able to alter the situation, should the message be misinterpreted.

The principle is, therefore: *personal contact when it is important, and when you want to be able to adjust the interaction during the communication.*

5. Plan and prepare
When it comes to the actual communication, at least prepare yourself mentally. What people are you dealing with, to which target group do they belong, what do they find important, what do you have to watch out for? These are all matters which, in a general sense, you can prepare for.

1.18 Communication

Then, just before you actually start to communicate, you ensure that everything is in order, and your material, if required, has been well prepared, In this instance, 'material' also includes the clothes you wear e.g. in an environment where people always wear ties, you also wear one, whether you like it or not. On the other hand, in environments where it is not appropriate, then you do not wear one.

In your mind, you go through the whole process once more, thus ensuring that you are well prepared for the communication.

6. Check the infrastructure

The infrastructure has already been briefly mentioned in the choice of the means of communication. This, however, goes a bit further insofar as you ensure that everything is technically in order. The more complicated the infrastructure, the more that can go wrong, and this is something you have to consider when choosing it. You have to ensure that all those parties involved who in one way or the other make use of the infrastructure, are aware of how things work. The infrastructure is a means, and is not intended to be an objective.

7. Measure the effectiveness

Does the communication work as intended? The best way to find that out is by checking if the message has come across, and you can tell that from people's behavior. If that is what you wanted to achieve, then apparently your method of communication is effective, but if people do not act in the way you intended, then obviously it is not.

Obviously, this is a tense situation, because it could be that the chosen form, together with the content, has not resulted in what you were expecting. So, you have to have the courage to seek out your weaknesses, and where necessary correct them.

8. Evaluate and take action

Be brave enough to really take action. Discuss with your team what is, and what is not, working. You must ask yourself the question whether or not there is an issue of miscommunication, and how this can be solved. Many evaluations of failed projects blame the failure on poor communication.

Which action you take depends on the situation, particularly when you are dealing with differences in culture, but it is clear that you have to take action.

9. Apply lessons learned

Learning to communicate is possibly one of the most difficult things to do, but without it, as people, we are doomed. When you communicate, there is not only a message concerning content, but also always an underlying, and more emotional, layer addressing the subconscious. We often try to suppress the emotions this evokes, because nobody enjoys it when the other person becomes angry or does not understand us (or does not want to understand us).

It is, however, the emotions in our communication which offer the pointers to learning new skills.

1.18-4 Special Topics

1. The communication model

A communication model can be of help in understanding what can go wrong in the communication between people. The most straightforward model looks like this:

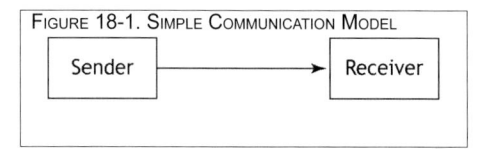

FIGURE 18-1. SIMPLE COMMUNICATION MODEL

Sender ──────► Receiver

There is a "right-minded" person who decides to send a message to another "right-minded" person. He does this by formulating well considered words, possibly written down. We all know that in practice it is not as simple as we would like, and therefore, we expand the above model:

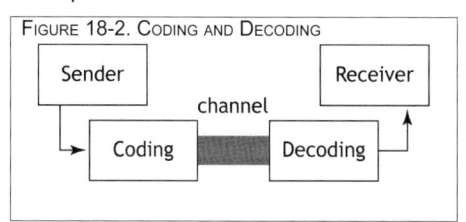

FIGURE 18-2. CODING AND DECODING

Sender   Receiver
         channel
  Coding ──── Decoding

Two right-minded people make contact, and one sends a message to the other. To do that, he first has to translate his message (code) into a language the other person understands. This may be Arabic or English, but could just as easily be: Morse code, drums or smoke signals. In order to get the message to the other person he needs a channel; a means or a channel. He might go to someone and speak to him, or he might send a letter, e-mail or SMS message, or pick up the telephone. When the message reaches the other person, that person has to understand it. He interprets (de-codes) the message and the communication has taken place.

This model immediately shows where problems might occur. It is possible that the message is not coded correctly, because it is not easy to put thoughts, intentions, or opinions into words. Another potential problem is in the de-coding of the message at the receiver's end, as he may interpret certain words differently than the way the sender intended them.

Take for instance: *"Whatever the cost, this project must be a success!"* Does this mean that you as project manager do not have to keep track of the costs? Of course not, but I do remember a situation in which the project manager did indeed think that he no longer had to watch the costs.

But also the channel has an effect on the way in which the message is received. If you say something to someone in a café, it is possible that it is not heard properly because of the noise. When you write a letter, this comes across differently than when you send an e-mail message. An important e-mail message in an inbox containing another hundred messages, is read differently from that same e-mail message in an empty box. The (negative) influence of the channel on the message is called bias.

One person sends a message which is received by another person. During coding, during the transport and during de-coding distortion in the message may occur. The other person reacts, codes his message, chooses a channel, which may also contain bias, and then this message also gets decoded by the receiver (the original sender). This gives a total of six points where distortion is possible.

To make it even more complicated, whilst the sender is still coding parts of his message (he is talking), the receiver is already busy de-coding and reacting. He can do this by saying something, but more likely, he will show it through a non-verbal reaction, which

1.18 Communication

initiates a second flow of information. Each of the persons then becomes a sender and a receiver.

But that is not all, because the message induces a certain (internal) reaction from the receiver. In diagrammatic form, this is illustrated as follows:

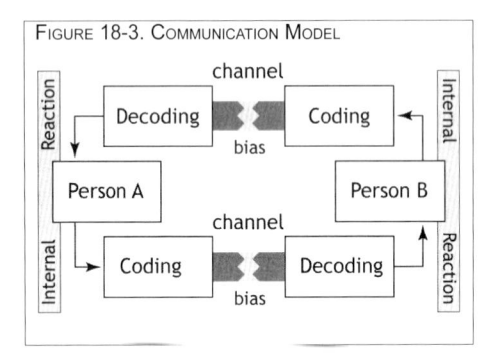

FIGURE 18-3. COMMUNICATION MODEL

This internal reaction from the receiver influences the way in which the receiver interprets the message (de-coding). The interpretation depends on someone's background, culture, family origins and life story. It is the frame of reference someone uses to approach the world. When you bring a team of ten people together, you have ten different frames of reference and when these ten people start talking about the project, they are really speaking about ten different projects.

Because the speed of our awareness is restricted with respect to the amount of information presenting itself to our senses, we are selective in what we observe. Partly this is intentional (we subscribe to one newspaper only, or none at all), and partly we do this unintentionally. We then talk of *selective perception*; we only observe what we want to hear. A good example of this is reporting to your project sponsor that there will be a delay. If this is unexpected, then the project sponsor does not want to, or cannot, hear this, so you try to bring it gently resulting in it not coming across.

Therefore, you area never completely sure if a message has come across, and so you always have to check this somehow. One way of checking this is by asking the receiver what he has understood from your message.

2. Verbal and Non-Verbal

In general, the various communication channels or media are sub-divided into *verbal* and *non-verbal*, whereby the former is that what you say, and the latter is that what you do. Researchers estimate that approximately 70% of our communication is non-verbal, but when we communicate about our feelings, then about 7% is verbal, 38% is in the sound of the voice, and as much as 55% is the body language[1].

Verbal communication

Verbal communication can be carried out in writing, electronically and orally, each one having its advantages and disadvantages. We have made a distinction between electronically and in writing. If you write a letter you do that differently than when you write an e-mail, or are chatting on MSN, or tweeting short messages.

The advantage of written communication is that you can take your time to think about your words, and the receiver has all the time necessary to let the information sink in. Furthermore, it is documented, so you can always look at your letter again later to see what was written. If the letter is handwritten, you can also create an impression of the writer from the handwriting. Written communication is a precise way of communicating; the sender reflects and the receiver reflects.

---

1 www.lichaamstaal.nl

1.18 Communication

That is the reason that contracts are usually in writing; the argumentation is easier. Manuals, and of course project management plans, are also examples of where written communication is the most obvious method. Written communication, however, also has its disadvantages, mainly the speed at which the sender obtains feedback from the receiver. If the receiver misunderstands the letter, the sender is not able to correct it, and with contracts for example, when lawyers are involved, the language used is often not even understood by the writers themselves. Later in court, it can sometimes turn out completely differently than expected.

Electronic communication falls between oral and written communication, because even though it looks the same communication, it is very different in nature. Just think about how e-mail works. You want to ask someone a question through e-mail, so you type in text, sometimes using the spelling checker but often not, and quickly press send. The standards regarding the use of spelling and style for e-mail are much lower than for a letter. Within seconds the receiver receives your e-mail. Sometimes he reads it immediately, but it may also take while. To be sure that someone opens your mail, you switch the reading confirmation on, but what you don't know is if this is also switched on in his e-mail program.

The receiver keys in the answers between your text, possibly with emoticon. Examples of emoticon are:

:-)   I am happy

:-(I am sad

;-)   wink

The receiver presses send and almost immediately you have your answer. When the receiver mails a lot, and his post box is full, there is a chance that he won't even see your mail. E-mail also has an 'escalating' dynamic which, once it has commenced, is hard to control. Rule: use e-mail to share information and NOT to enter into discussion!

Another form of electronic communication is chatting, where several "discussions" are held simultaneously, and in which you receive immediate feedback (though only verbal). Furthermore, we see more and more special intranets being set up, especially on international projects, in which all communication on the project is placed. The participants are then expected to regularly visit the relevant pages.

Non-verbal

Understanding non-verbal communication is a skill in itself. It is possible to make a list of body language "expressions", and attach a meaning to them. It would then be sufficient to learn them, and armed with that knowledge, interpret the other person.

This list could be long, but this is not what it is about in recognizing non-verbal communication. What is important is that you learn to observe better, initially with regard to yourself, and then with regard to others. The problem with non-verbal communication is that you are never completely sure what a certain pose means, and therefore we do not provide a long list here with an explanation of every body sign.

It becomes especially interesting when the verbal and non-verbal communications do not match. The project member who says he will be finished on time, but continuously looks the other way, or a business relation who says he is not angry, but who has red blotches on his neck.

1.18 Communication

Incongruence may be a sign that someone says something different to what he means, and because the body really never lies, you know that you have to ask some more questions. This technique is also useful for selection interviews.

Another way to look for non-verbal signals is to follow eye movements. Nissink[2] provides a simple method for doing this, based on the assumption that when people are speaking the truth, they look briefly to the left or right, and if they are not speaking the truth, they firstly look the other way. As this is different for everyone, the first thing you have to do is calibrate the eye movements of the other person. To do this you ask five clear, unambiguous questions related to events in the past, whereby in answering, the other person has no reason not to tell the truth (e.g. was it easy to find?). Observe which way the person looks. Then repeat this using questions related to the future, and again watch the eye movements. Because you have to "make up" the future, the eyes move in the same direction as when someone is lying.

3. The five axioms of Watzlawick

Paul Watzlawick (1921-2007), an Austrian-American psychologist, is one of the foremost communication scientists in the World, and has 18 books (in 85 different languages) and over 150 articles and chapters to his name. He has become well known predominantly for the five communication axioms[3] he formulated:

1. One cannot not communicate.
2. Every communication has a content and relationship aspect such that the latter classifies the former and is therefore a meta communication.
3. The nature of a relationship is dependent on the punctuation of the partners communication procedures.
4. People communicate in both digital and analogue modes.
5. Every communication exchange is either symmetric or complementary, depending on whether it is based on equality or difference.

These rules are very helpful in unravelling miscommunications. I will briefly discuss each of these five, and what they mean for communication in projects.

Axiom 1: One cannot not communicate

> EXAMPLE 18-3 AXIOM 1
> The project team is working hard to meet the agreed deadlines, and the project manager is completely focussed on the team to ensure that everything is being dealt with. In dealing with the everyday issues, he completely forgets the progress report. A week later the project sponsor calls him to account.

There is no such thing as anti-behavior, even if someone does nothing, his behavior will be interpreted by the (often unintended) receiver, usually unfavorably. This means that as project manager you have to be aware of the effect of everything you do and do not do, because generally interested parties will interpret it just slightly differently to what is desired.

Note that in the theory of communication, all forms of behavior are considered to be communication, including speaking, although this is not essential for communication. People interpret behavior in a certain way. An interesting observation is that in general people explain behavior in others that they do not understand by saying that the person in question is the problem, and they often explain their own behavior as being a consequence of the environment.

---
[2] (2002) *Je bent sprekend je lichaam*, Ed Nissink, ANKH-HERMES, Deventer
[3] (1967) *Pragmatics of human communications*, Watzlawick, NORTON & COMPANY, New York

For example: When others get into financial difficulties, it is their own fault, but if we encounter these problems ourselves, it is due to the situation. People have more consideration for themselves than for others. This phenomenon is called the *fundamental attribution error*[4]. It means that when people interpret behavior, this is usually unfavorable for the person whose behavior is being interpreted.

Axiom 2: Every communication has a content and relationship aspect

> EXAMPLE 18-4 AXIOM 2
> It is the first day at work for a new project member, and after meeting her new colleagues she meets with the project manager. The project manager tells her about the purpose of the project and what he expects of her. After the meeting she realizes that the project manager is not someone you should get into an argument with.

Initially communication seems just to be about the content; the information (content) you want to convey to the listener. However, but that thought is a bit too simple. There is always a hidden second message, which involves the behavior you expect from the other person.

This second message says something about the relationship, about how the other person should take the message, for example:
- This is an order.
- This is a joke.
- This is a plea.
- Who are you to say this?

You see the last example happening when two team members have a profound discussion concerning content they cannot agree on. The content hides a message of: *"Who are you that I should listen to you?"* In short,

---

4 (1977) *The intuitive psychologist and his shortcomings: Distortions in the attribution process in Advances in experimental social psychology (vol. 10, pp. 173–220)*, Ross, L. New York: ACADEMIC PRESS.

if the relationship has not been agreed on, the content will not come across.

The message at the relationship level contains several components simultaneously:
- This is how I see myself.
- This is how I see you.
- This is how our relationship towards each other is.

A description of yourself, a description of the other person, and a description of the relationship are all three expressed both verbally and non-verbally. It is a message to the other person containing a behavior assignment: *"See me as I see myself and join me in this relationship"*. The other person can react to this by accepting, refusing or ignoring. The first two are clear for both parties, and in the case of ignoring, the receiver avoids the choice.

You can ignore by using disqualifications, such as: silences, or starting to talk about something else, feigning a headache, not finishing sentences, making jokes, talking incoherently etc. *Disqualifying* is a technique with which you can say something without really saying it; you really want to say no, but instead of saying no, you display it.

Axiom 3: The relationship depends on the punctuation

> EXAMPLE 18-5 AXIOM 3
> The project manager carries out a performance appraisal with one of his employees. The discussion runs as follows:
> PM : *I want you to take more initiative!*
> Employee: *I would like to do that but you are so directive, I don't know what I can, and what I can't, do.*
> PM : *I am so directive, because you do not take any initiative.*

There is a punctuation problem when the people involved interpret each others behavior as a reaction to the behavior of the

1.18 Communication

other. When there is a different interpretation, both parties have sown the seeds for an ongoing conflict. The relationship suffers from this, with the result that also the content does not come across properly. In this case there is only one good solution: let bygones be bygones, and in clear language say what you expect of each other and how you plan to carry on together in the future.

Axiom 4: people communicate in both digital and analogue modes

EXAMPLE 18-6 AXIOM 4
The employee is red in the face when he leaves the project manager's office.

Digital communication is concerned with the rational message, the information one person wants to convey to the other. Analogue communication is everything to do with the relationship. Initially, we think of non-verbal communication i.e. the body language, but there are other forms of analogue communication, for example: speaking in metaphors and the intonation of the words used. Furthermore, "having a dig at someone" is also a form of analogue communication.

Digital information is very concrete; an extensive progress report with Earned Value numbers is a form of digital communication. However, a remark of the type: *"The changes are streaming in through every nook and cranny."* says a lot more than the digital EVA numbers. In the latter case something resounds through the message such as *"Help, I can't handle it anymore."*

Axiom 5: Communication can be symmetric or complementary

EXAMPLE 18-7 AXIOM 5
There is a heated discussion between the CEO and the project manager. The former demands that the latter leaves certain information out of the public report, but the project manager refuses to budge.

This axiom is concerned with how parties react to the relationship message. There are two options each with two poles. We call a reaction symmetric when the exchange is aimed at achieving as much equality as possible, whereas complementary is characterized by as big a difference as possible.

A symmetric reaction is about "together" compared to "against". A complementary reaction is about "above" as opposed to "below".

4. Four aspects - Schulz von Thun

Schulz von Thun (1944) has further elaborated on Watzlawick's second axiom, and differentiates between four layers in a message[5]:
- The matter layer (Watzlawick's "content").
- The expressive layer.
- The relational layer (Watzlawick's "relationship").
- The appealing layer.

By recognizing the different aspects in a communication it is possible to prevent, unravel and possibly resolve, miscommunication. I shall briefly discuss these four aspects by looking at what each aspect means for, and what can go wrong, in a project management situation.

The matter layer

Similar to the content aspect and the digital communication we already came across with Watzlawick. The sender has to ensure that he clearly brings his message across. The receiver listens attentively and asks questions when he doesn't understand something. Von Thun differentiates two possible problems here where, with regard to this aspect, it might go wrong: content only and comprehensibility.

---

5 (1977) *Kummunizieren lernen (und umlernen)*, F. Schulz von Thun,

1.18 Communication

PROBLEMS WITH CONTENT ONLY
Wouldn't project management be easy if we could focus on the rational side. Matters would be clear and measurable, and many technical project management competence elements focus on exactly that. Whether this makes the profession more enjoyable remains to be seen. Projects are people and people make projects successful and enjoyable (or boring).

In difficult team meetings it is tempting to say: *"Let's stick to the content and behave professionally"* (i.e. without emotion). Usually such a request works counter-productive, and all kinds of hidden agenda's occur.

However, you have to do something with this, because, as we saw with Watzlawick, as well as "*content*" you also have "*relationship*", and as long as the relationship has not been settled, the content will not come across properly. A solution is to now and again discuss what is happening conversationally, i.e. consciously communicate about communication itself. Both the sender and receiver constantly have to ask themselves: *"Is this about the content, or do I have a hidden agenda?"*. One of your tasks *as* project manager is to carry out such interventions when "*relationship*" causes miscommunication with regard to the business aspects.

PROBLEMS IN THE COMPREHENSIBILITY
In his research, Von Thun establishes that on average, no more than one third of the information comes across to the receiver, with the main cause being that the text used is too complicated. There are four means to improve comprehensibility of text: simplicity in style, structure, conciseness and attractiveness. These are skills which would not go amiss for project managers, and you should make time for these aspects.

The French scientist Blaise Pascal (1623-1662) wrote[6]: *"The current letter is rather long, and that came about because I did not have sufficient time to shorten it."*

Even though the above statement referred to written text, the message is clear, take your time! For both oral and written communication, preparation time is required before the definitive communication (sending the letter or starting the conversation) can take place.

For a project management report, this means providing insight into the current status by using simple words and easy to understand numbers. Not, therefore, as one of my course participants did, including an Earned Value Analysis in the progress report without any prior notification.

The expressive layer
What does the sender show of himself? How much does he hide, and how much of what we see is, in fact, our perception. The word personality is derived from the Latin word *persona,* the term for the mask the actor, in ancient classical times, wore during his performance. Does our personality then have something to do with the mask behind which, for our environment, we hide? And is this because we are afraid to show too much of ourselves?

There is some truth in that. There are two types of techniques both of which are concerned with "the fear of exposing yourself": *impress* and *façade* techniques.

TECHNIQUES TO IMPRESS
We often see this when colleagues call top managers by their first name, use elitist language, or casually say very positive things about themselves. It may be the sub-project manager, who recently *"talked to Bill (the CEO) at a reception about the completion of*

---
6 (1656) *Lettres Provinciales XVI*, Blaise Pascal

his 75 million dollar project". Another often used technique to impress, is moving the conversation towards a subject that one has a lot of knowledge of. I have the tendency to tell people how many books I have read; I'm wondering what effect this has on the receivers, and what I actually achieve by it.

Impressing techniques are aimed at showing off your best side.

TECHNIQUES TO MASK
The so-called façade techniques do the opposite; they mask someone's negative aspects. Pretending to be calm when inside you are turbulent, not showing any weaknesses, not asking any questions, obeying, etc. This can be either conscious or unconscious.

A lot has to do with how we were brought up, what our parents disapproved of, and what not.

A project manager who acts tough, but muddles on when he really should have asked for the help of his project sponsor, uses a façade technique which is harmful to the project and, if he does it often, also in the long run for his career.

THE CONSEQUENCES
So, neither of the techniques mentioned advance the communication. Awareness and self-knowledge are the first steps in doing something with this, but do realize that these techniques often try to protect painful aspects of someone's psyche, and that you have to be careful with interventions at this level. It is better to correct this in yourself when necessary, and only if you have a good, trust based relationship with employees, can you confront them with this.

The relational layer
This is similar to a part of Watzlawick's relationship message, and it is about what the sender thinks of the receiver, and what he thinks of the mutual relationship. You can differentiate two dimensions in the relational aspect of the message:

- Appreciation - Contempt.
- Steer – Give a free hand.

APPRECIATION – CONTEMPT
The way in which a project manager expresses himself with regard to his employees determines how they feel, and how they will behave in the team. If you speak to your employees in a tone, which allows them to speak to you in the same tone without jeopardizing the relationship, then there is equality. Togetherness incites togetherness.

As opposed to contempt, appreciation ensures this reversibility in the communication. A sentence like: "*The least you can do is be on time.*" does not invite constructive communication and when the other person feels offended, then "the shutters close". It is difficult for the other person to carry on the conversation in the same tone. He now as to choose between yielding, with the accompanying feeling of inferiority, or protesting and entering into the conflict. Opposition incites opposition. In any case, the business aspect of the communication will be completely lost.

DIRECT – GIVE A FREE HAND
By directing, you strongly try to influence the actions of others. Many project managers have little time and are very busy, because they confuse being results oriented with directing. The more you direct, the more the employees remain incompetent. Remember that you also want your project sponsor to give you a free hand. Above incites under, with all the uneasy feelings that brings.

1.18 Communication

The appealing layer
This is the second part of Watzlawick's relationship message and the way in which the receiver reacts to it. Now it is about that what motivates the receiver's behavior. When a project manager clearly states that all changes have to go via him, the question is whether that appeals sufficiently to the motives of the employees to heed his request.

The appealing aspect can take place either openly or it can be hidden. In the latter case it is not clear to the receiver that he is being influenced, and he is, in fact, being manipulated. With manipulation, it is important for the receiver to realize what the appealing aspect of the message is in order for him to then determine whether or not he is going to comply with it. In most cases, when someone else manipulates you, it gives you an uneasy feeling, and it is important to be aware of this. What is your body doing? What are you feeling? What are you thinking? What are you inclined to do?

The sender, or the manipulator, normally does this unconsciously, as it is behavior he acquired in his development and somehow it is effective. You always have people in a team who complain, and in this way manage to gain attention. By looking at the (unconscious) purpose of the behavior, you get an idea of what actually appeals. The question is then, what does this evoke in me? Do I want this? After this, you make a conscious choice.

5. Levels in group discussions
The levels that play a role in Group discussions are more complex. Among other things, Remmerswaal[7] differentiates the following levels:

- *Content* of the group task.
- *Procedure*, concerning the way in which the group members work together.
- *Interaction*, about the relationship pattern (relationships) within the group.

The above classification helps when:
- A team meeting is not running smoothly.
- The energy level falls.
- Some points take a lot of time.
- No decisions are being made.
- It seems as if there are issues at play, which have not been brought onto the table.

When this is the case, the above classification assists in finding the right interventions.

Content
Questions you then have to ask are[8]:
- Is all relevant information known by everyone?
- Should we invite a specialist?
- Are we all talking about the same thing?
- Is the objective clear for everyone?

Interventions that work when the problem is concentrated on the content are aimed at clarifying the task, content or solution. You ensure that every team member has his say, the necessary information is supplied, etc.

Procedure
Questions, and we again quote from Oomkes, that you pose are:
- Have agreements been made about the procedure?
- Is the procedure clear for everyone?
- Is everyone in agreement?
- Is there a chairman?

---

7 (2000) *Handboek Groepsdynamica,* Jan Remmerswaal, NELISSEN, Baarn

8 (1994) *Training als beroep,* Frank R. Oomkes, BOOM, Amsterdam

1.18 Communication

- How do we ensure that everyone get the chance to make his contribution?
- How are decisions made?
- Will a vote be held or not?

At this level, it is about the way in which everyone in the group co-operates with one another. It is, for example, important in meetings to have an agenda, to ensure someone takes minutes and that there is a chairman. The way in which decisions are taken, and when these can later be challenged, must be clear. The larger the group, the more rules that are required to organise the communication properly. Interventions at this level are concentrated on the one hand on the structure of the communication process, and on the other hand on providing the right conditions for everyone to be able to communicate well with each other (room, frequency, infrastructure, etc.)

Interaction
Where the previous level is about the extent to which the 'formal' side of the communication has been arranged, in this level it is more about the actual interaction with each other. It has to do with the relationship level mentioned earlier, but now with the effect it has on the group interaction, something we often forget about.

Questions arising here, and we shall stay with what Oomkes had to say about this, are:
- Do people have respect for each other?
- Do people react to each other, and how?
- Do some people ignore each other?
- Are certain people's suggestions always dismissed?
- Is there a fight for influence?
- Are there power blocks?

Interventions, which are now aimed at the content or at the procedure, will not work when people have no belief or trust in each other. These examples possibly point to a 'storming' stage which was not properly completed. Now it is important to say something about the two-way communication, and to make it a subject of discussion. Initially, this is the responsibility of the project manager, but he has to be aware that he is also part of the two-way communication, and that people may not want to see him as leader. In such a case, an external facilitator may provide a solution.

6. Presentation Skills

Objective and target group
Just as for a project, the preparation for a presentation is important. Especially when a lot is depending on it, a good preparation is vital. Planning a presentation starts with a draft and moves to fine-tuning.

Initially you think about:
- The *purpose* of the presentation, is it about information transfer, or do you want the listeners to change their behavior?
- With respect to *the target group*, what is their level of education, what are their expectations, and what is your position in relation to them?

Don't go into detail until you are able to describe in one sentence what the objective is of want you to achieve. That, together with your knowledge of the people who will be listening to your presentation, determines your strategy, so try to describe this in one sentence as well. This test ensures that it stays simple; it is only entertainers and trainers who know how to captivate their audience over a long period of time. As people can only remember a restricted amount of information, you should not want to achieve too much at a time.

Another question you have to ask yourself during this stage is who will be giving the presentation. It is the final result that counts, and so here too the rule is the right man or woman in the right place. Obviously, it is true that when you are the person giving the presentation, you might be noticed in a positive sense, but of course no one wants to be reminded of someone who, with a red face and gasping for breath, stammers on for thirty minutes. You waste a lot of your time if you insist on doing the presentation yourself, and then make a complete mess of it, although on the other hand, the only way to learn is to practice a lot.

As well as this, there is also the consideration as to who the best person is to bring across the message in question, and again it is the result that counts. In some situations it is smarter to have the project sponsor bring the message, and in other situations it will be you, as project manager.

Preparation
Once the choice of the speaker has been made, the preparation commences. A good title is essential, as it will provide all the invitees the opportunity to decide whether or not to come. In any event the title has to be catchy, and this can be achieved by conveying concisely what the presentation is about. The latter does present the risk that people will come with expectations which are different to what you, as presenter, are able to meet.

EXAMPLE 18-8 SENDER - RECEIVER CORRESPONDENCE
A young personnel officer told a department, consisting mainly of people aged fifty plus, how good it was that early retirement was being replaced by a pre-pension scheme. His age alone was reason enough for the presentation to fail.

All good presentations have an opening, a core (the "body") and a conclusion.

THE OPENING
- Points at the objective.
- Connects with the audience.
- Connects to your approach.
- Is catchy.
- Has both a verbal and a visual aspect.

During the opening the listeners mentally make the decision whether or not they want to listen to you, and in any case, that has to do with the topic. The preparation is, therefore, important, so you can connect with the expectations of your audience. If you know who the speaker before you is, you can start to empathize somewhat with that presentation, which will help you if you need to build a bridge across to your own presentation.

Also adapt your attire to the audience and the message you are bringing! In general you should wear the same, or a similar, style of clothing as your audience. However, this is not a hard and fast rule, and you might decide you want to make a big impact through the clothes you wear.

THE CORE
- What do you want to get across.
- Describe what you want to do.
- Does the language used match to the audience.
- Use as few words as possible.

The opening is the bridge to the core of your argument. It is possible to write the text out in full, but reading from a script during the presentation does not provide a strong impression. Once you have written it in full, it is better to make summary, and use this as a guideline during the actual presentation.

If you are certain of your content, you can be confident that you can present it in front of a group of people. You must adjust the language you use to your audience, so you must think about the words with which you are going to put the message across. This is also the usefulness of writing it down, because it helps you with the formulation. Think about the arguments you will use to make your point, and use arguments that match to your audience.

THE CONCLUSION
- Three short sentences summarizing the presentation.
- What actions should be taken as a result of the presentation.

Just as the opening provides a bridge to the core of the presentation, so the conclusion is a bridge to the future, and particularly to what you want to achieve from the presentation.

Tools, design and environment
Even though the core of your message is the most important, the design also plays a part, whereby you must always bear in mind that the design has to be supportive of the text.

TOOLS
- Support the core.
- In compliance with the available time.
- Connect with the video beamer.
- Are any slides properly arranged in the folder.
- Are there handouts of the presentation.

An American saying goes: *"The cheaper the merchandise, the higher the gloss"*, and that certainly applies to presentations. When preparing a presentation, it is tempting to put the most energy into the design, but this is a trap you have to avoid.

If the story is good and you are a good presenter, the design is less important.

Powerpoint has inundated us with many slides and even more text. The best thing is not to make the slides until after your story is ready, after which you look for text and illustrations that support your story. This is different text from the one you are presenting from, and consists of short keywords, which are easily readable.

Even though they provide almost unlimited possibilities, it is best to use sound and animations sparingly, because it is difficult to adjust your pace to these.

TIMING
Also make sure your timing is good.
- Is there a time estimate?
- Every slide approximately 3 minutes
- Do you have a margin of at least 10%

If at all possible, explore the room where the presentation will take place. You can then begin to somewhat mentally prepare yourself for the presentation.

ENVIRONMENT
- Where is everything?
- Readable from all corners of the room?
- Is the room big enough?
- What sources of distraction are there?

Mental preparation
This depends on the importance, and the pressure you experience at the presentation, but we list a number of points you can think about beforehand:

- Anticipate questions:
  o Which questions can you expect.
  o What answers do you have to these.
- How do you involve the audience.
- How are you going to move about.
- What are your feelings with regard to the presentation.

- What are your feelings with regard to the people in the audience.
- Who do you find sympathetic.
- Who do you find unsympathetic.
- Which questions do you fear the most.
- How motivated are you.
- Is it your idea or someone else's.
- What is your biggest fear.

The presentation itself
The best way to learn how to present, is through practising a lot. Obviously, you must then learn from what happened.

- What happens to you during a presentation?
- How do you react to questions?
- Does it come across?
- Preparation time versus presentation time.

Always try to be honest about these matters, because if a presentation is not going as planned, it requires courage to acknowledge it. Be self-critical, as only then can you learn from the experience you gained during the presentation.

7. Meeting
In a project environment, we are frequently involved in meetings and, as project manger, you will often experience someone who, at the end of a meeting, says with relief: "Now we can get on with our work again". Project teams benefit from meetings that take place only when they are necessary, and when they are also run efficiently.

Meetings in projects
Each project has a formal meeting structure, which is described in the project plan. The following is described for each meeting: the frequency, the objective, the participants and who the chairman is.

Examples are:
- Steering Committee meetings.
- Project (management) team meeting.
- Team meetings.
- Discussions with the end users.

Based on the organization chart, the project manager determines in advance what discussions and meetings are necessary and desirable. In addition he has to consider what the normal way of holding and running a meeting within an organization. The basic principle is that everyone from the top to the bottom is involved in one or other form of meeting ("linking-pins"). This ensures that everyone receives the necessary information, and is in a position to report on the progress of his or her work.

As well as the formal meeting structure, an informal discussion structure also exists, which is dependent on peoples needs. This can be a positive, but also a negative, sign. Positive, when the employees in the project develop a certain form of self-management that is complementary to what has been thought out beforehand, but negative when it arises out of necessity, because the formal structure is lacking. In the latter situation, it is advisable to change the formal structure in such a way that this does satisfy the need.

When we look at the nature of meetings, we can make the following differentiations:
- The meeting serves to *transfer information* from the management to the underlying levels or vice-versa.
- The meeting serves *to provide a picture* of the current situation, in which the higher levels of management are looking for information on particular issues.
- The meeting serves to *(collectively) arrive at a decision or a solution.*

1.18 Communication

INTERVENTION TABLE

In the table below, we describe a number of problems during meetings, and which interventions you, as chairman, can carry out:

Problem	Intervention
A team member lapses into a long-winded story.	Stop the participant and summarize essence of what he has said.
A team member strays off the subject.	Consciously ignore the participant, or stop him, remark on the digression and ask if he was aware he had started on a different subject. If so, park the subject and come back to it later (if necessary, in another meeting).
A team member talks about a subject that will be covered later anyway.	Stop and point out the agenda content.
A team member gets onto his hobbyhorse.	Stop the team member, recognise that it is an important issue for him, and refer to the agenda.
A team member initiates a non-urgent discussion, but one which involves a matter of principle.	Stop the discussion, indicate that the meeting is not intended for the subject matter initiated, and point out other urgent points. If necessary, plan another session to address this subject.
A team member raises a procedural question.	Request a proposal, try to discover what the precise issue is, and then make a proposal yourself.
The discussion stalls.	Summarise the most important points and ask open questions.
Smouldering conflicts that are not brought to the surface.	Bring the conflict onto the table. Express the feelings of the group: *"I thing that there is more happening under the surface than we are prepared to discuss with each other; maybe we should take a short break."*
Participants do not take the meeting seriously.	Tackle someone about their behaviour by giving some positive feedback. Formalise the meetings more.
The meeting goes slowly.	Continuously provide short summaries and pose closed questions.

Depending on the status of the team members not all interventions are applicable.

1.18 Communication

In general you can state that meetings should not last too long and must not try to cover too many points in one go. In the event of the latter, it is better to split up the meeting.

A meeting is necessary when:
- Mutual communication, back and forth, is needed.
- Available knowledge and information is fragmented.
- The problem to be solved is unclear.
- There is otherwise a risk that a conflict will arise.
- The group has to come up with a solution.
- Support within the team is necessary.
- Team building is desirable.
- Everyone needs to acquire the information at the same time.

There are situations for which it is not necessary that the whole team meets, for example when:
- It is only relevant for a part of the team.
- It is routine and/or extremely urgent.
- It is above the competence level of the group.
- Preliminary investigation or discussion is necessary.

The alternatives for a discussion can be:
- Memo, letter, e-mail, intranet
- Telephone or one-to-one discussion
- Video

From the start, it is important to work on an effective meeting habit. We can describe a number of symptoms of a meeting culture that is not effective:
- Necessity for, and objectives of, meetings are absent.
- Meetings regularly overrun.
- There are no breaks.
- People table new agenda items.
- The participants are badly prepared for the meeting.
- The agenda is not completed.
- There is a small group who do the talking, and the rest are just onlookers.
- The participants talk mainly about the mistakes of others.
- Too many debates, discussions, digressions and repetitions.
- Emotions regularly flare up.
- A pursuit of consensus is crippling.
- Decisions are taken too quickly.
- The agenda item "any other business" takes too long.
- There is no list of actions and decisions.
- Actions are not completed.
- Agreements are not adhered to.

The basic principle is that we do not hold a meeting if it is not necessary. If you decide to hold a meeting, ensure that it is well prepared.

Preparing for meetings
During the preparation, you should decide on, and arrange, the following:
- What is the objective?
- Which subjects are to be covered?
- Who is present and in which role?
- The drawing up and sending out of an agenda.
- Are there any guest speakers?
- Who is the chairman and who will take the minutes?
- The time and location of the meeting.
- Requirements for the location.

The objective of the meeting determines the attendees and the agenda. When compiling the agenda, you must take account of the priority of the agenda points; the most important at the top, the less important ones lower down. It can also be useful to firstly have one or two agenda points, which will have a positive effect on the atmosphere.

1.18 Communication

There is a difference between:
- Closed agenda points, such as announcements and facts.
- Half-closed agenda points, about which the chairman will ask for advice from the participants, but ultimately will make a decision himself.
- Open agenda points to collect opinions and ideas, and then possibly to make a collective decision.

The chairman, conscious of the objectives and of the participants, decides which strategy is best. Just as with negotiations or presentations, a meeting can be seen as a small project. The key question is always: what is the objective, what do I want to achieve, and what am I willing to do for that.

If it is a long meeting, you should beforehand ensure there is enough variation and sufficient breaks, coffee, tea, soft drinks and maybe even a snack in between. For the smokers, in the current climate of anti-smoking, you should pay extra attention to smoking breaks. All these are issues you can consider beforehand.

You also decide beforehand who will take the minutes. The person chosen also prepares for the meeting by studying the various subjects, pondering how the meeting is structured and in what form to record the minutes. Preferably, he discusses this with the chairman.

The other participants should receive the papers for the meeting some time beforehand, so that they have the opportunity to study them sufficiently. In fact, you should only start a meeting if all the participants have prepared themselves adequately.

Traditional meeting
In general, the agenda looks as follows:
- Opening.
- Agree the meeting procedure.
- Incoming correspondence.
- Announcements.
- Minutes of the previous meeting.
- Go through the action list.
- The subjects.
- Other points for discussion.
- Any other business or questions.
- Summary of the most important decisions and actions.
- Close.

The meeting itself
You should always start a meeting on time; if you wait until everyone has arrived, you *reward the latecomers, and punish the people who were on time*. Further, you try to ensure that the different subjects are allocated sufficient time.

The action list
A meeting must al least result in a number of actions being removed from, and a number of actions being added to, the agenda. Every action must be allocated a number, a start date, a planned completion date, who is responsible for it, and a clear description of the action.

When checking the status, the meeting constantly asks itself to what extent a particular action must remain on the list. Actions that are continuously slipped, have a very demotivating effect, and if this happens each time for certain actions, you can better remove them from the list.

Post meeting action
Following the close of the meeting, someone produces the minutes and distributes them. It is important that this is done quickly, whilst the meeting is still fresh in the participants' minds, and they, based on the action list,

can transfer the actions for which they are responsible, onto their own action list.

In addition, it can be necessary to quickly incorporate the decisions taken into the plan.

A cultural perspective on meetings
In some cultures in which relationship building is important, like in the Middle East, informal meetings may be more frequent than formal meetings. Regardless of any official meeting structure, people will get together anyhow. Personal relationships are the basis for trust. And without trust there will be no business. To sort out problems, brief chats or telephone calls are preferred to memos or e-mail. Formal meetings do take place of course, but are mainly for the transfer of information or to provide a picture of the current situation rather than for decision making on the spot. Major decisions or solutions to complex problems are often prepared during small and more or less informal get-togethers involving managers and key stakeholders before being tabled at the formal meeting. If this informal process has been successfully completed (in some cases this may take a rather long period) the discussion during the formal meeting may be just a formality.

So a Dutchman, being a product of a task-oriented culture, may get confused when attending a meeting in the Arab world. Instead of the somewhat rigorous and highly structured approach he is used to in meetings at home, the atmosphere he encounters will be more relaxed. For example, there may be more small talk at the start of the meeting which may be seen by the Dutchman as a waste of time ('let's move on and get the work done'), but may be considered by his Arab partners as a useful way to tune the mood in the meeting room into a positive atmosphere before making decisions. Here an atmosphere of trust rather than a binding action list is the best guarantee that people will actually stick to the agreements and promises that have been made.

1.18 Communication

1.19 Start-Up

A GOOD BEGINNING IS HALF THE WORK

In contrast to the work in the line organization, initially, little or nothing has been organized for a project.

The start-up is the first 'real' stage of the project.

During this stage, the project sponsor, the project manager and his team ensure that the plans are expanded with more details, and that the business case is finalized.

Furthermore, they ensure that everything is ready, so that the employees can immediately start carrying out the work.

1.19 Start Up

1.19-1 DEFINITIONS

Decision document	Document, on the basis of which the project sponsor decides whether or not to continue with the project.
Kick-off	Meeting at the commencement of the project, or a stage in the project, to stimulate an effective and efficient execution of the project or stage.
Project contract	The agreement between the project manager and the project sponsor to carry out the project.
Project decision	The decision of the project sponsor to initiate the project.
Project definition	Outline description of the project.
Project initiation	The first stage of the project in which the foundation is laid for the execution.
Project preparation	The work prior to the project decision.
Project Start Up (PSU)	A structured meeting to draw up in draft form the decision documents for the start of the project initiation or project execution.

1.19-2 INTRODUCTION

The project development stage precedes a clear agreement on the content of the project, and the relevance of it for the organization. The moment the project manager becomes involved, is the beginning of the start-up. In order to start, there has to be a management request including an approved budget for this stage (decision to justify). This is the project contract together with the global project definition.

Often, the project contract that the project manager receives is insufficient, and he then has to work it out further into a, for him, acceptable level. The important elements of the contract are:

- The reasons for the project.
- The global project definition.
- The solution direction, described functionally. This is, therefore, not the definitive solution, but that which the project result has to do for the organization.
- Constraints that the approach and result have to comply with.
- The resources available to him during the project start.

During this stage, and in consultation with interested parties, the project manager works out the project definition in more detail, whereby as a minimum, the following issues must be discussed:

- What the position of the project is in the organization's strategy.
- The business case, or another formulation, of the costs and benefits to be achieved.
- A definition of the quality level, with clear and measurable acceptance criteria.
- Important risks.

Another important output document from this stage, is the project management plan containing a description of the way in which, the costs for which, and the time within which, the project team will deliver the required results.

1.19-3 PROCESS STEPS

1. Initiate the project start up.
2. Communicate project goals.
3. Develop a mission and vision.
4. Draw up a PM plan.
5. Gain acceptance for the plan.
6. Ensure co-operation.
7. Secure all resources.
8. Ensure a start up per stage.
9. Apply lessons learned.

1. Initiate the project start up
The project start up process takes place at least once per project. For projects with multiple stages, it may be necessary to hold another project start up prior to the decision to commence a following stage.

The main reason for this process is to draw up a (number of) decision document(s), on the basis of which, the organization can decide whether or not it is wise to start this project, or to continue with it.

2. Communicate project goals
All participants in this process must be aware of the overall goal of the project. By this we mean the goal the project sponsor wants to achieve with the result delivered by the project team.

At the start of the project, this goal is translated into a result, which the project sponsor and the other parties involved can agree to. Bear in mind that this is one step removed from the original goal. As project managers, we translate this result into sub-results, schedules, working methods and all kinds of other structures. Each breakdown is a step away from the original goal, and it is not unthinkable that during this structuring process, the project team loses sight of the ultimate goal, as sometimes even the project sponsor does.

It is, therefore, absolutely crucial for the applicability of the result, that you keep communicating the goals, and thus ensure a result is produced that the organization is expecting.

3. Develop a mission and vision
Based on the goal that forms the reason for existence (mission) of the project, the parties involved set up a vision of what they want to achieve, when the project will be finished, and what the best way of achieving this is.

A vision is:
- Expressive
- Directive
- Focussed
- Flexible
- Achievable
- Desirable
- Communicable

When all members of the project organization share this mission and vision, it provides a motivation, which will keep the parties involved alert during the execution.

4. Draw up a PM plan
During the project start, the scope of the work must become clear. This often means that an initial specification of the project result must be made, and the level of detail in this specification determines the accuracy of the budget. It is therefore important to clearly indicate in the project contract, the level of detail required when drawing up the specifications.

In order to make the right decision on this, the following must be clear:
- What is being delivered?
- How it will be made?
- What it will cost?
- When it will be finished?

Both to a high degree of accuracy.

1.19 Start Up

In order to make these pronouncements, the project management plan must at least contain the following elements:
- Project definition.
- Specifications.
- Conditions, dependencies and interfaces.
- Project plan.
- Reference to the Business Case.
- Risks.
- Project organization.
- Resources.
- Quality agreements.
- Project library set up.
- Control agreements.
- Communication plan.

A major pitfall in making the project management plan is copying parts of earlier projects, without critically asking yourself whether or not these are also relevant and required for the current project.

5. Gain acceptance for the plan

One part of gaining acceptance for the plan is the official acceptance by the project sponsor and the steering committee. But we also mean specifically obtaining support for the plan. That is also the reason why the main interested parties are involved during the start-up process.

This acceptance of, and support for, the plan is important, because during the execution you will regularly have to remind the interested parties of the promises they have made in the project management plan.

6. Ensure co-operation

These interested parties, or their representatives, form a team which draws up the decision documents during this stage, and the project manager ensures that there is a good co-operation between all these people.

The project manager summarizes the results of all discussions, meetings, negotiations and suchlike in an overall project management plan. The project management plan should be the result of this co-operation.

7. Secure all resources

A plan is just a plan and "*the proof of the plan is in the execution*". When the signatures have been placed, as project manager you must ensure that all parties actually comply with the agreements made. You can't start early enough with this, as it does not happen automatically by itself.

In addition to your communicative skills, the project management plan is now the best means to achieve this security. As people have agreed to it, by reminding these stakeholders, who must provide people, finances, resources and facilities, of their promises, you are heading in the right direction. When the promises are not kept, the plan (and the schedule) has to be amended and approved by the steering committee, where the "*real fight*" has to take place if you cannot find a solution. As project managers, we often have to educate the organization on the meaning of project based working.

8. Ensure a start up per stage

An acceleration of this whole process can be achieved by a Project Start Up (PSU). Together with the team members, the draft decision document is drawn up here in a brainstorm like setting. During this process, all kinds of negotiations take place between the participants.

The project manager is leading, sometimes supported by a moderator. Every team member (also suppliers) makes a contribution, and also gives his own commitment to it.

1.19 Start Up

Critical Success Factors for the PSU:
- Good preparation.
- All important parties present.
- Mandate for the participants to be allowed to make decisions.
- Firm leadership.
- Quick follow-up.

A Project Start Up is useful if:
- Many parties, who do not see each other regularly, participate.
- A lot of choices have to be made in the initial stage.
- There is little time before the start of the project.
- The risks of the project are high.
- There is a suspicion of insufficient support among the project participants.

9. Apply lessons learned

During the start up, a number of people might be working together for the first time. In this case, it could be a good plan to start evaluating this co-operation with each other right from the start, and to see where things can be improved.

10. Other standards and guidances

The process steps as identified by IPMA are only a suggestion. The process steps described in the *ISO 21500 Guidance*, the 'guide to the Project Management Body of Knowledge' (the *PMBOK Guide*) from the Project Management Institute, and in the popular PRINCE2 Project Management method are much more "binding". Without discussing it in detail I shall name, as a comparison, a number of items from these standards that are related to this competence element. What will be noticeable is the high level of similarity and overlap.

Both the ISO Guidance and the 5th edition of the *PMBOK Guide* contain a subject which cannot easily be fitted into the IPMA framework. It is the subject of Integration, which, because of its importance for project management success, will be discussed here.

ISO 21500
The Guidance deals with this topic in the process groups:
- Initiation
- Planning

PMBOK Guide
The processes of the 5th edition of *PMBOK Guide* are identical to those of the Guidance:
- Initiation
- Planning

PRINCE2
PRINCE2 covers this in the processes:
- Starting up a project
- Initiating a project

In Starting has the same purpose as Initiating in ISO and *PMBOK Guide* and Initiating the same as Planning in the other two standards.

1.20 Close-out

ONLY WHEN IT WORKS, DOES IT WORK

Finally, the delivery is followed by the commissioning of the result.

"*The proof of the pudding is in the eating.*"

This, of course, takes place in a planned and structured way.

It is desirable that an evaluation is carried out as to how the project went, and also that lessons are learned from the experience.

We often see that a subsequent project is started, before firstly carrying out an evaluation of the previous one.

1.20 Close Out

1.20-1 DEFINITIONS

Close-out	Completion of a stage, project or programme once the stage, project or programme deliverables have been provided.
Commissioning	Putting the project result into operational use.
Delivery	The legal handover of the project result to the customer.
Transference	The physical handover of the project result to the customer.

1.20-2 Introduction

The final stage in the project should be the "crown" on the work. It is at these times that the project sponsor states his agreement, and the customer puts the delivered result into use.

Everything that happens in the project is aimed at achieving this.

In this respect, it is extremely relevant for a project manager, during the project, to look at all decisions, actions, events, issues and changes in the light of the question:

"Will it ultimately work?"

But this is somewhat too simple, because the close-out is not a one-off event. It is good practice to divide a project up into a number of stages, and to precede each stage with a short period, in which de project manager works out the schedule further in a detailed plan for the next stage, allowing the steering committee to decide whether or not to continue with the project. This is a decision which, for a major part, is dependent on the progress made in the previous stage.

Therefore, we close-out a project a number of times. At the end of each stage, we look back and process the insights acquired into a new plan. Ultimately, we reach the final stage in which the team delivers a working product, something that the customer can accept, but above all else, use. If sufficient evidence for the latter has been collected together, the project sponsor can discharge the project manager. If there is then good reason for a party, we celebrate the success achieved with the team members.

1.20 Close Out

1.20-3 Process Steps

1. Start to use the deliverables.
2. Formalise the completion.
3. Obtain customer feedback.
4. Plan the handover.
5. Assure warranty conditions.
6. Close contracts
7. Finalize financial transactions.
8. Hold a close-out meeting.
9. Release resources and assets.
10. Archive the Project file.
11. Issue final report.
12. Record and apply experience.

1. Start to use the deliverables

In each stage the team delivers something that is required in the following stage, and ultimately, in the last execution stage, the definitive and final result. Delivery is not a matter of simply chucking something over the wall, but something that happens in a number of steps, whereby the users continuously ensure that the correct project result has been delivered.

The essence of this process step is that the makers of a (sub) product realize that there are users, who need this product for their work. Therefore, I believe that the team member, the team, and the project manager are responsible for ensuring the next party in the chain is in a position to use what has been delivered in the way intended. The maker of the product is at least morally obliged to provide a form of "guarantee" for the work he delivers.

The last step is commissioning it, that is making the product work for the first time under operational conditions, and a planned approach to this is essential. Often the acceptance and commissioning is a separate stage of the project, sometimes followed by a period of shadow runs or a so-called pilot stage.

2. Formalise the completion

In order for him to start on the next stage, or close-out the project, the project manager needs to be discharged from his work at the end of a stage. Both the end of a stage and the end of a project should be formalized.

A formal completion is important as this motivates the stakeholders involved to carefully consider their decision to accept. Asking for a signature compels those involved to consider this decision thoroughly, and this is certainly necessary at the close-out of the project. Whether or not this is desirable at the end of a stage is dependent on the contractual obligations between the project sponsor and the project organization.

Before this can happen, it is necessary to determine whether or not everything has been delivered. To do this you compare the products with the specified Work Breakdown Structure, and in addition, by studying the acceptance documents and quality registers, you also need to assess whether or not the agreed quality has actually been delivered. If all the work has been carried out, you can initiate the formal completion.

Completion of a stage

In principle, the project manager produces two reports:
- Review
- Preview

In the review, which is sometimes also called a stage end report, he outlines in broad terms how the project has progressed, compares the actual situation with the original schedule and describes the lessons learned from the experience gained. This is the most important reason: learning lessons! He also gives his recommendations for the continuation of the project.

1.20 Close Out

As the project has not yet been completed, a preview or future outlook is also necessary. This translates itself on the one hand into the detailed plan for the next stage and the updating of the overall project plan, and on the other hand into an updated business case. Because we have progressed in time, there is now more information available, and this is much more accurate than at the start of the project. It is even possible that on the basis of the progressively more detailed insights, the management decides to stop the project or to radically change it. The advantage of this approach is that these choices can now take place in a structural manner planned in advance.

Completion of a project
This can only take place if the project manager has ensured that the most important stakeholders have agreed to what has been delivered so far. In the following processes, I shall explain this in more detail.

As well as the delivered product or result, the project manager also provides a project end report which includes an evaluation of the total project and also references the statement of acceptance for the delivery.

3. Obtain customer feedback
The term "customer" can have a broad meaning, but in this context we mean the people who are going to use the product, the end users. In a good project organization, these are represented in the decision making, but they often have less power than the project sponsor, who represents senior management.

The project sponsor must be continuously weighing up between costs, delivery times, quality and expected returns, whereas the users are predominantly interested in quality and ease of use. The choice of the project sponsor, therefore, is more difficult than that of the end user, but it is the end users who will soon be complaining about the product delivered, and possibly even refusing to use it.

Therefore, as project manager, you must ensure that the users have sufficient input into the project, for example by involving them in the specification and acceptance. In addition, you should also listen to what the users are saying when the project is in the end stage, and observe how they react to the delivered results.

4. Plan the handover
The handover to the end user implies that they have been well trained and aware of any changed work procedures. This training should be a part of the project scope.

As well as the end users, there is a second group of users of the delivered product, and this consists of the people that have to carry out the support and maintenance. This group can be easily forgotten, or become involved too late. You must realize that this is the group that has to resolve all the errors and problems that are still in the delivered product.

The planning of the handover should take place when it becomes clear which technical solution has been chosen and preferably even slightly earlier, by involving user representatives at the time the decision is made on the choice of the technical solution.

Before a handover to support and maintenance can take place, you must ensure that they have been sufficiently trained, and have sufficient resources, to carry out their tasks. To this end, and apart from the documentation, an updated configuration database should be available. It is my belief that you, as project manager, are responsible for

1.20 Close Out

this and that you cannot place it outside the scope of the project.

Another relevant point here relates to the issues that are still open, and which the project team can no longer resolve, such as problems that are still with the suppliers. If these issues are going to take some time to resolve, it is inefficient to keep the project team intact. A solution is then to hand over these points to support and maintenance, or another department in the line organization. Those responsible must then formally accept this list of open points.

5. Assure warranty conditions

If a supplier has managed the product, the project manager (and the responsible commercial people involved) must ensure that it is clear to the customer, which problems fall under the warranty, and for which problems a maintenance contract is necessary.

If the project has been internally managed, the project manager must ensure that good warranty agreements are made with the suppliers. Within the organization, there are often guidelines indicating how these matters must be handled and arranged.

Following the commissioning, end users will raise questions with the departments that are responsible for support and maintenance, and for the latter it is possibly the first time that they have to answer such questions on the product. It is useful, therefore, that a number of project team members are put on call for a few months for 2nd line support.

6. Close contracts

Insofar as you have not already done so, you must determine whether everything has been delivered according to contract before the completion of the project. This presents a number of possibilities:

- Everything has been delivered according to expectation.
- Something has been delivered according to expectation.
- There has been insufficiently delivered according to expectation.

Each of the above outcomes requires its own approach.

Everything
The ideal situation is when the supplier has delivered according to contract compliance. In order to verify this, you have to formally check and accept the supplier's deliverables, and this way of acceptance is something you should agree with the supplier and include in the contract clauses, thus preventing any subsequent surprises.

Something
If, during the project execution, the supplier has not delivered according to expectations, you must ask yourself how serious this is. If necessary, you discuss this with project sponsor and the user. It can then be that you accept anyway, but that you want compensation from the supplier. The possibilities that you have, are partially dependent on the clauses in the contract, partially on the benevolence of the supplier, and partially on prevailing legislation.

Insufficient
If, in your opinion, and that of the other decision makers in the organization, the delivery has been unacceptable, then a dispute situation exists that has to be resolved. Firstly, you try to come to an agreement with the supplier yourself, but if that does not succeed, it is possible to involve mediation, arbitration or even the courts. It is good practice to record in the contract what both parties do in the event of such a conflict.

1.20 Close Out

Formal termination

You should formally terminate each contract, whereby you discharge the supplier from his responsibilities. For straightforward deliveries, this can take place verbally or by e-mail. For more complex situations the supplier will require an acceptance document and, in this way, formally conclude his delivery.

7. Finalize financial transactions

This process step consists of more than the description implies. On the one hand, you are concerned with outstanding invoices, and on the other hand you are concerned with the handover of the financial aspects to the line organization.

Outstanding invoices

At the end of the project you must check whether or not all financial obligations have been completed according to the contracts in force. You have to hand over the invoices that are still outstanding, or still to be expected, to the responsible departments. A supplier's project manager must ensure that his organization knows which invoices still have to be sent. Furthermore, it is best to make a final overview of the ultimate costs.

The handover of financial aspects to the line organization

If you have used a time recording system, you must remove the project accounts, to which the team members have logged their hours, in order to ensure you do not get further hours booked against your project once you have completed it. In addition, the project possessions must be booked against the correct accounts in the bookkeeping.

This is dependent on the manner in which you deliver the project result. There are two possibilities:
- *Add* to the organization.
- *Integrate* in the organization.

When adding, a new part of the organization comes into existence as a result of the project, and when integrating, an existing department takes on the project result and subsequently starts using it. In the former situation, the bookkeeping adds a new cost centre to the general ledger. In both situations, any project possessions are transferred from the project administration to the regular administration, and it must be ensured that the correct booking of costs and receipts against the relevant cost centres takes place.

8. Hold a close-out meeting

Organizing a close-out meeting is a good way of making the completion of the project visible. The content of such a meeting is dependent on the way in which the project has come to an end.

EXAMPLE 20-1 CELEBRATING THE END

At the end of the last century, I was involved in a project that had a chequered history. It had already been stopped four times, and the project manager had been changed just as many times.

Together with a few colleagues, we had to get the project back on track, and this was only partially successful. Even before the end, I decided to go and work elsewhere.

I remained in contact with a number of colleagues and was, therefore, kept informed of the actual progress of the project.

About a half year after my departure, I received an invitation to an end-of-project celebration, together with all employees (about 300) who had ever been involved with the project. It was a luxurious party, although I had heard corridor chat that the project was nowhere near finished.

At the same time, a large reorganization was taking place, in which thousands of employees lost their jobs.

I declined the invitation – if you celebrate something, there has to be something to celebrate.

1.20 Close Out

Two scenarios (adding or by integration) have already been discussed. In the context of this process step, it is interesting to mention two other scenarios: *premature* end or the *slow death*. The role of this close-out meeting is dependent on the way in which the project ends.

Adding
In this situation, the majority of project employees often go and work in the new part of the organization. A project close-out meeting is then not suitable, as the team continues to function. It is then better to hold a meeting, in which the formal start of the new department (or sometimes the new company) is celebrated.

Integration
In this situation, the project team is disbanded and the team members return to their "home base". The break up of a group of people, who have worked together intensively, requires extra attention in whatever way you provide it. No one finds bidding farewell enjoyable, and it is a good idea, therefore, in this close-out meeting to dwell on the mutual experience, to thank everyone for his or her efforts, and to celebrate the success together.

Premature end
When the management decides, for whatever reason, to end a project prematurely, it is even more important than after a successful completion, to spend time with the team looking back over the project.

It is almost inevitable that a premature end leads to some disappointment and de-motivation, and by paying attention to these negative feelings, you can ensure that de team members understand senior management's decision, and, however painful it may be, leave the project behind.

It is desirable, therefore, to hold a close-out meeting, which does not have celebrating success as its theme, but which does have "therapeutic" value.

Slow death
This situation arises when no one dares (or will) recognise that the project is in reality, no longer viable. This is an undesirable situation, because somewhere in the background of the organization's consciousness it is still there, although in the operation, it no longer plays a meaningful role. It is then much better to disband the team, and put the project formally on hold. This seems a bit like the previous situation, with the difference that the project will be started up again, if feasible, at a later stage, but then as a new project and with a new team.

9. Release resources and assets
Normally, you work with people from different departments and suppliers. Near the end of the project you will release the people in a phased manner.

People
When you are going to release people, you inform them of this beforehand, the right thing to do is to hold an evaluation with the individual team members on their performance on the project. Dependent on the policy prevailing, you ensure that this evaluation reaches the responsible line manager.

You give the line managers of your team members a timely warning of when you will release people, and in this way you allow them to organise new assignments for those released. The same is valid for external suppliers, only more critical, as you are involved with the terminating of contracts.

Assets
The latter is also, of course, valid for tools and facilities you have hired. By terminating

1.20 Close Out

these agreements on time, you prevent incurring additional costs.

10. Archive the project file
The prevailing policy of the organization, for which you have carried out the project, is leading for these process steps. We have already seen that a project file can consist of the following parts:
- Management documents.
- Project plans.
- Technical plans.
- Technical documentation.
- Contract documentation.
- Minutes and reports.

The documents related to (legal) commitments have to be kept. Make a note in the project file of where the relevant documents have been archived. The technical documentation necessary for the use and maintenance of the product forms the handover documents, and you hand these over to the responsible departments. You record this in a handover document that also stays behind in the remaining project file. These records are necessary in case the documents are mislaid by the recipient. You have then covered yourself against such an eventuality.

You archive the other documents according to the available procedures related to this. For that matter, I know several project managers, who, for complete certainty, make a copy of all documents and retain these for a number of years. If you believe that doing this could be useful for some point later, then you should certainly do it.

11. Issue final report
It is tempting, when your project is finished, to directly start work on a new job and to just leave the final report for what it is. This is not a smart move, as the preparation of a final report is more than just a piece of bureaucracy. The process of writing something down forces you to dwell on what has happened, which ensures that you build up a better understanding of what has taken place. Putting the experience gained into words makes it sink in, because you cannot write something down if you do not understand it, and you should look at the final report as a moment of self-reflection.

The project's final report forces you to consider the history of the project. Of course, you are not the only person who provides information for this, and a number of interviews with others involved will enhance the value of this final report. In this report the following subjects are covered :
- Review by the project manager on the project performance.
- Evaluation of the business case (look back and look ahead).
- Evaluation of the project objectives.
- Evaluation of the team performance.
- Evaluation of the products delivered.
- Description of the lessons learned.

12. Apply lessons learned
It has already been mentioned in the previous process step, the recording of the experience gained and lessons learned in a final report. The recording of it is one thing, but applying it is quite another. I look at this from the following viewpoints:
- Organization.
- Project manager.
- Individual team members.

Organization
In this, the professional companies differentiate themselves from their weaker brethren. We often see a project management office that transforms the lessons learned into instructions for the organization for when they take on new projects. The aspects that went wrong can be seen back in a customized Risk Breakdown Structure, which can be reused in other projects.

1.20 Close Out

To facilitate this process, the project manager must provide a collection of recommendations that brings the project management office's attention to the improvement possibilities. When such a continuous improvement cycle is effectively implemented, you see that an organization delivers increasingly more successful projects.

Project manager
Even if the organization does not have a formal process to transfer the experiences gained across into subsequent projects, the project manager, himself, can do that. In the less professional organizations, which do have professional project managers in employment, we see that as time progresses, the latter develop their own sets of templates, checklists and suchlike for personal use, thus also creating a form of learning.

When the critical mass of project managers has reached a certain size, a call goes up for professionalization on an organization-wide scale, and when the management pays heed to this call, the organization grows in its maturity.

Individual team members
How do we now ensure that team members learn from their experience of working on projects? Generally, their attention is focused on gaining technical experience, as this is directly linked to their profession.

As project manager, how do you now make use of their experience of working on projects. You do that by, at the start of a new project, evaluating with your team members their last projects. The team then together looks at how you can apply these lessons in the current project.

13. Other standards and guidances
The process steps as identified by IPMA are only a suggestion. The process steps described in the *ISO 21500 Guidance*, the *'guide to the Project Management Body of Knowledge'* (the *PMBOK Guide*) from the Project Management Institute, and in the popular PRINCE2 Project Management method are much more "binding". Without discussing it in detail I shall name, as a comparison, a number of items from these standards that are related to this competence element. What will be noticeable is the high level of similarity and overlap.

ISO 21500
The Guidance deals with this topic in the process group Closing: and differentiates between the following processes:
- Close project phase or project
- Collect lessons learned

PMBOK Guide
The processes in the 5th edition of *PMBOK Guide* have some differences with the Guidance. The following processes are included:
- Close Project or Phase
- Close Procurements

PRINCE2
This is described in the processes "managing a stage boundary" and "closing a project".

Managing a stage boundary:
- Plan the next stage
- Update the project plan
- Update the business case
- Report stage end
- Produce an Exception plan

Closing a project:
- Prepare planned closure
- Prepare premature closure
- Hand over products
- Evaluate the project
- Recommend project closure

1.20-4 SPECIAL TOPICS

1. Project evaluation

The line management must use and translate the lessons we learn on projects into better ways of working. If a project management office exists, then that is the obvious department to carry out this task.

Projects often seek out the limits of the line organization, and because they transcend departments, they have a unique view of the organization. The experiences of a project, therefore, relate not only to the project, but also the complete functioning of the organization.

In order to learn the lessons as quickly as possible, it is not sufficient to just evaluate at the end. A review is worthwhile holding at each stage end, otherwise learning points get forgotten. Improvements in small steps is more effective (and more lasting) than an implementation in one big organizational improvement project.

Reflections when evaluating projects

It is clear that we want to learn from the past, but we all know the saying: *History teaches us that we learn nothing from history.*

This is the danger facing us when we evaluate the project. There are two forces at work, which can hinder a good project evaluation. One has to do with the project manager himself, and the other with what people are like. I mean:

- The project manager wants to start with his new project.
- No one enjoys being confronted with mistakes they have made.

How do you counterbalance these forces?

By keeping it simple and non-threatening, and by carrying out the evaluation directly after the completion; a short meeting with everyone involved, followed by an analysis and a short report containing conclusions and recommendations. This evaluation, consisting of a few pages, highlights experiences instead of mistakes made. A positive report, therefore (see insert).

The evaluation report does not provide any solutions, but describes experiences. By describing experiences in this way in the evaluation report, we provide the organization with a positive stimulus to develop itself into an environment in which projects become increasingly more successful.

The evaluation report is sent to the members of the steering committee, the project manager's manager, the project management office and all other job holders, who have an interest in the experience gained (other project manager colleagues).

EXAMPLE 20-2 WHAT'S WRONG?

During a project, it has repeatedly become apparent that one of the chairmen (Mr. X) of the workgroups was not able to effectively manage his part of the organization. As a result of this, the project overran by several months. One of the reasons for this was that the person in question did not have sufficient line authority to manage his part of the organization.

WRONG: The project has overrun by several months because the workgroup run by Mr. X frequently did not produce the required results. This is because Mr. X had insufficient line authority. Senior management must ensure that in future projects, Mr. X receives enough authority to manage his part of the organization.

RIGHT: Chairmen of workgroups with sufficient line authority to manage their part of the organization work better than when this is not the case.

1.20 Close Out

2. Behavioral Competences

2.01 Leadership

DOING THE RIGHT THINGS RIGHT

Being a leader is doing the right things, managing is doing things right. A project manager is both a leading manager and a managing leader.

Doing the right things is about courage, insight, passion, with the personality of the project manager.

Doing things right is about his professionalism; knowing how to apply different techniques in a way that is effective.

We sometimes say that you win the project with attendant leadership and lose it through absent management.

2.01 Leadership
2.01-1 Definitions

Coaching	Guiding an employee to independently find a solution to a work related problem.
Consensus	Decision forming method, whereby all participants share their knowledge and experience, in order to reach an agreement.
Delegate	Transferring own tasks, responsibilities and authorities to others.
Give an assignment	Telling an employee what he has to do.
Leadership	Providing direction to, and stimulating, others in the scope of their task and/or role fulfilment in order to achieve specific goals.
Motivate	Freeing up the individual responsibility, energy and effort of project members.

2.01-2 Introduction

Both managers and leaders are involved in directing and motivating people but there are many differences:

Managers	Leaders
Keep	Innovate
Copy	Create
Maintain	Develop
Focus on system and structure	Focus on people
Control	Trust
How and when	What and why
Short-term focus	Long-term focus
Take the status-quo as given	Challenge the status-quo
Do what is instructed	Follow their inner self
Do things right	Do the right things

A project manager will both manage and lead; the latter in particular when the reality differs from the plan.

Furthermore, we also use leadership when we mean initiative, daring, and perseverance, and that is not only required for project managers. Even though there is only one project leader, we expect leadership from all team members.

2.01-3 Process steps

1. Determine the leadership style.
2. Know your own abilities.
3. Apply the chosen style.
4. Modify the style if required.
5. Develop your competence.
6. Develop this also in your team.
7. Continuously improve.
8. Apply lessons learned

1. Determine the leadership style
When you lead people you have to be able to adapt your style to the person and the situation. A common misconception is that leadership is an inherent quality. Leadership is working hard, stumbling, getting up again and carrying on. The same applies to finding the right style of leadership.

Determining the appropriate style:
- The style has to fit you as a person.
- The style has to fit the persons you are leading.
- The style has to fit with the situation.

Fitting you
When the chosen style does not fit you as a person, you come across as being unauthentic. This is something you often see when people have been on a "Leadership" training course, where they have learned some tricks which they then apply. This will be perceived as not genuine and is, therefore, ineffective. People more easily follow a leader whose style is authentic, or at least appears to be so. Authenticity has a lot to do with self-knowledge, and therefore you can only become an effective leader when you develop sufficient self-knowledge through your life experience.

Fitting them
Yet, this is not enough. When the style does not suit the person you are leading, recognizable by the fact that the person doesn't do what you intended, then as leader, you are the one who has to change and not the other person. This requires a humble and flexible stance, which can only be achieved if you work on your own self-awareness.

Very often we become stuck in a particular style of leadership. This style is a strong reflection of our character. You notice this through statements such as the following:
- "I have a coaching style of leadership".
- "I am a political animal; I know which way the wind blows".

Both are examples of management: the first is a 'trick' that you possibly learnt on a training course, and the second relates to a 'game' that you play. Providing leadership is, however, not a trick and also not a game, but has to do with:
- The future.
- The profession.
- The person.

Real leaders go further where others stop, and years after they have left a company, or have retired or died, they are still remembered for the everlasting impression they have left behind.

Fitting the situation
Another dimension has to do with the situation in which you have to provide leadership. In a crisis situation, you use a different style from when everything goes according to plan. Another style is used in extensive reorganizations compared to the one used in the implementation of an ICT system, and for an infrastructure project, a different one to one used in a merger situation. For this third dimension, it is useful for you, as project manager, to have knowledge of the business aspects of the organization(s) in which the project takes place. You can then assess the necessity of certain actions, and their re-

lated urgency, much better than when you do not have this knowledge.

2. Know your own abilities

Self-knowledge and consciousness form the basis of the leader, who is prepared to understand and explore his intellectual, social and physical limits. It is not really a problem that there are limits, as long as he understands them and surrounds himself with people who are better than he is in a number of aspects. It is better to work for someone who knows himself, than for someone who thinks that he is "the president of the United States of America".

The hard work referred to in the previous paragraph, is related to the development of self-knowledge. This is a process of trial and error, and the experience you gain from this is something that takes place over a number of years. It is something you cannot learn at school or university, and something that an MBA or thesis does not add to. A leader is 'branded' by life itself.

Based on this learning and the knowledge from the previous step, we determine (for ourselves) the most effective style of leadership, which we then apply.

3. Apply the chosen style

This can mean that, in certain situations, you have to choose a style which is not exactly the one you prefer.

4. Modify the style if required

People and situations change, and sometimes we assess a situation wrongly. As "situational" leader, you firstly take a look at yourself. When a particular style of leadership does not work, it is apparently not effective, and you should modify the style until it does work.

That doesn't always mean you will get your own way. The situation, in which you have tried all the leadership styles and the employee still does not do what he should do, means that you have to "take your leave" of such a person; that is also a leadership style (directive).

5. Develop your competence

Dependent on the way in which you answer the following question, I can predict whether or not you, as a leader, will differentiate yourself from the rest.

Question: *Are you prepared to take the responsibility for a continuous development of yourself, and are you prepared to spend an average of one hour a day on doing this?*

If your answer is YES, then in one way or another you will differentiate yourself and be a cut above the average.

Stephen R. Covey[1] gives seven habits of effective leadership:

1. *Be proactive:* a part of your life is determined by your genetic makeup and the way in which you have been brought up, something that you cannot escape from. But between 'stimulus' and 'response', there is the opportunity to make choices of your own free will and, therefore, to move in a certain direction.

2. *Begin with the end in mind:* where do you want to be in 25 years time? Leadership requires a long-term vision, and retaining a firm hold on that vision. Be aware that this is something other than the pursuit of unachievable dreams.

---
[1] (1989) *The 7 Habits of Highly Effective People*, S.R. Covey

3. *Put first things first:* do what is important, above what is urgent but not important. Refuse to obey the tyranny of urgency.

4. *Think in terms of win/win:* leadership is winning together, and for this you need:
   o Character (integrity, maturity and the mentality of abundance).
   o A positive emotional bank account.
   o Partnerships to work together with.

5. *First understand and then be understood:* leaders are oriented towards their followers and capitalise on them, and because they do this, people follow them.

6. *Synergize:* whereby you have trust in someone else; built on that trust, you can work together.

7. *Continuously develop yourself:* if you do not take the time to do this, then you reach a point where you and your views become obsolete.

6. Develop this also in your team

Managers are busy with power and they protect their own 'kingdom', whereas leaders are busy with other people and accumulate power through the influence that they have on the life of their team members (followers). A manager looks at what he can take with him; a leader looks at what he leaves behind.

Leadership, therefore, also means that you are busy with the development of your team members.

For team members, leadership means that they:
- Take responsibility for their deeds.
- Look beyond the borders of their own work.
- Are accountable, and rectify mistakes.
- Have a proactive attitude.

Your first aim must be to bring your team members as quickly as possible to the level necessary that you are able to delegate the required work packages to them. You can read how you do this later in this chapter, when the model for situational leadership is covered.

Once you have brought the team members to the required level, you have to ensure that they remain at that level and this has everything to do with the atmosphere within the team. When, as project manager, you involve yourself with everything and don't trust anyone, you will never be any good at delegating. You can only trust competent people when you bestow trust on them.

7. Continuously improve

Your competence develops over a number of years. Experience is something that comes with time, but of course you have to make sure you pick up lessons from your experience and put them into practice. Practice makes perfect is the saying, and that means that you must begin at an early age to improve on your competence.

Good leaders always remain open to learn from their experiences. In 2000, Jim Collins[2] published a number of findings from research into successful companies. One of the most important findings was a particular type of leadership that he recognized in the successful companies. We can describe this

---

[2] (2001) Good to Great, Jim Collins, HARPERCOLLINS PUBLISHERS, New York

type of leadership, which he called level 5, in the project situation as follows:

> *Project leaders who make their own ego secondary to the larger objective of their project in order to multiply the value of both their own organization and that of their customers.*

The window and the mirror
When successful, level 5 leaders have the tendency to look outside, and accredit their success to factors outside their scope. On the other hand, they look in the mirror when things turn out to be less successful. This is an attitude of being prepared to continuously learn from your experience.

8. Apply lessons learned
Consider for a moment what I said before, that leaders look at what they leave behind. The least they leave behind is an impression, but there is more. When we look back into history, we see that most leaders of any significance have, in one way or another, recorded their experience in a book or in their memoirs. Now, this does not mean that every one of us has to write our memoirs, but you can ask yourself if your professional life is interesting enough. The least you can do is share your experiences with other colleagues. You can do this through a lecture, an article in a professional journal and possibly also through a book.

2.01-4 Special Topics

1. The development of management

Management was "invented" at the beginning of the 20th century and began with F.W. Taylor's *Scientific Management*[3].

His management philosophy was based on the following basic principles:
- Scientifically determine what the best method is for a particular task.
- Select and further develop employees in a way that is scientifically responsible.
- A close and friendly co-operation between employee and employer is ultimately the best.

In most Western cultures, regretfully, the first two principles have gained more credence than the last one.

A second name we should mention when we talk about the founders of the management profession is H. Fayol. Whereas Taylor concentrated on the implementation of primary processes within the organization, Fayol concentrated to a greater extent on the management of large, complex organizations.

He named fourteen management principles:
- Work redistribution.
- Authority.
- Discipline.
- Leadership unity.
- Unity of direction.
- Individual interests are secondary to the common objective.
- Reward.
- Centralisation.
- Hierarchy.
- Order and neatness.
- Fair treatment.
- Stability of the personnel.
- Initiative.
- Team spirit.

Each management philosophy gives rise to another reaction. Thanks to the scientific approach, effects were discovered that originally were difficult to explain. The so-called *Hawthorne experiments* carried out by Elton Mayo (1880-1949) in the nineteen twenties and thirties are well-known.

Although his research was originally intended to ascertain under which working conditions employees would be at their most productive, it was discovered that when people feel that they are providing an important contribution, they are more productive. This has become the basis for the so-called Human Relations movement. Here, we find names such as Argyris, Likert, Maslow and McGregor, who we shall come across in another chapter.

Note that the philosophies mentioned had an internal focus; they are concerned with production, managing and human capital. A reaction that had an external focus was also bound to occur, and this was the so-called System Approach, whereby the way managers acted was deemed to be dependent on: organization size, available technology and the individuals in relation to the environment. This approach sees the organization as a system that tries to survive in equilibrium with its environment (the market).

What remains of these philosophies and is there anything we still can learn from them? A lot, only we have learnt that each management philosophy has its valuable points, and an eclectic approach is desirable. This can be credited to Robert E. Quinn[4], who incorporated the best points from all the philoso-

---
[3] (1911) *The Principles of Scientific Management*, Frederick Winslow Taylor

[4] (1996) *Becoming a master manager: a competency framework*, Robert E. Quinn, JOHN WILEY & SONS, New York USA

phies mentioned in one model. He describes eight management roles, namely:

- *Mentor*: Advance the personal development of your team members. Here we see a coaching style of leadership; the project is now an environment in which team members develop themselves into professionals. The project manager facilitates this development process.
- *Facilitator*: Ensure a good team spirit. The project manager is the team builder, who ensures that the various team members co-operate well with each other, are motivated, and provide effort.
- *Monitor*: Follow and monitor the work of the team members. The task oriented manager, who has implemented a control cycle and keeps a close eye on the progress.
- *Co-ordinator*: Produce realistic plans and ensure that these are implemented.
- *Director*: Develop a vision for the project. The project manager designs an approach which contributes to the success of the project.
- *Producer*: Create a productive work environment, in which the team members can carry out their work optimally.
- *Broker*: Ensure the organization co-operates, and develop support. The management of the stakeholders.
- *Innovator*: Manage changes and provide leadership to innovative projects.

A manager has to fulfil each of these roles one way or another.

2. Leadership in a multicultural perspective

In the most comprehensive survey into leadership[5] across cultures, research was carried out into qualities that are universal. The researchers started out with the supposition that leaders are most effective when they display the behavior that their followers expect from a leader. They recognized six leadership profiles:
- Charismatic/Value-Based Leadership
- Team Oriented Leadership
- Participative Leadership
- Human Oriented Leadership
- Autonomous Leadership
- Self-Protective Leadership

Of these, the charismatic value-based leader was the global favorite. This profile contains the following characteristics:
- Visionary
- Inspiring
- Self-sacrificing
- Displays integrity
- Decisive
- Performance driven

The vision already commences during the project start, where you develop a vision and relay this in an inspiring story. In this way you gain the necessary support for your approach. Such a story is many times more important than any business case or project management plan. The researchers Keller en Price[6] came to the conclusion that change programmes, which are able to communicate an emotional and compelling story, are almost four times more likely to succeed than programmes that do not have that. But with just inspiration you are not there yet; employees expect a certain level of self-sacrifice and integrity, a form of

---

5 (2004) *Culture, Leadership, and Organizations, Globe,* SAGE PUBLICATIONS, California, US
6 (2011) Beyond Performance, Keller & Price, JOHN WILEY & SONS, Hoboken, New Jersey, US

2.01 Leadership

serving leadership, which would be suitable, therefore, for a project manager. The leader is there in the service of others, and not only to serve his own career and interest. Not a softy, of course, because a business-like attitude to making difficult decisions and also delivering tangible results is a part of this leadership profile.

Because these values are apparently universal, it is worth the trouble when developing leadership, to focus on these areas. In this way, you can differentiate yourself as an inter-cultural leader, because your style corresponds with what is expected of leaders worldwide.

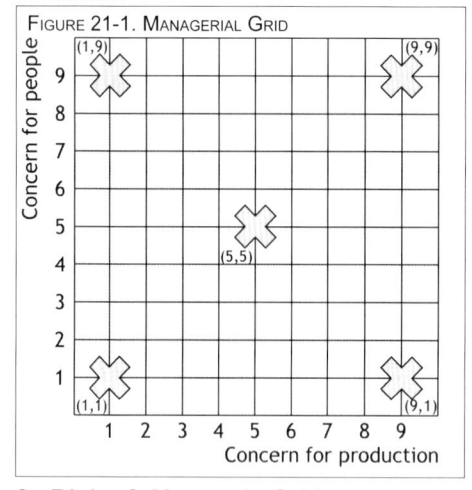

FIGURE 21-1. MANAGERIAL GRID

3. Blake & Mouton's Grid

When you ask people what they expect from a leader, their answers can be divided into two groups:

- Consideration
- Structuring

Consideration: the emotional-social behavior of a leader; the extent to which he relates to his employees in a pleasant, empathetic way. How he gains their trust, his willingness to explain things, the involvement in their needs and the mental support he provides.

Structuring: the behavior the leader displays to focus on the objectives and the structure of the group. The way in which he sets his priorities and makes his employees aware of the goals to be achieved.

A lot of project management activities will also have to do with the structuring side of leadership. Helping with the setting up of a business case, the estimation of the time, the planning of people and resources, the carrying out of a risk analysis. All of these are aspects that are related to structuring.

However, this is not enough, as it is ultimately the people who have to carry out the work. When people have to work overtime to achieve an important milestone, then you can motivate them by pointing out the planning to them (*structure*), but you can also listen to what they have to say (*consideration*) and so come to the realization that certain planned dates are no longer realistic, or that employees are not happy.

Leaders, therefore, can be *task oriented* or *people oriented*. A number of leadership models are based on this, and *Blake & Mouton's Managerial Grid* is one example.

In 1964, they described these dimensions[7] on a nine point scale, which resulted in 81 different management styles.

Five of these are important:
- (1,1) impoverished.
- (1,9) country club.
- (9,1) task manager.
- (9,9) team manager.
- (5,5) middle of the road.

Their view is that, looked at theoretically, the team manager (9,9) functions the best.

---

[7] (1964), *The Managerial Grid: key orientations for achieving production through people,* Blake and Mouton

2.01 Leadership

We look at the five main styles from the Management Grid:
- *Impoverished (1,1)*, poor management; a form of management which does not care much for the people in the organization, and provides a minimum of effort to induce the team to perform.
- *Country Club (1,9)*, manager of a holiday park or a tour guide; a lot of attention for the people aspects, relationships and fun, but little attention for production.
- *Task Manager (9,1)*, authoritarian; aimed at achieving results with little focus on the needs of the individual employee.
- *Team Manager (9,9)*, this manager builds a relationship based on mutual trust with his employees; people experience a mutual interest leading to an on-going improvement in performance.
- *Middle of the Road (5,5)*, a little of everything; the employees are contented but not overly enthusiastic, the work is done but no more than that.

You have to see the model for what it was in the time it was produced. It encourages managers to search for a balance between the human and task aspect. According to this model, the team manager is the best. From their nature, project managers are very result oriented and often tend more towards the task manager, although most of them will recognise that the people side is the most important.

Although the Managerial Grid has already been used in training for many years, there is little evidence available showing that the team manager is the best in all situations. The best style is very dependent on the situation in which the team finds itself. Another drawback with this model is that it encourages a certain level of inflexibility in the choice of your management style. You simply have a particular style, and that will be your style forever. Growth is no part of this theory

4. Situational Leadership - Fiedler

Each manager knows from experience that the best style of leadership is strongly dependent on the situation. The basis of Fiedler's theory[8] is that the effectiveness of leadership is dependent on the leader himself, and the situation in which he provides leadership.

There are three situational factors that play a role:
- The personal relationship between the leader and his team.
- The structure of the task.
- The position of power of the leader.

This is also the order in which these factors influence leadership effectiveness. It says a lot about the aspects which you, as project manager, have to give priority to; the relationship with your team members is more important than your position. Most of the project management techniques are concerned with structuring the project task and documenting the formal tasks and responsibilities.

When you combine these three factors with one another, you get in total eight different combinations, and when we rank this combination from left to right from favorable to unfavorable, we obtain the Fiedler table.

From the 800 or more investigations that Fiedler and his colleagues have carried out, they discovered that the task oriented manager is effective when the circumstances are either very favorable or very unfavorable, and that the relationship oriented manager is more effective in the middle area.

---
8 (1967), *A theory of leadership effectiveness*, E.F. Fiedler, New York, MCGRAW-HILL

2.01 Leadership

One of the underlying thoughts in this theory is that a leader is either task oriented or relationship oriented and cannot change his style. Dependent on the particular situation, the project sponsor looks for a suitable leader and by using the above table, he can assess how effective someone will be as a leader.

For example: you are a task oriented leader, and there are unclear goals, you have little positional power, and furthermore the relationship with the team members is good. From the table, you can conclude that you can best do something to *clarify the task structure*. However, if you are a relationship oriented manager, then you will decrease your effectiveness as a leader when you start clarifying the task structure.

As already stated, this model assumes that there are only two leadership styles: the task oriented style and the relationship oriented style. This simplified assumption has lead to many criticisms.

5. Hersey & Blanchard[9]

Where Fiedler assumes that you cannot change the leadership style, Hersey and Blanchard assume that this is possible. With Fiedler, the emphasis is on changing the situation, or on selecting a leader who fits the situation. With Hersey and Blanchard the emphasis is on changing the style of leadership.

In their research, Hersey and Blanchard looked at situations where particular leaders either perform well or not so well. Based on their findings, they developed the model of situational leadership, which is based on the combination of the following factors:

- The ability of the employee.
- The willingness of the employee to undertake the task.

These two dimensions determine the extent to which someone is prepared to undertake a certain task. This extent of this 'readiness' as they call it, says something about the competence of the employee. An older term for this is 'maturity'.

In this case, there are four levels of employee competence[10]:

Level of competence	R1 Low	R2 Moderate
Ability:		
Relevant work experience	None or little	Insufficient
Know-how	None or little	Incomplete

---

9 (2001) *Management of Organizational Behavior* (8th edition), Hersey, Blanchard, Johnson, PRENTICE HALL, Upper Saddle River

10 Reworked (2000), *Handboek groepsdynamica*, Jan Remmerswaal, NELISSEN-Baarn

Fiedler Table								
	\multicolumn{4}{c}{Favorable circumstances}			\multicolumn{3}{c}{Unfavorable circumstances}	
Relationship	Good	Good	Good	Good	Bad	Bad	Bad	Bad
Task structure	Clear	Clear	Unclear	Unclear	Clear	Clear	Unclear	Unclear
Position of power	Strong	Weak	Strong	Weak	Strong	Weak	Strong	Weak
Effective style	Task oriented		Relationship oriented					Task oriented

2.01 Leadership

Level of competence	R1 Low	R2 Moderate
Insight into the task	Little	Reasonable
Willingness:		
Sense of responsibility	Reserved	Hesitant
Need to perform	Does not get into action	Little
Commitment	Indifferent	Variable

Level of competence	R3 Considerable	R4 High
Ability:		
Relevant work experience	Available	Ample
Know-how	Available	Ample
Insight into the task	Sufficient	Full understanding
Willingness:		
Sense of responsibility	Willing	Very willing
Need to perform	Available	Great need
Commitment	Enthusiastic	Very committed

The way in which the leader makes his 'diagnosis' of the competence levels, is by looking at the extent to which both the dimensions ability and willingness are visible. Assumptions alone are not sufficient.

Each of these four levels requires its own style of leadership:

Demonstrated willingness	Demonstrated ability	Matching style
Low	Low	S1 Telling
High	Low	S2 Selling
Low	High	S3 Participating
High	High	S4 Delegating

You estimate an employee's level of ability for each task you assign to him.

> **EXAMPLE 21-1 HERSEY & BLANCHARD**
> The inexperienced employee joins his project; he is eager, but does not yet know what is expected of him. The project manager makes clear what he expects of the employee; a *directive* style.
>
> After some time the project manager spends more time on the employee; instead of saying how he has to do something (*directive*), he says how something can be done (*selling*). There is room for input from the employee. The project manager uses a *selling* style of leadership and they play a *negotiating game*.
>
> The employee grows in his task until the project manager thinks that he is able to carry out his task independently. The manager keeps his distance. The employee still hesitates. The manager *helps, participates*. More and more input is expected from the employee himself, who has to be encouraged to complete the task on his own.
>
> Then comes the time when the employee and the manager both know it, the point at which tasks can be *delegated*. Agreements are made on what, when, against what budget, and how progress will be reported. The manager uses a delegating style of leadership, where he is only present at a distance.

> **EXAMPLE 21-2 DIAGNOSING LEVEL OF COMPETENCE**
> So, it is possible that an employee has a moderate level of ability for producing specifications, whereas his level for writing minutes is high.
>
> According to the model of situational leadership, you apply a different style in each case. In the case of the specifications, this is a *selling* style. For the minutes, a *delegating* style is sufficient.

In the following table on the next page the various styles have been elaborated further.

2.01 Leadership

Leadership styles

Level of competence	Appropriate Leadership Style
Low	telling, Synonyms: guiding, directing or establishing Task oriented OR directing: high Relationship oriented OR supporting: low
	A determined, ambitious task oriented style of leadership. The leader is more concerned with the result than with the employee. Is cost conscious. It is a form of one-way traffic; he gives specific assignments, monitors progress, checks and controls, adjusts and has clear rules.
Moderate	Selling, synonyms: explaining, claryfying or persuading Task oriented OR directing: high Relationship oriented OR supporting: high
	A motivating leader who makes the power difference as small as possible, and is able to unite the interests of the project and his employee. He provides direction, stimulates two-way traffic, explains decisions, is interested in the employee, listens, shows understanding, motivates and is task oriented. Notwithstanding all of this, however, he ultimately decides what will happen.
Considerable	Participating, synonyms: encouraging, collaborating or committing Task orientated OR directing: low Relationship oriented OR supporting: high
	Puts the emphasis on the personal development of the employees, creates a safe atmosphere of trust. People come first. Gives a lot of space, finds it important that the employees support the decisions, points out the personal responsibilities, has a supporting role.
High	Delegating, synonyms: observing, monitoring or fulfilling Task oriented OR directing: low Relationship oriented OR supporting: high
	A meticulous, well-organised leader, who delegates responsibilities to his employees. Agrees procedures and keeps a certain distance. Listens, has understanding, shows interest, but lets the employee solve his own problems .

The Hersey and Blanchard model is a development model, in which the leader allows the employee to grow. He does this by situationally applying the appropriate leadership style.

There is a remark to be made on situational leadership in a project, and this has to do with the time pressure which occurs in projects. Often, there is not enough time to let the employee progress through all levels of competence "naturally". To fill vacant positions, you look for experienced people so that they can progress through the first two levels quickly.

Every leader has his preferred styles with which he feels more comfortable than with the other options. Such a preferred style often carries with it one or more pitfalls:

- With the *directive style*, these are nagging, acting without consultation, top-down communication, enlightened despotism and impatience.
- With the *selling style,* these are compliancy, looking for compromise

where that is not advisable and waiting too long before making decisions.
- With the *participating style,* these are avoiding conflict, dependency on recognition, identifying too much with the employees and not giving enough direction when needed.
- With the *delegating style,* these are avoiding involvement, not expressing his opinion enough, sometimes too much focus on the procedures and lack of creativity.

6. Power - Hersey & Blanchard

Power is unavoidably connected with management. My own simple definition is:

Power is the potential to make people do things against their own will!

This definition is too simple and needs to be deepened[11]:
- Power is determining the behavior of a person by another person.
- Power is a relationship between at least two people.

It always involves at least two people, and the less powerful person has to accept his role in relation to the more powerful person, otherwise the latter is 'powerless'.

Hersey and Blanchard cite the difference between positional and personal power, whereby positional power is the amount of responsibility and authority managers are willing to delegate down; this power, therefore, flows from downwards. Personal power flows upwards, and has to do with the extent to which the employees are willing to dedicate themselves to their leader, as they feel good doing so, and because in this way, they can achieve their own goals.

We see the use of these two forms of power in the styles of leadership applied positionally by the manager. The styles S1 and S2 will have more to do with positional power, whereas the styles S3 and S4 make more use of the personal power.

Positional
There are four types of positional power, namely:
- Coercive power.
- Connection power.
- Reward power.
- Legitimate power.

COERCIVE POWER
This power is based on someone's ability to do something unpleasant to someone else. The employee 'obeys' for fear of punishment. A certain amount of this power is needed to use the directive style (S1) of leadership. When managers never make use of this power, they run the risk that it erodes and thereby becomes ineffective.

CONNECTION POWER
Connection power is based on the relationships someone has with other influential people within the organization. Employees do what their manager tells them to do, because they hope to make a good impression higher up in the organization, which will have a positive effect on their career. It is not about the actual connection someone has, but about the perception people have. You see managers use this when they talk about more senior managers and call them by their first name, as this gives others the impression of a closeness which is not necessarily there. But with power, a lot has to do with the impression created; if the employee believes it, then the power relationship has become a fact.

---
11 (2004) *De logica van macht,* Mauk Mulder, SCRIPTUM, Schiedam

2.01 Leadership

REWARD POWER
Reward power is based on the ability of a leader to provide employees with things that are of value for them: a pay rise, promotion, recognition etc. Employees give in to the demands of their leader in the hope that this will result in the reward they want.

LEGITIMATE POWER
This power is based on the difference in rights and obligations linked to a more senior position. Based on his senior position, the manager has the right to expect or demand certain things of his employees. As he is "the boss", they will carry out his assignments and orders.

Personal
There are three forms of personal power, namely:
- Referent power.
- Information power.
- Expert power.

REFERENT POWER
Referent power is based on certain individual characteristics the employee admires (e.g. handsome, intelligent, charismatic, expertise). The wishes of a manager with a lot of referent power are complied with, because the employees find him 'nice', 'admirable' etc., and they trust him, identify with him and want him as a reference.

INFORMATION POWER
This power type is based on the difference in the possession of information. Employees allow themselves to be influenced by a manager with information power, because they are dependent on his information or because they like to belong to the 'inner circle'. Inexperienced managers sometimes hesitate to share information with their employees, but in order to support employees in moving from an R3 level of competence to R4, this form of power is an effective tool.

EXPERT POWER
The title speaks for itself: knowledge is power. The basis for this power lies in knowledge, expertise and experience. From a manager with a lot of expert power, employees accept something out of respect for his knowledge and expertise. His advice and help are accepted on the basis of this respect.

7. Manfred Kets de Vries

Of all the leadership theories, that of Manfred Kets de Vries takes a special place. Kets de Vries is a practising psychoanalyst and also professor in Management and Leadership at the Institut Européen d'Administration des Affaires (European Institute for Business Administration) or INSEAD located in Fontainebleau/France.

What makes the approach of Kets de Vries different, is that he specifically searches for the subconscious factors at play in organizations and with leaders. He makes three assumptions[12]:

- What you see isn't necessary what you get.
- All human behavior, no matter how irrational it appears, has a rationale.
- We're all products of our past.

The world is more complex than that which the human eye and mind can accommodate. Even though we like to preserve the illusion that we see what we see, in practice the truth is more complicated. Ask two people to describe a piece of artwork and then compare the descriptions. Although both are looking at the same piece, the descriptions are different, and this also occurs in projects!

The reason is that the reality is too complex to comprehend or to describe, and, therefore, we simplify this reality into a compre-

---
12 (2001), *The Leadership Mystique,* Manfred Kets de Vries, FT PRENTICE HALL, London

hensible model. From that model, we interpret this reality, and for us a personal reality is created having its own expectations.

When we, in project management, talk about *managing expectations* that is exactly what we mean. Our project sponsor has expectations, and with those expectations in mind, he looks at our project, but that does not necessarily mean that he will actually get what he sees.

As a leader you are also involved with this, and you may therefore be blind to signals you have no room for in your own inner theatre. Effective leaders are able to look outside of their own boundaries and view their project from a different angle.

As human beings, we like to have a self-image in which we are rational, civilised and intelligent. We tell ourselves that we are fun to be with, and are loved by the people around us. This already begins at a young age when we try to please our parents, teachers and later our bosses. Inevitably our self-image gets frustrated, for we are not always obedient, or a perfect pupil. Sometimes (or often), our emotions run away with us. We can burst into a rage and call someone everything under the sun, or we can become overcome by grief.

The work of Kets de Vries provides ground for research; every irrationality has a working principle. It is a search for those patterns which repeat themselves in someone's life. Every time you say to yourself: *"There is another one of those types"*, there is apparently something which activates your emotions. That something is the leading principle you have to go and investigate further, in order to improve your leadership effectiveness.

Often this principle finds its origin in your past; how you were brought up, how your school years were and also your first job appear to have a big influence on your professional life. This is where the psychoanalytic background of Kets de Vries resounds through his theories on leadership. His book *'The Leadership Mystique'* contains almost 50 questionnaires for self reflection.

He encourages us to take a journey into our personal history and to discover where our outlook on the world, our behavior, was created, and which deeper emotions drive this behavior.

8. Delegating

An organized desk and an almost empty task list are a good indicator of the extent to which you are able to delegate. However, we often see overfull diaries and inaccessible managers. One of the skills a project manager must have, is that of delegating.

As well as the specialist work that has to be carried out by the employees, there are also management tasks you, as project manager, can delegate to your employees, for example certain reports and control work.

When delegating, there are a number of things you have to take account of:
- Be clear (SMART) about what you delegate.
- Agree how you want to be kept updated on the progress.
- As well as responsibility, also delegate authority.
- Delegate to the right people, they should be able to carry it out.
- Have high expectations of your employees and make that known.
- Look out for "delegating back"; point out the responsibility of the employee.
- Reward success.

There are two basic forms of delegation; management by objectives and manage-

ment by exception, which are explained as follows:
- Management By Objectives (MBO): in advance, clear objectives are negotiated and agreed, on the basis of which the employee gets to work. All the aspects mentioned above are included, and with respect to the progress, there are agreements as to how, and how often, the reporting will be carried out.
- Management By Exception (MBE): the same as in MBO, only now, reporting is only carried out when it is clear that the agreed objectives can not be achieved, and so there is only contact with one another when something is wrong.

Delegation is only possible when your employees are capable, and know what you expect of them. Furthermore, you have to be able to put your trust in them.

9. Feedback

You will have to provide your project members with regular feedback on their performance. The problem with giving feedback is that the receiver, certainly in the event of negative feedback, takes it as a reprimand, and starts behaving 'childishly' by going onto the defence. What does not help in such a case, is making a comment such as "*you do not have to defend yourself*", as that only results in the other person becoming even more defensive.

Providing feedback in an effective manner attempts to prevent the other person from becoming defensive or offering resistance.

There are some basic rules:
- *Describe the behavior,* what is the other person doing.
- *Describe your own reaction,* and leave the other person free to do something with it.
- *Make it specific,* what has happened.
- *Only give feedback it is useful,* if the other person cannot do anything with it, leave it.
- *If required,* the more the receiver is waiting for it, the more the chance that he will accept the feedback.
- *At the right moment,* speaks for itself.
- *Accurate*, obviously it has to be right.

When giving feedback in other cultures, you should be aware of the effect your words may have on your project members and your relationship with them. For example, giving feedback or being critical of a colleague in public is something nobody will appreciate, but it can be disastrous in Asia and the Middle East where loss of face plays an important role. It may ruin your relationship with your colleagues forever! In these cultures, you can be critical of someone of course but take care that you tell him in private and never in public.

As well as giving feedback, receiving it is also a skill. We have already briefly talked about defending yourself, or offering resistance. Nobody enjoys receiving negative feedback, but when it does happen, the following tips are useful:
- *Thank the other person.*
- *Let it sink in,* and if necessary ask for an explanation when you don't understand something.
- *Decide later whether or not you are going to do something with it.*

We often think of criticism when we talk about feedback, but it is also possible to give someone positive feedback. This is less common, but very powerful, and when you tell someone how well he carried out a certain task, his motivation will only increase.

2.02 Engagement

IF THE ATTITUDE IS RIGHT, MOTIVATION WILL COME AUTOMATICALLY

What use are people, who do their job without feeling committed.

How about you, do you feel some sort of emotion when you work? Or are you biding your time until your retirement? That can't be true, how you must be suffering.

Engagement, involvement with the project and the staff, makes working enjoyable!

2.02 Engagement

2.02-1 DEFINITIONS

Approachable	Someone is approachable when he shows willingness to listen to comments about his functioning.
Engagement	The personal 'buy-in' of a project manager or a team member.
Empowerment	The extent to which someone feels capable of doing certain things.

2.02-2 Introduction

It is sometimes the case that team members promise to carry out a certain project task, but in practice make something of a mess of it. According to Ofman[1] [2] this happens because people didn't really choose to do it. He sighs:

> "Unfortunately project based working is in practice
>
> often synonymous with project based trying."

It is not, therefore, just about willing, but also about making a well thought-out choice. This creates a tension between the current reality and the future that someone has chosen. It also forms the energy from which someone achieves their choice. Therefore, a team member must:

- Know what he wants.
- Dare to face reality.
- Make a conscious choice with regard to the future.

Ofman elaborates this into the following steps: listening and hearing, aiming and finding, looking and seeing, checking and feeling, choosing and knowing, following and being.

For project managers, this means that they have to stimulate their team members to make a choice, which increases their involvement. That is only possible when the project manager has made similar choices himself:

- What do I want with this project sponsor; how is my relationship with him, and together with him, am I willing to make the project a success?
- What are the chances of success for this project? Do I want to, and can I, give it my all?
- What do I want with my team? What type of culture? Can the team handle it? Am I also prepared to make a choice for my project team?

This view leads to an increased energy level that you, as an individual, apply to your project, and that is exactly what this topic is about.

---

[1] (1992) *Bezieling en kwaliteit in Organisatie*, D. D. Ofman – SERVIRE, Cothen
[2] (1998) *Projectmatig Creëren*, Jo Bos e.a. SCRIPTUM BOOKS, Schiedam

2.02-3 Process steps

1. Be aware of those involved.
2. Explain your ability to 'serve'.
3. Investigate the possibilities.
4. Understand the engagement.
5. Appreciate and communicate.
6. Be proud of achievements.
7. Identify changing requirements.
8. Apply lessons learned.

1. Be aware of those involved

Information on the parties involved has been gathered through a stakeholder analysis.

The project manager is also aware of:
- The (personal) circumstances.
- Their interests.

Of the parties involved

This relates to both the team members and the stakeholders in the project environment. The ICB uses the word "engagement" that means as project manager you are interested 'from inside' in the skills, experiences, personal attitude, circumstances and inner motives of the people involved. Engagement is an authentic form of involvement, which motivates the other person to follow the project manager.

2. Explain your ability to 'serve'

Engagement is also about clarity. You know what you can, and what you cannot mean for another person, and you are clear about that. This clarity, however, is not an blunt rejection of the other person, but consists of an 'empathizing' explanation why you cannot, or do not want to, do something. This clarity shows itself inwardly (aimed at the team) and outwardly (aimed at the environment).

Inwardly with respect to the personal wishes of the team members, or suppliers, who deliver a contribution to the project result. You do not string people along, but you tell them truthfully what can, and what cannot, be done. Such an attitude ensures that the team members know exactly where you stand, and prevents disappointment during or after the execution of the project. As they know beforehand where they are heading, they also know what they are saying 'yes' to. Therefore, a conscious and informed choice is being made.

Outwardly is concerned with the expectations of all other parties involved, such as: project sponsor, senior management, users and suchlike. The same mechanism also applies here; if they know beforehand where this is leading to, they will be more committed when they agree, than when they are confronted with all kinds of surprises during the project. Clarity in advance increases the involvement, also when there is disagreement, as you could view opposition as a form of involvement.

3. Investigate the possibilities

Project management also means integrating interests. Good project managers see opportunities to bring parties together, and, alongside the differences that manifest themselves, also to see the similarities.

This basic attitude determines how you, as project manager, view the world. Is the world for you:
- A collection of people with conflicting interests, OR

EXAMPLE 22-1 COVERED SADNESS

A project is under a lot of time pressure, and one of the team members wants to take the next day off. The project manager refuses.

The following day, the team member reports in sick, and does not come back until a month later.

What emerged was: he wanted that particular day off, because it was the date at which his child died.

- A collection of people who want to be happy and enjoy their work.

By anticipating the interest of the parties involved, as project manager you show your engagement, and prevent many conflicts in advance. It is obviously very clear that this is sometimes not possible.

Involvement can be expressed in two ways:
- Support when people are in agreement.
- Opposition when people are in disagreement.

Both are forms of engagement, which are to be preferred over a wait-and-see attitude in which it is not clear how the project is being viewed. In such cases it may be helpful for you to draw people out into the open somewhat.

4. Understand the engagement

Another aspect is to develop a sense of how engaged the different team members are. What is their involvement? Are they still motivated, or is this changing? Because motivation declines very slowly, you often notice it much too late and therefore you have to be alert. With hindsight, what went wrong can often be explained, but when you are in the middle of things, it is very hard to notice changes in motivation.

There is actually only one good way to find this out, and that is by being present and communicating with your team members. A chat between times, having lunch together, being attentive when someone is about to marry, sending an e-mail wishing your Muslim colleagues a happy Ramadan, disclosing personal issues; it all seems so obvious, but there are more project managers than you would think, who go from one meeting to the next and communicate with the team via their PDA. This is not effective.

As you have more information and opportunities to control things as project manager, you are obviously much more involved than your team members. Don't underestimate the unique position you have in your team. Through your positive and enthusiastic attitude, you must bring a degree of involvement across to your team members, and that is only possible if you stay in contact with them.

5. Appreciate and communicate

Most people appreciate it when managers and colleagues voice their appreciation about the results they have achieved. To stimulate involvement, you communicate the results and show your appreciation, both informally and formally, when it is justified.

Informally through the proverbial 'pat on the back', and formally by naming milestones achieved in the progress report. When project sponsors see that the project deliverables contribute to their own objectives, they will feel positively involved. To put it briefly, tie the results to the objectives of the project sponsor.

6. Be proud of achievements

Pride increases the cohesion within a team, and the team is now more than satisfied with the results they achieve. This gives an almost euphoric feeling, which increases both the effectiveness and the efficiency of the team.

One comment we do have to make is that there has to be something you are actually proud of. When you celebrate something, there must be something to celebrate. If this is not the case, you achieve the opposite and staff distance themselves emotionally from the project.

> EXAMPLE 22-2 CELEBRATING THE UNFINISHED PROJECT
>
> A project has faced difficult problems several times already, and in fact nobody knew the actual status of the project any more. Everybody wanted it to be finished, but the staff on the work floor knew that this was not the case. The project management knew this as well, but refused to believe it. It was finished is what they reported to their project sponsors. The project office organized a party to celebrate the conclusion, and 300 people were invited at a time the company had to fire people because of the disappointing company results.
>
> In this way, you create an atmosphere in which people will not commit to your project any longer, because deep down they know that the party was a form of a 'scam' which they had taken part in.

7. Identify changing demands

There are two areas for attention where demands develop:

- The project environment.
- The project team.

The environment

See the project as a 'black box' (the system approach), which receives support from the environment in exchange for the results it delivers conforming to the demands. The level of engagement displayed by the project sponsor and other interested parties may be either positive or negative. Positive increases the support, and negative increases the demands. When the project does not offer the right answer to this negative involvement, the project will become more and more difficult to manage.

The project team

Here, the team members provide their support to the project manager in the form of commitment to the plans. The involvement and their engagement increases when they think that the project contributes to their own personal objectives. As soon as they lose this feeling, it manifests itself in the form of criticism or opposition. As project manager, how do you deal with this? If you do not notice that something in the demands/support balance is changing, and ignore this, then the opposition will initially increase until such time that the employees lose their confidence. They may then attempt to leave the project, and if that is not possible, there is a significant chance they will distance themselves emotionally. Involvement and motivation decrease, and apathy takes over.

8. Apply lessons learned

There are several reasons to emphasise the purpose of evaluation. You can only explain a particular experience properly when you understand it. That understanding increases the engagement and evaluation, therefore, is also important for this competence element.

When you take the time to brainstorm together with your team on the way things are going in order to develop possible initiatives for improvement, you increase the engagement. People appreciate it when you listen to them, and when they get the feeling that they can contribute to something that is important, their motivation increases.

2.02-4 SPECIAL TOPICS

1. Being Accountable
A part of engagement is the willingness to be accountable for the way you provide leadership. You want to do it well, and according to the agreement. If someone challenges you, it gives you a certain feeling, and you are not indifferent to it, particularly when it contains criticism. What makes someone challengeable for the consequences of his actions?

How often doesn't it happen that when you tackle someone on his conduct this person will defend himself?

In most cases this is a sign that you have touched a nerve, because the person feels involved. In general it is a fact that the more confidence you have, the more you can be challenged. A good principle is that when someone criticizes you, you listen to it carefully, ask any questions for clarification, and afterwards think about what you can, want to, or must change.

2. Delegating and empowerment
Delegating is one of Hersey and Blanchard's[1] four leadership styles, and you can see it as a means to increase the engagement of your staff on the project. When people are ready for it, you delegate work to them, and this increased responsibility acts as a stimulus.

> EXAMPLE 22-3 ACCOUNTABILITY EXERCISE
> Think of a recent situation in which you felt attacked, and you defended yourself.
>
> What was it about? How did you feel? How did you react? Have you been attacked before on this topic? How did you find that?
>
> You can probably think of more questions yourself, which would give a better picture of the situation concerned. One question is not important and that is:
>
> Was the other person right?
>
> What this exercise is about, is that you develop an image of what you can be challenged on, and what not. A piece of self-knowledge, therefore.

Empowerment is the giving and finding of the power to carry out the activity in question. Empowerment, therefore, comes from two directions: from outside and from inside.

From outside
Seen formally, this is providing sufficient powers and means for someone to be able to carry out the task he or she is responsible for. If you delegate a task, the member of staff needs to have the means to carry out the task properly.

But there is more to it than this! It is also about expressing confidence in a persons functioning, and for that reason, you start using the participating style of leadership, while working on the confidence of the employee. Because you express your trust in his abilities, you empower his self-confidence. When this trust is visibly present, the time has come when you can delegate.

From inside
Empowerment also has to come from inside. To have team members who carry out work, not because they have to, but because they want to, as the work they do also contributes to their personal objectives.

3. Motivating
When you know how to motivate people you will obviously be more successful than when you do not know how. In any event, you have to be aware of how your people feel, what moves them, and how you can use this to get them into action. When you are involved with your people, this will be easier than when it does not really bother you. In addition, some knowledge of the psychology of motivation comes in handy to deal with this appropriately. The following will be covered successively:
- Maslow needs hierarchy.
- Douglas McGregor X and Y theory.
- Herzberg motivation hygiene theory.

4. The Maslow needs hierarchy[2]

To find the explanation of human behavior, in the first half of the twentieth century people looked for the subconscious motives of a person (psychoanalysis), and also investigated the patterns of human behavior (behaviorism). Man was studied distantly, with a "negative" undertone.

Abraham Maslow's (1908-1970) theory belongs to the humanist psychology theories which evolved in the second half of the twentieth century, as a reaction to the then main streams in psychology. The humanist view has a positive outlook on people, and a number of common thoughts we come across[3] in those theories are:

- By nature, man is *good*.
- Attention for the *uniqueness* of the person, his thoughts and feelings.
- Man is studied as a *whole*.
- Man is a *developing* creature.
- An emphasis on the *conscious perception*.
- Man is a *self-regulating organism*.
- A view of man such as this has enormous consequences for how leadership is interpreted and implemented. Abraham Maslow produced the following summary list[4]:
- Trust the people to whom you provide leadership.
- Give people the right and relevant information on the situation.
- Assume that people want to achieve goals.
- The organization is not a place where laws of the jungle reign.
- Irrespective of their place, people identify themselves with the objectives of the organization.
- Employees are foremost of good will in preference to tending towards rivalry.
- The staff involved are sufficiently healthy mentally.
- The organization is healthy enough.
- People can objectively look at themselves and others.
- People are not driven by fear.
- People want to continuously develop.
- Everyone enjoys teamwork, friendship, group feeling, etc.
- Animosity is more a reaction than a personality characteristic.
- People are strong enough.
- People can improve themselves.
- A person would rather feel important and successful than the opposite.
- A person would rather respect his boss than not.
- Nobody wants to be afraid of someone else.
- A person would rather be active than passive.
- People are inclined to improve things.
- Growth evolves from both pleasure and boredom.
- People are rather a person than a means (resource).
- A person would rather work than not.
- All people would rather work on something useful than something useless.
- A person would rather be somebody than nobody.
- People can handle a new style of managing.
- People have a strong spirit.
- A person is sensible enough to make his own choices.
- Everybody wants honest appreciation in public.
- Every positive movement of growth has a dark side.

---

[2] (1943) *A Theory of Human Motivation*, A.H. Maslow, PSYCHOLOGICAL REVIEW nr. 50 (blz. 370-396)
[3] (1997), *Klinische Psychologie,* Molen e.a., WOLTERS NOORDHOFF
[4] (1998), *Maslow on Management,* A. Maslow, JOHN WILEY & SONS INC.

2.02 Engagement

- People prefer responsibility over dependency.
- People get more pleasure out of love than out of hate.
- Educated people would rather create than destroy.
- Most people do not want to be bored.

This list exudes a positive outlook on people, and assumes that people in the proper environment are inclined to do good, and will strive to further develop themselves and the organization.

The central assumption is that man is a need satisfying creature, and that his behavior is partially predictable from his search to fulfil unsatisfied needs. Literature usually speaks of a hierarchy of five groups of human needs, and there are also some sources that use seven groups. We shall firstly study the generally known model and then, for completeness, we shall extend it to the seven layers.

The pyramid starts at the bottom with the physiological. When these are not satisfied, a human being will be motivated mainly by these needs. He will start looking for food, for drink, for clothing, etc. Safety is the next motivation, which expresses itself in the looking for protection, comfort, reassurance and security.

When the lowest of the two bordering groups have been satisfied, a layer directly above it will start motivating, that of social needs. People start looking for solidarity and love, for a group of people to belong to. This is done, for example, by becoming a member of a club, a church, or by entering into an intimate relationship. Once a layer has been satisfied, it will no longer motivate. The order in which this takes place is from the bottom to the top.

FIGURE 22-1. MASLOW HIERARCHY OF NEEDS

(pyramid from bottom to top: Fysiological, Safety, Belonging, Esteem, Self-actualization)

Maslow also called the social need *the need for love and affection*. We often see that authors allocate sex a place in the layer of the primary essentials of life, but that is not completely right. Sex can be physiological (like a normal 'hormonal storm'), but can also arise from someone expressing his affection, and in that case we are dealing with satisfying a need in the third layer.

After that people go looking for respect in the form of appreciation by other people and recognition for performances achieved. An interaction between, on the one hand a sense of self-respect, and on the other hand the respect you get from other people for being who you are and for doing what you do. Once this layer has been fulfilled, then the need for safety will not motivate anymore.

2.02 Engagement

People then go looking for self-actualization or self-realization, in which the most important motivating factor is self-development. In his time, Maslow stated that less than one percent of middle-aged people arrive here, and according to him, this is due to the fact that this need can be slowed down significantly by unfavorable environmental factors. When someone is in danger of losing his job, he will immediately be motivated to look for safety, and when he is bound by a high mortgage, we can also state that he might be threatened in his physiological needs.

In his original article Maslow states that the extent to which someone's needs have been satisfied during childhood, is determined by the extent to which someone 'later in life' is able to endure hardship.

At the beginning of the 21st century, a new phenomenon occurs (in the western world) in people who have been "satisfied" in all Maslow layers, and who have problems with the choices they can, and have to, make. In many young people this creates a form of "choice stress".

In his somewhat more extensive variant, Maslow places two more needs between respect and self-actualization.

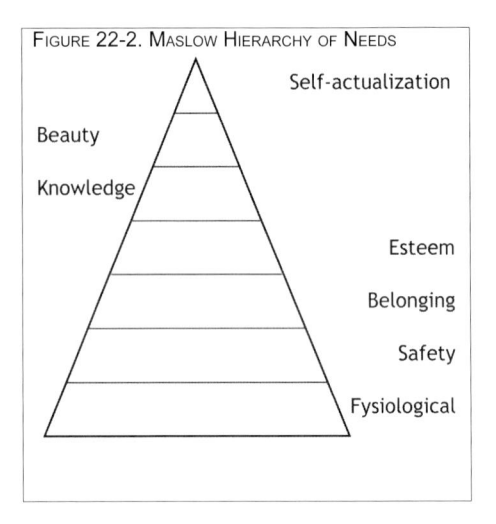

FIGURE 22-2. MASLOW HIERARCHY OF NEEDS

(Pyramid from top to bottom: Self-actualization, Beauty, Knowledge, Esteem, Belonging, Safety, Fysiological)

Cognitive needs to know how things function and why they are as they are, and also the need for variety.

The need for beauty, order and symmetry, enjoying art, etc. In our opinion a more complete model, although less known.

5. Theory X, Theory Y[5]

A contemporary of Maslow is Douglas McGregor(1906-1993). The core of his theory is that your *outlook* on people strongly determines the style of leadership you use.

Just as Maslow, McGregor challenges leaders to ask themselves the following questions[6].

Do you believe that people:
- Can be trusted.
- Look for responsibility and want to be accountable.

EXAMPLE 22-4 MOTIVATING

One team member on your project has a key position. He works enthusiastically on the project, has indicated several times that he is able to fully enjoy himself, and that he is learning a lot of new things doing this job.

You would think he is high up in the Maslow pyramid. In order to motivate him to work through the weekend to achieve a deadline, you can appeal to his need for respect by voicing your appreciation and saying that the senior management think highly of him.

However, if he has marital problems due to him hardly ever being at home, then this appreciation will not really motivate him any longer to work through the weekend. What would help is to offer him and his family a weekend in away once the deadline has been met. In this way, you appeal to the social needs that are at play.

---

5 (1960) *The Human Side of Enterprise*, Douglas McGregor
6 (1998), *Maslow on Management,* A. Maslow, JOHN WILEY & SONS INC.

- Search for meaning in their life.
- By nature, want to develop themselves.
- Do not resist change, but do resist being changed.
- Would rather work than do nothing.

In his *theory X and theory Y,* McGregor describes two ways you can look at people, and he argues that this image determines how you provide leadership.

Theory X is based on the assumption that the average person would rather not work than work, and therefore he must be forced to do his work. He would rather hear what he has to do, and try to avoid responsibility.

Theory Y is based on the assumption that the average person wants to work, and is motivated by both satisfaction and obligation. He prefers, however, to seek his own direction, as long as the right conditions are available to do this.

Leaders who support theory X are more directive and more authoritative than their counterparts who strongly lean on the own responsibility of the employees.

Just as Maslow, McGregor was, of course, a supporter of theory Y. Now in the 21st century it looks as if you are just kicking at an open door, but you have to to position this in the time it was written. McGregor came out with this theory at the beginning of the 1960's, a time in which this was far from being a matter-of-course.

It is important to realize *that the image you have of your employees has a significant impact on your style of leadership.*

6. Motivation-Hygiene Theory

The theory of Frederick Herzberg[7] (1923-2000) is aimed at those factors which have an influence on employees' motivation.

Fundamentally, people have two kinds of needs:
- Avoiding pain.
- Psychological growth.

If we translate this to the workplace, then there are elements of the work that make employees either unsatisfied or satisfied. The first group demotivates, whereas the second group motivates.

The first group **demotivates**, when the items are not well organized. What is then mentioned is the lack of a good or proper: policy and management, direct manager, relationship with the direct manager and colleagues, working conditions, salary, influence on privacy, relationship with subordinates, status and safety. The order in which the items are mentioned relates to the extent they *demotivate* when absent. These are so-called *hygiene* factors.

The first group is mainly concerned with the work *environment*, whereas the second group is about the actual *content* of the work. These include: goals achieved, recognition, the nature of the work, responsibility, progress, personal growth. This is also the order in which they contribute to the **motivation.**

---

[7] (1968) *How Do You Motivate Employees*, F. Herzberg.

2.02 Engagement

The combination of the hygiene and motivation factors leads to four possible situations:

Hygiene	Motivation	Description
High	High	The most ideal situation, resulting in motivated staff who go for it.
High	Low	Employees have few complaints, but are also not super motivated; there is an "as long as my salary gets paid" attitude.
Low	High	Employees are very motivated, but have many complaints.
Low	Low	The worst situation: unmotivated employees with many complaints.

To ensure that your team members are motivated in their work, you look at two symptoms:
- *Complaints*, which say something about the hygiene.
- *Effort*, which says something about the motivation.

In order to ensure that the environment in which the staff have to do their work is not demotivating, you initially look at what you can do about the complaints, something that is often not easy to change. How do you change issues such as: company policy, management and suchlike, as it is hard for a project manager to have an influence on these. This does not imply that you cannot do a lot in the area of the working environment (e.g. ensure that the team sits together), and in the development of an own stimulating culture.

Secondly, you look at the work the team members have to do, and you ensure that they can personally develop themselves further whilst carrying out the work. As project manager you certainly have a number of options to influence these factors. According to Herzberg, the most important motivator is achieving objectives, and that is exactly what it is about in projects. You can also control and influence such matters such as giving recognition, the nature of the work itself, and responsibility.

7. Dealing with opposition

Opposition is an unavoidable factor of change projects. Kurt Lewin[8] pointed out that opposition develops out of the habit formed within the group process. Within a group, there is a certain balance and people feel comfortable with that, and want to keep it that way. Every change then results in a certain opposition. Roderick Gilkey[9] points out the importance of how the life story of the individual employee determines the reaction to this type of stressful events.

He refers to the work of the development psychologist E.H. Erikson[10] who states that the way in which someone knows how to solve important life story conflicts in his or her life, determines the outcome between the following poles:

- *Trust* versus *Mistrust*.
- *Autonomy* versus *Shame & Doubt*.
- *Initiative* versus *Guilt*.
- *Competence* versus *Incompetence*.
- *Identity* versus *Role confusion*.
- *Intimacy* versus *Isolation*.
- *Generativity* versus *Self-absorption*.
- *Integrity* versus *Despair*.

Every one of the different eight life stages identified by Erikson results in a basic at-

---

8 (1951) *Field Theory in Social Science: Selected Theoretical Papers,* Kurt Lewin
9 (1993) *Organisaties op de divan – ch 14,* Manfred Kets de Vries en Partners, SCRIPTUM BOOKS, Schiedam
10 (1959) *Identity and the Life Cycle,* Erik H. Erikson, INTERNATIONAL UNIVERSITIES PRESS

titude of someone's outlook on life. In this way, everyone builds an inner décor, against which background the reality is given a personal interpretation. An own 'inner theatre' in which others play a part that fits in the person's own version of reality.

The uncertainty, which accompanies changes or complex problems, activates the unsolved conflicts from people's own personal life story. This invokes (conditioned) behavior corresponding to the respective life stage in which the original conflict took place.

> EXAMPLE 22-5 SHAPING YOUR FUTURE
> A child, who at primary school has difficulties connecting with children in his peer group, develops a sense of incompetence. As an adult employee, he is faced in a reorganization with a tougher function content. He reacts to this with an attitude of lack of involvement, and obsession with the process instead of the content; behavior which fits with the sense of incompetence he has developed as a child.

This phenomenon is called **regression**; it seems as if history is repeating itself, and instinctively this is true.

Regression is subconscious and in the change projects usually undesirable. Employees experience a mixture of feelings such as mistrust, shame/doubt, guilt, incompetence, blurring of identity and isolation. In general there is no room for these feelings, which only increases insecurity. Employees feel misunderstood, and unintentionally, 'childishly' irrational behavior is activated, ranging from the helpless behavior of a newborn to the rebellion of a adolescent. The most likely management reaction is to 'stamp this out', which, however, only inflates the regression and turns adult employees into 'helpless children', who are dragged from one reorganization to the next.

Everybody is susceptible to regression, and so this a phenomenon that is always present in change situations. As the forms and the causes of regressive behavior in a change situation are limited, this can be dealt with in a 'simple' way.

Because reorganizations have a high urgency, a conscious choice has to be made between the possible interventions. By including the underlying needs in the intervention carried out, the regression can be softened somewhat. Below is a list of possible interventions, each one on its own addressing the underlying conflicts, named by Erikson:

- By providing a clear insight in the objective, and how to achieve this, the *confidence* will grow.
- Promises have to be fulfilled to avoid feeding hidden *mistrust*.
- Give everyone the opportunity to participate in the change process, in order to boost *autonomy*.
- Make clear what is expected of the employees, so they can check the way they are *functioning*.
- In the event of a downsizing, explain to the employees why they are the ones allowed to stay, and teach them how to deal with the *feelings of guilt* people who remain often have.
- Provide a vision of the future, so they know which *initiatives* they themselves can develop.
- Voice clear expectations on how they can **function** *successfully* during the change process.
- Outline clearly the tasks, expectations and structures of the new organization, so employees *know* which role they will play in the new organization.
- Help the employees with drawing up career paths and *understanding* the job appraisal and promotion systems.
- Put the emphasis on the joint approach, which supports feelings of *togetherness*.

- In individual contacts clearly show how important the employee's *contribution* is for the organization.

These precautionary measures ensure a smooth implementation of the changes, because the stimulating triggers are transformed into messages which arouse less opposition. This reduced opposition allows the line managers to communicate with employees at the individual level about dealing with the consequences of the change.

8. Coaching leadership

Coaching leadership is a form of leading in which the project manager uses insights and techniques from the world of counselling. In coaching leadership, a good relationship is the key factor for success. In some situations, this makes coaching leadership potentially the most suitable form, especially in those cases where there is little time to work on relationships. When the ship is sinking, coaching leadership is not the best style.

Coaching leadership assumes that the manager focuses on releasing the potential qualities of his employee, so that he can perform to the best of his ability. In a way, it is as if the manager stands next to the employee and supports him in discovering, developing and using his qualities. The project is then more of a means than a goal.

As a side-effect, the project benefits from this as well, because the employee is able to develop himself and become motivated. The roots of coaching leadership can be strongly found in the ideas of Rogers and Maslow, and also in those of Senge's 'The Learning Organization'.

The question is, how this can be applied in a project. Hersey & Blanchard's situational leadership model is often used as the basis for developing a coaching leadership model; the manager helps the employee to develop himself into an independently working team member. The difference with the "traditional" form of leadership is that it is no longer only concerned with the content, but also with how it is carried out; the skills of the employee are consciously coached.

The starting point for the coaching is a package of objectives agreed between manager and employee. These are the objectives, which are documented in the work packages. The manager diagnosing the competence level, and he adjusts his style accordingly. The development of the employee is what is important. At the start, you still have to provide a lot of instructions (telling), but very quickly, you move on to independence (selling – participating – delegating), by distancing yourself more and more from the actual content of the task.

Louis Cauffman[11] has further developed coaching leadership in what he calls solution oriented management, an approach which is particularly suitable for a project environment.

He names ten pillars:
- *Solutions, solutions and solutions:* The manager points the employees in the direction of a constructive solution, and encourages them to think further in that direction. The focus is always on the solution, not on the problem.
- *Solutions belong to another world than problems:* The cause of the problem does not have to be removed; the problem is only a reason for coming to a better solution.
- *Attention for the exceptions:* A problem is never a problem for 100% of the time, there are always exceptions. In the exception you find the solution. If it

---
11 (2001), Oplossingsgericht management, Louis Cauffman, LEMMA - Utrecht

is not a problem, what else is it, and how can I make use of that?
- *Look for "tools":* In coaching we assume that the team members themselves have sufficient options for solutions, and as the manager, you help them to find them.
- *The right context:* Help the employee to see the problem in his context, and form a relationship in which solutions can be created.
- *Use solution oriented language:* Discuss what is going well; talk in terms of presence and aim at the end of the solution cycle.
- *Focus on the future:* Not the why, but how can I make changes to prevent the problem from occurring again in the future.
- *Co-creativity:* Solutions are created within the work relationship with the employee; the idea that as manager you know everything is a sign of haughtiness.
- *Modesty:* Realize and accept that, as project manager, you never have complete control over other people and situations.
- *Create stability during change:* Employees choose for the dynamics and the pressure of a project, but on the other hand they also need clarity. As a coaching leader, you have to ensure that employees experience sufficient stability to develop themselves despite the daily pressures.

Coaching leadership is a form of leadership based on the good in employees, and creates for them an environment in which they can develop to the full. It is more encouraging than controlling.

9. Enthusing

Enthusiasm is derived from the Greek words enthousiasmos and enthousiazein, which mean ecstasy and possessed by a god, or being beside oneself. It goes a step further than motivating; motivated people do their job, but also promote their job.

Enthusiasm expresses involvement of the employees with the project. The ICB states that the following behavior is fitting for a project manager: *enthusiastic, positive, with a smile, service oriented without losing sight of the project objectives*. Good project management, therefore, is also about passion and emotional movement, and this enthusiasm has a positive effect on the cohesion of the team.

10. Positive attitude

The two most extreme ways of looking at the world have been captured in the proverbial glass being **half full** or **half empty**. The ICB is clear about this, and states that a project manager demonstrates positive realistic behavior, and always looks for solutions to problems when they occur.

For a large part, this attitude finds its origin not only in the belief in his own capabilities (self-confidence), but also in the conviction that he has the right people in the right place. A positive attitude towards the project members stimulates their involvement, and the following research[12] illustrates this. The research question was what the effect would be if you would always approach children as being neat and cheerful.

---

[12] (1975) Attribution Versus Persuasion as a Means for Modifying Behavior, Miller, Brickman, and Bolen, Journal of Personality and Social Psychology nr 31

2.02 Engagement

> **EXAMPLE 22-6 RUBBISH BIN**
> Firstly, the researchers handed out sweets in the school playground and then they counted the number of wrappers in, and next to, the rubbish bin. For some time, different people (headmistress, teachers, cleaners) complimented the children (without there being a real reason), by saying how tidy the class was. This lasted two weeks, after which the researchers again handed out wrapped sweets, and again counted the number of wrappers in, and next to, the rubbish bin. The difference was significant, the children were a lot tidier than before.

All the researchers had done was to credit children with positive attributes and, as project manager, you can also use such a technique. It is the working factor of the positive attitude which is expressed in the form of positively labelling your employees and the environment.

11. Images

Images have a big impact on the motivation of people. By describing the goals, the results and the plan expressively, you take people with you in their perception of the project. As an example, take the *"Images of organization"* that Gareth Morgan[13] describes in his now classic book as follows:

- The organization as organism.
- The organization as brain.
- The organization as culture.
- The organization as political system.
- The organization as spiritual prison.
- The organization as flux and transformation.
- The organization as instrument for domination.

As soon as we read these, we immediately know what type of organization we are dealing with, because the images are so powerful. Creating an image that appeals, increases the involvement of the employees. On the other hand it 'reveals' something of the project manager's involvement with the project.

12. The Creation Spiral

The creation spiral[14] is, as Knoope himself says in the subtitle of his book of the same name, "*the natural path from a wish to actuality*". I doubt whether this is the only path, but the spiral does contain insights, which do indeed increase the chance that you achieve what you want.

Before we look at the spiral´s twelve steps, you must realise that it is not a technique for solving problems. It is about creating something, and as opposed to problem solving, which has a negative orientation (removal of the problem), here you do something positive and in the creation process, you leave something behind.

Knoope differentiates the following steps, which you go through in sequence in order to create your wishes:

- *Wish*, the wish is the beginning: what do you want?
- *Imagine*, make a vivid picture of it.
- *Believe*, if you believe in it, then you also have a greater chance of achieving it.
- *Share*, now you tell others that you believe in it.
- *Research*, look for ideas that will help you achieve your wish.
- *Plan*, take a practical first step towards reality, and plan what you are going to do.
- *Decide*, now you decide to act in accordance with your plan.
- *Act*, here you carry out concrete actions that bring your wish closer.

---

13 (1986) *Images of Organization*, Gareth Morgan, SAGE PUBLICATIONS

14 (1998) De creatiespiraal, Marinus Knoope, KIC NIJMEGEN

2.02 Engagement

FIGURE 22-3. INSIDE-OUTSIDE

	Appreciate	Rest	Whish	Imagine	Believe	
Receive	\multicolumn{5}{c	}{INSIDE}	Share
Receive	\multicolumn{5}{c	}{OUTSIDE}	Share
	Persevere	Act	Decide	Plan	Research	

	Appreciate	Rest	Whish	Imagine	Believe	
Receive	INSIDE					Share
	OUTSIDE					
	Persevere	Act	Decide	Plan	Research	

FIGURE 22-4. SURRENDER-WILLPOWER

	Receive	Appreciate	Rest	Whish	Imagine	
Persevere			SURRENDER			Believe
			WILLPOWER			
	Act	Decide	Plan	Research	Share	

FIGURE 22-5. CREATURE - CREATOR

	Persevere	Receive	Appreciate	Rest	Whish	
Act			CREATURE			Imagine
			CREATOR			
	Decide	Plan	Research	Share	Believe	

FIGURE 22-6. PRESENT - FUTURE

	Act	Persevere	Receive	Appreciate	Rest	
Decide			PRESENT			Whish
			FUTURE			
	Plan	Research	Share	Believe	Imagine	

FIGURE 22-7. REALITY - FANTASY

	Decide	Act	Persevere	Receive	Appreciate	
Plan			REALITY			Rest
			FANTASY			
	Research	Share	Believe	Imagine	Whish	

FIGURE 22-8. BEING YOURSELF - DISSOLVING

	Plan	Decide	Act	Persevere	Receive	
Research			BEEING YOURSELF			Appreciate
			DISSOLVING			
	Share	Believe	Imagine	Whish	Rest	

- *Persevere*, if you encounter setbacks, you persist with your decision and carry on.
- *Receive*, when results manifest themselves, you accept them.
- *Appreciate*, be thankful for, and pleased with, the results.
- *Rest*, following success, take a rest before beginning with your next wish.

When you follow these steps without missing out any, then, according to Knoope, the achievement of your wishes will proceed naturally.

You can view these twelve steps as points on a spiral of upwards circles and if you each time draw a line through two opposite steps, then these sub-divide the spiral up into a number of different domains.

Inside-Outside
This sub-division is about finding a good balance between your inner self (inside) and the world around you (outside). If you allow yourself to be led by what is happening in the world around you, then you neglect your own wishes. But too much emphasis on the inside results in unachievable wishes, with all the associated disappointments.

Surrender-Willpower
There is a lot that you can control, but not everything. The thesis "everything you want is possible to achieve" is not true; sometimes you have to accept your "fate", but not just like that.

Creature - Creator
That you can be both the creator and the creature makes you modest and humble. Too much emphasis on the creature makes you subservient, and too much on the creator makes you arrogant.

Present - Future
The present is certain, the future still unclear. Achieving your wishes is finding the balance between certainty and uncertainty.

Reality - Fantasy
Achieving your wishes is also about finding the right balance between fantasy and reality.

Being Yourself - Dissolving
The last sub-division is about having the right balance between on the one hand guarding your boundaries, and on the other hand being dissolved.

2.03 Self-control

No project control without self-control

You want to keep your project under control. That is a good thing, because you have been hired in to do just that.

But what happens if you cannot even keep yourself under control?

Self-control, well … that is something very useful for a project manager to have.

2.03 Self-Control

2.03-1 Definitions

Self-control	The ability to manage your own behavior, in order to be able to work in a conscious, systematic and disciplined manner and to be able to handle concrete situations, changing requirements, and stressful situations.
Self-knowledge	The picture someone has of the way in which his own thoughts, feelings, and attitude are made visible in his own personal behavior and the effect this has on the environment.

2.03-2 Introduction

A good leader also applies leadership to himself, and, in line with the meaning of the word self-control, has himself under control. This is the pit-bull mentality which enables project managers to keep sight of the goal, remain calm and carry on in times of adversity. Listening to the complaints of a disappointed user; parrying the antics of a "rat", without becoming a rat himself; accepting setbacks and remaining focussed on the goal.

2.03-3 Process steps

1. Analyze a stressful situation.
2. Analyze working behavior.
3. Provide adequate resources and skills to the project team.
4. Produce a SWOT of the team.
5. Act to reduce stress.
6. Communicate open and honest.
7. Share tasks, responsibilities and authorities.
8. Be well organized yourself and demonstrate appropriate behavior.
9. Apply lessons learned

1. Analyze a stressful situation

As compared to working in a department, a project is all about results the team has to deliver within a restricted timescale. By definition, a project is dynamic and aimed at the short term, and the project is, therefore, hectic and under time pressure. As the costs of producing the result have to stay within the agreed budget, there is also a significant focus on the costs.

You can say that a project team, in one way or another, is always involved with stressful situations, and a good project manager can always handle these effectively. In the ICB definition, a number of key words stand out:
- Own behavior.
- Systematic and disciplined manner.
- Changing requirements.
- Stressful situations.

Even before you are in a position to judge a stressful situation, you must be able to control your own behavior. This is needed for the way in which you provide leadership, how you deal with conflicts and how you negotiate; everything begins with self-control.

But now a project management "flavour" must be added to this: *systematic* and *disciplined*! You frequently look not only at yourself, but also at the situation in which your team finds itself. Is it stressful, and if so, what are the causes of this?

2. Analyze working behavior

Stress is not so bad, as long as it does not bring the work performances into danger. When people are under pressure for a long period of time, their performance will decrease, and that also applies to you! Therefore, you need to look at your own functioning when under pressure, and ask yourself the question "*which patterns of behavior do I follow*"?

The ICB considers the following behaviors to be undesirable:
- Moody.
- Irritated.
- Unreasonable.
- Offended by criticism.
- Aggressive.
- Denial of stress.
- Workaholic.

These behaviors require courage to recognise, but it is self-evident that such behaviors to a greater or lesser extent are responsible for a stressful atmosphere in your project. Only when you can recognise one or more of these in yourself, can you also recognise them in your team members.

3. Provide adequate resources and skills to the project team

There are various means of reducing stress. However, when your personality (i.e. behavior) is the cause of the stress, you have a 'tough struggle', because you cannot easily change your personality. It is, therefore, a good idea to have a person of trust in your project team, who can point out your stressful behavior to you.

Reduce stress, and start with yourself.

2.03 Self-Control

The question now is, next to this, what skills and means do you also have to offer to the project team? In general, you can say that people expect both structure and consideration from their leaders.

A clear structure
Nearly all technical project management competences have to do with applying a structure. Once you have identified and analyzed the stakeholders, it is easier to keep the working conditions stable. The same is valid for defining the scope; the better this is carried out at the start, the fewer changes are likely to be needed. Once you have described achievable objectives in the area of duration and the necessary hours, this has a stress reducing effect, as people are then under less pressure, as compared to impossible timescales which they have had no say in. Also, when it is clear who has to do what, the risk of stressful situations occurring is significantly reduced.

In short: *a clear structure reduces stress.*

Consideration
When, as group leader, you show understanding for the ups and downs of your team members, they will feel more at ease. Certainly when you adapt your style of leadership to their own personal abilities, they can develop on the project, and that is something that significantly increases motivation. This applies to both the team members (inwards looking), and to the important stakeholders (outward looking). When the latter group feels that they are being understood, they will lend more support to the project, which makes the environment more stable and again reduces the risk of stressful situations.

In short: *consideration with the ups and downs of those involved reduces stress.*

4. Produce a SWOT of the team
Self-knowledge is a key to success, and that is also true of the knowledge a team has of itself. In the first instance it can, therefore, do you no harm as project manager, to make a strengths and weaknesses analysis of your team, both the team in total, and the team members as individuals. Based on this analysis, you can determine which actions you should take to prevent stress.

When you do what you are good at, the risk of stress reduces, but if you do something you are not so good at, the risk of stress increases. This seems obvious, but it often happens that we allocate a task to a team that they are, in fact, unable to do.

5. Act to reduce stress
Reducing stress starts at the source. Take away the cause and the stress reduces. We can identify the following stress factors within organizations:
- Too much work, work that is too difficult or too easy.
- Roles that are too heavy, unclear or conflicting.
- 'Nervous people' in the team.
- Unfavorable working conditions.
- Unhealthy (internal) competition.
- Large changes.

The project manager can seize upon all these sources to intervene. There may also, of course, be sources of stress in the employees' personal lives, and these are much harder to deal with. Being considerate is often the only tool you can use.

6. Communicate open and honest
Most people would rather not admit that they are 'burdened' by stress, and that makes it even more difficult to deal with it. As project manager, you have to accept a responsibility for this, and creating an atmosphere in which people can communicate openly and

honestly with each other, makes it possible to talk about the stress and to do something about it.

7. Share tasks, responsibilities and authorities

If you do everything yourself, you also carry the whole of the burden yourself. That, however, is not necessary, and you can, of course, ensure that you delegate certain tasks to team members. This provides them with an opportunity to develop further, maybe even to the level of project leader. Delegation allows you to focus on the important issues in your project.

Together with the task and the responsibility, you also delegate the authority. If you do not do this, people will have insufficient room to carry out the task, and giving responsibility without the associated level of authority is also a source of stress.

8. Be well organized yourself and demonstrate appropriate behavior

This is one of the effects of self-control; it is that which is visible, also outside of your work. Self-control shows through in someone's overall conduct. There isn't a knack to it, but denotes someone who has his life in order, and behaves appropriately.

The behavior also depends on culture. What is accepted in one culture can be inappropriate in another, and so when, as project manager, you are dealing with different cultures, you have to investigate those cultures and not do anything that is not really appropriate.

9. Apply lessons learned

You learn the most from situations in which you have lost self-control. It is very useful to analyze those situations, to look at what happened, and how you reacted.

You then keep asking yourself the following questions:

- What did I feel?
- What did I think?
- What did I do?
- What would I have wanted to do?

The difference between the third and fourth question is the difference between conditioning and will. When you analyze the first three questions integrally, you can discover signs which will warn you the next time you may be starting to lose your self-control. If you are aware of what is happening, you will be able to steer away from it, and ultimately you will notice that your attitude changes somewhat. In actuality, this means that you have re-conditioned yourself.

2.03-4 SPECIAL TOPICS

1. Emotional Intelligence

Next to the various forms of intelligence in the areas of language, spatial thinking, music, and movement, there is also *emotional intelligence*, a term that has been popularized by Daniel Goleman[1]. In his book with the same title, he provides examples of how this form of intelligence can be the key to success.

The core is about how someone deals with his own emotions and those of others, i.e. whether someone is capable of empathizing with the lives of others. In his book, Goleman argues that we are dealing with an emotional malaise, and on the basis of research carried out amongst American school children, he ascertained deterioration in the following areas:

- Reservedness or social problems.
- Fear and depression.
- Problems concentrating.
- Aggressive behavior.

He advocates emotional schooling in the following areas:
- Emotional awareness.
- Regulation of emotions.
- Productive use of emotions.
- Empathy.
- Dealing with relationships.

As leaders, emotional intelligence is one of our tools for dealing with stressful situations.

2. Personality

Personality is the result of someone's aptitude and development. Personality is derived from the Latin word **persona** which means **mask**. If we philosophize further on that, personality is that which you show of yourself to the outside world. It is the totality of all your behavior with respect to other people, and is just the outside, but has its roots deep in the core of who you are.

Personality is that which you show, and only a part of who you are.

It is carefully constructed and enables you to live in balance with your surroundings. There are a lot of different models, and one of the oldest classifications comes from ancient Greece, in which four temperaments or types of personality were recognized:

- *Sanguineness*: fiery and energetic.
- *Phlegmatic*: calm and slow, the bookkeepers and diplomats.
- *Choleric*: hot-tempered, the leader types.
- *Melancholic*: the members of state, poets and artists.

As well as these, there are many others such as the Myers-Briggs Type Indicator, the Eneagram, etc. Most of these models often have a conviction as their basis, rather than a thorough scientific foundation, and come under the so called Big-V model, which originated in a series of investigations carried out from 1936 onwards.

In this research, a language study has been carried out to find words to use to describe personality characteristics. After much research, these words could be classified into five categories:
- *Extraversion* (versus Introversion).
- *Agreeableness*.
- *Conscientness*.
- *Emotional stability* (versus Neuroticism).
- *Openness to experience*.

This model offers leads for starting a discussion about someone's behavior and the impact of it on other team members. It is clear

---

[1] (1996) *Emotional Intelligence,* Daniel Goleman, OLYMPUS

3. Cognitive dissonance

> EXAMPLE 23-1 EXPLAINING THE SCORES
>
> In the context of his personal development, a 360 degree test was carried out on Gerard's competences. He could not recognise himself in the results of the test.
>
> The evening before the meeting with his manager, Gerard is busying himself looking for explanations as to why the questions in the test were not unambiguous, because that must be the reason for the fact that he absolutely did not recognise himself in the results.

Cognitive dissonance[2] is the tension experienced when someone is confronted with events that shake their self-image. This results in an uncomfortable feeling (often subconscious), which the person then tries to ignore or reason away. Not uncommonly, you then see that people become much more fanatical than they were previously.

There are various ways in which people try to get rid of the tension:
- By developing new convictions.
- By changing existing convictions.

An example of the former is the smoker, who is confronted with the damaging consequences of his addiction, and defends himself with the argument that smokers have less chance of contracting Alzheimer's disease. An example of the latter is when he says he would rather die young and happy, than become old and grumpy (comment: the dying process of a lung cancer patient is not a pleasant one, and his argument is a fallacy).

There are different reasons why it is useful to discover cognitive dissonance in you and in others.

Each time someone says something that makes the view you have of yourself, or of a particular situation, look foolish, a learning point is created. Normally, this then subconsciously creates a certain amount of unpleasant tension, which is a possible sign of cognitive dissonance. It is better not to defend yourself, but to listen to the conflicting facts, and then to determine for yourself what you want to take from it for your own development. You could call this cognitive relaxation.

It is different when you are confronted with cognitive dissonance in those involved in your project, and which expresses itself in a form of resistance. You must then realize for yourself that the more you try to convince someone, the more resistance you will meet. It is then better to leave the subject in question alone.

Here, we also have the issue of cultural differences[3], which predominantly play a role when people either come from an individualistic, or from a collective, culture. In terms of the former (individualistic), people will strive for a consistent self-image, and cognitive dissonance arises particularly when something happens that challenges the image that someone has of himself. People from a collective society, experience this from the viewpoint of the group image. As project manager, if you are not sensitive to this, then it forms an obstacle to the project team's acceptance of your decisions. If you then also have the wrong self-image of your own cultural skills, then you begin to suffer from cognitive dissonance, and you will, perhaps, begin to grumble and run down the people from the other culture. You then land yourself back and forth in a negative downwards spiral of cognitive dissonances.

---

2 (1956) *When Prophecy Fails*, Leon Festinger

3 (2007) *Handbook of Cultural Psychology*, ed. Kitayama and Cohen, THE GUILFORD PRESS, London

Many of the sensitivities back and forth between cultures are related to cognitive dissonance. In order to develop your intercultural skills, self-acceptance and self-analysis are then the way to go.

> EXAMPLE 23-2 MY WAY OR THE HIGHWAY
> A successful project manager from an individualistic culture carries out an international project in an Arab country.
> A difficult co-operation exists. Frustrated, he says: "*It's my way or the highway.*" The situation never resolved itself completely, and he never even realised it.

4. How people learn

When we really want to learn, self-control can be learned. There are several methods of learning, and Wierdsma and Swieringa[4] differentiate between three of these:
- *Single-loop learning:* when we change our behavior.
- *Double-loop learning:* when we change our insight.
- *Triple-loop learning:* when we change our principles.

Single-loop learning is about the outside e.g. we clear up our desk because we have to. Double-loop learning is about our thinking e.g. we now clear up our desk because we know a clear desk creates less stress.

With triple-loop learning we go even further into the area of emotional matters, about the person we are. You can change your behavior and also your insight, but if, by nature (as I am), you are a slob, after some time your desk will be a mess again. Triple-loop learning is about a change in your personality and that is difficult but not impossible to achieve. Sometimes a big crisis is needed to motivate people to change from the inside out.

---

[4] (2011) *Lerend Organiseren,* Wierdsma en Swieringa, NOORDHOFF, Groningen

2.03 Self-Control

2.04 Assertiveness

W̲ʜᴇʀᴇ ᴛʜᴇʀᴇ's ᴀ ᴡɪʟʟ, ᴛʜᴇʀᴇ's ᴀ ᴡᴀʏ ꜰᴏʀᴡᴀʀᴅ

If I know what I want

If I believe in what I want

I tell others what I want

Others believe what I want

Others do what I want

I want and therefore I am

2.04 Assertiveness

2.04-1 DEFINITIONS

Aggressiveness	The coercive conveying of a vision, without taking account of the interests and view of others.
Influence	The ability to convey a vision in such a persuasive and authoritative way that others are prepared to accommodate this.
Persuasiveness	The ability to achieve agreement about common goals through discussions, or the power of argument.
Project assertiveness	The ability to convey a vision persuasively and with authority.
Self-assertiveness	The recognition of your own wishes, needs and values and finding a suitable way of expressing these.

2.04-2 Introduction

In a general sense, assertiveness means that you recognise your wishes, needs and values, and you seek out a suitable way of expressing these. It is the willingness to stand up for yourself, to be open to who you are, and to treat yourself with respect in all encounters you have.

This description pre-supposes someone who is in contact with his inner motives and who, from his own self-confidence in his contacts with other people, stands up for himself. Someone who is well organized.

In the project context we use a tighter definition:

The ability to convey a vision persuasively and with authority.

We have to predominantly view this competence element in the light of effectively daring to fight for the interests of the project. This tighter definition, though, does not mean that "project assertiveness" has nothing to do with "self-assertiveness". Self-assertiveness is a pre-condition for project assertiveness. Project managers should have enough of both in their personal baggage.

2.04-3 PROCESS STEPS

1. Determine and record project goals and results.
2. Determine what can lead to discussion.
3. Prepare counter-arguments.
4. Assess viewpoints, interests and relationships.
5. Prepare meetings and discussions.
6. Present project interests in a calm and self-assured manner.
7. Value others.
8. Build up sustainable relationships with others.
9. Apply lessons learned

1. Determine and record project goals and results

Just as self self-confidence is one of the pillars under self-assertiveness, project goals and projected results are the foundation under project assertiveness.

I shall briefly repeat the terms result (the project goal in narrow sense) and goal. Result is that which you (in the project plan) have agreed to deliver, and the goal is that which the project sponsor and/or the users want to achieve, or effect, with this result. The goal is the justification for the result to be delivered.

As project manager, you are focussed on the project result. When you stand up for the interests of the project, it is because of the result you have to achieve. A thorough knowledge of what you want, i.e. the result, and why the organization wants it, i.e. the goal, allows you to substantiate what you want to achieve. The goal and the result underpin every argument.

You are already busy with this during the planning of the project, when you clearly specify which results lead to which goals. This goes a step further than only an involvement with respect to content. You have to, as it were, imagine yourself in the roles of your project sponsor, the suppliers and the users, a position which gives you a strong basis for being project assertive and to stand up for the project interests.

2. Determine what can lead to discussion

Foresight is the essence of government. Initially, this process step happens during the stakeholder analysis. Sometimes this takes place very formally during a meeting, but it is also possible that the project manager considers it gradually, eventually arriving at a list of potential discussion points per stakeholder.

By doing this at an early stage in the project, the stakeholder analysis gets more depth, and it is possible in advance to obtain a picture of the inherent resistance. Discussions take place when we are confronted with:

- Opposing interests.
- Conflicting personalities.
- Complex communication channels.
- Technical problems.
- Unclear boundaries.
- Unclear or conflicting responsibilities.

These form a part of the risk analysis, which takes place both beforehand, and then continuously throughout the project.

3. Prepare counter-arguments

On the subject of counter-arguments, it is useful if you already know beforehand what you can best say in certain situations. As this is about convincing someone else, the basic principle is to connect to the other party, and this only works when you present arguments the other person can accept.

This means that you must have some insight into the way of thinking and the interests of the other person. What does he find self-

2.04 Assertiveness

evident, from which frame of reference does he reason, and more considerations such as these. This knowledge broadens your possibilities of striking the right chord during the discussion. You repeat this in your thoughts and make notes to see where certain arguments can lead to in a discussion.

This thorough preparation increases your self-confidence and prevents you from becoming confused during the discussion so that you can no longer react adequately.

4. Assess viewpoints, interests and relationships

Counter-arguments only work when they are legitimate for the other party. For this reason, you must be in touch with the different viewpoints and interests. In this way, you are in a position to justify your own standpoints, but this alone is not sufficient.

You also assess the relationships between the different people involved. How dependent they are on each other, who the informal leaders are, how they influence each other, what coalitions have been formed, etc. Counter-arguments work in the directions of content, relationships and the influencing through third parties.

Content
The arguments you use to prove you are right must fit with in with the interests of the opposing party, who, by agreeing with you, is in a position to better achieve his or her requirements.

Relationship
Arguments regarding content are normally not enough. There must also be a relationship between you and the other person, and if this is not good, content based arguments will come over weaker than if you have a good relationship.

Influencing by third parties
If a party can be better influenced through other third parties, then, with respect to content, you can first try to influence the latter. When they have been turned round, they can win over the other party to agree with you.

Cultural considerations
When you are involved with people from different cultures, it is also important for you understand how these people do business with each other. There are countries where the emphasis is put on content and result, but just as many countries where the emphasis is on the relationship. First build a good relationship, and only then talk about the content.

5. Prepare meetings and discussions

The previous process steps are very general. This one is more specific in nature and is about preparing the actual discussion. This preparation no longer needs to take much time, because you have both the project interests and the interests of the others in your sights, and you have already immersed yourself in the discussion points and the associated counter-arguments.

It is preferable to choose your own arena, as it concerns looking after the interests of the project. Beforehand, you think about the possible courses the discussion can take, how you handle these and what you are prepared, and are not prepared, to yield. The greater the importance, the more time you spend on the preparation.

2.04 Assertiveness

> EXAMPLE 24-1 PREPARATION
>
> A number of years ago, I had to negotiate on a specific subject that was very important to our company. If it did not go our way, it would cost us a lot of money.
>
> I can still clearly remember that I spent a whole afternoon with my business partner investigating all possible directions the discussion could take.
>
> With a certain amount of tension, I went to the negotiations the next day, and because of the preparation I was able to represent our interests extraordinarily well.
>
> Good preparation is more than half the work.

6. Present project interests in a calm and self-assured manner

Now comes the crunch. Despite all the preparation, if you clam up during the discussion, you cannot represent the interests of the project well. This is where self-control comes into play. As long as you remain calm, you are able to direct the discussion towards your aims.

Calm is something other than cool or unemotional. It indicates the condition, whereby someone has his or her feelings under control, but does show them. It is tempting in the heat of the battle to become fanatical, and to force the other party on the defensive. Or the other way round, when the opposing party is fanatical and puts you on the defensive, it is not unthinkable that you recoil from it. The effect of both scenarios is that the discussion is no longer constructive, but has more to do with the "top or under dog" question (who is actually the boss of this situation?). It is then no longer about being right or co-operating, but about being proved right, which is an undesirable situation.

You prevent this by remaining calm, whereby you are in a better frame of mind to put forward your arguments.

7. Value others

When other people like you, it is easier to take care of your own interests. Most people prefer to associate themselves with likeable rather than unlikeable people, and this is so in all cultures. Assertiveness is about taking care of your own interests (and those of your project), and as you can imagine, this is easier when people like you. You can influence this by appreciating other people and expressing this as well.

Therefore, make sure the others have the feeling that they have provided a worthwhile contribution to a discussion. You can do this by explicitly thanking them, but non-verbal communication, such as nodding or smiling approvingly and suchlike, can be just as effective. The extent to which this comes across is strongly dependent on your own (cultural) background. If it is not customary to give a compliment, it can come across as being false.

Also, if it does not match with your normal personal style, people could, in the first instance, be surprised, but if you "practice" often enough, it will gradually become more a part of your personality.

8. Build up sustainable relationships with others

> EXAMPLE 24-2 CARPET
>
> A consultant working in the Gulf States had already been negotiating for half a year about a beautiful carpet, and each time he was in the neighbourhood he went along for a visit.
>
> The price had already been reduced somewhat, and it led to a lasting relationship with trader.

Here, we build further on the previous process step. When people have good mutual relationships, they feel safe together, and they will have less of a tendency to become defensive. You could say that, when the relationships are good, you need less assertiveness.

The building of a sustainable relationship has an influence on future discussions, and for this reason alone, as project manager, you should work on this.

9. Apply lessons learned

With respect to all behavioral competences, it holds good that you learn by:
- Awareness of your behavior.
- Repetition of new behavior.

Therefore, you must always evaluate important meetings and discussions afterwards, and look at which arguments worked and which did not. Also, how you reacted to the other party, in which situations you were able to do so, and under what circumstances you were not able to remain calm. This knowledge allows you to be more effective the next time.

Repeating new (desired) behavior feeds your self-confidence (and with this, your assertiveness) and your effectiveness as a project manager.

2.04-4 Special Topics

1. The cultural dimension

When we talk about assertiveness in a project environment, we cannot escape the fact that we must also consider the situation from a multicultural viewpoint. Behavior that a fellow-countryman considers to be acceptable, can be interpreted by someone from a different culture totally differently, with all associated misunderstandings.

I will keep to both the definitions of assertiveness:
- Self-assertiveness: The recognition of your own wishes, needs and values and finding a suitable way of expressing these.
- Project assertiveness: The ability to convey a vision persuasively and with authority.

In the first instance assertiveness is, therefore, about the effectiveness of behavior; can you find a "suitable form of expression", and do you come across as "persuasive and with authority"? Both definitions, therefore, force you to take account of the other party. Both you, and the other party, are strongly determined by the culture in which you have grown up. Certain behavior can be assertive for one person, whereas the other person will view it as being rude.

The extent of assertiveness in a culture
One of the most extensive studies on the cultural dimension of assertiveness is the GLOBE study[1], in which not less than 62 societies were researched with respect to cultural differences. One of the dimensions investigated was assertiveness. The study looked at:
- How assertive people experienced the society.
- How assertive people would like the society to be.

The practice, therefore, versus the desired values. Before I go into this, we first consider what the researchers understood by assertiveness.

In an assertive culture there is sympathy for the stronger members, competition is encouraged, there is the belief that everyone can be successful when they apply themselves, direct communication is expected, initiative is valued and performance is rewarded. Of the 62 cultures investigated, there are 29 that belong to this group, including, for example: Nigeria, Germany, Greece, USA, and Turkey.

In less assertive cultures there is sympathy for the weaker members, co-operation is encouraged, competition is associated with defeat, success is dependent on the circumstances, it is ensured that no-one loses face, and integrity, loyalty and co-operation are valued. Of the cultures investigated, French-speaking Switzerland, New Zealand and Sweden were some of the lowest scoring countries for assertiveness.

Assertiveness also has a lot to do with how we view nature. High scoring countries often assume that nature is controllable, whereas low scoring countries realize that nature is too complex to be subdued. It would be interesting to look at the discussion on climate in this light.

We find this also in the extent to which people are convinced they have control over

---

[1] (2004) Culture, Leadership, and Organizations – the GLOBE Study of 62 Societies, Robert J. House and others, SAGE PUBLICATIONS, London-New Dehli

their own destiny[2]. In countries such as Saudi Arabia, Oman or Kuwait, about 50% of the people think they can influence their own destiny, whereas in the USA or Australia about 80% of the population think that. The result is that what the average American experiences as suitable behavior, is experienced by the average Omani as uncontrolled and pointless. As has been said, assertiveness is culture dependent.

Another finding from the GLOBE study is that nearly all assertive societies investigated expressed the desire for less assertiveness. An explanation of this can be that it is a lot more strenuous to live in an assertive society. In a non-assertive society, you do not have to stand up for your rights so much, as the interaction with other people is not as hard.

A suitable form of expression
With assertive behavior, we immediately think of how you express your:
- Views
- Emotions

But this is a misunderstanding, as directness is not the same as assertiveness. It is not always necessary to stand up for your opinion, or always to express your emotions, and further on I shall briefly deal with diplomatic skills. What is permitted is strongly dependent on the culture in which people find themselves at that point in time.

We see that, for example, in the way in which people express themselves verbally. We can then differentiate between direct, clear and explicit use of language, whereby people are always to the point, versus indirect language, or use of words which can be construed in more than one way, whereby the other party must try to find out what the implicit message is. In this latter situation, assertiveness also means you ensure that someone else does not lose face.

You can envisage that someone from a direct culture has a lot of trouble recognizing the subtle hints that a colleague team member expresses with respect to his "rude" behavior. The person from the direct culture is handicapped by his upbringing, in which he has never learnt to recognise these subtle hints.

> EXAMPLE 24-3 PUBERTY IN SYRIA
>
> In 2008 I had a discussion with a Syrian project manager about bringing up children.
>
> He told me: "I hated my father! But now I understand him better."
>
> When I asked him if he had many arguments with his father, he said: "No".
>
> Instinctively, I though about the puberty years of my own Dutch children.

2. Persuasiveness
This is about the difference between being right and being proven right. It is not always so (unfortunately) that being right is the same as actually being proved to be right. Assertiveness and persuasiveness are two sides of the same coin. For the former, the project manager must stand up for his view, open his mouth, react when necessary, and that is assertiveness. Thereafter, it depends on how he packages the message i.e. either persuasively or incoherently.

Persuasiveness is unrelated to the content, and is the extent to which you are able to present your arguments to the other person, which convince him of your standpoint.

In ancient times, people were already busying themselves trying to find the right words

---
[2] (1997) Riding the Waves of Culture – Understanding Cultural Diversity in Business, Fons Trompenaars & Charles Hampden-Turner, NICHOLAS BREALY PUBISHING, London

2.04 Assertiveness

to strengthen their position. They differentiated between:
- Inventio: determine what you want to say.
- Dispositio: set out your argument.
- Elocutio: look for the right style/words.
- Memoria: mental preparation.
- Actio: practice and deliver your argument.

In searching for the arguments, you will initially make use of correct assertions. You can train yourself in this by thinking about it beforehand, and practicing what you are going to say.

3. Diplomacy

Diplomacy has to do with tact and sensitivity. Being right does not always mean that you have to be proved right; there is an element of give and take involved. Diplomacy is necessary when there is a difference of opinion on a sensitive subject. Silent diplomacy gives both parties the possibility of exploring opinions and seeking out solutions.

There is a hint of caution in the communication that prevents the other party from feeling he has to defend himself. As soon as people have the feeling they have to defend themselves, arguments related to content will no longer work. Even if you win the argument on content, the other person still believes that he is being manipulated. Diplomacy and assertiveness, therefore, should go hand in hand with each other.

The lists below[3] contains a summary of a series of behaviors that evoke defensive behavior, and behaviors that reduce this significantly:

Reduces defensive behavior:
- A description of what you have observed.
- Showing preparedness to come to a solution together.
- Making your opinion and intention clear in an open and honest way.
- Empathise with the feelings and interests of the other person.
- Let the other person see that you are both on an equal footing.
- Not being dogmatic.

Evokes defensive behavior:
- Expressing a (negative) value judgement.
- Forcing the other person to accept a particular opinion.
- Leading the other person to adopt a different behavior in a concealed or indirect manner.
- Ignoring the feelings and interests of the other person.
- Showing that you are superior to the other person.
- Taking on a pedantic attitude.

In every cultural setting, diplomacy is one of the key competences that a project manager must have.

4. Pillars of self-esteem

Nathaniel Branden[4] lists six pillars of self-esteem (or self-respect) and has developed a simple programme to work on these. He names the following six:
- Live consciously
- Self-acceptance
- Take responsibility
- Live purposefully
- Be assertive
- Integrity

---

3 (1961) *Defense Level and Influence Potential in Small Groups*, J. R. Gibb in Leadership and Interpersonal Behavior, HOLT, RINEHART AND WINSTON, New York

4 (1995) *The Six Pillars of Self-esteem*, Nathaniel Branden, BANTAM BOOKS

It begins with living consciously, meaning that someone is prepared to see himself or herself as he or she is, preferably without a value judgement, which immediately gives us the second pillar, which Branden calls self-acceptance. A lot of people find this difficult, and speak about faults or weaknesses they want to improve, whereas they could also talk just about the behavior they want to change. Talking about faults is a fundamental attitude that does not further self-acceptance, but quite the contrary.

Self-acceptance is a call to no longer live at odds with yourself. If you clam up, and become angry and aggressive in discussions, then that is just how it is. It is not a fault if you act differently to how you, perhaps, want to act. You could even say that people can only change properly when they dare to accept themselves and, without judging themselves, see what the effect of their behavior is. Only then can they really learn. Carl Rogers[5] formulated this as follows:

> "The curious paradox is that when I accept myself just as I am, then I can change."

Then, the third pillar, taking responsibility for your deeds, and setting in motion a change in your behavior. You set goals (the fourth pillar) to move onto the upwards road. Taking responsibility gives you self-confidence, and your assertiveness (the fifth pillar) increases, whereby you achieve more objectives, and set a self-fulfilling prophecy in motion.

The fifth pillar introduces an interesting chicken-and-egg problem. Self-esteem leads to assertiveness and assertiveness leads again to self-esteem, and this can develop into either an upwards spiral, or a downwards spiral.

The latter source is about integrity. When you are not honest, then this gnaws subconsciously at your self-confidence and, therefore, also at your assertiveness. Subconsciously you are very well aware that you are cheating on matters, and a 'gnawing conscience' eats away at your self-confidence, all of which affects your assertiveness.

5. RT, RET and REBT

Introduction

This technique, which is predominantly known as RET, was developed in 1955 by the American cognitive psychologist, Albert Ellis (1913 – 2007). Originally this was known under the name Rational Therapy (RT), but with continuing insights, in 1961 he changed the name to Rational Emotive Therapy (RET), and finally again in 1994 to Rational Emotive Behavioral Therapy (REBT). He would rather have changed the name into cognitive emotive behavioral therapy, but REBT and RET had become so well-known, that he decided against it[6].

The technique looks at how thinking and feeling exert an influence on behavior. Although first developed for a therapeutic setting, it is very suitable to employ for your own personal development. The approach of the so-called irrational beliefs that people harbour about themselves and others, makes it a useful technique for further developing your assertiveness, and that is also the reason why it is discussed in this chapter.

---

5 (1961) On becoming a person, Carl Rogers, HOUGHTON MIFFLIN COMPANY, New York, USA

6 (2001) Overcoming Destructive Believes, Feelings and Behaviors, Albert Ellis, PROMOTHEUS BOOKS, New York USA

2.04 Assertiveness

In Dutch management literature[7], an attempt has even been made to make this applicable for managers. I shall do the same for project managers.

Cause and effect

As humans, we always want to see a cause and effect relationship. We want to understand why things go the way they do. As this puts us somewhat in a position to "predict" the future, it has a lot of advantages. When you, as project manager, are busy doing a risk analysis, in order to minimize or prevent the negative consequences, you look for the possible causes. Cause and effect are anchored in the human mind.

But there is also another side. Something happens, we react to it and very quickly the connection is made: "because this happened, I reacted in this way". We do this right from childhood, and in this way certain beliefs are born. When you carry out self-analysis, you come to the conclusion that, as well as a direct cause, there are also more deep-seated assumptions and beliefs that, as it were, form a justification for the behavior displayed. Normally there is nothing wrong with this, until such time that the behavior is no longer effective. Then so-called development points originate, which in practice, are difficult to change. There are a number of ways to work on yourself, and we have already seen that one of these is the way of self-esteem.

REBT adopts a different direction, and this is a rational approach, in which you seek out the underlying beliefs and call them into question.

The way of self-esteem

In order to understand REBT properly, then, according to REBT, we first have to consider the downhill way of self-esteem. Self-esteem is ascribing yourself a rating, meaning in fact that you pronounce a judgement on yourself, preferably positive, whereby your feeling of self-esteem increases giving a high level of self-esteem, thereby supporting assertive behavior. The danger, however, is in the rating, as a positive rating goes hand-in-hand with a negative rating. In the following, you can see what effect this can have.

I AM A UNIQUE PERSON

This sounds good, but when you exaggerate, you soon think that you are a very special someone, in fact better than other people. Through this self-image, you set a high bar for yourself. If you cannot then satisfy that self-image, you create an unnecessarily stressful situation for yourself.

> EXAMPLE 24-4 I'M BETTER
> Gunther considers himself better than all his colleagues, and has, therefore, taken on a project that is too difficult for him. He can hardly keep his head above water and is not open to positive feedback.

IT ALWAYS COMES RIGHT

That is often the case, but not always. Suppose your motto is: "Luck is a choice and failure is not an option". This can quickly lead to a situation, in which you need the universe to work for you (as if that has a will of its own). When luck then deserts you (as if luck is a partner that can leave you), what then?

> EXAMPLE 24-5 HOLDING ON
> Nico believes in a good ending, and will not give up easily. Whilst he is still holding on, he does not inform his project sponsor. Ultimately, the project cannot be saved and it is stopped.

---

[7] (1992) Rationeel Emotief Management, Jan Verhulst, SWETS & ZEITLINGER, Amsterdam/Lisse

2.04 Assertiveness

I AM A GOOD PERSON

This remains to be seen, in the same way that you can put a question mark behind the supposition "I am a bad person". If you now also put your behavior on a par with who you are, then you must always be good, which is not sustainable, and it will ultimately lead to disappointment.

> EXAMPLE 24-6 I'M GOOD
> "I am a good project manager", Amil says to his colleagues. When, halfway through the project he exceeded his budget, he did not dare to say anything about it.

Working on your personal development quickly leads to the development of irrational expectations about yourself, which, when you cannot for some reason satisfy them, ultimately impedes your development. Often they will have a negative effect on your feeling of self-esteem.

The basic flow

If we then translate the above into REBT terms, we obtain the first three parts:

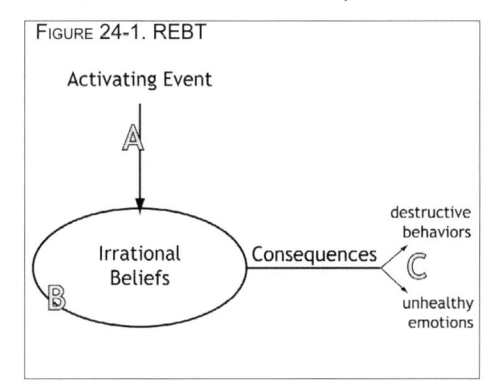

FIGURE 24-1. REBT

Activating Event

A

Irrational Beliefs — Consequences — destructive behaviors C / unhealthy emotions

B

A: is the activating event. B (from beliefs) is a relevant belief that someone has. C is the consequence of A and B in the form of destructive behavior or unhealthy emotions. Ellis names the following as being unhealthy emotions: depression, nervousness, anger, shame, hurt feelings, jealousy and guilt. Destructive behavior can then be: you withdraw into yourself, you tear into someone, or you no longer dare to express your opinion.

In his practice, Ellis now makes three important observations, which form the basis for REBT. These are:
- A is only part of the cause.
- The irrational beliefs (B) always remain present.
- Insight alone is not enough, and you must continue to work at it.

If we realize that our behavior (C) is dependent, on the one hand on (activating) events (A), and on the other hand on our irrational beliefs (B), then we accept that the cause of our behavior is in ourselves, and we no longer blame the environment for why we behave the way we do. This helps you to come out of a victim role, and to behave assertively.

The second observation means that these beliefs never go away completely. At the most they reduce somewhat in intensity as we get older, but they will always remain in the background. Therefore, and that is the third observation, we have to constantly work at it, which in REBT means that we must continuously seek out our irrational beliefs and call them into question (the third observation).

Irrational beliefs

The irrational beliefs can be divided up into the following groups:
- Dogmas
- Exaggerations
- Frustrations
- Judgements

We study these groups for their relevance to project managers.

2.04 Assertiveness

DOGMAS
This is about beliefs that we accept as being true, without calling them into question. For example: I have to be liked, every project must have a business case, I must always be ready on time, etc. You find them by looking for where you use obligatory words in your use of language.

EXAGGERATIONS
These exaggerations make certain issues bigger and worse than they actually are in practice. For example: This is a terrible project, the political situation here is impossible, this project is really sick, etc. Again, you pay attention to the words you use, and when, for example, you use dramatic metaphors, there is a high chance that you are exaggerating.

FRUSTRATIONS
Sometimes you find yourself in a situation, which reminds you of unpleasant events from your past that you have not yet properly dealt with. The activating event (stimulus) induces the old feeling, and before you know it you become just as clumsy as you once were (response). For example: I cannot stand those types of people, I am being driven completely crazy by this, etc.

JUDGEMENTS
Especially when you are dealing with cultural differences, beliefs will again and again get in the way of functioning properly. For example: the Dutchman who says of the Indian "*they say yes, but you can never rely on it*", or the Arab who thinks "*what rude people those Dutch are*". Although this is all understandable, it is better to detach the observation and the judgment from each other, or even better, to postpone judgment.

Discussion (dispute)
When you are on the track of your irrational beliefs, follow the next step, and call these beliefs into question (D).

You then look for:
- Preferences.
- Objectification.
- Frustration tolerance.
- Acceptance.

We study these on the basis of their relevance for project managers.

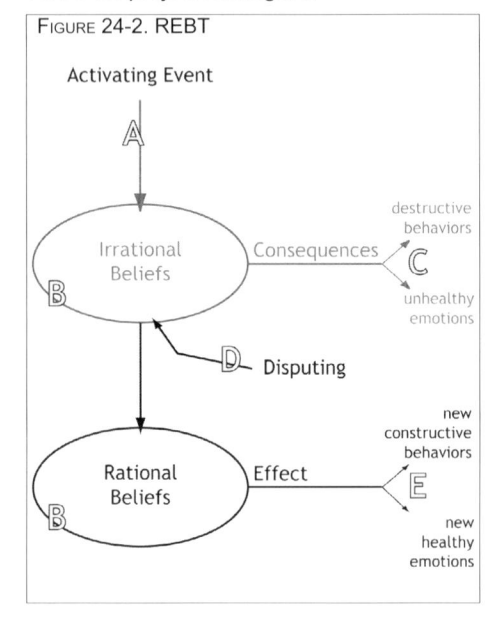

FIGURE 24-2. REBT

Activating Event
A

Irrational Beliefs
B

Consequences
C
destructive behaviors
unhealthy emotions

D Disputing

Rational Beliefs
B

Effect
E
new constructive behaviors
new healthy emotions

PREFERENCES
Whereas the dogmas were more obligatory in nature, here you look at what you would really want.

Based on the same examples: I really want to be liked, a project preferably has a business case, I always want to be ready on time, etc. If you now realize that it is unthinkable that you get everything you want, you develop a much more realistic image of reality.

OBJECTIFICATION

Now try to describe in neutral terms what is going on. Again, we take the same examples: The difficulty with this project was, the political situation here is as follows, this project is not healthy with respect to these points, etc.

> EXAMPLE 24-7 DEADLINES
> I have had this myself with deadlines I had to achieve. Often, I muttered in terms of: "I am being driven completely crazy by this." If I looked at it objectively, however, I achieved every deadline. I have now stuck a saying on my desk: *"Even when the clock is running fast, the deadline is the one I reach at last."*

FRUSTRATION TOLERANCE

You can also consider frustration as a situation, which you already have a lot of experience with. Viewed in this way it is not really as bad as it seems; the last time it turned out alright, so why not now?

For example: I have the following problems with these types of people, but they are not insurmountable, I become agitated with these situations, but I manage to survive.

ACCEPTANCE

This is about taking people the way they are. Every person has his own unique background that has made him what he is and when you are involved with different cultures, this certainly plays a role.

For example: Indians have different ways of saying "yes", and the Dutch are very direct. Both have their advantages and disadvantages, but it is never a case of good or bad.

Effect

Calling into question your irrational beliefs has an effect on both emotions and behavior. New healthier emotions and behaviors emerge. Ellis then mentions emotions such as disappointment, concerns, boredom, sorrow and remorse. In themselves, these are not positive emotions, but compare these with the unhealthy emotions mentioned earlier, such as: depression, nervousness, anger, shame, hurt feelings, jealousy and guilt. You straightaway place both the cause and the solution in yourself.

6. The will

Roberto Assagioli lived from 1888 to 1974. He obtained his PhD in 1910 through a critical study of the psychoanalytic theory. In "The Act of Will[8] he describes the different aspects of the will, which are:

- The strong will.
- The skilful will.
- The good will.
- The transpersonal will.
- The universal will.

A strong will

This is the best known aspect of the will, in which we set our minds on achieving a particular goal. You can train this aspect in different ways, for example:

- By visualization.
- By arousing feelings with the visualizations.
- By aimless will exercises.
- By physical exertion, for which perseverance is necessary.
- By practicing in daily life.

Project managers can use this as the basis of their own development. Quite often, we have to follow a long road to achieve what we want. The first two exercises (visualization and arousal of emotion) can be directly applied.

We can apply the last three continuously. The aimless will exercise can be a puzzle, where you continue just long enough to complete it. The physical exertion can be

---
8 (1973) The Act of Will, Roberto Assagioli, PENGUIN

2.04 Assertiveness

in the gym, carrying out a boring, repetitive exercise for a long time. As well as the fact that it is healthy for body and limbs, you also train the will.

A skilful will
Practice makes perfect. With as little energy as possible, a skilful will achieves the greatest possible result. The will influences perception, emotions, feelings, impulses, longings, imagination, thoughts, intuition and ultimately also itself again.

What is special in exercising the will, is that at a certain point, you set an upwards spiral in working, just as with the previous story about the pillars of self-esteem and calling into question your beliefs. In short, you become cleverer in wanting something.

Another question you can ask for the development of a skilful will is: "What do I put my energy into to fulfilling my will?"

It is useful to consider those matters which:
- You are involved in.
- You have an influence on.

Covey[9] talks about the Circle of Concern and the Circle of Influence. You are involved in more matters than you can influence. It is smart to channel your energy in those matters, which you can influence, as you then have a greater chance that your energy really will deliver something.

If you do that, there will be enough left over to work on your personal network, whereby, after a while, you enlarge your circle of influence. More influence means more possibilities to fulfil your will.

_____
9 (1989)The 7 Habits of Highly Effective People, Stephen Covey

A good will
This aspect goes so far that, in what we want, we do not inflict any damage on others. If we only have a strong and skilful will, we can lose sight of the interests of others. Big obstacles to developing this aspect are:
- Selfishness, the longing to possess and to dominate.
- Egocentricity, whereby we relate everything to ourselves.
- Lack of understanding for others.

A good will has everything to do with personal integrity and ethics. You do not then only want what is best for yourself, but also what is best for others. For project managers, this aspect of the will is strongly linked to project success, because success means that everyone involved is satisfied with the project result (and with the way in which this is achieved).

The good will is present in the project manager, who, from deep down in his soul, wants to satisfy those involved (comment: this is something other than keeping others satisfied).

A transpersonal will
The transpersonal will is about the need for significance, which we find in relation to other people. In his book, Assagioli mentions the story of Sakyamuni (Gautama Buddha) as an example of someone who, after a long search, found an answer to human suffering. This will for significance brought him to endure great suffering, in order to eventually arrive at a deep insight that has inspired countless people after him. This aspect of the will has been strongly developed by real leaders.

It is a will that strives for unification with another person (Romeo and Juliet), or one that pursues an ideal matter (environmental activists or development aid workers), or the creation of art, which survives through the centuries (Sistine Chapel – Michelangelo), or leaders who have changed a nation forever (Mahatma Gandhi). It is an aspect of the will, which we generally do not think about when we are talking about project management.

Although….?

What about the project manager, who is responsible for organizing the Roman Catholic Church's World Youth Day, for which annually millions of young people come together? Without doubt, this person is carrying out this task based on an inner passion, which we can rank under the transpersonal aspect of the will. History is full of religious architects, who have left behind magnificent places of worship for posterity, sometimes inspired by God, but always based on an idea from within.

Universal will
With the previous four aspects of the human will, there has been a movement from inner to outer. It is a need that, sooner or later, summons up a corresponding will. The Universal Will is about the need to bring this will in line with universal values, as these are assumed. We often see this aspect in deeply religious people, although it is not only reserved for them.

We can find a fitting example in the Bible, where Jesus, just before he is seized by Roman soldiers, prays[10]: "*My Father, if it is possible, may this cup be taken from me. Yet not as I will, but as you will.*"

It is from this aspect of the will that martyrs have given their life for their belief. When the personal aspects of the will correspond with what someone himself sees as the Universal Will, then we are dealing with one of the strongest forms of will power.

---
10 Matthew 26:39

2.04 Assertiveness

2.05 Relaxation

GOVERNING A GREAT STATE IS LIKE COOKING SMALL FISH[1].

When is it ready? In a week!

I need to know for certain!
Oh, in three weeks then!

The more pressure, the later it is ready.

You should not let people get stressed, but let them relax.

---
1 *Tao Te Ching*

2.05 Relaxation

2.05-1 DEFINITIONS

Burnout	A buzzword for the feeling of being totally exhausted, and no longer able to find the energy or motivation for work activities.
Relaxation	The capacity to reduce or remove physical, rational and/or emotional stresses and strains.
Role content	The execution of tasks, behavior, attitude and external characteristics that fit with the execution of a particular function.
Role expectation	The implicit and explicit expectations of the environment with respect to the way in which the role content should be shaped and defined.
Role interpretation	The personal way in which someone gives substance to the content of a role.
Role mingling	The unconscious taking over (of parts) of other peoples role content.
Stress	A long-term or sudden, severe disturbance of the balance between pressure and workload capacity.
Stress management	The capacity to create a healthy balance between pressure and workload capacity.
Tension	An incidental disruption of the balance between pressure and workload capacity.

2.05-2 Introduction

"A project is a collection of work that, with too few people and an insufficient budget, has to be finished within an impossible timescale."

By definition, projects are under pressure, and, as project manager, you want to be finished on time, so you have to get out the whip. However,…

When you put pressure on people, ultimately they will perform less. Every hour of overtime then becomes an hour of 'undertime', because people need time to relax. When you, and your project team, are under great pressure to achieve certain deadlines, you have to ensure that there are times for relaxation.

I believe that if your project is the cause of stress, then it is you that has to do something about it. In the chapter on self-control, a number of things have already been discussed about how to handle your own tensions. This chapter builds more on this, but the emphasis will be put on the relaxation within the team.

The reason, according to the Competence Baseline, is simple: *De-escalation of a tense situation is important in maintaining fruitful co-operation between the parties involved.*

This is a very pragmatic approach, which the Competence Baseline[2] continually returns to. We apply all the behavior competencies for the good of the project, and a project always benefits from a fruitful co-operation between those involved, and also, therefore, from *relaxation.*

---

2 IPMA Competence Baseline version 3

2.05-3 Process Steps

1. Detect tensions or fatigue.
2. Be proactive in discovering the reason for tensions.
3. Remove the cause, and set up an action plan.
4. Relax at a location away from the workplace.
5. Meet regularly as a team, and involve everybody.
6. Apply lessons learned.

1. Detect tensions or fatigue

Research by Golembiewski[3] showed that significantly more cases of burnout happened under certain managers. Burnout is, therefore, partially determined by manager type, and based on this, we can now add the project manager to the list of stress causes as being one of the stress factors. This places a huge responsibility on us.

You should take care of your team and recognise tensions when they arise.

For example[4]:
- Increase in absenteeism.
- Team members being less committed.
- A lot of people resigning.
- Declining performance.
- Increase in unsafe working practices and accidents.
- Users complaining.

These are general indicators. Individual signs are when someone:
- Adopts an attitude of dependency.
- Expresses having vague physical ailments.
- Talks of concerns about his health.
- Is impatient towards others.
- Displays frequent mood changes.
- Complains about small things.
- Is restless and sleeps badly.
- Is timid.
- Makes excessive use of stimulants.

These signals are especially important when there is a sudden change in the behavior of one or more team members. You have to be alert to this, and do something about it. If you observe the above symptoms, then you are, in fact, already somewhat too late, as prevention is better than cure. Anyway, you have to find out the cause or causes, which can be just within the person himself, or the way in which the project is organized.

2. Be proactive in discovering the reason for tensions

When setting up the project, there are many possibilities to prevent the risk of overstress. Causes of overstress have to do with:
- The type and amount of work.
- Lack of clarity about someone's role.
- The level of control that someone has.

The type and amount of work

When people have a reasonable amount of work, for which they have to exert themselves, but which is not impossible to do, then real stress will not occur. There is a healthy amount of tension that only serves to motivate. When, however, someone has the idea that there is too much work, or even too little work, then after a while stress sets in.

Another cause of stress can be the environment in which someone must work, or the tools he has at his disposal. An office without an outside window, a pc that is too slow, or complicated bureaucratic procedures, are all things that can contribute to an increase in the stress that someone experiences.

---
[3] (1988) Phases of Burnout, R.T. Golembiewski, PRAEGER, New York
[4] (2004) Work, Organization & Stress, Protecting Workers Health Series, WORLD HEALTH ORGANIZATION

work, we also look at ways to constructively help each other during work.

It is a good thing to talk regularly with each other about the work pressures, and what options are available to handle this together as a team. Also when the work pressure cannot be directly resolved, the fact that everybody wants to talk about it, provides the necessary relaxation.

6. Apply lessons learned
How do you learn from your experience? By looking at the effect of your style of leadership. How do people react to it? Is there a cheerful atmosphere? When you have a pattern of overtime, deadlines and suchlike in your projects, then there is a good chance that you, yourself, are the biggest cause of all the tensions in the project. You learn by recognizing this in yourself.

Relax your team by starting with yourself.

2.05-4 Special Topics

1. From tension to overstressed

The road from tension (or stress) to overstressed (or burnout) is long. Knowledge of the causes, the way in which people handle stress, and how burnout ultimately shows itself, enable you to do something about stress management for yourself, and your team members.

The first scholar, who wrote about the physical consequences of stress, was Hans Selye[6] (1907-1982). He discovered that when someone experiences tension, it causes an increased level of alertness in the body. There is an increase in heart rate, blood pressure and muscle tension, and extra stimulant chemicals are released in the body to prepare it for fight or flight, dependent on the situation. These are the basic mechanisms for coping with stress.

When stress lasts for too long, this increased state of alertness has a damaging effect on health and the so-called General Adaptation Syndrome occurs.

The adaptation syndrome consists of the following stages:
- Alarm Reaction.
- Stage of Resistance.
- Stage of Exhaustion.

During the alarm reaction, the total resistance of the body starts to decrease. When the stress cannot be warded off, the resistance stage develops, in which more energy is spent in removing the factor causing stress. The person in question, therefore, becomes more effective in doing this, but the total resistance continues to reduce, making the person more susceptible to illnesses (and potential new stress factors). If, for example, a new flu epidemic comes along, the person in question is much more susceptible to catching it. Ultimately, the stress takes its toll and the exhaustion stage appears, which we could call a burnout.

We investigate this phenomenon more deeply in the following subjects:
- Sources of stress.
- Link between personality and stress.
- Link between culture and stress.
- Symptoms of burnout.

Sources of stress

In a general sense, you can say that, on the one hand stress is connected with how someone experiences a physical or psychological threat as stressful, and on the other hand, with the idea that someone has on the extent of influence he or she has on the situation in question. There is, therefore, only a question of a cause of stress, if someone experiences it as such.

Sources of stress can then be:
- Important life events.
- Small irritations.
- Chronic tension.
- Unresolved conflicts.

The most important life events are of a different order than the other three sources, in the sense that they concern once-only major happenings, such as: the death of a loved-one, a separation, a re-location and such-like. The Holmes and Rahe[7] Social Readjustment Rating Scale enables you to make a prediction on the probability of developing an illness as a result of reduced resistance caused by stress.

---

6 (1950) *Stress and the General Adaption Syndrome,* Hans Selye, BRITISCH MEDICAL JOURNAL

7 (1967) *The social readjustment rating scale,* Holmes and Rahe, JOURNAL OF PSYCHOSOMATIC RESEARCH

2.05 Relaxation

The table below shows the ten life events having the highest scores:

Life event	Score
Death of a life partner	100
Divorce	73
Legal separation	65
Prison sentence	63
Death of a family member	63
Serious injury or illness	53
Marriage	50
Dismissal from work	47
Matrimonial reconciliation	45
Retirement	45

The higher your score, the more chance you have of developing an illness.

The scores in this table are based on research carried out in the western world, and it is possible that the scores differ according to culture. It appears, for example, that in South Africa, violating or breaking a taboo carries a high score. As project manager, it is therefore useful to become acquainted with which important events in a particular culture cause a lot of stress.

The other three stress factors are related to the saying: "a lot of small things make one big one", and in these factors it relates to continual exposure to them.

> EXAMPLE 25-2 HERPES INFECTION
> Within a period of three years, Charles lost his own parents and his mother-in-law, and also changed jobs. In the winter he contracted a serious herpes infection of his eye.

Connection between personality and stress

How someone handles stress is highly dependent on that person's personality, and some people suffer more from it than others. Neuroticism is one of the five dimensions we can use to describe the personality[8]. It indicates how great the need of someone is for stability, and at which point the adaption syndrome starts to take effect.

People who score higher on this scale will more quickly experience a particular situation as being stressful. Personality is difficult to change, and, therefore, also someone's susceptibility to stress. The Rational Emotive Behavioral Therapy mentioned in another chapter is a good tool for changing the underlying convictions with respect to stress.

Connection between culture and stress

Someone's personality is formed by the culture in which he has grown up. This leads to the supposition that there must also be a connection between culture, and how someone experiences stress, and handles it. From research carried out by Hofstede across different cultures, it appears that there is a culture dimension that influences the way in which people handle stress. This dimension is uncertainty avoidance[9], and inhabitants of cultures scoring highly experience either more stress at work, and/or have a greater need for rules, and they work, on average, longer at the same employer.

The culture in which someone has grown up in and in which someone is working, can

---

[8] (2001) *The Owners Manual for Personality at Work*, Howard and Howard, BARD PRESS, Austin – Atlanta, USA
[9] (2001) *Culture Consequences - Comparing Values, Behaviors, Institutions and Organizations Across Nations*, Hofstede, SAGE PUBLICATIONS, Thousand Oaks, USA

have an influence, in the following manner, on the way in which he handles stress[10]:
- The sources available in a society.
- The way in which people view events.
- The choice of how someone handles the situation.
- The institutes available to someone.

> EXAMPLE 25-3 SULTAN QABOOS BIN SAID
> "I promise to dedicate myself to the speedy establishment of a modern government in no time. My first aim will be the abolition of all unnecessary restrictions that overburdened you."
> Sultan Qaboos bin Said of Oman, when he came to power on the 23rd of July 1970.

As project manager, when you work together with team members, who have a different background to you, it is in your best interests to delve into the above four aspects, and to amend your strategy for stress management accordingly.

Signs of burnout
The Maslach Burnout Inventory[11] is an instrument consisting of three dimensions for measuring burnout:
- Emotional exhaustion.
- Personal performance.
- Depersonalization disorders.

Symptoms of emotional exhaustion are: a total tiredness that does not disappear after a good night's sleep, a feeling that someone must continuously push himself to the limit, a lot of internal tension when co-operating with people, and when someone is at the end of his tether.

Having doubts about one's own performance is another symptom of a possible burnout. Someone does not understand any more how others think about certain matters and has the feeling of no longer being able to face work related problems.

Depersonalization reveals itself in an impersonal approach to others, having a feeling of being blamed by others for being the cause of their problems, an emotional hardening, and not being interested in the ups and downs of others.

Not all countries recognise burnout as a real illness, although recognition has been brought a step closer by recent research at the Radbout University[12], which demonstrates that burnout has a specific brain pattern.

2. Possible Causes of Stress[13]
The list below comprises a number of possible causes, which can cause tensions at work:

Job Content:
- Monotonous, under-stimulation, meaningless tasks.
- Lack of variety.
- Unpleasant tasks.
- Aversive tasks.

Workload and Work pace:
- Having too much or too little to do.
- Working under time pressures.

Working Hours:
- Strict and inflexible working schedules.
- Long and unsocial hours.
- Unpredictable working hours.
- Badly designed shift systems.

---

10 (1999) Stress, coping and development: An integrative approach, C.M. Aldwin, GUILFORD, New York
11 (1981) *The measurement of experienced burnout*, Maslach en Jackson, JOURNAL OF OCCUPATIONAL BEHAVIOR, JOHN WILEY AND SONS
12 (2010) *EEG Findings in Burnout Patients*, Gilles van Luijtelaar e.a., THE JOURNAL OF EUROPSYCHIATRY AND CLINICAL NEUROSCIENCES, American Psychiatric Publishing Inc.
13 (2004) *Work, Organization & Stress, Protecting Workers Health Series,* WORLD HEALTH ORGANIZATION

2.05 Relaxation

Participation and Control:
- Lack of participation in decision making.
- Lack of control.

Career Development, Status and Pay:
- Job insecurity.
- Lack of promotion prospects.
- Under-promotion or over-promotion.
- Work of 'low social value'.
- Piece rate payments schemes.
- Unclear or unfair performance evaluation systems.
- Being over-skilled or under-skilled for the job.

Role in the organization:
- Unclear role.
- Conflicting roles within the same job.
- Responsibility for people.
- Continuous dealing with other people and their problems.

Interpersonal Relationships:
- Inadequate, inconsiderate or unsupportive supervision.
- Poor relations with co-workers.
- Bullying, harassment and violence
- Isolated or solitary work.
- No agreed procedures for dealing with problems or complaints.

Organization Culture:
- Poor communication.
- Poor leadership.
- Lack of clarity about organizational objectives and structure.

Home-work interface:
- Conflicting demands of work and home.
- Lack of support for domestic problems at work.
- Lack of support for work problems at home.

By removing these causes, you present yourself with a number of valuable intervention possibilities.

3. Humour

Humour has a releasing effect and in this sense is a good instrument for creating a relaxed atmosphere in and around the project team. The development of a sense of humour is both an enjoyable and a worthwhile activity. You have to realize that what people find amusing is dependent on both personality and culture, and what one person may find amusing, another person finds feeble or offensive. In the latter situation it actually works counter-productively.

Whether or not a joke works, is dependent on a number of things[14]:
- Content
- Structure

It seems that regarding *content* it makes a difference if the joke does or does not contain a sexual connotation, and regarding the *structure* it is about whether or not the joke solves an incongruence that has been raised, or whether it comes with a nonsensical punch line or solution.

Joke 1
Question: *How can we reduce the pregnancy of a woman to one month?*

Answer: *By letting a woman be impregnated by nine men.*

This is a joke with a sexual connotation, which also has a nonsensical punch line.

---

14 (1992) *Assessment of appreciation of humor: Studies with the 3 WD humor test*, Willibald Ruch in Advances in Personality Assessment (Vol. 9)

2.05 Relaxation

Joke 2
Then you have those project sponsors who think that they can shorten the duration by using more people. Do you know them? They do not understand that you really cannot make a baby in one month by using nine couples.

This is the same joke as before, but without a sexual connotation, and in which the incongruence raised is solved.

Another point we learn from this example is that it is not difficult to transform existing jokes into a statement, which works for our own project.

> EXAMPLE 25-4 A JOKE WITH THE BUSINESS CASE
> The consultant advises senior management to produce a business case for every project. People start grumbling about the bureaucracy. Disappointed, he leaves the room.
>
> In a subsequent discussion with his coach, the coach tells him he must approach it differently the next time, and propose that each business case must have a project.

The receiver
The previous two were concerned with the person thinking up the joke, but we of course, are also concerned with the listener, who finds the joke:
- Amusing or not amusing.
- Offensive or not offensive.

For the "joker", this means that he has to attune the joke to his public. The best jokes are the ones that the receiver finds amusing and does not experience as being offensive. Make sure you realize that when making a joke, the intention in the first instance is about relaxing the receivers, and not about how funny you are yourself.

> EXAMPLE 25-5 DANISH HUMOUR
> In 2005 a Danish cartoonist made a cartoon of the prophet Mohammed. What was intended as a joke led to worldwide protests and a high level of international tension?
>
> Moral: If you want to apply humour to aid relaxation, then match this to the group you are targeting at.

It is clear that culture and personality influences the type of jokes people appreciate.

4. Balancing private life and work

There are 24 hours in a day, and this is the same for everyone. In these 24 hours you have to make choices about what you are, and are not, going to do, and we often talk about finding the right balance between our private lives and work. What we then often do not realize is that making that differentiation creates more tension than it solves.

Both our private life and the work situation puts demands on us. Your private situation is dependent on your direct family, relatives and social network, who all, to a greater or lesser extent, require your attention, and dependent on what you find important, you give them that attention. If you live in an individualistic society, it is acceptable for you to give your own interests a higher priority than the interests of your family or the group. In a collective society, this can be exactly the opposite, and the interests of the family and group prevails above your own interests.

In both cultures, the application of a balance between private life and work is linguistically deceiving, because the balance metaphor implies an equality (of time) and that can, of course, never be the case. If you search for an (equal) balance, then the balance quickly gets lost. The quest must be for a steady or stable situation, in which the various factors that exert a pull on you, exercise a "healthy tension".

2.05 Relaxation

Dependent on the way in which you have organized your life, the following factors can demand your attention:
- Your life partner.
- Your children.
- Your family.
- Your friends.
- Your colleagues.
- Your manager.

In addition you have:
- Your ambitions.
- Your dreams.
- Your possibilities.

Of the 24 hours a day available, you have to spend a part on eating (at least one and a half hours) and sleeping (seven and a half hours), leaving 15 hours in which to do all your other activities. As a lot of research has shown that long-term sleep deprivation leads to a deterioration in both mental and physical bodily functions[15], the solution is not to sleep less. Otherwise, before you know it, you find yourself in a downwards spiral, in which, as a result of clumsy decisions, you create more problems than you solve. Also missing breakfast because you are in a hurry, is unhealthy, according to much research.

What then? Everything is about making choices; not everything can be done, and not everything has to be done. If you are married and have children, then you have to devote your attention there. If you do not do that, then the time will come when your partner, or your children, demand this attention, with all the resulting stress. If you work a lot of overtime, eat unhealthily and sleep little, there comes a time when your body demands the time from you in the form of a burnout.

It is about choices, and if you do not make these, then the balance is a long way off.

---

15 (2007) *Sleep deprivation: Impact on cognitive performance*, Paula Alhola and Päivi Polo-Kantola, DOVE MEDICAL PRESS LIMITED

2.05 Relaxation

2.06 Openness

WITH YOUR EYES OPEN, YOU SEE MORE THAN WITH YOUR EYES CLOSED.

You are a project manager and result oriented.

Sometimes you run to the finish wearing blinkers.

During this spurt you sometimes forget that the road you follow is just as important as the final destination.

2.06 Openness

2.06-1 DEFINITIONS

| Openness | The ability to make others feel they are free to express themselves, so that the project will benefit from their contributions, suggestions and concerns. |

2.06-2 INTRODUCTION

Openness is the ability to make others feel they are free to express themselves, so that the project will benefit from their input, suggestions and concerns. The saying teaches us that:

Two know more than one.

It is, of course, stupid not to make use of the knowledge and insights of all people involved in the project, but you do need an open atmosphere to do that. There are two types of openness, which we are dealing with:

- The partaking openness.
- The introspective openness.

The first (partaking), is visible in the participation of the different team members. Everyone opens his mouth during the meetings, and that is a good sign. Apparently everyone feels safe, people have their say, and after the necessary discussions, we reach a consensus.

But there are also a number of objections, which can be made for this partaking openness:

- Consensus delivers mediocre solutions.
- There are always (extravert) people, who put their mark on the meeting.
- Every group has its taboos.

Therefore, in addition to partaking openness, there is also a need for introspective openness. This is about the individual willingness of the people involved to change their insights and principles, which makes them open to change instead of just talking about it. When these two types of openness are present in a project you can talk of a learning project organization.

2.06-3 PROCESS STEPS

1. Develop a policy on openness.
2. Start with informal contacts.
3. Welcome information.
4. Ask open questions.
5. Create opportunities.
6. Praise positive input.
7. Apply lessons learned.

1. Develop a policy on openness

Openness does not just happen, but has to be designed into the culture of the project. This is the first goal of this first process step: think in advance about how you want to make openness happen in your project. Chris Argyris[1] specifies the following conditions to stimulate this:

- Providing the correct information.
- People making a free choice based on that information.
- Stimulating internal commitment.

He calls this action model II as opposed to model I (see further on).

Model II means a direct communication without hidden agenda's, no mean tricks or dirty manipulative political games. We see various other competence elements, which contribute to this required openness, such as:
- Engagement and motivation.
- Consultation and advice.
- Reliability.
- Values appreciation.
- Ethics.

The problem with openness is that nobody will deny the need for it, and in some cultures it is also socially desirable to think that. Therefore, you often do not find a chapter on openness in a project management plan and even though nobody will deny the importance of it, we often a lack of openness in our projects.

You have to see the development of a policy concerning openness in the daily practices, in which, as project manager, you set the example and stimulate people to be open. The following process steps explain this further.

2. Start with informal contacts

An often heard complaint from employees is that their manager does not know anything about what they actually do. The reason for that is that the managers are seldom seen on the work floor. Instead, they run from one meeting to the next, without looking after the people who do the actual work.

This is undesirable, and it is better to give some attention to the team members as one of your first activities of the working day. You can do that by getting coffee, making a phone call and talking about non-work related issues. In this way, you get to know whether or not people are married, have children, what their hobbies are, etc. That is one thing, but often you also get valuable information that will not appear from the formal progress reports.

3. Welcome information

A big trap you can get caught in, is that your employees get the idea that you are not receptive to them. This means that in the way you communicate with them, you have to send out signals that you are listening and that you understand what they are talking about. The next process step addresses this.

4. Ask open questions

An open question gives the other person freedom in choosing his answer. For other questions, such as closed, rhetorical and suggestive questions, this is much less the case.

---

1 (1992) *On Organizational Learning,* Chris Argyris

When you have asked an open question, you have to give the other person the opportunity to answer it. It is not very clever to ask a new question halfway through his answer. This interrupts his argument. Let someone finish first and listen actively. You only ask a new question after the previous one has been answered.

There are a number of techniques for this:
- Follow verbally.
- Silence.
- Parroting.
- Paraphrasing the content.
- Reflecting the feeling.
- Summarizing.

We sometimes summarize these under *"active listening"*. These and other techniques will be explained further in this chapter.

5. Create opportunities to stimulate openness in the team

Every time people come together in the team, there is a chance to be open with each other. So the first thing you have to take care of, is that the team members regularly meet each other. If people are not in contact with each other, stereotypes have all the room they need. An "us" versus "them" mentality will then develop, and that almost always has a negative effect on the mutual communication.

> **EXAMPLE 26-1 VIRTUAL TEAMS**
> The team was spread over two locations, London and Amsterdam. The long distance strengthened the stereotypes which existed back and forth between the British and the Dutch cultures.
>
> When the project managers at both locations had a webcam installed and projected what was happening on the other side via a beamer projection onto the wall, the openness towards each other increased.

Obviously, team outings (diner, adventure, etc.) help to stimulate the openness. It is better, however, to do this within the daily project work, as openness is something which should not only take place during team outings, but continuously during the planning and execution of the project. By anchoring openness in the daily project work, you educate the team, and as project manager, you must be a strong role model in this.

There are more than enough possibilities to stimulate openness in daily procedures. For example:
- Ask for criticism on the planning.
- Have the progress report read, before it goes to the project sponsor.
- Evaluate with your team during stage transitions.
- Walk around, and put your ear to the ground.
- Make a suggestion box.

Wrong type of question			
Question	**Example**	**Effect**	**Alternative**
Closed	Did you find the meeting useful?	The number of answers is restricted. The only options are yes or no.	What did you think of the meeting?
Rhetorical question	Do we not consider these meetings to be useless?	The speaker does not really expect an answer at all. He has given the answer himself: "This type of meetings is useless."	I found this meeting useless. What is your opinion?
Suggestive question	What did you *really* think of this long-winded meeting?	If the other person did not find the meeting long-winded, it is difficult for him to now admit this.	What did you think of the meeting?

2.06 Openness

6. Praise positive input

To stimulate openness, you have to honestly praise people when they are open. In that sense 'whistle-blowers' are welcome. This will stimulate them to also be open in the future.

7. Apply lessons learned

Accepting openness from someone else is, of course, also a form of learning. By seriously listening to the other person, you learn from his insight and experience, and you prevent falling into traps that he has already been able to avoid. This requires a certain level of humility towards the other person, because implicitly through listening, you admit that the other person knows best.

On the other hand, openness is also needed to learn from things that do not go so well. As real mistakes do not exist, I consciously do not use the expression *"to learn from your mistakes"*. It is better to speak of things which are awkward, or which you can better not do in a certain situation. An open attitude towards things as they happen, the results of this, and the willingness to learn, on the one hand prevents you having to re-discover the wheel over and over again, and on the other hand prevents the repetition of deep rooted patterns.

2.06-4 SPECIAL TOPICS

1. Skills to improve openness

For a large part, our communication is subconscious and unprepared. We just wait and see where we shall end up in the meeting. We shall now cover a number of communication techniques that you can use consciously to constructively influence the discussion.

Following verbally (parroting)

You do this by encouraging the sender to continue his discussion, by giving, for example, a short reaction to something he just said:

Other person	After that meeting a small conflict arose about the delivery time …
You	Small conflict?

You show that you heard the message of the other person. Other examples are hm, hm; yes .., and then, carry on.

Silence

Silences can be an encouragement to carry on with the story, and it can be very effective to make conscious use of that. In order to use this technique well, you must of course be able to cope with silences. It is good to keep in the back of your mind the fact that most people cannot cope with silence, so when you consciously let silence descend, be aware that the other person will usually start talking. When this does not work, you can always say: *Now there is a silence, tell me …* and then see what happens

Ask questions

By asking questions you can direct the discussion. There are open and closed questions. The open question gives someone room to voice his opinion, the closed question is like a multiple choice question, often it can only be answered with yes or no.

You	Tell me what you think of the plan?	Open question
Other person	I have a number of comments on ….	
You	Do you agree?	Closed question
Other	No.	

Both type of questions have advantages and disadvantages, you use them depending on what you want to achieve. Open questions have the tendency to open the discussion, and the other person will provide more information. Closed questions close the discussion, and a number of closed answers one after the other kills the discussion. This is convenient if you have someone opposite you who is rather wordy, but less useful if you want to find out exactly what happened. On the other hand, if you just want to know whether someone agrees or not, the closed question is a good technique.

When choosing the question, you have to know what direction you want the discussion to move in. Asking questions appeals to someone's rational abilities, enabling them to think. When you speak of feelings, it is better not to ask questions, but to use another technique (mirroring and paraphrasing, see further on), because by asking a question you divert people from their feelings.

Then there are also suggestive questions, in which the answer is already enclosed.

Other person	Obviously it is important that we all agree. What do you think?
You	Eh ..

It is actually best to avoid suggestive questions because it is a form of manipulation. It is better to tell someone what you think, and what you expect from the other person.

2.06 Openness

Another question you have to be careful with is the **why** question.

Other person	A conflict occurred, for which I didn't have a solution straight away, I then …
You	Why did you do that?
Other person	Come on, there was no other way … (becomes defensive)

The danger with the **why** question, is that if you use the wrong emphasis, it may be perceived as an accusation, with the effect that the other person becomes defensive.

Paraphrasing the content
When the other person tells a long story, it is sometimes difficult to keep paying attention, although you do want to listen to the other person. This dilemma can be solved by regularly summarizing the content in your own words. You then say something like: *"hold on, I just want to check that I have understood you properly"* and then you give a paraphrase of the content as you understand it. It is different from following someone verbally, or to repeat (parrot) to him. You express it in your own words, and give the other person the opportunity to check that you understood it properly.

This has two advantages: if you understood it wrongly, the other person will tell you so, and possibly he will explain it again. If you understood it correctly, the other person will react cheerfully with *"exactly and …"*, and he will then carry on secure in the knowledge that someone is listening to him. He will also carry on with the subject he was talking about. The danger of a new question is that you will then switch to another theme, so in general, it is best not to ask extra questions, particularly if a certain theme has not yet been explored in depth. Once the other person has finished with his story, you can get the missing information on the table by asking some good questions.

Summarizing
This looks a bit like paraphrasing, except that you do it at the end of a certain topic of discussion. Where paraphrasing is at paragraph level, summarizing is at chapter level. For example, at the end of a discussion about a certain subject, you give a succinct summary of the decisions you took and the agreements you made. After such a summary, you can carry on with a new subject.

Mirroring the feeling
What paraphrasing does with the content, mirroring does with the feeling. You listen attentively between the lines of what is said, and you watch for the non-verbal signs; for the incongruence between word and behavior. Whilst you are doing that, you try to ask yourself how the other person should be feeling. This almost always has an effect on your own emotions.

In order to mirror well, therefore, you have to be in contact with your own feelings. At a certain moment, you mirror that feeling back e.g. when someone has given a number of disqualifications, you could say *"if I understand you correctly, you do not like it at all"*. Or when you are speaking to an angry customer, you acknowledge the anger by saying *"I can understand that you are angry with me, I would like to help you …"*. By mirroring the feeling, the other person feels understood, and in a number of cases you can show him how he feels, without him being aware of it.

Provide and receive feedback
You will regularly have to provide your project members with feedback on their performances. The problem with providing feedback is that it embarrasses the receiver, particularly in the case of negative feedback. What definitely does not help in such a case, is making a comment like *"you don't have to defend yourself"*, as that only results in the

other person becoming even more defensive.

When providing feedback effectively, you try to prevent the other person from becoming defensive or offering resistance. There are a number of basic rules for this:
- *Describe the behavior,* what is the other person doing.
- *Describe your own reaction,* and give the other person room to do something with it.
- *Make it specific,* when did what happen.
- *Only if it is useful,* if the other person cannot do anything with it, then leave it.
- *At the right time,* speaks for itself.
- *Accurate,* obviously, it has to be right.

As well as providing feedback, receiving it is also a skill. We have already talked about defending yourself or offering resistance. Nobody likes to receive negative feedback.

When this does happen, the following tips are useful:
- Thank the person providing the feedback.
- Let it sink in, ask for an explanation if you do not understand something.
- Decide later if you will do something with it.

2. Model I versus Model II

Because people are not open enough over their experiences, they do not learn enough from them. According to the previously quoted Chris Argyris, this is because they act in accordance with the following model (Model I):

- *Stay in control* when something unexpected happens.
- Ensure that in all cases you are on the *winning* side, and you are always proved to be right.
- *Suppress all negative emotions.*
- Put the emphasis on the *ratio and the content.*

What happens if you act in accordance with model I?

Stay in control
This is expressed in you wanting to dominate the discussion, and therefore either not noticing other suggestions, or actually discouraging them. You no longer listen to anyone else.

Win
This creates competition in the group, and becomes more about being proved right, rather than about being right. People do not listen to one another anymore.

Suppress all negative emotions
And with that, also your intuition, which even though not perfect, does indicate that something important is happening. You do not listen to either the other person, or yourself, anymore.

Emphasis on ratio and content
By doing this, you also discourage others from following their intuition, with the effect that they also do not listen to themselves anymore.

The action model II mentioned in process step 1 is much better to use.

3. Defensive Routines

During their development, people build defence mechanisms to protect themselves against unpleasant situations. Many of these mechanisms were very useful during childhood, but cause internal blockages

2.06 Openness

when people have to function as adults in a professional environment.

The following defensive routines are often seen:
- Transference
- Projection

Transference
Transference has the following symptoms:
- You do not behave as if, or feel as if you are free.
- Somehow, you feel blocked.
- There is an unpleasant tension in the contact.
- You let the other person determine your behavior.
- You display behavior, which does not really fit the situation.
- You react as a child (rebellious or good).
- You react indirectly instead of directly.
- You cannot apply your qualities properly.
- You use your qualities wrongly (distorted).
- You find it difficult to, or cannot, distance yourself, and you lose the overview.
- Emotionally you become very involved.

What is wrong? The first contact you had as a growing child was with your parents. However, it is not just your parents who bring you up; all important people in your childhood contribute to your upbringing or conditioning. In your contacts with these 'important others', a certain type of behavior becomes ingrained, as an almost ineradicable pattern. You don't even think about it anymore, it is completely automatic. There is nothing wrong with this, but a number of these routines can be very awkward. This conditioning also has the effect that following proficiency training, you always fall back into your old and trusted behavior.

Transference was discovered by Sigmund Freud (1856-1939), who discovered that his patients transferred their parents' characteristics on to the therapist, whereas he himself did not have these characteristics. The patients started behaving towards the therapist, as if he was one of his parents. An important part of the psychoanalysis he developed was based on researching these transference feelings, because these hindered the patient in interacting with other adults on an equal level. "Healthy" people also have to deal with this, but they are not bothered by it. This phenomenon and also the next topic discussed on projection, has been further developed by the nineteen years younger Carl Gustav Jung (1875-1961), who worked with Freud for some time. Carl Jung was of the opinion that people have the task in life to develop themselves by, amongst other things, taking back transference situations and projections.

Projection
Projection is a phenomenon which is related to transference. It has to do with the subconsciously holding back (often non-permissible characteristics) of the psyche, which is projected onto other people. Jung states that everything that is subconscious, is projected onto other people. Projections find their origin in youth.

A child who was very sloppy (a possible expression of creativity), but whose parents did not allow him to be like that, has been conditioned to be a tidy person. But deep in his heart (i.e. subconsciously), there still is the urge to be sloppy. When a colleague now makes a mess of his desk, we speak of projection with our test subject, when this irritates him. Actually he is not angry with his colleague, but with his own need for sloppiness, only he is not aware of this.

2.06 Openness

In the table below, freely interpreted from Ken Wilber[2], these symptoms of projection are displayed in the left column, and the possible cause of it the right column:

Symptom	Original form
They make me …	I make myself, but cannot …
They find me incompetent …	I cannot handle this …
I feel guilty …	I cannot stand your demands …
Shyness …	I find it important what people think of me, much more important than I realize …
Fear (they want to get me) …	I am angry and aggressive, and I could do something to them …
Withdrawn …	I actually want nothing to do with you, but unfortunately I have to …
Obligation (I have to …)	Desire (I want to …)
I despise (hate) you for characteristic XXX …	I despise XXX in myself …
You are incompetent …	I am extremely competent, much more than I realize …
I admire YYY in you …	I have never been able to develop YYY …

Note: With projection there always is a "strong" emotion, just as with transference there is a certain lack of freedom (your behavior is determined by the other person). The strong emotion and the lack of freedom are signals to help you to become aware of things.

Step out of the transference, or take back the projection

Transference and projection are inevitable, but often undesirable. Fortunately there are things you can do to make them manageable. For example:
- Saying stop (in your mind).
- Consciously anchoring, settling and leaning back.
- Making what happens discussable.
- Asking yourself the question: "*If the other person would not be there, who would it be?*"
- Being aware that the behavior and the feeling go together with baggage from the past, and that both have nothing to do with the present situation.
- Diversion tactics: consciously move to another track, and try to take the initiative.

4. The skilful discussion

The skilful discussion comes from the literature on the learning organization[3], and is one of the ways to improve openness. Many meetings appear to be a coarse debate, or in the most favorable case, a polite discussion. The skilful discussion goes a step further, in which we can say of the participants that they:
- Pay attention to their own intentions.
- Keep a balance between pleading and active listening.
- Build a common meaning with others.
- Are consciously aware themselves.
- Want to explore impasses that have developed.

The effect of this form of discussing, is an enormous improvement in the team. The team members tackle the problems and solve them. Everyone can speak his mind, giving the team access to the best ideas, in contrast to compromise proposals.

---

2 (1981) No Boundary, Ken Wilber, SHAMBHALA, Boulder

3 (1994) *The Fifth Discipline Fieldbook,* Peter Senge, DOUBLEDAY, New York

2.06 Openness

2.07 Creativity

GOD DOES NOT PLAY DICE (QUOTE OF EINSTEIN). HE (EINSTEIN) WAS WIDE OF THE MARK.

I once talked to someone who had followed a course in creativity.

He became angry when I said that you cannot learn creativity, because being creative is just something that you are.

Apparently, this idea had never occurred to him.

A number of years later, I learned that you in fact can learn it a little.

2.07 Creativity

2.07-1 DEFINITIONS

Converge	Selection of applicable ideas.
Creativity	The ability to think and act in original and imaginative ways.
Diverge	Thinking of as many ideas as possible.

2.07-2 INTRODUCTION

I have come across the most creativity during my trips to countries around the world. If you travel across the upland plains of Tibet, or through the deserts of North Kenya, there are no emergency telephones and no motoring organization that comes to your help if you break down. If something goes wrong, you have to improvise, and you automatically become creative. Over time many of these creative solutions become embedded in the culture of a society.

Creativity originates from shortages, from people fighting to make life comfortable and endurable. My supposition is, therefore, that the more shortages disappear, the scarcer creativity becomes. Many countries in the world that, looked at economically, lead the way, will probably no longer do so in the future. Where excess increases, creativity diminishes, but there is even more.

Well-known research by Sulloway[1] states that the youngest children in large families are more open to renewal (are more creative) than the oldest children. The same study shows that the children who are the youngest in a line of children in a family, are more likely to become a revolutionary than their older brothers or sisters. I ask myself what effect the small families in the western world will have on creativity in general?

Where are the rebels, the people who dare to walk outside the well beaten track?

There are now courses where you can learn creativity; in fact what they do is provide you with those techniques that deliver creative solutions. However, after the training, are the participants really more creative or does it just seem that way?

Very few people are genuinely creative and really do leave behind something new in the world.

Despite this pessimistic view, for those of us who are the less creative spirits, I shall attempt to lift a corner of the veil, so that we can at least appear to be more creative.

---

[1] (1997) *Born to Rebel*, Frank J. Sulloway, VINTAGE

2.07-3 PROCESS STEPS

1. Recognise situations.
2. Determine contributors.
3. Bring people together.
4. Generate many ideas.
5. Prioritize ideas.
6. Make a choice.
7. Plan and execute.
8. Apply lessons learned.

1. Recognise situations

Just as all the competence elements in this book, creativity is related to matters <u>inside</u> the project requiring an original and imaginative way of handling them. If we restrict ourselves to this, then we need this skill for:
- Thinking up the approach.
- Planning the different activities.
- Implementing efficient project processes.
- Solving difficult dilemmas.
- Mediating between conflicting interests and parties.
- Etc.

This is a whole list that has to do with the uniqueness of a project. Compared to standard line activities, the project is nowhere near as predictable, and the team has to think up many of the ways of working. Creativity, therefore, is of vital importance in nearly every project.

Just as with many matters around project management, it is useful to quickly get a feel for which points we need original and imaginative ways of working. Is it new, or is it similar to something we have done previously.

Two heads are better than one, and can also produce more solutions, and so we go looking for a team.

2. Determine contributors

We look for people who are creative. From the research on team roles by Meredith Belbin[2], two roles emerge, which are about creativity, and these are:
- PLANT, suggests his (own) creative solutions for problems, and is of particular value when the team must solve an unknown problem.
- RESOURCE-INVESTIGATOR, has a good view of what has been thought up and invented. Team members with this role come with solutions that have already been proven to work elsewhere.

Which of the two we use is dependent on the sort of problem we have to solve, whereby we must realize that the intelligence of the participants must match the complexity of the problem. There are resource-investigators and inventors that are not so intelligent, and you then get a lot of creativity, but little usefulness.

As well as these two roles, there are of course still the other roles which you have to fill, dependent on the type of problem. In particular, the leadership roles:
- CO-ORDINATOR, this person knows how to get the best out of the various team members, and is necessary when there is sufficient time, and when new, well-considered and thorough solutions need to be generated.
- SHAPER, this person brings tempo and energy into the team, takes quick decisions and can function well under great pressure. This person is necessary when the team has to solve a number of crises quickly.

As project manager, when you have to lead such a team, you can ask yourself what the

---
2 (1981) *Management Teams*, R. Meredith Belbin, BUTTERWORTH-HEINEMANN, Oxford

2.07 Creativity

best role is for yourself, and this is a completely separate question from which role is most suited to you as a person. The competence element "creativity" we are investigating here concerns the creation of an environment, in which the team comes up with original and imaginative solutions. This is your task as project manager, and sometimes a co-ordinating role is needed and sometimes that of a shaper; you just choose the role that matches the situation.

As well as these roles, there are also the operational roles, which are covered in another part. The only role I want to review here is the MONITOR-EVALUATOR, who checks the feasibility of ideas. Getting a process that generates new ideas up to speed, often results in an excess of alternatives. There has to be someone, in this case the monitor-evaluator, who exposes the feasibility of all of the ideas

3. Bring people together

When you bring the people together, you need to have an open atmosphere. Openness is a competence element in itself, and we are not going to examine it in more detail here. As more people know more and can come with more solutions than a single person, the emphasis is now on bringing people together.

Many of the techniques that generate new ideas make use of the fact that people together stimulate each other to think of new ideas. The brainstorm technique is also based on this; everyone can call out what comes into their mind without fear of that being corrected by someone else.

4. Generate many ideas

This is the diverging stage of a creative process, in which the team thinks up as many solutions as possible. Many techniques have been thought up to achieve this, and they all have the goal of getting you to think outside of your existing concepts ("out-of-the-box").

To be able to do this, all participants have to put their own beliefs on hold, because these prevent us finding the solution we want. If we think along restricted lines, then that is what we also get. A simple technique for investigating your own notions is to write these down and then pose yourself the following question:

What would happen if this notion is not true?

You remove, as it were, the restrictions that you put for yourself on the solution. Of course, if you do this, all sorts of alarm bells will start ringing in your head. A real storm of thoughts get a clear run in your consciousness, together with their objections. You have to resist them, or even ignore them, or even better, say to yourself that these thoughts are just for this moment not true. After a while, a creative idea will appear.

Another question that can have the same result is: Should a miracle happen tonight, what will then have changed tomorrow? This question ensures you focus on the solution instead of on the problem.

The result of this phase is a whole list of ideas, and the next step is to submit these ideas for further investigation.

5. Prioritize ideas

Now we begin the converging stage of the creative process. We have come across this in the risk analysis, where, following the identification (diverge) we reduce (converge) the number of relevant risks to a manageable number in two analysis steps.

For all the ideas from the previous diverging stage, we investigate which ones could contribute the most to the solution. Be aware that you still take no account of other potential limitations such as costs, duration and necessary resources. So do not converge too strongly, that comes after this.

The result is an ordered list with ideas that could each be a solution to the problem.

6. Make a choice
The first converging steps have already been taken, but the test of each idea, of course, is the ultimate implementation, and we do that in a project-based and structural way.

We assess the feasibility, costs and duration of executing each of the remaining ideas on the list from the previous step. If necessary, you must go through the formal change procedure.

The completion of this step is a choice of the solution direction to be followed, if necessary approved by the most important people involved (steering committee members).

7. Plan and execute
Once the solution has been chosen, it is placed in the project team's regular work process. It is possible that existing work must be re-scheduled, or that you have to hire people in. In any case, the implementation of this solution is carried out according to the project's standard work procedures.

8. Apply lessons learned
Why do we have to keep on re-inventing the wheel?

That has to do with the inadequate way in which we share experiences with colleagues, and with the fact that the current technology has still not found suitable solutions for recording our experiences in a quick and accessible manner. Perhaps it is best to share our experiences with creativity, in lectures, in intervision and other fraternal activities. It is, therefore, your professional duty to actively do this.

2.07-4 Special topics

1. Culture

I define culture as 'what is left over from the historical learning process of a society'. During its development, a society has experienced problems, but by being creative, people have found solutions to the problems they came up against. When solutions become available, it is no longer necessary to constantly keep re-inventing the wheel, and the necessity for a creative solution disappears; the solution has become a part of the culture.

Parents and their environment socialize their children as to how they should behave. In this way, they do not have to solve the same problems that their forefathers endured. These patterns settle deep in the sub-conscious of the culture's members. You must realize that this behavior has often been gained at the cost of great sacrifices, and therefore, people will defend them with great passion.

There is nothing wrong with this, until the situation changes and the solution (embedded in tradition) is no longer sufficient; it is then very possible that what once was a solution, now becomes an obstacle. Many creative ideas are nipped in the bud, because cultural beliefs did not allow the expression of these. A study of such occurrences provides both humoristic and painful examples.

The cultural framework determines (from history) the most obvious solutions, but that is precisely what creativity is not. Creativity is about the ability to look at the same thing in a different way and in this sense, people who have been brought up in different cultures, or who have knowledge of different cultures have an advantage[3].

One way of developing creativity is to learn from another culture and to see which notions are applicable to your projects. Questions you can then pose are:

- How does an American solve this?
- How does an Iraqi solve this?
- How does a Frenchman solve this?
- How does a Chinese solve this?
- How does a Mexican solve this?

By putting on multicultural glasses you obtain a more complete view of the situation and its possible solutions.

2. Think holistically

When we try to understand a complex problem by dividing this up into small parts, we approach it in an analytical manner. This is diametrically opposed to the holistic approach, which tries to understand the whole by looking at the cohesion and the patterns that the whole exhibits. Holistic thinking is the same as thinking in systems, and assumes that the whole is slightly different to the sum of all the parts; sometimes more and sometimes less.

Many project management techniques get in the way of thinking holistically. Take, for example, the WBS (Work Breakdown Structure), in which we break down the project result and ultimately assign these elements as control accounts to the responsible team leaders. By breaking down in this way, we create, in any case, interface risks on the borders of each work package. In this case, holistic thinking means you can "zoom out" and overlook the whole; the so-called helicopter view.

---

3 (2007) *Multicultural Identities* (ch 13) in Handbook of Cultural Psychology, Kitayama and Cohen, GUILFORD PRESS, London

2.07 Creativity

This breaking down into work packages has another risk, and that has to do with the effect of estimating at a detailed level. Often, everyone who makes an estimate will "conceal" a safety margin in it, and the project manager also does this for the final picture. The result is that the actual contingency is many times greater than the visible contingency and is much too high in total. If you now consider that people are most motivated by activities with a 50% chance of success[4], you can make a reasonable prediction about what they will do with this much too generous schedule. Here, holistic thinking means that you are able to remove all contingency out of the work packages and manage them as a whole, and that in addition, you ensure everything starts on time (also, therefore, when a previous activity finishes earlier).

What do you think about the long list of risks that we have brainstormed, which contains potential mutually dependent risks, and for which we develop risk measures. The result is a large table with events, probabilities and consequences. By focusing on this, you possibly do not see the early warning signs of unrecognized risks. Holistic thinking, then, means regularly distancing yourself and cleaning up, re-arranging and renewing the risk table.

Developing holistic thinking

Already mentioned is the in-depth studying of other cultures, and looking at how things work in them. There are other possibilities, however, that all have their roots in the basic quality "inquisitiveness" and the desire to immerse yourself in many different subjects. The more ideas that you absorb into your brain, the broader your insight becomes.

If you now apply this in your project, you should acquire not only an in-depth knowledge of the project, but also of the figures, the details of the schedule, the stakeholders of your project sponsor, the companies where they work, the culture that prevails there, etc. Be open and, when you enrich yourself with new insights and ideas, you get a feel for systems, and you develop a holistic view.

3. Intuition

In the Meno[5], Plato compares the acquisition of knowledge to remembering what the "eternal spirit" has already seen, and indeed, when we suddenly understand something, it provides that same excitement as when we remember something. The application of intuition gives the same sensation; it is as if you have knowledge, which cannot be directly explained, but which is adequate in a certain situation to take a decision which is not obvious.

I want to investigate the following questions:
- Can I trust my intuition?
- How can I develop it?

Can I trust my intuition?

The answer is yes, but not just like that. Different studies[6] have shown that experience has an important influence on whether or not a decision is the right one. The way in which this works is described[7] in the so-called 'Recognition-Primed Decision' model. When someone is in a situation that forces him to make a decision, he draws on the experience of a familiar situation.

---

4 (1987) *Human Motivation*, David C. McClelland, CAMBRIDGE UNIVERSITY PRESS, New York - US

5 (380 VC) *Meno*, Plato
6 (2004) *The recognition-primed decision model*, Ross e.a. in July/August MILITARY REVIEW
7 (1998) *Sources of Power: How People Make Decisions*, Gary A. Klein, MIT PRESS, CAMBRIDGE, MASS.

2.07 Creativity

This recognition has a number of by-products:
- Expectations.
- Relevant indications.
- Logical goals.
- Possible actions.

From the last of these, a choice is made, firstly by imagining it in thought, and then possibly adapting it. The more experience someone has, the more frequently he initially makes a right choice. It even happens that when someone reconsiders the choice and considers other options, it often leads to a worse choice. Intuition is, therefore, only of value (often better than analytical decision-making), when someone has experience in the matter on which he has to make a decision.

Dependent on the amount of time available, you can still consider rationalising your decision by using a decision tree.

Developing intuition
Intuition can be learnt, and we have already come across one way, which is experience. A number of other options are:
- Reviewing
- Previewing
- Trust

REVIEWING
Think of a particular decision from not so long ago that you had to make quickly, and that turned out well. Try to remember how that went, how you felt, in what sort of environment it was, and what stimulating factors were present. Often, you can develop some general guidelines you can apply the next time you have to take an intuitive decision.

PREVIEWING
This technique is very easy to apply, by, just before you do something, imagining how this action will work out. You can do this at the beginning of a meeting, before opening an e-mail, or before you read a team member's progress report. The idea is that you try to guess what happens, in this way training the intuitive abilities of your brain.

LETTING GO
This is a process that consists of the following steps:
- *Name*, what you want to develop an intuitive thought about.
- *Collect*, information on the theme and fill your brain with it.
- *Instruct*, your brain to come up with an idea.
- *Ripen*, now you let go, and trust that an intuition will come.
- *Harvest*, after a while, a thought will automatically come up.

This is the closest to what Plato meant by 'learning is nothing other than remembering'. By filling your brain with information on the theme for which you want an answer, and trusting your intellectual abilities to work well, you can let go and let the search go on subconsciously until you suddenly come up with an idea.

4. Creativity techniques
In general, the human brain follows the path of the least resistance. Certain thoughts, notions and beliefs stand in the way of real, creative thoughts.

A way of coming up with new ideas is to do this in a group. Two heads are better than one, three even better, and so on. There are many techniques that can stimulate this, and they broadly follow the same pattern:
- Formulate the phrasing of the question.
- Diverge.
- Converge and choose.

Firstly, the phrasing of the question is thought up, followed by generating, almost without criticism, as many answers as possible. The answers are then clustered and prioritized, in order to ultimately make a choice from the possible options.

Formulate the phrasing of the question
The creative process starts with a clear formulation of the question in the form of a stepping-stone, or springboard. The stepping-stone is a sentence that begins with the word "How ..." followed by the question, to which we must find an answer.

We begin with diverging on the basis of a positive formulation. If certain parts of the project are overrunning, the stepping-stone should be something like "How do we finish on time?" rather than "How do we make up the overrun?" In this way, you are already in a more positive energy than when you direct your attention to the problem.

Diverge
On the basis of the stepping-stone, we generate as many ideas as possible with the team. We can do this using:
- Classical brainstorm techniques.
- Helicopter technique.
- Climbing technique.

CLASSICAL BRAINSTORM TECHNIQUES
These are the most well-known; the participants sit around a flipchart and call out ideas. A facilitator ensures that everyone has a say, that there are no discussions on, or criticism of, an idea, and he writes the ideas up so everyone can see them. In doing this, the participants stimulate each other to come up with new ideas. After a while, the process dries up, no new ideas are forthcoming, and that is the time to start the converging.

HELICOPTER TECHNIQUE
This is about considering a problem from a different viewpoint, and letting go of the existing logic.

You begin by letting go of the problem, and embracing a different line of thought. You can do this, for example, by thinking about a story that you have read recently, or to think about your holiday. Try to sketch a clear picture of what happened. After a while, and on the basis of the stepping-stone, you go through the story, and look to see if the story contains any answers to the question.

> EXAMPLE 27-1 VISION QUEST
> At the start of this century, I did a so-called Vision Quest.
> I walked onto a path signposted "access forbidden". Frustrated, I turned back, and not long afterwards, this pattern repeated itself twice more.
> The ensuing result was an interesting self-reflection about the rules that I sub-consciously imposed on myself.

CLIMBING TECHNIQUE
As opposed to the helicopter technique, the climbing technique does take the problem as the starting point, but then goes looking for the underlying suppositions that prevent the finding of a solution. The REBT technique already discussed is an example of such a climbing technique.

Take the situation, for which a solution is not readily available. One way of climbing out of this, is to first look at the reasons why something cannot be done, and then directly open this up for discussion with the question: "What if we actually can do this?" This often provides a new lead to finding a solution.

Converge and choose
A disadvantage of nearly all creativity techniques is that they deliver a large number of ideas, from which you then have to make a choice. Sometimes I say that creativity techniques are not really creative, but can be likened to a scattergun approach; you do not have to aim carefully and there is always a pellet that hits the target.

The step of reducing (converging) to a number of usable alternatives is, therefore, unavoidable. When there are many different alternatives, it is advisable to cluster them into the following categories:
- Nonsense.
- (Currently) Not achievable.
- Existing idea.
- New idea.

We cross out both the nonsense and non-achievable ideas, leaving the existing and new ideas. We then put both categories into sequence, and there are a number of different techniques to achieve this:

- Everyone is given ten points to divide up across the ideas.
- Everyone can vote for three ideas.

Then select two or three good ideas with the highest scores, and work these out further in order to come to a rational choice.

5. Edward De Bono
When we talk about creativity, we cannot avoid mentioning Edward de Bono (1933). If there was ever a management author, who has enriched the world with ideas about creativity, then it is him. He is the person who thought up the term "lateral thinking", and also the six thinking hats sprouted from his brain.

I shall now cover the following in succession:
- Lateral thinking.
- Thinking course.
- Six thinking hats.

Lateral thinking
Experience is about pattern recognition, and is the way in which our brains work. Everything we observe, we observe through the eyes of our experience. This has big advantages, as we do not have to keep re-inventing the wheel. The disadvantage is that we stay in a certain pattern, and approach a changed situation with old solutions.

Perhaps you have heard the following saying: *"you cannot solve a problem with the same way of thinking you used to cause the problem."*

This saying shows great wisdom, and lateral thinking is about breaking out of the standard pattern. Although it is related to creativity, it is something else. With creativity, we are often talking about the result, whereas according to de Bono, with lateral thinking it is about the process[8]; a process of restructuring, escaping, and the provocation of new patterns.

It has to do with:
- Generating new ideas.
- Escaping from the conceptual prison of the old ideas.

Let's apply them to the problem of the traffic jams. You could ask yourself: What if all birds were driving cars? Most people would immediately say that that is not possible. But that is precisely what you want to break out of with lateral thinking, birds driving cars provides new insights, and to name a few others:

1. Use Zeppelins.
2. Stimulate short flights (planes) between the big cities.
3. Have separate lanes in which drivers can drive very fast.
4. Etc.

Make sure you give your ideas free rein.

---
8 (1970) *Lateral Thinking*, Edward de Bono, WARD LOCK EDUCATION

> EXAMPLE 27-2 WATER SUPPLY[1]
>
> A big problem in a country such as Jordan is the water supply. The traditional way of looking at this is to estimate how great the future demand will be, and to make an attempt to meet this.
>
> If we think laterally, instead of solving the problem from the supply side, we could consider approaching it from the demand side.
>
> ---
> 1 (1999) *Introduction of Lateral Thinking to Civil and Environmental Engineering Education*, Ode Al-Jayyousi.

Thinking course

De Bono states that thinking is a skill that we have to develop[9], and in his thinking course he provides a rich collection of techniques, which allows the user to generate new ideas. There is a relationship between intelligence and thinking, whereby the former is the potential, and the latter the skill to make use of that potential. There are a lot of intelligent people, who are not so good at thinking.

Six thinking hats[10].

The six thinking hats technique is probably what he is best known for.

This is a technique in which you give the team members the assignment to approach a problem from a particular point of view (thinking hat). You have now got the following hats:
1. *White*: Think virgin white, in the form of facts, numbers and information.
2. *Red*: A 'red mist' in front of the eyes, in the form of emotions and sentimental judgments, as well as presumptions and intuition.
3. *Black*: The 'devils advocate', negative assessment; why something won't work.
4. *Yellow*: Sunshine, clarity and optimism: positive assessment, constructive input, search out opportunities (opportunism).
5. *Green*: Fruitfulness: creativity, seeds germinating and blossoming, movement , provocation.
6. *Blue*: Detachment and control: the conductor of thinking, think about thinking.

It is because you give the team members the assignment to think with a certain hat on, that you also give them the freedom to think of everything within it. The result is a broad range of possible solutions.

6. The Cartesian Product

This technique, which, by way of an example, I shall apply to a strengths and weaknesses analysis (SWOT), generates a large number of ideas and can therefore be seen as an effective creativity technique. The example I want to use is as follows:

We have here a small successful company with a product portfolio that is doing well. When the senior management takes stock of its situation by brainstorming, the result is as follows:

Strong Points:
- S1: Sufficient money.
- S2: Superior Product.
- S3: Fast innovation cycle.

Weak Points:
- Z1: Too few staff.
- Z2: Reputation – not well-known.

Opportunities:
- K1: Potential abroad.

Threats:
- B1: Economic circumstances.
- B2: New market entrants.

---
9 (2009) *Thinking Course*, Edward de Bono, BBC ACTIVE, UK
10 (1999) *Six Thinking Hats,* Edward de Bono, BACK BAY BOOKS

2.07 Creativity

A Cartesian product comes into existence, when we pair together the findings of the SWOT (S1xZ1, S1xZ1, S2xZ1, etc.).

We then get the following table of possibilities:

S1xZ1	S1: Sufficient money. Z1: Too few staff.
S2xZ1	S2: Superior Product. Z1: Too few staff.
S3xZ1	S3: Fast innovation cycle. Z1: Too few staff.
S1xZ2	S1: Sufficient money. Z2: Reputation.
S2xZ2	S2: Superior Product. Z2: Reputation.
S3xZ2	S3: Fast innovation cycle. Z2: Reputation.
S1xK1	S1: Sufficient money. K1: Potential abroad.
S2xK1	S2: Superior Product. K1: Potential abroad.
S3xK1	S3: Fast innovation cycle. K1: Potential abroad.
S1xB1	S1: Sufficient money. B1: Economic circumstances.
S2xB1	S2: Superior Product. B1: Economic circumstances.
S3xB1	S3: Fast innovation cycle. B1: Economic circumstances.
S1xB2	S1: Sufficient money. B2: New market entrants.
S2xB2	S2: Superior Product. B2: New market entrants.
S3xB2	S3: Fast innovation cycle. B2: New market entrants.

The fifteen possibilities are now stepping-stones for generating new ideas. As an example, I shall work out S1xZ1 and S2xZ1 further.

S1xZ1:
- S1: Sufficient money.
- Z1: Too few staff.

First idea:
As we have sufficient money, we can recruit new staff through a recruitment campaign.

Second idea:
By positioning our economic situation well, we can be an attractive employer.

Third idea:
As we have sufficient money, we can ask our part-timers if they are prepared to work more hours.

S2xZ1:
- S2: Superior Product.
- Z1: Te few staff.

Fourth idea:
The superior product means that people will want to work for us. We can use this in our recruitment campaign.

You can see that by using a traditional method, a whole list of ideas can be created, and you can now go a step further by combining ideas using a common approach.

393

2.07 Creativity

2.08 Results orientation

IS IT ALRIGHT IF IT IS A LITTLE BIT OVER FOR THE SAME PRICE, MADAM?
OF COURSE, BUTCHER!

A colleague said to me:
"I am better at planning."

I thought:
"That is a pity, because, as important as planning is, ultimately the result is what counts."

Progress means nothing more than delivering results according to a plan.

If you do not have a plan, you do not know how much progress you are making. But you do deliver a result.

If you do have a plan, but no result …

Well, what should I say?

2.08 Results Orientation

2.08-1 DEFINITIONS

Result orientation	The ability to focus the attention of people and/or a team on the goals to be achieved, in order to arrive at the best possible result for all parties involved.

2.08-2 Introduction

The definition used in the ICB on result orientation mentions the following topics:

- Focus attention on the main goals of the project.
- Achieve the best possible result for all parties involved.

According to research[1] quoted before, result orientation is one of the biggest success factors, Van Aken correctly states that: *"A goal oriented style of working has a big influence on project success."* This is further elaborated here; project managers focus all parties involved on the bigger goals of the project, and by doing this, they continuously build on the foundations for success already laid down in their plans.

Another definition[2] of result orientation I want to mention here is:

*Being actively focused on achieving results and objectives,
and the willingness to intervene in the event of disappointing results.*

This definition adds a number of extra dimensions to this competence element, namely:

- An *individual* orientation towards results and goals.
- The willingness to intervene.

This comes prior to the elements the ICB attributes to this element. The latter is especially important, as result orientation means that as project manager, you are willing to intervene when something is falling short. This requires courage by which you can differentiate yourself, as most people hesitate to take such (sometimes drastic) action, and often are not keen to disturb the routine.

---

1 (1996), *De weg naar projectsucces"*, T. v. Aken, ELSEVIER/de Tijdstroom
2 (2004) *Coachen op gedrag en resultaat,* PIMEDIA, Utrecht

2.08-3 PROCESS STEPS

1. Define results unambiguously.
2. Arrange results into interest groups.
3. Explicitly manage expectations.
4. Determine and communicate the critical path.
5. Make the project plan definitive, communicate it and get it approved.
6. Repeating the previous steps for as many times as is necessary.
7. Striving for a continuous result improvement.
8. Communicating project performances and results.
9. Compare project performance and results against the plan.
10. Apply lessons learned

1. Define results unambiguously

The motto here is clarity in advance. There are two ways to formulate results, of which only one is really suitable for projects.

ER/RE[1] formulation

These are results in terms of: *better, faster, more efficient, more user friendly,* etc. Such formulations work well during the project development stage, but are insufficient for managing a project successfully, as an ER/RE result cannot be measured.

What is *better, faster, more efficient and more user friendly?* On what basis will the project sponsor at the end of the project be able to say that he is satisfied with our results?

SMART formulation

With this formulation, it is possible to define the result as being: *specific, measurable, acceptable, realistic and timely*. This is necessary, because only with this, can we also give form to the next process steps.

The formulation of the results must be unambiguous, and not open to more than one interpretation. This seems to be obvious, but our language is tougher and unintentionally more ambiguous than we would like. For many decennia now, project management literature mentions SMART as being the guideline, but still I seldom see a result formulation (however clever it may be), which is not open to at least two interpretations.

It is, however, important to at least make an attempt, as in the process of defining "unambiguously", you point all parties involved in the same direction. The co-operation process which produces results that are recorded in writing, proverbially points all the noses in the same direction, and that is precisely what it is all about.

2. Arrange results into interest groups

You know it already, one of the first things you do as a project manager, after you have met the project sponsor, is look around for who else has an interest in the project. You have: the line management, the users, the maintenance departments, the works council, unions, environmental movements, etc. All of them have an interest.

If politics takes over in your project, you must be aware of the fact that in nine cases out of ten, this happens because you do not have a clear picture of the different interests. Therefore, you have to start with a focus on the interests, and you try to find an answer to the question as to why interested parties either support or frustrate the project.

Politics is easy to understand when you know what the underlying interests are. The next question you then ask is, which result

---

[1] (2006) *Programmamanagement – Sturen op samenhang,* van der Tak en Wijnen, KLUWER, Deventer

belongs to which interest, and you must try to identify that relationship. Maybe, you can serve the same interest with a different, much more realistic result. Maybe the contrasts are less than they appear. Such a concept and proactively anticipating makes annoying politics 'melt' away.

This is then also the reason why a project manager has to have knowledge of the contextual elements the ICB describes. By this, I mean issues such as: permanent organization, business, systems, technology, personnel management, health, safety, security and environment, financial management and legal aspects. This does not mean he has to be an expert on this, but he does have to have knowledge of it, because in that way, he can build up a better understanding of all the different interests.

3. Explicitly manage expectations

Explicit means visible. All interested parties have to see that you, as project manager, are actively looking after their expectations. Project management does not happen behind the notebook, but in communication with others. The management of expectations has two directions: inwards and outwards.

Inwards

Here you translate the expectations into concrete results, and work processes. You ensure that the project team and the result delivered comply with these.

Outwards

This involves ensuring the parties involved stay informed of the ins and outs of the team, and the results that it delivers. Sometimes faster and cheaper, sometimes later and more expensive, but in both cases, you keep everyone informed.

4. Determine and communicate the critical path

The classical definition of project management is to deliver on time, within budget and in accordance with the specifications. Many versions of this definition have already been documented, and almost all writers agree that the project manager is responsible for managing time, costs and quality. I agree only partly with that, because time cannot be managed.

If you do nothing, you do not deliver bad quality, and you also do not spend any money, although the clock keeps ticking! So you do not have to manage time, as it will go by itself, meaning that all the definitions mentioned are wrong. What you can manage is progress, which means the same as: *delivering on time.*

The ultimate instrument for doing this is the *critical path*, which we have already discussed under the topic: *Time & Project phasing*. Many project managers do this from their gut feeling, but that is much too inaccurate. The best approach is to carry out a real critical path analysis, and then to communicate this critical path very clearly, so that everybody knows that his contribution to this is essential for achieving the promised result on time.

In concrete terms, this means that when someone is busy with a certain non-critical activity, he lets go of this immediately, when he is needed for the critical path. This is obviously only possible when he knows this, and therefore communication is essential.

5. Finalize the project plan, communicate it and get it approved

Definitive is a strong word, as a plan only becomes definitive once it has been carried out. However, that is not what I mean here. The large part of the plan has been established in consultation, and the most important interested parties have had their say. The project manager has summarized all these agreements and thoughts in a project management plan, and he now presents it to the decision makers.

The approval by them has a ritual function, and it is, therefore, important that you have the plan signed. Signing for most people is a deed with a deep meaning; you do not sign your name under just anything. The signing of the plan means that with these agreements, and with you as project manager, they commit to giving it their all to achieve the defined result. Ensuring all interested parties are result oriented is what it is all about.

6. Repeating the previous steps for as many times as is necessary

You keep repeating the previous five steps for as long as necessary, both in advance, and also during the project, when the result orientation is lacking. You continuously provide direction with respect to agreements on work processes, and work results.

7. Striving for a continuous result improvement

Once the plan has been approved, one of the first things you do as project manager, is to look for improvements. Is it possible to do it faster, cheaper and better?

From experience we know that it often is more difficult and takes longer than planned, that it costs more than estimated and that it does not go as well as was expected. From the beginning, and with that knowledge, you start looking in advance for room in the budget and plan, to cushion setbacks. However, you do this only when the plan has been approved, and not before, because otherwise, you will be putting the whole project under too much pressure.

You stimulate the team members to come up with improvement initiatives, and you discuss the feasibility of these. Wherever possible you implement them, as long as you do not go outside the scope of the project, as you have no mandate to do so. You must also ensure that team members look to improve their own efficiency. This attitude of both result orientation, and improvement, has to be present in the project organization from top to bottom.

8. Communicating project performances and results

Results only count when they are visible! You have to handle this, because the team members are busy delivering the performance and do not have the time for it. The communication plan of a project ensures that the parties involved are informed, and will therefore continue to give their support to the project.

Many project teams retire back into their offices or remote bunkers, and are very busy with achieving beautiful results, but during the execution, nobody notices this. Unknown is unloved, and this provokes political manoeuvres from the bystanders. In their ignorance, they then assume that there is no progress, and they begin to feel insecure (depending on what is at stake for them). This leads to them intervening in order to turn the project around 'for the better'.

If the project manager also communicates the intermediate results of the team, the latter should become unnecessary. Where people have a sense that things will work out, they will provide support, and they will only make demands when there is doubt.

9. Compare project performance and results against the plan

You can only know something, if there is something to measure. For that you need a plan, or as we often say, the baselines against which we measure the real performance. You provide a result if you do it on time, and within the budget. Baselines are, for example, the budget, the planning, the agreed capacity, the quality specifications, and suchlike.

The project management plan is not a document which is somewhere in an inaccessible place on a network server, but it is a manual that you check against continuously in order to see to what extent you are actually achieving the previously defined results.

10. Apply lessons learned

Short term result orientation versus long term result orientation. This process step is one for the long term. What do we learn from what we are doing, and are we now doing better than ten years ago, and in ten years time will we do better than now? Let's hope so, because someone who does not want to develop is actually someone who is only biding his time.

2.08 Results Orientation

2.09 Efficiency

SMART, SMARTER, SMARTEST

Things can always be done smarter and faster and give the same result.

But why do it differently if we have been doing it this way now for years?

Could this be the reason that we more frequently hear about people becoming burned out?

2.09 Efficiency

2.09-1 DEFINITIONS

Efficiency	The ability to deploy time, people and resources cost-effectively, in order to deliver the agreed results, and meet the stakeholders' expectations.

2.09-2 INTRODUCTION

Things can always be done better and smarter. You can continuously improve your own work and that of your team members, and you have to look for ways to achieve this. It has always surprised me how many people there are, also amongst our colleagues, who hardly ever look for new ways of doing their job smarter and more efficiently.

For example, you can do this by copying what your colleagues do and interpreting it in your own style. Another way is to read books on the profession, and convert your theoretical knowledge into practical experience. When used at the right time and properly, many of the techniques covered in this book can make your work as project manager easier. You have to want to do this and actually do it, but when you start working on the content, you will soon discover the power it brings.

I find efficiency to be a professional assignment that I really like carrying out, as in this way my project sponsors obtain the most benefit from the effort I put in, compared to the rate or salary I receive for it. It is a pitfall to look at experience as a reason for not carrying on with a continuous development process, in which we improve our personal method of working.

Once we have started the project, do we keep to the planning and the agreed budget, or do we try to do it better, more cheaply and faster?

That is precisely what this competence element is all about.

2.09 Efficiency

2.09-3 PROCESS STEPS

1. Actively seek to improve.
2. Plan, obtain and assign.
3. Determine priorities.
4. Look for sustainable efficiency.
5. Look for improvements.
6. Follow, monitor and compare.
7. Estimate resources.
8. Report, and propose measures.
9. Propose and evaluate.
10. Apply lessons learned.

1. Actively seek to improve

You can interpret this process step either in a narrow, or in a broad sense. By narrow sense, we mean improving the work and the results within the scope of the project, so that right from the start of the project, we question whether or not we can achieve the same result faster and more cheaply, and we check whether or not we can deliver better quality than agreed. We continuously scrutinize the work processes, and by so doing, search out methods to make them more efficient.

Project management then means faster, smarter, cheaper and better.

In a broad sense, however, it is about 'bettering the world' with the results of the project. People are the stewards and inhabitants of this planet, so does this also apply to project managers? The answer is yes, and you can read about it in the fourth process step.

The ICB mentions a number of topics for this competence element, which should be points to focus on, such as:
- Efficient use of capacity and energy.
- Social and environmental costs.

Actively seeking is a motivation which should come from within, and in this, the 21st century, where there is a lot of focus on sustainability, we should include these considerations more and more in the way we manage our projects.

2. Plan, obtain and assign

On the hard side of the profession, we have techniques to ensure we can plan to have the right man, at the right place, at the right time. However, you can plan as much as you like, but if you do not stay on top of the situation, something often happens that is completely different to what you want. Most successes do not just happen by themselves.

This means working pro-actively, and coming to agreements with the resource managers and suppliers. Implement a work authorisation system, so that the work is placed with the right person at the right time, at the same time ensuring that the tools someone needs to do his job properly are also available on time. If people have to wait three days for a pc, you do not make efficient use of their time.

This also means that you have to keep a close eye on the critical path, so that when an employee has to work on it, he can start immediately and make efficient use of the limited time.

This is about creating a work environment in which people can work effectively, and thus provide an efficient contribution to the project. They have the right to a work environment which is created with thoughtfulness, attention and care; not a big noisy room, but one in which it is enjoyable to work.

The work is adapted to the competences of the employees, but the different project procedures should also be there to help, and not to degenerate into bureaucratic procedures, which sometimes make it impossible to carry out the work.

2.09 Efficiency

3. Determine priorities

It has to be clear what the current priorities are; managers set these because only they can oversee all work activity areas. Therefore, you should communicate these clearly to the members of your team, because if you do not, they will determine their own priorities, often deviating from those of the project, with all resulting consequences.

Obviously, you also have to ensure that they have some room for manoeuvre, because if they frequently have to wait for your decisions, you will lose valuable time and efficiency will deteriorate. Beforehand, you determine and agree what deviations are reasonable with respect to the agreed plans.

4. Look for sustainable efficiency

Make smart use of the different resources on the project, so not only a plan for people, but also for the resources they will be using on the project. Also, as doing it well is better than doing it again, ensure that everything required is available on time.

You can often see from the project organization whether or not the lines of communication are efficient; if this is not a top-down construction, something is wrong. If the duration of meetings gets out of hand, you have to find the cause, and possibly put certain people into one and the same team, or merge two teams into one team.

There are limitations to the technology you can use, as you have to be aware of the longer term, and therefore, you make use of durable technology where this is relevant... We all know the stories of ground becoming polluted, because companies, often due to ignorance, have made use of non-durable production techniques. In the short term this can be efficient, but not over the long term.

5. Look for improvements

Here we are continuously looking for improvement. The principle you use is the so- called Kaizen[1] concept, which was developed by Masaaki Imaai.

Kaizen means: "*change for the better*".

It is a philosophy about what the best way for us is to change, which is fundamentally different from the 'western' way of innovation. In the West people are inclined to make a big change every so often, work with it for a certain period of time until it no longer meets requirements, and then start along a new path for change once again, in order to be able to cope with the new situation. The graph below shows the difference between this approach and the Kaizen approach.

EXAMPLE 29-1 MEXICAN GULF 2010

Different choices with respect to design and safety led to the oil spill in the Mexican Gulf in 2010.

Possibly many of those choices were made from a cost viewpoint, but looked at from the point of long term efficiency, these choices have resulted in prohibitive costs for nature, society and ultimately also the oil company itself.

---

1 (1986) *KAIZEN* Masaaki Imai, THE KAIZEN INSTITUTE LTD.

2.09 Efficiency

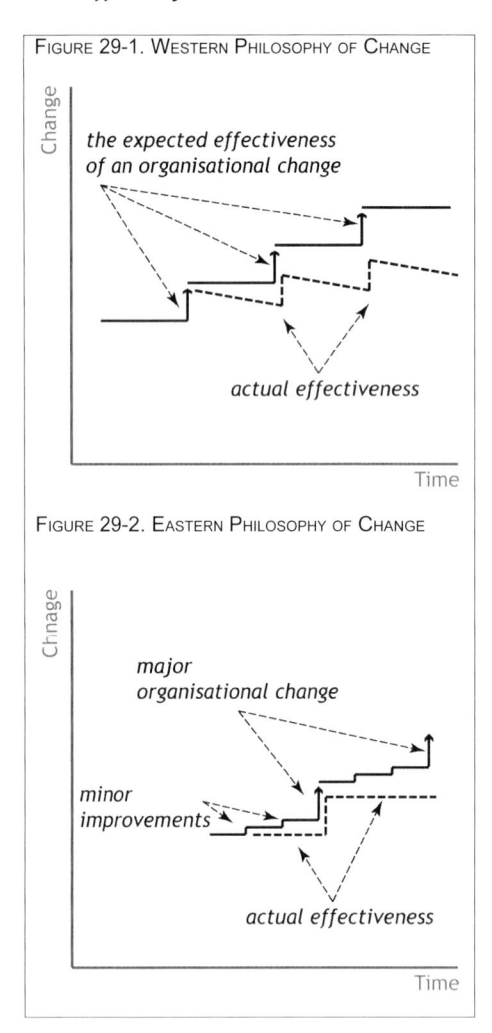

FIGURE 29-1. WESTERN PHILOSOPHY OF CHANGE

the expected effectiveness of an organisational change

actual effectiveness

FIGURE 29-2. EASTERN PHILOSOPHY OF CHANGE

major organisational change

minor improvements

actual effectiveness

What it comes down to, is that instead of a big change now and again, we continuously make small improvements in the way we carry out the work. We continuously improve processes in small steps.

This also means that you delegate part of the responsibility for the improvement to the people who actually carry out the work. Improvements now come from the bottom instead of being laid down at the top and this creates a lot more support. You stimulate the continuous activity of looking for improvements in your project. This method is more efficient than the 'big steps' approach of the western version.

6. Follow, monitor and compare

If you do not measure, you do not know anything and efficiency has to be measurable. A hard technique you can use for this is the Earned Value technique, which contains the following indicators, each of which says something about the performance compared to the plan:

- CPI (Cost Performance Indicator), says something about the use of resources.
- TCPI (To Complete Performance Indicator), says something about the required improvement in efficiency.
- SPI (Schedule Performance Indicator), says something about the use of the available time.

You can consider determining the SPI and the CPI for each individual employee. You then replace the employees who continuously have low scores.

It is a fact for this technique, just as for all other techniques, that it is not the technique itself that makes the improvement happen, but the pre-conditions required to be able to apply the technique properly. These are also pre-conditional to achieving an efficient use of resources and time during the project.

In order to apply the Earned Value Technique you have to decide beforehand:
- What progress is.
- How this becomes apparent.

This is only possible if you structure the project efficiently and effectively.

7. Estimate resources

At two levels! Which resources, and in what numbers, do my employees need, in order to complete the project within the timescales set?

2.09 Efficiency

Resources are:
- Instruments and tools.
- Office space and furniture.
- Infrastructure and IT.

But also:
- Workable project procedures.
- Clear work package descriptions.
- Clear information on project objectives.

And further:
- Financing in order to make project payments on time.

As project manager, you have to make a prognosis of these beforehand, because only then can you start everything up on time and not be confronted with waiting times for resources your employees need. Time on the critical path is lost by not organizing resources properly.

8. Report, and propose measures

You carry out all improvements within your scope, and this will result in an increase in project performance. It is possible, of course, that you see improvements outside your boundaries of tolerance, and for these you will need the project sponsor's approval.

For every improvement outside the scope of the project, you produce a cost-benefit analysis, which you present to the project sponsor, and ultimately it is up to him to decide whether or not you can actually implement it.

9. Propose and evaluate

You and your team members are continuously (in accordance with the KAIZEN principle) working on making improvements based on the experience gained during the execution. You assess the different alternatives in consultation with your sub-project leaders. You implement those improvements which are feasible, desirable and within the tolerances.

10. Apply lessons learned

Share your experience with other colleagues in the organization, because why should others have to re-invent the wheel you discovered? The whole organization should profit from your input and every suggestion is a new small step.

2.09-4 Special Topics

1. Long term efficiency

Efficiency has been defined as: "The ability to deploy time, people and resources cost-effectively, in order to deliver the agreed results, and meet the stakeholders' expectations".

In economy bad times, the concept of efficiency comes more into the spotlight than when organizations are doing well. For this reason the concept has been degraded into a cost-cutting measure, because "cost-effective" will be interpreted by the senior manager, staring at his spreadsheet, as "doing more with less money", and this will inevitably lead to a short term focus; when results are produced quickly, everyone is happy. This may seem attractive, but efficiency in the short term is almost always inefficient in the long term.

That this is one of the competence elements, has to do with the dilemma the project manager sometimes finds himself with. On the one hand, his boundary is the delivery of the project result, whereas he also (in any case) is morally responsible for the long term effects, for which, however, he often does not have any authority to decide on. This situation demands that you, as project manager, develop a vision which you propagate in a convincing and substantiated fashion.

We strive for "long term efficiency" because this is ultimately better for everyone. I shall successively substantiate this proposition for the following topics:
- Use of natural sources.
- Organizational effects.
- Reputation damage and social effects.

Use of natural sources

How clean is your project? That is the key question for this aspect of efficiency, and it is about:
- The "clean" raw material used in the project.
- The amount of raw materials used by the project.
- The extent to which the production process causes pollution.
- The amount of waste generated by the project.

It is tempting to think no further than the boundaries of the project, i.e. as cheaply as possible. In the long term, however, this will lead to higher costs when natural sources are exhausted, pollution turns out to be unacceptable, and the company has to pay damages afterwards. When you then draw the boundaries for the project (within scope), you can talk of efficiency, but when you look over the boundaries, then for the totality you can no longer speak of efficiency at all.

Organizational effects

Here we are talking about the effects of the project after delivery has taken place. Is it also an improvement in the long term? You should then think about the cost of maintenance, management and ultimately dismantlement at the end of the life cycle. To what extent does this counterbalance the quick solutions, which are chosen in order to stay within budget and the time frame.

Reputation damage and social effects

Another aspect, the effects of which can continue to work through in the long term, is the social effect and the reputation damage caused by wrong choices during the project (see previous text insert on the oil spill).

2. Benchmarking

This is an instrument for discovering where you can improve the efficiency. At a project level, this can be used by looking for similar projects and comparing them to yours. If you work in a large company, there may be colleagues who are up for the challenge. You then get a competition to find out who is the most efficient. When your project consists of sub-projects, you can compare these with each other, and in this way, the different sub-project teams keep each other on their toes. What is possible with sub-projects, is, of course, also possible with individual team members.

3. Time management

It is important to manage your own time effectively. When you start, you look back at the time spent and you evaluate how you spent it. Dependent on the result, you may decide to arrange your time differently.

In planning this, there are two aspects you have to keep looking at: *urgency* and *importance*. Often the tyranny of the urgency rules, which makes it look as if you are running from one fire to the next.

A task is *urgent* if it has to be finished quickly, for example in one day, and when you realize this, and have to work overtime to finish it, you experience the urgency. This is especially true, when you have to complete several tasks within a short timescale. So, **urgency** has to do with time, and tasks are usually urgent because we have started them too late or overlooked them.

A task is *important* if it is an essential contribution to the end result of the project. *Important* is not so much to do with time, but more with the contribution to the result. A question you may ask yourself to find out whether or not something is important is: *What would happen if I don't do it?*

EXAMPLE 29-2 URGENCY AND IMPORTANCE
Urgent can be the report to the project sponsor, which has to out in the afternoon.
Important however, is to check a contract for the small print.

the priority of an activity, and you can then make the following matrix:

	Not urgent	Urgent
Important	2 Plan in, and start on time	1 Start immediately, and report any delays when they occur
Not important	4 Do not do it	3 See if someone else can do it

That which is important obviously depends on the project management plan, but also on your view as a professional. Personal time management, therefore, starts with setting goals, i.e. what do you want to achieve? You use that when assessing the different tasks you have to carry out.

For people who feel they are always short of time, all work falls into the first quadrant. Everything is important, and has to be done immediately, meaning that the work is never completed as you always let the circumstances dictate what you do. For project managers, the aim is to always put the bulk of the work into category two, allowing you the time to sort out important issues. For personal goals, it is useful to make a monthly, quarterly, and annual plan, and to reserve the time necessary to achieve this planning in your diary.

2.09 Efficiency

Time management means a good planning and administration of the work you still have to do. On this basis, you are able to carry out the required work according to the *DTM* principle (Diary, Tasks and Mail): firstly you study the *Diary* to get an idea of the urgency and the appointments in the coming period. Then you study the (prioritized) *Tasks*, the order of which may change based on what is in your diary. Finally, you open the *Mailbox* to see if you can maintain the current priority, and then you plan the order in which you will carry out the different tasks.

You do this at the end of every day for the following day, on Friday, at the end of the week, for the next week, and at the end of each reporting period again for the next period. The leading principle is that at the end of one period you always plan the next one. This means that you can go home with an '*empty*' head, which obviously does imply that an empty-headed person goes home.

When planning, also take account of the activity '*time management*' itself, as on average, it will take you 15 minutes per day. But also take into account unforeseen activities, which also take your time. It depends somewhat on the type of work you do, but if you do not do this, you will consistently find yourself being short of time.

If you do not yet make use of time management techniques, you will gain at least one hour of net time in a working day by starting now. At least, that is my personal experience.

4. Take account of your rhythm
Another point is your personal efficiency, and this concerns taking account of your own physical rhythm.

During the day
People do not have the same amount of fitness all day long. The diagram below shows how their energy fluctuates during a working day. You can clearly see that you are fitter in the morning than in the afternoon.

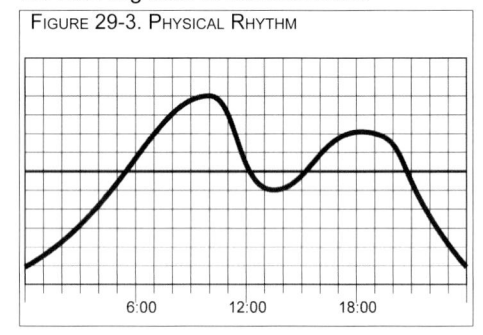

FIGURE 29-3. PHYSICAL RHYTHM

By aligning the time at which you have to carry out difficult issues with the times when you are at your best, you achieve an efficiency gain. Although everyone has his own rhythm, for most people it will look like the diagram above.

Night rest
Working efficiently is one thing, but sleeping efficiently is just as important. An old proverbial saying is: hours before twelve count double. But there is even more in the area of sleeping. A complete night rest is built up of about five short periods of sleep, each of ninety minutes. Every short sleep consists of a slumber time, followed by an increasingly deeper sleep, a period in which we dream (REM sleep), and then we wake up, which is something most of us do not really notice, only to fall asleep again.

When we are woken up during the deep sleep, for example, by our alarm, we feel tired and as if we have hardly slept at all. Sleeping efficiently now means that the total sleep is always a multitude of ninety minutes, because with this pattern, you wake up well rested. It is better to sleep six hours than seven hours, and similarly, better to sleep seven and a half hours than five hours.

5. Core Quadrants

Core Quadrants are not only a useful aid to your self-development, but also to start a discussion with team members about behavior, or analyzing the culture of an organization. They have been developed by Daniel Ofman.

It is a simple principle, which assumes that everybody has so-called core qualities, or in other words things they are good in and that they really want to exploit. When the task at hand fits the available core qualities, you will achieve an increase in efficiency. Something to take in account when dispatching the assignments. Examples of such qualities are:
- Firmness
- Decisiveness
- Improvisation ability

Because people really want to exploit such qualities, there is also, in fact, a pitfall associated with each core quality when the latter goes too far. Firmness, for example, can lead to obstinacy, decisiveness to insistence and improvisation to changeability.

Ofman asserts that the opposite of the pitfall is an interesting development opportunity, or challenge, which you should strive for. If we arrange the previous examples in a table, then this looks as follows:

Quality	Pitfall	Challenge
Firmness	Stubborness	Adaptability
Decisiveness	Insistence	Patience
Improvisation	Changeability	Firmness

If you now compare improvisation ability with firmness, a form of "mirroring" appears to be possible. When someone with improvisation ability is involved with someone who displays too much of the first person's challenge (firmness), i.e. stubbornness, the latter is then called the allergy. We can now make a core quadrant.

Quality	Pitfall
Improvisation	Changeability
Stubbornness	Firmness
Allergy	**Challenge**

The good thing about this is that the drawbacks in our personality, whereby I mean the pitfalls and the allergies, are leads to finding qualities. They also teach me something about the behavior of the other person, or about the culture of another organization.

2.09 Efficiency

2.10 Consultation

HE, WHO KNOWS BETTER, CONSULTS MORE THAN HE ADVISES.

Who knows better?

The consultant or the customer?

The consultant or the employees on the work floor?

It is sad but true: we often forget, that our employees can tell us more about the company than expensive consultants.

2.10 Consultation

2.10-1 DEFINITIONS

Consultation	The competence to reason, put forward sound arguments, view an issue from a different angle, negotiate and find solutions.

2.10-2 Introduction

The fifth big secret[1] in medicine is:

> *Ensure they pay you enough to do what you say.*

This secret also applies if we look at consultancy practice. Quality costs money, and subconsciously we all know that. Someone who wants something for nothing will sometimes get a bargain, but mostly he will buy rubbish. A similar assumption applies to advice; if it comes cheap, it can't be any good, and many consultants make grateful use of this. The extent to which the project sponsor accepts advice, strongly depends on the rate the consultant charges.

This gives rise to the suggestion that the project sponsor is subconsciously more concerned with having a certain amount of security, than about an actual solution. Someone, an expert with a lot of knowledge and experience (translated in his charge rate) provides a confirmation of what the project sponsor deep down already suspected.

This is because providing advice is no more than holding a mirror up in front of someone's face, instead of listening to what the customer has to say, reformulating the question, and returning it. In order to be able to this, you have to be in consultation with your customer.

Good consultation consists of:

- Mutual respect.
- Systematic and structured thinking.
- Analyzing facts and arguments.
- Formulating and presenting decisions.

Does a project manager need this skill? Yes he certainly does, because he advises his project sponsor on how the project has the best chance of success.

---

1 (1985) *The Secrets of Consulting,* Gerald M. Weinberg, DORSET HOUSE PUBLISHING, New York

2.10-3 Process Steps

1. Analyze situation and context.
2. Identify goals.
3. Listen to arguments.
4. Determine similarities and differences.
5. Diagnose problems and choose solutions.
6. Come to an agreement on differences.
7. Consider consequences; document and communicate them.
8. Apply lessons learned

1. Analyze situation and context

I have said it more often, think before you act. When you have to give, or want to give, advice, always start with an analysis of:
- The situation.
- The context.
- The project sponsor.

The situation
What is the problem for which advice is wanted or required? What attempts have been made to implement previous advice, and with what results? Remember that every solution could be the cause of a new problem.

You also have to make a distinction between problems and limitations. The big difference is that for a problem there is a solution, for a limitation there isn't. A problem without a solution doesn't exist, that is a limitation.

The advice to be given is, therefore, about:
- The solution to a problem.
- Handling a limitation.

The context
In which environment does the organization, or person you have to advise, operate. What is the influence of this environment on this particular problem, and to what extent can the environment be ignored. Some problems actually resolve themselves if you do nothing about it.

The project sponsor
What does the project sponsor expect from you as consultant, and particularly when he has asked your advice, it is interesting to know the role he expects you to play.

There are three possible roles[1]:
- *Expert*, where you as consultant take the lead, and solve the problem.
- *Accomplice*, where you, as consultant, work alongside the project sponsor to do his 'dirty' work, with the project sponsor maintaining control over the proceedings.
- *Partner*, where, in consultation, both think of and implement a solution.

The last of these roles always takes preference, because it does the most justice to the qualities and responsibilities of both of you. This, however, is not always feasible, and as advising project manager, you will have to ask yourself the question whether or not you do want to function in one of the first two roles. It depends on your own ambitions and abilities.

2. Identify goals

There are main goals and personal goals; the main goals are often explicitly voiced, and the personal goals not. Sometimes, with respect to certain points, the two can be contradictory. When you are able to unravel the personal goals of the various players, you can be effective in formulating advice that will create sufficient support.

There may also be alternative goals that can be identified, which may be just as ac-

---

1 (2000) Ed Schein cited in *Flawless Consulting: A guide to getting your expertise used, Second Edition,* Peter Block, JOSSEY-BASS/PFEIFER PUBLISHERS, San Francisco

2.10 Consultation

ceptable as the main objectives voiced. You need a broad knowledge and interest in your project sponsors situation to be able to give sensible advice, which must also be in the language of the receiver.

3. Listen to arguments

As you want to base your advice on as much information as possible, you have to talk with the various different people involved. One of the most important skills of the advising project manager then is being able to listen to the other people's arguments. To be able to do that, the other competence elements such as sincerity, respect and empathy have to be well developed.

When you listen to the arguments of someone else, you have to temporarily defer what your view of it is. Therefore, only ask questions for clarification, but still better is to follow the list of *'hm, parrot, paraphrase and summary*' in order to allow someone to tell his complete story. By understanding the arguments of the other person, you are also better able to identify the underlying personal goals. You can then base your own arguments for the advice you give on that.

4. Determine similarities and differences

Active listening provides a large collection of opinions and arguments. The trick is to determine the similarities and the differences, as these provide the leads for the advice. You continuously ask yourself the question: *"Can it be that these different points of view arise when all these people involved look at the same problem?"* As long as the answer to that is negative, you have not yet managed to get all the relevant information onto the table.

5. Diagnose problems and choose solutions

When all information is on the table, you can start researching the cause of the problem, and try and find a remedy for it. Don't forget that within the organization, there is usually already an idea on the direction to finding a potential solution, and it is, therefore, essential to find that out.

Actually, advising really is simple, it is about discovering the solution that unconsciously already exists in the organization, and presenting in an acceptable manner.

6. Come to an agreement on differences

There are always more roads that lead to the same destination. The best advice is that which can count on receiving the most support. But there is more, and the effectiveness dimensions of advice can be mapped out using the following formula:

$$Effectiveness = f^2(Quality \times Acceptance \times Management)$$

The effectiveness depends on:
- The quality of the professional content of the advice.
- The acceptance of the advice.
- The management of carrying out or implementing it.

It is, therefore, not just the content of the advice, but also how the message is packaged and implemented, and there is a chance that you will be faced with resistance (lack of acceptance).

---

2 *f , is a function of (*Quality x Acceptance x Management)

2.10 Consultation

Peter Block mentions three steps in dispelling the resistance[3]:
- Pick up the signals.
- Name the resistance.
- Say nothing, and let the customer react.

Nathans[4] goes deeper into this, and mentions the following techniques to deal with resistance:
- Naming.
- Recognizing.
- Inquiring.
- Treating it seriously.
- Judo.
- Avoiding.
- Reverse intervention.

It is clear that Nathans names a broader collection of techniques than Block. Both contain the milestone of **naming** the resistance. What is striking is that in Block's approach, the consultant leaves the work with regard to the resistance with the customer (a non-directive style), whereas Nathans does the opposite, and in this approach, the consultant has the active role. Something can be said for both approaches, and it depends strongly on your own preference.

7. Consider consequences; document and communicate them

All advice has consequences which you have to document in a report, but you also have to explain it verbally. Everything that has been put into writing cannot be considered to be automatically and unambiguously understandable. During the personal explanation you can keep track of the customer's reaction and adjust your approach when you see it is not being understood as you intended it. You provide the advice verbally; the accompanying report serves as a written reference for the customer.

8. Apply lessons learned

When your advice has been successful, the temptation will be to adapt the advice somewhat, and offer it again for similar problems at another customer. There are consultants who conclude all their assignments with the same advice, with only the name of the customer being changed. This is not a clever approach. As you are already prejudiced with respect to the possible solution, you will probably overlook a number of details.

The best thing is to have a completely open mind about every situation requiring your advice. It is possible that solutions from the past can be applied again, but you first have to make certain of that. That is only possible, if you repeat the previously mentioned process steps again and again.

---

3 *Flawless Consulting: A guide to getting your expertise used, Second Edition*, Peter Block, JOSSEY-BASS/PFEIFER PUBLISHERS, San Francisco

4 (2006) *Adviseren als tweede beroep*, Hannah Nathans, KLUWER, Deventer

2.10-4 SPECIAL TOPICS

1. Build up arguments

An important part of all communication is the content of the message. This is about putting the content across properly, and, when you want to convince someone of something, you do this in a well-founded way. Ever since the ancient classical times, philosophers have tackled this subject, and there are three means[5] people use to convince others:

- *Ethos*, by referring to one's own authority in this area.
- *Pathos*, by playing to the emotions of the audience.
- *Logos*, by making use of logical reasoning.

Although people often use the first two to be proven right, the latter, the logos, is preferable. It is now about backing up the things you say and want to have done. With logical reasoning we are always looking for the answer to questions such as:

- Why something is as it is?
- Why do we have to choose a certain approach?

and more of these sort *'why' questions*. I shall take a simple example to clarify this. What do you think of the remark "*I shall die.*" Your first reaction might be something like, *"that is obvious."* But why is that so, what is the underlying warrant for such a definite pronouncement? Something which is so obvious, suddenly seems difficult to back up, but it is possible though, for example:

People are mortal + *I am a person* and from this follows *that I shall die*.

This type of reasoning is called a *syllogism* and always consists of three elements:

The conclusion	I shall die.
The maior	People are mortal.
The minor	I am a person.

The argumentation for the conclusion, therefore, is built up from a general quotation (the maior) and a number of facts (the minor), which when you apply the general quotation to them, leads to the conclusion you want to prove.

No we apply it to a project management situation. In your progress report you have put the planned milestones next to the actual dates, and from that you conclude that the project is running on schedule. The underlying reasoning is:

The conclusion	The project is running on schedule.
The maior	When actual dates of milestones match with the planned dates, the project is running according to plan.
The minor	The actual dates for this project match the planned dates.

The next question you could ask yourself is whether or not the maior is right. Why is it that when the actual milestone dates match the planned dates, the project is on schedule? In this way, you have to further unravel a particular argument further, by, for each maior, asking the same question each time, 'why is this so'?

---

5 (4th century BC), *Retorica*, Artistotle

2.10 Consultation

2. Toulmin

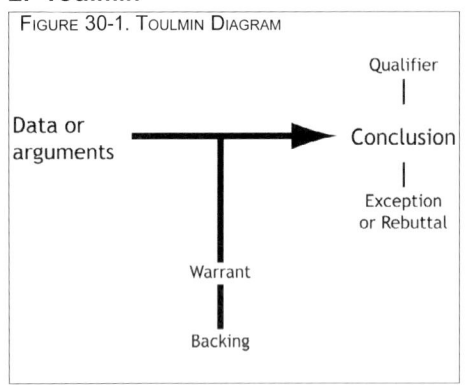

FIGURE 30-1. TOULMIN DIAGRAM

The conclusion	This project delivered quality.
Arguments	The products delivered have been approved during the acceptance test.
Warrant	When the project deliverables have been approved during the acceptance tests, the project has delivered quality.
Backing	It has been agreed in the project management plan that quality will be checked by using an acceptance test.

Stephen Toulmin[6] formulated a useful model for drawing up or analyzing certain arguments. At the core we find classic syllogism again in the data (minor) and the warrant (maior). But a number of new elements have been added, which on the one hand is backing the warrant (maior), and on the other hand, weaken the conclusion.

Backing of the warrant

The warrant from our first example is: *"People are mortal."* We can support this with the argument that all people so far have died at some stage. We can point to the fact that currently there is nobody alive who is older than 150 years, so all people born more than 150 years ago, have also died. That is the majority of people who have ever lived, and on that basis you can expect that all people who are now alive are mortal.

The warrant for our project management example is: *"When the actual milestone dates match the planned dates, the project is on schedule."* We could support this by referring to a book on project management which explains the principle of baselines.

Another example of a warrant with the accompanying backing is:

In the examples mentioned above, three types of support for the warrant have been used:

- *Regularity*, when something occurs often (all people born over 150 years ago have also died), there is a high chance that this is also true for the situation at hand.
- *Authority*, when prominent writers (reference to the literature), or thinkers, say that it is true, it probably is.
- *Rules*, the warrant has been proven to be true (recorded in the project management plan) according to a rule.

The support can also be a combination of all three of these. The more support, the stronger the reasoning and also the ultimate conclusion.

Qualifying the conclusion

Depending on the strength of the warrant and the backing, you can apply some reservations, or not, in respect of the conclusion or statement you advance. One way to do this is by giving a *qualification* of the conclusion.

---

6 (2003) *The uses of argument – Updated Edition*, Toulmin, CAMBRIDGE UNIVERSITY PRESS

2.10 Consultation

Again we look at the examples given:

Conclusion	I shall die.
Maior	People are mortal.
Minor	I am a person.
Qualifier	I will definitely die

In view of the evidence (warrant and support) nobody will probably deny this as we are dealing with a very strong argumentation. The qualification in this example is the word **definitely**.

With the following example, it is somewhat more difficult, because it is not completely clear what we mean by 'on schedule'. Suppose there is a discussion about some quality requirements.

The old conclusion	The project is on schedule.
maior	When the actual milestone dates match the scheduled dates, the project is running according to plan.
minor	The actual dates for this project are the same as for the scheduled dates.
New conclusion with qualification and exception	The project is largely on schedule, with the exception of a number of points of discrepancy regarding the quality requirements.

The new elements added to the argumentation are:
- A *qualification* of the conclusion, giving the listener an idea of the scope of the conclusion.
- An *exception (or rebuttal)*, so where the conclusion does not meet the set reasoning.

This underpins the whole argumentation, apart from the qualifier, much better, and it will make the listener feel much more comfortable.

Checking in practice

When you want to argue your assertions, then as well as the facts (minor) and the warrant, you also show you have researched the weak points by providing a qualification and an exception (if they exist). In this way, you show your listeners that you work very conscientiously and carefully.

For each argument, whether it is your own, or someone else's, you always ask the following critical questions:
- What is the conclusion?
- Is the information leading to the conclusion correct?
- Does the information match with the warrant?
- Is the warrant correct?
- Have exceptions been made?
- Is the (certainty) in accordance with what has preceded?

New elements in these six questions are the questions 2. and 3. What you have to be careful of is the difference between logical syntax and the content. The syntax of the warrant is always:

If <<information>> then <<conclusion>>.

But let us now assume the information is wrong. For example, the actual dates do not at all comply with the planned dates, or the acceptance tests have absolutely not been concluded positively. In that case we are dealing with a twisting of the facts, or put bluntly, lying. In using this form of reasoning, it seems as if the reasoning is solid, whereas this is not the case. You then have to contest the correctness.

Another issue is when information is being used which does not match the warrant at

423

2.10 Consultation

all. In the quality example, for example, this could be referring to a certain (lesser) standard norm which was never a part of the quality requirements, and this should then also be contested.

Fallacies
Next to true arguments, there are also the fallacies. I will list a few of them, not so much as a recommendation to use them, but more to help you recognize them when they are used by an opponent:

- The inclining plane, wrongly suggesting that a measure will lead from bad to worse. For example: *"If we do not implement this change, the system ultimately won't work…"*.
- Misrepresenting the point of view or the argumentation of the opposing party. For example: *"Saying this is a sign of incompetence, what blunderers."*.
- The personal attack, by getting personal and ignoring the point of view or argument that is being discussed. For example: *"Your last project also ended badly …"*.
- False dilemma: suggest two opposite options (while there are many more). For example: *"What do you prefer: function A or function B? You have to choose now."*.
- The circular reasoning or begging the question: here, the argument put forward is identical to the point of view it has to support. For example: *"We must carry on with the project because this is what is in the original plan."*.
- Populist fallacy, where the opinion of others has been offered as sole evidence for argument. For example: *"everybody agrees that …"*.
- Authority fallacy or naming names, by wrongly quoting the authority of someone else to support the point of view. For example: *"The general manager has also said this …"*.

2.11 Negotiation

ONLY IF YOU ASK FOR SOMETHING, WILL YOU GET IT.

Line managers and suppliers must provide the people and resources you need, as project manager, in order to be able to achieve the agreed results.

Negotiation, therefore, is one of the skills you need to have.

2.11 Negotiation

2.11-1 DEFINITIONS

BATNA	Best alternative, no agreement.
Breaking point	The minimum outcome, also called the breaking point.
Negotiation	An activity, whereby two or more mutually dependent parties having both conflicting and common interests, and coming from different positions, try to reach an agreement.
Target figure	The outcome a party wants to achieve.

2.11-2 Introduction

When negotiating, parties, who in one way or another depend on each other and who have both conflicting and common interests, try to reach an agreement through negotiating.

Van Osch[1] defines negotiating as: *effective communication with the focus on reaching agreement and acceptance.* Therefore, on closer analysis, negotiating is a collection of communication techniques.

During a negotiation, each party puts forward its own views and arguments in order to obtain agreement and acceptance from the other party. Project managers negotiate with:

- The project sponsor on the definition of the project.
- A resource manager on the resources to be used.
- A supplier on the price of a contract.
- The purchaser on the suppliers to be contracted.
- The team members on the solution to a particular problem.

It has almost always to do with differences of opinion and/or conflicts, which have either a positive or negative impact on the progress of the project.

---

[1] (2001) *Competent communiceren*, van Osch en van de Wiel, KONINKLIJKE VAN GORCUM, Assen

2.11-3 Process steps

1. Determine the desired outcome and the absolute minimum.
2. Develop a negotiation strategy.
3. Explore and analyze the situation.
4. Address issues and suggest alternatives.
5. Consider alternatives for a win-win situation.
6. Focus on the agreements.
7. Discuss viewpoints of both parties.
8. Apply lessons learned.

1. Determine the desired outcome and the absolute minimum

A proper preparation is a pre-condition for a successful negotiation. This starts with obtaining a clear picture of the following issues:
- The target figure.
- The breaking point.
- The best alternative no agreement.
- The room available for negotiation.
- The balance of power.
- Self-knowledge.

Target figure
What the negotiator preferably wants to achieve is the so called target figure, clearly formulated in terms of:
- Requirements with respect to the product.
- A certain level of service provision.
- Guarantee provisions.
- The price.
- Support.

A negotiator can only start developing a strategy, if he knows what he wants to achieve. If he wants to be successful, he reflects on this in advance.

Breaking point
As well as a target figure per aspect, there is also the breaking point. This is the worst offer by the opposition you are still willing to accept. Such a point is necessary, because during the negotiations there must not be too much depending on the emotion of the moment. The breaking point ensures that the negotiator does not lose sight of his objectives.

The breaking point is also about how keen the negotiator is to reach a result. If one party has something the other party would like to have, it is difficult to negotiate about it. Even though they may have defined a breaking point, inexperienced negotiators often let go of this during the negotiations. A breaking point really has to be a breaking point, when the opposition goes beyond that, there are only two options left: stop or suspend.

The best alternative no agreement
Just having a breaking point, however, is not enough. What do you do when, as negotiator, you want to stop the negotiations, but you do not have an alternative? This is a situation that limits your options. A fixed part of the preparation, therefore, is that you think hard about the Best Alternative No Agreement, abbreviated to the BATNA.

I sometimes say: *"you can only start to negotiate about something if you don't want it"*.

Determining the target figures and breaking points
When determining both the target figure and the previously discussed breaking point, the **baselines** form the starting point. The following information is available to you:
- The description of the work (WBS) covering the scope.
- The budget for various work packages.
- The planning and margin in the activities related to setting deadlines.
- The quality requirements for purchase decisions.

There may be different target figures and breaking points in a negotiation, one for each aspect.

The room available for negotiation
Both negotiating parties have a breaking point, and the area that lies between these points is the room available for negotiation. This is a theoretical concept, because both parties usually do not know each others breaking point. You can make some assumptions on where it roughly might be, but these remain just assumptions that you have to test during the negotiation.

Balance of power
The position someone takes during the negotiation depends on how the power is divided between the parties. The more unequal, the harder it is to negotiate, and the less it deserves that title. The principle of negotiating is that it takes place on a voluntary basis.

Power can come from two sources: the power someone holds based on his position, and the power someone exercises on the basis of his personal authority. The positional power of the project manager mainly stems from what he has arranged in the project management plan, and the position his project sponsor holds in the management hierarchy, whereas his personal power is based on his professionalism as project manager and his personality as a human being.

Power may also evolve because of the time a party has to negotiate. The party under the most time pressure has less power than the party which has all the time in the world to either come to an agreement or not.

Self-knowledge
As well as the concrete issues, there are also less tangible issues that you as a negotiator want, such as: someone who listens, respect, recognition, manners, etc. The difficulty with these issues is that they are usually subconscious, but they do play an important role and can undermine the effectiveness of the negotiations. Therefore, gaining self-knowledge is an on-going preparation for the negotiations still to come.

2. Develop a negotiation strategy
The desired target figure and the breaking point, the expected room for negotiation, and knowledge of the balance of power, are the starting points for the development of a good negotiating strategy, but they are not sufficient.

You also have to know where the opposition stands:
- What target figure does the other party have?
- Where would the breaking point be?
- What power (mandate) does this party really have?
- Who is it?
- What are the preferences?
- How does he negotiate?

You cannot really develop a proper strategy if you do not know anything about your opposition. In a win-win situation, you search for common areas, in a win-lose situation for the weak points in order to achieve the optimum result for yourself.

Firstly, you choose the basic strategy:
- *Dividing strategy* (win-lose); you determine where you will start to force, and where you will give in.
- *Problem solving strategy* (win-win); you take on an open attitude and you initially look for agreement.
- *Mixed form;* you determine where both win-win and win-lose are possible.

2.11 Negotiation

Dividing strategy
Dividing has three positions: forcing, compromising or giving in. The issues which can be pushed through, and the ones on which you will give in to, are decided in advance. It is often possible to push some issues through if you give in on others, and in this way, the totality will be seen as a compromise by both parties.

The negotiator determines the position he will take, and how he will open (be the first to put his wishes on the table, or not). If he has lot of power, the opening may be closed (this is what I want, the opposition no longer has much choice), and if he doesn't, he adapts a more open position (this is what I want, what do you want?).

Solving strategy
In the case of a solving negotiation, you create a good climate in advance, for example by arranging informal meetings in which you explore each others ideas, without any party yet committing itself. Both target figures and breaking points are less 'written in concrete' than with the dividing strategy. Beforehand, consider the different alternatives well, because in these types of negotiations there is a completely different atmosphere; it is far less about winning than about working together.

Mixed strategy
This is the most used negotiation strategy. Beforehand, the negotiator has divided his wishes in: **want-to-have** and **nice-to-have** and **exchangeable** and **non-exchangeable**. During the negotiation, you then try to negotiate about win-lose packages. Afterwards, both parties have the feeling of having achieved a win-win, when in fact they have negotiated several compromises.

Channel choice
I can be very short and direct on this. Only personal contact, face-to-face, is suitable for negotiation, both dividing and solving. Telephone, written or electronic tools are unsuitable channels for effective negotiations.

This is because you won't be able to keep an eye on the non-verbal communication of the other party. The non-verbal aspect is the main source of information in communication, especially when emotions come in to play. Because this feedback is absent via the telephone and in written negotiations, it is difficult for both parties to interact with each other.

Language
Another problem related to this, is the language used for the negotiations. When it is not your mother tongue, you have only a limited vocabulary. It is even more tense when two negotiators negotiate in English, and it is the mother tongue of neither of them. They believe they have understood each other, but the misunderstandings can be very comical (or dramatic).

3. Explore and analyze the situation
This sub-process takes place during the whole of the negotiation. Depending on where the negotiation takes place, the host prefers to pick up the other party himself if he has chosen for a resolving strategy, as this gives him the opportunity to get used to the other party. Conversely, the party, who is the guest, pays good attention and observes how the office is decorated. He watches the passers-by in the lobby, and creates for himself a picture of the opposition's organization. If it is a nice office, he comments on that to the host. Authentic compliments are concessions that cost nothing, and have a positive influence on the atmosphere.

Things are different if the choice has been made for a win-lose style; the visiting party is left waiting a bit longer in the lobby to make him feel insecure, causing him to be less effective during the negotiations. For example, you have your guest picked up by a secretary or have the doorkeeper or receptionist tell him to take a lift to a certain floor, where a secretary then collects him, which can be very intimidating. If it happens to you, the only thing you can do is remain calm and just let it all happen, remembering that it does say a lot about the opposition's strategy. Later on, I shall discuss the various manipulation techniques, and how to deal with them.

This exploring and analyzing of the situation gradually takes on a more serious character. Between each other, both parties will "fly balloons" to find out where the similarities and differences lie. During this exploring stage they test their assumptions, and adapt their approach accordingly.

4. Address issues and suggest alternatives

This is where the creativity of both parties comes into play. Differences and similarities are known, and these form the core of the negotiation, in which the negotiators show patience and perseverance to come to an agreement.

If he is well prepared, the negotiator does not lose sight of his own interests when he gives in to his opponent, and alternatives are developed together. Win-win is possible by not committing to a certain alternative too quickly, but by firstly coming up with a few different ones. This whole process can be spread over several sessions.

A condition for developing acceptable alternatives is to actively discover where the interests of the other party lie and with this knowledge, options can be thought up to satisfy these interests.

5. Consider alternatives to achieve a win-win situation

In almost all project management literature, the authors prefer a win-win style of negotiating.

During the exploration stage, a picture has been formed of the topics where, and the topics where not, a win-win outcome is possible. The latter can be bundled into packages for which both parties give in as much as they win. Strictly speaking that is not a win-win, but more a collection of small compromises. As both parties feel they lose as much as they win and this is evenly balanced between both parties, it is called a win-win anyway, which fosters the relationship.

I don't agree with this preference for win-win, as it is not suitable for all negotiations. Price negotiations, for example, are by definition dividing in nature. The consideration for choosing a particular strategy depends on various factors:
- The importance of the relationship.
- The need to have certain issues agreed.
- The time pressure.
- The position of power a party takes up.

What is important is that both parties have the feeling they have benefited from it, and that their interests have been represented in the agreement in the best possible way.

6. Focus on the agreements

As the ultimate goal of the negotiation is an agreement, the recommendation is, from the beginning of the negotiations, to put the emphasis on the similarities. Differences, of course, do get discussed, but then just as a bridge. The general tenor, however, is one of "*together, we shall come to an agreement*".

2.11 Negotiation

The differences are discussed in a business-like manner.

A good negotiator then pays attention to:
- Creating a constructive climate.
- Preventing loss of face.
- Separating issues and the person.
- Preventing a debating atmosphere.

When the negotiations are successful, they lead to an agreement. Usually we document these, sometimes in a contract, and sometimes in a memo containing:
- The obligations of both parties.
- When both parties have to carry these out.
- How these are to be done.

Sometimes, who is going to do something, and why a certain solution direction was chosen, is also documented.

7. Discuss viewpoints of both parties

The pitfalls in the negotiation can normally be found in the differences. The predominant technique is that of active listening and of postponing assumptions. The essence of this technique is to allow, and to help, the other party to clarify his point of view. The technique is a collection of communication techniques consisting of: *'ahem'ing, parroting, paraphrasing, summarizing and asking questions'*. When you apply these techniques well, you allow the other party to clarify his point of view, without your own point of view being pushed aside.

8. Apply lessons learned

Good preparation is half the battle of a negotiation, and as well as the preparation, a good evaluation is also strongly recommended. You can also consider this to be a preparation for the next negotiation, and particularly when both parties intend to do business more often with each other, a mutual evaluation of the whole negotiation process is very useful.

2.11-4 Special Topics

1. The Harvard Method[1]
Also called the Mutual Gains approach.

We can differentiate between two fundamentally different negotiation strategies:
- Positional Negotiating.
- Principled Negotiating.

Positional Negotiating
What I covered in the first process step is positional (or dividing) negotiating. Both parties take up a position and try to get the most out of the negotiation, which has a number of limitations:
- It leads to *unwise* agreements, because your ego becomes entwined with your position, and everything you surrender feels like a personal loss.
- Arguing about positions is *not efficient*, because certain motives remain below the surface.
- It *jeopardizes relationships,* because parties are inclined not to give in anymore.
- When there are a lot of parties involved, you soon reach an *impasse*.

All in all, these are sufficient reasons for considering an alternative way of negotiating, which has become known as Principled Negotiation or the *"Harvard Method"*.

Principled Negotiating
This approach is based on four basic elements:
- Separating the PEOPLE from the problem.
- Focusing on INTERESTS, not on positions.
- Looking for SOLUTIONS in the common interest.
- Pressing for objective CRITERIA.

---
1 (1981), *Getting to yes*, Fisher, Ury and Patton

We shall briefly look into these four elements.

PEOPLE
The problem or the issue you are negotiating is *objective,* whereas both you and your negotiating partner are *subjective*. Therefore, you have to separate the person from the problem, because as soon as you mix both (which easily happens with positional dealing), you are no longer effective. However, because people are creatures with emotions and strong convictions, it is almost inevitable that these issues will play a part, and therefore you pay extra attention to this subjective aspect of human factor.

We can do this by approaching the human factor, and the associated problems, from three categories:
- Viewpoint
- Emotion
- Communication

In the following table possible interventions are mentioned for each category.

> **Example 31-1 Expectations**
> Negotiating with other cultures can be difficult because the parties involved may have a completely different reading of the situation. As was the case with a European airline company that wanted to increase the frequency of its flights to Damascus, in Syria. Before plunging into full-scale negotiations, the airline company first wanted to explore the situation and the willingness of the Syrian authorities. So before wheeling in their top negotiators from main office and maybe an official from the Foreign Office, they sent a middle level manager to Damascus accompanied by the local station manager. Just to test the waters. They were amazed to be received by eight Syrian high officials, including the deputy minister. The meeting had already failed before it had started. If the Europeans had wanted to find out if there was something to negotiate about, the Syrians had already concluded that the Europeans were not serious about negotiations because they had sent such a low-profile delegation.

2.11 Negotiation

Viewpoint	Emotion	Communication
Put yourself in his shoes.	Observe and understand the emotions of both parties.	Listen actively, and show that you hear it.
Do not derive his intentions from your fears.	Bring up emotions for discussion, and recognise them as justified.	Speak in such a way that you are understood.
Do not blame him for your problems.	Give the other party the chance to blow off steam.	Speak about yourself, not about the other party.
Look for opportunities to act in contradiction to his point of view (about you).	Do not react to emotional outbursts.	Speak with an objective in mind.
Involve him in the realization of the result.	Make symbolic gestures.	
Present your proposals in accordance with his standards.		

INTERESTS

In any negotiation, it is ultimately about you protecting the interests of your project, and obviously the other party also wants to protect his interests as far as possible. Also, when positions seem to be irreconcilable, there are both opposite and common interests. By putting them on the table, you can together search for a solution.

When discussing interests, you can make use of the following techniques:
- Describe your interests clearly.
- Recognise the interests of the other party, you are not the only one involved.
- Start with the problem, and then give an answer.
- Focus on the future, the past cannot be changed anyway.
- Be specific, but exercise some flexibility.
- Be tough in handling the problem as opposed to the people, whom you treat mildly.

SOLUTIONS

There are four big obstacles to solving problems:
- Judging too quickly that certain solutions will not work.
- Looking for the best solution.
- Thinking in or/or options.
- A one-sided focus on your own problems.

To overcome these obstacles you have to:
- Separate the thinking up of solutions from the deciding on them.
- Extend existing solutions by thinking up new ones.
- Look for mutual advantages.
- Make the decision making easier for the other party.

CRITERIA

Whatever you do, differences will always arise, and with positional dealing, both parties throw their strong wills into the fray, which delays the negotiation. It is better to look for objective criteria, on the basis of which you both come to an agreement.

Objective criteria can be:
- Market value.
- Precedents.
- Scientific assessment.
- Industry specific standards.
- Efficiency.

2.11 Negotiation

	Fighting Pursues his own interests, possibly at the cost of the other party. Applies means of power such as: expertise, position, etc.	Co-operating Always goes for the relationship, and in the event of conflicting interests, will be prepared to give in.
Styles according to Mastenbroek.		
Exploring Tries to find a solution taking all interested parties into account. Takes his time to explore the topic further.	Agile – aggressive Will take the initiative, engages in new directions, keeps the negotiation going.	Jovial – cooperative Actively provides a positive contribution to the atmosphere, builds on relationships, and is open to the arguments of others.
Avoiding Does not face the confrontation, is diplomatic, would rather postpone difficult issues, or sticks to a certain way of reasoning.	Analytical – aggressive Is strong in figures and on the procedure, makes things clear and keeps track of the bigger picture.	Ethical – convincing From his trust of the other party, he focuses on the common interests, but keeps thinking independently.

- Costs.
- Judicial decisions.
- Moral standards.
- Equal treatment.
- Tradition.
- Reciprocity.
- Etc.

If these form the starting point for solving differences, the relationship will also remain undamaged, which is an important advantage. Because the criteria are objective, they are also reasonable, and ultimately both parties will experience the outcome as a WIN-WIN.

2. Negotiation styles

According to Mastenbroek[2], the attitude of negotiators can be divided in four basic styles of negotiation:
- Co-operate or Fight.
- Explore or Avoid.

Note that the first pole is about the relationship, whereas the second pole is aimed far more towards the content. In addition, there are some mixed forms, for example a negotiator who co-operates and also explores, or someone who fights and avoids. We can now supplement the four basic styles with another four mixed forms, which brings us to a total of eight negotiation styles (the grey ones are the mixed forms).

3. Rapport

Rapport is a technique which was originally developed in the field of hypnotherapy[3] and later popularized via NLP, and made available for a larger area of application. Even though it is initially meant for a therapeutic setting, the technique is very valuable in negotiations.

Rapport can best be compared to tuning a radio or television receiver to the right channel. The parties in the negotiation have a rapport when they are on the same wavelength, and this allows the negotiation to run more smoothly. You have both verbal and non-verbal rapport, and the former has already been addressed in the discussion on *active listening*, which is really a form of verbal rapport.

---

2 (1992) *Onderhandelen*, W.F.G. Mastenbroek, HET SPECTRUM/MARKA, Utrecht

3 (1996) *Essenties van NLP*, Lucas Derks & Jaap Hollander, SERVIRE, Utrecht

2.11 Negotiation

Another way of creating verbal rapport, are the so called *Meta programmes,* which is the way in which people interpret messages. As negotiator, by adapting your message to the *Meta programme* of the other party, the communication is more efficient.

A number of examples of such programmes are:
- *Proactive/reactive*, the first thinks in terms of taking action; the second thinks in terms of reflecting and waiting.
- *Internal/external reference*, the first does not need advice, and knows what he wants; the second seeks advice from the expert.
- *Similarity/difference*, the first looks for mutuality; the second for what is differentiating.
- *Global/specific*, the first looks at the big picture; the second at the detail.
- *Visual/auditive/kinesthetic*, the first thinks in images, the second in words and the third in movement.

By attuning your use of language to the other party, you more quickly arrive on the same wavelength, and the understanding grows.

The second dimension of creating rapport is non-verbal, in which parties 'mirror' each others non-verbal behavior. This is all about:
- Body language.
- Movements.
- Gestures.
- Breathing.
- Tone of voice, and volume, speed and rhythm of speech.
- Mood.

This mirroring ensures there is a subconscious contact, allowing people to better interact with each other. However, a word of warning is necessary here, as this 'mirroring' of behavior does not work if you use it as a trick. It then becomes too obvious, and is not authentic. From a basic attitude in which you want to understand the other party, you try to empathise as much as possible with the other party. Rapport then becomes a natural process during the negotiation.

Non-verbal Communication
As well as mirroring the non-verbal communication, understanding it is also a skill which will come in useful whilst negotiating. In "*Je bent sprekend je lichaam*[4]", Nissink discusses this in more depth. It is possible to make a list of body expressions, and to give them a meaning. It would then be sufficient to learn these, and to interpret the other party using this knowledge.

Such a list could read as follows:
- Someone says yes, but shakes his head meaning no.
- Letting the head hang down.
- Chest out; overconfident but having an underlying uncertainty.
- Big steps; steamrollers over people and things.
- Foot hooked behind the calf; completely closed off to others.
- Hands open, nothing to hide.

The list can be much longer, but in recognizing non-verbal communication, studying these types of lists is not what it is about. It is important that a negotiator learns to observe, initially himself and then others. The problem with non-verbal communication is that you are never completely sure of it, and therefore, a long list explaining the meaning of different body expressions is useless.

You have to be particularly careful when the verbal and non-verbal communication are not congruent. The project member who says that he will be finished in time, but looks the

---
[4] (2002), *Je bent sprekend je lichaam,* Ed Nissink, ANKH-HERMES, Deventer

other way. The business relation, who says he is not angry, but has red blotches in his neck. Incongruence is a sign that someone is saying something different from what they mean and as the body never lies, you then know that you have to ask more questions.

4. Dealing with manipulation

Manipulation is influencing other people without them realizing it, in such a way that they make certain choices that they really did not want to make. From an ethical point of view, manipulation is not acceptable, and most people will not easily admit using it, but nevertheless it happens more often than we care to admit.

The manipulator is cunning, so that the other party does not actually realize what is happening to him or her. Sometimes there are indefinable feelings such as: inferiority, guilt, feelings of incompetence, fear, etc. and because these feelings are not pleasant, we deny and suppress them. The energy this takes makes us unable to resist or respond sufficiently.

In the table on the next pages, which I have compiled from Mastenbroek[5], Ritsema van Eck/Huguenin[6] and Tipler[7], I mention a number of possible counter-actions.

5. Developing this competence

In daily life there are many options to practice negotiating, and it is worth making use of these. When you start in a somewhat easier context, you can already start practicing with newer forms of behavior without too many risks. For example:
- If you have children, you can negotiate with them about: holiday destinations, pocket money, the time they have to be home by, etc.
- Do the negotiations for a club where you are a committee member.
- When you buy something in a shop, try to negotiate.
- Pretend to be the other party, and write an essay on what you want to achieve from the negotiation, and what you expect from the opposing party.

6. Thirty-Six Stratagems

The thirty-six stratagems originate from the history of the Chinese empire. It is not completely clear when, and by whom, they were written[8], but they have still not lost any of their topicality, and you still see them in use in China. Because a culture consists of the results of the learning process that a society has progressed through, they offer a treasure of wisdom for project managers over the whole world. Some will sound familiar to you; they are thirty-six sayings about stratagems, applicable in war, politics, normal life, but certainly also in the negotiations that you, as a project manager, have to carry out. They can be sub-divided into six categories:
- To enforce superiority (1-6)
- Dealing with enemies (7-12)
- During the attack (13-18)
- In confusing circumstances (19-24)
- Conquering an area (25-30)
- When you are the underdog (31-36)

You will always have to make a consideration yourself whether or not you find something ethically justifiable or not, because you will not be thanked for some of these stratagems.

---

5 (1999), *Vaardig Onderhandelen*, Mastenbroek, HOLLAND BUSINESS PUBLICATIONS, Heemstede
6 (1992), *Conflicthantering & Onderhandelen*, Ritsema van Eck/Huguenin, BOHN STAFLEU VAN LOGHUM, Houten/Diemen
7 (2000), *Onderhandelen*, J. Tipler, TFC TRAININGSMEDIA, Velp

---

8 (1998), Chinese Business Negotiating Style, Tony Fang, SAGE PUBLICATIONS, London

2.11 Negotiation

Manipulation	Counter-action
Salami tactics The opposition successively introduces a number of reasonable, "small" demands, which you really have to agree to. However, many small ones make one big one.	Ask the opposition if he has any more demands or wishes. State your own boundaries. Explain what it will cost you.
Last minute escalation You have reached an agreement, and the opposing party suddenly increases his demands at the last minute.	React indignantly, but do not respond to it. Point out that this is the last time you want to do business this way.
Good Guy - Bad Guy The opposing party comes with two people, one blunt and one friendly. You agree to the demands of the latter, but probably you give in much more than desirable.	Listen carefully to what both have to say, and come with your own proposal.
Limited authority You have reached a compromise, then the opposing party mentions that he does not have sufficient authority and has to check things with his boss. The next day he communicates that the negotiations have come a long way, but a few concessions will still have to be made.	Ensure that you clearly know the authorities of the opposing party in advance. If it happens to you, react indignantly, as the other party is often bluffing. Play the ball back into the opposition court, and state that if he wants to reach a decision, he has to agree now.
Emotional outbursts The opposition reacts very emotionally towards you by being accusing, blaming, etc.	Recognise the emotion, look for the cause, and apologize if necessary. If there is no reason to apologize, explain how you want to negotiate. In all cases, recognise the emotion.
Belittling, intimidating The opposing party tells you that you see things wrongly, and that you have little experience, etc. The other party keeps you waiting, gives you a seat looking straight into the sun, writes whilst you are talking, laughs sardonically after you have said something, etc.	Indicate that it is unacceptable to you, and you want to sit somewhere else. Do not accept bad treatment from the opposing party, see it as a clumsy form of manipulation. Focus on the issues at hand.
Playing off The opposing party points out the differences between you and your followers, between you and your colleague, etc.	Indicate that you don't appreciate this, and deny the differences. Explain again how things really are. A proper preparation, of course, is important in ensuring that in this situation, you are not surprised.

2.11 Negotiation

Manipulation	Counter-action
Bluffing The opposing party remarks: "That is how it is", "Everybody knows that things work like this." Especially the last remark is difficult to refute, you might even be considered as being stupid.	Ask for proof, and don't be afraid to be "stupid". Ask questions.
Appeal to decency When you are persistent, the other party will appeal to your decency to remain constructive. In the case of issues sensitive to the other party, you are requested to remain businesslike.	Honour decency standards; say that you want to resolve the situation in a decent manner. Indicate that it is in both your business interests to apply care when dealing with sensitive issues.
Acting pathetically You have made your offer, and the opposing party acts pathetically, by saying, for example, that they cannot afford it.	Agree that you find it difficult and unpleasant for them. Keep talking in terms of interests.
Acting incompetently The opposing party acts as if he does not really understand, causing you to underestimate him, or to provide him with more information than you intended.	Ask what he does not understand, and why it is not clear.
Suspicious units A large final sum is divided up to make the costs look more reasonable.	Focus on the total amounts. If the final sum is above your budget, it does not matter how it is divided up.
Black on white When discussing the price, the opposing party refers to the price list, and implies that it is non-negotiable.	Together with the opposing party, check what the price is based on. Do you need everything, check if you can change the criteria. Propose a new price.

2.11 Negotiation

In the translation of these 36 lists for project managers, I have allowed myself to be inspired by Tony Fang[9], Kenrick E. Cleveland[10] and Harro Senger[11].

1. Hide behind your openness
The original saying is: *"Cross the ocean without the emperor knowing"*. By acting as if you are laying all your cards on the table, people think that there is nothing wrong. In reality, however, you are hiding the actual intention. By talking, for example, in a friendly manner with a supplier, and giving him the feeling that he is the only one in the picture. Because you are in discussions with several suppliers, you are able to negotiate a very keen price.

2. Find the Achilles heel
Originally: *"Besiege Wei to rescue Zhao"*, where a friendly ruler, instead of joining with Zhao to wage war against the armies of Wei, instead targeted the unprotected cities. When waging war, you do not lay siege to the enemy directly, but you try to find a weak point of your enemy to exploit.

In a negotiation for instance, you can start by opening up an attack on the weak points of your opponent. This will not only surprise him, but also give you an advantage over him.

3. Make use of someone else
The direct translation from this stratagem reads: *"Defeat your opponent with a borrowed knife"*. You create a situation, in which someone else cleans up the mess. This could be an interim manager, but an extra PMO employee can also function just as well as a borrowed knife. Using a loan to finance a project is also an example of this stratagem.

When you entice the other person to disadvantage himself to gain benefit for yourself, you are making full use of this stratagem. A manager, who during the end of year discussion with his employee asks how he himself thinks he has functioned, makes use of this stratagem.

4. Relax whilst the other person exhausts himself
Before you start the attack, you restrain yourself, and when the other person is exhausted you strike. For example, in a meeting you let the other person put forward his arguments, then firstly show interest by asking some questions (stratagem 1), followed by more and more critical questions. The other person has to use more and more energy to present his arguments, and then when he becomes quiet, you present your proposal.

When the other person becomes exhausted, he will fall more quickly into his trap, allowing you to gain an advantage. This means, of course, that you have to be very aware of your own weaknesses, as these will surface when you are under pressure.

5. Take advantage of someone else's problems
"Loot a burning house" is the original description. It is based on the assumption that when people are having problems, they will agree more readily than they otherwise would.

When the economy is under pressure, you can negotiate keener prices with suppliers. Some large companies have used this stratagem to put pressure on suppliers to reduce their prices retrospectively.

---
9 (1999), Tony Fang, Chinese Business Negotiating Style, SAGE PUBLICATIONS, London
10 (2001), Kenrick E. Cleveland, How To Use The 36 Chinese Stratagems To Win
11 (2004), Harro Senger, The 36 Strategems for Business, MARSHALL CAVENDIS BUSINESS, Singapore

Another way is to ask someone what he would do if a particular risk manifests itself, and then see how this insight helps you to put him under even more pressure. In this manner, "the house of the other party" is actually not on fire, but it puts you in a good position to use what he tells you.

6. Provide a diversion
The original stratagem reads: *"Shout in the west and then strike in the east"*. This is what happens when we think that people have a hidden agenda; they do one thing, but they really have other intentions. By creating the diversion, it is not exactly clear what the other party wants. Suppliers use this tactic by, for example, arguing a higher price by pointing out the superior quality. I once spoke to a car salesman who said: *"I am not a salesman, I advise someone to make a choice."*

7. Create something out of nothing
This involves creating a convincing illusion, whereby others do something that they originally were not planning to do. A supplier, who creates the idea that he is investing in certain new technology, but who is really just going to use existing technology, can attract the unsuspecting customer to do business with him.

When people have a particular view of you, for example that in the past you have managed every project successfully, then they will also have that view now. In this way, you are your own brand, and the image that you have radiates from you, making you successful in this project as well.

8. Act as if you are taking the royal road, but take a shortcut
Show that you find particular subjects important, and then during the execution you just do your own thing. For example: the supplier, who puts the emphasis on how much his organisation is investing in the training and development of the consultants, whereas he actually only employs inexperienced people.

If there is a lot of resistance to a particular approach, you can just pretend that you are considering the objections. Your opponents are pleased, and think that you represent their interests, but in fact you just carry on with what you were already planning to do.

9. Watch a fire burning on the other side of the river
When people are in trouble, in the first instance they will not want to admit it. It is then better to wait until the seriousness of the situation gets through to them. The situation exhausts them and they will request help, and that is the time to step in.

If the project sponsor will not listen to your advice, you must wait patiently until such time as he can no longer avoid it. If, at that point, you again bring forward your arguments, you are in a much stronger position, because he then has the necessity to listen to your solutions.

You see this stratagem applied in commercial situations when a supplier is waiting with his offer until the customer encounters problems, whereby the supplier can ask for a higher price. Or what do you think of a small supplier who patiently waits while the two main players are involved in a fierce competitive battle. The patience pays more than an extensive marketing campaign.

10. Disarm your opponent with a smile or with gifts
The actual saying reads: *"Hide your dagger behind a smile"*. You can use this both negatively and positively.

Be friendly while you hide strong will, in this way win someone's trust and strike when

2.11 Negotiation

that someone is off guard. For example: A potential customer is very friendly and accommodating, giving you the impression you are building a good friendship. When you start negotiating, this customer turns out to be a tough negotiator and you only realise this after you have granted the necessary concessions.

When you give an interest group something in exchange for something very important for the project, you are making positive use of this stratagem. You could call this the Principle of the Reciprocity.

11. Look for a scapegoat
This concept comes from the Bible[12] where once a year, the High Priest would symbolically transfer all the sins of the people to a goat, which was then sent into the desert; a small sacrifice in order to pay off a large debt. Or as the Chinese say: *"Sacrifice the plum tree to preserve the peach tree"*, meaning rather the crop of peaches than plums. You make a small sacrifice in order to achieve a high return.

Sometimes, in order to protect senior management, we see that people lower down in an organisation take the blame. Sometimes it is better to suffer a small loss, if in so doing you prevent something more serious from happening.

12. Take advantage of the opportunity when this occurs
Literally translated, this stratagem reads: *"Lead a goat away in passing"*. It alludes to the picture of someone who walks through a herd of goats and nonchalantly takes a goat and leads it out of the herd without anyone noticing.

This conforms to one of the positive risk responses, in which you consciously utilise certain opportunities, however small they may be. But also during negotiations when you have already achieved agreement on certain aspects, if someone then makes a slip of the tongue, it is sometimes possible to gain something extra out of it.

13. Beat the grass to startle the snake
An example of this stratagem is to threaten that you will resign from your position. This can shock or frighten people in such a way that they may accept your proposal. Acting as if you are angry can work in the same way. When the police announce in the media they are going to hold a large speed check, they are also making use of this stratagem.

When a small case of fraud is discovered in an organisation, senior management sends out a strong signal by dismissing the fraudster with immediate effect. At that point in time, this seems to be an excessive reaction, but it is highly effective, because it warns off the other employees.

14 Borrow a corpse to resurrect the soul
This is about giving something that is outdated a new look, and this can be done in a number of ways. When trying to get a new idea accepted repeatedly fails, it sometimes does succeed by packaging it up differently. We also see it when, following very negative publicity, a company changes its name. A number of years later, the public at large has forgotten the original name and with it all the negative publicity.

A young company that merges with an older, well-established company also makes use of this stratagem. Through the merger, the young company profits from the name recognition, and the older company from the innovation that the merger partner contributes. Also, when you give new meaning to an existing department, you introduce "soul"

---
12 *The Bible, Leviticus 16*

2.11 Negotiation

into it, and you can prevent the necessity of closing it down.

15. Choose your own arena
Or as the Chinese say: *"Entice the tiger to leave its mountain lair"*, because as a human being you have the advantage if you are not on the mountain, but lower down. To ensure your opponent leaves his safe environment, you take away his advantage. This also holds true when you have to negotiate over scarce resources with a line manager. You can do that during lunch in the company restaurant, or in his office. In the first situation, you are on a more equal footing than in the second situation.

In football, playing at home is always easier than playing away. That comes about through both the familiarity with the surroundings, and the presence of supporters. By ensuring that your opponent can gather as few supporters as possible around him, you make your own position much stronger.

When you are involved in a conflict, this stratagem can provide a solution by bringing the parties in conflict to a neutral location.

16. Let someone escape in order to capture him again
By letting go of something, you often increase the chance of achieving your goal. Every parent, who has children going through puberty, understands this. The stricter you are, the more you distance your child from you. It is better to allow something, and in this way maintain contact with your rebellious child.

When a disciplinary measure is necessary, a first step can be to tell someone you believe they have earned it, but that you will give him the benefit of the doubt. This will frighten the person off (stratagem 13), but also put him at ease, because you wait with the actual measure. In this way, you will win someone over more quickly.

17. BAIT PEOPLE WITH A SMALL GIFT
The saying reads: *"Toss out a brick to attract a piece of Jade"*. This stratagem is based on the principle of reciprocity. When you receive something from someone, you experience the need to do something in return. You can do this consciously by winning the heart of the other person through a small gift, which could be anything. But small concessions also stimulate the other person to do something in return.

In order to gain the support of a user, a project manager could, for example, accept a small change to the scope. But also by acting favorably to the requests of your team members, you increase their motivation to apply themselves to the project. Many such things cost less than the returns they generate.

18. To catch the villains, firstly catch the gang leader
The extent to which this stratagem works is dependent on the influence the (gang) leader has on his followers. If the top management of a large organization has a lot of influence, then in the event of a major change, it is essential to have their support. This is less essential, if their influence is low. The power that top managers apply only works when the people on the shop floor accept it.

You can view it in a broader context by looking to see who has the real influence, ignoring the hierarchical structure. It is these opinion leaders and informal leaders that you have to win over to your point of view. If you succeed in this, you have powerful allies for your project.

2.11 Negotiation

> EXAMPLE 31-2 PRESIDENTIAL ELECTIONS
> The 2012 presidential elections in the USA were characterised by the negative way in which the campaigns were carried out, whereby both camps tried to discredit the candidate of the other party.

this. It seems somewhat similar to stratagem 18, only you now look for the people offering the most resistance. By discrediting these people, you break the resistance, and you can achieve this by expanding on the bad qualities of such a person. Although, from an ethical standpoint, you can put a question mark against doing this, it is a strategy that competitors use against one another.

As project manager, you can apply this when there is a conflict in the team. Usually, such a conflict arises between only a few people, and sometimes it is possible to calm the situation down by locating people in different rooms. If this is not possible, you can even decide to remove someone from the project. By keeping the conflict under control in this way, you prevent other people from choosing sides, which would increase the conflict to something bigger than it actually is.

20. Take advantage of confusing and chaotic situations

Or as the Chinese say: *"Fish in troubled waters"*. People under pressure do not think things through well enough, and are more quickly inclined to listen to advice. In general, confusing and chaotic situations make people more receptive to change, meaning that you can best implement a change when there is already confusion. You can make good use of this when problems have arisen on your project. If you are then able to come up with a solution, there is a greater acceptance of it.

There are in fact people, who use this stratagem to create the confusion themselves. The top manager, who, whilst there is still a profit being made, says that no matter what a reorganisation must be carried out, makes use of this. Just the pure announcement that some people will lose their jobs is sufficiently threatening and confusing for them, that as a result they offer less resistance.

21 Act just as if you are somewhere else

"The golden cicada sheds its skin." is the literal translation of the stratagem. It refers to a story in which Lu Bu, a general from Chinese history, acted as if he was somewhere other than where people thought he was, and in so doing saved his life. When a team member says he is ill, but in fact is not, he is making use of this stratagem. When you say you are not implementing a change, but in fact you secretly do so, you are also applying this stratagem. You also do this when you quote someone in order to be proved right. You do not then have to accept any responsibility for what you have said, because they are not your words.

It sometimes happens during negotiations that you do not want them to go any further, but for some reason or other you cannot directly say that. An option is then to set increasingly difficult requirements, and in so doing force the other party to stop. You pretend you want to continue, but you ask for more, whereas you really want to walk away from the negotiations altogether.

22 Lock the door to catch a thief

If someone has no way out any more, he is imprisoned. When your option is the only one, or when the other party thinks it is the only one, then you are making use of this stratagem. The other party can do nothing else than agree you are right. In a competitive tender, you can submit a very low price in the hope that your competitors offer a still lower price. In fact, you really do not want the order at all. When the competitor does win the contract, he will run into serious

2.11 Negotiation

problems, which, in fact, is your real objective.

Large organizations also make use of this when they threaten a smaller party with legal proceedings. The smaller party does not have the time, nor the money to contest such a lengthy court case, and because of this, the smaller party is forced to comply with the demands of the larger organization.

To prevent yourself becoming the victim of this stratagem, you must never let it be seen that you have limited options. For example, when you go to an important meeting, ensure that you do not have another appointment directly afterwards, because if your opponent knows that, he can use it towards the end of the meeting to extract certain concessions from you. The time pressure you experience causes you to give in on points that you would normally never give in to under other circumstances.

23. Enter into tactical alliances
"Befriend a distant state while attacking a neighbor" is the literal translation of this stratagem. You sometimes have to work tactically to achieve your goals, and that can mean pragmatically making use of different parties to achieve your goal. A good relationship with someone higher than yourself in the organization's hierarchy can help you to obtain the necessary priority for your project. A good project management saying is: *"If you know the right address, you can get everything you want done"*.

During your stakeholder analysis you should also look at the strategic alliances you can enter into with the different interested parties. At the end of the day, it is people who either provide support, or voice their opposition. By entering into a co-operation with a party who has already achieved a certain amount of success, you too can benefit from that success.

24. Use a springboard
This stratagem seems very similar to the previous one, but here you make use of the friends you already have. In achieving your goal, you do not have to work alone, because in your network there are always people who can help you. That means when you build up your network of friends, you must always look further than the boundaries of the project. After all, in the current project you lay the foundation of the friendships you may need in a future project.

Another application of this stratagem is initially to aim for small successes, and then build on these further. The small successes then act as a springboard for the larger ones.

25. Replace the beams with rotten timbers
Triumph over your adversary by increasing your influence at the cost of his. Many consultancy companies make use of this stratagem by making themselves indispensable at their customer. The result is that such an organization becomes fully dependent on them, whereby such companies can place junior consultants with them, and train them at the customer's cost. Also, when someone gives large donations or gifts to an organization in order to gain influence, he is making use of this stratagem.

A project manager does the same thing when he takes on activities in his project that really do not belong there. By gaining control over these, he can look after his projects interests better. By making other people dependent on you in this way, you destroy the structures present in the other party, in order to solve particular problems and gain influence.

2.11 Negotiation

26. Set an example
The saying reads: *"Point at the Mulberry Tree but Curse the Locust"* and relates to the story of a ruler who enforced obedience by setting an extreme example. You can apply this in both the negative as positive sense.

In a negative sense, by acting angrily in a particular situation. Because people do not like that, they will try to prevent it the next time by immediately agreeing. Some negotiators make frequent use of this.

> EXAMPLE 31-3 TOO EXPENSIVE
> The project manager went with his account manager to his future project sponsor. When they handed over their proposal, the project sponsor leafed through to the pricing page and reacted furiously: *"This is far too expensive. Go away and do your homework again."*

In a positive sense, by rewarding people for good performance or effort. The recognition that you award, motivates others to also deliver good work.

27. Remain sensible, act stupid
With this stratagem, you do not speak your mind. By talking more slowly than you normally would, and by frequently saying nothing for long periods, you tempt the other person into being more talkative, and providing you with more information that you can turn to your advantage. By asking many (obvious) questions, you can also achieve the same result. It is possible that by doing this, people underestimate you, and do not realise your strength. When the time is right you then seize your opportunity.

28. Entice someone onto the roof and then remove the ladder
When you make it impossible for someone to reconsider their choices, you are applying this stratagem. But you can also apply it to yourself. When you want to bring about a particular change in your behaviour, tell it to everyone who will listen to you, and once you have declared this publicly, it is difficult to go back on your word. A stratagem, however, that can go very wrong.

The stratagem also works very well when someone is short of time. By delaying your decision until the very last moment, it is easier to extract a concession from the other party.

29. Deck the withered tree with false blossoms
When you present things as better than they are, you are making use of this stratagem. For example, by putting the emphasis in a difficult project on the positive points where progress has been made, you gain support for a following phase.

Although it is tempting, this stratagem can soon lean towards lies and deceit. Everybody makes things sound more positive than they really are, but before you know it, you end up a long way from the truth. A photo on a brochure that shows you in front of a large office building that is not yours is a form of misrepresentation. Making the contracts on your CV bigger than they actually were, and therefore making it appear that you have more experience than you actually do, is also a variant of this stratagem.

> EXAMPLE 31-4 A TRUE STORY
> In the beginning of the 1990's, Workflow applications were only just appearing. A computer manufacturer took its first steps in this area, but could not get the software to work on its platform. A competitor's computer was used and provided with its own logo.

In general, the reality exposes the lie, and if you are made out to be a liar, even if that was not your intention, it will seriously damage your image, which will hinder your work. You must, therefore, be careful with the use of this stratagem.

30. Make the host and guest exchange roles

In a customer/supplier relationship, the customer is the host and the supplier the guest. When the supplier finds out that his customer does not have any alternatives, it gives him a strong position in the negotiations. This can even extend so far that the supplier determines how the negotiations will proceed. The application of this stratagem is based on the exchange of roles.

31. Make use of beautiful women

A stratagem that is used a lot in advertising campaigns, which are nearly always accompanied by beautiful people, irrespective of whether the target audience is men or women. Most people would just rather look at beautiful people than ugly people. In the advertisement for a sporty car, we see a beautiful woman sitting next to the man, whereas in a cosmetics advertisement, we generally see models or cover girls playing the main role.

In its most immoral application, we see this stratagem applied in the form of visits to clubs of dubious origins, in order to lavishly entertain the other party. This is an ethically discreditable manner, in which men treat women more as instruments than as human beings. It capitalizes on the weakness of men for feminine beauty, making them susceptible to blackmail.

32. Conceal your vulnerability by showing your weakness

> EXAMPLE 31-5 NEGOTIATE
> During one of my first negotiations, I said: *"We now have to do something I am not very good at."* I meant this, but my opponent reacted with: *"Those are the most dangerous people."*
> Ever since, I have never said that I am a poor negotiator.

Or as the saying goes: *"Swing open the gate of the empty city"*, which refers to a story from Chinese history where the ruler's army was involved in a battle, and not in a position to defend the capital. Opening up the gates made the enemy think that this was an ambush, and it abandoned the attack.

There are all sorts of descriptions of what a good project manager should be able to do. By openly admitting certain weak points, people will quickly jump to the conclusion that you are joking, and be more likely to acknowledge the opposite. Displaying vulnerability is viewed in many cultures as a quality.

33. Mislead the spy with information

> EXAMPLE 31-6 OPERATION NORTH POLE
> In the 20th century in Europe during World War 2, the Germans used captured spies to mislead the British. The British realized this and continued to send spies, who in turn then misled the Germans.

With this stratagem, you feed the opponent with wrong information, by making use of his own employees. It does not matter whether they realize this and consciously disadvantage their own employer, or whether they are unaware of it. Dissatisfied employees are more receptive to this than satisfied employees.

When a supplier offers free services to help you achieve a certain deadline, you must ask yourself what he has in mind. In any case, there are sufficient reasons to be careful with the information you share with the employee in question. By supplying the information carefully, bit by bit, you can wrongfoot the supplier.

34. The stratagem of the self-inflicted pain

You can make use of this stratagem in a number of ways. In its most extreme form, you can inflict pain on yourself in order to gain the sympathy of other people. Some-

2.11 Negotiation

one who goes on a hunger strike, or sets themselves on fire, does this to gain attention for their case.

A lot less extreme is trying to arouse sympathy in the other party. By pointing out a physical ailment, emotional or financial problems, you increase the chance that people are willing to help you. The thing that is clever about this is that you make use of your weaknesses in order to achieve your goal.

35. Combine
If you apply a number of stratagems together, the effectiveness is obviously much greater. This is the 35th stratagem.

36. Retreat
Mao Zedong said: *"Fight no battle you are not sure of winning[13]"*. You do not have to win all battles; sometimes it is wiser to just depart from the battle scene.

---

13 (1938), Mao Zedong, *Problems of Strategy in Guerilla War Against Japan, Selected Works Vol. II*

2.12 Conflicts and crisis

A PARTY GAME WITH A GUN TO THE HEAD

We can jokingly say that a conflict is a party game for at least two people, which ends when there is just one person left in the game.

What then is a crisis?

A crisis is more a runaway flock of sheep plunging into the ravine.

2.12 Conflict and Crisis

2.12-1 Definitions

Conflict	A situation in which two or more parties with conflicting interests or ideas are opposite each other.
Crisis	A serious emergency situation, whereby the functioning of a system (of any nature) becomes severely disrupted.

2.12-2 INTRODUCTION

Conflicts can occur at various levels, and within projects we have to deal with conflicts:

- Between people.
- Between teams or departments.
- Between organizations.
- Between societies.

Conflicts are inevitable and have positive and negative aspects. Well managed, they create energy in a team, can be a source of innovation and change[1], and can strengthen the bond between team members.

It is more to do with how you look at conflicts. Even though, initially there may be a tendency to cover them up, it doesn't hurt to wait and see how a particular conflict develops. The question you have to keep asking yourself as project manager is to what extent the conflict may endanger the project result.

The other side of conflicts, especially when they become drawn-out and do not lead to a solution, is that relationships become disturbed, there is loss of energy, and through the increase of stress in the organization, a distortion of reality occurs.

The same can be said about a crisis, only to a much greater extent, and with a much higher level of intensity. A crisis turns everything upside down and demands a lot of leadership by the project manager who is involved with it.

---

1 (2000), *Conflicthantering & Onderhandelen*, Ritsema van Eck, BOHN STAFLEU VAN LOGHUM

2.12-3 PROCESS STEPS

1. Predict reactions.
2. Don't become involved.
3. Consider all points of view.
4. Choose a suitable approach.
5. Balance interests.
6. Agree upon solutions.
7. Apply lessons learned.

1. Predict reactions

Risks, which have a conflict or crisis as impact, are a special category requiring particular attention. Both the conflict and the crisis may severely disrupt proceedings. There are conflicts in the:
- Work and task areas.
- Social field.
- Economic field.
- Ideological field.

If you do not pay enough attention to these, any latent conflicts present at the start of the project will ultimately develop into emotional conflicts. Wherever possible, you have to try and prevent this from happening, as emotion is difficult to manage.

Furthermore, we know from group dynamics that shortly after the team has started to work together for the first time, it can be predicted that there will be a period of conflict, the so-called *"storming"* stage. As this is predictable, you can take it into account at the start and anticipate it.

What is valid for conflicts is even more important for crises, whereby you must think of events of such magnitude that everything becomes disrupted.

Crises come in the form as:
- Disasters.
- Explosions, fires.
- Transport accidents.
- Riots, disturbances.
- Terrorism and hostage taking.
- Psycho crises.
- Managerial crises.
- Reorganization.
- Company disaster.
- Product recall.

It is clear that crises are more difficult to predict than conflicts. Depending on the type of project, you determine which reactions to conflicts and crises you will include in the plan.

2. Don't become involved

Now it is important to keep a cool head. Both conflicts and crises are accompanied by a lot of emotions, which can cause you to quickly lose your rationality, and if there is ever a moment when the adage *think first act later* applies, it is with one of these events.

Think first and act later does not mean that you should not act quickly, but that you have to act in a well thought-out way. Furthermore it is difficult to cope with such a situation if you let your own opinion play too much of a role. That is what the next process step is about.

3. Consider all points of view

Due to the tension, which slowly builds up, all parties involved experience restricted awareness, and as such, we need to simplify the situation. The result, however, may be that we are not able to decide properly what the best approach is, and you listen, therefore, to all people involved.

Two know more than one, and so by listening to the different points of view, you get a clearer picture of the situation enabling you to react much better. As project manager, you are expected to have a calm and emotionally stable attitude from which you lead the team. During a crises or a conflict you use a directive style of leadership.

4. Choose a suitable approach
Of all possible approaches, a few can always be discarded as not being workable. It may be because we do not have the resources, or because they are not feasible, but those that are workable have to be investigated further.

In the event of a conflict, you may now decide whether or not it is useful to involve a third party to mediate between the parties. If you are a stakeholder yourself, or when parties involved find you biased, this really is the only option.

5. Balance interests
All possible options have to be set against each other, and you look at those solutions where all the interests are in balance. For solutions such as these, you can later also count on the support of the most important parties involved.

6. Agree upon solutions
You then choose the solution that has the most support, and ensure that everyone has the same picture of what has to be done and the expected effects. Then the solution can be carried out.

7. Apply lessons learned
During crises and conflicts, so much happens that you do not have time to sit down and reflect on all that has happened. You only do that after it is all over, and together with your team you discuss the events and the effectiveness of the chosen solutions.

2.12 Conflict and Crisis

2.12-4 SPECIAL TOPICS

1. Diagnosis of conflicts

Before you can effectively deal with a conflict, you have to be aware of its existence. Conflicts have a certain incubation time between the cause and when it becomes visible. At a certain point in time, the conflict becomes apparent and the need arises to do something about it. Making a diagnosis is a first step.

What is it about, who are the parties involved, what was the cause, what are the consequences, and what has been tried to resolve it. These are all questions you would like answers to, and there are two different ways to make such a diagnosis.

- The *process approach:* which looks at how the behavior of the one party invokes certain behavior in the other party (the dynamics of the process). The various alternating episodes in the conflict are looked at.

- The *structure approach:* in which the conflict is described and explained in terms of the more or less stable characteristics (the structure) of the circumstances in which the conflict takes place. What fixed forces have an impact on the situation.

It is not a case of one or other approach being better; they are additional perspectives from which the conflicts can be viewed, and an attempt can be made to understand the conflicts. It is true that everyone sees the conflict from his viewpoint, and you can best use both approaches in order to come to a complete diagnosis of the conflict.

Diagnosis according to the process model

Every conflict has at some time had a cause, which one of the parties became aware of. This awareness brought with it feelings which were ultimately transformed into specific behavior. That behavior in itself brought on feelings in the other party, which were then again transformed into certain behavior.

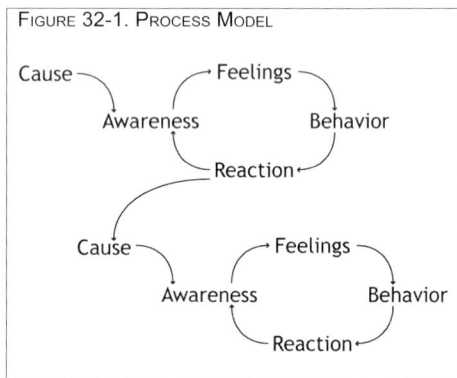

FIGURE 32-1. PROCESS MODEL

Cause → Awareness → Feelings → Behavior → Reaction → Cause → Awareness → Feelings → Behavior → Reaction

In itself, this is a very normal cycle, be it that in the conflict every cycle is another step further in the escalation. When you start working this way, you will see that both parties disagree on the way in which the conflict should be described. We call this a battle around the differences in punctuation. Each party has its own structure (punctuation) and places the emphasis somewhere else.

Note that this approach is strongly about the conflict as experienced (often felt) by the participants. An attempt is made to understand the communication backwards and forwards between the two parties, thus breaking the escalation cycle.

We look at the causes, and these are both internal and external, which are at the foundation of both parties behavior.

For instance, an internal cause is how much success is expected from a certain style of

2.12 Conflict and Crisis

handling a conflict. What is possible, and what are the risks you run using a certain style. In short, will I achieve what I want, and at what price. So far this looks very calculated and rational, but the reality is more complex.

Certainly when conflicts have already matured somewhat, emotions come more into play, and these have a much stronger impact on behavior, both directly and indirectly. Negative emotions lead to a simplification of the reality, to black and white thinking, whereby the ability to find a solution in a constructive manner is far less likely.

External causes have to do with the quality of the relationship. A conflict between friends will, in general, develop differently to a conflict between people who do not trust each other anyway. The current conflict will only serve to stoke the fire of old (never solved) conflicts.

Another external cause is the behavior of the other party, as certain behavior evokes other behavior. There is a kind of reciprocity of conflict behavior: competing evokes competing.

The way to get out of this is to go back along the same road, to make both parties aware of their conflict process. It does not matter where you start i.e. what your pretext is, you can start with the behavior or with the feelings, and each one has its advantages and disadvantages. If you start with the behavior, you can describe in a very businesslike fashion what one party does, what the effect is on the other party, and what he will do in return. In this way you go through a chain of cause and effect, although one of the disadvantages is that when it is very emotional for one of the parties, he feels misunderstood. If you use feelings as a pretext, then someone will feel seen and recognized in his being, and in that way he will be able to work on the conflict more freely. The best approach is a combination of both. Where issues are threatening to become too emotional, you focus on the behavior of the parties in conflict, and, where possible, you recognise that emotions are involved in the conflict.

This is no easy task in a process which has escalated.

Diagnosis according to the structure model

In this model, the cause of the conflict is shown in the stable features of the objective reality: the cause, the characteristics of both parties and their relationship, and furthermore, on how conflicts are usually solved in the environment concerned (regulatory mechanisms).

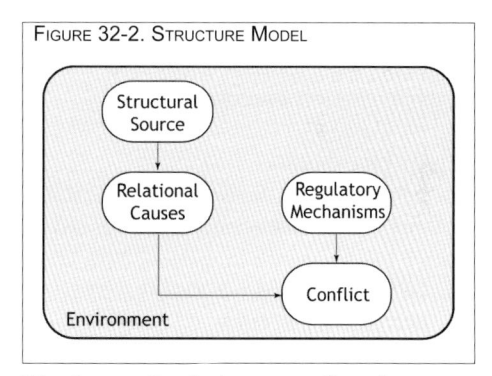

FIGURE 32-2. STRUCTURE MODEL

We discuss the features mentioned.

STRUCTURAL SOURCES OF CONFLICT
Conflicts can develop on the priorities of objectives and resources when, between the various units, these have not been co-ordinated with each other properly. Sometimes there is even a *negative goal dependency* when the one unit will only achieve its goals at the expense of the other unit. You really do then have an insoluble conflict.

Usually it is not so black-and-white, and there is a *mixed goal dependency* in which

2.12 Conflict and Crisis

some goals are positively, and some negatively, linked to each other.

There may also be lack of clarity with regard to the responsibilities and authorities in an organization. When tasks and roles overlap, this can be a permanent source of conflicts.

Within the project, the project manager can prevent many of these types of structural sources of conflict by setting out a clear and simple organization structure, by splitting up results clearly, by dividing up tasks in such a way that there are no overlapping responsibilities and also by making the prioritizing of the various activities clear for all parties involved.

The relationship with the project environment is less practicable than you would like it to be. Here, the project manager is dealing with conflicts about people and resources, and about administrative procedures, which hinder the project execution.

RELATIONAL CAUSES

Conflicts can also develop from the stable features of the relationship itself, for example:
- Differences in personal style, characters that clash.
- Lack of communicative skills.
- Cultural differences.
- The duration of the relationship.
- Reciprocal power relationships.

I shall cover the last one of these in more detail. Someone has power over another person when he is in a position whereby he can force the other person to do something against his will. It is obvious that this has consequences for the way in which a conflict manifests itself. It may also explain why a conflict is latent for a long time, and then suddenly manifests itself with great intensity (e.g. an employee hands in his notice), without there being anything that can be done about it.

Someone may have power and not use it, but nevertheless having power (as seen through the eyes of the other party), has an impact on the course of the conflict.

We know the following sources of power[1] that can play a part in conflicts:
- Formal power.
- Access to information.
- The importance of the task carried out by the job holder.
- The replaceability of the job holder.
- The expertise of the job holder.
- Referent power.
- Power of the rank and file.
- Reputation and status.
- Personal characteristics.
- Relationship with other authorities.
- Political sensitivity.

REGULATORY MECHANISMS

These are (temporary) procedures which prevent the escalation of a conflict, and sometimes enough of these already exist in an organization. There are (unwritten) rules such as *'do not let your emotions get the better of you'* or *'romances at work are not allowed'* and, of course, it remains to be seen to what extent you can enforce these types of matters, but strong standards within the group should regulate such things.

You may also be dealing with rules agreed on in advance, in which parties have laid down how conflicts are to be solved, such as, for example, the contract clause which legal system applies, or that disputes will be submitted to arbitration.

In projects, the change procedures, the pre-established way in which reporting takes

---
1 (2000), *Conflicthantering & Onderhandelen*, Ritsema van Eck, BOHN STAFLEU VAL Loghum

2.12 Conflict and Crisis

place, the budgets and tolerances are examples of formal regulatory mechanisms.

When two people involve a level of senior management to make a decision, this has the advantage that afterwards both parties will be able to carry on in good harmony and submit themselves to the judgment made by the senior manager.

Making objectives SMART and agreeing them in advance is another mechanism to prevent conflicts. In the same way that the goal and the result are defined in the scope of the project, at the level of the work packages, what has to be delivered by whom and when, is described very precisely.

ENVIRONMENT FACTORS
No project stands on its own, and so a number of the conflicts that occur will have to do with the larger environment. A number of these are: working terms and conditions, legal position, meeting culture, inadequate communication, unclear policy, etc.

2. Stages of the conflict

In general
In common parlance, we usually talk of a conflict when it has become visible. The milder variant when people disagree at a business level, and the heavier variant when it is has become an escalated conflict with a lot of emotion between the parties involved.

When you look in more detail at how conflicts develop, you can already speak of a conflict at a lot earlier stage; often a latent, slumbering conflict has preceded it.

There may already be a latent conflict, without parties being aware of it. At a certain moment both parties notice that their interests are not synchronous, or even worse, that they are actually contradictory, and particu-

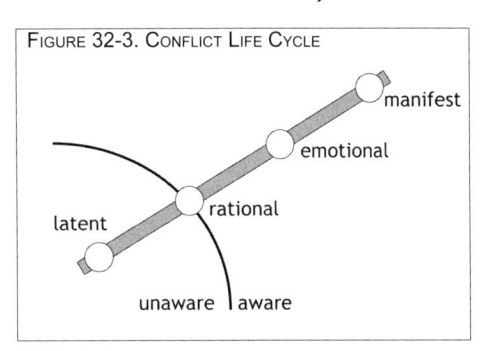

FIGURE 32-3. CONFLICT LIFE CYCLE

larly when two groups are in conflict this is reinforced even more. The content aspect is accompanied of an emotional conflict. Up to that point in time, there is not really a question of something threatening to get out of hand, but if it is not dealt with carefully, it could go that way. The conflict develops into an open battle, in which the conflict has manifested itself.

Initial stage – or latent
A latent conflict, or a conflict that is in its initial stage, is not consciously experienced as such. There are, however, various different sources that can lead to a conflict.

In projects, it is often predictable which type of conflicts you will have to deal with, and in general they concern[2]:
- Priorities.
- Administrative procedures.
- Plans.
- Application of resources.
- Costs.
- Technique.
- Personalities of the team members.

Good project management means that you take account of this in advance and adjust your leadership style accordingly.

---

[2] (1989), *Project Management, A systems approach to planning scheduling and controlling*, Harold Kerzner, VAN NOSTRAND REINHOLD, New York

2.12 Conflict and Crisis

The conflict subjects are also strongly dependent on the stage in which a project is, and in the below table[3], we give an overview of the ranking for each stage in the lifecycle:

Start	Initial stages	During execution	Towards the end
Priorities	Priorities	Planning	Planning
Procedures	Planning	Technique	Personality
Planning	Procedures	People	People
People	Technique	Priorities	Priorities
Costs	People	Procedures	Costs
Technique	Personality	Costs	Technique
Personality	Costs	Personality	Procedures

As project manager, the structure model is a good way of acting pro-actively. When developing the project organization, you ensure that a negative goal dependency does not exist. The term "*all noses pointing in the same direction*" is more than a motivating kick-off, it is also actually ensuring that the various different deliverables lead the team in the same direction. It has already been said earlier, but when dividing up the work in the WBS and allocating work packages, you ensure that tasks and responsibilities are clear and disjunctive.

The research quoted provides some advice to the project manager how to prevent a number of these conflicts in advance: "*One of the tasks of a project manager is to take account in advance of the inevitable, and to implement a structure in which conflicts have less chance of thriving.*"

MEASURES DURING START
Priorities:
- Clear plans.
- Decide together.
- Consultation of parties.

Procedures:
- Develop good procedures for the project administration in consultation with those responsible.

Planning:
- Obtain commitment to the plan in advance.
- Assess which aspects in the line organization will have an effect on the project.

MEASURES DURING INITIAL STAGES
Priorities:
- Provide feedback on project plans by means of review sessions.

Procedures:
- Contingency planning for the most important administrative problems.

Planning:
- Produce the WBS in cooperation with the line organization.

MEASURES DURING THE PROJECT
Planning:
- Keep continuous track of the execution.
- Think about alternatives when something overruns.

Technique:
- Solve technical problems as quickly as possible.
- Put the emphasis on thorough testing.
- Obtain approval in a previous stage for the specifications.

People:
- Make a timely assessment of the required manpower and communicate the need.
- Carry out the assessment together with the line organization.

---

3 (1975), *Conflict Management in the Project Life Cycle,* Thambain en Wilemon, cited in *Project Management, A systems approach to planning scheduling and controlling,* Harold Kerzner, VAN NOSTRAND REINHOLD, New York

2.12 Conflict and Crisis

MEASURES TOWARDS THE END
Planning:
- Reallocate people in order to ensure critical activities are completed on time.
- Ensure quick solutions for technical problems.

People:
- Ensure there is a plan for people to stream out of the project.

Personality:
- Be aware of the mutual relationships.
- Keep stress to a reasonable level.

Rational stage - or recognized

The moment the parties involved recognise the fact that there are conflicting interests, then this marks the transition to a new stage in the conflict. Even though the conflict is experienced more as being a "point of issue" rather than as a real conflict, we do see a hardening of the positions. The parties distance themselves somewhat from each other. When there is a conflict between two organizational units, the group feeling will grow during this stage. Because of the differences, the identity gets stronger and one of the disadvantages is the potential for the development of "groupthink" or group blindness. During this stage, we also see the rise of the leaders (in the conflict), who, as so-called opinion leaders, are a key factor in steering the conflict in the right direction.

This does not mean, however, that the conflict has to be suppressed. During their development, each team will go through a stage in which they will have to deal with characters and opinions challenging each other, and this is a condition for becoming a team that performs well.

An annoying incidental phenomenon in the development of a conflict is, that under the stress of the conflict, people pay less attention to their similarities than to their differences. This stress has to do with insecurity, and it is then up to you as manager of the team to display firm leadership.

When there are differences of opinion between two groups with regard to content, it may be tempting to eliminate this through discussion. You have to be careful with this, however, as shown by the example. The danger of a discussion, therefore, is a polarization of the viewpoints.

EXAMPLE 32-1 DISCUSSIONS CAUSES POLARISATION

There is a difference of opinion in the team. There are four team members, and the discussion is about any random topic XYZ. In the table below, we give a summary of the different arguments supporters and opponents have.

Supporters	Opponents
John has the following arguments in support: Argument A Argument C Argument D	Mary has the following arguments against: Argument 1 Argument 2
Petra has the following arguments in support: Argument B Argument C	Abdul has the following arguments against: Argument 2 Argument 3

The supporters have a total of four arguments in support of the discussion, but each individual has no more than three. The opponents have a total of three arguments against, but each individual has no more than two. When both parties try to resolve things through a discussion, there is a chance that the supporters will become even more supportive, and the opponents will disagree more. This is because afterwards, all participants in the discussion will have more arguments to support their point of view.

This does not imply you should not start the discussion, but you must be aware of this risk. In this stage of the conflict, it is still mainly about the content of the conflict and you can use the energy in the conflict to intrinsically resolve the underlying problem, or

459

2.12 Conflict and Crisis

to prevent it turning into an emotional conflict.

Because there is pressure on the team, irritations between both parties may occur quickly. As project manager, you have to keep an eye on which behavior is fuelling the conflict further, and if necessary, you call the team members to account if you think they cannot resolve it themselves.

Examples of behavior that escalates conflicts are:
- Not letting someone finish speaking.
- Asking suggestive questions.
- Naming names ("*the director agrees*").
- Telling long stories.
- Mentioning non-arguments.
- Bringing up the matter of someone's integrity.

As chairman of meetings, you have to ensure that people listen to each other, and also understand each other before bringing in their own arguments. A technique which is very suitable for that is paraphrasing. Before someone brings up his own point of view, you encourage him to summarize what the other person has said in his own words. A new point of view is then only introduced once the other person has been fully understood.

A number of tips to de-escalate a conflict[4]:
- Speak in *I-term*.
- Speak for *yourself*.
- Ask the opinion of others.
- Do not state the obvious.
- Separate the person from the issue.
- Don't use the words: *never and always*.
- Keep the door open.
- Do not stop the negotiations.
- Make proposals for reaching a solution.

---
[4] (1996), Gesprekken in organisaties, Gramsbergen-Hoogland, van der Molen, WOLTERS-NOORHOFF

Emotional stage - or felt
This is the stage in which the conflict becomes more emotional and the conflict challenge is no longer the content. We often see a long discussion about the content, without a solution being found, because the underlying message is one of a relational and emotional nature, whereby one party feels better about the situation than the other.

The group cohesion, which already increased in the previous stage, will increase further, and within both the teams the mutual differences will decrease, whereas between the teams these will increase. In discussion, the opposition's weakest argument will be swept off the table and with that, also all the other (stronger) arguments. When the conflict is between two individuals, we see that both parties will go looking for allies, thereby increasing the conflict.

In this stage, it doesn't help anymore to talk only about the content, as there is now a chain of cause and effect which has to be sorted out. As project manager, you ask yourself the question whether or not it is useful and desirable to give mediation a try, and that is dependent on the state your project is in. Because, by definition, a project is temporary in nature, you may ask yourself what the advantage is of solving the conflict at a relational level. If both parties are not going to see each other again after the project, you do not have to put so much energy into this.

Much more than in a line management function, you can put pressure on both parties, if the conflict concerns individuals, or on the opinion leaders if it is a conflict between groups, and demand that they solve the conflict in a businesslike manner. If one of the two is not willing, you can replace him, and if that does not work because the person in question plays a key part, you have a real

2.12 Conflict and Crisis

problem. Even then, if you bare your teeth, you will be surprised.

We provide a model for "businesslike" negotiating in a conflict situation, which stems from the relationship therapy[5], and you can use it to support two parties in solving a conflict together.

The numbers are corresponding with the sequence to be followed.

	Person A.	Person B.
Separate	1) A and B prepare the agenda with the requirements for the other person.	
Together	2) A reads out the list.	3) B listens, repeats and takes notes.
Together	5) A listens, repeats and takes notes.	4) B reads out the list.
Separate	6) Both make the (false) assumption: If I get everything I want from the other person, what am I willing to give.	
Together	8) A listens, repeats and takes notes.	7) B reads out the list.
Together	9) A reads out the list.	10) B listens, repeats and takes notes.
Separate	11) Both wonder: If I get this and this from you, then I am willing to give you that and that.	
Together	12) A reads out proposal.	13) B listens, repeats and takes notes.
Together	15) A listens, repeats and takes notes.	14) B reads out proposal.
Together	16) Each in turn comes with a new proposal until a decision is made.	

---

5 (1994), *Helpen bij partnerrelatie problemen*, Alfons Vansteenwegen, BOHN STAFLEU

As starting point for this discussion model, both parties have to be prepared to park the emotional aspects. As project manager, you play the role of mediator. Firstly, you obtain consensus on this procedure, and when both parties agree to that you can carry on. During the discussion it can happen that both parties want to deviate from the procedure, but you don't allow that, pointing out the agreements made at the start.

When you decide to take the time to also address the emotional aspect, you have to instruct both parties to listen to each other, and just as with the previous approach, you have to ensure you remain impartial. Particularly where emotions are involved, this is not easy, because during the discussion your own emotions also become involved. It may then be helpful to ask someone in the team, who is trusted by both parties, to do this.

Listening to each other and speaking with each other about what is irritating, demands a lot of the communicative skills from the people involved. Already a few times we have mentioned paraphrasing what the other party said, speaking in I-messages, naming behavior and refraining from being judgemental. As mediator, you must ensure that both parties understand why this is important, and then you help them to enter into discussion with each other.

Fight stage - or Manifest
When the conflict enters this stage it has got out of hand, and parties threaten each other (either verbally and/or physically).

Then there is not much more left for you to do apart from separating the fighting parties, or maybe even considering which party has to be "sacrificed" for the good of the project objective. Maybe even both have to be sacrificed, and if you have let this happen in the

2.12 Conflict and Crisis

project, there is a big chance that you yourself are one of the first to suffer this fate.

3. Conflict styles

Every person has developed a number of styles for handling conflicts, which he more or less consistently applies when resolving a conflict in which he finds himself. The styles developed depend strongly on someone's personal life story.

You can imagine that someone who grows up in a family in which the parents were often fighting, develops different styles from an only child or someone from a family of six children.

When resolving conflicts, there are always two considerations in play, and these are:
- The need for relationships.
- The need for autonomy.

Therefore, there are two dimensions at play in dealing with a conflict. On the one hand there is the contradiction between working together or against each other, and on the other hand the contradiction between assertiveness and effacing oneself.

This results in five basic styles:

FIGURE 32-4. THOMAS-KILMANN CONFLICT STYLES

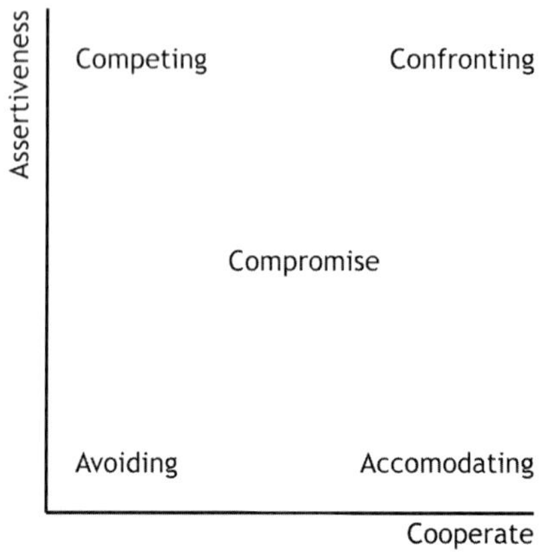

(Assertiveness vs Cooperate axes showing: Competing, Confronting, Compromise, Avoiding, Accomodating)

As alternative dimensions, we also see care for the relationship and care for the task. The accompanying conflict styles are then the same.
- *Confronting*, also called collaborating, integrating or problem solving. There is a direct and open communication, in which a realistic solution acceptable to both parties is searched for. The target is a win-win situation.
- *Accommodating*, also called giving in or smoothing over; all energy is put into holding on to a good relationship with the opposition. The other wins everything, whereas you give up everything that is needed to maintain the relationship.
- *Compromising*, it is a situation of "you win some, you lose some, I win some, I lose some".
- *Competing*, also called forcing or fighting. Only your own objectives are important and are imposed at all costs. A real win-lose situation.
- *Avoiding*, whereby the conflict is avoided; the relationship is no longer that important, people are indifferent about it.

This so-called conflict grid has been the subject of study for various researchers, the best known of whom are Thomas and Kilmann[6].

Even though you might be inclined to say that confronting and looking for a compromise are the best styles, this is not the case. Handling a conflict the right way depends on the situation. Just as with providing leadership, you have the most effect when you adapt your style to the situation.

---

6 (1974), *Thomas-Kilmann Conflict Mode Instrument*, K.W.Thomas, R.H.Kilmann, XICOM Inc.

Competing

This style is best applied in the following situations:
- A quick decision is required; there is little time.
- You find the topic vitally important, are convinced of being right, and you want to protect yourself against misuse of your own usual giving-in style.
- It is an important issue, and others hesitate or are not motivated.
- It is an important issue, whereby unpopular measures have to be taken.
- You have sufficient power.
- You have to build up power.
- You are not dependent on the other party.
- You are dealing with people who misuse non-competitive behavior.

Confronting

This style can best be applied in the following situations:
- There is sufficient time (and money) to be able to decide.
- The 'commitment' in execution by the other party is required, an in depth consideration of what both parties have in mind is required.
- The problem is too complex for a compromise.
- Both parties intend to work on the underlying relationship.
- Voicing emotions is important for the follow up, people want to get to know the expectations, wishes and so on of the other party.
- If your main aim is to learn from the cooperation.
- To handle feelings which have hindered the relationship.

Accommodating

This style can best be applied in the following situations:
- You are wrong (and want to show that you can learn from your own mistakes).
- To minimise the loss when you are on the losing end.
- You want to build credit with the other party by showing your own good will and reasonableness.
- It is an insignificant topic for your own party (but not for the other party).
- The relationship is more important than the issue.
- A competing strategy will inevitably lead to a breach, which is not desirable.
- You have insufficient power.
- You are very dependent on the other party.

Avoiding

This style can best be applied in the following situations:
- The topic is trivial or not important.
- Currently you do not yet have the power to achieve your own goal.
- The feelings have become overheated (cool down).
- You can better postpone an issue and discuss it at another time(for example: not enough information, there are people present who have nothing to do with it).
- There are more essential problems to discuss.
- If collecting information is more important than an immediate result.
- Someone else can better raise the issue.

2.12 Conflict and Crisis

Compromising
This style can best be applied in the following situations:
- You have little time, and have to come to a decision quickly.
- Parties who have equal power are fighting over a divisive issue.
- In order to reach a temporary agreement for a complicated issue.
- Other styles have failed.

4. Solving conflicts

We have briefly spoken about the mediating role a project manager sometimes has to play in resolving a conflict, and this will especially be the case with conflicts within the team.

Within a project, it is about recognizing, exploring and acknowledging the conflict. This requires a good balance of observation skills and discipline from the project manager. Early intervention in a latent or recognized conflict may lead to it escalating further. *"A dead dog moves if you kick it"*, and that can also happen with conflicts. Therefore, after recognizing the conflict there is a period in which you explore the conflict by asking the following important questions: can the different parties resolve it themselves? Are they capable of doing that? What consequences does it have for the project? Is the planning threatened? These are the considerations you have to make before you intervene.

On the one hand discipline has to do with patience (do not intervene too early), but is also about the courage to intervene when it is really necessary. When you decide to intervene, you also decide how you are going to do it.

Approach for a conflict within the team
Initially you will try to solve conflicts within the team by using a co-operating or a compromising style. If that does not work, as project manager you have to force a solution, but only after you have come to the conclusion that both parties cannot come to an agreement (accommodating or avoiding the conflict).

It begins by preparing both parties for your approach, and for a potential confrontation. You tell them what the cause is, how you see the conflict, and the consequences for the project itself. When you apply the negotiating model that we described earlier, you explain how this works.

In addition, you explain the basic rules for the confrontation:
- The mediator is the chairman and controls the rules of the game and the procedure.
- Everyone keeps their own view to themselves until the viewpoint of the other party becomes clear.
- No one talks over anyone else.
- Discussion is held directly with each other.
- Everyone is as specific as possible.
- Everyone listens actively.
- Revealing emotions is allowed, but blaming others is not.

As mediator, you prepare yourself thoroughly for the conflict by:
- Having the conflict points clear yourself.
- Listing and understanding the underlying interests.
- Having a clear view of the parties perceived priority.
- Forming your own opinion of the priority.

In "normal" mediation situations, the mediator is an independent third party, who has no self-interest in the ultimate resolution of the conflict. Of course, in a project situation, this is not the case, as it is in the project manager's interest that the conflict does not endanger the achievement of the project result. Therefore, you try to be as impartial as possible, but you set additional pre-conditions on the resolution of the conflict by applying you own authority with respect to the priority of the various points.

During the discussion, you look for a solution which both parties can agree to (co-operation) or you look for a compromise. Together with both parties, you list the possible solutions and pick out one that both parties can accept. You record the chosen solution in a document, and you ensure that both parties explicitly voice the fact that they agree with it.

5. Crisis approach

In crisis management, communication is key, as in such situations people have a great need for information, which you should supply them with as quickly as possible.

There are a number of fundamental rules[7], which you must take account of, and these are:
- Act quickly.
- Determine the policy beforehand and then keep to it.
- Always put the safety of people first.
- Demonstrate responsibility and sympathy.
- Take the initiative.

---

[7] (1996) *Crisiscommunicatie*, Gerard F. Boulogne, KLUWER

2.12 Conflict and Crisis

2.13 Reliability

Trust arrives on foot, and departs on horseback

Peter, we are not going to lie to the customer, are we?

Because if we are, you should not have brought me with you.

When I lie, I turn bright red.

(A true fragment from a conversation between a project manager and his sales director)

2.13 Reliability

2.13-1 DEFINITIONS

Dilemma	An almost impossible choice from various alternatives, which meets several contrasting interests.
Reliability	Keeping the agreements that someone has made.

2.13-2 INTRODUCTION

I can still hear him say: *"Project management is lying, cheating and stealing."* He just stopped short of saying murder. It was an experienced and successful manager, who was making an attempt to explain project management to me, but I thought: *that's not for me.*

Project management is all about trust; it is the driving force your credibility runs on. If you are caught lying once, you have had it.

Reliability is the skill to deliver in line with planning and specifications. That means that you can also look at many of the techniques covered as tools for being reliable. Yet more reason for you to gain more knowledge about the difficult side of the profession.

Someone is reliable if:

- There is consistency between words and actions.
- His behavior is consistent in different situations.
- His behavior is coherent in different situations.
- He is authentic and transparent.

Reliability is not something that just happens; it requires: perseverance, decisiveness, reason, assertiveness and a good memory to remember the promises made.

2.13-3 PROCESS STEPS

1. Use good planning techniques.
2. Communicate to stakeholders.
3. Know their dilemmas.
4. Be respectful, honest and open.
5. Engage stakeholders.
6. Mitigate and clarify.
7. Reach agreement.
8. Work systematically.
9. Apply lessons learned.

1. Use good planning techniques
It is, perhaps, strange to mention good planning techniques as the first process step with respect to this competence element. However, if you think about it for a while, it really is very logical.

We can interpret the word reliable in two ways:
- Someone is reliable as a person.
- What someone says is reliable.

Even though both are obviously related, someone who is reliable will more often provide a reliable statement than someone who is not. When a reliable person does not have the right information, however, then he is (however much he would like to) not capable of giving reliable statements.

In essence, reliability in a project management context means that you deliver what you have agreed on time, in accordance with the specified quality and within budget. This is only possible if, during the planning process, you make use of good planning techniques and if you have the right control tools during the execution.

2. Communicate to stakeholders
As well as making use of the right techniques, which are fundamental to obtaining a reliable insight in the actual status of the project, there is also a need to communicate this properly to the different stakeholders.

The extent to which the parties involved experience the project and the project manager and his team as reliable, strongly depends on how the team communicates with them. When there is little communication, they might get the idea that the team is hiding something, and therefore is unreliable. It is important to always communicate some kind of progress.

When making an agreement, you must ensure that all parties have the same view of what has been agreed. If this is not the case, it will stimulate a perception of unreliability. Adequate communication means that you document the agreements as concretely as possible.

3. Know their dilemmas
The contrasting interests people often have, provides them with difficult dilemmas, and from those dilemmas, the temptation arises to be less reliable than we appear. According to Kaptein[1], there are three types of dilemmas, which below have been related to projects:

- *Dirty hands*: the interests of the stakeholders are opposite to the interests of the project.
- *Many hands*: line managers, project managers and staff involved in the project, have opposite interests and visions.
- *Intertwined hands*: the personal interest of a stakeholder can be the opposite of the project interest.

Generally, people will act according to the interests that weigh the most heavily for that

---
1 (2002) *De integere manager – Over de top, dilemma's en de diamant,* Kaptein – KONINKLIJKE VAN GORCUM

person at a certain time. What does this then mean for us as project managers?

Insight into the other person's interests and dilemmas allows us to prevent our staff being placed in situations that pose impossible dilemmas to them.

> EXAMPLE 33-1 ONE YEAR AGO
> The project had a fixed deadline to meet, and it was touch and go whether or not this would be achieved. One of the employees wanted a day off (exactly one year ago his child died). The project manager (who was not aware of the tragic background for the request) refused to give the employee a day off.
>
> The next day the employee reported in sick, and out of ill-will he did not come to work for some time.
>
> Unreliable or not?

4. Be respectful, honest and open

Respect is the ability to recognise the intrinsic qualities in others, and to understand their standpoints. It also is the ability to communicate with them, and to be open to their opinions, value judgments and ethical standards.

> EXAMPLE 33-2 CLOSING THE DOOR
> The employees repeatedly told the project manager that the current date was not achievable. However, he had no other options, and stated that this date was non- negotiable.
>
> As they were not listened to anyway, they stopped reporting approaching problems.

This step elaborates on what has been previously addressed about dilemmas. It is impossible to have respect, if you do not understand the dilemmas people face.

Respect requires a basic attitude, whereby we are able to separate the person from his actions. You could speak of an unconditional acceptance of someone as a person. This does not mean that you always have to agree with him, and this is not easy. Try, for example, to have respect for a suicide terrorist. That is difficult when you do not share his political motive, whereas his own people will honour him as a hero.

In any case, respect is the basis for creating an atmosphere of honesty and openness, both of which are essential in the project team in order, as project manager, to be reliable in your own reports to the project sponsor(s).

5. Engage stakeholders

All stakeholders must co-operate in creating the best solutions for the project. Only when everybody joins in, can you talk of a reliable project organization. A chain is as strong as its weakest link, and the reliability therefore, extends over the whole of the project organization.

6. Mitigate and clarify

There are projects where reliability is an important theme e.g. projects having a commercial interest, whereby it is undesirable that certain matters become known. Also projects, which solve certain problems in the organization, must also not become common knowledge.

Obviously, these sorts of risks have already been addressed during the project set-up. Tight agreement must then be made with the employees, with respect to the secrecy expected of them. This ensures that from the start of the project, they know which matters they can, and which matters they cannot, make common knowledge.

7. Reach agreement

For an important part, the ICB sees reliability also as delivering what has been agreed on time, and the latter is what this process step is all about. Otherwise, how will you be able to deliver, if it has not been clearly agreed what will be delivered at a certain time. It is,

2.13 Reliability

therefore, necessary for you to have agreement on the essence of the project.

8. Work systematically
Carrying out the work systematically and structurally is possibly one of the best guarantees that you will actually deliver what has been promised. The scope is defined and structured in the WBS, there is a tight planning, and the critical path is known. Periodically, you check whether everything is going according to plan, you report on this, there are no surprises, and you deliver what you have promised.

9. Apply lessons learned
Reliable people are not afraid to face what, according to the plan, they have not done.

2.14 Values appreciation

If you respect me, then I matter

As boundaries are diminishing,
we've to stretch our own.

2.14 Values Appreciation

2.14-1 DEFINITIONS

Values appreciation	The ability to recognise the intrinsic qualities in others, and to understand their point of view. It is also the ability to communicate with them and be open for their opinions, value judgments and ethical standards.

2.14-2 INTRODUCTION

Respect and empathy go together. Respect without empathy becomes a collection of rules and clear boundaries of what is, and what is not, allowed. If, next to empathy, I do not have respect, then I lack the skill to protect my own values and standards, and I blend in with the other person, so losing my own identity.

Because that is, of course what it is about; the need of respect for my values. If someone takes that from me, life becomes unbearable.

Why, when the honour of his family has been tarnished, would a father kill his daughter? Does he not love his daughter? Of course he does, with all that is in him, but the core of his identity has been harmed, and that is unbearable for him.

I, as a westerner, cannot accept this, because one of the core values of my identity is "the individuality". Even if my children do something which tarnishes the family honour, I shall have to carry this shame myself.

Who is right? What is the truth?

That truth, according to my convictions, does not exist. The lack of it is ultimately one of the attainments of that so much praised Enlightenment in the western world, which according to some of the so-called enlightened souls, all people have to experience. That to me seems to be in contradiction to the Enlightenment.

Better for me is to postpone my judgment until the final one is at hand.

2.14 Values Appreciation

2.14-3 Process steps

1. Communicate your values.
2. Look after values, opinions, ethics and interests.
3. Comply with the values.
4. Include values in discussion.
5. Amend viewpoints.
6. Respect and value others.
7. React quickly to changes.
8. Apply lessons learned

1. Communicate your values

Respect and empathy begin with clearly communicating your own values. You have to make a distinction here between values and norms. Values are things we find important, such as: love, honour, equality, independence, etc. These are characteristics our lives have to satisfy.

In order to protect the values, we develop norms, which are specific codes of conduct. It is prohibited to kill someone, because we want to protect the value of life. The current legislation on abortion and euthanasia in some western countries, and the discussion which sometimes flares up on these subjects, has to do with the conflict between the values *power of decision,* and the *sanctity of life.*

Legislation is a norm, and norms are always compromises which, often subconsciously, have been made in a group.

Norms are what is visible of the underlying values. Norms are only useful in a group, because they have to protect the values of the group members, and without a group, that is not necessary. Organizations are large groups, and, therefore, they have their norms, which have grown over the period of existence of the organization. In the project environment, where we actually always work together under a certain time pressure, there is insufficient time for the team to let the group standards evolve naturally from the underlying values. Clashes are then inevitable, and the project manager has an important part to play in these situations.

This brings us back to the first sentence of this narrative: *Respect and empathy begin with clearly communicating your own values.*

When you are dealing with many different values, which may lead to conflicting norms (codes of conduct), you need to spend more time in managing this area. You provide the example by laying your own values on the table, and remember not norms but values! It is then clear what you stand for, and you open the discussion on this and the respect for it.

2. Look after values, opinions, ethics and interests

As there is not enough time to let norms develop naturally in the project team, you, as project manager, have the responsibility to look after these matters. As well as the values, there are also opinions, ethics and interests.

Values

You need some knowledge of your employees; their background and what is valuable to them. You try to find out what they think about certain issues, and stimulate the defence of these values. Every team member is ultimately responsible for protecting his own values, but each one has to be given room to do that.

In order to be able to function successfully in a multi-cultural team, all team members have to be aware of the fact that there are different values, and that there is no one Truth, but there are various truths.

Looking after values does not mean that we have to, or another person has to, adapt other values than our (his) own. That is not even possible, because we have no absolute frame of reference we can check against, so adapting is what you do to the norms. What it does mean is that an open discussion must be held about this subject, indicating that we accept the difference, and respect the other person unconditionally, but need to discuss the required norms.

Opinions

There are opinions on values and norms, and everyone must be allowed to have his opinion. Whether he vents it or not, has nothing to do with the question of to what extent this is useful and contributes to the project result; it is about looking for a balance.

Ethics

Ethics is the philosophy of acting properly. But because there is no Truth, at least not in a group of people with different philosophies on life, it is impossible to define a right way of acting. Let's just keep to the project results, because that is what we are striving for, and is, therefore, the interest we all have together.

Interests

When interests are key, we almost automatically stay in the safety zone, because it is the interests that have brought us together as a team. All these interests may be different, but it is a fact that the project result apparently offers enough common ground to remain in the team.

3. Comply with the values

The values of the society, in which the project is carried out, are leading. Further on in the text, I have listed a number of different customs in the business sector for a number of countries, and these are the sorts of things that are meant here. Matters that are common practice in business transactions, including topics such as: the way in which visiting cards are handed out, how presents or gifts are given, how invitations are dealt with and suchlike.

They are norms which are customs, and with which you can quickly turn people against you, if you do not take account of them.

4. Discuss about values

In a multi-cultural team, values (and norms) play a strong role, and for this reason, you bring them into the discussion, when they are jeopardizing the project progress in one way or another. You have to realize that values are very hard to change, as at a very early stage, they have already become ingrained in our conditioning pattern, but just the recognition that they play a role, is sufficient.

5. Amend viewpoints

This knowledge can help us to change viewpoints, without having to change the underlying value. As project manager, you have to keep pointing to the project result and the extent to which a certain viewpoint contributes to that.

6. Respect and value others

Appreciation is the verbal expression of the respect we have for someone and we should really visibly show our appreciation of the uniqueness of certain values. By voicing this appreciation, we motivate the employee concerned at an existential level, his identity. Actually, we then confirm the uniqueness of his being, which will make him feel wanted and appreciated. As project manager you have a responsibility in this.

7. React quickly to changes

Changes can take place not only in the project, but also in the environment. In the beginning of the 21st century, values and

2.14 Values Appreciation

norms have become explosive stuff, and if it is ignited, it may endanger the progress on your project. This, therefore, requires a certain level of alertness. It says react quickly, but I doubt whether a quick intervention will always be the right action.

Observe what is going on, and assess whether or not the employees in your team will be able to resolve issues themselves. If that is the case, it is better not to intervene, but you should train your team in making potential conflicts regarding value discussable.

8. Apply lessons learned
Learning from each others values and norms is motivating and stimulating. It deepens your own development and life experience, and through the confrontations, deep bonds develop between the team members. The multicultural solutions we discover, and share with the rest of the team, are valuable learning experiences.

2.14-4 SPECIAL TOPICS

1. Building a relationship

By consciously building on a good relationship with your project employees, you can motivate them to deliver the required results within the agreed time. Such a relationship has the biggest chance of success, if it is one which improves their personal development. We are now moving more in the direction of coaching leadership, where you get the best out of them, including the underlying cultural values.

In his essay "*Some hypotheses on advancing personal growth*", Carl Rogers[1] addresses the three principle constituents of such a relationship.

- *Authenticity*, the ability to be yourself.
- *Acceptance*, take the other for who he is.
- *Empathy*, being able to empathise with another person.

Even though Rogers mainly attributed these three characteristics to successful counsellors, they would also be fitting for project managers.

Authentic project managers are aware of their own feelings, and are prepared to show these feelings to their employees. They do not play manager, but they are the manager, with all their doubts and beliefs. These types of leaders are perceived as being real.

Authenticity has everything to do with consistency between word and deed. When the project sponsor asks about progress, he gets a realistic answer on the status. An authentic project manager will also not keep to a date that, deep in his heart, he knows is unachievable.

In the de *Project Management Institute's Ethical Standards,* the following text has been included:

Members will provide customers, clients, and employers with fair, honest, complete and accurate information concerning:
(a) their qualifications;
(b) their professional services; and
(c) the preparation of estimates concerning costs, services, and expected results.

Authenticity and integrity go together hand in glove; they create an atmosphere of mutual trust.

The *second principle* is accepting the other person as he is, which is what, as project manager, you do with the team members. You give him the opportunity to live through the project as he experiences it, and he will enjoy the room he has to live up to his personal values. This makes him feel stronger and experience the project as a warm environment in which, also if things are difficult, he can work with pleasure. Trust in you as leader grows, and you create a team that, of its own accord, will go through hell for you.

Acceptance is something different than approval. When someone botches up a task, from your authenticity, you call him to account, but you leave him free in the way in which he emotionally deals with the bad news talk. The person and the matter are separated. His work may be below par, but as person he is certainly not.

The *third principle* has to do with empathizing with the employee. Sensing how the other person is feeling and visibly show that, so that the employee feels understood. Exhibiting empathy by summarizing in your own

---

[1] (1961), *On becoming a person, a therapist's view on psychotherapy,* Carl Rogers, HOUGHTIN MIFFLIN, Boston

2.14 Values Appreciation

words what you have heard the other person say, by showing that you listen and pay attention, and by naming difficult subjects.

2. Ethics and Cultural dimensions

What is acceptable in one culture is not acceptable in another culture, and so with ethics you must always look at the cultural dimension. There are various models which describe this culture, and one of the best known is Hofstede's[2] five dimension model:

- Power distance
- Individualism
- Masculinity
- Avoidance of uncertainty
- Long/short term orientation

Hofstede, a Dutch organizational psychologist, has derived his cultural model from research IBM carried out under its personnel in the 1960's, which provided a clear insight into cultural differences. It is because of cultural differences that what is unacceptable in some societies, is very normal in other societies. In northern European countries it is not advisable, nor desirable, to favour friends and family for a certain function, but in a collective society, this is a matter of course.

1. Power distance

The relative recognition of social equality and hierarchy: the higher the score, the more distance people experience from those in power. Countries in Latin America and the Arab countries score highly on this, meaning that employees experience a big distance between themselves and their manager. Countries such as the United States, the United Kingdom and, for example, Austria have a low score. In these countries, a manager has to explain a lot more of his decisions to his employees.

---

2 (2005) *Allemaal andersdenkenden,* Hofstede en Hofstede, UITGEVERIJ CONTACT, Amsterdam

2. Individualism

Everyone is expected to look after themselves, whereas with collectivism, from birth an individual is included in a large group, which will protect him for the rest of his life in exchange for his unconditional loyalty. The level of individualism is high in the United States and low in Japan. A Japanese top manager who, because he has to fire so many people, apologizes in tears, is an example of this collectivism.

3. Masculinity

The level of masculinity or femininity indicates to what extent the society values traditional male and female qualities. Male values include competitiveness, assertiveness, ambition and amassing wealth and luxury, and opposing these are the female values of modest behavior, servitude and solidarity. Note that in a masculine society, women will also be more masculine than in feminine societies. As project manager in a masculine society, you have to take up a strong position, whereas in a more feminine society a more coaching role is expected from you.

4. Avoidance of uncertainty

The extent to which uncertainty is protected by rules, formal procedures and rituals. The higher the score, the more calculating people act when doing business internationally. Mediterranean countries and Japan score highly here, and the United States and the United Kingdom have a low score. In a country such as Greece, which has the highest score, drawing up a contract will take a lot more time and effort than in a country with a low score.

5. Long or short term thinking

This dimension did not come out of the original IBM research, and has been added later by Hofstede. In this dimension, the (Eastern) perseverance in the development and application of innovation is matched against the

(Western) pressure for truth and immediate results. This cultural dimension also explains why a concept such as Kaizen has been developed in Japan (4th on the list), because this requires a much more long term vision than the fast Western innovations.

Countries such as Nigeria (16) or Pakistan (0) score extremely low, compared to China (118), which has the highest score.

3. Customs

Customs vary from country to country. In the tables following, for a number of countries, I have compared some customs[3] with each other on the next pages.

---

[3] Source: www.evd.nl and www.executiveplanet.com

2.14 Values Appreciation

Netherlands & Oman

Custom	Oman	Netherlands
Exchange visiting cards	Business cards are essential in Omani business culture. They should be presented at the start of the meeting. Study it for a short while before putting it away or in front of you on the table.	It is usual to hand over a visiting card the first time you meet a business partner. There are no real guidelines for the layout, as this is dependent on the company standards and guidelines.
Presents	Gifts are highly appreciated, especially something from your own country. The gift should be according to status, e.g. you cannot give the same pencil to both manager and his assistant. It is impolite to refuse a gift.	Promotional gifts are usually given around Christmas time. These are usually small gifts. Over the past few years there is a trend towards employees no longer being allowed to accept these in order to prevent any semblance of bribery.
When someone invites you	Omanis desire to build personal relationships and establish trust with potential business partners before entering into business. They may invite you to their home at night. When invited, always accept and show your gratitude by bringing a gift. Be prepared to meet unexpected guests and enjoy your time in getting acquainted with them.	Dutch people will seldom invite you to their home, as there is a strict dividing line between business and private life. If they do offer a business partner an invitation, then it is usually to a restaurant for lunch or dinner, or to a big event, such as a football match.
Speed with which business is carried out	In Oman people have fluid agendas. So make sure to confirm your meeting the day before. Although visitors are expected to arrive on time, don't get upset when your counterpart is arriving late. The meeting will start with coffee or tea and small talk which may last quite a while. In Oman it is important to build a positive atmosphere before plunging into business.	Dutch people are fast and to the point, and move almost immediately on to the order of the day. They spend little time on making someone's acquaintance.
Company culture	There's a strong vertical hierarchy. Decisions are made top-down. Status within the company is related to relationship with CEO, tribal background, status of the family in society, educational background and job title. If first names are used, it is mostly preceded by Mr, Mrs or Dr. Expect to be addressed likewise, e.g. "Dr. John".	The distance between a manager and an employee is very small. Managers are usually addressed by their first name, and managers will normally discuss important decisions with their employees. Dutch people are averse to all forms of status.

2.14 Values Appreciation

China & Belgium

Custom	China	Belgium
Exchange visiting cards	After the greeting, visiting cards are exchanged immediately. The cards must be presented with both hands. During the meeting the cards stay on the table. You show a lack of respect if you put them away without looking at them properly. An important sounding title helps increasing the speed of the negotiations.	About 60 percent of the Belgium population speaks Dutch (Flemish). The rest speak French (Walloons). Language problems can play a role, not only when entering into a contract, but also for instance with offers, labels and advertisements. Adapt your documentation and possibly also visiting cards to cater for this.
Presents	Previously, it was normal to give presents. Nowadays it is no longer permitted, and a present is considered as an attempt at bribery.	It is not customary in Belgium to give presents, or to receive them.
When someone invites you	In China you have to take account of copious banquets and dinners, with which a lot of local alcoholic drinks are consumed. Shaking hands, something imported from the West, is a generally accepted greeting, although the Chinese shake the hand more lightly and keep hold of it longer than in the West.	It is important to display the necessary modesty and reservedness when making contact with Belgians.
Speed with which business is carried out	The bond of friendship is important for a Chinese person. Building up such a business relationship takes time. The success is partly dependent on the preparation. Doing business is a question of patience and persistence. In order to Carry out business successfully, the Chinese business partner wants an offer of something concrete and you have to be very clear in this. They are known as being hard negotiators, and it can take months or even years before a contract is concluded.	In negotiations, it is important to know who your discussion partner is. The person with whom you talk, is not necessarily the person who makes the decisions. Do not expect that at the end of the discussion, a final decision is made, because normally further time to think is necessary. Belgium is a 'contact country', for Belgians trust is a condition of doing business.
Company culture	Of old, China is bureaucratic. The philosophy of Confucius had and still has a significant influence on the social order and structures in China. Confucius emphasized obedience and respect for the authorities and government. Great value is still attached to the social ranking order.	The relationship between a Belgian employer and an employee formal.

2.14 Values Appreciation

USA & Germany

Custom	USA	Germany
Exchange of visiting cards	Use the smaller format American visiting cards and pay sufficient attention to the layout and titles. It is normal to use business titles, but it is not recommended to use "foreign" titles on the visiting card. Except for Ph.D., University titles are normally not used. Generally initials are used on the card, rather than first name(s).	Although the complete first names are generally used on German visiting cards, this does not mean that German business relations should be called by their first name. In discussions, the surname is always preceded by 'Herr' or 'Frau'. When someone has a title ('Doktor' or 'Professor'), this should be used before the surname ('Herr Doktor…'). Always leave your visiting card behind, even if the person you want to speak to is not available.
Presents	Although a present is a nice gesture, it is not expected. When offered, it is not wrapped, and is in sight of everyone present. The best presents are ones that come from your own country.	Small presents for a first contact. Make sure they are not too expensive, as your intention may be misinterpreted, particularly if you do this in private.
When someone invites you	If you are invited by a business contact to his home, then it is customary to take a small gift or trinket, and to send a short thank-you letter the next day.	The agreed time should be kept to punctually.
Speed with which business is carried out	The fast and smooth way of doing business verbally, and the personal contact can be misleading. Due to the relaxed and jovial behavior of an American partner, foreign business people sometimes overlook the fact that the American counterpart, from a business perspective, remains level-headed and will always try to gain an advantage. The 'easy going' partner is extremely formal when it comes to elaborating on commitments in contracts.	Contract negotiations can often take a long time in Germany. All factors must be defined and specified in detail. Germans work on the basis of well thought out plans and according to strict policies. They take decisions on the basis of hard facts; a prospectus is only convincing when it is accompanied by figures, product analyses, results of market surveys and other research.
Company culture	Small and medium-sized companies have a flat organization structure, whereas for large companies this is not the case. Individual initiatives are appreciated, but the manager or senior manager makes the decisions and takes the responsibility. Employees are valued for their specialities. Responsibilities are strictly defined and tasks clearly described. Americans often work long days during the week and reserve the Friday evening and the weekend for family and leisure activities.	A German company is strongly hierarchical with clearly defined responsibilities. Each has his own area which is prohibited to other people. In the same way, others are left alone in their own territory. Because of the strong hierarchy, you have to enter in at the right i.e. corresponding level.

2.14 Values Appreciation

Morocco & Poland

Custom	Morocco	Poland
Exchange of visiting cards	Visiting cards should preferably be made up in the French language. English language letters and documents are normally not reacted to.	Visiting cards are used a lot. Preferably printed on both sides in Polish and English or Polish and German. Make sure you are first to hand over your card.
Presents	Giving a small present or gift, such as chocolate or a typical souvenir from the country itself, can assist with building up a relationship. Never offer alcoholic drinks. With business contacts, promotional gifts are often not unpacked in the presence of the giver.	You give presents at the beginning of a relationship during the first meeting, and at the end of collaboration. The best presents are ones that typify your own culture.
When someone invites you	It is a good custom at a meeting to shake the hand of everyone present, also the youngest employee. Moroccans are well-known for their hospitality and will quickly move on to inviting you to their home.	When you enter the meeting room, wait until the host indicates your place. If you do not know the people, then wait until someone else introduces the attendees. When someone invites you to his home, it is customary to give a small token, such as a bottle of wine or bunch of flowers. Afterwards, send a short handwritten thank-you letter.
Speed with which business is carried out	Business is arrived at, only once a relationship of trust has been built up. In general patience is a virtue when doing business in Morocco. Ample time should be allowed for appointments. It is advisable to confirm appointments a short time beforehand. Business is usually carried out in the office, and less so during a lunch or a dinner.	Polish negotiators are reserved and patient. Periods of silence during a negotiation are not abnormal. Remain conscious of not filling these silences with unnecessary talking.
Company culture	The Moroccan business culture is typified by a mix or Arabian and Mediterranean influences.	The etiquette is reasonably formal. The feeling for hierarchical relationships is fairly strongly developed, and it is advisable to take account of this in business contacts.

2.14 Values Appreciation

2.15 Ethics

MORE CATHOLIC THAN THE POPE

Hypothesis 1:

Man is good and tends towards evil.

Hypothesis 2:

Man is evil and tends towards good.

Final Conclusion:

Man is as you want to see him. In both situations he contains something good.

2.15 Ethics

2.15-1 DEFINITIONS

| Ethics | Acting properly with respect to other people, animals and nature. |

2.15-2 Introduction

Ethics is the philosophy of acting properly. But what is acting properly? Perhaps, as it is so difficult to answer this question, it is, therefore, a philosophy. There are a few things we can say about it.

Ethics relates to the following three value domains:

- People
- Profit
- Planet

Ethics is about having a proper relationship with our employees, about our selection procedures, the daily management, the rewards they get, the way in which we assess them, the working conditions, and so I could go on with a number of other points. If we translate this into a project environment, then you are faced with issues such as: working overtime to achieve deadlines, playing political games, the extent to which you have to take account of the personal interests of your employees, etc. Ethics is concerned with all human aspects; it is the people that ultimately make a project successful, and ethics is, therefore, an essential part of projects. How far, or how much further, are you prepared to go?

It is also concerned with how we deal with money, what costs we make, and how we forecast and calculate profits. So why, when we talk about accounting, do a lot of employees snigger and sneeringly refer to the term "creative accounting". Apparently, there are many ethical challenges here, both inside and outside the project. What about polishing up a progress report, or giving gifts to a prospective customer? Ethical dilemmas you may have to deal with as project manager.

It makes me think of an administrative employee who told me the following story: *"I was responsible for signing the time sheets. One of the employees declared more hours than he was actually present. I took it up with my immediate manager, who told me not to complain, as it would only disrupt the atmosphere in the department."*

At a much higher level it has to do with the way in which we treat the planet, as we also have a responsibility there. Ethics is about care for the environment. You do not have to become an environmental activist, but of course it is not the idea that your project leaves a mess behind. Ethics is relevant in projects which, during and/or after delivery, have an impact on the environment.

2.15 Ethics

Classically with projects, we are talking about the triple-constraint, whereby we talk of the trade-off between time, cost and the quality of the result. From an ethical point of view that is not enough, a second triple-constraint can be added to that: people, profit and planet.

How ethical are we really? Are we then not more catholic than the Pope, because talking about ethics soon results in fundamental codes of conduct which nobody can adhere to. When acting ethically itself becomes unethical, we really have a problem.

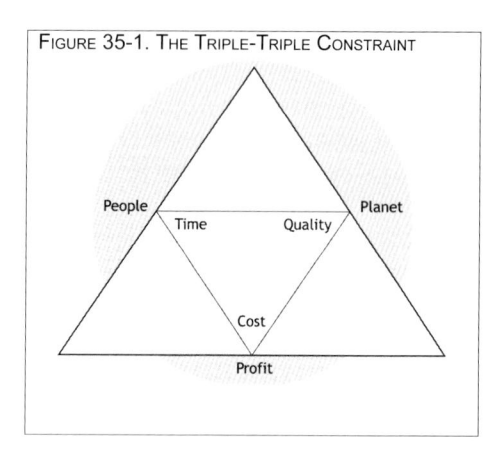

FIGURE 35-1. THE TRIPLE-TRIPLE CONSTRAINT

2.15-3 Process steps

1. Ensure conformity.
2. Address ethical issues.
3. Involve interested parties.
4. Be explicit.
5. Escalate when needed.
6. Deal with the consequences.
7. Apply necessary actions.
8. Apply lessons learned.

1. Ensure conformity

If ethics is about acting properly, it immediately raises the question: *What is properly? And does that mean properly, always and everywhere?*

Even though you define and scope a project, it is not an island. There is a project environment consisting of suppliers and customers, there are several departments and organizations involved, and there are cultures that rub up against one another. Somewhere in that tangle you have to go looking for a framework.

When something is a given with respect to what a group sees as appropriate behavior, for instance in the form of a code of conduct, then that is a starting point from which we can base our further actions. Obviously, there are also laws which may legally define the possible choices. In addition, there are the standards that the organization has imposed on itself, or which have come into existence subconsciously, and which have an influence on your project. For this you need yet another competence element that has to do with values appreciation, in order to recognise these unspoken standards.

As project manager you are obviously also faced with the codes of conduct of the various project management associations and bodies. At the start, a project manager has to establish to what extent this already applies to a project, and he must ensure that from the very beginning of the project everything is clear to everyone. Employees may also be subject to their own professional code of conduct.

2. Address ethical issues

Ethics is always concerned with values and norms, usually mentioned in one breath.

They have to do with what we, as individuals or as a group, find important (values) and how we want to protect this (norms). They have to do with our background and our personal development. It looks as if many of the values we have are innate, and form part of our "cultural package of genes". Another part we learn from our environment, how our parents raised us, how the culture we live in values certain issues, or disapproves of them. All of this taken together determines the development and the preservation of our package of values and norms.

Some values are universal. Most people agree that you should not kill someone, and in most religions you find the commandment "*Thou shalt not kill*" in one form or another. Other values, however, are not universal, for example bribing someone, or as a manager in the Third World told me "*this is an act of gratitude*", a token of appreciation for the police who co-operated. Even though, in most literature you will read that this is not allowed, it is questionable whether or not such a purist attitude works and this is where ethical dilemmas come to the surface and create a problem.

The values may differ per culture. In many western countries individuality is an important value, and many of the norms that developed there have the value of protecting the right of self-determination of the individual. In the Arab World, collectivism is an important value, and we see completely dif-

2.15 Ethics

ferent norms develop. You will not find problems with waiting lists for care homes there, because there you take your elderly or sick mother or father into your own house to look after. In the West, the privacy of the child is often more important than the collectivism of the family, and mother or father is put into a care home.

It is good to realize that norms protect underlying values, and that is the reason discussions about the "proper" norms are often very emotional. Standards say what is *right* or *wrong* for a person or a group, and one of the pitfalls is to put your norm above that of another. This is an understandable pitfall, as your norm protects an underlying value that is very important to you, and which is being challenged by someone else's conflicting norm.

But how do you deal with that? At least discuss the differences, without expressing a judgment.

The big problem with ethical dilemmas is that there isn't really a right or wrong, but often you still have to make a choice. Philosophers through the ages have racked their brains over this, and one of the best known is Immanuel Kant's[1] (1724-1804) *categorical imperative*, which can be formulated in two ways:
- Act in such a way that it could serve as a universal law.
- Don't just look at people as a means, but also as a purpose.

Even though "purists" may have some reservations about this, it gives the project manager a useful handle for solving ethical issues within the project. The *categorical imperative* is especially useful when there is no legal or regulatory framework, as it provides direction for finding a solution for those issues where it is not yet clear what to do.

3. Involve interested parties

As you have to deal which a rich mix of interested parties in a project, it is essential to involve them in an ethical dilemma. During the introduction, I already made a reference to the three value domains you have to protect: people, profit and planet. You discuss the effect on these domains with the interested parties, bearing in mind that you need to find the optimum balance between the size of the group, and how fast you have to "resolve" a certain dilemma.

Furthermore, within the framework of the project, you obviously also have to deal with the scope, quality of the deliverables, duration and costs to be incurred. In a certain way, you can interpret these as norms within which you, as project manager, have to realize the project. The business case is then the value that has to be achieved with the project.

Together you determine whether or not the circle of interested parties is large enough. The problem with a circle that is too small is that it can be oblivious to its own actions, and the problem with of a circle which is too large, is that as everyone wants to have his say on the matter and the ethical problem becomes bigger than it actually is.

By involving interested parties in this way, you consider people both as a means for finding a compromise, and as a purpose, by listening to their vision and the values they wish to protect. It now is about interests, and not about positions.

4. Be explicit

As project manager you have to do with the values and norms that apply to the project, and to you personally. The values and

---

[1] (1785) *Grundlegung zur Metaphysik der Sitten*, Immanuel Kant

norms for the project have been explained in the previous three steps. As project manager, you are one of the guardians of the required ethical standards, and you have to call people to account with regard to their behavior, when certain norms (of others) are being violated.

For personal values and norms, it is more difficult, because there isn't such a thing as a superior set of values and norms. It is, however, a requisite for your own conscience that you are clear in what you as a professional and as a human being stand for. When the behavior of people involved is related to certain ethical aspects, you have to call them to account in whatever way you can. The objective must be that people involved can function within the project, as far as possible without moral conflicts. If there are regulations, you have to ensure that you, and your team members, do not avoid them by using any form of ingenuity or slyness. Later in this chapter, we shall go deeper into a number of codes of conduct for project managers.

Due to the sensitivity of nobody wanting to be known as being unethical, you have to handle this carefully and dynamically. Calling someone to account due to unethical behavior is difficult and it is best to clearly state to what extent the problem affects you personally, and what you want to see change. Together, you discuss how this improvement will be effected, and you agree on how you will measure the progress.

5. Escalate when needed
Initially, confronting someone about unethical behavior is done on a one-to-one basis. If that doesn't work, especially when the unethical behavior has developed into a group norm, you have to escalate the situation into the group.

Usually, people quickly conform to the existing group norms. A classic is the experiment of Asch[2] in which a test subject, together with the scientist's accomplices, was shown three lines, one of which had a different length. The accomplices claimed that the length of the three lines were the same. Of the test subjects, one-third went along with the wrong group judgment.

Another investigation by Allen[3] names the following circumstances as increasing the tendency to conform:
- Group members are acquaintances of each other.
- If people are attracted to the group.
- In the case of difficult or unclear tasks.
- The absence of supporters.

Festinger[4] determined the mechanism that this pressure from the group to conform decreases in situations where the group member does not change his deviating opinion, and changes to the group ignoring the person concerned. This illustrates that it is difficult not to give in to the pressure of your colleagues.

When you apply the outcome of this various research to unethical behavior within a team, it is not difficult to imagine how complicated the matter is. Before you know it, you are out, and it is, therefore, very important during the development of the team, to pay sufficient attention to ethical behavior, and to act immediately when the team, or an individual team member, looks to be heading in the wrong direction. If you find yourself in

---

2 (1951) *Effects of group pressure upon the modification and distortion of judgments, S.E.* Asch in Groups, leadership, and Men, Pitsburg, Pa, CARNEGIE PRESS
3 (1975) *Social support for non-conformity,* V.L. Allen in Advances in experimental social psychology (Vol 8.), NEW YORK, Academic Press
4 (1950) *Informal social communication,* L. Festinger in Psychological Review 57

a group culture that already exists, then in view of the above, it is a lot more difficult. Escalating then no longer works, and you maybe have to go a level higher.

If your own management is not receptive to this escalation, you have to consider taking on the role of whistle-blower. It is clear that such a role is even more difficult than the previous one. Whistle blowing in itself is an ethical dilemma, in which you consider the loyalty to the organization against your own (professional) conscience.

When can you whistle blow in a morally justifiable way? Wirtz[5] mentions the following considerations:
- There is a threat of serious damage to the environment.
- There is a clear indication that certain interests are being threatened.
- Do the interests that are harmed counterbalance the protected interests?
- All other means of internal whistle blowing have been tried.
- Your motives as whistle-blower are sound.

This requires courage.

6. Deal with the consequences

As opposed to the previous step, the first four process steps are preventive. They are concerned with preventing ethical dilemmas and contain measures to ensure that team members and other people involved experience as few ethical dilemmas as possible. When certain behavior has aggrieved others, it is your responsibility to address these consequences and where necessary inform the people involved and look for a fitting atonement. Honesty is the best policy and takes the longest time, but it is required.

Again, you look at the effects on the three named value domains: people, profits and planet.

With respect to the people
Consequences may occur in the working conditions of both the internal and hired in people, who are working on the project. As project manager you can address the first immediately, and with regard to the working conditions at your suppliers, you can enforce these during the selection process.

In addition, your project may have an impact on the local community. To what extent does the project execution and the ultimate result bring changes to their living conditions? Is this impact reasonable and fair?

With respect to profits
This is about an equitable distribution of costs and benefits. A well-known example is the cost benefit analysis of a minor adaptation ($11 per vehicle) to a car, which would make it a lot safer. The social cost of a death was estimated at $200,000, and of an injured person at $67,000. A cold calculation did not justify the minor adaptation, but it does not take a lot of effort to substantiate that this decision is unethical.

When looking at the costs and benefits, it is necessary that the apportionment here is also reasonable and fair.

With respect to the planet
Modern thinking concentrates on the long term effects. However, judging by the many environmental groups on the world stage, you may ask yourself the question whether thinking about the environment is actually put into effect in most of the projects we carry out.

---
5 (2006) Morele verantwoordelijkheid in organisaties, R. Wirtz in Bedrijfsethiek: een goede zaak, Assen, VAN GORCUM

The consideration of profit versus planet is one of the short term versus the long term. As conclusion, it is easy to say that you have to go for the long term option, but what do you do when you can also use the money for a less effective short term solution? Then you have a dilemma.

7. Apply necessary

Ethical actions must be both pro-active and reactive. As prevention is better than cure, it could be part of the risk analysis to determine whether or not the project can expect problems in this area. If that is the case, you can take measures in advance, which will ensure that employees and managers involved are not tempted into displaying unethical behavior.

In the unlikely event that unethical behavior does occur, you do what is described in the previous process steps on reversing the consequences.

8. Apply lessons learned

You learn from your mistakes, and it is important that you share that experience with others. You can, for example, put a supplier on the black list if he has offered you a bribe, or make suggestions to amend certain procedures in order to prevent unethical behavior.

2.15-4 Special topics

1. Declaration of Human Rights

The first process step talked of a framework within which we can test ethical issues. The treaty of Human Rights[6] is such a framework. It consists of the following articles

- All human beings are born free and equal and have the same rights.
- Everyone, without distinction of any kind, is entitled to these rights.
- Everyone has the right to life, liberty and security of his or her person.
- No one shall be held in slavery or servitude.
- No one shall be subjected to torture, or to cruel inhuman or degrading treatment or punishment.
- Everyone has the right to equal protection and recognition by the law.
- Everyone has the right to equal protection by the law.
- Everyone has the right to legal aid for acts violating the fundamental rights granted to him or her by the constitution.
- No one shall be subjected to arbitrary arrest, detention or exile.
- Everyone is entitled to a fair, public and impartial hearing.
- Everyone is presumed innocent until proved guilty.
- No one shall be subjected to arbitrary interference with his privacy.
- Everyone has the right to freedom of movement and to return to his country.
- Everyone has the right to asylum.
- Everyone has the right to a nationality (or to change his nationality), of which he cannot be deprived.
- Everyone has the right to marry.
- Everyone has the right to own property.
- Everyone has the right to freedom of thought, conscience and religion (and the freedom to change it).
- Everyone has the right to freedom of opinion and expression.
- Everyone has the right to freedom of assembly and association.
- Everyone has the right to take part in the government of his country.
- Everyone has the right to social security.
- Everyone has the right to work and free choice of employment.
- Everyone has the right to rest and leisure, and periodic holidays with pay.
- Everyone has the right to an adequate standard of living.
- Everyone has the right to education.
- Everyone has the right freely to participate in the cultural life of a community.
- Everyone is entitled to an international order, which maintains these rights.

Following on from the rights, there are two articles at the end of the declaration, which are concerned with the duties of human beings:

Article 29
Everyone has duties to the community, without which the free and full development of his personality is not possible.

In the exercising of his rights and freedom, everyone shall be subject only to such limitations as are determined by law solely for the purpose of securing due recognition and respect for the rights and freedoms of others and of meeting the just requirements of morality, public order and the general welfare in a democratic society.

These rights and freedoms may in no case be exercised contrary to the purpose and principles of the United Nations.

---

6 (1948) *The Universal Declaration of Human Rights,* UNITED NATIONS DEPARTMENT OF PUBLIC INFORMATION.

Article 30
Nothing in this Declaration may be interpreted as implying for any State, group or person, any right to engage in any activity or to perform any act aimed at the destruction of any of the rights and freedoms set forth herein.

With regard to these matters, it is clear that you may not deviate from them. Maybe you are asking yourself how this relates to project management. Well, if someone has a different opinion, is he allowed to voice this, or do you pressure him to follow the majority opinion? And what about freedom and safety? To what extent are employees able to exercise influence on their own functioning and is the environment he or she is working in, safe enough?

Universal accepted?
It should be mentioned that this declaration has been criticized by some Islamic countries for not taking into account the cultural and religious values of non-Western countries.

2. Cairo Declaration
In 1990, the Organization of the Islamic Conference adopted the Cairo Declaration of Human Rights in Islam[7] which represents the Islamic perspective on human rights and affirms Islamic Law (Sharia) as its sole source.

Apart from the strong religious component in this declaration another major difference is that next to rights, obligations are mentioned.

Article 1
Quote: *"All men are equal in terms of basic human dignity and basic obligations and responsibilities, without any discrimination on the grounds of race, colour, language, sex, religious belief, political affiliation, social status or other considerations."*

Rights
In general both declarations cover the same human rights. Extra are some explicit rights like:
- Both the fetus and the mother must be protected.
- Living in a clean environment, away from vice and moral corruption.
- Living in security for himself, ... , his honour, ...
- Privacy in the conduct of his private affairs.

Some obligations
In the following list I have summed up the main obligations:
- Protecting the (unborn) live.
- The husband is responsible for the support and welfare of his family.
- It is prohibited to force someone to convert to another religion or atheism.
- Supporting peoples in their struggle against colonialism.
- Information may not be used to violate sanctities and the dignity of Prophets.
- It is not permitted to arouse nationalistic or doctrinal hatred.

There is a special article (3) on the protection of nonbelligerents, the environment, livestock and civilian buildings during an armed conflict.

Article 23
Covers an interesting ethical issue on authority. Quote: *"Authority is a trust; and abuse or malicious exploitation thereof is absolutely prohibited, so that fundamental human rights may be guaranteed."*

---
[7] (1993) *The Cairo declaration on Human Rights in ISLAM*, THE ORGANIZATION OF THE ISLAMIC CONFERENCE

2.15 Ethics

This article can be a strong guideline for project managers when showing leadership.

3. Project Management Ethics

Project management associations often also have codes of conducts, which can help with resolving an ethical dilemma. We shall look at a few codes of conduct.

PMI

The largest project management association in the world is the *Project Management Institute*. The introduction of their Code of Ethics and Professional Conduct[8] reads:

> "As practitioners of project management, we are committed to doing what is right and honourable. We set high standards for ourselves and we aspire to meet these standards in all aspects of our lives—at work, at home, and in service to our profession."

The codes of conduct are now sub-divided into:
- Responsibility
- Respect
- Fairness
- Honesty

This code of conduct differentiates between what is worth striving for, but often difficult to obtain, and that what is absolutely compulsory.

IPMA

At the time of writing this book, the International Project Management Association does not yet have a code of conduct, but some of the affiliated members do. As the author comes from the Netherlands, we shall further discuss the IPMA Netherlands code of conduct.

The Code of Conduct[9] aims to provide clarity and insight in:

- The professional position and attitude of the members of IPMA-NL in society, as well as the standards the members, as project managers, have to abide by with respect to project sponsors and other parties involved.
- The way members treat and deal with one another.

As well as some general issues on enforcement, the codes of conduct have been grouped into the following categories:
- Independence
- Expertise
- Confidentiality

Some rules are just common sense, such as article 5 *"striving for constructive and collegial relationships"*. Others such as article 25 *"Does not replace a project member without consultation with his/her project sponsor and …"* are in many cases unworkable, and makes you wonder what the underlying reason must be for such an article. Without wanting to discredit the author of such a code, I sometimes get the feeling with these codes of "one judges others according to one's own standards."

4. Ethical dilemmas

An interesting case, which positions the consultancy agency in an ethical dilemma with respect to the "profits" domain. The consultancy agency could suggest to the freelancer that he stretches out his work to four days a week (which they actually did, thus transferring the dilemma to the freelancer) in order to achieve the planned margin in that way.

---

[8] *Code of Ethics and Professional Conduct,* THE PROJECT MANAGEMENT INSTITUTE

[9] (2005) *Projectcode IPMA Nederland*

2.15 Ethics

> EXAMPLE 35-1 SUBCONTRACTORS
>
> A consultancy agency is carrying out a large project for a certain public body. The project sponsorship leaves a lot to be desired. On the basis of actual costs incurred, a certain deployment and accompanying charge rate have been agreed for the employees hired in by the consultancy agency as sub-contractors. The consultancy agency has a margin of 25% on all the sub-contractors hired in.
>
> One of the sub-contractors, a freelancer, has been planned for four days a week, but only needs two days for his task and the consultancy agency, therefore, misses out on the margin for two days.

Let us apply Kant's *categorical imperative* to this. What does this mean when we make it a universal law? It has an impact on two of the three domains mentioned.

- *People*: it is an encouragement by the main contractor to work less fast, and make more costs than necessary. Put very bluntly, it is an invitation to practice fraud. If we were to make this universal, then all sub-contractors would be allowed to practice fraud. If everybody was to practice fraud, however, no-one could be trusted anymore, which is obviously not desirable.
- *Profits*: in the short term, the consultancy agency's profit will increase, but if sub-contractors were to take the same approach with their customers, the ultimate costs would increase, and the profits of the contractor would decrease, which is undesirable from this point of view.

Furthermore, the freelancer has been used as a means to make a lot of money, which is an unethical choice. The freelancer concerned could not work under these conditions, and terminated the assignment. There were no winners, just losers.

In the example above, a lot of money has been falsely charged by the organization involved. I suspect that this happens on a large scale, given the many government projects which either overrun their time, and/or overspend on their budget.

Kaptein[10] provides a number of tests we can use to test our actions:

- The *spectacles test*: what does the choice look like through the spectacles of each party involved?
- The *front page test*: if it reaches the press, what will the headlines in the papers look like?
- The *shoes test*: what would my biggest role models do in this situation?
- The *mirror test*: will I be able to look myself in the face following this action?
- The *slippery slope test*: if everybody would do it, would we all slide downhill?
- The *scales test*: will everyone profit from it equally, or is there a difference?

We shall will look at another example, and see how these six tests can be applied to that.

> EXAMPLE 35-2 BUILDING SITE
>
> The example takes place at the building site of a project in Nigeria. The question is, do we have to fire a construction worker because he ignores the safety regulations? If we fire him, he will probably not find new work. He has a family of six children, and looks after his parents who are ill.

A dilemma, and looking through the **spectacles** of the project manager, it is clear that the construction worker should be fired, as the rules are there for a reason. Looking through the spectacles of the construction

---

10 (2002) *De integere manager – Over de top, dilemma's en de diamant,* Kaptein – KONINKLIJKE VAN GORCUM

worker, or his family, you reach a different conclusion. With these six tests, it is now important to reserve your judgment until the end. After you have looked at it through the eyes of the different players involved, you do the next test.

How would this appear on the **front page**, either if you fire him, or if he has a fatal accident? What would the local newspapers write, and how would the other newspapers in the country report it? Let the thoughts that come up with these types of questions sink in, but do not yet make a choice. And what about firing? If that would appear on the headlines? What would that do to your reputation.

With the **shoe test**, we look at important role models from our own past or from history. What would Mahatma Ghandi have done, or what would my father do or have done? Let yourself be "advised" by these silent witnesses in making your final decision.

Ultimately you have to look at yourself. Could you still look at yourself in the **mirror** after all of these different choices? How well could you look yourself in the face if the building worker loses his job because of your intervention, or if he should fall to the ground and die.

What if everybody were to make that one particular choice? This test strongly corresponds with Kant's categorical imperative. But what if that puts us on a **slippery slope**? Where do we slide off to? Would the effect not be that other building workers would also ignore safety?

The last test is to weigh up the **costs and benefits**. Who will ultimately benefit most from it?

All these questions result in an intuitively correct feeling to make the decision. What would you do in the above case? I did this exercise with a dozen Nigerian project managers and they unanimously chose to fire the building worker.

3. Contextual Competences

3.01 Project orientation

MORE OR LESS DEFINED INCIDENTAL ACTIVITIES,
WHICH ARE RECOGNIZABLE BY A PROJECT NAME

There are projects
which are well managed.

There are projects
without a project manager.

There are project managers who do
not carry out project management.

There are line managers who
carry out project management.

There are jobs, which are
managed on a project basis.

In short a great field of expertise.

3.01-1 Definitions

Project	A totality of related activities in a temporary organization to deliver a pre-defined result, within specified conditions.
Project Management	The planning, organizing, monitoring and controlling of all aspects of a project and the management and leadership of all people involved to achieve the project objectives safely and within agreed criteria in the areas of time, costs, scope and performance/quality.
Project Orientation	The orientation of an organization to managing by projects and the development of project management competence.

3.01-2 INTRODUCTION

What is project orientation? Before answering this question, I will firstly explain what a *project* is and what *project management is*. Many authors have already made an attempt at doing this. The previous definition (from the ICB) is one, but there are more:

- A temporary undertaking to achieve a unique product, service or result[1].
- A totality of related activities carried out to achieve a pre-determined result, which has a start and end date, uses limited manpower, and is usually of a non-recurrent nature[2].
- A project is a management organization set up with the objective of delivering one or more business products based on a defined Business Case[3].

The first two definitions are the more traditional approaches: a *beginning*, an *end*, *unique* and limited resources. The third definition has become known over the last few decades, mainly under the influence of the PRINCE2 methodology. It is a more restricted definition than the previous one, because it talks of a '*company result*' and a '*business case*'.

There are also various definitions for project management. Here, we compare the definition from the ICB with the previously cited *PMBOK Guide*.

In the ICB we read that project management concerns all managerial tasks containing, and I quote: *"The planning, organizing, monitoring and controlling of all aspects of a project and the management and leadership of all people involved to achieve the project objectives safely and within agreed criteria in the areas of time, costs, scope and performance/quality."*

The *PMBOK Guide* is much shorter and talks of *"applying knowledge, skills, instruments and techniques to project activities in such a way that the requirements are met."*

This (Anglo-Saxon) definition leads to a much more instrumental approach than the management definition mentioned in the ICB (Rhenish). Neither of them is the only one that is right, and as far as I am concerned we do not have to make a choice, as it is all about what is needed to achieve a particular project result.

---

1 (2008) *PMBOK Guide: A guide to the PROJECT MANAGEMENT BODY OF KNOWLEDGE 4th edition,* the Project Management Institute, USA
2 (1996) *De weg naar Projectsucces,* Teun van Aken, ELSEVIER/TIJDSTROOM, Utrecht
3 (2005) *Managing Succesful Projects with PRINCE2,* the Office of Government Commerce

3.01 Project Orientation

Project orientation is now about a choice, and the willingness, of the management to carry out work in the form of projects, alongside other work in departments. This means a number of things:

- It is a conscious choice; people realize that the power is now divided over the projects and the line organization, with all the disadvantages this brings.
- The willingness means that a programme is now being implemented in which people consciously work on improving project management competence.

When an organization has a project orientation, you see this in the career paths in project management, supporting systems, project management office, etc.

3.01-3 PROCESS STEPS

1. Assess whether there is a need to carry out projects.
2. Culture and process analysis in relation to projects.
3. Make the business case for project management.
4. Implement project management.
5. Monitor progress and record learning experiences.

1. Assess whether there is a need to carry out projects

There are three ways we can organise work:
- Routines
- Improvisations
- Projects

Routines
Based on the business processes from which the organization has a right to exist, the senior management designs an organizational structure, consisting of departments which carry out repetitive work (the routines). Each year the senior management agrees what results (performance indicators) they want to achieve in the coming year. This is then delegated down, so that ultimately the employees on the 'work floor' achieve these objectives.

Improvisations
Routines are about predictable work, but in the daily reality this is difficult to plan, and things often do not go according to plan. Sometimes the management starts up an initiative, for which the existing departments are not equipped, and a team is then formed, which gets to work. Using improvisation, this team then designs on-the-flight the way in which the initiative is to be carried out.

Comparison: Routines; Improvisations and Projects
The following table provides a summary of the differences between these three.

Routines	Improvisations	Project
Aimed at efficiency	Less efficient but pragmatic.	Aimed at effectiveness.
Managed hierarchically.	Both are possible.	No hierarchic power present with the project manager.
Standard rules (sometimes rigid).	Flexible, few rules.	Rules, but geared to the project.
Circumstances and resources used are constant.	Just carry out each job.	Staged, balanced use of resources is difficult.
Tasks evenly spread over time.	As long as necessary.	Specific results within a time span.
Little preparation, the way of working has already been thought of.	Get to work immediately.	Think first, act later.
Example The service department follows the existing procedure to the letter. Treats customers with a very service oriented mentality.	**Example** Two service engineers are on location at an important customer, they are looking for the cause of the breakdowns in a particular machine.	**Example** On the 25th of February, a team of software developers hands over an implemented complaints system. A planning and budget was made in advance, which was approved by the management.

3.01 Project Orientation

Projects
For a large part, this is similar to improvisations, but also contains routine elements. Under the leadership of a project manager, a team of interested parties takes time to formulate a well thought out plan containing its objectives, the duration and budget for the required solution, which it submits to management for approval. Following approval, people work in a structured and systematic way on carrying out the plan, and thus achieving the agreed result. To a large extent, each project follows just such a (routine) approach.

Project orientation
Working in projects means that the organization incurs extra costs for the project manager and his team. To justify these costs, it has to be clear that the extra effort provides added value, otherwise it is better to carry out the work according to the fixed rules in the existing organization. Senior management, therefore, has to make a conscious choice.

When an organization carries out a lot of projects, there comes a time when there is a need for a standard working method, and career paths for employees who are good at project management. When senior management acknowledges this, and is prepared to invest in it, then **project orientation** exists within the organization.

2. Culture and process analysis in relation to projects
Before an organization chooses for a project orientation, it has to realize that this has a significant impact on the existing way of working, and that the methods it chooses have to fit in with the existing culture and processes.

Culture and project orientation
Research by Quinn and Cameron[1] recognizes two cultural dimensions:
- Flexibility and freedom of action *versus* stability and manageability.
- Internal orientation and integration *versus* external orientation and differentiation.

Four main cultural forms for organizations can be derived from these two dimensions:

Flexibility	Manageability	Internal orientation	External orientation	Main form
X		X		Family
X			X	Adhocracy
	X	X		Hierarchy
	X		X	Market

Main form	Management theory	Effectiveness criteria
Family	Participation, stimulates involvement and commitment.	Cohesion, moral and personal development.
Adhocracy	Open to innovation, stimulates tapping into new sources.	Producing the newest of the new, creativity and growth.

---
1 (1999) Diagnosing and Changing Organisational Culture, R.E.Quinn, K.S. Cameron, Addison Wesley

3.01 Project Orientation

Main form	Management theory	Effectiveness criteria
Hierarchy	Manageability, stimulates the efficiency.	Efficiency, timeliness and smooth functioning.
Market	Competition, stimulates the productivity.	Market share, achieve objectives and beating competitors.

The success of how you wish to shape the project orientation depends on the culture within the organization. The four forms of culture mentioned each require a different implementation. A project management methodology, which does not fit, will quickly lead to failure and disappointment.

Process analysis in relation to projects
We want to achieve clarity in a project orientation. The worst that can happen to you, is that after implementing a certain project management methodology, the lack of clarity has only increased. A methodology available in the market is all too easily "purchased", after which all project managers are sent on a training course, with the resultant conclusion that nothing further is needed. This is a big misconception; it is far better to firstly carry out an analysis of the existing processes, and to look where small changes can achieve big results. Taking account of the culture, these changes must then be in line with what is desirable and achievable.

3. Make the business case for project management

There are financial consequences attached to a project orientation, and the organization has to invest in:
- Selecting and training project managers.
- Adapting the function structure.
- Opting for, or developing, a project management method
- Amending existing processes and procedures.
- Communicating new processes to the line organization.
- Additional consultation as a result of the project control.

These costs must be balanced against the results the orientation will provide. These can be:
- Less work that overlaps.
- Clearer control being possible.
- More complex innovations being possible.
- Insight into the costs of ad hoc jobs.
- Etc.

When an organization only carries out a few projects per year, it is not very useful to do a large-scale roll-out of this orientation. Instead the project leader can be sent on a course, which is quite often sufficient. However, if the organization carries out dozens of projects or more, then it pays to think about this, and to investigate if there is a need for standardization. This is the case when there will also be a large number of projects in the future, because the expectation is that:
- The organization will have to be able to react more flexibly to market circumstances.
- The primary process will consist more and more of projects.

It then pays to start up a professionalization programme, ensuring it takes account of what I said in the previous process step about cultures and processes.

509

4. Implement project management

The following is normally carried out when implementing a project orientation:
- *Choice:* For a project management method and embedding. Often there are reasons to choose for a certain method, and this is especially so when the most important customers specify clear requirements for one.
- *Pilot:* Of the new operating method in a first project. This will show how it all turns out in practice.
- *Amendment of the method:* Based on the assessments of all parties involved. The input of the project sponsor, project manager, project controller and project members is important.
- *Setting up guidelines:* For the follow-up projects. These can now be finalized.
- *Organise assurance and support:* Having good intentions alone usually means that after a while, an organization falls back into the old way of organizing things, often with the original quality problems that formed the reason for doing something about it in the first place.
- *Application:* Whereby the intention is that all projects reap the rewards of the effort that is carried out only once.

5. Monitor progress and record learning experiences

The users of the new approach still have much to learn, and there is a high chance that the method and the changed processes have to be further amended in order to get them working. It is highly desirable, and advisable, not to begin immediately with this, but to first give the method a chance to find a prominent place in the minds of the employees. If we immediately begin to change things, there is a threat that the implementation, packaged as an improvement, will meet with significant resistance.

In addition, the company management must monitor this matter. Just blindly implementing a method and amending the processes is not sufficient. At certain specified times, the management must assess whether the chosen direction is still in line with the strategic objectives that they had in mind at the start.

Questions they then ask are:
- Has the approach solved the original problem?
- Do the amended processes work?
- Does this approach really fit in with our culture?
- Do the benefits outweigh the disadvantages?

If the answers are largely negative, this can be because of (the combination of) the following two factors:
- There is no culture fit.
- There is no synergy with the current processes.

The latter is easy to change, as you just have to change the processes, but the former is more difficult because it is much more difficult to change the culture.

3.01-4 SPECIAL TOPICS

1. The Project Management Office

When an organization carries out enough projects, there is a need for support of the projects in the areas of administration, professional development, standards, etc. This can justify the establishment of a Project Management Office.

In its simplest form, a project office supports project managers with drawing up plans, budgets and other administrative issues. In its most complex form, we see it as centre of expertise in the area of project management, and as a home base for all project managers within the organization. The manager of the office is a member of the organization's MT.

A project office can have one or more of the following functions[2]:

Management of the profession:
- Develop, implement and maintain the project management method.
- Select, develop and implement instruments.
- Develop and implement standard metrics.
- Knowledge management in the area of projects.

Maintaining the infrastructure:
- Setting up and maintaining project control.
- Assessing the effectiveness of the control.
- Facility management for projects.

Staff management:
- Recruitment, selection and deployment of project staff.
- Training and professional development.
- Career development for project staff.

- Development of the project office team.

Support:
- Providing professional support.
- Providing technical planning support.
- Carrying out project audits.

Business alignment:
- Project Portfolio Management.
- Management of customer relationships.
- Management of supplier relationships.
- Management of the business performances of the office.

2. Project management Methods

Introduction

A project management method[3] is a collection of guidelines or principles, which can be adapted to a specific situation. As an organization focuses on the professionalization of project management, the need arises for a standard approach, in which the experiences from the past are bundled, and in which agreements are made on a uniform approach. This makes reports comparable, and ensures a common language. You often see that large organizations develop their own method, which is sometimes based on methods available in the public domain. The most important methods currently available, are discussed in this section, and I have distinguished between the international and the Dutch methods.

International Methods

When you study the various project management methods, it is striking that there is a group, which strongly focus on how the project planning is established, such as:

---

2 (2004) *The Complete Project Management Office Handbook,* Gerard m. Hill, AUERBACH

3 (2003) *Project Management Methodologies: Selecting, Implementing, and Supporting Methodologies and Processes for Projects*, Jason Charvat, JOHN WILEY & SONS

3.01 Project Orientation

- Critical Path Project Management.
- Critical Chain Project Management.
- Event Chain Project Management.

And methods which are a lot broader, and which also include the control of projects in their approach, such as:
- PMBOK Guide.
- PRINCE2.
- Extreme/Agile Project Management.

CRITICAL PATH PROJECT MANAGEMENT
Just as in the following two methods, the emphasis is on estimating durations, and determining those activities which are critical for the total duration of the project. When the planner takes account of the uncertainty of the estimates, he uses the PERT technique. The durations are then a measured average of optimistic, pessimistic and probable. With the help of a statistical analysis, a statement can be made on the probability that the project will be completed before a certain date. This method is applicable in most cultures, but the least in the "*Adhocracy*", because here, working systematically will be less appropriate.

CRITICAL CHAIN PROJECT MANAGEMENT[4]
The Critical Path Method does not take sufficient account of the human factor, and the way in which people deal with estimates. People are inclined to plan ASAP (as soon as possible), and to work ALAP (as late as possible), and furthermore, they estimate generously, causing all time contingency to be used up during the execution. It is claimed that applying this method will result in a gain in time of between 10% and 50%.

The method does require a radical culture change, in which project members are no longer put under pressure, and indicate on time when they are ready. The way of reporting is also fundamentally different, as reports are made on the use of the available contingency in the duration. You can discuss whether it is the method, or the culture change, which is responsible for the success, and just as with the previous method, this one is less suited to the "*Adhocracy*" culture.

EVENT CHAIN PROJECT MANAGEMENT[5]
Event Chain Project Management is one of the last real innovations in the area of project planning. Much more than the other methods, this method takes account of uncertainties. In this method there are also critical activities, but they do not have to be the activities on the critical path. An activity not on the critical path, but one which is very uncertain, may become critical in a pessimistic scenario and may, therefore, have an impact on the ultimate duration.

The method links uncertain events (risks) to activities, and using a Monte Carlo Simulation calculates the probability and the consequences. The project manager now has many handles for carrying out a thorough quantitative analysis. During the whole project (in the planning), the focus on risks remains. What is special about this method is that, as opposed to the solutions from the previous two, it is easy to apply and provides a much more realistic planning model. Although this method, just as the other two, is less suited within the "*Adhocracy*", it provides a model that takes the most account of the fickleness of the environment.

PMBOK Guide
PMBOK Guide is short for "*a guide to the Project Management Body Of Knowledge*", which means the total collection of knowledge of the profession, as present both in

---

[4] (1997) *Critical Chain,* E.M. Goldratt, GOWER PUB.CO

[5] (2006) *Schedule Network Analyses Using Event Chain Methodology,* Lev Verine, PROJECTDECISIONS.ORG

3.01 Project Orientation

practice and in literature. It has been developed by the *Project Management Institute* (www.pmi.org), the biggest project management association in the world.

The *PMBOK Guide* does not dictate a specific set of procedures and guidelines, but leaves it to the project manager and his team to choose the best practices they think they may need for the successful management of the project. Strictly speaking, therefore, it is not a method.

The *guide* consists of a core document which applies to all types of projects, and in addition there are extensions, which concentrate on specific sectors, such as government, the construction industry and defence. Together with these extensions, the *guide* is a standard work which is consulted by a large group of readers when they want to know more about project management.

It consists of three main sections:
1. The project management framework.
2. The project management standard.
3. The project management knowledge areas.

The first section is a general description of the profession, and the key areas a project manager has to deal with. In the other two sections, the *PMBOK Guide* describes round 40 management processes.

The first section divides these processes into five main groups:
- Initiating processes.
- Planning processes.
- Execution processes.
- Control processes.
- Closing processes.

These processes return in every stage. In the last section, the same processes are described once more, only now divided into nine knowledge areas:
- Integration
- Scope
- Duration
- Costs
- Quality
- HR
- Communication
- Risks
- Purchasing

Knowledge areas is the most extensive section, and covers just under 200 techniques the project manager can apply in the various key areas. The *PMBOK Guide* is very instrumental, and that is also expressed in the previously cited definition it provides for project management:

The application of knowledge, skills, tools, and techniques to meet project requirements.

In my opinion, this is also at the same time its weakness, as there is little attention paid to the behavioral aspects of project management. They are discussed in the knowledge areas "*Communication*" and "*HR*" but all too briefly.

As the *PMBOK Guide* is not a method in the sense that it dictates certain actions, in principle it could be applicable to all previously mentioned organization structures. However, I do have some reservations in this regard, and precisely because of the instrumental approach I believe it is less applicable in the *"Family"*, and that the *"Adhocracy"* will have difficulties with the clear scope definition that *PMBOK Guide* assumes. I do, however, see it's application in the other two; the "*Hierarchy*" and the "*Market*".

3.01 Project Orientation

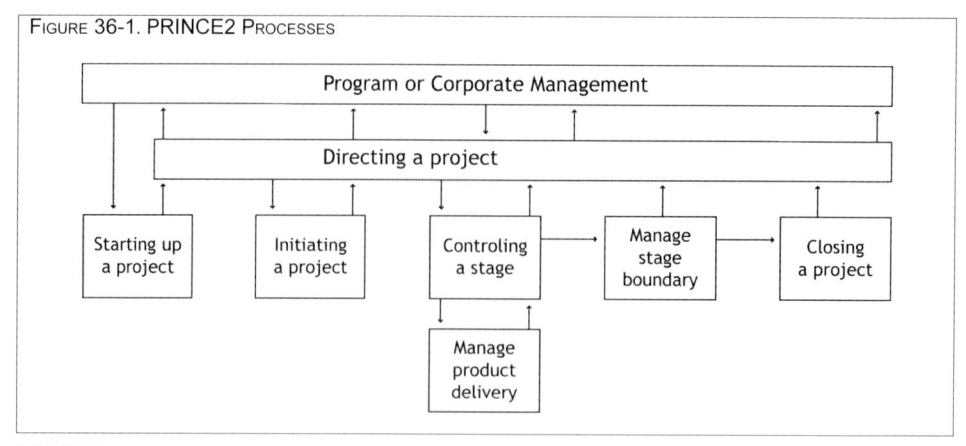

FIGURE 36-1. PRINCE2 PROCESSES

```
Program or Corporate Management
        ↓
Directing a project
  ↓       ↓         ↓            ↓             ↓
Starting  Initiating Controlling  Manage stage  Closing
up a      a project  a stage      boundary      a project
project
                        ↓
                     Manage
                     product
                     delivery
```

PRINCE2

PRINCE[6] means 'Projects IN a Controlled Environment'. The method was designed in 1989 by the British government. Initially aimed at ICT projects, in 1996 PRINCE2 was made more general, and adapted for all types of projects, or at least that is what is claimed. There is a process approach, which is shown in the diagram.

In addition to these processes, PRINCE2 also contains principles and themes.

The seven principles are the foundation on which the method is build:
- Continued business justification.
- Learn from experience.
- Defined roles and responsibilities.
- Manage by stages.
- Manage by exception.
- Focus on products.
- Tailor to suit the project environment.

The *themes* are the knowledge elements the project manager needs when going through the life cycle of the project:
- Business case
- Organization
- Quality
- Plans
- Risk
- Change
- Progress

The driving force in PRINCE2 is the business case which is already evident from the definition the method gives for a project:

A project is a management approach with the objective of delivering one or more business products conforming to a specified business case.

The management approach requires a Management-by-Exception culture (MbE), and furthermore the method uses an "extremely heavy" administrative system, which as the saying goes, keeps the project manager "on the right track". If there is no MbE culture, however, we see a lot of attention being paid to filling in forms and documents, and less to the project result. Many so called PRINCE2 implementations are PINO (PRINCE In Name Only).

---

6 (2009) *Managing Successful Projects With Prince2,* OGC, London

3.01 Project Orientation

With respect to existing processes, components and techniques, and based on the cultures, the method would fit perfectly in the *"Hierarchy"*, but it is actually here that an MbE culture is not obvious. For the *"Family"* and the *"Adhocracy"*, the method can be tailored. Maybe it is most applicable in the *"Market"* where it actually is about reaching the higher objectives, and because the method is strong in keeping the project deliverables in line with the business case.

EXTREME/AGILE PROJECT MANAGEMENT
This method is developing fast. The underlying thought is that the traditional linear (cascade) methods are insufficient to bring (complex) projects in complex environments to a successful conclusion. Instead, various "lightweight" methods have been developed, providing the project manager with handles to approach this complexity structurally. In general, these methods come from the ICT world.

Agile is a family of methods such as: Scrum, Crystal Clear, Extreme Programming, Adaptive Software Development, and Feature Driven Development. Agile, therefore, is more than a method; the driving forces (a number of prominent figures from the software development world) are trying to start a movement in the area of project management.

There is a manifest[7] based on the following principles:
- Our highest priority is to satisfy the customer through early and continuous delivery of valuable software.
- Welcome changing requirements, even late in development. Agile processes harness change for the customer's competitive advantage.
- Deliver working software frequently, from a couple of weeks to a couple of months, with a preference to the shorter timescale.
- Business people and developers must work together daily throughout the project.
- Build projects around motivated individuals. Give them the environment and support they need, and trust them to get the job done.
- The most efficient and effective method of conveying information to and within a development team is face-to-face conversation.
- Working software is the primary measure of progress.
- Agile processes promote sustainable development. The sponsors, developers, and users should be able to maintain a constant pace indefinitely.
- Continuous attention to technical excellence and good design enhances agility.
- Simplicity--the art of maximizing the amount of work not done--is essential.
- The best architectures, requirements, and designs emerge from self-organizing teams.
- At regular intervals, the team reflects on how to become more effective, then tunes and adjusts its behavior accordingly.

In 2005, the manifest was followed by a statement of independency[8]:
- We increase return on investment by making continuous flow of value our focus.
- We deliver reliable results by engaging customers in frequent interactions and shared ownership.

---

7 (2001) *Principles behind the Agile Manifesto*, www.agilemanifesto.org

8 (2005) *Declaration of Independence*, www.pm-doi.org

3.01 Project Orientation

- We expect uncertainty and manage for it through iterations, anticipation, and adaptation.
- We unleash creativity and innovation by recognizing that individuals are the ultimate source of value, and creating an environment where they can make a difference.
- We boost performance through group accountability for results and shared responsibility for team effectiveness.
- We improve effectiveness and reliability through situationally specific strategies, processes and practices.

Agile is a protest against strict methods, and the wish to control all uncertainty existing in many organizations. It will probably work best in a *"Market"* or an *"Adhocracy"* culture.

Dutch Methods[9]

INTRODUCTION
In the Netherlands, we see the Agile and PRINCE2 methods and the *PMBOK Guide* approach being used. Of these, the PRINCE2 method is by far the most used. Furthermore, the Netherlands has an additional two methods which compete with PRINCE2:
- Project-based working.
- Project-based creating.

PROJECT-BASED WORKING
Project-based working is one of the oldest of the Dutch methods for project management. As early as 1984, the first version of the book with the same name was published. This method left its mark in almost all project management methods which have been developed in the Netherlands since. Sometimes knowingly adopted by the developers, but also often not.

Project-based working consists of four processes[10]:
- Staging
- Controlling
- Deciding
- Working together

The approach divides the projects in the following standard *stages*:
- Initiative stage.
- Definition stage.
- Design stage.
- Preparation stage.
- Realization stage.
- Aftercare stage.

Staging uses four principles[11]:
- Think first then act.
- Thinking from front to back and from back to front.
- Working from general to detailed.
- Working sequentially and simultaneously.

The *control* of projects is now based on five aspects (in the jargon called MOQIT):

- Money
- Organization
- Quality
- Information
- Time

The most important *decision points* are at the stage boundaries, where the project sponsor then always has to make three decisions:
- Is he satisfied with the result up to now?
- Is he satisfied about the plan for the next stage?

---

9 (2006) *Wegwijzer voor methoden bij projectmanagement,* Baardman e.a., VAN HAREN PUBLISHING, Zaltbommel

10 (2006) *Wegwijzer voor methoden bij projectmanagement,* PMI Nederland, VAN HAREN PUBLISHING

11 (2001) *Projectmatig Werken,* Wijnen, Renes en Storm, SPECTRUM, Utrecht

3.01 Project Orientation

- Does he, in view of the current state of affairs, want to carry on with the project?

He makes the decisions, depending on the stage the project is in, based on one of the following decision documents:
- Project contract, project management plan and a detailed plan for the first stage.
- Project programme, and definitive requirements set for the project result.
- Project design, and elaboration of the project programme.
- Execution programme, implementation plan.
- Aftercare programme, delivery documents.

The method pays a lot of attention to the factor *working together*, and topics discussed are:
- Project environment.
- Politically complex environments.
- Organization and project culture.
- Teamwork.
- Project leadership.

This method is very applicable in the various different organization cultures. In the definition of a project:

*Projects are temporary, result oriented collaborations between people,
who make use of scarce resources*

Attention is also paid to the behavioral competences, and in the details we can find a good balance between hard and soft. As the method assumes that the project result can be clearly defined, it will probably be less effective in the "*Adhocracy*" culture.

PROJECT-BASED CREATING
Project-based creating[12] ("Projectmatig Creëren) is a project management method that, as well as the hard and soft aspects, also pays attention to the "inside" of the project manager and others involved. There are four facets that the project manager and his team have to take account of:

- IT-part, what are we going to solve.
- WE-part, how are we going to work together.
- I-part, how will I, and how am I going to, apply myself.
- THEM-part, the stake-holders in the project environment.

IT is about: formulating, staging, controlling and deciding. These are issues we already came across in previous methods. In *WE*, the emphasis is on: working together, team spirit, managing relationships and culture, whereas *I* puts the emphasis on inspiration, personal development, core qualities and leadership. *THEM* involves those interested parties that can influence the project. The method covers these four facets for all important project management activities.

The definition speaks of a '*flexible deployment of people and resources*':

Projects are temporary structures based on a flexible deployment of people and resources, but aimed at realizing a concrete result within clear agreements on time, money and quality.

We see that this contains a lot of project based working, only the IT-WE-I-THEM approach differentiates it as a method, which, as a project manager, you should have at least studied.

---

12 (1998) *Projectmatig Creëren,* Jo Bos, Ernst Harting, SCRIPTUM MANAGEMENT, Schiedam

3.01 Project Orientation

I believe the method is perfectly suited to the cultures *"Family", "Adhocracy"* and *"Market"*. It is less suited for the *"Hierarchic"* culture, as this culture pays far less attention to the personal component.

3.02 Programme orientation

YOU NEED THE SUPPORT OF YOUR FAMILY

A rigid scope definition is often not sufficient to head in a strategic direction.

If the whole of the individual projects seems to be less than the sum, then you need programme management.

3.02 Program Orientation

3.02-1 DEFINITIONS

Managing change	Managing and providing leadership on change.
Programme	A temporary whole of connected projects and activities aimed at achieving a strategic goal.
Programme management	Managing and providing leadership for a programme.
Programme organization	A temporary organization for achieving a programme with defined roles and a meeting structure
Programme orientation	The decision of an organization to apply and manage the concept of managing programmes, and to develop this competence.

3.02-2 INTRODUCTION

Programme management is still a relatively new field of expertise, and under this title, we can find several variants. In this book, I am following the ICB definitions.

When an organization wants to make certain strategic changes, it often starts up a number of projects to achieve this. The danger which now arises, is that each of these projects will start leading its own life and causing an amount of suboptimization within the projects. Because it is the cohesion which is important for achieving the required change, it is also better to manage these projects in cohesion.

Programmes have a much more flexible management than projects. Whereas a project relates to a product delivered by the team, in a programme it is more often about a strategic change, something which comes with much more uncertainty. The scope of a project is "rubber", that of a programme "elastic", making it more difficult to define.

It can also happen that a decision is made to combine a number of projects already running into a programme.

The most important difference between projects and programmes can be summarized as follows:

Topic	(Complex) Project	Programme
Resources	The project manager has a clear picture of all of them.	Less easy for the Programme manager to keep an overview.
Responsibilities	Only for project product.	Additionally for the actual implementation of all the products.
Changes	Try to prevent them.	Manage and control the change.
End	Delivery of products.	Implementation of products (delivery of benefits).
Success	Within time, budget and specification.	In terms of ROI, and benefits achieved.
Scheduling	Detailed.	In outline.

3.02-3 PROCESS STEPS

1. List and prioritize improvements.
2. Confirm there is a justification.
3. Quantify benefits.
4. Align with the strategic goals.
5. Assess the benefits.
6. Change the organization, culture and processes.
7. Initiate relevant programmes.
8. Apply lessons learned

1. List and prioritize improvements

With programmes, we manage in a co-ordinated way a number of initiatives for improving the functioning of the organization.

When we now manage the above in the traditional way, the responsible project managers will each carry out their own scope definition, and you are faced with some sub-optimization, which is undesirable for this strategic goal. In such a case, programme management is justified. The various projects each have their own project manager, but they report to the programme manager, who is then, as well as for the project deliverables, also responsible for the goals or benefits.

The starting point for such a programme is the totality of the related goals or **benefits**.

2. Confirm there is a justification

There is a justification for programme management, if there are strategic goals, and when there are so many dependencies between the different projects that an extra management level is needed, and which, therefore, justifies the investment. According to Van der Tak and Wijnen[1], the follow-

---

[1] (2006) *Programmamanagement – Sturen op samenhang – herziene druk,* Tak, Wijnen, KLUWER - Deventer

---

EXAMPLE 37-1 MANAGEMENT OF CHANGE

An organization wants to improve its customer satisfaction. The average mark currently is a six, and has to improve to an eight within two years. That is the assignment the Board of Directors has formulated, and the line management have to investigate what the customer complaints are.

The top three are:
- The organization is hard to reach by telephone.
- Outside office hours, the organization is not contactable at all.
- The staff consider a customer who asks questions to be an irritating disturbance of their daily activities.

The line managers involved translate the assignment into the following goals or **benefits**:
- We have to be contactable day and night.
- The customer has to immediately come into contact with someone who can answer and/or solve most of the questions.
- The culture has to change from internally orientated into customer orientated.

To achieve this, a blueprint of the required changes is made:
- The organization will set up a separate account management unit, responsible for all customer contacts.
- A call centre will be implemented with 24 hour coverage, and reporting to the account management.
- All managers will be assigned targets linked to customer satisfaction.

After this, the following projects and activities will be defined:
- Set up a call centre and make it operational.
- Set up and structure the account management.
- A culture project to make the organization think in terms of customers.
- A knowledge project enabling answers to the questions most frequently asked by customers to be directly available.
- Set up an internet portal and associated organization, to deal with questions on-line.
- A one-off action to amend the balanced scorecard with targets which match with the new business model.

3.02 Program Orientation

ing issues make the consideration for a programme orientation beneficial:
- There is a unique and temporary assignment.
- There is a complex assignment.
- If it has to be goal oriented (**benefits**).
- If co-operation with others is necessary.
- When there are limited resources available.

I would like to remark here that being goal oriented is the only real difference from a project. They proceed through the list with considerations that are distinguishable from projects:
- Goals are complex or vague.
- The object to be improved is complex and not enforceable.
- Top-down realization of an important strategic change.
- Prevention of fragmentation.
- A very dynamic environment.

Drawing up a business justification (or **business case**) is much more difficult in a programme than in a project. Often, it is more a case of entrepreneurial "must", or a strong conviction that this is the right direction to go. The programme manager gets a "large kitty" with money and a number of goals and with theses, he gets going.

3. Quantify the benefits
To quantify all different benefits you can make use of the following five criteria:

- *Speed* in which the results have to be visible.
- *Feasibility* of the required results.
- *Efficiency* of the effort in comparison to the benefits.
- *Flexibility* between benefits, and the deployment of resources.
- *Goal orientation* of the effects.

4. Align with the strategic goals
This, and the 7th process step, correspond with the 1st process step of the portfolio orientation. It is important that the organization uses the limited resources it has, for those programmes and projects which assume the largest contribution to the organizations's strategy.

This all looks so simple and rational, but the opposite is true. Projects and programmes are often started up from the personal vision (or pet topic) of one of the more senior managers, without a balanced decision being made. In the higher regions of our organizations, there is often much display of power, and so called *"hobby horse riders"*. Therefore, it is desirable that, as well as a project and programme orientation, organizations also have a portfolio orientation, thus ensuring that all activities always stay in line with the organizations's strategy.

5. Assess the benefits
The line managers are much more involved with a programme than they are with a project. Only they can make a rough assessment as to what extent the proposed results will deliver the required effects. Furthermore, with this process step, you also achieve an increase in the support for the results delivered in the scope of the programme.

6. Change the organization, culture and processes
Just as with the project orientation, the organization, culture and processes have to change. Because programme management is more closely aligned to the daily operations, this is a lot less complicated than with project management. Furthermore, organizations that are ready to apply programme management, have usually already been working with project management for some time, and are used to such improvements in the professionalism of the organization.

7. Initiate relevant programmes

This step, together with the 4th one, correspond with the 1st step of the portfolio orientation, in which the management puts together a balanced portfolio of programmes and projects based on the overall strategy.

8. Apply lessons learned

Within programmes we use the experience gained at two levels:
- Within the projects of the programme.
- Beyond the programme boundaries.

Learning within the programme boundaries, is one of the reasons why we apply programme management at all. Through the combined management of all these projects, we achieve a certain synergy, both in execution and in managing.

Learning beyond the programme boundaries, is mainly about the fact that programmes increase the potential of the organization through the results delivered. A programme, therefore, is already a form of organizational learning.

3.02-4 SPECIAL TOPICS

1. Available Standards
There are a number of standards for programme management, which give an insight into the different stages in a programme, and in the table below, you will find the two most important ones:

Managing Successful Programmes[2]
- Programme identification:
  Making a proposal.
- Programme definition: Working out a programme plan.
- Programme Governance:
  Planning & control.
- Portfolio Management:
  Optimal planning and execution of the projects.
- Managing Benefits:
  Achieve the results, the change works.
- Programme close-out: Discharge.

PMI Program Management standard[3]
- Management of the programme
  o Pre-Program Set Up.
  o Program Set Up.
  o Setting up the Programme infrastructure
  o Incrementally delivering programme benefits
  o Programme close-out

- Management of the benefits
  o Identifying
  o Analyzing
  o Planning
  o Execution
  o Transition

---
[2] (2003) *Managing Successful Programmes*, OFFICE OF GOVERNMENT COMMERCE, TSO Norwich
[3] (2006) *Program Management Standard*, the Project Management Institute (www.pmi.org)

Both have their own approach, the most important similarity is that it is about managing **projects** and managing **benefits**.

There are three themes which play a part in successfully managing a programme:
- Management of the Programme Benefits
- Management of the Programme Stakeholders
- Programme management and control

Management of the Programme Benefits
The management of the programme benefits is the driving force under the programme, and ensures that:

- The organizational value of the programme is determined.
- The consequences of the programme are known to the organization.
- The required benefits are identified.
- The mutual dependencies between the benefits have been identified.
- The goals set are realistic.
- The responsibilities for applying the programme benefits have been determined.
- It is clear how the benefits are being achieved and verified.

The management of the programme benefits happens partly during the programme under the responsibility of the programme manager, but is carried out by the line managers. As it is often the case that programme benefits have a longer life cycle than the programme itself, it is necessary to make a transition plan for the transfer of this responsibility.

The MSP method differentiates between the *business change manager(s)*, who is responsible for applying the programme results and achieving the programme benefits, and the *programme manager*, who is

3.02 Program Orientation

responsible for managing the different projects in the programme. The latter is one individual, whereas the change managers are often a group of line managers.

Management of the Programme Stakeholders

Stakeholders are all the individuals and parties, who, in one way or another, are involved in the execution and the use of the programme results.

This large group consists of: the programme director, programme manager, project managers, project sponsors, customers, users, permanent organization, team members of the programme and the underlying projects, programme and project offices, steering committee, suppliers, government authorities, competitors and potential customers.

Sometimes, organizations who have no interest in the results, but who can have an influence on them, also fall within this group. Good stakeholder management means that the different interests are known and that the programme organization (as far possible) makes use of this fact. It is an important success factor.

A number of the stakeholders mentioned are part of the programme organizations, and have a specifically described (in the programme plan) role. The MSP method contains the following roles for programme management:

- *The Programme director,* supplies the vision, and makes the programme definition together with line management.
- *The Programme manager,* delivers the blueprint, through good coordination of the projects and the project sponsor.
- *Business Change Managers*, make the blueprint operational, execute the continuity of the transition (making use of the programme benefits), and manage operational risks.
- *Programme Office*, spider in the information web, supplies infrastructure and a lot of data.

Programme management and control (governance)

The main topic of programme management and control is controlling the investments made in the scope of the programme. It involves the development, communication, implementation and monitoring of the policy and procedures, which ensure an effective management.

A programme board, consisting of the project sponsor and other representatives of the different interests within the organization, is responsible for directing the programme.

The decisions they take include the following:
- Initiation of the programme.
- Go/no go decisions.
- Approval of plans.
- For escalations, which the programme manager cannot solve.
- Allocation of resources.
- Etc.

It is good practice to have a number of so called "gate reviews", in which the programme board assesses to what extent the programme is still in line with the expectations and any changed circumstances. The PMI standard specifies the following:
- Assess to what extent the programme is in line with the organizations's strategy.
- Assess the business justification of the programme.
- Assess the programme start up.
- Assess the deliveries.

3.02 Program Orientation

- Evaluate the programme benefits and experience gained.

To ensure that the organization gets an idea of the programme results as quickly as possible, and then especially to what extent the programme benefits deliver that what was expected, it is advisable to work with so called tranches or plateaus.

In advance, it is determined when sufficient projects have been concluded and when the use of the project deliverables gives the organization enough handles to see the first benefits. It is possible to group projects together in terms of time, and sub-divide them into tranches.

2. Kurt Lewin[4]

The basis of many models on Management of Change is still the well-known stages: *Unfreeze – Change – Freeze,* described by Kurt Lewin (1890-1947). In his model, he advises leaders, when confronted with change, to look at two forces that resist change.

The first force is concerned with the *'habits'* people develop in groups, and the second is concerned with the internal *'opposition'* of people to change. To overcome these, the manager has to employ stronger forces which, as it were, eclipse this opposition.

This happens during the *Unfreeze* stage of the changes, with the objective of breaking the habit and challenging the employees. Examples of unfreeze interventions are: creating a crisis, authoritatively telling employees they have to change, restructuring the organization, etc. These types of activities force people out of their comfort zone. The biggest virtue of many crisis managers is not so much the change they start up, but the fact that they ensure that the organization stops with a certain practice, which got it into trouble in the first place.

When employees have been forced out of their comfort zone, they will stop their opposition more easily, and that is the time to set the change in motion. After this has taken place, management has to once again ensure stability. Many organizations make the mistake of continuously changing, whereas it is better to give an existing change the opportunity to take shape.

This is the *Freeze* stage of the change. Interventions are: burn your boats, prove that the change was a success by using figures, reward employees for the changes they have brought about, ensure the change is anchored in the formal structure of the organization, and keep a focus on the future.

3. Kotters Eight Stage Process

For change projects, Kotter differentiates[5] the following eight stages:

- *Establishing a sense of urgency*: Complacency prevents an organization from seeing the necessity of a change. By naming a crisis, employees will be jolted and prepared to change.
- *Forming a leadership coalition*: by putting together a group of managers with sufficient power, expertise and credibility, who will manage the change, the engine for change is established.
- *Developing a vision and strategy*: Is crucial for communicating and achieving the change successfully.
- *Communicating the change vision*: What keeps coming back as an omission during change processes, is adequate communication. The vision

---

4 (1951) *Field Theory in Social Science: Selected Theoretical Papers,* Kurt Lewin

5 (1996) *Leading Change,* John P. Kotter, HARVARD BUSINESS SCHOOL PRESS, Boston

and the strategy have to be propagated and explained repeatedly.
- *Creating a broad basis for action through 'empowerment'*: As soon as possible give people the opportunity to take the future in their own hands; this reduces the uncertainty and increases the motivation to change.
- *Generating short term successes*: As evidence that the direction being taken is the right one, in order to remove uncertainty and create trust for the future.
- *Consolidating the improvements and bringing about more change*: The short term successes increase the support for the change, making it possible to bring about even bigger changes.
- *Anchoring new approaches in the organization culture:* The changes have been implemented successfully.

The model concentrates on the steps that have to be taken to achieve a successful change. In the eight steps we also see Lewin's *Unfreeze – Change – Freeze* stages.

4. Change in Five Colors

Projects, and still many more programmes, concern changes in organisations. You would think this is quite obvious, but what do we understand by the word "change"? De Caluwé provides a number of examples:
- I change the policy
- The building is changed
- I change the organisation
- I change Pete
- Pete changes

All five examples use the word change with a different meaning. When change agents are in discussion with each other, they very often use different meanings, and this creates confusion. In 1999 De Caluwé and Vermaak further elaborated on this in a framework of five colours: yelow; blue; red; green; and white print thinking.

By the way, these colours are not related to De Bono's thinking hats. They stand for a certain way in which the change agent, in general, views changes. The advantage of this classification is that people can name their view explicitly, thus opening it up for discussion. The disadvantage, and that applies to each characterisation, is that you quickly place someone into a specific category, e.g. "This is typically blue print thinking", which then kills off any further discussion. Obviously, this is not the intention.

Every colour has its own set of characteristic interventions, and for his reason the book Learning to Change), as well as containing an extensive description on change processes, also embodies a collection of many possible interventions. What the PMI "guide to the Project Management Body of Knowledge" is to the project manager, the above book is to the change manager. Although De Caluwé's book is primarily aimed at change agents, it can also be applied readily by project and programme managers, who can also be categorised as yellow, blue, red, green or white.

YELLOW PRINT THINKING

Saying: *It is better to talk to the king, than to the minister.*

Yellow is the colour of the sun and symbolically stands for power. It is the view of organisational change as seen through the eyes of politics and power. People look for coalitions and consensus. The power can be formal and informal, and is more about who you know, than what you know (or can do).

As project manager, you have to play the political game of influence, at the same time working on the assumption that others are doing the same. As you, yourself have little formal power, you will be predominantly busy with identifying the different interested parties and the people with a say in the project, and trying to combine these together as much as possible.

Possible interventions:
- Personal Commitment Statement
- Confrontation Meetings
- Improve the quality of Work

PERSONAL COMMITMENT STATEMENT
In a dialogue with team members, produce a form of contract covering what they expect from the project and what they personally will contribute to it. During the execution, you can then challenge or confront them about this.

CONFRONTATION MEETINGS
A team of people involved list the issues that are present, and order and prioritise them. Together, everyone sets to work to resolve these. Regular meetings are held to discuss the progress.

IMPROVE THE QUALITY OF WORK
Involve the employees by giving them a say in matters, provide them with sufficient information, train them so they are capable of carrying out their task and reward them both materially and non-materially.

BLUE PRINT THINKING
Saying: *An honest man's word is as good as his bond.*

Blue is the colour of the "blueprint"; the change agent works on the principle that a change is best effected by a planned, structured and rational approach. The approach is, of course, through a project and makes use of best practices, as these have already been proven.

As project manager you define the scope very clearly and precisely, and ensure a good WBS is produced with an associated schedule and budget, both of which have been approved by the project sponsor. With a tight change procedure and good risk management, you ensure you deliver within time and budget what was agreed at the start. PRINCE2 is the pre-eminent example of a "blue" approach.

Possible interventions:
- Management by Objectives
- Working in projects
- Strategic Management

MANAGEMENT BY OBJECTIVES
Together with employees, determine objective, measurable objectives and manage to these.

WORKING IN PROJECTS
Is self-evident.

STRATEGIC MANAGEMENT
Carry out a SWOT analysis and based on this, develop and implement the correct measures.

RED PRINT THINKING
Saying: *A happy employee is a productive employee.*

Red is the colour of blood, and this way of looking at changes is predominantly concerned with the human factor. The change agent will look at ways to motivate the employee to go along with the change. He will try to involve people in the project, and in this way, to "get the best out of them".

Here, the project manager is a real people manager, who predominantly focusses on the personal development of people, and ensures that everybody really is to the proj-

3.02 Program Orientation

ect, and with each other. If people are feeling good, they also work better together.

Possible interventions:
- Career development
- Social Activities
- Reward in organisations

CAREER DEVELOPMENT
Discuss thoroughly with the employees how the project will contribute to their personal development and ensure that this is also actually the case.

SOCIAL ACTIVITIES
Many social activities with the team. Discuss the team roles and how these function in everyday practice.

REWARD IN ORGANISATIONS
Ensure they are well rewarded for the work they carry out.

GREEN PRINT THINKING
Saying: *Practice makes perfect.*

The leading principle with this is "growth", thus the colour green. Changing means learning, and the reverse is also true. The change agent assumes that an organisation is chiefly a "learning organisation". It is about providing feedback, reflecting on the functioning, experimenting with new work forms, exchanging experience and creating the right amount of safety in order to be able to learn.

The "green" project manager sees his project as a system that, in contact with the environment, adapts itself to that environment. In particular, the project is a common learning experience, with much attention paid to the hidden assumptions that lie locked up in the team's culture, and how these assist or hinder.

Possible interventions:
- Coaching
- Team building
- Open Systems Planning

COACHING
Hold regular meetings in which you provide feedback on how they are functioning and help them to further develop themselves.

TEAM BUILDING
Together with the team, investigate the way in which people work together, and which areas of the group dynamics have to be improved. This is a somewhat heavier instrument than the "social activities" in the red print thinking.

OPEN SYSTEMS PLANNING
The team regularly looks at the project environment and takes stock of the various expectations, which together determine what the project mission should be.

WHITE PRINT THINKING
Saying: *It is the way it is*

This form of thinking is a reaction to Newton's linear world view. This change is concerned with self-direction, but in fact, it is not that easy to direct the change. The change agent facilitates by removing blockages and addressing people's own knowledge and wisdom. The colour is white, because white consists of all colours.

As project manager you are more a facilitator than a manager, and you ensure an ideal working environment within which your team members can get to work.

Possible interventions:
- T-Group
- Self-directing Teams
- Search conferences

T-GROUP
In this, a person practices a specific new behaviour with people he doesn't know. He can then move the new behaviour across to another (real) setting.

SELF-DIRECTING TEAMS
The group itself largely determines the goals and how they are going to achieve these.

SEARCH CONFERENCES
Involve as many as possible in looking for the right direction for the organisation.

5. Change is inevitable

There are different ways of looking at changes. We often see it as a necessary reaction to something happening in an organisations environment. This could be an economic development, the competition, or new innovative possibilities and so on. Based on that event, we modify the strategy of the organisation, and as a logical consequence of this, we also amend the structure. Structure follows the strategy; something happens "outside", to which we react "inside".

With a totally different view, Greiner[6], after studying various different research, came to the conclusion that the history of the organisation had a much greater influence on the problems that the management are confronted with than was assumed. The point of time in the lifecycle determines the style of leadership more than what is happening outside the organisation.

In his model, Greiner recognises lengthy periods of evolution, during which the organisation grows without too many problems. The end of such a phase is accompanied by turmoil and revolution, whereby the management solves a particular management problem, which is integral to the phase, before moving into a new phase of evolution.

Each phase has its own management style, which, due to the growth of the organisation, becomes no longer adequate, and thus provokes certain types of (inevitable) crises. When the management sees the opportunity to solve these, then again a period of calm and evolution will follow. In the table on the next pages, you can see the different stages with their characteristics.

The speed in which an organisation moves through these stages is dependent on the following five dimensions:
- Age
- Size
- Current phase of evolution
- Current phase of revolution
- Growth rate of the industry segment

For a large part, the age of the organisation determines in which phase the organisation finds itself; the older, the higher the phase. The larger an organisation is, the earlier it will reach a particular crisis, and after solving it, move into a following phase. It is obvious, then, that the faster the growth rate of the industry in which the company operates is, the faster this process takes place. The phase in which an organisation finds itself predicts the next crises, and the crises it is in predict the following phase, which is entered into after solving those crises.

For the managers of organisations, Greiner provides the following guidelines:

- Know the phase of the organisation.
- Recognise the limited range of solutions.
- Realise that solutions create new problems.

---

[6] (1972) Evolutions and Revolution as Organizations Grow, Larry E. Greiner, HARVARD BUSINESS REVIEW

3.02 Program Orientation

Stages in the organizational change[7]

	Stage	Characteristics of Evolution	Characteristics of Revolution
1	Growth through creativity	The founders, often management averse, lead the organisation starting from the service or product. There are many informal communication channels, the people work long hours, are extremely dedicated and have modest earnings. Customers react, and the management reacts back immediately.	Due to the growth, directing informally doesn't work any longer. The newer employees are less motivated to invest in a lot of overtime. There is often a need for extra capital, resulting in the founders becoming overwhelmed by management tasks.
	The solution that many organisations now choose is the appointment of a strong senior manager, who is acceptable to the founders and who concentrates on managing the organisation.		
2.	Growth through direction	This manager takes a firm hold on the organisation and implements a functional structure, separating production and marketing, and professionalising the administration. He introduces budgeting and work standards, building up a formal hierarchy. Decision-making lies with the management team.	When the organisation grows further and becomes more complex, this directive style is no longer sufficient. In the lowest levels of the organisation, a so-called autonomy crisis develops, and part of the operational management and some of the original employees leave the organisation due to this frustration.
	The obvious solution, although difficult for managers to accept, is through delegation, or as Greiner later wrote, decentralisation. In short, allow autonomy lower down in the organisation.		
3.	Growth through delegation (or decentralisation)	There is a real management-by-exception culture where the responsibility sits with the decentralised parts of the organisation. Profit centres are set up, and bonuses used as motivation. Management now often concentrates on acquiring new business units and incorporating these into a divisional structure. Communication with top management is mainly written or by telephone.	Now, a type of kingdom forming develops, with its own sub-optimisation. Top management gets the feeling it is losing the control. Some organisations try to regain control of things again through centralisation, which often does not succeed.
	The solution is now found in the implementation of more formal reporting systems, through which the company management can obtain more insight and give direction.		
4.	Growth through co-ordination	The decentralised units are merged into product groups, which senior management consider and assesses as separate investment centres. There is an increase in the number of decentralised staff functions, which plan more formally and also develop new (extra) procedures. As motivation, share option plans are introduced.	After a while, the formal procedures develop into a top-heavy bureaucracy and a large gap is created between the HQ staff and the managers on the work floor.

---

[7] (1998) Evolutions and Revolution as Organizations Grow, Larry E. Greiner, HARVARD BUSINESS REVIEW

3.02 Program Orientation

	Stage	Characteristics of Evolution	Characteristics of Revolution
	\multicolumn{3}{l	}{The solution is now found by putting a lot more emphasis on spontaneous collaboration and skilfully reconciling the differences in perception. Social control and self-discipline now take over from the formal control systems.}	
5.	Growth through collaboration.	The organisation reduces the number of staff functions and formal control systems and starts to work more and more in a matrix type structure. Inter-disciplinary teams quickly solve problems.	In 1972 Greiner still thought that the following crisis consisted of what he called a "psychological saturation" of employees, resulting from the intensive collaboration. In 1998 he reflects back on this, now judging that the crises arise from the realisation that there is no solution, and that organisations must look more for partners outside the organisation.

3.02 Program Orientation

3.03 Portfolio orientation

CASH IS KING

Every element of expenditure by an organization is an investment.

Therefore, so is a project.

When you now look at all the projects in an organization, you can say that you are actually looking at an investment portfolio.

Therefore, you have to manage it as such.

3.03 Portfolio Orientation

3.03-1 DEFINITIONS

Management by projects	Method of working, whereby the primary process of an organization is, to an important extent, being achieved through the execution of projects
Multi-project	A totality of projects using the same resources.
Multi-project management	The management and leadership of a totality of projects using the same resources.
Net Present Value	The discounted future cash flows.
Payback Period	The time that elapses before the initial expenditure can be received back through the operational receipts.
Portfolio	A totality of projects and/or programmes which realize one or more common goals, and possibly make use of the same resources.
Portfolio management	The management and control of a portfolio.
Portfolio-orientation	The orientation of organizations on managing through portfolio's, and the development of portfolio competences.

3.03-2 Introduction

Project portfolio management is the decisions taken by the senior management with respect to the projects to be started up. They are the go/no go decisions, which have the objective of ensuring that the organization starts only those activities, which are in line with the strategic choices of the organization.

The portfolio management process has three objectives[1]:

- Maximizing the added value.
- Balancing between the different strategic goals.
- Bringing in line with, and keeping to, the strategic goals.

These decisions take place on the basis of a business justification. This justification contains, as a minimum, a financial underpinning of the project costs and benefits. In this chapter, I shall discuss the techniques you can use for this.

---

[1] (2001) *Portfolio Management for New Products,* Cooper, Edgett, Kleinschmidt, BASIC BOOKS, Cambridge

3.03-3 Process steps

1. Identify and prioritize.
2. Balance and allocate.
3. Standardize processes.
4. Track and monitor.
5. Remove components.
6. Add components.

1. Identify and prioritize

Once the company management has decided on the strategic direction for the organization, various initiatives arise in order to achieve the specified objectives. All these initiatives place a demand on the organization's resources, including investment amounts, people, machines, tools, space and suchlike. Obviously you want to make as efficient and effective use of this as possible. There are likely to be more initiatives than available resources, and therefore the company management will have to make choices. This is the portfolio orientation.

To be able to do this well, we provide the various initiatives with criteria which can be mutually weighted, allowing us to compare the different projects with each other.

The easiest criteria are those that are easily quantifiable such as:
- Profit growth.
- Cost savings.
- Cost avoidance.
- Returns.
- Net Present Value.
- Payback period.
- Costs.
- Effect on the cash flows.
- Claims on available resources.

However this is not enough, because otherwise there will be too much focus on finance, so as well as the above, we also have to take account of:
- In line with the strategy.
- Competitive advantage.
- Customer satisfaction.
- Opportunities and threats in the environment of the organization.
- Impact on the current company operations.
- Chances of a successful implementation.
- Staff satisfaction.
- Availability of the required knowledge and experience.
- Conformance with standards.
- In line with choices already made in the past.
- Consequences if we do not do this.

In contrast with the previous group, this one is difficult to quantify, and you have to make use of the Likert scales, whereby for each programme and project an indication is given as to what extent they meet a criterion. For the criterion "*in line with the strategy*", you may then have the following Likert scale:
- Very positive contribution to the strategy.
- Some contribution to the strategy.
- Neutral.
- Negative contribution to the strategy.
- Very negative contribution to the strategy.

We now provide the various criteria with weighting factors and we can now score all projects and programmes and mathematically compare and prioritize.

I do want to make a small comment on this, because no one priority system can take the place of real entrepreneurship. It is only intended to support it.

During research[1], Crawford, Hobbs and Turner established a series of problems,

---

1 (2005) *Project Categorization Systems,* Crawford, Hobbs en Turner, PROJECT MANAGEMENT INSTITUTE, Newton Square

3.03 Portfolio Orientation

which occur when classifying projects on the basis of such a system:
- Criteria can be explained in different ways.
- Classification leads to bureaucracy.
- The priority setting can be manipulated.
- Some work remains invisible.
- There are doubts about the necessity.
- Negative impact on innovation.
- Customer confusion on the priority setting used.

I want to add one further objection to these:

- Not all projects can be compared the same way.

Let's look at these objections:

Criteria can be explained in different ways

This is because the meaning of certain concepts is taken for granted. Although the people from different job functions, who are involved in the "ranking", speak of the same category, they think differently about the meaning.

Classification leads to bureaucracy

Organizational inflexibility can be a result of a wrong classification, or a classification which leaves little room for flexibility, and the latter is a requirement for a workable classification.

The priority setting can be manipulated

This can take happen in two places: at the establishment of the classification, and whilst actually classifying. This is an unavoidable phenomenon.

One of the causes, of course, is power and politics in the organization, but another, often disregarded, reason is that manipulation takes place because the system just does not function, and then you have to do something to still achieve your result anyway.

Some work remains invisible

The classification provides visibility of the projects. If a project falls within the set criteria, it is visible and included in the portfolio process. When there is work to be done, which should be carried out as a project, but which does not come within the existing classification, it remains "invisible", which of course is undesirable as these projects do put a demand on the organization's resources.

There are doubts about the necessity

This and the following problems often have the side-effect of there not being any support for the classification used by the organization. Implementing such a prioritizing system is, of course, a project in itself.

Negative impact on innovation

There is a tension between the bureaucracy that unavoidably evolves from such a system, and the necessity to innovate. This is

---

EXAMPLE 38-1 PRIORITY SETTING

Strategic goal 1	Strategic goal 2	Strategic goal 3
Cost reduction of 25% on maintenance work.	Invest 10% of the turnover in innovation.	Outsourcing all non-critical processes.
Improve design process	Xipion v3 Project	Facility management
Training maintenance staff	Xenofio v4 Project	Training
Renew quality system	Recruiting new staff	Company restaurant

As there are not enough resources (money and people) available to carry out all these projects, a choice has to be made which scenario is desirable. This happens in the following process step.

a much heard objection against these types of systems.

Customer confusion on the priority setting used

Customers are not involved in the internal priority setting. Suppose you have done business with a certain customer for years now. Through the classification used, his projects always get a high priority. When a new project for this customer now falls into another category, it is possible that the project gets a lower priority than he is used to, and this is incomprehensible for the customer and difficult to explain.

Projects cannot be compared the same way

A priority setting system assumes that all projects can be compared in the same way, but in reality the opposite is true. How, for example, can you compare *"the implementation of a legal requirement"* with *"the introduction of a new product"* or a *"process improvement with an FTE decrease"*.

The only good solution for this is defining categories within which the different projects and programmes can be measured the same way.

The categories are now directly linked to a strategic goal such as:
- Financial benefits.
- Market share.
- Process improvement.
- Innovation.
- Etc.

Within the different categories, different weighting factors apply. For innovation, cost savings will have a lower priority than it will have for process improvement, etc. So, this approach results in a number of categories containing prioritized projects.

2. Balance and allocate

When balancing the portfolio, the various scenarios are looked at to choose the most desirable. This is an entrepreneurial choice.

This approach is very similar to the management of a securities portfolio, where you also provide a balanced portfolio consisting of securities with high, medium and low risks spread over different sectors and regions.

Balancing the portfolio brings a piece of reality to the strategic process, because it is there where the options of the organization and the expected results of all investment

---

EXAMPLE 38-2 PRIORITY SETTING

There are two possible scenario's which fit with the existing resources (financial, people, tools, etc.) of the organisation. It is a choice of the one or the other.

Scenario 1:
- Training maintenance personnel.
- Xipion v3 Project.
- Recruiting new staff.
- Outsourcing facility management, training and company restaurant.

Scenario 2:
- Improve the design process.
- Renew the quality system.
- Xenofio v4 Project.
- Recruiting new staff.
- Outsourcing facility management, training and company restaurant.

proposals, are being considered. Not everything is possible within the existing resources, but once the choice has been made, the resources can be allocated to the different projects. The company management obviously must communicate this.

3. Standardize processes
These first two process steps are necessary to get the whole process going. Also, if an organization does not have an official portfolio process, this does actually happen, for instance at the end of the year when the budgets for the next year are determined. Each go/no go decision is a form of portfolio management.

However, this is insufficient to speak of real portfolio orientation. This consists of the following processes:
- Identify and prioritize (process step 1).
- Balance (process step 2).
- Track and monitor (process step 4).
- Remove (process step 5).
- Add (process step 6).

The last three steps will be discussed later. When an organization does much of its work through projects, a certain form of standardizing of the processes mentioned will take place.

4. Track and monitor
Tracking and monitoring the portfolio has on the one hand to do with the actual results compared to the original assumptions of the programmes and projects which have been started up. On the other hand, changes in the organization's environment must be taken into account, and to what extent this is still reflected in the current priority model.

Is the organization still pursuing the same strategic direction, or are existing projects and programmes no longer opportune? If this is confirmed, it is a waste to spend more time and energy on it, and the company management must stop them.

So, tracking and monitoring the portfolio is about:
- Keeping track of all projects and programmes that have been started.
- Continuously checking the correctness of the priority model used.

There is a difference between the progress cycle of a portfolio, and that of a project or programme. Weighing up and evaluating the portfolio will take place once a year, half year, or quarter, whereas for a project, this is based more on the technical staging, and for a programme, on the implementation plateaus. In order to achieve a connection, we can make use of the management phasing as opposed to the technical staging.

The difference between both is:
- *Technical staging*, dependent on how the project team produces the result.
- *Management phasing,* dependent on the points in time at which the company management (or the portfolio management) wants to be informed about the actual status.

For the project managers, this means an extra complication in their reporting activities.

Projects under the parapet
The larger an organization, the higher the chance that the line managers, using their departmental budgets, start up projects, which are not in line with the strategic goals of the organization. This is inevitable, and based on the "*empowerment*" philosophy, you should not want to prevent this. However, when these projects avoid the portfolio attention, and lay a significant claim on the resources, we also arrive here at an undesirable situation.

3.03 Portfolio Orientation

The organization must find a certain balance in this. Therefore, it is necessary every so often to go through the organization with a "fine tooth comb", take a closer look at all the projects, and bring them under portfolio management.

5. Remove components

A result of the previous process step may be that a programme or project has to be stopped, and that means:
- Informing the project sponsor.
- Informing the project/programme manager.
- Informing the project team.
- Stopping the project/programme.
- Returning resources to the line organization.

This is always a painful decision, but *"desperate diseases need desperate remedies"*. Certainly when it is a project in which a lot has already been invested, the emotions will run high because people will think that the decision to stop is a form of capital destruction. This is, however, not what it is; it is much more a decision to not fritter away any more capital. All costs already spent, have gone anyway, and these are the so-called **sunk costs.** Money already spent never comes back, whether you carry on with a project or not. Therefore, you cannot include these in any consideration as to whether to stop a project, or keep it going.

6. Add components

New programmes and projects come under portfolio management, and will be included in the total portfolio.

3.04 PPP implementation

THE PROJECT "THE IMPLEMENTATION OF PROJECT MANAGEMENT"

Implementing professional project management is a change process.

Core to this, is that the promise of dynamism and flexibility is fulfilled.

After all, procedures that appear to be embedded in concrete, together with a multitude of forms, are contradictory to the organizational agility that can be achieved with project management.

3.04 PPP Implementation

3.04-1 DEFINITIONS

Capability	Proven capacity to apply knowledge and skills in practice.
Management through projects	Method of working, whereby the primary process of an organization is, to an important extent, achieved by carrying out projects.
Managing change	The management and control of a change.
Multi-project	A totality of projects, which make use of the same resources.

3.04-2 Introduction

Not infrequently, project managers complain that the organization never learns anything, and that everything to do with project management is badly organized. They have a point here, because that often is the case.

But is that a problem; do not project managers obtain a part of their motivation from the hectic environment and the unpredictability of their profession? Would there actually be project management, if everything was well organized? I don't think so; chaos precedes the professionalizing of the profession.

But anyway, the profession exists, and that means that we are 'obliged' to professionalize. This competence element is about the ability of the organization to carry out projects that are in line with, and stay in line with, the strategic choices of the organization. It is about properly organizing project management processes.

As well as an individual employee's capability in project management, there is now also the capability of the organization in project management. By this I mean the combined action between line and project managers in successfully starting up, executing and concluding projects, and also the learning capacity of the organization to not get into a rut with a chosen methodology, but to continuously adapt this to the evolving requirements.

This now relates to the choice of senior management to carry projects out professionally, and not to view them as a necessary evil, but as a critical success factor.

3.04-3 PROCESS STEPS

1. Decision to consider PPP as a continuous improvement process.
2. Determining the current capability of the organization.
3. Developing the PPP concept for the organization.
4. Proving the feasibility through a pilot.
5. Assessing the pilot.
6. Determining the implementation speed of the maturity path.
7. Implementing company wide.
8. Apply lessons learned.

1. Decision to consider PPP as a continuous improvement process

The project, programme or portfolio orientation can be implemented without actually taking a decision to consider the complete PPP construction as an on-going improvement process.

There are two lines along which the organization implements its strategic choices:
- Through the line.
- Through the three-pronged approach: portfolio, programme and project.

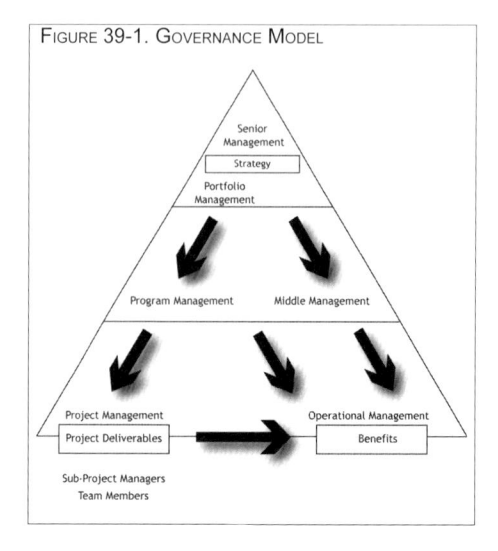

FIGURE 39-1. GOVERNANCE MODEL

Implementing the strategy through the line will be explained further in the competence element "Business"; here I am explaining how this should be carried out for projects.

A management model for projects

Because projects are temporary, the permanent organization is not sufficiently equipped to provide management. The interface with the line is where it goes wrong in projects time after time. At the start, as well as during the execution and acceptance, the line has to check on the project manager and provide him with the required resources.

When several projects are aiming for the same goal, or are dependent on each other, or use the same resources, it is advisable to make this into a programme or multi-project. What a programme is has already been explained earlier. A multi-project is a precursor of the portfolio, but you apply it for those parts of the projects which use the same resources.

The portfolio consists of all projects (possibly clustered in programmes or multi-projects), and the portfolio manager is a senior line manager who takes decisions on the projects, thereby taking into account the value of the complete portfolio.

The PPP improvement process

When an organization is continuously on the move, and it is impossible to implement all the improvements through the line, it is desirable to standardize the project processes and bring them in line with the strategic needs that exist. This is a choice which actually means that the management appoints process owners with sufficient authority to improve the project processes.

After that, the standardization and the improvement cycle the management has committed to commences.

2. Determining the current capability of the organization

To do this, we can make use of the so called maturity models, which give an accurate description of those matters that, at a certain level, have to be organized. Many of the available maturity models for project management have been 'copied' from the Carnegie Mellon's Software Engineering Institute's (SEI) Software Capability Maturity Model (CMM). The model gives the level of maturity of the software development process in an organization, and recognizes the following levels[1]:

- *Initial process,* there is a process, but it is ad hoc and chaotic.
- *Repeatable process,* availability of project management processes for time, costs and functionality.
- *Defined process,* as well as the management processes, the software process has also now been documented, standardised and completely integrated.
- *Controlled process,* there exists a process which keeps within the specified boundaries.
- *Process optimization,* the organization innovates and adapts the process to the requirements demanded by the environment.

The success of the CMM model caused it to be adopted in the project management literature, for example, in the Project Management Maturity Model of Project Management Solutions[2], which related the above mentioned levels with the *PMBOK Guide*[3]. For each level is described what from the *PMBOK Guide* has to be organized. This model has been adopted by many organizations, and given a personal flavour.

At the end of 2003, the Project Management Institute attempted to introduce some standardization with the Organizational Project Management Maturity Model (OPM3[4]). This model is an ANSI standard, and because the model is supported by the largest project management association in the world, it stands a good chance of becoming the global standard. The model is very extensive and provides a detailed view of all best-practices available in the area of project management.

Apart from the model you use, each PPP implementation begins with carrying out a baseline measurement, on the basis of which, the organization can develop a plan to further professionalize the organizational capability in the area of managing projects, programmes and portfolios.

3. Developing the PPP concept for the organization

With the baseline measurement mentioned as starting point, and the strategic direction of the organization as goal, the organization develops a number of standard processes for project, programme and portfolio management.

In doing this, they take account of the market requirements. When, for example, quality is one of the unique sales arguments, more attention will be paid to the quality processes than to the others. For an organization where safety is an important issue, more energy will be spent on that.

This results on the one hand in an adaptation of the existing standards and guidelines,

---
1 (1993) *CMU/SEI-93-TR-024 ESC-TR-93-177*, SOFTWARE ENGINEERING INSTITUTE
2 (2002) *Project Management Maturity Model*, J. Kent Crawford, MARCEL DEKKER INC.
3 (2004) *A Guide to the Project Management Body of Knowledge*, The Project Management Institute

4 OPM3 Organizational Project Management Maturity Model

and on the other hand in a number of new ones. Processes are also developed to introduce the required improvement loops.

4. Proving the feasibility through a pilot

Implementing such a construction in one go is asking for problems. First of all, the new and adapted processes have to be tested, and this can be done in steps, firstly, for example, by taking one programme as a pilot, and implementing and applying all project processes to it. Within the programme, the feasibility can then be tested, and the required adjustments defined.

5. Assessing the pilot

When the pilot is finished and the recommendations have been evaluated, an assessment can be made as to whether or not this is the way to continue in the future. It is now essential to take a well considered decision. Project management is a practical profession, and even though a lot has been written about it, it is not an exact science. There are more roads that lead to Rome, although if you now and again hear the experts preaching, you would think there was only one road to salvation.

6. Determining the implementation speed of the maturity path

A blind application of the CMM steps that I previously listed, is not advisable. There are three orientations against which the PPP maturity has to be compared: portfolio, programme and project.

Each of these orientations may have a certain level of maturity, whereby the professionalizing of project management will usually come first.

It is possible to use the five CMM steps, but also those out of the OPM3 model, which have been used in the next illustration, are very well applicable. The meaning of the different levels is discussed further on.

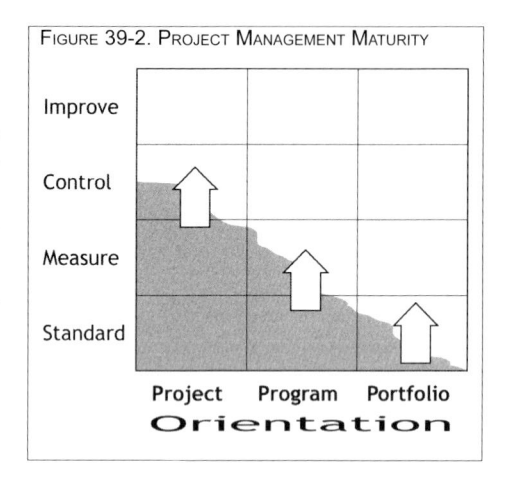

FIGURE 39-2. PROJECT MANAGEMENT MATURITY

A PPP development takes years, implementing a standard is not enough. There has to be a consistent use of that standard, it has to be in line with the critical success factors of the organization, and there have to be guidelines referring to what is good and what is not. In short, it is necessary that the operational management actively provides direction on the various project management processes.

7. Implementing company wide

If there is a long term plan for the PPP implementation, a start can be made with the company wide implementation. This is a change programme in itself with all the perils such as opposition, and everything that comes with that. Therefore, it should be managed as such. It is a heavy programme and, therefore, needs a strong programme manager.

8. Apply lessons learned

The environment changes, the market changes, and people change. All factors which put pressure on the PPP processes.

To keep improving, the organization needs to have the following capabilities:
- Identify the core causes of problems with processes.
- Develop improvement initiatives across the organization.
- Show that the improvements are in use.

This process step is about the capability of an organization to face the actual situation, and to recognise the core of the problems.

3.04-4 Special Topics

1. OPM3[5]

OPM3 is a model for *organizational project management*. Here, we mean organizations for which the service provision to customers is mainly carried out through projects (for example a software house or a construction company) and/or organizations which are continuously undergoing changes, and where strategic choices and programmes are being implemented. OPM3 describes what you have to organise in order to translate strategic choices into concrete projects and programmes, how you have to set up the line to make this possible, and how you get a standard or norm working as it should.

OPM3 distinguishes between three domains (orientations), for which it describes standard processes:

- The *project domain,* a collection of activities providing a concrete result, within a fixed time and budget using limited resources.
- The *programme domain,* in which projects and line activities are managed in cohesion, usually because this has to do with a communal theme or resources.
- The *portfolio domain,* in which all projects, programmes and possible line activities in a company, or part of it, are managed as being investments, which contribute to the strategic choices of the organization.

---

5 (2003) *Organizational Project Management Maturity Model – knowledge foundation* – PROJECT MANAGEMENT INSTITUTE INC, Newton Square - USA

Example 39-1 Best Practices in OPM3

We check how this works out for the *project initiation process*. The best practice is:

1010 Project Initiation Process standardised
1010.10 Active Process Management body
1010.20 Project Initiation Process developed
1010.30 Standardised Project Initiation Process

The three components of the best practice are, in OPM3, called capabilities. A number of outcomes have been defined for each capability which has to be available before you can conclude how capable people are. This availability can be demonstrated during an assessment.

Firstly the best-practice OPM3 "1010 Project Initiation Process Standardised" contains the component, 1010.10 an Active Process management governing body, which regularly meets to discuss the process management to ensure that (in this case) the *Initiation Process* runs smoothly, and where needed, apply improvements. This is the first step, even before a standard has been thought of and implemented.

This group of process owners is responsible for the development of a standard, and they can decide to develop it themselves, or possibly to purchase this method and customise it to their requirements. This is up to the organization, and you only implement what is needed. As OPM3 is completely in line with the PMBoK, it will quickly become clear if you have forgotten anything. When you have acquired this standard and have also communicated it to all parties involved, then the second component, 1010.20 Project Initiation Process developed, is also ready.

To develop this complete best-practice in al its maturity, it is necessary that all project managers in the organization consistently use the working methods described in the standard. Only then can you say that the third and last component of this best-practice, 1010.30 Standardised Project Initiation Process, is finished.

3.04 PPP Implementation

Per domain there are management processes available, which can each be one of the four possible capability levels:
- The process is *standardised*.
- The process has been made *measurable*.
- The process is *controlled*.
- The process is *continuously being improved*.

As opposed to the maturity models based on the CMM, there is a level for each process. The organization can choose for itself which processes it wants to professionalize, and also to what extent. I find this flexibility an important advantage in comparison to other models.

For each combination, a best practice has been described with an implementation route. So, in total about 500 best practices, which say something about the standards to be used. This appears to be a lot, but in practice it is not as bad as it looks.

The knowledge bank of OPM3 has also described the mutual dependencies, as a result of which you automatically also get presented with the *best practices* that are conditional for getting the *costs* practices in order. It is not possible to forget anything.

As well as the best-practices for the management processes there are some supporting ones, which ensure the right staff, management support, ROI calculations, etc. They are, indeed, important for a successful implementation of *organizational project management*, but in this explanation I shall leave them out of the consideration and continue with the levels mentioned.

THE PROCESS IS STANDARDISED

The maturity of a process starts with policy. As one of the first steps in a maturity programme, the organization determines which processes it will standardize, and which they plan to maintain. The latter is important, because, contrary to a one-off implementation of a standard, a maturity programme is a development model. This choice means that there have to be process owners with sufficient knowledge and authority to make decisions on the processes, and this is the group responsible for the process control.

MAKING THE PROCESS MEASURABLE

How do you make the quality of a process measurable? OPM3 bases finding the right indicators on the needs of the customer. The first capability for this maturity level of all project management processes states that the process *focuses on the customer needs* and ensures that all projects also do that. The *PMBOK Guide* defines the customer as being the person, or organization, who will be using the results of the projects.

By knowing what customers find important, it can be determined which characteristics of the process are critical, and how the customer's needs can be met.

A further capability in making the project management processes measurable, is that the effect of the feeding processes on the

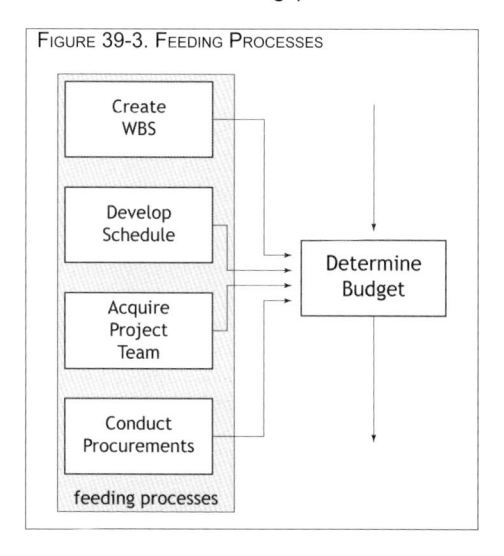

FIGURE 39-3. FEEDING PROCESSES

feeding processes: Create WBS, Develop Schedule, Acquire Project Team, Conduct Procurements → Determine Budget

3.04 PPP Implementation

quality of a certain process has been evaluates. Take the process Setting up the cost budget (see figure).

The figure includes a number of feeding processes, which provide our process with input. Garbage in means garbage out. When it is clear how the quality of the input influences the quality of the process, then, for example, entry checks can be carried out prior to starting the process. In our example it makes no sense to set up a good cost budget, when there are no contracts for which the agreements on rates are known, or when the agreements in the contract are not clear. If you do go ahead and set up a cost budget anyway, the reliability will be less than desired.

CONTROLLING THE PROCESS

The controlling of a process means that this functions between the lower and upper limits that have been set. But what does this mean exactly?

> EXAMPLE 39-2 CONTROLLED PROCESS
> Take for instance the process *Human Resource Planning*. The PMBoK indicates that this produces the following output:
> - Roles and responsibilities
> - Project organization chart
> - Schedule of the resources to be obtained
>
> Now suppose that experience proves that for a certain type of projects, there is an urgent need, to, in advance, unambiguously record certain roles and responsibilities. This is because this regularly leads to uncertainties in the organization. You now start counting how many project plans this paragraph contains. You apply the necessary statistics to that in order to determine whether or not this is a controlled process. For a number of readers the picture of doom will appear of a bureaucratic, measuring organization. That remains to be seen, if it is costing you turnover you have to do something, and apparently, judging by our example, this does not happen automatically.

When processes have been made controllable, you start a cycle of continuously improving and amending.

CONTINUOUSLY IMPROVING THE PROCESS

Only after the preceding processes have been implemented, can you start thinking about a continuous improvement cycle. The organization has now developed knowledge and experience for each sub-process to:
- Identify the main causes of problems in processes.
- Develop improvement initiatives across the organization.
- Prove that the improvements are being used.

2. ISO 21500 Guidance[6]

On the 1st September 2012 the first edition of the ISO 21500:2012 *"Guidance on project management"* was published. This standard

---

[6] (2012) *ISO 215000, Guidance on project management*, ISO

> EXAMPLE 39-3 IMPROVING THE PROCESS
> Imagine the following situation (probably recognizable). The process *Cost Budgeting* is known as a controlled process. One of the criteria this is measured by is a clearly described limit, above which project sponsors have to ask the management permission to enter into commitments with suppliers. This limit was determined at a time when the liquidity of the organization was under a lot of pressure. After a time, the economy starts growing again, but this limit has not been amended in line with the average size of an order. In order to anyway make some progress in project contracts, the contracts are split in such a way that amounts are not above the set limits. All measurements show that the *cost control process* is controlled. Through the management information systems, another picture develops, namely that the liquidity is again coming under pressure.
>
> What is the main cause, over expenditure, or a wrong limit? In the example, this is for now not important. But what is important, is that the organization learns to recognise and improve such basic problems, and can identify improvements to the process and implement them.

3.04 PPP Implementation

looks very similar to the *"guide to the Project Management Body of Knowledge"* published by the Project Management Institute, and their influence on the ISO publication is clear to see. The overlap with IPMA is primarily in the area of technical competences. Where possible, I have indicated this in the relevant elements.

The Guidance contains, just as the *PMBOK Guide*, five process groups with a slightly different naming convention:
- Initiating
- Planning
- Implementing
  (in the *PMBOK Guide* Executing)
- Controlling
  (in the *PMBOK Guide* Monitoring and Controlling)
- Closing

The essence, however, is the same. Where the *PMBOK Guide* differentiates knowledge areas, this Guidance talks of subject groups, which are:
- Integrate
- Stakeholder
- Scope
- Resources
- Time
- Cost
- Risk
- Quality
- Procurement
- Communication

Compared to the *PMBOK Guide*, there is one additional topic (stakeholders). There are 39 processes, which are classified under the process groups, and the subject groups.

It is expected that, through this Guidance, IPMA with its technical competences and PMI with its *PMBOK Guide*, will grow closer together.

3.04 PPP Implementation

3.05 Permanent organization

STANDING, AS LONG AS IT GOES WELL

The permanent organization is one which exists when the project starts, and still exists when the project ends.

The permanent organization is the "mainland" where the project result ultimately has to be anchored.

Projects don't stand on their own, but in the permanent organization.

3.05-1 Definitions

Authority	Have the right to carry out certain actions.
Customer organization	Organization, for which the project is being set up and carried out.
Infrastructure	A system of facilities, equipment and services necessary for the functioning of an organization.
Management system	System to determine policy and objectives, and to achieve these objectives.
Organization	Group of people and facilities with a hierarchy of responsibilities, authorities and mutual relationships.
Organization structure	Hierarchy of responsibilities, authorities and mutual relationships between people.
Permanent organization	The line organization, within which the project/programme is running.
Responsibility	Obligation to ensure that something functions well, progresses, and can be accounted for.
Senior Management	Person or group of people managing and controlling an organization at the highest level.
Suppliers organization	Organization that supplies the required resources and services.

3.05-2 INTRODUCTION

In an old definition an organization is described as *"every form of human co-operation for a common goal"*.[1] New definitions do not substantially deviate from this. In practice the word organization is used in different ways:

- *The institutional organization concept:* an organization is now a group of people and resources who purposefully work together as one (system), without the individual people being recognized. In the legal sense, this is legal entity. Sometimes an organization is attributed almost (in)human characteristics, for example, a certain organization is treacly, aggressive or American.
- *The instrumental organization concept:* something is not just an organization, it also has an organization. This is about the structure, with which relatively stable relationships between people are defined. The different parts, and the people, are attuned to each another. The organization can now be seen as an instrument.
- *The functional organization concept:* this is about organizing. Organizing something usually means that we establish the work to be done, and carry it out to achieve a certain goal. It is the opposite of waiting for. It is about such things as co-ordinating, liaising, allocating resources, stimulating co-operation, etc.

When we now look at the organization as a collection of people who work together, we can differentiate the following main processes[2]:

- Formulating goals.
- Organizing.
- Realizing.

A project manager is appointed by an organization. What we look at in this chapter is the permanent organization(s) within which the project that the project manager is responsible for, takes place.

---

1 (1931) *Onward Industry*, Mooney JD & Reiley, HARPER, New York.
2 (2001) *Ondernemen in de onderneming,* Weggeman, Wijnen en Kor, KLUWER, Deventer

3.05-3 PROCESS STEPS

1. Understand the structure, goals and working methods.
2. Take account of structure, goals and working methods.
3. Monitor the project- line interface.
4. Identify similarities and differences.
5. Consider the different options and their consequences.
6. Discuss, decide, communicate and implement.
7. Apply lessons learned

1. Understand the structure, goals and working methods

In order to be able to organise a project smoothly, it is important that the project manager understands the different organizations involved. He is involved with[1]:

- The culture and the architecture of those organizations.
- The standards and conditions that apply for the project.
- The existing (technical) infra structure.
- The available staff.
- The guidelines for personnel policy.
- The way in which the organization allocates work.
- The market conditions or the political climate.
- The risk tolerance of the parties involved.
- Historical data on the cost estimates and the risks to be run.
- Project management Information Systems.

Furthermore, he has to deal with the way in which different organizations have organized their processes, such as:

- Standards in the area of security, safety, health and environment.
- Project management and quality standards.
- Manner of progress reporting and producing reports.
- Financial and administrative procedures.
- Procedures for change and configuration management.
- Procedures for risk management.
- Procedures for recording and archiving information.
- Etc.

As the project does not take place on an island, all these issues provide input for designing the project organization.

2. Take account of structure, goals and working methods

As far as possible, you have to ensure that there is a connection between the permanent and the project organization. This is not always easy, and especially when you are dealing with several organizations, it is often difficult to design a structure and develop working methods, which satisfy all of the parties. It is advisable, therefore, to focus on the communal goals, and to derive the structure and working methods from that.

3. Monitor the project-line interface

"The more the merrier" is a saying which does not apply to the project organization, there we can better speak of: *"The more parties involved, the more work."* Also the goals of parties involved may change during the project, leaving you to think there still is agreement, but the situation is actually far from that. It is crucial that the project manager keeps an eye on these "moving targets" and reacts adequately to them.

Here are two extremes:
- Keep to the situation as seen at the start.
- Move in line with every change.

---

[1] (2004) a Guide to the Project Management Body of Knowledge, THE PROJECT MANAGEMENT INSTUTUTE, USA

The initial reaction is the result of confusion between the concepts scope and environment. At the start, you determine the scope and aim for that. However, the environment is, by definition, what changes, and the project manager has little influence on that. You will have to move along with it flexibly. The latter however, does not mean that you go to the other extreme, and end up continuously chasing events.

When the environment continuously changes, it is better to split the project up in into short stages, whereby each stage then defines a time period of "some certainty".

4. Identify similarities and differences
When the project has started, it is best to look at the stakeholder analysis in order to determine to what extent the different interests still remain the same. When these start changing for the most powerful stakeholders, it is high time to intervene and take action.

Just as you would if you come onto a project for the first time, you then carry out a new stakeholder analysis, and look to see what they expect from the project. If this would mean a big change in approach and the result to be delivered, you draw up an amendment or change, which you then present to the new stakeholders.

5. Consider the different options and their consequences
There are often different options for arranging the common ground between the project and the permanent organization. In consultation with the project sponsors involved and the line managers, you choose which option is best for both the project and the organization itself.

6. 6. Discuss, decide, communicate and implement
This consideration results in the decision of which control mechanisms to implement, and the implementation must go hand in hand with good communication towards both the line and project.

7. Apply lessons learned
The unique temporary nature of the project makes it almost inevitable that the interfaces with the permanent organization will not progress smoothly, nor as a matter of course. Both during and after the project, we can learn from the experience.

3.05-4 SPECIAL TOPICS

1. Formal and informal

The organization can be described as a *formal organization,* by which is meant the official framework. Function descriptions, procedures, guidelines and rules are all part of this. They are impersonal in nature and restrict the individual freedom and autonomy. This formal organization is based on organization principles such as management unity, unity of authority, distribution of work and co-ordination. This leads to combined action on optimized activities, which are aligned to each other. On paper, anyway.

There is also an *informal organization.* Under this, we mean rules of conduct, which people develop in addition to the official framework of the formal organization. This results in an additional communication network as people who feel restricted in their work by the formal side of the organization seek out one another. Talking about it offers a certain amount of comfort. Informally all kinds of issues are taken care of, which, by following the formal procedures, would take up a lot more time.

2. The organization architecture

An organization structure shows how the work, which has to be carried out in an organization, is divided into tasks and functions. The authorities and responsibilities which are associated with the tasks are also shown.

The organization structure is represented in an organization chart. This consists of a number of boxes and lines.

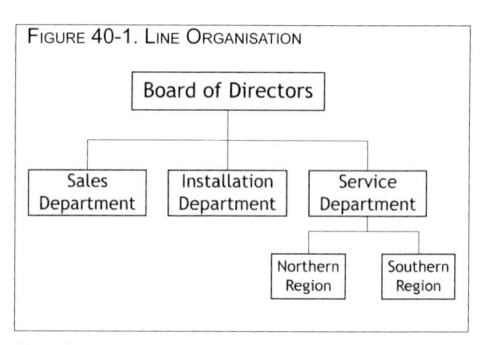

FIGURE 40-1. LINE ORGANISATION

The figure above illustrates a *line organization*. There is an unambiguous pattern of authority relationships. The person with a line function is directly responsible for parts of the production process.

The following figure shows a *line-staff-organization*. Someone in a staff function has no authority to make decisions, and can only advise. In practice, however, this is often different. Staff employees (in the next figure, the executive secretary and the planner) often have information, and direct access to senior line managers, so their influence may indeed be compelling. The differentiation of authority between line and staff is often a recurring organization problem.

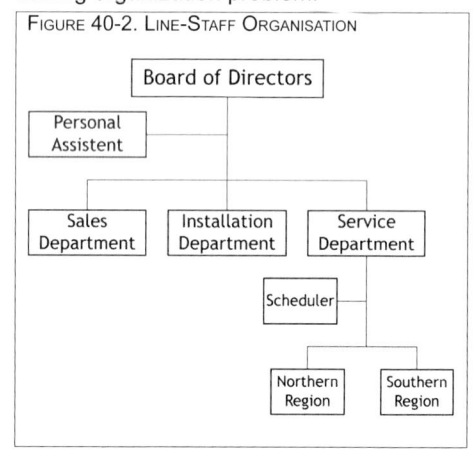

FIGURE 40-2. LINE-STAFF ORGANISATION

A *functional relationship* exists when a jobholder (or a department) can, from his function, give binding guidelines to someone else, even though there is no hierarchic connection between them both. A personnel department, for instance, can draw up binding guidelines regarding job evaluation systems. Another example is the soldier, who stops the general at the barrack gates, and asks him for identification. He is then exercising the functional authority granted to him in that position. A functional relationship is sometimes represented in an organization chart by a dotted line.

Tasks & Functions
By a *task* we mean work built up of a number of operations or activities. The *tasks* form the content of a function. A *task* always involves *authority,* and as a result of this, also *responsibility*. These three elements are inseparable from each other.

A *function* is a grouping of a number of tasks. This grouping can take place on the basis of a number of criteria, such as the goal the tasks are aimed at, the type of tasks, the skills required for the task, the place where, or the time at which, tasks are carried out, and the resources needed to carry out the tasks. An organization has primary functions, which are directly aimed at external service provision, and secondary functions, which take care of internal support.

A *function analysis* investigates the content of a function. A function has a goal which should be achieved through a number of tasks. The function analysis indicates which task characteristics are important, and which are less important. These are the function requirements, which are about characteristics like personal qualities, such as leadership abilities, creativity, knowledge, for example training and/or experience, skills, for example manual skills and/or social skills, and special requirements such as unusual working hours.

The **function description** consists of the list of the above mentioned function requirements and the function content. It concerns the function designation or function name, the place of the function in the organization, the core tasks of the function, the authorities and the responsibilities associated with the tasks. Through function descriptions, the organization chart gets content and takes on meaning. We use function descriptions for recruiting and selecting staff, and recognition and reward. As the functions are subject to change, the personnel department has to periodically amend the function descriptions.

An *authority* is a right someone has to take certain decisions. It is often unclear in organizations who, and at what time, is authorised to take a certain decision. The definition of the tasks and the accompanying authorities is then unclear. The most important authority is usually having availability of a budget.

Responsibility means the obligation to ensure that something functions or proceeds well, and to render an account of that. Put in an unfriendly way, the person with responsibility gets blamed when thing go wrong. Carrying responsibility without having authority is not possible, but often required.

The responsibility for a certain matter should not reside with a group of people, but preferably with one, and no more than one, person. Dividing responsibility over a number of jobholders always leads to vagueness and uncertainty.

Separation of functions
In addition to the co-ordination mechanisms mentioned above, the organization has to take some additional measures to ensure that it will discover mistakes (intentional or unintentional) as early as possible. The means it uses for that is function separation, based on the premise you cannot check your own work, but also that someone else has to

make sure you only carry out investments on your project which fall within the budget. Separation of functions always leads to bureaucracy, and this is both inevitable and necessary.

One of the areas where project managers are faced with function separation, is the deployment of people. The function separation looks as follows:

- *Decide:* the *operational management* or the *portfolio management* determines whether or not a project has sufficient priority to deploy certain people.
- *Keep:* the *line manager* takes care of the training and professionalizing of the staff, and he agrees the details with the project manager. He also does carries out the end of year assessment, and coaches and supports the employee in his professional development.
- *Use:* the *project manager* allocates the work to be carried out, and focuses the employee on achieving the project result.
- *Register:* the project office keeps track of whether or not the employee works on the project for the agreed number of hours, and reports any deviations.

Because the different functions have separate responsibilities, we achieve the situation that the one checks the other. In this way, possible mistakes or misuse can be discovered faster.

The example above can be applied generally. You achieve function separation by ensuring that the *deciding, keeping, using* and *registering* are carried out by different employees.

Delegating the responsibility
Delegating is the transfer of authorities and responsibilities by an authorised jobholder or manager, to jobholders lower down in the organization. This now gives the manager the opportunity to concentrate on other tasks, but it is still the case that many managers have a lot of problems delegating. You have to *want* to do it, and *be able* to do it. A proper transfer of information is essential. Which tasks, and accompanying authorities and responsibilities, are being transferred has to be documented. A part of the responsibility, the *end responsibility,* will remain with the person who is doing the delegating.

> EXAMPLE 40-1 CAPTAIN
> The captain who has the responsibility of steering the ship delegates this to the navigating officer. The navigating officer also gets the authority to act independently. Should an accident happen then the navigating officer is responsible to the captain. However, the captain remains responsible to the shipping company and statutory authorities. The captain cannot hide behind the navigating officer by saying that he might have made a mistake and not the captain himself. The navigating officer acts under the responsibility of the captain. If the navigating officer makes mistakes he apparently is not capable to carry out the task, and so the task should not have been transferred to him.

Span of Control
This is the number of staff a manager can still manage directly. For more senior functions this will only be a few employees, but for more junior functions and especially similar types of employees, this number can be a lot higher. As general guideline, you sometimes hear of a maximum span of control of seven plus or minus two. This has implications for the size of the total organization.

> EXAMPLE 40-2 SPAN-OF-CONTROL
> 7
> 7x7=49
> 7x7x7=343
> 7x7x7x7=2401
> 7x7x7x7x7=16807

y a part here are, as well as the type of organization and the work that has to be done, the personality characteristics, and the expertise of the manager and the staff. If the number of employees the manager manages is higher than the number of staff that the manager can effectively and safely manage, problems will arise. A possible solution is delegation of a number of tasks. Other options are: creating an assistant function, involving a staff service, or dividing up over more departments.

Depth of Control
This is the number of levels, which can be managed effectively. You can translate this to be the depth of control. This concept is aimed vertically, whereas the span of control is clearly aimed horizontally. The greater the number of levels, the more difficult the functioning of the communication. Information from higher levels is received in a distorted way, and is no longer understood. The estimate is that for each additional level, 40% of the essence of the information provided is lost. Similarly, information which goes from bottom up is either blocked, or distorted somewhere on its route.

3. Line verses Project
Depending on the number and the type of projects an organization carries out, and the primary process of that organization, certain organization architecture is decided on. For a large part, this choice determines to what extent the organization can be successful in carrying out projects.

There are two basic questions:
- Where do we put the project manager?
- How do we split the authority over the resources?

Functional Organization
The architecture of a functional organization can be called stable. The organization is divided into departments such as Procurement, Warehouse, Research & Design, Production and Sales. There is a clear authority structure; each employee has only one manager.

The projects carried out in such organizations often fall within the borders of the departments, and are managed by the line manager or an employee.

There is no need for a formal portfolio management process here, because this falls under the responsibility of the line manager. The most important control aspects of such an organization are scope and time, because money and capacity are already being controlled in the existing departmental budget.

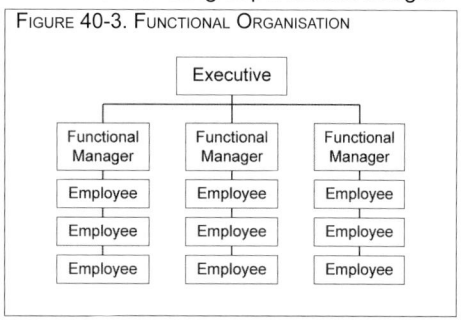

FIGURE 40-3. FUNCTIONAL ORGANISATION

Project-Based Organization
The project-based organization is precisely the opposite of the functional organization. Project managers report directly to a more senior manager.

From the project manager's point of view, this is an ideal situation, as he is completely responsible for, and has authority over, all the resources on his project. Just as with the functional organization it is clear what the lines of authority are.

There are also important disadvantages recognizable in this architecture. The different skill disciplines are divided over the projects, and there is suboptimization because in each project, the 'wheel' has to be invented again.

3.05 Permanent Organization

The latter of these can be solved by standardizing the approach and the various functions. There is a small supporting staff, which carries out the 'repetitive' work, such as administration, personnel department, and senior management etc. We then also see (virtual) centres of expertise coming into existence for the various disciplines, in which staff from different projects come together in order to further develop their field of expertise.

FIGURE 40-4. PROJECT BASED

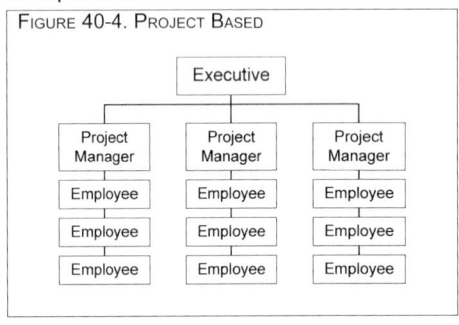

The project manager is often a line manager or another jobholder, who additionally takes on this task temporarily (sometimes alongside his permanent function).

FIGURE 40-5. WEAK MATRIX

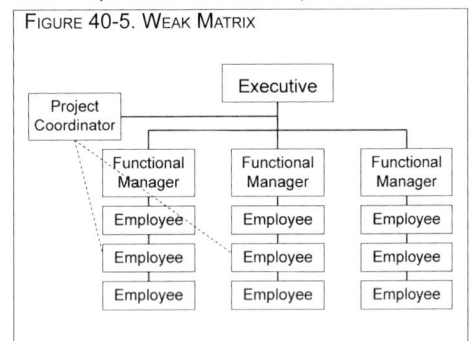

In the following form, there is a jobholder whose profession is project management.

In the *balanced* matrix, for the first time there is a situation of a multi-project environment.

FIGURE 40-6. BALANCED MATRIX

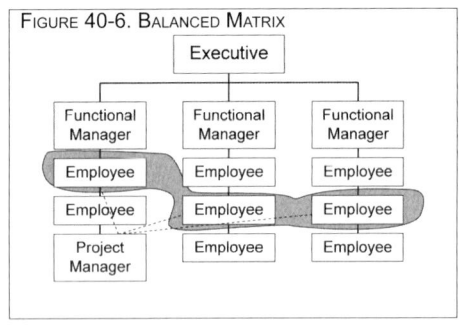

Matrix Organization

The matrix form as organization architecture tries to couple the best of two worlds with each other. In the matrix structure, employees still have two managers; a project manager and a functional (or resource) manager. There are three forms, whereby the difference between these forms is primarily determined by the power balance between the project manager and the functional manager.

In many aspects, the *weak* matrix resembles the functional matrix. The project manager has a co-ordinating role and reports to someone in the higher management.

He has limited authority, and to get things done he has to rely for an important part on his powers of persuasion.

Projects now transcend departments. This form is especially suited to organizations which have a limited number of projects.

Project managers have operational responsibilities and authority, and decide what has to be carried out and when.

The functional line managers then determine how and by *whom*.

In the line, the discipline and the employees are both further developed. In this form, the biggest objection to the matrix organization definitely applies, that of the dual authority relationship. Matrix organizations often display the characteristic of a lot of tussles around people and resources. Because higher management has the tendency to listen to the functional management, project managers often feel that they are not understood.

In the *strong* matrix, the project manager has much more say. The difference with the project based organization is small. In the heavy matrix, the employee has a 'home' in the form of the department to which he belongs, and in the project based organization, that is not the case.

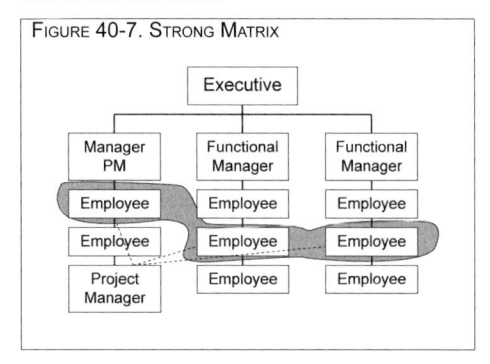

FIGURE 40-7. STRONG MATRIX

There is a separate project management department or division that manages all projects within the organization and also carries out portfolio and capacity analyses.

4. Henry Mintzberg

Co-ordination mechanisms

To ensure that the organization's employees do what is intended, an organization will have to anchor a number of mechanisms in the structure. Mintzberg[2] differentiates five basic mechanisms, which can also be applied within a project.

- *Mutual adaptation,* where the employees during their work, gear their work activities to each other. Suitable for small organizations, or for complex tasks for which it is impossible to determine in advance how the work can best be carried out.
- *Direct supervision,* one person is responsible for the work of other employees. He gives instructions on the execution, and monitors the progress.

What the following three co-ordination mechanisms have in common, is that certain aspects of the work are standardised:

- *Standard work processes,* the way in which employees have to carry out the work is laid down in procedures.
- *Standard output,* a clear description of the result to be delivered, how it is done being less important.
- *Standard skills,* there is a specification of which training and exams passes are required before being allowed to carry out this work.

Mintzberg states: *"As the work of organizations becomes more complex, the co-ordination mechanism used the most appears to shift from mutual adaptation to direct supervision, and from there to standardizing, preferably of work processes, or otherwise of output or of skills, and then returns to mutual adaptation."*

When the organization is growing, there is work specialization. A sales department and a procurement department will be set up, divisions, subsidiaries and more management layers emerge. The linking-pin principle ensures that each layer is represented in a higher layer. Responsibilities are then delegated top down.

---

2 (1983) *Structures in fives: designing effective organizations,* Henry Mintzberg, PRENTICE HALL

3.05 Permanent Organization

Configurations

Mintzberg has written a lot about the structure of an organization. He differentiates between five parts in each organization.

These five parts, which are shown in the next figure, vary in size depending on the type of organization. They are:
- *The Strategic Apex,* have ultimate responsibility, and determine the strategy of the organization.
- *The Middle Line,* is the link between the strategic top and the operational core, and consists of the operational and middle managers of the organization.
- *The Operating Core,* these are the employees that carry out the primary process of the organization.
- *The Technostructure,* takes care of the different forms of standardizing (for instance the quality department) in the organization.
- *The Supporting Staff,* specialised services (accommodation, restaurant, repro, etc.) providing support to the other parts of the organization.

Based on their position within the organization each part will influence the evolution of the organization.
- *The Strategic Apex,* towards centralization.
- *The Middle Line,* towards decentralization.
- *The Operating Core,* towards professionalization.
- *The Technostructure,* towards standardization.
- *The Supporting Staff,* towards cooperation.

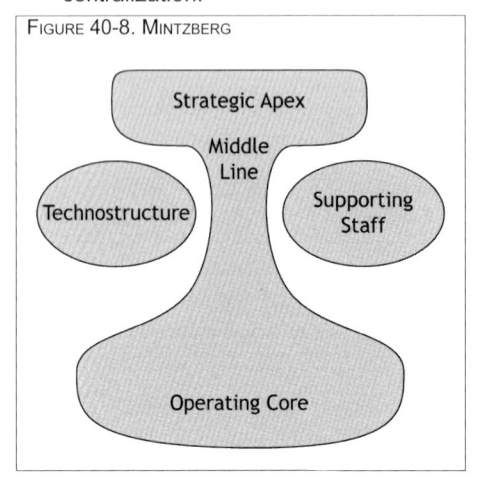

Mintzberg describes seven different configurations[3]: the entrepreneurial, machine, professional, diversified, innovative, missionary and political organizations. Each has its own specific configuration, whereby the size of the different parts differs in relation to the others. Each represents a resulting force that captures much of the essence of the managerial processen:
- *Entrepreneurial,* direction.
- *Machine,* efficiency.
- *Professional,* proficiency.
- *Diversified,* concentration.
- *Innovative,* learning.
- *Missionary,* cooperation.
- *Political,* competition.

Each has its own specific configuration, whereby the size of the different parts differs in relation to the others.

Organizations do not stand alone, and need to adapt themselves to the influence of the environment. For commercial organizations, that is the market, and for public organizations it is politics and the social field of influence.

FIGURE 40-8. MINTZBERG

[3] (1989) *Mintzberg on Management,* Henry Mintzberg, THE FREE PRESS, New York

5. Porters Value Chain

Commercial organizations have to adapt themselves optimally, in order to achieve their strategic goals, and it is important that they do this better than their competitors.

Organizations are faced with: customers who want to pay less, suppliers who want a higher price, more competitors causing the price to drop, the existing competition and newcomers in the market.

According to the value chain theory of Porter[41], an organization consists of five primary activities:
- Inbound logistics.
- Operations.
- Outbound logistics.
- Sales & marketing.
- Services.

Plus four supporting activities:
- Firm infrastructure.
- Human Resource Management.
- Technology.
- Procurement.

According to Porter an organization can only gain a competitive advantage by systematically carrying out its strategically important activities better or cheaper than the competition.

The value chain contains the primary activities, the supporting activities and the margin of the organization. The margin is the difference between the total value of the organization and the total costs incurred for the primary and supporting activities.

6. Management of change

In the pioneering phase, an organization tackles things pragmatically and efficiently. It goes for its goal, is flexible and also prepared to take risks. Such an organization, however, experiences growth, becomes more professional, and the pioneering attitude, therefore, is no longer suited. The organization then often starts to follow a more 'conservative' course. New staff, who have not experienced this pioneering stage, have other motives than the people who have been there from the start, and they also often take less risk.

The necessity arises to standardize and to implement procedures and quality improvement. Function descriptions and salary systems emerge, and slowly, the organization becomes less efficient, particularly

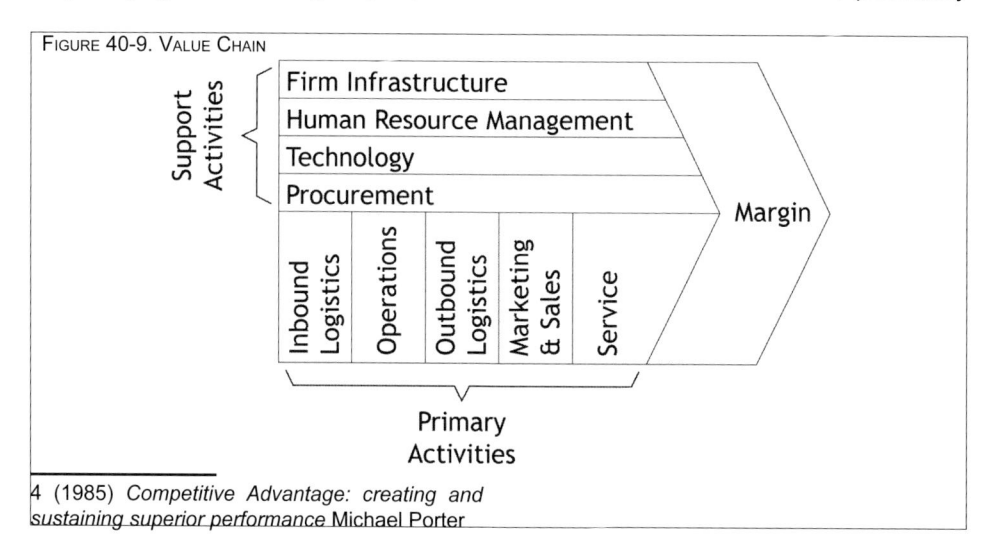

FIGURE 40-9. VALUE CHAIN

Support Activities:
- Firm Infrastructure
- Human Resource Management
- Technology
- Procurement

Primary Activities:
- Inbound Logistics
- Operations
- Outbound Logistics
- Marketing & Sales
- Service

Margin

4 (1985) *Competitive Advantage: creating and sustaining superior performance* Michael Porter

when these developments are ignored. An organization, which does not consciously change, will automatically start working less efficiently. More and more rules are added, and no rules are discarded. The overhead automatically goes up, and the productivity goes down.

> EXAMPLE 40-3 QUOTE FROM 'THE PRINCE" BY MACHIAVELLI:
> He (the king) should never turn his mind away from warfare. And in times of peace he must become even more skilled in it than in war itself. He can do this in two ways: on the one hand through action and on the other hand through study. With respect to the first point, apart from organizing and training his troops well, he has to...etc...

Also from the organization's own environment (for profit organizations, this means the market), there are forces that make it necessary for the organization to adapt itself. Kotter[5] mentions four:

- *Technological changes*, such as faster and better communication (internet) and transport possibilities, whereby it is possible to easily connect people all over the world.
- *International economic integration,* the evening out of trade barriers, the solidarity of currencies and an increase of the global cash flows.
- *Saturation of the markets in 'developed' countries,* decreasing domestic growth, more aggressive exporters, more deregulation.
- *Collapse of the communist and socialist regimes,* whereby more countries start to privatize communist systems and state enterprises.

According to Kotter this globalization of markets and competition on the one hand leads

---
5 (1996) *Leading Change,* John P. Kotter, HARVARD BUSINESS SCHOOL PRESS, Boston

to more opportunities, and on the other hand also to more risks, with the result that organizations feel the need to further adapt. Apart from these causes mentioned by Kotter, there is another phenomenon which occurs when a profit organization is successful. The success will attract competitors, whereby what is making the organization successful will soon be imitated. For this reason, an organization has to keep innovating.

You can distinguish, roughly, between four types of innovation:
- *Product Innovation*, developing new products which are differentiated from those of the competition.
- Process Innovation, improving the way in which products are made, or services provided.
- Market Innovation, newer ways of marketing.
- Organization Innovation, renewing the organization structure.

Bottom-line, these innovations can always be brought back to, on the one hand increasing the turnover, and on the other hand reducing costs. When we make the business case for a project, then it often directly, or indirectly, involves these two issues. The project based form of working is pre-eminently suited to designing and managing innovations.

That is because:
- The innovation is, by definition, something new, and therefore happens outside of the permanent operation.
- There is more than one discipline needed to design and achieve the innovation.
- It has to be carried out in a limited time.

7. The learning organization
The learning organization is a concept which in the nineties of the 20th century strongly

3.05 Permanent Organization

influenced the thinking about changes in organizations. Particularly Peter Senge[6] and Chris Argyris[7] have published much about this.

According to Senge, a learning organization must possess five disciplines:
- Personal skills mastery within the staff of the organization.
- The fathoming of the underlying mental models related to our attitude.
- Common vision on what the future of the organization should look like.
- Teaching employees in teams to improve themselves and improve the team (team learning).
- Being able to see the organization as a system in its context.

This last fifth discipline is the most important, and is about the skill of the organization to see itself as a whole in its context.

Organizations can learn at three levels[8]. At the first level, the single loop learning, an organization adapts its rules. The underlying insights remain intact. The change comes down to the organization doing the same thing, but better.

When the organization now changes its insights, we speak of double loop learning. The management and the staff now go into debate, questioning the 'why' of the rules. This form of learning is needed when it becomes clear from the environment of the organization that the existing working methods are no longer adequate.

However, if the essential principles of an organization do not change, there will be no triple loop learning. With this form of learning the 'what for' question is also being asked. The mission of the organization is being questioned.

The essence of the theories on learning organizations is always about the skill of an organization to adapt to the ever changing environment around it. According to this viewpoint, collective learning is equal to organizational change.

8. The coping curve

A number of models for change projects are based on how people cope with big changes in their life.

They are often based on the ideas of Dr. Elisabeth Kübler-Ross (1926-2004), a psychiatrist who carried out pioneering work in the area of terminal care. The people involved in a major change process are faced with similar problems as people who have just heard that they are terminally ill. These are, just as with Kotter, stage models, but with more emphasis on the emotional side.

We describe what these different stages could mean:
- *Denial and isolation*: employees cannot accept it, and they shut off from the reality. The situation is a matter of a complete sense of disbelief.
- *Anger:* after some time, the seriousness of the situation has sunk in, and the disbelief changes into a form of anger. Now it is important that the staff is allowed to voice this anger.
- *Bargaining:* employees recover their composure, and 'negotiate' with the situation that has arisen to see if something can be changed. All kinds of initiatives emerge to 'save matters'.

---

6 (1990) *The Fifth Discipline,* Peter Senge, DOUBLEDAY
7 (1996) *On Organizational Learning,* Chris Argyris
8 (2002) *Lerend Organiseren – als meer van hetzelfde niet meer helpt,* Wierdsma en Swieringa, STENFORD KROESE, Groningen

- *Depression:* people realize that they have to accept the situation. Initially this results in resignation, in grieving for the fact that things will no longer be as they were before. The coping has now properly started.
- *Acceptance:* the state of affairs has been accepted, and people resign themselves. People take their time to find themselves again, and make the best of it.

The importance of this model is the insight that staff must be allowed the time to accept a big change. Whether or not the company can allow that time, strongly depends on the necessity of the change and the time the organization has.

9. Adjusting change strategy to company culture

Most models for change are very much consistent with each other. Core concepts which keep returning are: urgency, opposition, gaining speed, culture and empowerment. Apparently, these concepts play an important role in changes, but nevertheless, many changes do not bring what was intended at the start.

Ten Have[9] states that when determining the right change strategy, account has to be taken of the 'temperature' of the organization and that of the change itself. There are cold and warm changes, and there are cold and warm organizations.

The core of his recommendations have been summarized in the table.

What usually is clear, is the type of change. The cold change is driven by the necessity, to which the organization must react. The warm change comes from inside. Depending on the type of organization, either warm or cold, a choice has to be made as to which strategy is the most natural.

---
9 (1999) *Gezond verstand in managementland*, Steven ten Have in Holland Management Review nr. 64, ELSEVIER, Amsterdam

Temperature of the organization	A **cold** organization interprets opposition as barriers, which have to be removed. The driving force is formed by the direction of the management.	A **warm** organization interprets opposition as involvement. Internal involvement of the staff is the driving force behind this organization.
of the change	Change strategy	
With a **cold** change, the necessity is no longer an issue. Change is **necessary,** because the continued existence of the organization is at stake.	*Intervening* on the hard side of the organization: figures, company processes, structure and systems. Opposition is broken through. There seems to be only one good way available.	*Interactive change* through which the top management can rely on the skill, cohesion, energy and vitality of the organization in arriving at the necessary changes.
With a **warm** change, it is not so much the necessity which is the driving force, but much more the ambition and the motivation of the management, who want to go in a different direction. This is more about a **voluntary** change.	*Implementing* the change is enforced top down. The vision and insights of the top management are translated into structures, which incites the required behaviour.	*Renewing* where the motivation to change comes from the organization itself. It is a matter of changing proactively, and anticipating on the future situations.

3.06 Business

WHAT IT IS REALLY ALL ABOUT

The business is
the organization's essential process.

Everything we do in an organization
has the ultimate objective of
supporting the business.

'Things' come into the organization
that the staff get to work on, and
add value to. This process of
adding value is the business.

Let me see the primary process, and then
I know what business
the organization is in.

3.06-1 Definitions

Input	Products and services that the organization involves and uses in its activities.
Output	Products and services that leave the organization for the benefit of the environment.
Primary process	The processes in the permanent organization that create the added value with which the organization serves its customers.
Procedure	Specified way of carrying out an activity or a process.
Process	The totality of connected or influencing activities that transforms input into output.
Product	The result of a process.

3.06-2 Introduction

We have already come across what the primary process is in the previous chapter, when handling Porter's[1] value chain. It consists of:

- Inbound logistics.
- Operations.
- Outbound logistics.
- Marketing and Sales.
- Service.

Any stagnation in one of these elements, leads to a stagnation in the organization's operational life. To an important extent, this fact drives the problems with projects that, in one way or another, have to do with the primary process.

There are a number of possibilities as to why this dependency exists:

- The *project results* interferes with the primary process.
- The *project execution* interferes with the primary process.
- The project *uses resources* from the primary process.

The problems that can arise now vary, from critical resources that are pulled off the project because there are production problems, to a complete standstill of the critical process as a result of a wrong project decision or project results that do not function.

This is the justification for including this competence element!

When, during the project start-up, a project manager is busy with producing the project management plan, he must realize where his project might interfere with, or be involved with, the organization's primary process, and that because of this, there is possibly an extra point for attention in his risk management plan.

---

1 (1979) *Porter on Competition,* Michael E. Porter, HARVARD BUSINESS SCHOOL PRESS

3.06-3 PROCESS STEPS

The ICB has chosen for a broad interpretation in the elaboration of this competence element in possible process steps. This leads to a certain overlap with other chapters, which I would rather avoid here. This is especially the case with element 3.04 PPP Implementation, and therefore, I will now only address the issues regarding the primary process insofar as these apply to an individual project.

The process steps are then:
1. Align project and line organization.
2. Understand the strategic standards and guidelines.
3. Verify whether standards and guidelines have been met.
4. Satisfy the business case requirements.
5. Provide feedback on the existing PPP implementation.

1. Align project an line organization

The ICB itself describes this process step as follows: *setting up the line organization and the organization for projects, programmes and/or portfolios.*

When, as project manager, you start setting up your project, you look at the maturity level that the organization has in the area of project management. Because when an organization has little experience with project management, it is probably not aware of the implications of project based working.

When you are clear about this, you look at to what extent your project interferes with the primary process of the organization. As mentioned in the introduction, this interference may be related to *results,* the *execution* or the required *resources*. The necessary agreements are made on:
- The way in which the results interferes with the primary process.
- The risks that the execution of the project impose on the primary process.
- The deployment of the required resources.

The basic pre-condition for all these points, is that the primary process must (never) be endangered, it is the organisation's lifeline.

When you are dealing with a mature organization in the area of project management, many of these problems will have been dealt with in one way or another in the form of processes.

2. Understand strategic standards and guidelines

The ICB describes this process step as follows: *Determine strategic standards and guidelines, for instance for legal issues, finance and economy, personnel, sales and marketing, ICT.* You have to understand that most of these standards and guidelines have been set up to protect the primary process. Project managers often complain about the amount of bureaucracy in large organizations, but (unfortunately) this is inevitable. They are not rules for the sake of setting rules, but they are there mainly to protect the primary process, and the fact that the "internal rule issuers" sometimes overdo this, is something we just have to accept.

For the individual project manager, who is setting up his project, this means that at the start he has to study the standards and guidelines, and the way in which they protect the organisation's primary process. By doing this, he will be able to find more acceptable solutions for problems during the execution of his project, than he would if he manages the project 'detached from his environment'.

3. Verify whether standards and guidelines have been met

The previous process step means that a project manager must immediately verify that the way his project has been set up complies with these standards and guidelines. The ICB describe this process step as: *initiate processes for determining appropriate standards and guidelines in the organization, and assess projects and programmes against these standards and guidelines.*

The word appropriate deserves extra attention, because this is often a problem project managers experience in an organization, which in their view, is too bureaucratic. Often, certain procedures do not fit, and creative interim solutions are designed. Is this desirable, you may ask yourself. I think we can once again find the answer by looking at the effect a possible amendment of these standards and guidelines has on the primary process. When the primary process is not endangered, an amendment is allowed, and if it would be endangered, it isn't allowed. Furthermore, there are also legal standards and guidelines, and for these it is quite simple, you just have to comply with them.

4. Satisfy the business case requirements

The business case has, over the last few years, deservedly enjoyed a growing interest. The ICB describes this process step as follows: *implementing a strategy for company changes, management reports and implementation of business case requirements.*

To do this, the organization devises a number of guidelines in the form of:
- Minimum rate of return.
- Payback period.
- Style (standard form).

With the aim of making the different projects comparable. We have already come across this in the topic covering investment decisions.

The assessment of projects as business cases is about the viability of the organization in the long term. Drucker[1] states that a company has the goal of making enough profit to be able to cushion future risks. In investment projects, therefore, we look more and more for a minimum return per project. The higher the risk, the higher that minimum return must also be. As there are also projects with no return (implementing legal requirements), the minimum return also contains sufficient room to finance those projects.

All that remains is the role of the project manager, which consists of providing the 'cost' side of the business case. In turn, the project sponsor handles the 'benefits' side. There are often financial professionals, who enter this into a spreadsheet model, in order to assess the extent to which the project is financially acceptable.

5. Provide feedback on the existing PPP implementation

The "proof of the pudding is in the eating", also with regard to the implementation of the various PPP processes. There is always something to be criticized in that regard, as every manager has his own hobbyhorse, but that is not what it is about in this process step. What is important, is that the processes implemented do not get in the way of the primary process. Therefore, at the end of the project, the project team evaluates to what extent this has been the case. This evaluation is carried out in consultation with the line managers from the departments that execute the primary processes, and who have

---

1 (1954) *The Practice of Management,* Peter F. Drucker, HARPER & ROW PUBLISHERS, New York

3.06 Business

been involved in the project. The evaluation delivers suggestions for improvement, which are included in the on-going PPP process improvement cycle.

3.07
Systems, products and technology

WE CANNOT DO WITHOUT THEM ANY MORE, HE SIGHED

There are systems, which we do not even know exist, but which imprison us.

Products we think we need,
but then again, not really.

And technology?

Without that, our society
would not exist.

And what of the architects of all of this, where are they actually hiding?

3.07 Systems, products and technology

3.07-1 DEFINITIONS

Interface	A system boundary, where different sub-systems can exercise influence on each other.
Integration	Making an entity from the various sub-systems that functions well.
System	The totality of related influencing elements. Or, the rules and procedures, with which the organization manages the daily operation.
System approach	An inter-disciplinary, holistic approach, whereby projects and programmes are seen as a system working together with other complex systems.
System management	The management of, and providing leadership for, a system

3.07-2 INTRODUCTION

This competence element is about the systems, products and technology that an organization uses to fulfil its mission and achieve its vision. These three elements determine whether or not an organization can survive within its environment. They form the real capital of the company.

However, with regard to the three concepts, the ambiguity of the words continuously plays tricks on us. This is because there are products which are part of a system, systems which in turn are part of a piece of technology and technology which may consist of a number of connected products.

But what is it really all about in this competence element? Without a definition for the three separate concepts, the essence is fairly simple: *an organization uses systems, products and technology to add value to the social traffic*. That applies just as much to a commercial company as to a non-profit organization. If, as an organization, you do not add value, you have no business being here.

Two important tasks then emerge, which an organization has to undertake:

1. Applying systems, products and technology.

2. The development and maintenance of systems, products and technology.

When the ICB mentions these two tasks, it talks of *system application* and *system development*, whereby with system, they mean systems, products and technology. This causes unnecessary confusion, because we use the word *system* twice, but each time with a different meaning. To avoid this confusion I choose to consequentially mention all three in this chapter.

So, there are:

- *Systems*: these are the rules and procedures, through which the organization manages the daily operations.
- *Products (or services)*: these are the things the organization delivers to its customers, or procures from its suppliers.
- *Technology*: the tools, working methods, machines and suchlike, used for adding value to the social traffic.

Together with the subject of personnel, which has been addressed in another chapter, these four determine the viability of the organization.

3.07-3 System Application Process

The *application of* systems, products and technology:

1. Analyze the structure, definition and environment.
2. Make a feasibility analysis, and produce a business justification.
3. Determine customers and functionality.
4. Determine goals and components.
5. Design production and supply-chain for the distribution.
6. Authorise the design and production.
7. Test and optimize .
8. Validate against the requirements in the "business case".
9. Put into operation.
10. Manage the life cycle.
11. Apply lessons learned.

1. Analyze the structure, definition and environment

The application starts with the definition of the system, product or technology in relation to its environment. It doesn't just stand alone, but has the objective of ensuring that it adds value to its environment, because only then will the organization have the strength to survive in a changing world.

> EXAMPLE 42-1 REWARD SYSTEM
> The application of the reward system involves:
> • The first design
> • The approval of the HR Department
> • The approval of Senior Management
> • Allocating employees
> But also the updating of it five years later, in order to stay in line with the labour market.

This may mean that we have to adapt systems, products or technology to:
- Legal requirements.
- Norms.
- Expectations.
- Progressive insight.
- Market demand or the lack of it.
- New possibilities for the organization.
- Competition.
- Strategic choices of the company management.
- Etc.

When you now look at it, schematically it looks as follows:

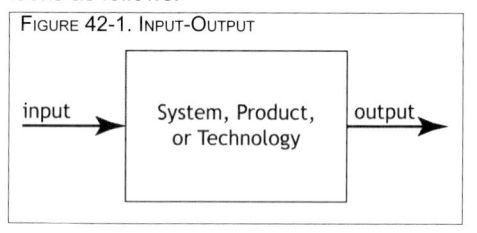

FIGURE 42-1. INPUT-OUTPUT

input → System, Product, or Technology → output

The environment puts demands on both the production and the output of the system, product or technology. If you can not comply with these, you will ultimately taste defeat.

It does not stand alone, but is part of a larger whole. The company management cannot allow itself not to include the environment in its considerations. The question is, however, how far can and should the organization go?

When we take the definition too tightly, we shall start suffering from a form of tunnel vision in which the larger whole is missing, and when it is taken to widely, we become bogged down in good intentions, ambitious visions and deceptive dreams, which change into nightmares.

Even before we are dealing with a project, we think about the application of the system, product or technology e.g. the profitability of the company. Of which larger whole are we a part? The supply chain of course, and for non-profit organizations one or other chain can also be found. This results in the following diagram:

3.07 Systems, products and technology

FIGURE 42-2. PART OF THE SUPPLY CHAIN

Suppliers → Our Organisation → Customers
input / output

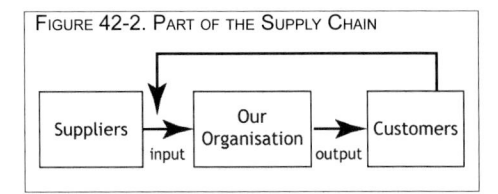

Indirectly the customers have an influence on the input into our organization; they make demands on the quality of our output (garbage in is garbage out), and the "raw materials" we use must make it possible to continuously comply with their demands.

What applies to the organization as a whole, also applies to a system, product or piece of technology, all of them have "suppliers" who supply the "input" and "buyers" who take receipt of "output".

When, as project manager, you are involved in the development or adapting of a system, product or technology, it is important that you know which part of the whole the result of your project will be taking.

2. Make a feasibility analysis, and produce a business justification

When an organization wants to develop or utilize systems, products or technology, this has to be based on a well founded feasibility analysis and business justification. Note, that this is something other than the business justification of a project. Here we are dealing with a choice for entering into a new market, for developing and marketing a new product line, or even changing the complete management philosophy.

3. Determine customers and functionality

Everything now starts with identifying the buyers or customers of the systems, products and technology. You have to take the concept customers in a broad sense; it is the people or other systems, products and technology in the environment (so not just people). The question is ALWAYS, what do they need, and what are their demands of it?

4. Determine goals and components

Based on the required functionality, you will be able to determine the added value the system, product or technology has to offer the environment. This added value is the determining factor for the goals we set. The management of the organization may for instance decide to:
- Enter a certain market segment.
- Develop a medicine.
- Design a faster computer.
- Initiate a change project.

We can then broadly determine the components. In the example of the change project, these could be:
- Reward system.
- Training programme.
- Set of instruments for the employees.

Note that we are now dealing with a system (*reward*), a product or service (*training*) and technology (*set of instruments*). Here some of the confusion concerning the concept 'system' surfaces, because often we also call the combined components outlined above a system (in the so-called *system approach*). Each component can ultimately result in a project.

5. Design production and supply chain for the distribution

Each system, product or technology is part of a larger whole, just as the organization is part of a chain. We still have to determine which role it plays in the whole chain. Before the actual system design and the execution of it can take place, we have to determine and design the dependencies on other systems, products and technologies in the chain.

581

3.07 Systems, products and technology

6. Authorise the design and production
If the results from the previous process step are satisfactory, we can move on to authorizing the designing and manufacturing of the system, product or technology. We then start with process step 2.1.

7. Test and Optimize the system
The system, product or technology in use proves its value in the application. Within the parts of the organization responsible, a continuous optimization will take place. Initially this is done with the existing possibilities, and if that is not feasible, it is done with the proposal to start a maintenance or innovation project. This means a repeat of process step 1.3 up to and including 1.6, possibly also followed by 2.1.

8. Validating against the requirements in the "business case"
The input costs money and the exploitation cost money, and against this is the output, which receives appreciation (in the form of money) from the environment, and which make the financial resources increase.

For a commercial organization, this is what the market will pay for it, and for a non-profit organization, this is what government or the 'generous giver' has available for it. Decision makers continuously consider whether or not there still is a business need, and if so, money comes in, if not, ultimately they (or the market) pull the plug on it.

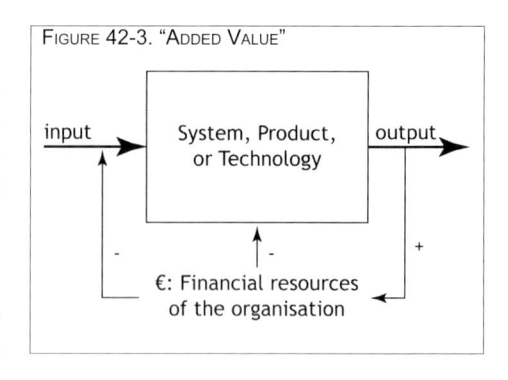

FIGURE 42-3. "ADDED VALUE"

9. Put into operation
Project teams provide systems, products or technology to the permanent organization. These now have an important responsibility, for they have to assess whether the delivered systems comply with the requirements they set. If not, then from their position of responsibility, they are not allowed to accept the 'goods' delivered. If you are project manager, that is not pleasing, but apparently the product, or result of your project, does not provide enough added value, and that is something you (and your team) should accept.

10. Manage the life cycle
All systems, products or technology have a life cycle, from the earliest idea (*conception*) up to the stopping, rejecting or elimination (*dying*).

Commercial products and/or services
For organizations supplying commercial products and/or services, I refer to the Boston Matrix[1]:
- *Stars*, products with a high market share, and high growth figures.
- *Cash cows* take care of the resources for financing growth.
- *Question marks*, using extra resources, turn into stars.
- *Dogs*, are not really necessary in the organization, and do not show growth.

---
1 (1998) *Strategy-Safari,* Mintzberg

Here we have the product portfolio of the organization, in which the different products together form the *financing system* of the organization. We find a useful addition in Collins[2] so-called Hedgehog Concept, in which he asks three questions regarding the products to be sold:
- What are you deeply passionate about?
- What can you become the best in?
- Where is the economic motor?

It comes down to doing what you are good at and what you can earn money with, or get financing for. The management continuously makes choices as to where the *stars* and the *cash cows* are, which *question marks* they can still make into a *star,* and which *dogs* have to be chased off the property.

As employees, we take up a small space in that bigger whole, and I think that each one of us must continuously question what our added value is, and will be in the future. Are you a *star* or a *cash cow*, or a *question mark?* If you are a *dog*, you had better go looking for another boss.

11. Apply lessons learned

There is a constant cycle of learning and applying in an organization. The five disciplines of Peter Senge on the learning organization have become well-known.

According to Senge[3], an organization should develop the following five disciplines in order to become a real learning organization:
- Think in Systems.
- Personal Mastery.
- Mental Models.
- Building Shared Vision.
- Team Learning.

The five disciplines of the organization form the basis for a continuous evolution in providing added value to the chain it is in. This process step goes further than the project evaluations that we say must be done, but which hardly ever are, and if they are, then nothing is done with them.

---

2 (2001) *Good to Great,* Jim Collins, HARPER BUSINESS, New York
3 (1990) *The Fifth Discipline,* Peter Senge, DOUBLEDAY

3.07-4 Systems Development Process

The *development* of systems, products and technology:

1. Define the development as a new project.
2. Define the customers and the required functionality.
3. Match up with existing systems, products and technology.
4. Design production and distribution.
5. Calculate costs.
6. Optimize in accordance with the requirements.
7. Hand over to the organization.
8. Determine opportunities for further strategic improvement.
9. Apply lessons learned.

1. Define the development as new project

The development of a system, product or technology is only a small part of what we are talking about in this competence element. But it is the main one that we, as project managers, are faced with. Never forget that where the work stops for us (transfer and discharge), it begins for the customers of the delivered result.

Many of the process steps described here, directly correspond with all competence elements that have been addressed in the first chapters on project management techniques.

This first process step of this competence element takes place in what we call the *project development stage*. It starts, even before the project manager is involved, when an initial idea develops in the line organization. When this slowly takes shape, the need arises to bring structure to the chaos of creative ideas and the often unrealistic expectations with respect to the feasibility. The project manager is the perfect professional to help with this. We expect him to bring structure into the situation, together with an eye for the larger whole.

The first stakeholder is the line manager with the mandate and the budget to decide on the project, and he is the project sponsor who, together with the project manager, sets to work to further develop the system, product or technology.

2. Define the customers and the required functionality

Before we can say anything sensible, we have to know the customers of the system, product or technology that the project has to develop (or adapt). Customers are, in any case:
- The end users.
- The maintenance staff.

But furthermore, it is good practice not to leave it at this, but to look at all the stakeholders. A stakeholder is then someone who:
- Actually has an interest.
- Believes to have a interest.

All these stakeholders are the '*living*' part of the project environment, who provide support and set requirements on the project. When they have been identified, we analyze precisely what they want.

Functionality is then related to:
- The things we deliver.
- How we deliver them.

3. Connect to the existing systems, products and technology

We live in a world and a time, in which everything depends on everything else. No system, product or technology stands alone,

3.07 Systems, products and technology

and even during the *project development stage,* we start looking for the common ground (or *interfaces*) with the environment. In parallel to that, we define the scope of the project, and what applies here is: not too broad, but definitely also not too narrow. Experienced project managers will confirm that if it goes wrong anywhere, it will be with the interfaces.

4. Design production and distribution

As well as the development of the system, product or technology, there is the use of it. During the execution the parties involved get an ever better picture of how it will all work out in practice. This allows them to customise the actual application of the system, product or technology (*produce and deliver*) and to identify how the organization will make use of it, and customise it accordingly.

5. Calculate the costs

The same clarity also arises with respect to all cost estimates, for both the execution of the project (the investment), and the expected revenues. There is continuous attention paid to the business justification for the project, whereby the investments still to be expected are offset against the revenue.

6. Optimize in accordance with the requirements

This is the execution of the project and optimization now works from two sides. From the project, the project manager provides enough motives to stimulate the team members to work more efficiently and more effectively. The project sponsor and other important stakeholders check what, in their view, is really necessary. In this way, the project and environment meet each other at set times to look for the optimum deployment of resources against the expected effects of the system, product or technology.

7. Hand over to the organization

Project teams have the responsibility to hand over the system, product or technology produced by them to the permanent organization, in such a way that the organization can work with it.

This means that:
- Systems have been tested and accepted.
- Manuals are available.
- End users have been trained.
- The system is maintainable.
- Maintenance and management documentation has been produced.
- Resources have been handed back over to the organization.

Handing over is not something that should be done at the end of the project, but it is something that is an area of attention throughout the duration of the project.

8. Determine opportunities for further strategic improvement

This is at odds with the change process that a good project manager has implemented in his project. We provide what is agreed, not more, and definitely not less, but indeed better, faster and cheaper. But as we work, ideas arise and this is called progressive insight. The danger now is that while we are working we get so many new ideas, that the project is never finished. I do not dare to give a statement on how to deal with this. The project manager in me says: *scope is scope*. The entrepreneur in me says: *opportunity is opportunity*. Each time we will have to make a choice on what has preference: the entrepreneur or the project manager.

9. Apply lessons learned

The learning in this competence element is about how the development project and environment are in contact with each other.

3.07 Systems, products and technology

Questions we can ask during the evaluation are:
- Are all stakeholders involved?
- Has everybody taken account of each other?
- Was the scope too small or actually too large?
- Are the deliverables useable?
- Has maintenance and management been taken into account?
- How could we improve our processes?
- Etc.

3.07-5 SPECIAL TOPICS

1. EFQM

The EFQM® model is a system model in which the relation between those aspects, which in an organization are involved in delivering excellent performances, are described. EFQM is an abbreviation of: *European Foundation for Quality Management.*

It describes the relation between leadership, people, policy and strategy, partnerships and resources, processes, human results, business results, social results and key performances. Organizations can use this model as a yardstick to measure their performances against.

In the introduction I stated that the essence of this competence element comes down to *an organization using systems, product and technology to add value to the social traffic.*

The central thought behind the model is that an organization, whether this is a company or a public organization, as well as anticipating what is going to happen in its environment, also continuously pays attention to how it is organized and being managed.

Central to the model are the processes, the things people in an organization do. When we look at these, we ask ourselves the question:

What is the effect of what we do (the processes) on our customers and our suppliers?

Without customers, we have no right of existence, and without suppliers no "raw materials" to deliver our products or services. Every organization is part of a bigger chain.

At the core of the organization are the chosen strategy and the policy developed for the management of the:
- Employees
- Resources
- Processes

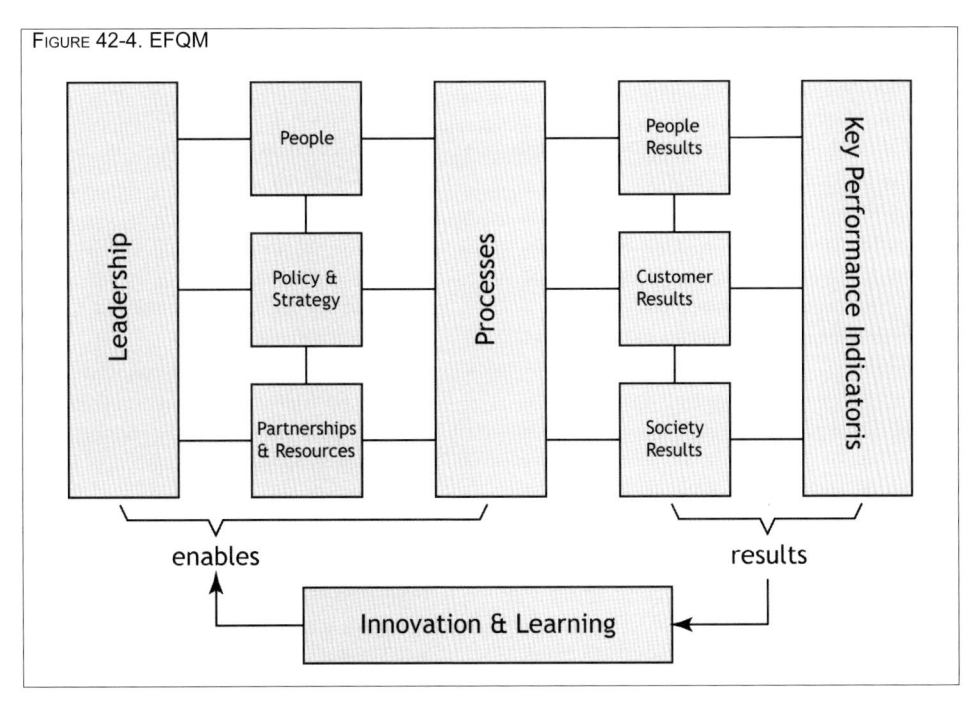

FIGURE 42-4. EFQM

3.07 Systems, products and technology

Without employees, resources and processes, we cannot provide added value in the chain we are part of. We find systems, products and technology in the latter two (resources and processes).

The nine areas for attention are sub-divided into:
- An enabling organization.
- Result.

In the *organization,* it is about what we do for leadership, strategy/policy and management (of staff, resources and processes). With *result,* it is about the effect this has on: employees, customers, suppliers, society and directors and financiers.

The EFQM philosophy stands for a continuous cycle of improvement, in which the organization consistently adapts itself to the requirements from the environment, in order to become an excellent enterprise. It is a development model containing five stages through which the organization develops itself, and these are:

- *Activity* oriented, the emphasis is on the result.
- *Process* oriented, as well as the result, the processes must also be under control.
- *System* oriented, the processes now work smartly together with each other.
- *Chain* oriented, agreement with suppliers and customers in the whole chain.
- *Transformation* oriented, striving for excellence in the long term.

2. Deming's[4] fourteen points

Deming's fourteen points are older than the EFQM model. They form the basic preconditions for his programme to bring the western industry out of the morass it was in during the last century in the 1970's and 1980's.

The points are:
- Continually strive for quality improvements in order to stay in the market, and create employment.
- Accept the new reality, in which management takes responsibility for delays, mistakes, faulty material and inadequate workmanship.
- Cease reliance on post-inspection, but instead demand the statistical proof that quality has been 'built into the product'.
- Do business on the basis of more than price, and work together with (a few) qualitatively high value suppliers, with whom a long standing relationship of mutual trust can be built up.
- Ensure a continuous improvement in the quality of products and services, and a decrease in costs through a lower amount of scrap.
- Institute on-the job training.
- Institute a form of leadership that is aimed at supporting staff in the improvement of their performance.
- Drive out fear, so that everyone can work effectively.
- Breakdown barriers between departments. Staff working in R&D, sales and production must be able to pro-actively latch on to problems and react to them adequately.
- Eliminate slogans, incentives and targets for better quality, when people do not have the necessary means available to achieve this.
- Eliminate judgement by numbers and Management by Objectives, but swap these for leadership, who take responsibility for quality.
- Remove the issues that rob people of their pride about their workmanship.

---
[4] (1982) *Out of the Crisis,* W.Edwards Demming, MIT, Cambridge

3.07 Systems, products and technology

- Institute a rigorous training programme for both management and the people on the shop floor.
- Involve everyone in the achievement of this transformation.

3. Standards

The establishment of Standards[5]

Standard can be specified by a standards institute itself, but it is also well possible that these can be set up by companies, organizations, governments, or individuals.

The relevant standards institute discusses such a proposal in a policy/advice forum, and decides if it is desirable to develop such a standard. If this decision is positive, a standards committee works out a draft. The committee's working method is one of discussion and consensus, whereby as much support as possible for the standard is created.

Over a period of time, the committee gathers criticism (through an internal and external criticism round) on the standard and processes this into a definitive standard. This standard is then made public via symposia, courses, and publications.

Project specific standardization

Regulation, standards, rules and guidelines in use determine the production systems, methods, procedures and processes. For project leaders, this means that they should be well informed about the standards and regulation available for the relevant specialist field. These are both the technical standards and provisions, and those related to processes. Taken together, all of these have consequences for what has to be made and how it is made.

Specific rules and regulation apply to the setting up and operational progress of a project. Often, general models with respect to project based working are translated into industry sector specific, or project specific, situations.

A project can be confronted with standards and regulation on products and processes originating from the customer organization, or the supplier organization. When many organizations take part in a project, an agreement must be made on which standards and regulation are valid for the project.

There where conflicting standards occur, the project organization must make a choice based on the standard with the strictest regulation, and this choice is included in the project quality plan. As an addition to existing standards and regulation, agreements that are only applicable within that project, can be made.

Deviation from (binding) standards and regulation generally means that dispensation must be requested from the relevant authority. Prior to this, this (intended) deviation should be covered in the related procedure.

Divergent interpretations of, and inconsistent descriptions of standards and regulation should be prevented. The formulation of standards and regulation in a project must be unambiguous.

During the planning stage of a project, the project leader must provide clarity on which standards and regulation are relevant to it, and to do this he undertakes the following steps:

- Determine the necessity for, and the existence of, public standards and regulation.
- The same applies to user standards.

---

5 *Wat is normontwikkeling,* NEDERLANDS NORMALISATIE INSTITUUT, Delft

3.07 Systems, products and technology

- Determine which of these standards are (potentially) not applicable.
- Achieve agreement with the project sponsor on the required standards.
- Apply these standards to the way of working.
- With respect to the standards, obtain approval for any deviations that might occur.

Regulation
A **regulation** is a mandatory stipulation with a legal basis, issued by an administrative authority. Provisions are, in fact, process oriented and say something about the consequences of the standards employed.

The objective of the use of standards and provisions is to arrive at a uniform application of terminology and sizing for products and processes (standardization), through which common terms and frames of reference are created. For this reason, standards and regulation often form the basis for, amongst other things, agreements, quality control and acceptance criteria.

Only a few companies have been able to set up their own norms or standards, and to mandate these for the rest of the world. An example of where this has succeeded is Microsoft with their operating systems and office applications. Specialization, and the acquisition of a massive competitive advantage, provides the possibility to establish generally accepted standards in this way.

Market forces (organizations and users) and the impact of regulatory measures issued by industry sector organizations and government, are two influences that lead to the creation of standards.

ISO
Partly as a result of globalization, scores of international user, supplier and government organizations have arisen, that are working on various forms of standardization. A very well-known organization is ISO, the International Standard Organization.

The most well-known standard is ISO 9000, which is predominantly related to quality management. Quality consists of all the characteristics of a product or service that are demanded by the customer. Quality management encompasses what the organization does to ensure that its products and services satisfy the customer's quality criteria, and conform to all the regulations that are applicable to the products and services.

ISO 14000 is primarily concerned with environmental management, or in common language, everything an organization does to minimise the harmful effects of its activities on the environment.

Both ISO 9000 and ISO 14000 require organizations to continuously improve their performance.

The standardization has recently been modernized. The amended version of the ISO 9000 series was issued in 2000, and among other things, consists of:
- ISO 9000:2000, concepts, terms and definitions.
- ISO 9001:2000, quality requirements.
- ISO 9004:2000, guidelines for performance improvement.

The previously existing standards, ISO 9002 and ISO 9003, have been withdrawn.

An ISO standard has also been appeared for the application of project management. The First version of this standard was ISO 10006: 1997; Quality Management Guidelines to quality in project management.

3.07 Systems, products and technology

The second edition of ISO 10006 is available in the English and French languages and this second edition has been completely revised and adapted to the ISO 9000:2000 series.

4. Process impeovement with Six Sigma

The quality of a process has to do with predictability of the outcome, and a process is good if you can trust it. There is always the matter of a certain variation in the outcomes. How do you know of a particular deviation is coincidence or indicates a structural problem. A measure of the variation is the standard deviation (sigma), and traditional process management assumed that when the spacing of three standard deviations below and above the average fell within the specifications, the process was controlled[6]. In concrete terms, this means that 99.73% of all outcomes fell within the specifications.

Over the last years, the Six Sigma method has been advancing strongly, which says as such that an area of plus/minus six standard deviations must fall within the boundaries set, and this is 99.99985% van all circumstances i.e. everything.

Six Sigma is a quality management methodology, or if you would prefer it, a management philosophy. It offers a framework for managing the quality of processes. You can see it as being the successor to Total Quality Management that made much use of Statistical Process Control (control charts), which we came across whilst handling the seven quality instruments.

Six Sigma uses a fixed methodology for investigating company processes. This approach has the name DMAIC (Define-Measure-Analyse-Improve-Control) and recognizes the following steps:

- *Definition* of the improvement project.
- *Measurement* of the existing process quality.
- *Analysis* of the relationship between the process characteristics and the result.
- *Improving* of the optimum tuning of the process.
- *Controlling* the situation achieved.

It begins with a clear choice of which processes you need to improve, en then you carry out measurements. For the project management planning process, you can, for example, measure: is there a standard, and if so, how many people use it, how well we estimate the duration, etc.? The essence is that this covers the total population of projects, and how project management delivers a positive contribution towards the organization's results.

You compare these measurements with the way in which the process is structured to determine the mutual dependence. The analysis must provide an insight into the relationship that exists between the way in which people work and the subsequent results that are produced. For a significant part, Six Sigma consists of statistical analyses on measurement data in order to reach conclusions on the quality of processes. This approach allows you to make well founded decisions on the best way to structure and tune the process. With these decisions in your hands, you can then determine changes, and apply these to the situation.

---

[6] (2001) *The Six Sigma Handbook,* Thomas Pyzdek, QUALITY PUPBLISHING

3.07 Systems, products and technology

3.08 Personnel management

WE WISH YOU A LOT OF STAFF.

It is sometimes said that people are the most important assets of an organization.

What I do not understand, therefore,
is why people are the first to go
in economically difficult times.

That must have something to do with
personnel management,
or maybe with the lack of it.

3.08-1 Definitions

Personnel management	Managing of, and providing leadership to, the personnel policy.
Personnel policy	Part of the company policy, which is directly related to the staff.

3.08-2 INTRODUCTION

People come and go. An organization, which ensures it has people who understand what it is all about, who have a good attitude to work, who are competent in their task and who continuously develop themselves, is prepared for the future.

The management has a responsibility towards its staff, and should ensure that the working conditions are such that the work can be done properly, and that all tools and safe working conditions are provided for.

The line managers regularly talk of the functioning of the staff, and annually, there is a job appraisal interview, in which manager and employee look at the extent to which they both have met the expectations.

Much of what applies to organizations, also applies to recruiting and selecting staff for projects, but there are differences:

	Permanent organization	**Project organization**
Determination of the quantitative and qualitative needs	In accordance with a complex process, in which the operational management determines the strategic direction of the organization.	In accordance with a simple process, where, on the basis of the capacity planning, an insight is gained into the required resources.
Recruiting staff	Free choice during the selection procedure.	Enforced "shopping", whereby staff must be recruited from within the permanent organization.
Staff development	Has a long term focus.	Has a short term focus (for the duration of the project).
Reward	A lot of influence.	Little or no influence.
Power	Hierarchic authority.	Functional authority with limited power.
Dismissing staff	Subject to the right to terminate employment.	Staff can easily be given back to the permanent organization, or an external supplier.

3.08 Personnel management

3.08-3 PROCESS STEPS

1. Set the requirements for employees.
2. Employ, or keep, the right people.
3. Explain your expectations to the team members.
4. Check the planned and actual performance per employee.
5. Monitoring changes in the staff.
6. Monitoring staff motivation.
7. Maintain contact with the responsible HR person.
8. Discharge the team members personally at close-off.
9. Document and apply learning points.

1. Set the requirements for employees

A project starts with the objectives it has to meet, followed by structuring the scope, the activities and the capacity schedule. You design the project organization and determine the required functions. For all functions, there is an idea of what they have to comply to.

It helps to ask the following questions per function:
- What are the important results the employee has to deliver?
- What results and behavior are absolutely not wanted?
- Which technical and which behavioral competences does the employee have to possess?
- What intellectual level must he have?
- What psychological profile are we looking for?

With this information in the back of his mind, the project manager starts looking for the right staff.

2. Employ, or keep, the right people

There are different ways to recruit people for a project position:
- From the permanent organization.
- Temporary hire from a consulting firm.
- Temporary hire of a freelancer.

Each of the three options has its own problems, which the project manager in consultation with his project sponsor has to consider. For each of the options mentioned, there are two possible agreements:

1. Obligation to guarantee a result.
2. An obligation to perform to the best of a persons abilities.

Obligation to guarantee a result
You make an agreement with the responsible manager, sales person or freelancer as to what results the employee will deliver, agree how the costs will be settled, and then you manage the employee concerned.

There are advantages and disadvantages:

	Advantages	Disadvantages
Permanent organization		In most organizations this is not possible, and you will only be able to agree an obligation to perform to the best of the persons abilities.
Consulting firm	As project manager you can be sure of getting delivery of the required result. The agreements have been laid down in a contract.	The agency will give you less insight into how things have been arranged, so you have less control.

3.08 Personnel management

	Advantages	Disadvantages
Freelancer		Most freelancers are not in a position to make such promises.

Obligation to perform to the best of a persons abilities

Now you make an agreement on the deployment of the employee, you agree a number of hours and a start and end date between which you can make use of him.

There are advantages and disadvantages:

	Advantages	Disadvantages
Permanent organization	Employees are more committed to the organization, and will comply with its interests.	If they are critical resources, and you need them longer than contracted, they cannot complete their work.
Consulting firm	Have a name to uphold up, and will do their best to achieve the required result.	May see your organization as a 'cash cow', and will possibly be inclined to drag the assignment out endlessly.
Freelancer	Are cheaper than consulting firms and easier to 'fire' than permanent staff.	Many freelancers act as mercenaries, and will quickly leave you when they can get a better rate somewhere else.

Selection of team members

We must dwell a bit longer on the recruitment of staff. An initial selection takes place on the basis of their CV, and from there you can form a first idea about the potential employee. This is not sufficient, but it is a first step, and I would not consider holding an interview, without first having seen a CV.

Next, you can start collecting references on the employee by making enquiries of former customers. Try to elicit from them how they worked with the employee and whether this was positive.

Then follows the selection interview, which obviously has been well prepared. Many managers are not sufficiently competent to conduct such an interview. They ask questions such as:

- What are your hobbies?
- What would you do in this case, and what in that case?
- What are your strengths and weaknesses?

These types of questions say little about the employee, who will be able to prepare the answers to these types of questions well, giving you an answer that is reasonably in line with what you expect to hear for the function in question. So they will not be very distinguishing.

There are two mistakes you can make when selecting:

- You hire someone who is incapable.
- You reject someone who is capable.

The first mistake is actually the worst one, and when you make the second one, you will not notice that at all, because you will probably never see the employee again. So we have to focus on preventing the first mistake.

You do that by asking questions on behavior shown in the past. The central questions from the previous process step are then leading. You ask the questions as openly as possible and listen actively in accordance with the well-known list: hmm, parrot, paraphrase and summary. You ask as few questions as possible, and interrupt the employee only if you want the discussion to go in a certain direction. In this way, the employee will ultimately tell you the information you need to know in order to make the right decision.

Ensure that every time you collect sufficient evidence for each competence so you can say:
- In which *situation* the employee has applied the competence.
- What his *task* was, and
- Which *actions* or behavior he displayed, and
- What the *result* was of that behavior.

The first letters of each of the four components mentioned together form the acronym *STAR*. Every time the candidate for a certain competence scores enough positive *STAR's*, you can move on to a new one.

This form of interviewing is friendly, but very intense. It is recommended that you first make the potential employee feel at ease, and later on slowly put on the STAR squeeze.

Preferably, selection interviews should be carried out by two people, because the amount of information the selector receives is large, and two get to know more than one. If a deployment or rejection follows, you always have to be able to justify this on the basis of a number of *STAR's*.

3. Explain your expectations to the team members

When a team member spends his first day on the project, we have to properly guide and coach him in what we expect of him. During the first weeks, a directive and selling style of management is best. Only after we see that the employee understands what we expect of him, and he delivers good work, has the time come to give him more responsibility. From a situational perspective, this then moves from telling to selling, through participating to delegating.

When you manage a large project where a lot of employees join at the same time, you or your sub-project leaders have to take the time with every employee to agree their work activities on an individual basis. This personal contact is part of the hygiene factors on the project, and when absent, this reduces motivation. If you do not make proper contact right at the start, you will notice that things becomes more and more difficult the longer you are together on the project.

4. Check the planned and actual performance per employee

The previous process step is a pre-condition for this one. You regularly check (the control cycle!) to what extent the employee is working according to plan. In the event of deviations you discuss this with him by using the proper leadership style.

The good thing about projects is that it is easier to take people off the project than it is for a line manager to fire someone. A question you have to regularly ask is:

If I could do the selection for this employee again, would I still take him on?

If the answer is NO, you have to replace the employee, and this is one of the luxuries a project manager can allow himself. If you would keep someone like that on, it almost always has a negative impact on the project result, and nobody is so indispensable that a replacement cannot be found.

5. Monitor changes in the staff

Certainly for large projects, where sub-project managers manage the actual projects, you must keep track of staff turnover. This

3.08 Personnel management

is a discussion topic for the periodic project management team meeting, and also has a lot to do with the next process step.

6. Monitoring staff motivation
As long as the employees are motivated, you do not have to worry very much. Demotivation, however, is like a fire in a dry forest; once the fire has started, it is very difficult to put out.

As project manager, you have to be accessible for your employees, also when there are sub-project leaders in between. There are projects, on which team members do not even know what the project manager looks like, which is not only undesirable, but also demotivating.

7. Maintain contact with the responsible HR person
In a matrix organization, this can be the resource manager, or if you are working with a consulting firm, the account manager. Never forget that you are one of the few links between the employee, who is working on your project, and his line manager, who in turn should be interested in:
- The development of the employee.
- His personal performance.
- Possible issues or problems.
- Illness and other domestic circumstances.

This information often is hard to come by for the line manager, as the employee is carrying out the majority or all of his work for you. It is good practice that, around the time of the annual appraisal, you provide the line manager with input. We do have to realize that this usually has a positive tint, because it will not do you any good, as project manager, if the employee loses his motivation, due to a bad appraisal which is based on information you provided.

8. Discharge the team members personally at close-off
Just as you spoke with the individual team members at the start, it is good professional practice to hold an exit interview with each of the team members. This can, of course, also be carried out by the sub-project leaders, and is dependent on how intensively you have worked with a certain employee. You can also do it together.

The following points are addressed in such an exit interview:
- The performance and points for improvement.
- What you both think of how the project went.
- The performance of the employee.
- The performance of the project manager.

As project manager, you end the allocation of the employee on the project team formally, and forward your conclusions to the line manager.

9. Apply lessons learned
What have we learnt, and what are the points for development of the individual employees. A meeting on these points allows us to express the learning experience explicitly. During the exit interview, as project manager, you have to adopt a vulnerable attitude, and accept all criticism with gratitude. What do you have to lose; the employee is leaving the project and you just have to accept his comments on how you have functioned as free advice. You can decide later whether or not you do something with it.

3.08-4 SPECIAL TOPICS

1. Competence development

The ICB defines competence as: *a collection of knowledge, behavioral characteristics, skills and relevant experience necessary to carry out a particular function successfully.*

The ultimate responsibilities for the development of the project management competence lie with the line-management, and they have to take care of two matters:
- Establishing the right processes.
- Staff development.

I shall discuss the establishment of the right processes in the chapter on the PPP implementation. Here I want to discuss staff development in more detail, especially for the project managers.

Based on this definition, it is important that there is enough knowledge, skill and experience available in the organization, such that we see concrete behavior in the required direction.

What the organization now has to ensure to make this possible is:
- Insight into the required competences.
- Training programmes to develop these.
- Assessment systems to measure progress.
- The evidence that the competence is available in line with needs.

Insight into the required competences

One of the most complete frameworks presently available is that of IPMA. IPMA distinguishes between the following project management competence elements.

The culture determines to what extent certain competence elements are important. For example, in the *"Hierarchy"*, the emphasis will be more on the technical elements and less on the behavioral elements than in the other cultures. In the *"Family"* and *"Adhocracy"* the emphasis will be a little more on the behavioral elements, whereas the *"Market"* and the *"Hierarchy"* will also require the contextual components.

IPMA Competence elements

Technique	Behavior	Context
Project management success	Leadership	Project orientation
Interested parties	Engagement & Motivation	Programme orientation
Requirements & Objectives	Self control	Portfolio orientation
Risks & Opportunity	Assertiveness	PPP Implementation
Quality	Relaxation	Permanent Organization
Project organization	Openness	Business
Teamwork	Creativity	Systems, Products
Problem resolution	Result orientation	& Technology
Project structures	Efficiency	Personnel management
Scope & deliverables	Consultation	Health, Security, Safety
Time & Project phases	Negotiation	& Environment
Resources	Conflict & Crisis	Finance
Cost & Finance	Reliability	Legal
Purchase & contract	Values Appreciation	
Changes	Ethics	
Control & Reporting		
Information & Documentation		
Communication		
Start-Up		
Close-out		

Training programme
When the required competence elements have been named, the organization has to develop a training policy with regard to project management, for both the initial training and maintenance and further development of the competence.

We now see individual development plans arising containing objectives for self-development as a project manager. In addition, there are career paths in project management, for example:
- Project co-ordinator.
- Project leader.
- Project manager.
- Programme manager.

Which often contain different degrees of junior and senior function specifications.

The policy is aimed at *'permanent education'*, which is necessary because many project management techniques can only be learned properly in practice, and because behavior is hard to change. Only through continuous repetition there is a chance that this properly sinks in.

Assessment systems
When the required project management competence elements have been named, there is the need to evaluate whether or not these actually delivers the required result.

This means that as well as an assessment of the individual skills, an assessment is made of the products delivered and their contribution to the results of the organization. After some time, it would be interesting to assess which project managers are the more successful for the organization, and this is only possible when you include the actual project performances in their assessment.

Evidence
After some time, there has to be evidence that the competence is developing, for example:
- There are local initiatives coming from the project management community.
- The company management supports these.
- An active project management community exists.
- Projects become more successful, having less extensions and overruns.
- There are sufficient project managers of the right calibre.
- The organization sees project management as one of its success factors.

2. Professional Development Plan
In the PDP, you make agreements with your manager on your personal and professional development, which go further than the annual appraisals. It may be best to view this as a long term contract, in which you promise to develop in a certain area, with your manager promising to do his best to provide you with the work that fits in with your development goals.

There is a big snag to this, and that is the one-sided obligation of the manager and the rights of the employee connected to this. I repeatedly hear the cynical remark: *"My employer has not been able to provide me with the right work, therefore I have not been able to develop in the required direction."* That is a wrong attitude with regard to personal development.

Initially there is only one person who is responsible for the professional development of the employee, and that is the employee himself. If you are actively working on that, the assignments will follow. This has to do

3.08 Personnel management

with certain patterns which are the result of applying a skilful will[1] namely:

- Images or mental pictures and ideas have the tendency to generate the matching physical circumstances and external actions.
- Attitudes, movements and actions have the tendency to invoke matching images and ideas.

There are a number of other patterns like that, which have the effect that someone who wants something strongly and skillfully enough, can also get very far in achieving his goal. That definitely applies to your career. If you are good, things will work out of their own accord.

What do we find in such a PDP?

- Where you are now.
- The goals for the coming year.
- The long term goals.
- The type of work you are going to do.
- The training required.
- Agreements on the support of your manager.

The power of the word can be felt in this document. If you are able to explain what you want to achieve, you are almost halfway there. Furthermore, the agreements you made help you not to forget them.

3. The appraisal cycle

The appraisal cycle is the annual concretization of the PDP. Annually, there are several function reviews, one appraisal and one salary review meeting. All three have a different function and can best be carried out separately, even though, in all fairness, it has to be said that for practical reasons the latter two are often combined.

Job function reviews

The frequency depends on the agreement and the necessity as a result of the employee's actual performance. When these are as expected, there will be between one and three meetings between the employee and his line manager on how he is functioning. The idea of this meeting is to support the employee in his professional development, and the working method used for that is coaching.

Appraisals

This interview has only one goal: a business and objective assessment of the past year, and the agreements for the next year. The pre-conditions for this interview are that the job function reviews have also taken place, and that the manager has built up sufficient insight on how the employee is functioning.

He can only do the latter, when, during the year, he has collected different STAR's of the employee to be able to justify his appraisal. Both for the manager, and the employees, this interview can be torture, and this is mainly because the following is strongly connected to this.

Salary reviews

In this interview we translate the employee's appraisal into the salary increase he will receive. On the one hand, that knowledge clouds the openness of the employee during the appraisal discussion, because in the back of his mind he will be thinking of his salary, but on the other hand, it also clouds the manager's assessment. The margin the manager has in awarding salary increases is fairly limited. The operational management sets an average percentage, and the line manager has to indicate to his manager who should receive an increase. This leads to a set increase, which has often already been determined before the review meeting takes place.

---

[1] (1973) *The Act of Will,* Roberto Assagioli, THE VIKING, New York

3.08 Personnel management

3.08 Personnel management

3.09
Health, Security, Safety and Environment

SAFETY BELTS ON AND DRIVE, BUT NOT TOO FAST

Let's ensure we work at keeping these subjects at an acceptable level.

These aspects are often organized within the line organization.

For specific projects, however, a tailored approach at a project level is necessary.

As project manager, you have to know which elements are important and which specific conditions will have an influence on your projects.

3.09 Health, security, safety and environment

3.09-1 Definitions

Environment	The social climate for humans, animals and plants.
Health	State of mental, physical and/or social well-being.
Safety	Social and technical systems are protected against external harmful effects.
Security	People are protected against personal harm, both physical and mental.

3.09-2 Introduction

Health, security, safety and environment are aspects which, when they play a role, you as project manager have to take account of, both legally and morally. As project manager, you have at least a legal obligation to provide for these, and even if there is no legal obligation, you certainly have a moral obligation.

- *Health* is concerned with the responsibility you have for the physical and psychological well-being of the people involved in your project, in particular the influence the project has on their health.
- *Security* is about protecting the people and organizations involved in the project against the wrongful actions of malicious people. Primary it is aimed at the protection of the social end technical systems.
- *Safety* involves preventing and protecting against dangers that might threaten the people involved.
- The last element, the *environment* is all-embracing. It relates to the protection of the earth in order to keep it safe for future generations.

These four elements have a lot in common, and sometimes it is not easy to make a clear distinction. In this chapter I will discuss the "technical aspects". Much has been laid down in statutory regulations and standards, which you need to be familiar with before you can responsibly take on the management of a project.

The ICB dictates that *"the project manager may also be required to be the highest level security agent for the project".* The explicitness of this position indicates just how important the professional body considers this role of the project manager to be.

3.09-3 Process steps

1. Determine applicable laws and regulations.
2. Determine the risks that are present.
3. Evaluate the actual situation.
4. Plan and develop processes.
5. Monitor and control effectiveness.
6. Report issues and risks.
7. Record and apply learning points.

1. Determine applicable laws and regulations

As early as the project start-up stage, you already determine together with the most important parties involved which laws and regulations apply. These provide important constraints on both the project execution and the project result.

Project execution

When carrying out the project, you have to consider the law with respect to working conditions, safety and environment. This applies predominantly to the safety of the employees and people in the vicinity, and also to the effect on the environment.

It is also possible that the project team has to work with confidential data or intellectual property rights. A system has to be in place to ensure that these particular interests are protected during the execution.

Dependent on the stakeholders and the various interests at stake, you will often have to deal with rules in these areas that are additional to the law, such as a level of security against undesirable events, which could endanger the execution and result.

Project result

During the execution, the project delivers a result which could be, for example, a factory, a stretch of motorway, an installation etc. When this result is commissioned, then its operational usage could, in fact, also have effects on the surroundings. This means that during the design and construction, the builders must consider the long-term effects.

Ethics

Ethics goes a step further than legislation and regulations. Ethics is concerned with "conscience"; there is a difference between keeping to the law and carrying out a project responsibly. This is analogous to the maximum speed limit in a built-up area; if a driver keeps to the maximum, it can still be dangerous when children are playing in the street. Responsible behavior normally goes further than just laws and regulations.

It may, therefore, be necessary for the project team itself to determine rules with respect to health, security, safety and environment, which they want to uphold on ethical grounds. This is a situation of "wanting to" and not "having to".

2. Determine the risks that are present

The above laws and (sometimes self-imposed) regulations, which have been laid down, form a part of the restrictions that the project has to satisfy, and are part of the project result. Because we are concerned with the well-being of people, it is necessary to explicitly pay attention to this subject during the planning and execution.

The risk analysis is the appropriate time to do this. Risks are uncertain events with damaging consequences, and they can have various causes.

The main groupings are:
- *Human error* (placing the ladder at the wrong angle, so that it slides away).
- *Technical problems* (a rung of the ladder snaps through).

3.09 Health, security, safety and environment

- *Misuse/sabotage* (someone deliberately drives into the ladder).

When determining the risks, we look at what can go wrong and how much of a problem that is. Dependent on this, we can take preventative measures.

Human error
This is related to the knowledge and skill of people who have to carry out particular tasks.

You can ask yourself the following questions:
- Does someone (still) know how to carry out the task safely?
- Is someone sufficiently proficient to do this?

The prevention of human error in this situation revolves around ensuring that the right people are included in the team, and that they have sufficient information on the safety risks that are present in the project. Not only is training an essential part of this, but also the work environment, which should stimulate the right behavior.

Technical problems
The previous risk was concerned about having "*the right people*", and this risk concerns having the "*the right material*". Technical problems can be caused by inferior material or tools, and the project management has to now weigh up the arguments for using more expensive material compared with the potential consequences if the problem occurs.

It is tempting here to make use of the expected value in money terms (probability times the cost of the consequences), but how do you determine the costs of personal injury, reputation damage or environmental damage?

Misuse/sabotage
This relates to the wilful interference of people (internal or external), with the intention of causing damage to the project. You have to investigate beforehand where the weaknesses lie and how serious these are, and then take the necessary measures. This is the aspect where the security aspect also becomes involved.

3. Evaluate the actual situation
In the previous process step, attention is paid to uncertain events in the future, and in so doing, you find an answer to the question: *"What can go wrong?"* which is, of course, an important question.

A more urgent question, however, is: *"What is already going wrong?"*

Here, we are not concerned with uncertainties, but with certainties for which we have to take direct action, because:
- People are in danger.
- Systems are in danger.

And, therefore, the whole project is endangered. We should provide an open and honest assessment of the situation, not only at the beginning, but also during the execution.

4. Plan and develop processes
Based on the risk inventory and the assessment of the actual situation, you develop your processes to monitor health, safety, security and environment. These processes contain the preventative risk measures, and in them we find the well-known plan-do-check-act cycle. Prevention is better than cure.

In an emergency or disaster plan, we define how, in the event of disasters, the communication is organized, and what specific measures should be applied (for example, standing upwind of the site to ensure that no poisonous fumes or particles are blown towards you). Once completed, these plans should be agreed with the relevant emergency services.

Within a contract, the project manager is responsible for keeping these risks to an acceptable level. He must take the initiative for carrying out the general steps mentioned earlier, and also ensure these are in line with the procedures in the line organization(s) to which the project participants belong. In the case of sub-contractors, the agreements are specified in the contract.

5. Monitor and control effectiveness

You continuously keep track of the extent to which the processes implemented are employed and remain suitable, and if the latter is no longer the case, you amend them to bring them back into line with what is required. The adjustment is made in consultation with the parties involved, and in addition, you also look at the attitude and behavior of the employees with respect to these aspects.

In order to monitor these areas, the project needs a measurement system that enables you to keep an eye on developments. A number of possible criteria are:
- Number of accidents.
- Number of near accidents.
- Number of observed "violations".
- Attitude survey of employees.
- Number of safety courses followed.

When evaluating the measurements, it is important to assess whether a certain result is coincidence, or whether there is a structural problem. You only need to act in the latter case, firstly by further analyzing the situation, followed by taking the necessary measures.

Apart from the desire to make the effectiveness as measurable as possible, statistics are not everything. It is, therefore, useful from time to time to provide employees with the opportunity to reflect openly and honestly on the measures that have been taken and their effectiveness.

6. Report issues and risks

Reporting on these aspects forces (or stimulates) you to work on these aspects. The report is primarily an aid to achieving the required level of safety for people, resources and the surroundings, and only secondarily as a means of control. When the completion of the reports make those responsible aware of the safety aspects for the environment, people, and systems, they will be less inclined to "massage" the figures than if these reports are experienced as being a burden, which certainly will be if employees view these reports as being a control tool.

Project management must also be willing to embrace what is reported, because if an employee reports on a risk and he is not listened to, then the next time he will be less inclined to say anything.

7. Record and apply learning points

Regular evaluation of the method of working leads to a better insight. By looking at the statistics and investigating the causes, for example by using a cause and effect diagram, you get a better grip on the most effective form of working for the project.

3.09-4 Special Topics

1. Sustainability

As long ago as the 18th century, Thomas Robert Malthus[1] warned of the consequences of overpopulation: *"The power of population is indefinitely greater than the power in the earth to produce subsistence for man"*. In the report published by the Club of Rome[2] in the last century, the researchers also warned about unlimited growth and the effects of this on our living environment. For decades scientists have pointed out to us the effects of human activities on the climate, although with variable success. Sustainability only really found itself on the agenda in 2006 through Al Gore's film: *An Inconvenient Truth*.

In the project setting sustainability is predominantly discussed in relation to all the laws and rules applicable to the environment and living conditions of those directly involved. In project management circles, we see an increasing interest in this subject. Silvius[3] outlines the contrast between sustainability and projects:

- Short term versus long term.
- Stakeholder versus future generations.
- Result oriented versus life cycle oriented.
- Scope, time and money, versus people, profit and planet.
- Simplifying versus increasing complexity.

The contrast demonstrates the gap between sustainability and classic project management. He arrives at the following conclusions:

- Sustainability is relevant to project managers.
- Integrating sustainability stretches the system boundaries of project management.
- Project management standards fail to address sustainability.
- Integration of sustainability may change the project management profession.

In the area of sustainability, therefore, there is still a very long way to go. Silvius states that we must apply the following principles to project management:

- Balancing or harmonizing social, environmental and economic interests.
- Short-term and long-term orientation.
- Local and global orientation.
- Consuming income, not capital.
- Transparency and accountability.
- Personal values and ethics.

He defines sustainability in projects as: *"the development, delivery and management of project-organized change in policies, processes, resources, assets or organizations, with the consideration of the six principles of sustainability, in the project, its results and its effects"*.

This is the reason that project management, as well as delivering within scope, time and budget, also now includes subjects such as environment and social justice.

---

1 (1798) *An essay on the principle of population*, Malthus T.R., Chapter 1, p 13 in OXFORD WORLD'S CLASSICS reprint.
2 (1972) *The Limits to Growth*, the Club of Rome, POTOMAC ASSOCIATES
3 (2012) *Sustainability in Project Management*, Gilbert Silvius e.a., GOWER PUBLISHING Ltd, Farnham, Surrey, England

2. Health

Relationship to the other topics

Health is strongly related to the other three topics:
- Systems are primarily put in place to protect people, and therefore the subject of *security* has an indirect effect on people's health.
- *Safety* ensures an environment in which people can carry out their work without fear for their health.
- Attention for the *environment* is attention for the living conditions and social environment of both people and animals, and can, in both the short and long term, influence peoples health.

As these three subjects are so strongly related to each other, it may be the case that certain aspects I cover for one topic, can also be applied to the other three subjects.

International Treaty on Economic, Social and Cultural rights

In 1966 a treaty[4] was drawn up and agreed in the United Nations in which various basic rights related to people's health were mentioned. It goes without saying that this can be translated one-for-one into the workplace. In the introductory text of this treaty, we can read that: *"the ideal of free human beings enjoying freedom from fear and want can only be achieved if conditions are created whereby everyone may enjoy his economic, social and cultural rights, as well as his civil and political rights."*

As far as I am concerned, the next text illustrates what this subject is about i.e.: *Creating the right conditions* in which employees can work, without unnecessarily bringing their health into danger. The mainstay of the treaty is that nations served by legislation and resources use these to create such an environment. Legislation as such does not guarantee the health of employees, as compliance with the legislation is also necessary, and that is primarily the responsibility of managers. We often find this at an organizational level in the policy with respect to this subject, but this is also not sufficient, as, after all, who is to say whether or not the managers observe this policy.

Ultimately it all adds up to the manager's responsibility and leadership, in our case the manager being the project manager. As this responsibility stretches further than just abiding by the law, you have to remain close to the source. I quote a number of pieces of text taken from the treaty in question.

	Text
6	… the right of everyone to the opportunity to gain his living by work which he freely chooses or accepts, and will take appropriate steps to safeguard this right.
7	… the right of everyone to the enjoyment of just and favorable conditions of work, which ensure, in particular: (a) … (b) Safe and healthy working conditions (c) … (d) Rest, leisure and reasonable limitation of working hours, periodic holidays with pay, as well as remuneration for public holidays.
10	2. Special protection should be accorded to mothers during a reasonable period before and after childbirth. … 3. Special measures of protection and assistance should be taken on behalf of all children and young persons … Their employment in work harmful to their morals or health or dangerous to life or likely to hamper their normal development should be punishable by law.

---
4 (1966) International Covenant on Economic, Social and Cultural Rights

3.09 Health, security, safety and environment

	Text
12	... the right of everyone to the enjoyment of the highest attainable standard of physical and mental health. ... (a) ... (b) The improvement of all aspects of environmental and industrial hygiene. (c) ... (d) ...

In practice, this means that as project manager, you must at the very least consider health risks, such as:
- Pressure of work.
- Working times.
- Lifting.
- Repetitive movements.
- Body posture.
- Dangerous substances.
- Temperature.
- Moisture / dampness.
- Light.
- Noise.
- Use of machinery.
- Vibration.
- Falling or slipping.
- Danger of suffocation or choking.
- Age.
- Vulnerable groups.

Some list, but where the health of your employees is concerned, you cannot afford to make any concessions.

3. Security

On the subject of security, we are involved with:
- The vulnerability of systems.
- The risks we run.
- The causes, which form a threat.
- The countermeasures we can take.
- The extent (level of safeguards) to which we can trust these aspects.

Vulnerability

Security is about the protection of:
- Social systems.
- Technical systems.

As opposed to safety, where the primary focus is on the protection of people, security concerns the protection of systems. A number of examples:
- A development department in which people are working on a new car model needs to be protected against industrial espionage.
- Computer data kept in the data centre must be protected against hackers.
- The public gallery in a court must be protected from undesirable persons.
- Etc.

The central question on this subject is: How serious is it when a particular system does not work any more or is harmed? This is related to the interests of the various people involved. The greater someone's interest, the louder his or her call for (more) security.

Risks

The extent of vulnerability is one side of the risk analysis, and the other side is the probability that a risk will occur! The chance that hackers will aim their arrows at a small business or organization is many times less than it is for a large business. For security, we also look at the chance that something will occur.

Before we can take the appropriate countermeasures, we have to look deeper into the causes.

Causes

If you know the cause, you can potentially remove it, thereby eliminating the threat. A possible classification is:

3.09 Health, security, safety and environment

Internal causes
- Deliberate: striking, sabotage, fraud, etc.
- By accident: data files are lost or mislaid, computer crash, fire, etc.

External causes
- Natural disasters: hurricane, earthquake.
- Human causes
   o Deliberate: break-in, terrorism, evacuation.
   o By accident: fire next door, environmental disaster, etc.

You can view the above breakdown as a Risk Breakdown Structure, which acts as a basis for carrying out a thorough risk analysis in the area of all the available security systems.

Countermeasures

A countermeasure is a way of preventing a particular threat resulting in a manifested risk. In terms of security, it is essential that you do not rely on only one measure.

Security measures can be taken at the following levels:
- Organizational: access, key holders, badges, etc.
- Constructional: fencing, strength of material, etc.
- Electronic: alarm installations.
- Reaction: speed of reaction to breaches.

Each countermeasure demands its own investment that has to be weighed up against the interests of the people involved.

Extent of trust

The extent of the trust that stakeholders have in the security systems will be indicative of the requirements they place on them. As such, you can have a good system, but when people mistrust it, then it has missed its goal.

> EXAMPLE 44-1 SCAFFOLDING ACCIDENT
> *"Considering the known risks of this large scaffolding collapsing, the verdict of the court was that it was a case of acting recklessly."*
>
> This is a quote from a verdict as a result of an accident with scaffolding collapsing during maintenance work on a power station. Five people working on the scaffolding died, and three workers were injured. A drama for everyone involved; for the victims, their relatives, but also for the staff responsible. I would not like to be in the shoes of the responsible project manager.

4. Safety

Organizing safety in the project

Safety is about protecting people against physical and psychological harm. During the execution of the project, but also afterwards when use is being made of the project result, the safety of all persons must be secured.

The thinking on safety developed strongly in the last century from one whereby the responsibility lay primarily with the employee, to a socially shared responsibility between management and staff.

In the following I show the differences between the old and new insights[5].

Old:
- Engineer instruments, environment and protective measures to be as safe as possible.
- Educate the employees.
- Enforce observance of, and compliance to, the safety procedures.

---

5 (2001) *The Psychology of Safety HANDBOOK*, E. Scott Geller, LEWIS PUBLISHERS, Washington/US

3.09 Health, security, safety and environment

New:
- *Ergonomics*: a careful and detailed study into the relationship between environment and behavior.
- *Empower* the employees to actively participate in the thinking about safety.
- *Evaluate* the existing safety system continuously.

Based on the new thinking about safety, we look at the three areas for attention that are stated.

ERGONOMICS
You can rest assured that the *engineering of the safety* is a part of the ergonomics, but it is more than that. In ergonomics, we look at both the safety of the project installations and at the effects that the environment has on the behavior of the project employees. A cluttered building site does not directly stimulate carefulness. In the same way, badly fitting safety clothing does not stimulate the wearing of it.

A way of engineering the safety in an installation is the so-called HAZOP analysis[6]. HAZOP stands for HAZards and OPerability. This method can best be compared with a risk analysis of the installation to be delivered and what could potentially go wrong. The method forces you to investigate the dangers in depth, which immediately also provides the disadvantage that the method is lengthy, expensive and requires the necessary expertise. Worldwide, however, it is the most used method for investigating the dangers with respect to safety.

As a *first step* all the relevant documents, plans and schedules for the installation are collected, and based on these, everything is divided up into manageable parts, which are then analyzed one by one.

The *second step* is the drawing up of two lists; one with control parameters and a following one with operations. For example:

Parameters	Operations
Pressure	Fill
Temperature	Move
Flow	Clean
Composition	Empty
Level	Ventilate
Reaction time	Maintain
Viscosity	Start-up
Degree of acidity	Close-off
Etc.	Etc.

In the *third step* you investigate what influence deviations to the design objectives have on the controllable parts, in other words, does the part still function as intended. You consider what effect a particular operation has on one or more control parameters. When, for example, it is not intended that a certain vessel becomes hotter than a specific temperature, you investigate what will actually happen when the temperature actually does rise to a higher level.

For this, so-called guide words are used, such as: *more, higher, larger, less, lower, smaller, invert, instead of, earlier, later, before, after, during, etc.* Going back to our example: *higher temperature in the vessel*. When the effects become dangerous, then you have an issue for which you have to work out what to do.

The *fourth step* consists of searching for causes for the list with potential deviations and the consequences such deviations can have. This forms the basis of the safety measures for preventing the cause and reducing these risks.

---

6 (2003) *Guidelines for Process Hazards Analysis, Hazards Identification & Risk Analysis*, Nigel Hyatt, DYADIM PRESS, Ontario/Canada

3.09 Health, security, safety and environment

This then covers the installation to be delivered. We now go a step further than the HAZOP study and address the effects that the project environment has on safety.

A number of points to consider:
- Make the human handling as simple as possible.
- Always choose the most simple solution to a safety problem.
- Are there factors that discourage safety
- Is risky behavior in one way or another rewarded.
- Are the employees competent.
- Is someone's personality suitable for the task.

So as well as the engineering of safe installations and the use of safe tools, we have now also to do with the design of a safe "project system" or a culture in which safety can develop.

EMPOWER
Measures alone are not enough. During the whole project, you have to encourage and enable your co-employees to think and act safely. The type of intervention that as project manager you should employ, is determined by the situation and, dependent on the competence of the employee, can be one of the following:
- Telling
- Selling
- Participating
- Delegating

This is completely synchronous with the leadership styles according to Hersey & Blanchard[7], which have already been covered. The essence is that, with respect to safety, employees develop themselves in their personal attitude and behavior. Until such time as they do that from within themselves, a more directive style is required. As project manager, however, the ultimate goal is to ensure that you do not only have to enforce an attitude of safety, but that this becomes an intrinsic motivation.

EVALUATE
Paying continuous attention to the various safety measures, and also to incidents that occur, ensures that eventually a safety system exists in which the optimum level of safety for the employees is guaranteed.

Europe: CE guideline
The European Machine (CE) guideline sets health and safety requirements with respect to engineering, construction, use and maintenance to protect users of installations delivered with the project. This is particularly important for the delivery of machines and installations.

For this, a risk analysis must be carried out under the responsibility of the project manager, whereby special attention should be given:
- Ergonomics of workplaces, which the users come into contact with.
- Access zones in and around the installation.
- Access for maintenance: platforms, walkways, ladders, stairs, clear passage, etc.
- Escape routes in the event of fire.
- Emergency stops and emergency stop zones.
- Protection from, or screening-off, of non-accessible zones.

As well as the risk analysis, a safety inspection should be carried out once the system has been electrically connected, but before the functionality of the system is tested. A certified safety expert will carry out such an inspection.

---

[7] (2001) *Management of Organizational Behavior (8th edition)*, Hersey, Blanchard, Johnson, PRENTICE HALL, Upper Saddle River

Based on the safety inspection report and in order to hand over a safe system to the user, any necessary changes to the system are implemented. At the very latest, a CE safety declaration must be issued together with the attachment of a CE label to the main control box when the system is handed over to the customer. Additionally, the user manual that is handed over must be in the local language. The project manager is jointly and severally liable for a safe delivery of the installation conforming to the CE standard.

5. Environment

It is important that the decision makers and people fulfilling the project take account of the effects their project has on the environment. Therefore, it is obligatory nearly everywhere in the world to produce an environmental effect report in advance. In each country, the laws will vary in the details, but in broad terms it all comes down to the same thing. The International Association for Impact Assessments[8](IAIA) has set up general principles. In relation to the effect reports, this organization founded in 1980, brings academics, the people operationally carrying out the work, and users of effect reports together in order to:
- Develop and improve methods.
- Promote training and understanding.
- Make available professional quality safeguards.
- Provide information.

There are more than 1600 members, who together globally represent more than 120 countries.

Principles of an environmental impact assessment[9]

The objective of such a report is to:
- Make environmental considerations a part of the decision making.
- Prevent, or at least minimize, negative effects.
- Retain functions of natural systems.
- Stimulate durable development.

A difference is made between so-called basic principles and the principles of operational fulfilment. The basic principles are general quality criteria which the fulfilment and the report have to satisfy, such as: goal-oriented, practical, relevant, effective, efficient, focussed, adaptable, etc.

The following fulfilment principles are related to the process that:
- We start up as early as possible.
- We use during the whole lifecycle.
- Concern all developments with (possible) effects on the environment.
- Involves both stakeholders and interested parties.
- Is in agreement with international standards.

It is enshrined in national legislation, which has to specify what type of project requires a report. Each report contains:
- An investigation into the alternatives.
- An impact analysis.
- Protective measures.
- Evaluation of the importance of the different consequences.

The report is subsequently assessed by the competent authority. This can result in a rejection or an approval. Following approval, a check on complicity is carried out.

---

8 www.iaia.org

9 (1996) *Principles of Environmental Impact Assessment Best Practice,* IAIA

3.09 Health, security, safety and environment

3.10 Finance

ACCOUNTING TO ACCOUNT FOR

Nowadays, the authorities demand a lot of an organization's financial administration.

Projects, with their temporary character, are part of a larger whole, and it is useful to have some knowledge of accounting processes, even though it is not a necessity for managing a project successfully.

3.10 Finance

3.10-1 DEFINITIONS

Added value	Turnover less purchase value.
Assets	An organisation's assets and accounts receivable. These are on the left side of the balance sheet.
Balance sheet	A representation of an organisation's assets and liabilities at a specific point in time.
Cash flow	The actual cash flow generated; the surplus of income over expenditure (including tax).
Cash flow (investment)	The balance of the annual revenue and expenses to be expected, linked with an investment project.
Credit	Right side of the balance sheet or the profit and loss account.
Creditors	Suppliers from whom goods are obtained using a suppliers credit.
Cumulated cash flow	The sum of the annual revenue and expenses to be expected, linked with an investment project.
Current Assets	Assets linked to the company for a short period. These can be used (stock, liquid assets), sold (end products, securities) or collected (accounts receivable).

3.10 Finance

Debit	Left side of the balance sheet or the profit and loss account.
Debtors	Accounts receivable from customers through sales on account.
Depreciation	Periodic decrease in value of a durable product or production resource.
Discount factor	The number with which you multiply a future cash flow, in order to calculate the present value.
Discount percentage	The percentage you use for present value calculations.
Financing costs	Costs, such as interest, which result from attracting liabilities.
Fixed Assets	Assets belonging to the company for a long period (>1 year).
Interest	Payment or fee, on borrowed money, to be paid over a certain period.
Internal Rate of Return	The internal rate of return for investment decisions is the discount percentage, which makes the Net Present Value zero.
Investing	Tying up of equity in assets.
Leverage	The extent to which the return on the owners equity is affected by the interest rate and the relative amount of liabilities attracted.

3.10 Finance

Liabilities	Equity which has to be paid back by the company to the provider of the equity within, or at, a certain time. For as long as this has not taken place, there is a debt.
Liabilities & Equity	The equity capital and the liabilities. These are on the right side of the balance sheet.
Liquidity	The ability of a company to meet its payment obligations in the short term.
Long and short term debts	Long term liabilities (> 1 year), for instance loans with mortgage security. Short term debts (=< 1 year), for instance current account and creditors.
Operating result	The added value less the total costs (excluding interest), or the turnover less the total costs (including purchases, excluding interest) of this turnover. This is also called the result from business operations.
Owners equity	Risk bearing equity that the owners (shareholders) have permanently made available to the company. The equity capital of a company consists of share capital and retained earnings.
Present Value of a certain amount X	The amount you now have to deposit in order to have saved the amount X after a number of years (based on a certain discount percentage).
Profit	The positive difference between receipts and costs.

Profit and loss account	The profit and loss account gives a specification of the revenue (benefits) and the costs (expenses) over a specific period.
Rate of equity turnover	The number of times a year the equity is first available in cash, is then put into goods, and ultimately becomes available in cash again through the sales of the end product.
Retained earnings	Retained earnings are the profit not distributed to the shareholders.
Return on own equity	Profitability of the equity invested in the company by the owners.
Return on total equity	Profitability of the total equity invested in the company.
Solvability	The ability of a company to meet its payment obligations in the long term.
Stock	The total of issues shares (at nominal value).
Turnover	The total amount for which invoices have been sent during the financial year.
Working Capital	The (net) working capital is the difference between the total amount of current assets and current debts.

3.10 Finance

3.10-2 INTRODUCTION

Projects are not stand-alone, but are part of a larger whole, and in one way or another, as project manager, you have to account for the funds made available to you by the organization. This has to fit in with the guidelines of the organization) that execute and the organization) that receive(s).

3.10-3 Process steps

1. Recognise the financial environment of the project.
2. Define the business case.
3. Implement the financial administration and reports.
4. Provide the financial reports.
5. If applicable, schedule financial audits.
6. Obtain financial discharge at close-out.

1. Recognise the financial environment of the project

The law is one of the reasons every organization keeps accounts in which it records all transactions, from which financial rights and obligations are derived, in such a way that it will ultimately be able to draw up a balance sheet and profit & loss statement. For us as project managers, this means that everything happening on the project, and which has an effect on the balance sheet, and/or the profit & loss statement of one of the organizations involved, has to be justifiable.

If this is not already prescribed by the organisation's financial departments involved, the project manager must ensure that from his project organization there is a link with the administration of the different organizations. In many cases this has not been organized and the project manager has to do it himself (off the books).

2. Define the business case

The "business case" is a document in which we balance the costs and benefits, and substantiate why we are carrying out the project.

The following topics are addressed:
- Reason and background.
- Alternatives considered.
- Expected benefits or returns.
- Summary of the most important risks.
- Budget.
- Duration and phasing.
- Investment assessment.

The justification has to be as objective as possible, and where possible supported by a financial justification, which gives an insight into the effect, the project has on the organization's cash flows.

3. Implement the financial administration and reports

Dependent on the current guidelines, during the project start, the project manager implements an administration which fits in with the existing administrations of the organizations concerned. The best tool for this is the Work Break Down Structure; what the general ledger is to the permanent organization, the WBS is to the project.

Ensure that the financial reporting fits in with that of the permanent organization, but take account of the fact that there are big differences. A number of these differences are:

Permanent organization	Accounts for a project
Required by law	Not required by law
Looks at the history	Looks at the future
According to strict (legal) guidelines	There is no legal regime
Subject to regular audits	Audits are sometimes carried out
Comprises a fiscal period	Comprises the whole (sometimes several fiscal periods) life cycle of the project
Reporting takes some time	Reporting takes a few days at the end of the reporting period
Contains accurate deferment entries deferment entries and accrual entries	Forecasts on rounded numbers
Depreciation costs	Total costs of the capital investment are part of the projects budget

3.10 Finance

It is mainly the actuality (or lagging behind) of the existing accounts which actually forces the project manager to keep his own accounts off-the-books, based on which he manages the future costs of his project.

4. Provide the financial reports

This is about the link between the project accounts and the financial function of the organization. This link is mainly aimed at the future, as the history is being kept by the accounting department itself.

The project will have to show what effect it will have on the future cash flows of the organization, as this allows the organization to have enough (but not too many) liquid funds, or cash, when required. This is especially important when, sooner or later, certain payments have to be made.

When the project budget is built up from several departmental budgets, the project manager has to report to the line managers involved on the budget spend, so that they can then take that into consideration when managing their own budget.

Another problem occurs when a project stretches over year-end boundaries, as it is then possible that the project using department budgets no longer has any budget, because it has been forgotten in the annual budget round. A similar situation occurs when the project has been stopped for some time (a certain decision took longer than planned), and as a result, has not spent any budget. If this project now goes over year-end boundaries, there is a high chance that less budget has been reserved than is needed.

In the case of a project that the organization is carrying out for one of its customers, the progress has an influence on the amounts that can be invoiced, or the value which can be included on the balance sheet (as an asset).

5. If applicable, schedule financial audits

The goal of the scheduled financial audits is twofold:
- Discovering a misrepresentation of matters.
- The 'deterrent' effect motivates the drawing up of a correct report.

The project manager and his staff can *consciously* present the financial situation to be more favorable than it really is, and in this case, it is justified to talk of fraud. Of course, it is also possible that they provide the wrong, or no figures because of *ignorance* or *unwillingness*.

There are three conditions, which can cause a more favorable representation of the project finances:
- The project manager is under pressure from his management (or the project sponsor).
- There are circumstances which make it possible.
- Making the report look better can be rationalized.

These three alone make it necessary that for financial audits to be effective, they must be carried out by an independent auditor. This auditor can then not be influenced by the project sponsor and/or project manager. Possibly this is a suitable task for the Project Management Office, and the auditor from this body can then investigate whether or not the above mentioned conditions are present.

In addition to the above, the auditor can also look at how project management processes have been implemented. the *PMBOK Guide*[1] mentions the following processes:

Costs process	Processes providing input
Estimate the costs	Define the scope Make the WBS
Budget the costs	Select the suppliers Estimate the required capacity Develop the scheduling
Manage the costs	Report on the progress Manage the project

The question will now always be: have these processes been implemented in such a way that the financial reports are a realistic representation of the reality.

How many financial audits per project? That should be a logical result from the risk analysis. It would be better to schedule an audit in advance, than to schedule it, only when there is a feeling something might go wrong.

6. Obtain financial discharge on close-out

After the project, there should be a formal close-out in which the project manager carries out a final project evaluation. One of the elements of this evaluation consists of a difference analysis between the original estimate, and the actual situation. The project sponsor or the steering committee can then discharge the project manager.

---

[1] (2006) *A Guide to the Project Management Body of Knowledge,* THE PROJECT MANAGEMENT INSTITUTE

3.10-4 Special Topics

1. The annual report
To comply with the obligations in the previously mentioned section of the law, the organization draws up the annual financial report and accounts. For a company these consist of:

The annual report
The *annual report* (*senior management or board of directors report*) with announcements on:
- The status on the balance sheet date and the affairs of the past financial year.
- Exceptional or special events in the new financial year, which have already taken place.
- The expected state of affairs for the coming financial year such as: planned investments, financing, manpower, activities of the company in the area of research and development, circumstances on which the development of turnover and profitability depends (for instance the exchange rate of the dollar).

The annual accounts
The *annual accounts* provide information on the equity position, results and activities of the company and consist of:
- *Balance sheet*: overview of the composition of the total equity of the company at a certain time, expressed in terms of money.
- *Profit and loss account:* overview of the positive or negative financial results of the company.
- The *explanation* on the balance sheet and the profit and loss account.

Other information
The *other information,* such as:
- Auditors report.
- Profit appropriation, important here is the statutory regulation.
- Information on special authorities regarding the control, such as priority shares.
- Special events with major financial consequences, which have occurred after the end of the financial year, e.g. a fire.
- A list of participations.

The Balance sheet
The balance sheet is an overview of the assets and the equity (how these are financed) of a company at a given time, and consists of:
- Active side (debit): the assets of the organization (buildings, car fleet, stock, debtors, bank, etc.) also called the "capital" of the company.
- Passive side (credit): the sources of finance (shares, reserves, provisions, long term loans, creditors, etc.) also called the "equity and liabilities" of the organization.

Because the capital (debit side) of the company has been obtained with the equity and liabilities (credit side) both are the same.

THE DEBIT SIDE OF THE BALANCE SHEET: THE ASSETS (CAPITAL)
The debit side is about the assets, which can be divided into:
- *Fixed assets*: production means which are fixed for a longer period:
  o *Material* (tangible) fixed assets: such as machines, buildings, terrain, cars and inventory.
  o Immaterial fixed assets. These represent a certain value, but have no tangible manifestation: for instance patents, research and development costs, concessions, licences, goodwill, publishing rights, trade marks.

- o   Financial fixed assets: mainly participation ratios (parent-subsidiary relationship).
- Current assets, the characteristic of this is that the appropriation possibility is limited until one production process and/or durable servitude is missing from the production process.
- Assets, which quickly become available in liquid form:
  - o   Stock.
  - o   Debtors (the accounts receivables).
  - o   Securities (the temporary investments).
  - o   Liquid funds.

However, the boundary between fixed and current assets cannot always easily be drawn.

THE CREDIT SIDE OF THE BALANCE SHEET: THE AVAILABLE EQUITY

The credit side of the balance sheet is distinguished by:
- Owners Equity (OE) is the equity brought in by the owners of a company. For a Private Limited Company (Ltd.) or a Public Limited Company (plc) this is in the form of company shares. We have:
  - o   The statutory share capital which includes the maximum amount of shares a company can issue in accordance with the articles of association.
  - o   The issued share capital which is the part of the shares which has been issued. The non-issued shares are still in the portfolio.
- The Equity is permanent. Usually the company is not obliged to pay the share capital back to the shareholders. The Equity is available to the company for as long as it exists.
- Provisions. The amount set apart on the credit side of the balance sheet for liabilities, which are to be expected. For example, a warranty provision indicating the amount of claims for damages that can be expected in the future for products which have already been delivered. As they are claims by third parties on the company, the provisions fall under liabilities.
- Liabilities: made available on the condition of repayment and payment of interest, irrespective of whether or not the financial situation of the company permits this. A distinction can be made between long-term debts (longer than a year) and short-term debts (less than a year). With liabilities you are dealing with temporary, non-profit and non-risk bearing equity. A subordinated loan is semi-enterprising equity, whereby in the event bankruptcy, payment is only made after other debts have been paid, but before the Equity providers.

The Profit and Loss statement

With respect to a certain period, the profit and loss statement shows the parts of the changes in the owners equity by means of an overview of income (credit) and costs (debit).

The various entries on the profit and loss account can also be presented following each other.

The main functions of a profit and loss account are:
- Providing insight into the causes of changes in the Equity by providing a specification of the net profit over a certain period.
- Forming a basis for the proposal in the general meeting of shareholders for appropriation of profits.

3.10 Finance

Other costs and benefits
Over a year, the profit and loss account provides an overview of the costs and benefits in that year which resulted from the primary, daily (operational) company activities. Activities, which do not happen regularly are, however, connected with the daily activities. The result of such activities are the other costs and benefits: profit/loss when selling production resources, equities, and interest received and paid.

The other costs and benefits are included in the operating results, as they are connected to the normal operations.

Extraordinary costs and benefits
There are also costs and benefits, which are referred to as extraordinary costs and benefits, and are not connected with the normal operations, such as:
- Results of expropriation.
- Results of a nationalization.
- Damages through the loss of assets which are unusual or impossible to insure.

These are not accounted for in the normal operating results.

2. Accounting
In order to comply with the statutory obligations to report, an organization has to record all its actions which lead to a change in the balance sheet or profit and loss account in its accounts.

The following concepts will be successively discussed:
- Accounting evidence.
- Daybook.
- Double entry bookkeeping system.
- Journal.
- General Ledger.
- Extended trial balance.
- Connection between the balance sheet and the profit and loss account.

Accounting evidence
All *financial facts* are described in *accounting evidence*, for example:
- Incoming invoices.
- Outgoing invoices.
- Bank statements.
- Etc.

The accounts department processes these documents as follows.

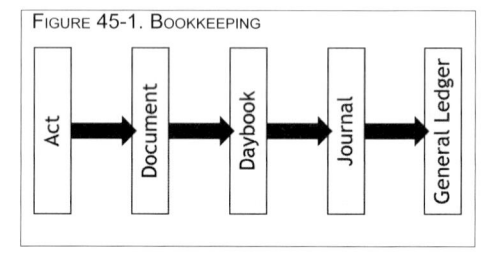

FIGURE 45-1. BOOKKEEPING

Act → Document → Daybook → Journal → General Ledger

Daybook
A piece of accounting evidence is the justification of a certain action, which has financial consequences. Accounting evidence of similar transactions come from the different parts of the organization to the responsible accounts department employee, who enters them in the relevant daybook, and then archives the accounting evidence.

Examples of daybooks are: Stock book, Sales ledger, Cash/Bank/Giro book, Creditors ledger, etc.

Double entry bookkeeping system
A financial fact always has an effect on more than one aspect of the organization. When a delivery van is bought, then on the one side the assets increase, and on the other side the creditor balance also increases. When the invoice is paid, the bank balance decreases, just as do the accounts payable.

3.10 Finance

This system of accounting is called double entry bookkeeping, every entry is booked as both debit and credit.

Journal
The accounting system makes a journal entry of every entry in a daybook, which ultimately ends up on a number of ledger accounts. The journal entry divides the amounts of the financial fact over the ledger accounts.

General Ledger
For every entry on the balance sheet or in the profit and loss account, there is a general ledger account, in which during the year, the accounts department enters the various financial facts.

In principle, there are two types of ledger accounts:
- Balance sheet account.
- Profit and Loss accounts.

At the end of the year, the balances on the balance sheets are the basis for the opening balance for the new year, whereas the total of the balances of the profit and loss accounts constitutes the profit or loss of the organization.

So every general ledger account is, therefore, an overview of the changes occurring over a certain period in an asset, debt or in the organisation's owners equity.

EXAMPLE 45-1 HIRING AND EXTERNAL CONSULTANT

The project manager hires an external consultant for two weeks, for which he charges € 20,000. The accounting evidence of this action is the invoice the project manager receives at the end of the two weeks. He signs it for approval, and sends it on to the credit department who enter it in the bought ledger. The accompanying journal entry is:

Consultancy costs   € 20,000
To Creditors   € 20,000

The general ledger account, Consultancy costs, is now debited for € 20,000, whereas the general ledger account, Creditors is credited with the same amount. The total of all ledger accounts is always in balance. A "double" entry has just been made, thus "double entry bookkeeping".

A month later, the invoice is paid, and a bank statement is received. Entering this statement in the Bankbook results in the journal entry.

Creditors   € 20,000
To Bank   € 20,000

The account Creditors is debited (debts are reduced) and the general ledger account Bank is credited (liquid assets have decreased).

The trial balance
A *trial balance* is a total lay-out of debit and credit amounts.

Per account, the difference is determined between the debit and the credit amount of the trial balance, and entered in the *Trial balance*. The profit and loss account and the final balance sheet are added to that, and the total forms the *Extended trial balance*.

The trial balance is the basis for composing the profit and loss account and the final balance sheet. The costs and income accounts are entered into the profit and loss account. The profit or the loss is entered into, respectively, either the debit column or credit column of the profit and loss account.

The trial balance shows whether or not the ledger is in balance, as the amounts come from the general ledger. The amounts on the trial balance are equal to the closing amounts on the general ledger accounts. The relationship between the profit and loss account and the final balance sheet is formed by the profit or the loss. The amounts of the final balance sheet are again equal to the general ledger accounts to be re-opened.

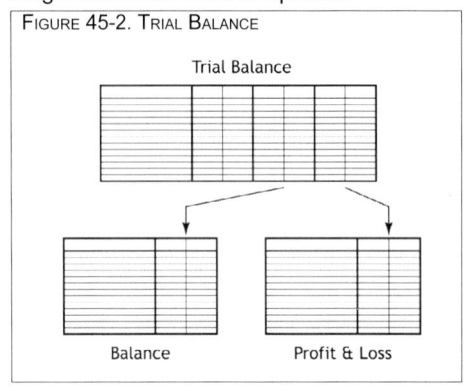

FIGURE 45-2. TRIAL BALANCE

Trial Balance

Balance   Profit & Loss

The connection between the balance sheet and the profit and loss account
With the double entry bookkeeping system, both the changes in the use of the equity and the changes in the size and composition of the equity are entered into the accounts. In this way, the balance sheet provides an overview of the available assets, debts and the Equity at a given time.

The profit and loss account then shows the change in the size of the Equity, which occurred in a certain period. In this way, the profit and loss account forms a more detailed representation of the balance sheet item Equity. It provides an insight in the cause of the decrease or increase of the Equity.

There is an important relationship between the balance sheet and the profit and loss account. The balance sheet gives an overview of the use of the invested equity, and the profit and loss account contains more information on changes in the Equity, i.e. the equity invested by the shareholders.

There is also an important difference between both. The balance sheet is related to a point in time, whereas the profit and loss account is related to a period.

3. Cost allocation

In order to be viable, a company has to somehow cover its costs through proceeds from the sale of its products, services and projects. You could say that these commercial activities carry the costs the company makes. Therefore, we sometimes also call these the *cost carriers*.

To be able to make the right decisions about the organization, the operational management has to have an insight into the profitability of the different cost carriers. The accounts department should be capable of doing this, and this is easier for some costs than for others.

We look at the way in which the organization has to do this. Successively, the following topics will be discussed:
- Standard lay-out of cost categories.
- Cost carriers.
- Fixed versus variable costs.
- Direct versus indirect costs.
- Allocation of costs.
- Activating costs.

Standard cost categories
Initially, you can make a lay-out matching the way in which costs occur during the company processes, and a frequently used lay-out is:
- Raw materials.
- Labour.
- Depreciation on fixed assets.
- Land use.
- Third party services.
- Taxes which increase the cost price.
- Interest on borrowed money.

Obviously it is also possible to break this down further according to need. The depreciations form a special cost category, as there are no direct expenses attached to them. After all, when the organization bought the fixed asset, it paid at that time the related price to the supplier. When the asset has been in use for several years, from a business economics point of view it is not right, and legally not permitted, to take all the costs in the year of purchase. The asset is then entered on the debit side of the balance sheet (is activated), and annually the depreciation is written off to the account of the book value.

Cost carriers
Cost carriers are the end products, services or projects an organization delivers to its customers. Note that a project is sometimes a cost carrier, sometimes a cost centre (see further on), and sometimes a collection of different costs attributed to one department.

Fixed versus variable
Another break down is that of fixed versus variable costs, whereby the latter is dependent on the production delivered by an organization. If the production increases or decreases, the variable costs also increase or decrease, as opposed to the fixed costs, which remain constant irrespective of the production delivered.

Direct versus indirect costs
The distinction between the direct and indirect costs provides the accounting department with a problem, especially if the operational management wants to know how profitable certain products or services are. The direct costs are unambiguously attributed to a product or project.

However, this is more difficult for the indirect costs, because how do you, for example, charge the salary costs of the senior management or the costs for the company restaurant to a product or project? There are several methods to do this, which I will explain later.

Allocating indirect costs
There are three methods the organization can use to attribute the indirect costs to a cost carrier:

- An overhead percentage.
- The cost centre method.
- Through "activity based costing".

OVERHEAD PERCENTAGE
This is the easiest method, which can be made clear by means of an example.

> EXAMPLE 45-2 OVERHEAD PERCENTAGE
> The organization rents a building for €150,000 per year. At the beginning of the year, the turnover is estimated at approximately €15,000,000. The cost price for each order contains a part of 1% of the sales price, in order to cover the rental of the building.

COST CENTRE METHOD
The cost centre method approach is a lot clearer, but also more complex to administer in the accounts. Cost centres are "transitional stages", where we initially collect the indirect costs before attributing them to the different cost carriers.

Traditionally there are three types:
- Main cost centres: independent departments, which supply products, services or projects to external customers (Factory, Shop, etc.).
- Independent cost centres: independent departments, which have no direct relationship to the products, services or projects provided (Senior Management, HR, etc.).
- Supporting cost centres: not independent departments, but in accounting terms can be considered as a unit (Accommodation, etc.).

3.10 Finance

In an organization that achieves many of its *internal* activities in a project based manner, there is a need for a fourth cost centre:
- Project cost centre, for those projects which deliver results on behalf of other cost centres.

This latter type can be compared to a type of supporting cost centre, but with the difference that the traditional supporting cost centre has a permanent character, whereas the project cost centre does not. The project cost centre is not used for external projects that the organization carries out based on customer contracts (an external project is a cost carrier).

The allocation of costs is now carried out as follows:
1. Collecting the costs per cost category.
2. Allocate direct costs to cost carriers.
3. Allocate indirect costs to the appropriate cost centre.
4. Cost centres x-charge services to the main cost centres.
5. Main cost centres x-charge services to the cost carriers.

All cost centres charge a rate for the services they provide. The supporting cost centre "Accommodation" may charge a rate per square meter, the "ICT" department a rental price for the software used, and the "HR" department a fixed rate per employee, etc.

On the assumption that the variable costs are proportional, the rate can be calculated using the following formula:

$$Rate = \frac{Estimated\ Fixed\ Costs}{Normal\ Service} + \frac{Estimated\ Variable\ Costs}{Expected\ Service}$$

When the services a certain cost centre can charge is higher than the estimate at the beginning of the year, it is called over absorption, and when it is less it is called under absorption.

The diagram shows how the allocation of costs is carried out. We break the cost categories down in direct and indirect costs and the direct costs go straight to the cost carrier. The indirect costs follow another route. Initially the costs go to a (supporting) cost centre, and from there to the main cost centre carrying out services on behalf of the

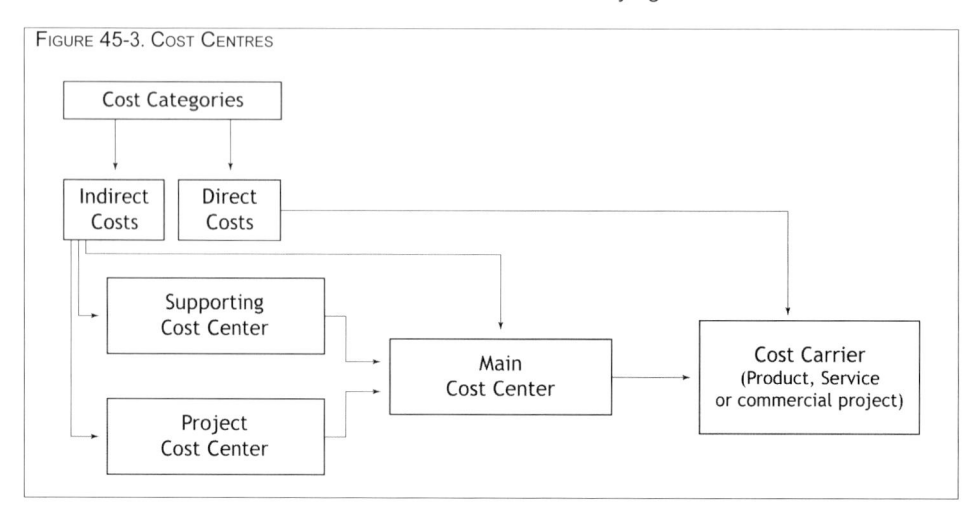

FIGURE 45-3. COST CENTRES

cost carrier. In this way, by using a number of interim steps, we have made direct costs from the indirect costs.

Note that administratively there are now two types of projects:
- The project as cost centre.
- The project as cost carrier.

As cost centre, the project can get costs charged to it from other cost centres, but in turn it can also charge costs on to other cost centres. The project functions as a cost carrier when it is a service for one of the organisation's customers.

The cost price of a product (i.e. cost carrier) is then built up of:

$$\sum \text{Direct Costs} \\ + \\ \sum \text{Rate Main Cost Centres}$$

ACTIVITY BASED COSTING

This method looks like the cost centre method on the understanding that now the cost allocation does not take place from the departments, but from activities required to deliver a certain product or service. The costs borne by a cost carrier are now the number of actions (activities) times the related rate.

Activating costs

Sometimes it is undesirable or not allowed to take a certain cost entry in a certain year. In such a case, it is included on the debit side of the balance sheet as active, and this is called activation of costs. There are clear guidelines for this; it is only allowed when it is likely that it will result in economic advantages for the company, and when it is possible to reliably determine the costs. The latter means that the valuation is equal to the purchase price or manufacturing price.

Examples of these types of costs are: software, patents, copyrights, feature films, customer files, market share, fishing rights, etc.

4. OPEX and CAPEX

OPEX

Is an abbreviation of Operating Expenditures. These are recurring costs for a product, system or company, or put another way, the exploitation costs of the product, system or company.

CAPEX

Is the counterpart, and means the Capital Expenditures (CAPEX). These are the costs for development or delivery of the non-usable parts of a product or system, and are actually the investment costs.

For example, the purchase of a photocopier is the CAPEX, whereas the annual costs for the toner and paper together with the maintenance, form the OPEX.

5. Ratios

Financial ratios, or financial indicators, are ratios that can be determined using the information from the balance sheet and the profit and loss account.

Ratios must be interpreted on the basis of:
- Internal comparison (previous and future years), or
- External comparison (of different companies).

The value of a ratio as criterion, therefore, is often specific for an industry, and, among other things, depends on the market sensitivity of the company.

Many ratios are susceptible to manipulation (window dressing to present a better picture

3.10 Finance

of the actual truth), which happens for different reasons, such as:
- Attracting finance resources more easily or cheaply.
- Better negotiation position in a merger or takeover situation.

Because the interpretation of a value of a ratio is not always easy, conclusions should never be drawn based on the outcome of one ratio. It is advisable to also take the underlying values into consideration.

Rate of return
Rate of return says something about the profitability of a company, however different approaches are possible, depending on the goal with which the rate of return is viewed.

PROFIT MARGIN

$$Profit\ before\ Tax\ /\ Turnover$$

RETURN ON EQUITY (ROE)
This is one of the most important rates of return figures, because it indicates what the owners of the organization gain.

$$Profit\ after\ Tax\ /\ Equity$$

Sometimes the average equity is used, that is the equity at the beginning of that year + the equity at the end of that same year, divided by 2.

RETURN ON TOTAL ASSETS (ROTA)

$$Profit\ before\ Tax\ /\ Total\ Assets$$

For as long as the interest on liabilities is lower than the rate of return on the equity, the attracting of liabilities will lead to an increase in the rate of return of the equity. This is called leverage. In periods of inflation and high interest, however, this does not apply, as due to the high costs of the liabilities, the rate of return of the equity goes down the drain. Suppliers of the liabilities will then, as compensation for inflation, receive a higher interest payment. The consequence can then be that the interest for the liabilities is higher than the rate of return on the equity.

PROFIT PER SHARE
For this option of measuring the profitability of the company, the profit available for the (ordinary) shareholders is related to the average number of issued shares in one year.

$$Profit\ for\ Shareholders\ /\ Number\ of\ Shares$$

The higher this ratio, the more favorable the profit position of the company.

PRICE/EARNINGS RATIO
For assessing the profitability of the company, use is also made of the:

$$Share\ Price\ /\ Profit\ per\ Share$$

This ratio is primarily used to assess whether the price of a share provides a reasonable reflection of the company's profitability. If the ratio is relatively low, then that can be reason for investors to invest in the company in question.

EBIT(DA)
EBITDA stands for Earnings Before Interest, Taxes, Depreciation and Amortization and is a yardstick for the Gross profit of a company.

It is used as a yardstick for the profit that a company achieves from its operations, without inclusion of the costs and income of the financing.

3.10 Finance

Liquidity

Liquidity the extent to which the organization is able to meet its short-term commitments from the on-going revenues. In order to deduce the liquidity of the organization from the balance sheet, use is made of:

- Current Ratio.
- Quick Ratio.
- Liquid Ratio.

And from:

- Net Working Capital

CURRENT RATIO

Current Assets / Current Liabilities

Short –term always refers to one year. The standard within which this ratio is healthy, is strongly dependent on the sector in which an organization operates, and sometimes CR>1.5 is adjudged to be a healthy ratio.

QUICK RATIO

If an organization has a lot of stock, the current ratio will suggest a larger level of liquidity than there actually is. The quick ratio then provides additional information, because the stock is now not included in the numerator.

(Current Assets - Stock) / Current Liabilities

As it is not certain whether or not the stock can be sold in the short-term, the quick ratio is a safer yardstick than the current ratio for assessing the organisation's liquidity position.

Also here, the standard is again strongly dependent on the sector, but it is, in any case, desirable that this is > 1.

LIQUID RATIO

For complete safety, the Liquid or Cash ratio is used:

Cash / Current Liabilities

(NET) WORKING CAPITAL

Current Assets - Current Liabilities

In normal language, the Net Working Capital the amount that remains (as contribution) when all short-term debts have been paid. Although it is possible to run an organization with a negative working capital, a positive working capital is preferable.

The absolute amount of the working capital, in fact, does not say very much, but the larger an organization is, the bigger the need for working capital. Therefore, you obtain a better picture by looking at:

Working Capital / Turnover

Also possible is:

Working Capital / Total Assets

The above key indicators provide insight to the liquidity at a certain moment in time, and as well as this insight, it also interesting to have knowledge about the speed with which an organization is in a position to acquire liquid resources.

For this, the following ratios have been thought out:
- The rate of stock turnover.
- The average collection time or turnover time of the debtors.

3.10 Finance

RATE OF STOCK TURNOVER
This ratio indicates how quickly the organization is able to sell its stock.

Costs of Stock Sold / Stock

The organisation's turnover is built up of cost price of the products sold, increased by a certain profit margin. If we now take the part of the cost price that relates to the parts or raw materials used from stock, and we divide this by the current warehouse stock, we know roughly how often per year we sell the stock in the warehouse. This rate of stock turnover is an indicator to how well the Sales department is performing.

AVERAGE COLLECTION PERIOD
This ratio say something about the speed with which debtors pay (or go cycle round in the turnover). The collection time is easier to fathom out than the speed of turnover, and, therefore, I give this first:

Account Receivables / Turnover per day

TURNOVER DEBTORS
We calculate the turnover speed of the debtors in a similar way to that of the stock. You could take the debtors balance as a form of stock of liquid resources that the organization still has to receive or collect.

Turnover / Account Receivables

If you compare both formulas with each other, then it becomes clear that both are measurements for the same thing. They are extremely suitable as performance indicators for the debt collection department.

Solvability
Solvability is the extent to which an organization is in a position to meet its total commitments in the long-term. This means that the company must be in a position to meet its total debts using of its assets, should the activities of the company be wound-up or suspended. There are two solvability ratios.

EQUITY MULTIPLIER

Total Assets / Liabilities

If this ratio is greater than 1, that indicates that in the event of a possible suspension or winding-up of the company, all debts (all claims from third parties) can be paid from the total assets. The company is then not insolvent.

DEBT RATIO

Liabilities / Total Assets

This debt ratio shows which part of the total of all of the organisation's assets is financed with the liabilities (debt ratio). This ratio will normally lie under the value of 1. The closer to 1, the greater the risk for the providers of the liabilities. These will then probably demand a higher interest payment, because the company is approaching the insolvability limit.

6. Investment appraisal

With investment decisions we usually look at the return from a project, and we have a number of calculation techniques available to work that out:
- Average return.
- Payback period.
- Net Present Value.
- Internal Rate of Return.
- Real Option Analysis.

Below, I briefly explain what the various methods are. What is common to all these methods, is that they all look at money which actually comes into, or goes out of, the organization – the so-called cash flows. The reason for this is that you can only invest money you have in "cash". You only include accounting or fiscal tricks for the annual accounts when they have an effect on the tax to be paid (and therefore on the cash flow).

Average return
The average return is the ratio between the cash flow a project produces annually on average, and the average capital invested in the project:

Nett Profit / Average investment

The average capital invested is equated to half of the original investment (if at the end of the project there is no residual value).

The average annual net profit is obtained by calculating all net cash flows and dividing this by the duration of the project. In doing this, the investments and the operational expenses (including tax) are counted as negative and the income as positive.

The objection to this method, is that no account is taken of the point in time that the cash flow comes into being.

Payback period
This is about how long it takes before the invested amount is completely paid back from the cash flows. The point at which the total of the cumulative costs are equal to the total of the cumulative income is called the Break-Even-Point.

The objection to this method is that the cash flows which come after the payback period are completely ignored. Another objection is that the payback period does not give a clear indication of the profitability of a project.

In practice the payback period is often used as a criterion of certainty, to show that the project will actually be profitable, and, the faster, the more certain. When you take the payback period and the average return together in the assessment, you are a lot more accurate, but not accurate enough.

Net Present Value
This is not yet the most accurate method, but it is the most used. The annual cash flows are discounted at a certain discount percentage. The essence of this, is that today's currency is worth a lot more than tomorrow's currency, as the currency today can be used immediately to invest and generate income with. This is the first basic rule for financial decisions, and stands apart from the fact as to whether or not there is inflation.

The value of a future cash flow can be calculated by multiplying the amount with a discount factor:

Discount factor = 1 / (1+r)

Suppose that after 1 year (so in year 2), a cash flow is expected:

*Present Value of a Cash Flow
= Expected Cash Flow x Discount factor*

> EXAMPLE 45-3 CALCULATING PRESENT VALUE
> The discount percentage r has been set at 10%. After one year (so in year 2), a cash flow of €150 is expected. The current value of this cash flow in the future amounts to €136.36 (=150/1.10).

For the third year the present value is:

$1 / (1+r)^2$

Annually, the cash flow of that year is calculated back to the present value:

$Cash\ Flow_n / (1+r)^{n-1}$

All amounts are now comparable, they have been calculated back to the present value, and because of this, we can add them all up

3.10 Finance

without a problem. These cumulative cash flows then are:

$$\sum (Cash\ Flow_n / (1+r)^{n-1})$$

This amount we abbreviate to NPV (nett present value).

> EXAMPLE 45-4 CALCULATING PRESENT VALUE
> The discount percentage r has been set to 10%. After one year (so in year 2), we expect a cash flow of €150, after two years (so in year 3), again €150. So the NPV of the two future cash flows is equal to €260.33 (=136.36+123.97).

This method is often called the discounted cash flow method.

WHICH DISCOUNT PERCENTAGE

The question now is, which percentage you use to make these calculations? It is normal to use a percentage that is equal to the return you would get in similar investments. The underlying thought is that the investors in the organization expect a minimum return on the capital they make available. For the company, this return is the *"cost of capital"* to attract capital, and note that this is different from the interest they have to pay for a money loan.

Every investment (project) an organization makes must provide a positive contribution to the return expected by the investors. When the net present value of the project is greater than, or equal to, zero, it provides the required contribution and it can be started. Projects with a high risk (for instance innovations) must satisfy a higher discount percentage than projects with a low risk.

Internal Rate of Return

The internal rate of return is that percentage for which the Net Present Value of the project is zero. In this way, the internal rate of return is the combined return on all negative cash flows which are yielded by the positive cash flows in the project. This return has nothing to do with a correction for inflation. The internal rate of return is a meaningful financial criterion for the attractiveness of projects.

You can only calculate the internal rate of return by estimating and trying out. There is no direct derivation method. You start with estimating the value, and then the NPV is calculated, with the objective of getting it to zero. If the NPV is still positive, apparently the percentage apparently needs to go up. If the NPV is negative the discount percentage needs to go down, and so on.

The internal rate of return has to then exceed the so-called **hurdle rate**. This is the same percentage (cost of capital) we use in the net present value calculation.

Luckily spreadsheet programmes have a function to calculate this. Within Excel, this function is called IRR. This is then calculated over a series of numbers (cash flows).

Assumptions with Net Present Value and Internal Rate of Return

Applying the Discounted Cash Flow method is usually based on a number of assumptions:

- The length of the period is one year.
- The expenses and receipts always take place in the middle of the period.
- The receipts are net receipts. The sales income from the products is reduced with all costs made for the production and sales.

Bang for Buck Index

One of the objectives of portfolio management is maximizing the value of the portfolio. If we just look at the NPV, we overlook the number of resources we have to use.

3.10 Finance

A better yardstick for prioritizing is the so called Bang for Buck Index:

Bang-for-Buck Index = NPV / # Resources

In other words, the NPV for each resource used. When taking portfolio decisions, the net present values are recalculated, and you do not include the **sunk-costs** in doing this. This means that the business justification becomes better and better as time progresses (negative cash flows decrease, causing the NPV and the BBI to increase, and the numbers of resources also decrease causing the BBI to increase).

Real Option Analysis

When a portfolio process has been implemented, in which the above calculations provide guidance for the decision making, a discrepancy quickly develops between the gut feeling of the entrepreneur (innovations), and the cold 'spreadsheet' calculation from which the priority setting is established. This is one of the biggest weaknesses of the NPV calculations, which often wrongly reject innovations.

This comes about because a number of assumptions lie at the core of the Net Present Value and/or the Internal Rate of Return, which do not comply with reality. These are for instance[2]:

Assumption	Reality
The decision for the complete project is taken once at the beginning.	In view of the uncertainty of many factors, some decisions cannot be taken until later.

Assumption	Reality
Projects are mini-companies and can be assessed as such on their contribution.	Projects are mutually dependent on other projects and/or decisions and cannot be assessed on the basis of separate cash flows.
When the projects have been started, management is hands-off or remote.	There is a lot of attention paid to projects during the whole lifecycle, including go/no go decisions, budget restrictions, etc.
Cash flows can be well predicted.	Cash flows are very uncertain, and actually not very predictable.
The discount percentage is equal to the capital costs for a similar investment with the same risk as the proposed project.	There are a lot more business risks that this project depends on, and has an effect on.
All risks can be offset in the discount percentage.	Project risks can change during the project.
All factors which might have an influence on the outcome of the project are offset in the net present value calculation.	Due to all of the uncertainties, it is not easy to offset all the factors in the cash flows and the discount percentage.
Unknown, intangible or immeasurable factors are valued at zero.	Many of the important benefits are intangible or difficult to qualify (and not quantifiable) strategic benefits.

For the real option analysis we draw a parallel with financial options in the stock exchange.

There are two types of options:
- Call option
- Put option

---
2 (2006) *Real Option Analysis,* Mun, JOHN WILEY & SONS, Hoboken, New Jersey

641

3.10 Finance

With a call option, you buy the right, during a certain period, to buy shares in the future at a price agreed in advance. The put option is the opposite, you buy the right to sell shares in the future at a certain price. When the actual share price is either favorable or unfavorable, you can decide to carry out the option, but here is no obligation to do that.

You can also see the start of the first stage of a project as an option, to, at the end of that stage:
- Stop the project.
- Wait a little longer.
- Carry on with the project.
- Order an extra investigation to be carried out.

Therefore, you can also look at portfolio management decisions as options you buy. There are then many more possibilities (real options) than in the financial market.

As well as the options mentioned above, you also have options to:
- Increase the scope.
- Outsource the project.
- Change resources.
- Take decisions in stages.

Using the real option analysis you can analyze and value all of these options. Just as in the net present value method, the outcome is an amount, no longer that of the total project, but of the option value of the decision you take. However, this value will be a lot more favorable with innovations than the traditional method. The disadvantage of this method is that it requires a lot of statistical knowledge and is very extensive.

3.11 Legal

TO BE RIGHT, TO BE PROVED RIGHT

An unavoidable aspect, which you would rather not have anything to do with.

A language for experts.

You do not have to know a lot about it, but just enough, and you only know that when you go more deeply into the subject.

3.11 Legal

3.11-1 DEFINITIONS

Contract	A voluntary agreement between two parties.
Legal	Everything regarding statutory provisions and regulations.

3.11-2 INTRODUCTION

Projects take place in a legal environment. This does not mean that every project manager also has to be a legal expert, but he has to ensure that the dealings and activities in projects are in accordance with the national and international legal rules in force. A legal contract often underlies a project that a supplier carries out for a customer. It is then one of the tasks of the project manager to determine:

- What the legal basis of the project activities is.
- Which legal principles and laws are applicable.
- At which points specialised legal experts must become involved.

It is also important to juridify as few conflicts as possible. The moment that contracts must be read with a magnifying glass and lawyers need to become involved, a lot has already been lost that, perhaps, could have been prevented by using social skills and by a careful consideration of interests.

Projects can become involved with a broad collection of legal aspects. The most common of these are:

- Employment law (social law)
- Contract law
- Health & Safety laws
- Intellectual Property Rights (IPR), patents, copyright
- Environmental law
- Expropriation
- Liability
- Permits and licenses

A project manager must have just enough knowledge of the specified areas in order to assess how much account needs to be taken of these in the project and when the advice of a legal expert is necessary.

3.11-3 Process Steps

1. Set up legal standards.
2. Identify legal aspects.
3. Initiate compliance.
4. Manage contracts adequately.
5. React to unions and works councils.
6. React to 'whistle-blowers'.
7. Record and apply learning points.

1. Set up legal standards

This takes place at two levels:
- Organization
- Per project

Each organization has its own standards and procedures, which projects are involved with. At the start of the project, the project manager must ask himself to what extent he is involved with the legal conditions for his project. In the introduction, I have already referred to:
- Employment law (social law).
- Contract law.
- Health & Safety laws.
- Intellectual Property Rights (IPR), patents, copyright.
- Environmental law.
- Expropriation.
- Liability.
- Permits and licenses.

If the organization has guidelines for these, that is a bonus, but if that is not the case, then the project manager has to determine these himself. One thing is certain, the more external parties and stakeholders there are, the more you will be involved with legal aspects.

Therefore, in the stakeholder analysis, it is useful to take into consideration the common ground between the project and parties involved.

2. Identify legal aspects

This concerns ensuring that everyone knows which aspects are relevant for him or her. By using control lists (if they exist), at the start of the project the project manager can determine which legal commitments the team members have to satisfy. The law is always part of the scope, and you should ensure that the team keeps to it.

When you are involved with suppliers, make sure you realize that contracts are risk instruments. When you draw up a contract, carry out a risk analysis beforehand, and where necessary, translate this into specific contract clauses.

> EXAMPLE 46-1 NIGERIA
> In a remote area of Nigeria, all expats came together in the only local hotel to relax. During the partying, a member of the local population fell into the swimming pool and drowned. That same evening, the project manager and a number of his team members were removed from their beds by the police, and spent five days in an overcrowded prison before the authorities were convinced of their innocence.

3. Initiate compliance

When you know which legal aspects you are involved with, you must develop measures which ensure that the team members comply with these legal requirements.

The extent of the legal complexity also determines in how far you need to ensure that there is a legal expert (or a whole team) available to you full-time. If parts of the project take place in countries which are unknown to the team members, you have to prepare them on this aspect.

4. Manage contracts adequately

A lot has been said about this in another competence element, but adequately managing contracts also means that you pay attention to the legal aspects of them. The contracts (agreements) with customers and suppliers generate legal obligations. Contract management is there to ensure that, on the one hand the organization itself honours all its commitments, and on the other hand to ensure that the suppliers also comply with their commitments.

You must ensure that you keep your project file well organized and up-to-date, in case a dispute arises. You must record important events in a log, and always confirm agreements in writing. If necessary, you should give a supplier notice of default in a timely manner.

5. React to unions and works councils

For those countries with trade unions and works councils, you must consider beforehand how you are going to handle this situation. Trade unions and works councils form separate areas of discipline, and both of them can significantly stand in the way of the project manager and his result orientation. When they become 'troublesome' during the project, you must handle them in the correct manner to prevent any (further) delays.

6. React to from 'whistle-blowers'

The affair in 2010 around Wikileaks provides a reasonably good picture of the sensitivity around this theme. With danger to their own reputation, whistle-blowers forsake their anonymity and provide information on:
- Intimidation
- Discrimination
- Safety
- Under performance

You have to also react to this type of situation with great care. Personally, I would like to receive every honest whistle-blower with open arms. If they share the leaked information to you, this can generate legal commitments. If something is unlawful or illegal, you must bring this out into the open and you then become, as it were, a 'whistle blowing associate', but to just ignore it is often a criminal offence.

What should you do, however, when a 'whistle-blower' is not honest, and is reacting out of vindictiveness or ill-will? The question is then how seriously you should take it. Doing nothing does not mean that the situation will then blow over, and it is normally better to remain in discussion with the person in question.

7. Apply lessons learned

Everything lends itself to learning experiences, including the legal aspects. In particular, where we have been disadvantaged because we did not fully understand the law, we must quickly make this known to the rest of the organization. We should also do this when we have a legal dispute with a supplier, otherwise it is possible that this supplier can just carry on as before elsewhere in the organization.

3.11 Legal

3.11-4 Special Topics

1. Law sources
The law consists of rules, which have the objective of regulating society. The rules can be found in:
- Legislation
- Case law
- Customs
- International treaties

Legislation
This refers to laws developed by Parliament.

Case law
General rules often provide us with a basis for resolving issues. In a specific situation, the courts must decide (interpret) what the meaning of a particular rule is.

Customs
Customs recognized by society and the legal system. These customs can be particularly found in commerce and the agricultural sector, and also in countries where religion plays an important role.

International treaties.
Such treaties normally contain only provisions that are directed towards the states that are parties to the treaty. There are no consequential citizens rights or duties emanating from treaties; these only come into existence if the provisions are integrated into national laws. Some treaties are self-executing and can bind citizens without the requirement for a national law.

2. Different Legal systems
Although people in everyday language talk about legal systems, it is better to talk about a legal tradition. The type of legislation in any particular country is a product of the history and, therefore, strongly linked to the culture in that country. For a project manager, who is internationally active, studying the legal tradition is an interesting starting point in order to get to know the culture better.

We can differentiate between the following traditions[1]:
- Chthonic, the unwritten law of a primitive tribe.
- Talmudic, based on the revelations of the prophet Moses.
- Civil, finds its origins in the laws of the Roman Empire.
- Islamic, based on the Sharia.
- Common, originating in England and later extended over the Commonwealth countries.
- Hinduistic, in India.
- New Asiatic, based on Marxism.

When you look at these different traditions, then in the 21st century, there are three large groupings that still play a significant role:
- Civil law.
- Common Law.
- Islamic Law.

Furthermore, these traditions influence each other back and forth.

Civil Law
The leading principle of Civil Law is the conviction of the legislator that a law can be drawn up in advance, and with that you can regulate social traffic. Legal precedence does play a role, but more as an example of what the law means. In Civil Law, legislation is an extensive system of law codes.

Common Law
With Common Law, more nuance is placed on the possibility of drawing up an adequate law in advance, and legal precedence plays a much greater role. In the arguments they use to underpin their case, lawyers will here

---
1 (2007) Legal traditions of the World, H. Patrick Glenn, OXFORD UNIVERSITY PRESS

make much more use of comparable lawsuits.

Islamic Law
An important religious component plays a part in Islamic law. There are a number of countries in the world where the Sharia is applicable. Just as with Common Law, much more customary law can be found here, in which the scholars interpret certain religious texts in their meaning for a particular case. The most important differences compared to the other systems lie in the area of family law, and the way in which something can be financed (no interest).

3. Contract law

Introduction
A contract is a legal relationship between two or more persons (or organizations), which is effected by way of a verbal or written agreement. This agreement contains at least one promise that is legally enforceable.

When, as project manager, you hire in a sub-contractor to carry out a piece of work, you must, of course, be able to assume that the work to be carried out will meet your expectations, and if it does not, that you can enforce this through the courts. Seen from a project management perspective, contracts, in the first instance, are risk instruments.

As project manager you are not a legal expert, and the involvement of a legal expert for complex contracts, certainly when they are international, is a necessity. However, to ensure that legal experts, who are pre-eminently risk averse, do not make away with your project, some knowledge of contract law is desirable. What is especially important, is that you develop a feeling for the different legal systems in the world, thereby enhancing your cultural insight.

The following provides a number of thoughts and facts about contract law, not with the intention of being complete, but to give you an idea of a number of aspects that could arise.

International contract law
In the last century, lawyers have put a lot of energy into making international contract law uniform, and this resulted in the UN Convention on Contracts for the International Sale of Goods[2], abbreviated to CISG. A large majority of countries, although not all, have ratified the CISG.

When individuals, or organizations, resident in these countries conclude an international contract, then the CISG automatically becomes valid. It is, however, possible for contracting parties to explicitly exclude these provisions.

Offer, Acceptance and Establishment
We now go back to the contract, and look at how this originates. There are two important milestones: the offer and the acceptance, whereby the law protects the parties in doing this with a free will, and well-considered. The legislator must then find solutions for:
- A party that misleads the other party.
- The mental inability of one of the parties.
- Duress that one party exercises on the other.

The different legal systems have developed their own (different) solutions to these points, and that makes it a risky business when you are not sufficiently informed about these.

---
2 (1980) www.unictral.org

3.11 Legal

5. Incoterms

Incoterms or International contract terms are international agreements on the transport of goods and how the costs and risks are divided between buyer and seller.

FIGURE 46-1. INCOTERMS

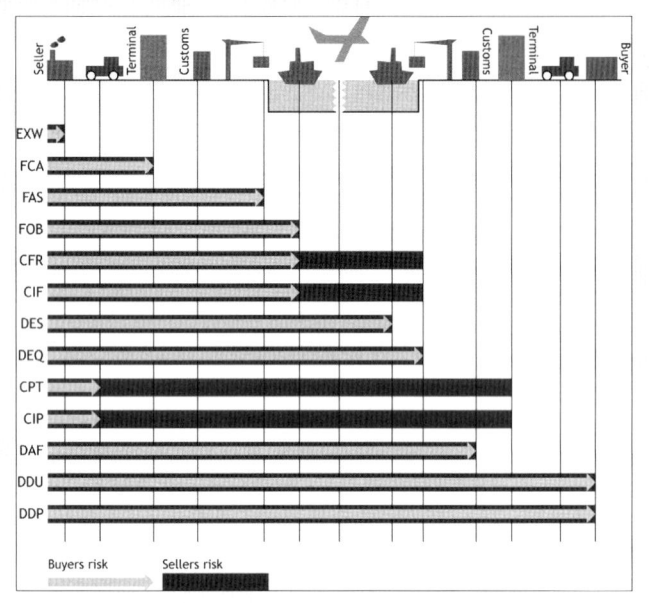

Incoterm		Description
EXW	ex works	Here the seller has the least responsibility. The delivery takes place at the location of the seller where the buyer can pick it up. The seller provides the goods with invoice and the minimum of packaging. The seller providers the goods with invoice and the minimum of packaging The buyer is then liable for loading or for clearance (the procedures at customs). When necessary, the seller can be responsible for "loading" the delivery and then we see the condition 'EXW loaded' applied. The buyer is responsible for all transport costs and risks from the company premises of the seller to the destination.
FCA	free carrier	In this case, the seller provides the goods with invoice, packaging, export license, export customs formalities and costs for delivery of the goods to the transport company stipulated by the buyer. The seller delivers the goods, cleared through customs, and transfers them to the carrier named by the buyer at the agreed location.
FAS	free alongside ship	The same as FCA only now up to the quay and alongside the ship. From there, the buyer has to enter into a transport agreement and he also carries all the risks for loss or damage to the goods. An extra obligation is that the buyer has to effect a sea transport insurance to cover the risk of the seller for loss or damage to the goods during transport. The buyer enters into an insurance contract and the seller pays the fee. The buyer must take note that the delivery conditions FAS only obliges the seller to an Insurance with minimum cover. The term FAS obliges the buyer to clear the goods!

3.11 Legal

Incoterm		Description
FOB	free on board	The seller ensures that the goods, including invoice, packaging, export licence and customs formalities, are loaded on board the ship. He pays the costs (clearance etc.) until the goods are passed over the ship's rails. The seller has complied with his obligation to deliver when the goods have passed over the ship's rails and are on board in the specified shipping port. From that point on, the buyer bears all costs and risks of loss of the goods.
CFR	cost and freight	The seller pays the costs and freightage to transport the goods to the specified destination port. The risk of loss or damage to the goods and any extra costs caused by events after the goods have been delivered on board the ship, is transferred from the seller to the buyer when the goods have passed over the ship's rails in the shipping port. The term CFR obliges the seller to clear the goods. This term can only be used for sea freight and inland shipping.
CIF	cost, insurance and freight	The seller has the same obligations as under CFR. An extra obligation is that the seller has to effect and pay for a sea transport insurance (with minimum coverage) to cover the risk to the buyer of loss or damage to the goods during transport. This term can only be used for sea freight and inland shipping.
CPT	carriage paid to	The seller ensures the clearance of the goods and pays the fee for freight costs for transport. The risk of loss of, or damage to, the goods, and the extra costs caused by events which occur after the goods have been delivered to the first carrier, pass over to the buyer once the goods have been transferred to the first transporter.
CIP	carriage and insurance paid to	The seller has the same obligations as under CPT. An extra obligation is that he has to effect and pay for a freight insurance (with minimum coverage) to cover the risk of loss or damage during transport.
DAF	delivered at frontier	The seller delivers the goods, cleared, at the customs border of the bordering country. The term "border" can be used for every border including that of the country of export.
DES	delivered ex ship	Only applicable to sea freight and inland shipping. The seller delivers the goods, not cleared inwards, on board of the ship in the destination port stipulated. All costs and risks of transport to the destination port are for account of the seller.
DEQ	delivered ex quay	The seller delivers the goods, cleared inwards, to the quay or loading quay of the destination port. All risks and costs, including rights, taxes and other expenses connected with the delivery of the goods, are for the account of the seller.
DDU	delivered duty unpaid	The seller delivers the goods to the stipulated town or city in the import country. He carries the costs and risks connected with the transport to there, with the exception of rights, duties and other official import levies, and the costs of the customs formalities to be fulfilled.
DDP	delivered duty paid	The seller delivers the goods to the stipulated town or city stated in the import country. He carries the risks and costs, including rights, duties and other levies connected with delivering inward cleared goods.

3.11 Legal

What all legal systems have in common, is the offer and the acceptance leading to the establishment of the contract, and we often see that the weaker party enjoys more protection than the stronger party. The differences can be found in what is enforceable by law, and what can serve as evidence.

In Common Law countries, the doctrine of consideration plays a part. This supposes that a contract is only legally valid when a promise is made with the primary objective of getting something back from the other party in exchange[3]. This means, therefore, that the promise to give someone a large gift is not enforceable by law. In a dispute about the validity of a contract under Common Law, an examination of whether or not there is sufficient consideration will be carried out - no consideration, then also no contract.

Another difference between Civil and Common Law is the point in time at which the offer can still be rescinded. In Common Law, that is no longer possible once it has been sent[4] (the so-called "mailbox rule"), but the CISG takes another approach and leaves the possibility of rescinding open until the accepting party has received the offer[5]. A telephone call whilst the offer is on its way, gives the proposing party the option of getting out of the situation.

In both systems, the acceptance does not have to be in writing, as activities indicating (e.g. payment) that a party has accepted the offer, are, as such, also valid. However, when the receiving party signs the offer, at the same time making amendments to it, the court sees this as a rejection of the original offer by means of a counteroffer, and there is then no question of there being an agreement.

Battle of forms

We are involved in this when the parties make use of standard purchase or sales terms and conditions, often printed in small letters on the back of a proposal or purchase order. When these differ from each other, a so-called "battle of forms" arises. The different traditions contain small nuances in the determination of which conditions are valid.

The sending of new standard terms and conditions means a counteroffer, and, therefore, no agreement. When one of the parties now delivers, in Common Law this is seen as an acceptance, and the most recent standard terms and conditions will apply. Under the CISG, the accepting party can even then make small amendments, which form a valid part of the contract.

For project managers the maxim in this situation is: "*Always involve a legal expert*!".

Breach of contract

When one of the parties does not comply with the agreements made, then to a lesser or greater degree, a breach of contract situation arises. The disadvantaged party can now try to obtain his rights in one or more of the following ways:

- Mediation, a voluntary process in which both parties try to come to a solution with the assistance of an independent third party. The result of this process is not binding.
- Arbitration, a more formal process that leads to a binding outcome. This allows the parties in an international affair to resolve the dispute on a more neutral terrain.

---

[3] (2004) Contract Theory, Stephen A. Smith, CLARENDON LAW SERIES –OXFORD UNIVERSITY PRESS
[4] (2005) International Business Law and Its Environment, Schaffer, Agusti, Earle, SOUTH-WESTERN CENCAGE LEARNING, Mason - USA
[5] (1980) UN Convention on Contracts for the International Sale of Goods, Article 18

- Litigation, where the parties try to obtain their rights in court.

For the last two, provisions can already be made in the contract about where the arbitration takes place, or under which law the agreement falls. This is important because the courts in different countries use different ways of finding out what the intention of the contract is.

A big difference between Common Law and Civil Law is the documents the court takes into consideration as items of evidence. According to the so-called "parole evidence rule", pronouncements (written or verbal) made before the actual agreements do not count as evidence under Common Law, whereas they do count as evidence in a Civil Law Court.

The basic premise of both traditions in the event of breach of contract, is to bring the situation back to the state it was in before the breach happened. In the CISG, the following solutions are then possible:
- Dissolve the contract (avoidance).
- The right to come forward with a remedy.
- Allow extra time to still deliver according to the agreement.
- Reduction of the price.
- A compensation payment for the damages suffered.

Bringing everything back to the original situation prior to the breach, therefore, means including the benefits that would have been derived from this contract.

4. Intellectual property

When someone has a good idea that, in economic or artistic terms, has value, there is a need for one form or another of legal protection, as ideas are difficult to protect.

We are talking about the legislation regarding intellectual property rights. Just as with contract legislation, a movement took place in the twentieth century to harmonize these rights internationally. To achieve this, in 1967 the WIPO (World Intellectual Property Organization) was established as part of the United Nations to specialize in this subject. According to their deed of formation[6], intellectual property is one or more of:
- Literary, artistic and scientific works.
- Performances of performing artists, phonograms, and broadcasts.
- Inventions in all fields of human endeavour.
- Scientific discoveries.
- Industrial designs.
- Trademarks, service marks, and commercial names and designations.
- Protection against unfair competition.

As project manager, you are involved with this when you hire in people or companies to carry out a part of the WBS, and you must then be aware of the possibility that the property rights of a particular delivery do not automatically transfer to the customer. This is something you have to arrange contractually.

The following forms of legal protection are available:
- Copyright and Design Rights.
- Patents.
- Registration of names.

Copyright and Design Rights
Copyright relates to literary, artistic and also scientific works produced by the maker. The protection of the author is on two terrains[7]:
- De economic rights.
- The moral right.

---
6 (1967) www.wipo.int, articel 2
7 (Downloaded in 2011) Understanding Copyright and Related Rights, WORLD INTELLECTUAL PROPERTY ORGANIZATION

The latter ensures that a relationship always remains between the author and what he has thought up. The author can authorise the reproduction or forbid it. As well as text, in some countries industrial designs are also protected under this title.

Patents

A patent can be used to protect an industrial idea. The inventor does this by making a precise description of the idea, and lodging this with the appropriate authorised institution. For a period of approximately 20 years, no one may use this idea without the permission of the inventor, and in this way he is protected. At the same time it is possible that, through this patent, another person may think up a more innovative idea, because another goal of the patent law is the stimulation of creativity. When you describe ideas precisely, you can protect them soundly, and on the other hand, the description is for other inventors a step towards a new (and perhaps better) invention.

In order to patent an idea, it must satisfy the following conditions[8]:
- Industrial applicability.
- Innovation.
- Not self-evident.
- Able to be patented in the country.

Both products and industrial processes can be patented.

The extent of the protection is dependent on the country in which the inventor applies for the patent, but generally the rule is that other parties cannot execute, offer, sell or purchase the idea, without his permission. It is possible, when parties so want, that the inventor licenses or sells the idea.

In addition to the patent, there is also another form which is similar; the so-called "utility models" used for less complex inventions. They offer less protection, have a shorter duration and are predominantly in use for inventions, which have a shorter economic life span.

Registering

When a patent is not possible, some protection can be gained by registering:
- A brand name.
- An industrial design.
- At an appropriate authorised office. The rules concerning these also differ per country.

---

8 (Downloaded in 2011) Understanding Industrial Property, WORLD INTELLECTUAL PROPERTY ORGANIZATION

Index

A
accommodating 463
accounting 630
activities 155
ACWP 228
adjourning 105
adversaries 26
Agile Project Management 515
Aken, Teun van 5, 8, 16
Allen, V.L. 493
allergy 413
allies 25
allocating indirect costs 633
analogue communication 258
annual report 628
arguments 421
Argyris 377
asking questions 375
Assagioli 351
assertiveness 337
assessment 80
avoidance of uncertainty 480
avoiding 463

B
BAC 229
BATNA 428
battle of forms 652
BCWP 228
BCWS 228
bedfellows 26
Belbin, Meredith 61, 108, 384
benchmarking 411
benefits 36
benefits realization management 36
Bertalanffy 118
Big-V 333
black box 118
Block, Peter 25
BLUE PRINT THINKING 529
Bono, Edward de 391
BOOT 192
Boston Matrix 582
brainstorming 116
Branden, Nathaniel 346
breach of contract 652
burnout 362
business 571
business case 34, 625

C
Cairo Declaration of Human Rights in Islam 497
Cameron, K.S. 508
Cartesian Product 392
categorical imperative 492
Cauffman, Louis 322
cause and effect diagram 81
CE guideline 616
change control 173, 215
Change in Five Colors 528
changes 211
checklists 53
check sheet 81
Civil Law 648
CMM 547
coaching leadership 322
code of conduct 17
Collins, Jim 583
Common Law 648
communication 247
communication model 253
communication plan 250
competing 463
concepts of time 162
configuration management 149
conflicts and crisis 449
conflict stages 457
conflict styles 462
conformance to specification 76
confronting 463
consensus 117
constraints 159
consultation 415
contingency reserve 187
contract changes 200
contract law 649
contract management 199
contract pricing 206
Contract Work Breakdown Structure 198
Control Account Managers 138
control accounts 134
control and reports 221
control chart 83
converge 390
coping curve 569
Core Quadrants 413
cost allocation 632
cost and finance 179
Cost Breakdown Structure 190
cost control system 186
cost of quality 76
Cost Plus Fixed Fee 207
Cost Plus Incentive Fee 207
Cost Reimbursable 206
Covey, Stephen R. 295

Index

CPI 229, 408
Creation Spiral 324
creativity 381, 389
Critical Chain 176
Critical Chain Project Management 512
Critical Path 157
Critical Path Project Management 512
Crosby, Philip 74
cultural dimensions 480
culture 387
custom 481
CV 228
cyclic phases 165

D

De Caluwé 528
decision points 159
decision trees 57
Declaration of Human Rights 496
defensive routines 377
delegating 307
Deming, W. Edwards 72, 74, 588
Deming cycle 74
dependencies 155
depth of control 563
digital communication 258
diplomacy 346
discussion 379
diverge 390
double-loop learning 335
duration 155
dysfunctional behavior 109

E

EAC 229
earliest start 158
Earned Value Method 227
efficiency 403
effort matrix 24
EFQM 587
Ellis, Albert 347
emotional intelligence 333
enforce superiority 437
engagement 309
environment 617
environmental impact assessment 617
Erikson, E.H. 320
estimation methods 166
ETAC 229
ETC 229
ethical issues 491
ethics 487
European Tender guidelines 208
Event Chain Project Management 512

F

failure costs 77
fallacies 424

Fayol, H. 298
Feedback 308
fence sitters 26
Fiedler, E.F. 301
finance 619
financial ratios 635
Firm Fixed Price 206
fishbone 81
fitness for use) 76
Fixed Price Incentive Fee 206
Fixed Price with Economic Price Adjustment 206
float 157
flow diagram 86
force field analysis 116
forming 104
forward pass 157
free slack 158
Full Analytical Criteria Method 203
Function point analysis 167

G

Gantt 162
GAP principle 37
General Adaptation Syndrome 362
general ledger 631
GLOBE study 344
goal 31
Goldratt, Eliyahu 176
Goleman, Daniel 333
Golembiewski 358
GREEN PRINT THINKING 530
Greiner, Larry E., 531
group blindness 110

H

Hall, E.T. 162
handover 147
Harvard Method 433
HAZOP 615
health 605, 612
Hersey & Blanchard 302
Herzberg, Frederick 319
histogram 82
holistic approach 387
horizontal analysis 24
humour 365

I

images 324
improvisations 507
incoterms 650
individualism 480
influence matrix 23
information and documentation 233
initiation documents 11
intellectual property 653
interested parties 13, 16
interest groups 23

Index

intuition 388
Ishikawa diagram 81
Islamic Financing 190
Islamic Law 649
ISO 590
ISO 21500 10, 19, 51, 73, 95, 148, 161, 189, 202, 218, 225, 242, 276, 286, 552
issue register 219

J
Juran, Joseph, 74

K
Kaizen 407
Kant, Immanuel 492
Kaptein, Muel 470, 499
Kets de Vries, Manfred 306
Knoope, Marinus
Kotter, John P. 527
Kübler-Ross, Elisabeth 569

L
latest start 158
law sources 648
leaders 293
leadership 291
Leadership in a multicultural perspective 299
leadership style 294
Leadership styles 304
lead or lag 159
legal 643
legal systems 648
Lewin, Kurt 320, 527
line organization 560
linking pin 97
long or short term thinking 480

M
make-or-buy 198
Management By Exception 308
Management By Objectives 308
management reserve 187
management stages 165
managers 293
Managing Successful Programmes 525
managing the expectations 17
manipulation 437
Mao Zedong 448
masculinity 480
Maslach Burnout Inventory 364
Maslow, Abraham 316
Mastenbroek, W.F.G. 435
Mayo, Elton 298
McGregor, Douglas 318
meeting 265
meeting intervention table 266
milestones 159
Mintzberg, Henry 565

mirroring 376
monochronic 162
Monte Carlo simulation 60
Morgan, Gareth 324
MoSCoW 220
Motivation-Hygiene Theory 319
multi-tasking 176
Mutual Gains approach 433

N
negotiation 425
negotiation strategy 429
negotiation styles 435
non-verbal communication 255, 436
normal distribution 57
norming 105

O
Ofman, Daniel 311, 413
openness 369
OPM3 547, 550
opponents 25
organization architecture 560
organization breakdown 138
organization chart 97
outsourcing 205

P
paraphrasing 376
Pareto analysis 87
parroting 375
performing 105
permanent organization 555
personality 333
personal power 306
personnel management 593
persuasiveness 345
PERT 168
PESTLE 20
phases 156, 164
PID 11
PMBOK Guide 5, 10, 19, 51, 73, 95, 148, 161, 189, 202, 218, 225, 243, 276, 286, 512
PMI Program Management standard 525
polychronic 162
Porter, Michael 573
portfolio 535
portfolio orientation 535
positional power 305
power 305
power distance 480
PPP implementation 543
Precedence Diagram 156
presentation skills 262
price risks 192
PRINCE2 11, 19, 35, 52, 73, 95, 98, 140, 148, 161, 189, 202, 218, 219, 225, 243, 244, 276, 286, 514

657

Index

principled negotiating 433
problem resolution 111
process approach 454
procurement and contract 193
product oriented planning 140
Professional Development Plan 601
programme orientation 519
project 7, 507
project approach 7
project assurance 98
Project-based creating 517
Project-based working 516
project controller 98
project environment 20
project evaluation 287
project financing 183
project goals 32
project management audit 80
project management information management system 236
project management method 511
Project Management Office 511
project management plan 8, 17
project management plans 244
project management success 3
project management team 21
project manager 98
project office 98
project organization 89, 93
project orientation 503
project procedures 94
project review 39
project sponsor 217
project start up 274
project structures 123
PSU 275
public private financing 191
public tendering 207
punctuation 257

Q

qualitative analysis 48
quality 65, 147, 413
quality assurance 71
quality control 71, 74
quality improvement 74
quality plan 71
quality planning 74
quality system 75
quality trilogy 74
quantitative analysis 48
Quinn, Robert E. 508

R

RACI 99
RAM 138
rapport 435
RED PRINT THINKING 529

relaxation 355
reliability 467
requirements 31, 146
requirements and objectives 27
resource diagram 172
resources 158, 169
responsibilities matrix 138
results orientation 395
RET 347
RFI 199
RFP 199
RFQ 199
risk analysis 47
risk and opportunity 41
Risk Breakdown Structure 53
risk identification 47
risk matrix 53
risk premium 187
risk profile 50
risk register 58
risk responses 48
Rogers, Carl 347, 479
role 359
roles 94, 97
routines 507

S

safety 614
Sarbanes-Oxley act 191
scatter diagram 82
Schulz von Thun, model van 258
Scientific Management 298
scope 145, 146
scope and deliverables 143
security 613
self-control 327
self-esteem 346
sensitivity 26
sensitivity analysis 61
seven habits of effective leadership 295
seven tools of quality 81
single-loop learning 335
Six Sigma 591
six thinking hats 392
slack 157
Slip Chart 230
SMART 398
span of Control 562
SPI 229, 408
stakeholders 16
stake matrix 24
Standish Group 6
start-Up 271
steering committee 97
storming 104
stress 330
structure approach 454
student syndrome 176
successful team 107

658

Index

Successive Principle 61
summarizing 376
suppliers 22, 199
suppliers selection 203
supply chain 580
sustainability 611
SV 228
systems, products and technology 577
system thinking 117

T
Taguchi, Genichi 75
Taylor, F.W. 298
TCPI 408
teambuilding 107
team lead 98
team structure 107
teamwork 101
tension 362
Theory X, Theory Y 318
Thirty-Six Stratagems 437
time and material 207
time and project phases 151
Toulmin, Stephen 422
transference 378
triple-loop learning 335
trust versus agreement matrix 25
Tuckman model 104

U
uncertainty 176
Unfreeze - Change - Freeze 527

V
VAC 229
value chain 573
Value Management 37
values 476
values appreciation 473
variance 56
variance analysis 188
verbal communication 254
versions 165
vertical analysis 24

W
waterfall 165
Watzlawick, Paul 256
WBS 128
WBS dictionary 134
WHITE PRINT THINKING 530
will 351
Work Breakdown Structure 133, 190

Y
YELLOW PRINT THINKING 528

659

Index